# THE UNIVERSITY OF LONDON, 1858–1900

In 1858 the University – in reality an examining board – opened its non-medical examinations to candidates irrespective of how or where they prepared themselves – thus consolidating what became known as the 'external' system. At the same time, graduates could join the newly established Convocation, which for four decades was empowered to veto changes in the University's Charter, and which chose a quarter of the governing body, the Senate. From 1868, Convocation elected the University's MP. Parliament provided financial support, and the University's expenditure and proceedings were subject to control by Government.

A sequel to the author's *Our Minerva. The Men and Politics of the University of London 1836–1858*, this book analyses the delicate and often stressful relations of Senate and Convocation, covering the long struggle over admission of women to degrees; the contribution of the University to secondary education; the establishment of the University's seat in the House of Commons, and the subsequent elections of Members. Later chapters describe the extended campaign to change the institution into an orthodox university, involving two Royal Commissions; the ambitions of all the institutions of higher education in London; the fierce attention of the medical profession; an aggressive professoriate; the concerns of the London County Council; the influence of religious and provincial interests; and much parliamentary and governmental manoeuvring. Convocation was deeply divided, those defensive of the existing 'external' system being apprehensive of the power which the new 'internal' system would give to teachers in London. Convocation exercised its veto once, and lost that power when the Charter of the University was replaced by an Act of Parliament.

F.M.G. WILLSON, sometime Principal of the University, was born in Carlisle and studied at Manchester University and Balliol and Nuffield Colleges, Oxford. He has retired from an academic and administrative career in Oxford, Zimbabwe, California, London and Western Australia.

# THE UNIVERSITY OF LONDON, 1858–1900

## The Politics of Senate and Convocation

*F.M.G. Willson*

THE BOYDELL PRESS

First published 2004

Published by The Boydell Press
An imprint of Boydell & Brewer Ltd
PO Box 9, Woodbridge, Suffolk IP12 3DF, UK
and of Boydell & Brewer Inc.
PO Box 41026, Rochester, NY 14604–4126, USA
website: www.boydellandbrewer.com

ISBN 1 84383 065 5

A CIP catalogue record for this book is available
from the British Library

Library of Congress Cataloging-in-Publication Data
Willson, F. M. G. (Francis Michael Glenn), 1924-
The University of London, 1858-1900 : the politics of Senate
and Convocation / F.M.G. Willson.
    p. cm.
Includes bibliographical references and index.
    ISBN 1-84383-065-5 (hardback : alk. paper)
1. University of London—Administration—History—
19th century.  I. Title.
LF403.W55 2004
378.421'2—dc22                                    2004000051

Typeset by Keystroke, Jacaranda Lodge, Wolverhampton
Printed in Great Britain by
Antony Rowe Ltd, Chippenham, Wiltshire

# Contents

# CONTENTS

## PART V: THE UNIVERSITY AND SECONDARY EDUCATION

## PART VI: EXAMINING AND TEACHING – THE LONG AND CROOKED ROAD TO COMPROMISE

# List of portraits

Numbers 1, 6, 8, 9 and 10 are reproduced by courtesy of the National Portrait Gallery; numbers 2, 3 and 4 by courtesy of the Courtauld Institute of Art; number 5 by kind permission of the Honourable Society of Lincoln's Inn; number 7 by kind permission of St Bartholomew's Hospital Archives & Museum. Photographs of 2, 3, 4, 5, and 7 by the Photographic Survey, Courtauld Institute of Art.

# Acknowledgements

I am most grateful to the University of London for generous financial assistance, which has made publication of this book possible; to Negley Harte, who has contributed, as he did in the compilation of a previous volume, expert scholarly advice, continuous encouragement, and invaluable help in the negotiations which precede publication; and to my wife, who has never ceased to indulge me with constructive support, careful criticism, and endless patience.

A large part of the data on which this study is based is contained in the archives of the University. I am specially indebted to Christine Wise, Head of Historic Collections, for permission to quote from them; and to the staff of the Paleography Room in Senate House, on whom I have made heavy and persistent demands. My thanks are also due to the Archivists of Imperial College, King's College, and University College, for assistance and permission to quote from items in their collections.

For help received, access to and permission to quote from other archives, I am indebted to the Duke of Devonshire, the Trustees of the Chatsworth Settlement, and Mr Peter Day, Keeper of Collections at Chatsworth; to Lord Cranbrook and the Ipswich Record Office of the Suffolk County Council; to the Trustees of Lambeth Palace Library and Dr Richard Palmer, Librarian and Archivist; to The Marquess of Salisbury and Robin Harcourt Williams, Librarian and Archivist at Hatfield House; to the National Library of Scotland and Dr Iain G. Brown, Principal Curator, Manuscripts Division; and to the Wellcome Trust.

I am grateful to the staffs of the Courtauld Institute of Art and the National Portrait Gallery for help with the choice and reproduction of portraits.

# Sources

Specific references in the notes to each chapter comprise a guide to relevant secondary material.

The printed Minutes of Senate and Convocation are major sources, and are lodged in the University of London's Library at Senate House. The University's archive includes all Convocation's limited official manuscript material outside the Minutes.

Selected portions of the manuscript material in the collections listed below were examined.

Bodleian Library: *Bryce and Kimberley Mss*
British Library: *Balfour, Cross and Lubbock Mss*
Chatsworth: *Devonshire Mss*
Corporation of London RO: *Mss relating to Gresham College*
Hatfield House: *Salisbury Mss*
Imperial College: *Huxley and Playfair Mss*
King's College London: *College Records*
Lambeth Palace: *Benson and Temple Mss*
Mercers' Company: *Minute Books*
National Library of Scotland: *Haldane and Rosebery Mss*
Public Record Office: *Education, Home Office, Privy Council, Treasury, and Granville Mss*
Suffolk RO, Ipswich: *Cranbrook Mss*
University College London: *Council and Senate Minutes, College Correspondence, Grote and Lodge Mss*
University of London: *University Records, Collins and Silvanus Thompson Mss*
Wellcome Institute, Contemporary Medical Archives Centre: *Sharpey-Schafer Mss*
The Women's Library, London Metropolitan University: *Elizabeth Garrett Anderson Mss*

# Abbreviations

| | |
|---|---|
| BL | British Library |
| BMJ | *British Medical Journal* |
| Bod | Bodleian Library |
| ED | Education Pps, PRO |
| HO | Home Office Pps, PRO |
| KCL | King's College London |
| LUM | *London University Magazine* |
| PC | Privy Council Pps, PRO |
| PP | Parliamentary Papers |
| PRO | Public Record Office |
| T | Treasury Pps, PRO |
| TNAPSS | *Transactions of the National Association for the Promotion of Social Science* |
| UCL | University College London |
| UL | University of London |

# Introduction

For two decades, since its establishment in 1836, the University of London made slow and often halting progress. Founded, primarily, to provide a route through higher education for those denied entry to Oxford and Cambridge, it was a peculiar institution. In effect, it was a Government department, in the form of a board of examiners with power to matriculate students and to award degrees. But this board was called the Senate; its chief officers were a Chancellor and a Vice-Chancellor; and its other members were Fellows. In fact it had the trappings of a university, but not its most obvious function – it did not teach. Candidates who took the degree examinations in Arts and Laws had to have attended courses, for at least two years, at colleges recognised by the Government: and those who were examined in Medicine had to have studied at a medical school recommended by the University and approved by the Government. The principal recognised institutions were the original University of London, renamed University College London (UCL) in 1836; King's College London (KCL), its Anglican counterpart; and the medical schools of the great London hospitals. These provided the bulk of the candidates for degrees, and many of the examiners, who were engaged annually. But by 1858 the other non-medical recognised institutions ranged from the universities of the United Kingdom to over thirty provincial colleges and schools, many of them Roman Catholic and Nonconformist seminaries. And there were some fifty recognised, provincial medical schools, though less than thirty of them had produced successful London graduates.

From the outset, the University was dogged by denominational suspicions and antagonisms which reflected the partisan conflicts of parliamentary politics; by bitter struggles with and within the medical corporations; by self-inflicted wounds over the employment of examiners; and by a prolonged, three-way argument between the Senate, the graduates and successive Governments, over how and when the graduates should be given a place in the University's governance.

None the less, by the end of 1857, 2707 candidates had passed the matriculation examination of the University. Only 1469 degrees had been awarded, however: because of the incidence of higher degrees, the number of graduates was probably no more than about twelve hundred, of whom a quarter were medical men. The LLB degree could only be taken by those who had already achieved a BA, and the total of legal graduates was only about eighty, of whom eight had been awarded the LLD. Those who took only the BA degree, or who went on to take the MA, comprised the clear majority of graduates, most of whom pursued careers in teaching, or as ministers of religion – particularly in the Nonconformist churches – or in the law, without taking any additional law degree. Though this was a modest output, it was one which was recognised, particularly after 1850, as being comprised of men who had succeeded in passing examinations of high standards. And undoubtedly, the University's reputation was strongest in the medical context.

After twenty years, therefore, the University was accepted, and was in a far stronger position than at its establishment. But a new Charter, in April, 1858, incorporated some significant constitutional revisions which reflected old controversies and new developments. Those revisions ushered in a major change in academic policy, and a new political force.

The requirement that students taking non-medical degrees had to be enrolled in recognised institutions was controversial from the outset. There were always those, including some on the Senate, who would have preferred non-medical degree examinations to have been thrown open to candidates, irrespective of how they had prepared themselves to take them. The Senate had no control over the approval of the institutions which prepared students for non-medical examinations, and by the late 1850s some Fellows had become alarmed at how many of them were really secondary schools with no proper facilities for teaching undergraduates. It also became obvious that the small number of approved institutions greatly restricted the number of potential degree candidates.

In the very last negotiations over the new Charter, a dominant group in the Senate achieved something of a *coup*, by persuading the Government to abandon the requirement of attendance at recognised institutions, thus throwing the University's future non-medical degree examinations open to all matriculated comers, wherever and however they prepared for them. This established, in fact, an early version of the Open University. Candidates for medical degrees continued to be required to attend medical schools.

But the decision to drop the requirement of attendance was strongly opposed by the colleges – especially UCL and KCL, which supplied a high proportion of the candidates – and by many of the graduates, who feared a drop in the quality and status of the London degrees. Those teaching institutions which had been recognised before 1858 remained listed in the new Charter, but this was merely a sop to injured pride and had little practical significance. The opposition to the breaking of the collegiate link ran deep, and was reflected later in the struggle to convert the University into a teaching, as well as an examining institution, which was to be the major focus of concern for the last quarter of the century.

The second major innovation, in 1858, was the recognition of the demands of graduates for the establishment of Convocation as an integral part of the University. The powers given to Convocation were far less extensive than the graduates, who had campaigned for a decade for its establishment, had wished, and their disappointment, like the opposition to the abandonment of collegiate connections, was a political factor in the years following 1858. But the new Charter did give Convocation an unusual power of veto over any major change in the University's constitution, and provided for the gradual selection, by Convocation, of a quarter of the Fellows who formed the Senate. The very existence of the veto power was, for forty years, to give Convocation a unique significance in the affairs of the University, and the presence of Convocation Fellows on Senate was a major influence in shaping the character and behaviour of the governing body during the period. The veto was to be used, only once, but with devastating results for both the Senate and for Convocation.

Ten years after the new Charter came into effect, Parliament provided for the representation of the University in the House of Commons. The Member for the University would be chosen by the members of Convocation. This was the last significant change in the main constitutional arrangements of the University until the end of the century. But a smaller change worth recording was the abolition, in 1858, of the right of members of the Senate to act as examiners. In fact a mere handful of Fellows had been examining in the years since the practice was savagely criticised by Government in 1841. Those still examining were allowed to go on doing so only until 1861.

The search for a fully appropriate and comprehensive system of higher education, whose origins can be found in the mid- and later nineteenth century, has not been fully satisfied more than a hundred years afterwards, and has long been a subject of investigation, recommendation and frequently acrimonious debate. There were, and still are, important arguments over the desirability and viability of separating responsibility for teaching from that for examining; over the virtues and vices of orthodox residential education; over the practical and social advantages of independent study, by people of all ages, subject to a system of external assessment. But in the 1860s and 1870s there was a freshness and an urgency about that search which carried the mid- and late Victorians forward into continuous and controversial innovation and expansion. In such an era the University of London could put behind it any fears of being unwelcome, possibly unviable, and an object of suspicion: its contribution was considerable, honourable – but difficult. It was, as an institution, *sui generis*, and, as such, particularly open to criticism, internal and external. Before examining its constitutional and political experience, it is as well to summarise, briefly, its educational achievements and some of its essential administrative and financial arrangements between 1858 and 1900.

Religious and denominational conflict over higher education had by no means disappeared by 1858, and it was to be another twelve years before Oxford, Cambridge and Durham opened their doors to non-Anglicans. But so far as London was concerned, justice had been achieved in this context for Nonconformists, Roman Catholics and Non-Christians, from the beginning.

In the last four decades of the century the over-riding objective, for London along with all the other institutions of advanced learning, was to meet the increasing, overall, national demand for highly educated men – and women. That demand was triggered by the remarkable growth of population, of industrialisation, of science and technology, and of concern to improve the physical conditions of life for the mass of people. And it was a demand enhanced by recognition of the significance, for all the providers of education, of the widening of the franchise. Robert Lowe was already a Fellow of the University of London when he famously told his colleagues in the House of Commons that 'It will be absolutely necessary that you should prevail on our future masters to learn their letters.'

Figures quoted earlier indicate that, by the end of 1857, some fifteen hundred pupils at the approved institutions had passed the matriculation examinations, but had not tried, or had tried and not succeeded, in taking degrees after further studies. The matriculation examination had not been designed as a measure of the successful completion of a secondary school career, and was in some respects by no means ideal for such a purpose. The Oxford and Cambridge local examinations, introduced much later, were designed, from the start, as school exercises. Nonetheless, the 'London Matric', like them, became a standard secondary school leaving certificate.[1] The compilation of precise figures of how many school leavers regarded the 'London Matric' as the end of their formal education is probably impossible, but an approximation is worthwhile. By the end of the century some thirty-nine thousand London candidates had matriculated. But only a quarter of them had taken degrees. Thus between 1858 and 1900 it would seem probable that at least twenty-five thousand candidates – the overwhelming majority of whom would have been boys and girls at secondary schools – left those schools with the matriculation as their final, formal educational qualification. The University, therefore, was a major participant in secondary education and was, inevitably, drawn into the world of school supervision and teacher training.

In 1863, the medical offerings were completed by the introduction of degrees in Surgery. The medical training provided by the London teaching hospitals, and the degrees awarded by the University of London, were widely accepted as prestigious offerings and awards, but even so it was not until the last decade of the century that between one hundred and two hundred graduates received the MB each year, while the MDs numbered on average about forty. The steady, but slow, growth went alongside a continuation, though at a rather more sophisticated stage, of the arguments and negotiations which had already marked the struggle of the Royal Colleges of Physicians

---

[1] For these developments see John Roach, *Public Examinations in England, 1850–1900* (Cambridge, 1971), and R.J. Montgomery, *Examinations: An account of their evolution as administrative devices in England* (Pittsburgh, 1967).

and Surgeons to retain their former monopolies, against the University's insistence on establishing an independent position in examining candidates and awarding qualifications to practice. Despite that persistent element of conflict, however, the University was thoroughly and importantly involved in the training of the medical profession.

But the University did not make similar headway in the context of the Law. Here efforts to bring the University more prominently into the training of lawyers were unsuccessful: the profession's own organisations – the Inns of Court and the Law Society – retained their attraction for the great bulk of aspirant barristers and solicitors. Although, from 1867, students who wished to take the LLB degree were no longer required to have taken the BA previously, there was no great increase in the number of candidates. Only a mere twenty-five or so degrees of LLB were awarded each year in the 1890s.

Those who matriculated after 1858, and did not aim to become doctors or lawyers, were offered a significantly wider choice of subject matter than had been available in the first decades of the University's life. By far the most significant innovation was the introduction of Bachelor's and Doctoral degrees in Science, consideration of which was going on alongside the final stages of debate on the 1858 Charter. The first Science degrees were awarded in 1860, and, in 1900, 28 per cent of all first degree graduates took BScs. In 1881 a postgraduate Teacher's Diploma was introduced, and in 1877, the University began to appoint Inspectors of those secondary schools which asked to be involved in a system of inspection and examination. Also in 1877, Bachelor's and Doctor's degrees in Music were established.

The first attempt by a woman to be accepted as a candidate by the University was made in 1856. Subsequent attempts led to the introduction of a special examination for women, roughly equivalent to the matriculation examination, in 1869, and after a Supplemental Charter had been granted in 1878 women were admitted to all the University's examinations. The first female graduates took their degrees in 1880.

The widened offerings and the steady increase in the numbers of candidates meant that by the end of the century the pattern of matriculation and graduation was very different from what it had been in 1857. In the latter year only 224 men passed the matriculation examination: in 1900, 1917 men and women matriculated. The total number of degrees awarded in each of the two years were, respectively, 120 and 536, distributed as shown below:

*Numbers graduating*

|      | BA  | MA | DLit | BSc | DSc | LLB | LLD | MB | BS | MS | MD | BMus | DMus |
|------|-----|----|------|-----|-----|-----|-----|----|----|----|----|------|------|
| 1857 | 66  | 5  |      |     |     | 6   | 1   | 30 |    |    | 12 |      |      |
| 1900 | 202 | 22 | 1    | 135 | 7   | 21  | 2   | 92 | 20 | 2  | 29 | 2    | 1    |

The rise of the scientific graduates and the still very restricted appeal of the law degrees are outstanding features of the 1900 figures. The typical non-medical graduate of the University in the 1850s was likely to be either a school teacher, a minister of religion, a man aspiring to one or other of those roles, or a man aiming to be a lawyer who was more likely to have taken a BA than an LLB. But the figures for 1900 imply strongly that the typical graduates of that year in the arts and sciences were men, and a minority of women, already or intending to be teachers in schools, or working or entering work in scientific or technological establishments, governmental or private.

This change in the characteristics of the examinees was paralleled by a very altered institutional pattern. The abandonment of required attendance by candidates at a limited number of institutions clearly boosted the growth of the sheer numbers of examinees after 1858. But the great majority of them, nonetheless, were enrolled in schools or colleges, most of them outside the London area. In March, 1865, it was reported that 27 per cent of those who had taken the matriculation examinations since 1858 had prepared themselves by 'Private study and tuition'.[2] But the registers of graduates later in the century suggest that the proportion of those who prepared for degree examinations entirely by private study was much smaller than at the beginning of the period: overall, it is doubtful whether it constituted as much as 10 per cent of the total. However, those who gained degrees either through private study or through attendance at provincial colleges were fiercely loyal to the role of the University as an examiner of 'external' students, and that loyalty was to be a major factor in decisions about the University's future.

The University undoubtedly gained the patronage, as it were, of a very large number of secondary schools who chose to prepare their pupils to go through the matriculation exercise. It was pressure of numbers which forced the University to arrange for examinations to be held at Owens College in Manchester and at Queen's College, Liverpool, as early as 1859, and later at various other provincial places. The growth in the number of those who took degree examinations was much less spectacular than the growth of those taking matriculation, and preparation for degrees took place, increasingly, in the well-established London colleges and medical schools and in new institutions of higher education, not least those enrolling women. Matriculation and degree examinations were taken in colonies, beginning with Mauritius in 1865, followed by Gibralter, Canada, Australia and the West Indies during the next decade.

After 1858, London was not alone in providing a school-leaving qualification. Nor did it continue to have for much longer a virtual monopoly

---

[2] Evid. of Carpenter to R. Comm. on Education in Schools in England, not comprised within HM's two recent Commissions on Popular Education and Public Schools [hereinafter referred to as the Schools Inquiry Commission], 14 March 1865. PP 1867–68 xxviii.

of the non-Anglican seekers after degrees. Local school examinations were introduced by Oxford and Cambridge in 1858; and, as a result of the abolition of religious tests at Oxford and Cambridge in 1871, it is probable that some of those who would have chosen to take London degrees if they had been barred from entering the ancient universities, preferred to take advantage of the residential facilities and the social and professional status which the Oxbridge colleges conferred. Much larger numbers of prospective candidates must have been lost through the establishment of the federal Victoria University at Manchester, Liverpool and Leeds in 1880.

Even so, the overall demand ensured that there was steady growth in the number of examinees. More important, for its future, than these shifts in clientele, was the increasing isolation of the University of London within the whole untidy, uncertain but dynamic growth of higher education. Despite the scale of its activities, it was an examining board which offered degrees, and was entirely detached from all the teaching institutions which prepared its examinees. But the majority of the 428 full and assistant examiners employed over the years between 1858 and 1900 were drawn from the teaching staffs of other universities, colleges, and medical schools – and many of them were based in London. The University's only activity in the field of research was also based in London, but in a very narrow field – the result of the private endowment of the Brown Animal Sanatory Institution, which began to operate in 1871.

As the size and complexity of the demand for and the provision of higher education in and around London increased, local arguments against the existing nature of the University were expressed ever more vehemently. Inevitably, the visions of what were the most desirable alternatives were, for a long time, matters of passionate disagreement. But, overwhelmingly, there was dissatisfaction and resentment in the colleges and medical schools of London, and there was widespread agreement, especially in the most prestigious institutions, that, whatever the relevance and success of what had been achieved since 1836, the case for having a university as a mere provider of examinations had outlived its welcome. What was wanted, it was claimed, was a 'real' university embracing teaching, research and examination; that it should not be a national and imperial, non-metropolitan institution, but the main focus of higher education in the capital city – a genuine 'University of London'.

But to bring about change was to be a tremendously complex and controversial operation, in no small part because, unlike the other institutions of higher education in England, London was answerable to Parliament and Government. The University was subject to the detailed control of the Treasury over every penny of its expenditure, while its considerable fee income was paid directly into the governmental coffers. Indeed, as numbers grew, the fee income came very close to covering the operational expenses of the institution. There was some discussion in the mid-1880s of the possibility of changing to a grant-in-aid system of financing, but that did not happen until

1901.[3] The Government provided accommodation, which involved moving from part of Burlington House to a new building in Burlington Gardens in 1870, and then, on the eve of the major change in its role, to the Imperial Institute in South Kensington, in 1900. In those quarters worked the tiny handful of civil servants, led by the Registrar, who organised the examinations.

After prolonged and often bitter confrontations, the Charter of the University was replaced by the London University Act, 1898. The Act and subsequent Statutes and Regulations brought into being, towards the end of 1900, a teaching, research and examining university of great complexity, incorporating within it, in a quasi-federal format, the major colleges and medical schools in or close to London, which were to teach 'internal' students. Convocation lost its veto, but retained overwhelming influence over the continuing 'external' side of the new institution, after a lengthy and determined struggle with Government and Parliament.

Any student of the experience of the University of London is heavily indebted to the comprehensive histories of UCL and King's College, respectively by Hale Bellot and Hearnshaw, which were published in 1929; and to Negley Harte's celebratory volume for the 150th anniversary of the founding of the University, which appeared in 1986.[4] Unlike those classic studies, this book, like the writer's *Our Minerva. The Men and Politics of the University of London 1836–1858*, published in 1995, to which it is a sequel, is not a general history. It is concerned with the internal and external politics of the University, and their relation, where relevant, to the political life of the country. It concentrates on the impact of Convocation on the affairs of the University, and especially on the relations between Convocation, Senate, Parliament and Government. And it does not try to cover all the areas of those relationships. In particular, it does not include any close scrutiny of the major controversies about medical and legal education. Both areas were dominated by the determination of the professions to safeguard their internal control of training and qualification to practise. Senate was necessarily involved, and the medical story is well told elsewhere.[5] Convocation was not a compelling influence in

---

[3] Sir Julian Goldsmid claimed that H.C.E. Childers, when Chancellor of the Exchequer in 1884, was sympathetic to the idea of changing to a grant-in-aid system, but Carpenter, who had been Registrar, told his successor, Milman, that he thought the move would be 'inexpedient' unless the grant was 'much more ample' than the Treasury would award. Goldsmid raised the matter in Parliament in 1886, but without effect. UL RC4/24, Carpenter to Milman, 11 June 1884. 3s Parl. Deb. vol. 302, cols 1228–34, 25 February 1886.
[4] H. Hale Bellot, *University College London 1826–1926* (London, 1929), and 'The University of London' in *Victoria County History of Middlesex* I (1969); F.J.C. Hearnshaw, *Centenary History of King's College, London, 1828–1928* (London, 1929); Negley Harte, *The University of London, 1836–1986* (London, 1986).
[5] See, especially, A.M. Cooke, *History of the Royal College of Physicians of London* (London, 1972), vol. 3.

the search for compromises in those particular professional areas. But medical and legal questions were highly significant in many other aspects of the University's progress, and doctors and lawyers played highly influential roles as members of Senate and Convocation.

Part I of the following text is an overview of the personnel of the Senate and of Convocation; an examination of their participation and their increasingly close inter-relationship; and a consideration of those within all camps who constituted the leaders and whose influence was crucial. Part II describes and analyses Convocation's early problems and its impact on the scene from 1858 to 1865. Part III is devoted to the struggle within both Senate and Convocation for the acceptance of women as students and graduates; Part IV follows the experience of the University as a Parliamentary Constituency up to 1886; Part V covers developments within the University concerning secondary education and teacher training. Part VI tells the story of the long-drawn-out search and struggle involving Senate, Convocation, Parliament and Government, which led to the change from an examining and degree awarding authority to a federal university, orthodox in its combination of teaching, examining and research, but still *sui generis* in its twentieth-century combination of internal and external study, and in the width and complexity of its metropolitan, national and colonial operations.

# Part I

*The Political Arena*

# 1

# *The Senate*

Neither the Charter of 1858, nor the subsequent Charter of 1863, nor the Supplemental Charters of 1867 and 1878, changed the overall size of the governing body, the Senate, which had been fixed in the original version, in 1836. Its formal composition continued to be a Chancellor and Vice-Chancellor plus thirty-six Fellows. The Chancellor and the Fellows were appointed by the Crown and held office during good behaviour: the Vice-Chancellor was elected by the Senate from amongst the Fellows, and was subject to annual re-election. However, from 1858 onwards, while all Fellows continued to be appointed by the Crown, the practice began of filling a proportion of vacancies from among persons elected by Convocation. Every other new Fellow appointed after April, 1858, was to be chosen, by the Crown, from three elected nominees of Convocation, until a quarter of the Fellowship – nine Fellows – consisted of Convocation nominees – a quota reached in 1866. Thereafter the elective device was employed to fill one vacancy in four. In what follows, the Fellows appointed after nomination and election by Convocation are described as 'Convocation-nominated'. Those Fellows appointed directly by the Crown are described as 'Crown-chosen'.

As significant as the formal change which brought Convocation nominees on to the Senate was the change in the attitude of Governments, after 1858, to the matter of filling vacancies. For the first two decades of its existence, the Senate had often been well below its full strength. Deaths and retirements reduced the Fellowship by almost a third in the 1840s. The Conservative Government of Sir Robert Peel, from 1841 to 1846, and Lord Derby's two short-lived Conservative Governments in the 1850s, made no appointments. But in Lord John Russell's Administration, six new members were added in 1849–50; and in Lord Palmerston's first spell in Downing Street a new Chancellor and six new Fellows were appointed in 1856–57. Among the latter were the first two London graduates to enter the Senate – Frederick John Wood and William Withey Gull. Just before the 1858 Charter came into effect, they were joined by Charles James Foster, one of the leaders of the graduates, who was to be the first Chairman of Convocation.

From then onwards, the tendency to leave vacancies unfilled for several years disappeared. This happened mainly, perhaps, because of the need to deal immediately with the nominees elected by Convocation. Partly, perhaps, it happened because of an acceptance by the Conservatives that the University could no longer be treated only as a place for Dissenters and as the exclusive concern of Whig/Radical/Liberal interests. Some lowering of the temperature in the religious atmosphere may also have contributed. In 1874, Benjamin Jowett was still very conscious of the divison of the nation, 'politically and socially', because of the 'cleavage between church and dissent'.[1] But as early as 1865 – six years before the final abolition of religious tests at Oxford and Cambridge – Grant Duff, later to become a Fellow, when pressing the claims of the University of London in the House of Commons, had remarked that

> There was a time when its name was a watchword of party, but that stage of its history has long passed by, and one would no more expect now-a-days to hear of any party opposition to its pretentions than to those of the Board of Customs.[2]

Whatever exact weight should be given to these and other factors, the Home Office was scrupulous, after 1858, in its early attention to keeping the Senate fully manned, irrespective of which political party was in office. Roughly equal numbers of new Fellows were appointed by Liberal and Conservative Administrations between 1858 and 1899.

Of the 119 senators who held office between 1858 and 1900, thirty-nine had been appointed before the new Charter took effect in April, 1858. Of the eighty who first served after 1858, twenty-four were Convocation-nominated: but additionally, among the Crown-chosen senators, another twenty were London graduates, and, as will be seen, on their appointment as Fellows they became *ex officio* members of Convocation's leading group, its Annual Committee. Thus, if Wood, Gull and Foster are included, forty-seven of the 119 members of the Senate, between 1858 and 1900, were London graduates and members of Convocation.

However, the growth of the proportion of home-grown graduates on the Senate was a rather slow process. It was natural enough that only as the early students of the University achieved professional prominence did their representation in the Senate increase. Foster, who had been appointed a Fellow in 1858, resigned in 1863. Gull and Wood, who had been appointed in 1856, were to continue as Senators until 1889–91. But from 1863 until 1875–76, they were the only London graduates, other than the Convocation-nominated. Then they were joined by a new, Crown-chosen London graduate, Julian Goldsmid, whose arrival meant that twelve Fellows – one third of the

---

[1] J.P.C. Roach, 'Universities and the National Intelligentsia', in *Victorian Studies* III, 2, December 1959, p. 136.

[2] 3s Parl. Deb., vol. 179, cols 1209–16, 2 June 1865. Grant Duff used the Board of Customs because the supply debate in which he was speaking was about government departments, and it was accepted that, in effect, the University of London was a government department.

Fellowship – were London University men – nine nominated by Convocation and three directly chosen by the Crown.

From 1883 onwards, though, the appointment of London graduates to fill vacancies became more frequent. Between 1883 and 1898 the Crown appointed eighteen London graduates as opposed to only eleven others. In 1892, shortly after taking office as Chairman of Convocation, Edward Henry Busk claimed that

> . . . three quarter of the Senate appointed directly by the Crown are very largely members of Convocation. The Crown does graciously take this into consideration, and of recent years it has appointed members of Convocation in almost every instance.[3]

This was a slight exaggeration: but at the beginning of the 1890s the Crown-chosen London graduates and the Convocation-nominated, together, constituted half the Senate: and, at the end of the decade, they filled almost two-thirds of the seats. The first London graduate to become Chancellor, Lord Herschell, held office from 1893 to 1899. The first London graduate to become Vice-Chancellor, from 1880 to 1883, was Sir George Jessel: two others, Sir Julian Goldsmid and Sir Henry Roscoe, served between 1896 and the end of the century.

There were no changes made in the membership of the Senate when the new Charter took effect on 14 April 1858. But in October, 1900, when the new constitution, authorised by the University of London Act, 1898, was introduced, only the then Chancellor and Vice-Chancellor, and twelve of the thirty-six Fellows, were included in the new Senate. All the other Fellows who served up to 1900 retained their Fellowships for life, but without any voting rights. There were sixty-six Senators whose total membership was completed between 1858 and 1900. Only one person spanned practically the whole period: Timothy Smith Osler was appointed in January, 1859, after nomination by Convocation, and served until October, 1900.

From the outset, the Senate of the University of London had been composed, very largely, of upper middle and professional class men. From 1858 onwards, professional representation became even stronger, and was equally dominant in each of the sub-divisions of Crown-chosen, Convocation-nominated, London graduates, and other members. With the exception of a small handful from aristocratic families, members of the Senate were usually the sons of bankers, merchants, clergymen, lawyers, and doctors, with a smaller contingent

[3] Evid. to R. Comm. on Draft Charter for the proposed Gresham University in London, with dissentient and other notes [hereinafter referred to as the Cowper Commission], 2 June 1892. PP 1894 xxxiv, 541.

who were the offspring of senior civil servants, colonial officials, army officers, architects, painters, publishers, scientists, engineers and academics.

Though their religious affiliations are not always easy to establish, it would seem that only a minority of them were Jews, Roman Catholics, Quakers, Unitarians, and members of other non-Anglican churches. Information about schooling is also incomplete, but we know that a few were educated privately; that only about a dozen attended the great public schools; that about the same number attended non-Anglican or strictly non-denominational schools – no less than seven of the London graduates were pupils at University College School; and that a sizeable contingent were enrolled in grammar and minor public schools.

Their higher education is fully documented. Of the eighty senators appointed after the 1858 Charter took effect, forty-four were London graduates. No less than twenty-six of those had been students of University College London: four came from King's; eight had studied for medical degrees at one or other of the great teaching hospitals. William Turner Thiselton-Dyer, Thomas Bateman Napier and William Augustus Tilden took their London degree examinations after private study; John Hopkinson, Grant Duff, and John Fletcher Moulton took them while enrolled as students at Oxford or Cambridge. Of the thirty-six Senators who were not London graduates and were appointed after 1858, twenty-two studied at other universities at home or abroad. Only four did not attend a university or did not take a degree. Sir James Paget, an eminent surgeon and teacher of medicine, who became Vice-Chancellor, trained at St Bartholomew's Hospital in the days before the University existed. T.H. Huxley studied at Charing Cross Hospital, but did not take a London degree.

Of the eighty Senators appointed after 1858, some twenty-five were judges, barristers, solicitors or teachers of law; and another twenty were medical men, almost all of whom were involved, to a considerable degree, in medical teaching. But perhaps the most striking feature of the Senate's membership was that well over half of it was made up of men who were directly involved in education and other intellectual and cultural pursuits, either as university professors, schoolmasters, or educational administrators; or were Government scientists, men of letters, or artists. Thirty of them had practical experience as examiners for the University before they joined the Senate.

There was, in fact, a steady growth of the professional educational contingent, helped in part by the fact that almost half of the Convocation-nominated Fellows were academics – mainly scientists or medicos. No less than thirty-eight of the eighty Senators appointed after 1858 were Fellows of the Royal Society, though six of them were not scientists. Of the forty whose careers were made very largely in university teaching or administration, fifteen were medical professors and another fifteen were scientists, engineers or mathematicians. While two or three Fellows who were heads of Colleges were theologians, and Lord Acton and Sir Henry Maine were distinguished historians and legal authorities, the only Senators who were unequivocally 'Arts' men were Sir Hubert Parry, the musician, and the Greek scholar Sir

Richard Jebb. Neither Parry nor Jebb was appointed until nearly the end of the century – Parry in 1895 and Jebb in 1899.

Despite the high proportion of lawyers appointed to the Senate after 1858, hardly any could be defined as having been a full-time university teacher of Law, though a small number of them served as examiners before their appointment as Fellows. Several of them, however, were politicians, primarily, and formed part of the group of over twenty MPs and peers who sat in Parliament during at least part of their tenure as Senators. Ten of them held ministerial office, seven at Cabinet level. No less than five of Gladstone's Cabinet, in 1868–74, sat in the Senate – Cardwell, Goschen, Granville, Kimberley (who had been appointed a Fellow as Baron Wodehouse, in 1859), and Lowe. This political and ministerial *cadre* was enlarged by the service after 1858 of several pre-1858 appointees, including Lord Granville and the 15th Earl of Derby (who had joined the Senate as Lord Stanley in 1856), who were Chancellors until 1891 and 1893, respectively, to name only the most prominent.

Though the professions were so well represented, there were very few members of the world of business. Lord Overstone, one of the country's richest financiers, had been appointed before 1858. After 1858 two bankers appeared – Robert Nicholas Fowler and Sir John Lubbock, 4th Bt.; but both had very mixed careers. Fowler was an MP for seventeen years, a major organiser of the Conservative Party in the City, and twice Lord Mayor of London. Lubbock, son of the first Vice-Chancellor, had serious scientific interests, became the fifth Vice-Chancellor, and was an MP for twenty-four years, twenty of them as the University's representative. In 1890 Sir Albert Rollit was appointed, but he, too, had a mixed career as a solicitor, a highly successful ship owner, and an MP.

The roll of the Senate thus continued, from 1858 until 1900, to be dominated by professional men, but with a steadily increasing representation of those whose principal occupations were in the practice or supervision of education. In effect, the professoriate became a significant group. Legal and medical practitioners were prominent, but there was a notable growth in the number of scientists. While there was a strong presence of men with non-Anglican affiliations, alongside a much smaller number of Anglican divines, religious concern appeared to become a relatively unimportant consideration in the matter of appointment. On the other hand, there continued to be a notable 'lay', or 'establishment', or 'political', or 'governmental' element in the overall membership, though smaller than had been the case from 1836 to 1858. In the national political context, the partisan complexion of the whole body was, throughout, more Liberal than Conservative; but particularly after 1885, there were many Fellows whose sympathies were clearly with Conservative and Liberal Unionist positions.

There is plenty of evidence, here and there, of Prime Ministers and Home Secretaries seeking names of suitable people to appoint to the Senate, and of Chancellors, Vice-Chancellors and Fellows themselves making suggestions. A typical example is a letter of Lord Stanley, who succeeded his father as Earl of Derby in 1869, and was made Foreign Secretary by Disraeli in 1874. In the following year he wrote to the Home Secretary, Richard Assheton Cross, that vacancies to the Senate should be 'filled by really competent men: we are weaker of late years than we used to be, especially in regard of scholarship'. And he commented on a list of names put forward by the Chancellor, Lord Granville:

> I don't think Carnarvon could attend. If out of office he would probably be out of London. The same applies to the Duke of Bedford, who is very seldom in town. Lord Lyttelton is rather more mixed up in ecclesiastical affairs than is desirable on the London University – Lord Aberdare you know better than I. He never seemed to me very competent. Arthur Russell would do. He is much in town, studies, likes that sort of work, and is a thoroughly cultivated man: very little of a politician, though an MP. Lord Rayleigh's degree is in his favour. He devotes himself to science altogether. He is young but might be suitable, if he would serve and attend.[4]

No doubt, too, there were people seriously keen to participate in educational matters who would have made their bids for places through whatever channels were available to them. But there is at least one case – and therefore it is reasonable to think that there may have been others – where the bid for a place was apparently made with an eye firmly on political advancement. Just after the 1858 Charter took effect, Fowler, a UCL graduate and member of the College's Council who, at the age of thirty, was partner in a City bank, wrote to the Conservative MP, Viscount Ingestre:

> I understand there are some vacancies in the Senate of the University of London which are to be filled up by Mr Walpole. Now being an MA of the University and having taken honours in both Mathematics and Classics I think I have a claim somewhat similar to one that was recognised by Sir George Grey in three appointments he made. [i.e. the appointments of Wood and Gull in 1856 and of Foster earlier in 1858.] I am aware that the Home Office is going to allow a member of the Senate to be elected by the graduates but they have other vacancies to fill up. In the event of the University ever being represented in Parliament the appointment might possibly give one some little influence. I should feel greatly obliged if you could help me in the matter.

Ingestre passed this on to the Home Secretary, Spencer Walpole. Fowler, he explained, was

> . . . a strong partisan . . . who subscribed very largely to Lord Chelsea's late election, and means to come into Parliament as a supporter of the present Government. He

---

[4]  BL Add Mss 51266, Derby to Cross, 9 August and 12 September, 1875.

is a Quaker but curiously enough strongly opposed to abolition of church rates . . .
Mr Fowler subscribed £500 to Chelsea's election fund and worked like a horse.[5]

But Fowler only reached the Senate as a Convocation-nominated Fellow in
1864, and sat until his death thirty years later. He fought two parliamentary
elections unsuccessfully in 1865, but sat in the Commons from 1868 to 1874,
and from 1880 to 1894. As we have seen, he reorganised the Conservative
Party in the City of London and became Lord Mayor. He received a Baronetage
in 1885.

It is clear that the Senate was a body which could call, in its membership,
on substantial elements of political expertise in the parliamentary and
governmental arena, and within the medical, legal and scientific worlds. It has
to be seen how such expertise was used in the Senate's devotion to educational
concerns, and in providing leadership to the University community.

[5] HO 45/6434, Fowler to Ingestre, 11 May, Ingestre to Walpole, 12 May 1858.

# 2

# Convocation: membership and participation

Convocation immediately became a major force in the University's affairs, continuing to exert the pressure which had been exercised for the previous ten years, with campaigning zeal, by the Graduates' Committee. But the early ambition of the graduates, which had been, in effect, to make Convocation the governing body of the University, had been severely disappointed. In addition to being authorised to regulate its own business, the significant powers given to the new body were to nominate candidates for up to a quarter of the seats on the Senate: to veto the acceptance of any new Charter or the surrender of the 1858 and any subsequent Charter: and to discuss and declare its opinion on any matter relating to the University. However, the new Charter also provided that 'Except, as expressly provided, the Convocation shall not be entitled to interfere in, or have any control over, the affairs of the University.' In addition, some basic services to Convocation, such as registration and the fixing and collection of fees, were handled by and in conjunction with the University's administration.

As many of those who had fought long and hard for the establishment of Convocation were to be prominent in its affairs for another twenty or thirty years, it is understandable that there was for a considerable period an underlying resentment of the relatively weak constitutional powers which the new body had been given. At the same time, the failure to achieve more, initially, probably intensified the efforts of the leaders of Convocation to make as much as they could of such opportunities as were offered to them. In fact, the considerable influence which Convocation did exert was due in part to the persistence with which they put forward demands and ideas about University policies. But perhaps it was due, even more, as we have already seen, to what might be called the infiltration of the Senate by members of Convocation, either through the electoral process, or through the increasing willingness of the Crown to appoint London graduates.

The Senate, essentially, was a small, executive group. Convocation, in contrast, was an organisation envisaged as becoming an increasingly large, representative body. At the outset, Convocation was open to all Doctors and Masters, to Bachelors of Laws and Medicine of two years' standing, and to Bachelors of Arts of three years' standing, on payment of a membership fee of ten shillings and six pence a year, or three guineas for life. In 1868 the annual fee was reduced to five shillings, and could be compounded for life for

£1, but there was no further change in the rules governing membership until well into the twentieth century, save for the admission of women graduates from 1882. The Senate was made responsible for keeping the register of Convocation and for controlling the removal or reinstatement of members. Graduates, when fulfilling the requirement for membership, did not have to apply, but were registered and sent a bill. Not surprisingly, quite a few objected and did not pay, but from 1859 to 1863 their names remained on the register for two years: thereafter the names of those who did not pay were removed after six months.[1]

Complete and exact figures of membership for each year are not readily available. The University printed a list of graduates eligible for Convocation, in 1858–59, which included the names of just under 950 men, alive and resident in the United Kingdom. That compares with the award, up to and including the year 1858, of 1561 degrees since the first were granted in 1839. The difference must be accounted for, largely, by the number of graduates who took more than one degree – BA and MA, LLB and LLD, MB and MD – and by the number who had not achieved the requisite years' standing. Given the later addition of new Bachelor's, Master's and Doctor's degrees in Science, Surgery and Music, and given the loss of graduates through death, it is reasonable to suggest that the number eligible for membership at any one time was always rather less than two-thirds of the total of degrees granted. Thus by 1900 the record shows that nearly 13,500 people had passed final examinations for degrees: and in 1903, when the last of the students enrolled under the pre-1900 regulations graduated, there were about ten thousand names listed, though duplication of entries in some degrees must have inflated the number somewhat. Overall, it seems reasonable to claim that those eligible for Convocation began at less than a thousand in 1859, and in 1900 numbered about nine thousand.[2]

Eligibility for membership was no guarantee of an intention to accept it, however. Though the University listed 950 as eligible in 1858–59, and though, according to the regulations, names were not removed for non-payment until two years had elapsed, Convocation's historians, Dunsheath and Miller claim, without quoting a source, an 'initial membership of about 400' – only some 42 per cent. Membership figures crop up from time to time in various documents, and some of the most reliable are those compiled for

---

[1] The details of the formal processes relating to Convocation are admirably summarised in Dunsheath and Miller, *Convocation in the University of London. The first hundred years* (London, 1958), ch. III.

[2] These figures are drawn from the detailed list of examinations taken and passed, published in Senate Minutes annually, and from the lists included in the official *History of the University*, published in 1912. The names of all graduates and undergraduates since 1839 are listed in three *Registers* published in 1890, 1899 and 1901 – the total is almost 39,000, of whom only a little more than a quarter are graduates, the rest being successfully matriculated.

each of the parliamentary elections from 1868 onwards. Graduates had to be members of Convocation to be eligible to vote. Thus we have membership of 1160 in 1868; 1225 in 1869; 1485 in 1874; 1570 in 1879; 2579 in 1886; 2700 in 1888; 3700 in 1893; at the beginning of 1896, 'about 4000', and at the change in the nature of the University, in 1900, 'nearly 5000'.[3] From this data it would seem that membership of Convocation floated between a little less and a little more than half of the eligible graduates.

In 1869 a list of Convocation members showed that, of the 1225, 347 had medical degrees, and 295 were ministers of religion. Only 130 boasted London law degrees, but from their addresses it is clear that many more were lawyers, who had graduated with BA degrees. No less than 520 lived in London postal districts, and a considerable additional number had homes within easy reach of London. A comparable list in 1894, with a total of 3818 names, showed that 858 had medical degrees, and that 485 were ministers of religion. 355 held law degrees, but because of the far larger proportion of members living and working outside London, there is no safe way of suggesting, more than roughly, what number of the members were practising law without having taken a London law degree. Some 1207 of the whole 3818 lived within the London postal districts.

Although their share of the total dropped nearly 6 per cent between 1869 and 1894, the medical people must have comprised about 25 per cent of the total membership throughout. It is impossible to claim a comparably accurate percentage for the lawyers, but an educated guess would give them not less than 20 per cent. The ministers of religion definitely lost ground during the period: they had almost 25 per cent of the total in 1869 but only 12½ per cent in 1894. Taken together, the medicos, the lawyers and the ministers of religion comprised nearly 70 per cent of Convocation in 1869 and about 55 per cent in 1894. The published list for 1869 does not give a satisfactory basis for identifying any other group: but the 1894 list contains clear evidence of the presence of at least 350 men and women engaged in school or college teaching. That number, representing only 10 per cent of the total membership, is almost certainly a considerable underestimate, and as with the lawyers, it is highly likely that the percentage could be doubled, safely, in attempting to calculate the distribution of members over professions.[4]

What opportunities were opened to graduates by the establishment of Convocation, and how much were those opportunities taken up?

---

[3] The figures given are taken and calculated from data in UL CN 2/1, 2/3/1–3. Evid. of E.A. Busk to Cowper Commission, PP 1894 xxxiv, 2 June 1892, 540, 549; 2 February 1893, 20780; Evid. of F.J. Wood to R. Comm. to enquire whether a new university is required for the Advancement of Higher Education in London [hereinafter referred to as the Selborne Commission], PP 1889 xxxix, 7 July 1888. Minutes of Convocation, 21 January 1896. Dunsheath and Miller, *Convocation in the University of London*, ch. XIII.
[4] UL CN 2/3/1 & 3, List of Members of Convocation, 1869 & 1894.

No doubt from the outset, for many graduates the major attraction of belonging to Convocation must have been the prospect, and then the privilege, of having a vote – for many of them a second vote – for a Member of Parliament. But though the University gained its parliamentary seat in 1868, there were only three contested elections during the next thirty-two years – in 1880, 1886 and 1900. In those elections, participation dropped steadily – from 79 per cent, through 71 per cent, to 61.7 per cent, the numbers voting on each occasion being 1549, 1830, and 2720, respectively.

After parliamentary elections, the next wide opportunities for members of Convocation to take an active part in its affairs were the elections held to nominate three candidates for each vacancy in a quarter of the Senate seats. Until 1863, though nominations of candidates could be made by any six members, voting was restricted to those who attended the relevant general meeting of Convocation. The mode of election was 'by open voting by means of signed voting papers', to quote from the original Standing Orders. There was no prohibition of plural voting, and it seems certain that, as was formally introduced later, each voting paper listed all the candidates, and the voter signed against those he approved. At the meeting on 10 November 1858, sixteen men were nominated for places on the list of six members whose names would be submitted to the Crown, and from whom two would be chosen to join the Senate. Less than two hundred members were present, but they cast 876 votes: the six winners, in order of success, each received 94, 93, 82, 78, 74 and 68 votes. The Home Secretary set a precedent, always followed thereafter, of recommending the appointment of the candidates who received the most votes. Thus Thomas Smith Osler and John Storrar became Fellows of the University as a result of the support of just less than half of those present and voting at Convocation's second meeting.

Postal voting was introduced in 1863, so that living well away from London did not pose an impossible barrier to participation. At the same time the Standing Orders were amended to include a specific procedure, formalising existing practice, whereby each member received a voting paper listing the names of candidates and a direction 'to write his name against the names of the Candidates for whom he votes and to strike out the names of those for whom he does not vote . . . ' There is some evidence that the second requirement was often not met, and that considerable numbers of voting papers were declared invalid as a result.

But there was no repetition of the scale of the competition for places on Senate in 1858. The number of candidates nominated for each of the subsequent elections varied only between three and five for the three places. However, the introduction of postal voting did encourage a substantial participation beyond that of those who attended meetings. From 1885 we have figures of members present at the meetings at which the voting was decided. Those figures can be laid alongside the votes cast from 1885 to 1896 in eight contests. The voters knew that the candidate who got the most votes would, automatically, be appointed to the Senate. When there were only three candidates – in seven of the eight contests – the major motive for voting was to express a preference as to which candidate should join the Senate. No doubt there was some plural voting, for any of a possible variety of complicated reasons – for instance, there may have been those who wished to object to one candidate but were indifferent as between two others, and so on. But the strong likelihood must have been – alas, there are no papers extant to prove it – that most of the ballot papers returned would have given a vote to only one candidate. If that was the case, then the extent of the postal vote was striking.

If we make the very conservative assumption that 80 per cent of the votes were cast for only one candidate, and that all those who attended the meetings voted, then the ballots which must have been posted constituted between 73 per cent and 95 per cent of the totals in the eight elections. Using the same percentage, 80 per cent, of the votes cast, as representing the number who returned their ballots, we can calculate, very roughly, that the 'turn out' varied from about 25 per cent to rather less than 40 per cent of the total membership. We have seen that participation in the parliamentary election of 1886 was some 71 per cent, but, if the above assumptions are valid, participation in the election of three nominees for a place on the Senate, in the same year, was only about 31 per cent.

Because of the lack of hard evidence, particularly as to the extent of plural voting, it is impossible to make a definite assertion about how many members of Convocation took part in the process of getting their nominees on to the Senate. In the early part of our period the number of votes cast was quite low – less than five hundred allotted to all candidates during the 1860s. In eight of the fourteen recorded elections from 1871, more than a thousand votes were cast, including the highest figure of 2070 in June, 1890. But these figures are inclusive of votes cast for all candidates – in 1890 the distribution between the four candidates was 990, 626, 274 and 180. In estimating the number of members who voted, that total of 2070 has been reduced by 20 per cent to allow for any plural voting.

Overall, it is probably safe to suggest that while a half to three-quarters of Convocation exercised their right to vote in the election for their Member of Parliament, not much more than a third were sufficiently interested to vote for their representation in the Senate of the University. These percentages of participation are by no means disreputable in any overall context of the practice of representative democracy. But if the numbers voting were modest, so were the numbers of those competing for places.

The twenty-three elections held between 1858 and 1898 produced three nominees on each occasion, except the first, in 1858, when six names were submitted to the Crown as prospective new members of Senate. The 1858 election was the only one which attracted numerous candidates – no less than sixteen. There were five contenders in 1860, and on six other occasions there were four. But for fifteen elections, only three candidates put themselves forward. Moreover, all but one of the contests which produced four or five candidates were held by 1882: at the remaining nine elections, there were only three candidates at each, save for the contest in 1890, which attracted four. And in the earlier years it was common for candidates to persist in their attempts to win nomination. Among those who won Convocation's nomination, eight made it at the second attempt. Up to about 1880, there is a certain suggestion of 'Buggins's turn' in the whole operation. Among those who never won the first place, six tried twice and one, three times. And among the defeated were five who subsequently were appointed to the Senate by the Crown.

In short, in twenty-three elections there were only fifty-seven candidates for the twenty-four places: sixteen of the fifty-seven stood in the inaugural exercise in 1858. Thus only forty-one men competed in twenty-two elections thereafter – those ambitious for Fellowships were not numerous. The twenty-four victors became Fellows, but so did five defeated candidates who were appointed Fellows by the Crown in later years. Just over half of those who stood, therefore, achieved membership of the Senate.

We can turn, now, to the two remaining exercises in participation offered by Convocation to its members – attendance at meetings, and involvement in the choice of leaders.

The Annual Meeting of Convocation was held in May, but there were additional meetings in all but eight years. There were two meetings in each of seventeen years; three in each of twelve; four in each of four; and in 1895 Convocation was called no less than seven times. On one or two occasions a meeting required a second session. It was not until 1885 that the number of members present was included in the minutes. Division lists were only published from 1874–75. Prior to 1885, therefore, the only indicators of the numbers present in the previous decade were the records of voting in divisions. In the few years before postal voting was permitted, attendance can be estimated from the counts of shows of hands in choosing the Chairman, the Secretary, and members of the Annual Committee.

The likelihood of numerous members travelling long distances to attend must be regarded as slight. But though exact figures are not available, we have seen that rather more than two-fifths of the members in 1869, and just less than a third of them in 1894, lived within the London postal districts. It is very probable that they, and those members who lived within an easy railway journey of the capital, comprised a half of the total membership. At the inaugural meeting, on 4 May, 1858, 153 members signed the attendance register, and it was reported that at the second there were 194 present.[5] If we accept the notion that the initial membership numbered only about four hundred, then those attendances imply that a very high proportion of the members based in and within easy reach of London were present.

---

[5] UL CN 1/2, Dunsheath and Miller, *Convocation*, p. 188; *LUM*, December 1858.

Thereafter, as membership grew, the percentage of those who turned out, whether from London or elsewhere, dropped steadily. Until the middle 1870s, while membership was still relatively small, it would seem likely that meetings rarely attracted more than a hundred, although in 1877–78 there were divisions which produced from 224 to 372 votes. A decade later, in July, 1888, the Chairman felt that two hundred would have been 'a full meeting', and in 1892 his successor stated that two hundred was an average attendance.[6] But there were great fluctuations in the years from 1885 to 1900: attendance exceeded 250 on only six out of forty-eight meetings, though twice it failed to produce a quorum. The lowest, quorate turn-out was sixty-six, but the two quite exceptional highest were 733 in 1891, and 784 in 1896. Those two very unusual meetings each attracted approximately 20 per cent of the total membership of Convocation. But no meeting between 1896 and 1900 was attended by more than 160, and an average of two hundred in the last decade of the century meant only about a 5 per cent turn-out, or perhaps 10 per cent of those members living in or within easy reach of London. Crises apart, attendance was very moderate.

[6] Evid. of Wood to Selborne Commission, 7 July 1888: E.H. Busk to Cowper Commission, 2 June 1892, 672.

# 3

# Convocation: the Annual Committee

Convocation devised its internal political arrangements in the months after its inauguration. The Charter of 1858 had provided that the Chairman should be elected for three years, and would be eligible for re-election. Convocation decided to elect its Clerk every year. In addition there was to be an elected Annual Committee, initially with thirty-two members, but enlarged in 1862 by the addition, *ex officio*, of any member of Convocation who was a Fellow. In 1862 this meant only seven additional, *ex officio*, members, but from the end of the 1880s onwards there were never less than twenty. From its inception until 1896, the thirty-two elected members of the Annual Committee were chosen by two groups of graduates – sixteen from those with degrees in Arts and Laws, and sixteen from those qualified in Medicine and Science: but the Science graduates only came on the scene in 1865. The two groups of sixteen operated as sub-committees to deal with most of the affairs of Convocation. From 1896, the title was changed from Annual to Standing Committee, and its total elected membership was increased to thirty-six, nine from each of the Faculties of Arts, Laws, Medicine and Science.

Any member of Convocation could be nominated to serve as Chairman, as Clerk, or to sit on the Annual Committee, but the choice from among those nominated was made only by the members present at the May meeting of Convocation.

Though there were four Chairmen and three Clerks during the years from 1858 to 1900, there were only two contested elections. In 1864 John Storrar became Chairman by defeating James Walter Smith: the voting was 121 to forty-two. In 1876, Henry Ebenezer Allen beat Talfourd Ely by two votes – 108 to 106 – to become Clerk. Once in office, no Chairman or Clerk was ever challenged when re-nomination was needed.

There was more competition for places on the Annual Committee, but in most years it was on a small scale. In 1859 and 1860, the nomination of exactly thirty-two candidates was moved on each occasion by Francis Sibson, and accepted without question. In time for the election of 1861, a Standing Order had been adopted whereby nominations should be made by five or more members. This procedure produced exactly sixteen medical men and seventeen graduates in Arts and Laws, nominated as a group by six members, all of whom were among the nominees. In addition, another five members nominated an eighteenth candidate – Thomas Dunbar Ingram – for a place among the Arts and Laws group. At the meeting, one of the Arts and Laws nominees withdrew his name. The medical group was then approved automatically, but the Chairman took a show of hands on each of the seventeen nominees for Arts and Laws places: Ingram was not elected.

In 1862, when Convocation agreed to put all its members who were Fellows on to the Annual Committee, *ex officio*, several members of the previous year's Committee, who were already on the Senate, automatically continued to serve. The timing of this innovation was probably responsible for the fact that only twelve medical men and thirteen from Arts and Laws graduates were nominated by the time the meeting began. Four more medics were nominated on the spot, and the whole sixteen were then approved. But six members were nominated for the three vacancies in the Arts and Laws group: each of them was voted on by show of hands, *seriatim*.

The process in 1863 produced only thirty-two nominees, automatically approved; in 1864 there were contests because eighteen were nominated for medical places and twenty-three for the Arts and Laws category. This was the last occasion when the choice was made by show of hands. Henceforward voting slips, in the form of complete lists of nominees, were issued to members attending, and they deleted the names of those they did not wish to see elected. Scrutineers were appointed, and voting slips accepted until late in the meeting.

In 1865 and 1866 elections were not needed for the medical group, for which only sixteen men stood. In the following year, only eighteen Arts and Laws men were nominated. During the next thirty years, there were no elections needed in the Medicine and Science group on seven occasions, and none for the Arts and Laws group on four occasions. This means that, in thirteen of the thirty-eight years, 1859 to 1896, there were no contested elections for Medical and Science places; and none for Arts and Laws places in seven years.

There was a very moderate amount of competition for the sixteen places in fifteen of the annual elections for Medicine and Science places, when there were from seventeen to nineteen candidates; and the same numbers stood in seventeen elections for Arts and Laws. There were elections to choose between twenty to twenty-four candidates for the sixteen seats, in seven years in Medicine and Science, and in eight years in Arts and Laws. But only in 1894 and 1895 were there twice the number of candidates than there were places to fill: thirty-three and thirty-one stood for the sixteen places for Medicine and Science, and twenty-nine and thirty-five for Arts and Laws, in those years.

When the Standing Orders were amended in 1896 to provide for the replacement of the Annual by the Standing Committee, the future election of nine members from each of the Faculties of Arts, Laws, Medicine and Science was so arranged that those elected would sit for three years, that one-third of the number would retire in rotation, and that members would have votes for not more than three names on each list of candidates. In the initial election of 1897, for nine places in each group, and in the three subsequent years for such vacancies as arose, there were only eight contests, and none of them attracted more than two candidates additional to the number of places to be filled.

These annual elections attracted 1528 nominations – 1435 up to 1896, which produces an average, over those thirty-seven years, of just below thirty-nine per year for thirty-two places. But long service and frequent re-election ensured that only 196 members served. Some of them were nominated several times before succeeding in being elected. There were only sixty-one others, sharing eighty-eight nominations, who never won a place, and twenty of the sixty-one only stood in one or more of the three years, 1893–95. Thus in the previous thirty-four years, there were only forty-one unsuccessful candidates – further evidence of the low level of competition for membership.

The rather high proportion of years in which there was either no need for an election, or only a need to choose between less than twenty-five people to fill sixteen places in each of the groups, implies that very often such jockeying for places as took place occurred before Convocation met, and that there was, in all probability, often a need to find enough people willing to stand. It was rare for there to be full-blooded competition. The number of votes cast at meetings when attendance was of average size usually reflected fairly closely the numbers present. But when major controversy brought larger than usual attendances, the numbers voting was near to the figure of average turn-out. In May, 1891, when 733 members were present, the range of votes for Medicine and Science candidates was only 181–131, and for the Arts and Laws candidates, 189–160. The choice of the Annual Committee was clearly left to those who were regular in their attendance.

The practice which emerges from these tedious statistics is that the choice of the Chairmen, Clerks, and members of the Annual/Standing Committee, which had to be made by those who attended the annual meeting in May, was dominated by a very small group of members. Those who tried to become, and those who did become Convocation's leaders, were selected – and to no small extent self-selected – from among the overwhelmingly London-based members who turned up, regularly, in May and comprised, on average, perhaps 5 per cent of the total membership. It might well be thought that no member who really wanted to join the Annual Committee would fail to do so, even if he, or she, were defeated once or twice and had to wait a year or two. One could conclude that Convocation was run, more usually than in many democratic institutions, by those who wanted to run it; and that at any one time the group from which effective leadership emerged was based in London and was never more than about forty to fifty strong.

The system of annual election, even from what we have seen was a very small pool of members, ensured that a much larger number of people served on the Annual Committee of Convocation than were members of Senate. It is possible to say 'people' rather than 'men', because Sophie Bryant, Grace Augusta Howell, Alice Elizabeth Lee and Mary Ann Scharlieb were elected to the Committee during the 1890s. No woman, however, reached the Senate during our period.

From 1859 until 1900, there were 221 members of the Annual Committee. There was, however, a notable overlap of membership with the Senate. Over the forty-one years, forty-seven men – over a fifth of the members of the Annual Committee – also served on the Senate. But twenty-five of the forty-seven were members of Convocation who only became *ex officio* members of the Annual Committee on joining the Senate. The other twenty-two were among the 196 members of Convocation elected to the Annual Committee: when they became Senators they, too, retained their Annual Committee places, *ex officio*.

It has been possible to find details of the occupations of the fathers of only about a quarter of the 174 elected members of the Annual Committee who were never Senators. But taken together with much fuller, though by no means complete, information about their schooling, it can be said confidently that the vast majority of the 174 came from social backgrounds similar to those of most of the Senators, already discussed. They were overwhelmingly the products of professional class homes, perhaps on average a little more modest than those in which many of the Fellows had been raised. Almost none of them was a pupil at any of the famous public schools: at least 10 per cent attended recognisably denominational schools of the Dissenting and Roman Catholic communities. Geography dictated that many would be Londoners: no less than twenty-five were students at University College School, and a dozen more were enrolled at other schools in the metropolitan area.

No less than eighty out of the 174 non-senatorial members of the Annual Committee were graduates of University College London. If to them are added the twenty-eight Fellows who also graduated from UCL, then the College supplied 108 men – just under half of the Annual Committee. King's College provided only twenty non-senatorial members: the London teaching hospitals, other than those associated with UCL and Kings, twenty-seven. Some nineteen took their London degrees after private study, using the 'external' examination route provided in the Charter of 1858. Most of the remaining group of about thirty were drawn mainly from graduates who had prepared for their examinations either at some of the Dissenting colleges long-connected with the University, or from the more recently created scientific institutions like the Schools of Chemistry and of Mines.

There is no definite data available about the occupations of some twenty-five of the 174 non-senatorial members of the Annual Committee. It is probable that many of the twenty-five were schoolteachers. However, for the others the information is clear, though to some extent complicated. Doctors and lawyers predominated – sixty-four of the first and forty-six of the second – accounting between them for 63 per cent of all the non-senatorial members. Another twenty-four had qualified in science, engineering or mathematics. The remainder – almost all of whom qualified with Arts degrees – are not easy to classify: some eight were ministers of religion – mainly

Nonconformists – several of whom combined teaching at secondary or tertiary level with their religious duties: another dozen were mostly men who had mixed careers in school or college teaching or academic administration; Sidney Webb, then a junior civil servant, is listed in this varied group.

What is most noteworthy about this collection of London graduates is the high proportion of them who were professionally involved in education. At least seventy of them taught in universities, or in medical schools and colleges preparing students for university degrees: and at least ten – and conceivably another fifteen or so – were schoolmasters. Within that group of possibly nearly a hundred, a third were London University examiners. The medical men formed by far the largest block, consisting of about fifty university teachers, almost all based at one or other of the London teaching hospitals. The lawyers, on the other hand, were far less involved: only four or five can be defined as university teachers, though nine examined for the University of London. At least seven of the scientists and engineers were university professors, and we have noted above some twenty graduates who had mixed careers as school or college teachers.

In addition, some twenty three of the Fellows who were *ex officio* members were also academics. Thus well over half of the total membership of the Annual Committee of Convocation were teachers – most at university level – and to them must be added a small group of scientists employed outside the universities and predominantly involved in research. Not far short of two-thirds of the members of Convocation's main committee, therefore, made their living by teaching and research.

# 4

# *Personages, officers, and examiners*

The Senate and the Annual/Standing Committee of Convocation provided the University with its political activists, from whom, in turn, were drawn almost all its political elite. But before analysing their relationship, their attendance and their participation, it is as well to consider other important figures in the University's affairs. Titular leaders – the Chancellors, Vice-Chancellors and Chairmen of Convocation – were particularly capable of being politically active; but nonetheless their special status did set them apart somewhat from the rest. The same could be said for those who won, or contested unsuccessfully, the University's parliamentary seat from 1868 onwards. The very small professional staff led by the Registrars carried the burden of the administrative work of the University and must, through that very activity, have had a very practical effect on the development and execution of policy. Similarly, some influence must have been exercised by the Clerk of Convocation, a salaried officer elected from and by Convocation. And the fundamental work of the institution was entrusted, over the period under review, to some 430 examiners and assistant examiners.

By no means all those who held the leading, formal positions in the University would find a place on a list drawn up strictly on the basis of long membership, combined with high and regular attendance at Senate and Convocation. Short tenures and the great pressure of more demanding interests affected the service given by several influential members. But in any event, it would be ridiculous to omit any of the four Chancellors, eight Vice-Chancellors, and four Chairmen of Convocation from consideration as very important members of the University, not least because, in addition to their experience of office, however brief, they had made significant earlier contributions. Nor can the salaried Registrars of the University and the Clerks of Convocation be excluded, especially as some of them subsequently became Fellows.

Of this score of officers, the four Chancellors, very different in their tenures, were all drawn from the highest of political circles. With one exception, each followed Lord Burlington, subsequently 7th Duke of Devonshire, who had filled the post from 1836 to 1856, in being a scion of the landed aristocracy, educated at public school and Oxbridge. None of the Chancellors was heavily involved in the routine running of the University, and some of their duties were ceremonial; but as the figures show, they presided over the Senate far more frequently than would ever be expected of their twentieth-century counterparts, and they were by no means mere passive chairmen. There were times when their influence on Senate decisions was obvious, and, as all of them were powerful members of the House of Lords, they were on occasion active in the relations of the University with Parliament and with Governments.

Granville George Leveson-Gower, 2nd Earl Granville, had been Chancellor since the end of 1856, and was to serve until his death in 1891. He had been Lord President of the Council in Palmerston's first Administration when appointed Chancellor, and had gone out of office just two months before the University received the Charter of April, 1858. He was back in the Cabinet in June, 1859, and, of the thirty-two years left to him, eighteen were spent as Lord President, as Colonial Secretary and as Foreign Secretary. Out of office, he remained a leading figure in political life. It is easy to understand why, during some of his years at the Foreign Office, he could find no time to attend the Senate, but it is a tribute to his interest and his sense of duty that, over the years from 1858 until 1891, he presided at 30 per cent of the meetings: in 1889–90, the year before his death, he was present at more than half the sessions.

Granville's successor was his close contemporary, Edward Henry Stanley, 15th Earl of Derby, who had begun life as a Tory, became a Liberal, and then a Liberal Unionist. He, like Granville, had joined the Senate at the end of 1856, and, again like Granville, held high offices during ten of the years from 1858 to 1885 – the Secretaryships of State for India, the Colonies, and Foreign Affairs – while pursuing what was, in partisan terms, a rather eccentric career at the top of politics. As a Fellow, Derby attended about a quarter of the Senate meetings; he came to the Chancellorship less than two years before his death, but presided during that time at half the meetings.

Burlington (Devonshire) had remained a Fellow, but never attended the Senate after 1858, and he, Granville and Derby all died in 1891–93. By contrast, in terms of social class, the last Gladstone Administration celebrated the success of the University of London in promoting not only the professional class, but those within it of Dissenting, foreign and exotic backgrounds, by appointing as Derby's successor the Lord Chancellor, Lord Herschell.

Farrer Herschell's father was a Dissenting Minister who had been born in Prussian Poland of Jewish parents, and had settled in England in 1830. Farrer was a student at Denmark Hill Grammar School, at UCL, and at Bonn; thence to Lincoln's Inn and a distinguished legal career. He was Liberal MP for Durham from 1874 to 1885, Solicitor General from 1880 to 1885, Lord Chancellor in 1886 and again from 1892 to 1895. Not only was he the first London graduate to become Chancellor: he had also been a politically ambitious member of Convocation. He was first elected to the Annual Committee in 1869, and altogether served for three spells, totalling nine years. In 1875 and 1880 he had come third and second, respectively, in the Convocation elections for nominating new members of Senate. And in 1883, while Solicitor General in the Liberal Administration, he became a Crown-chosen Fellow.

He was, therefore, a proven academic politician, who managed to attend a third of the Senate and Annual Committee meetings over the years, and presided at nearly 45 per cent of the Senate's meetings during his five years as its presiding officer.

The Chancellor who saw through the conversion of the examining into the teaching University was the first Earl Kimberley, who had joined the Senate as Lord Wodehouse in 1859. Like Granville and Derby, he had held several high offices: he was Under Secretary at the Foreign Office when appointed to the Senate at the age of thirty-three, and subsequently served as Lord Lieutenant of Ireland from 1864 to 1866. In Gladstone's Administrations of 1880 to 1885, and 1886, he was, successively, Lord Privy Seal, Secretary of State for the Colonies and then for India. He remained devoted to the Liberals, leading them in the House of Lords from 1891. In the Liberal Governments of Gladstone and Rosebery, from 1892 to 1895, he was again Secretary of State for India, then Lord President of the Council, and finally Foreign Secretary. Though, like Granville, he was not available in the busiest periods of his political career, over forty-one years he managed to attend not far short of a quarter of the meetings of the Senate, and in the eighteen months of his Chancellorship before the old regime disappeared, he presided over four-fifths of the sessions.

In the Government's gift, the Chancellorship remained, an aristocratic, high political preserve. The Senate elected the Vice-Chancellors from among their own membership: they chose mainly either politicians or eminent public servants, but increasingly tended to select within that category men who were scholars, teachers and proven educational administrators. Sir John Shaw Lefevre, whose twenty years of service as Vice-Chancellor ended towards the close of 1861, partly because of declining health, was a Senior Wrangler and a brilliant linguist; but he filled the office while being, simultaneously, Clerk of the Parliaments and a member of both the Civil Service and Church Estates Commissions.[1] His successor was the well-to-do banker, radical politician and famous historian of Greece, George Grote, a long serving member of the Council of University College, and a Fellow of the University since 1850, whose tenure of the Vice-Chancellorship ended only with his death in 1871.

For a year after Grote's death, the Vice-Chancellorship was filled, on a confessedly caretaker basis, by Sir Edward Ryan. Ryan had been an Indian judge who returned to England in the mid-1840s and was made a Railway Commissioner. This brought him close to Shaw Lefevre, who was at the time Joint Permanent Secretary of the Board of Trade: some years later Ryan became the first Civil Service Commissioner, where he was joined as a colleague by

---

[1] F.M.G. Willson, *A Strong Supporting Cast. The Shaw Lefevres 1789–1936* (London, 1993), ch. 15.

Shaw Lefevre, and also a Fellow of the University. Both men remained on the Senate after serving as Vice-Chancellor. Ryan died in 1875 and Shaw Lefevre in 1879.

Ryan's willingness to fill the post for a while only was, perhaps, an indication that the Senate was really hoping to find a candidate who would be cast in the same scholarly mould as Grote, but who would also be a well-recognised public figure. The man they chose, in 1872, was Sir John Lubbock, 4th Bt., who had been appointed a Fellow in 1865, on the death of his father, who had been the first Vice-Chancellor of the University, and had remained on the Senate since his resignation of that post in 1842. Like Grote, Lubbock was a wealthy banker; and he was a polymath, whose principal intellectual interests were scientific. Like Grote, too, he was a politician, had been elected for Maidstone as a Liberal in 1870, and was re-elected there in 1874. He thus sat in the House of Commons throughout his tenure of the Vice-Chancellorship, which ended in 1880 when, as will be described later, he succeeded Robert Lowe as the University's own MP, and retained the seat until 1900, though he switched his allegiance from Gladstone to the Liberal Unionists in 1886.

On Lubbock's exchange of the Vice-Chancellorship for the University's parliamentary seat, the Senate turned, for the first time, not merely to a London graduate, but to one who had been a founder member of the Annual Committee of Convocation in 1859, and at the third attempt had won nomination to the Senate by Convocation, in 1860. George Jessel, a UCL man, had risen to the top of the legal world: he was Liberal MP for Dover from 1868 to 1873, during which time Gladstone first made him Solicitor General, with the traditional knighthood, and then, in August, 1873, as the first Jewish judge, Master of the Rolls. He resigned his seat in the Commons shortly before the Mastership of the Rolls was made incompatible with membership. By the time he became Vice-Chancellor he was a member of the Court of Appeal. But he was not destined to have a long tenure, and died in his sixtieth year, early in 1883.

The intellectual calibre of the Vice-Chancellors appointed so far had been high, and all had made considerable contributions to the University's development and its political life. However, none had been a teacher or examiner, and rather strangely in view of the importance of the medical faculty, no medical man had served – perhaps, in part, for the reason given by Lord Burlington in 1842, that the high likelihood of medicos being called away from meetings of Senate, to deal with emergencies, made them ineligible for the Chair.[2] In 1883, Jessel's successor was Sir James Paget, Bt., who was sixty-nine years of age, and, like Sir John Lubbock, never boasted a university degree. The son of a brewer and ship owner, he had been Professor of Anatomy and Surgery at Barts, and the leading surgeon in London from 1861: but he

[2]  F.M.G. Willson, *Our Minerva. The Men and Politics of the University of London, 1836–1858* (London, 1995), p. 66.

was also, clearly, a medical politician, and had sat on the General Medical Council between 1876 and 1881, and on the Senate since 1860.

When Paget resigned, at the age of eighty, in 1895, the Senate apparently abandoned any intention of confirming the precedent set by the appointment of a professional academic in the person of Paget. Instead, they chose another politician with long-established connections with the University, with UCL, and with Convocation. Sir Julian Goldsmid, 3rd Bt., member of a family prominent in the support of University College, had been a Fellow of UCL since 1864, and served as Treasurer of the College from 1880 to 1887. He had been a member of the Annual Committee of Convocation since 1864, and was appointed to the Senate of the University by the Crown in 1875. He had been a Liberal MP from 1865 to 1868, and from 1870 to 1880, turning to the Liberal Unionists after returning to the House of Commons in 1885. Though he was only fifty-seven at the time, he died six months after his election as Vice-Chancellor.

The Senate then elected Sir Henry Enfield Roscoe, who had been a student at UCL, and had graduated from London in 1853. He had made his scientific reputation as Professor of Chemistry at Owens College, Manchester, from 1857 to 1885, and while there, between 1874 and 1878, he had been a London examiner. But like Lubbock and Goldsmid, he had also been lured into politics. He had been elected as Liberal MP for South Manchester in 1885, and sat until his defeat in 1895. Roscoe had only joined the Senate in 1894. As Vice-Chancellor from 1896 until 1902, he saw the University through the major constitutional changes at the end of the century.

Of the eight Vice-Chancellors between 1858 and 1900, three – Grote, Jessel and Roscoe – had been MPs before they took office, and two – Lubbock and Goldsmid – held office while sitting in the House of Commons. Jessel was a senior judge while he was Vice-Chancellor, but did not sit in the Lords. When the four Chancellors are added, all of them peers and ministers, nine of the twelve men who shared the duty of presiding at the Senate during the last four decades of the nineteenth century were or had been parliamentarians. But only two – Paget and Roscoe – had earned their livings as university teachers.

What proportion of their working days had to be devoted by Vice-Chancellors to their university responsibilities cannot be demonstrated, and certainly not quantified, from the records – which contain very little of their correspondence – except in terms of their attendance. When Mrs Grote learned, in 1862, that her husband had been elected Vice-Chancellor of the University, she wrote in her Journal:

> I regret this, since he will I fear be called upon to exert himself even more actively, in the administration of that body, than he has done already for many years past. I hope however that he will draw off from the labour of attending the meetings of the Council of the University College (of which he is, also, Treasurer) and that his time and services will be consecrated chiefly to the direction of the concerns of the

British Museum (of which he was nominated a Trustee in 1859) and London Senate.[3]

Grote, like his predecessors and his successors, were all busy, public men, and the Vice-Chancellorship – totally unremunerated – is unlikely to have been always given top priority in their demanding schedules except, perhaps, by Paget and Roscoe, who were, in effect, retired professors, though very active ones. Nonetheless, the office clearly carried with it an obligation to attend, and, on a high proportion of occasions, to preside. And as the figures show, their willingness to meet their obligation was remarkable. Four of them attended 95 per cent or more of the meetings during their tenure as Vice-Chancellor: three of them were present at 81–84 per cent. Lubbock, who was a very active MP while being Vice-Chancellor, was able to manage attendance at only 73 per cent of meetings.

The beginnings of the Graduates' Committee, formally constituted in 1848, has been traced back to 1841.[4] Once formed, the Committee carried on the campaign for the establishment of Convocation, which succeeded in 1858. In terms of personnel, the significant fact is that the Graduates' Committee and Convocation formed a continuum whose leaders were a close-knit, long-lived group. They were not always agreed among themselves, but they were able, persistent advocates of their cause who had about them the aura of pioneers, and several of them became so prominent as to be the obvious candidates to represent Convocation in the Senate. Indeed, recognising the inevitability of the establishment of Convocation, the Crown had appointed three of them – Charles James Foster, William Withey Gull, and Frederick John Wood – to the Senate in 1856 and 1858. There was no provision, in the Charter of 1858, that the Chairman of Convocation should be a member of the Senate, but in practice the first three Chairmen were Fellows of the University before their elections to the Chair, and the fourth entered both offices almost simultaneously.

Charles James Foster, a lawyer and Professor of Jurisprudence at UCL, joined the Senate in February, 1858, and was unopposed for election as the first Chairman of Convocation in the following May. He resigned both the Chair and his Fellowship in 1863 and emigrated to New Zealand. He and his successor, John Storrar, a medical man, were both quite controversial characters whose involvement in the University scene will emerge fully in the narrative to come. Storrar, however, survived as Chairman and Fellow until shortly before his death twenty-two years later. Even then, in the mid-'eighties, he was followed by a third representative of the original group of graduates from the 'forties – the successful London solicitor, Frederick John Wood.

[3] UCL, MS ADD 266, C1.1, Harriet Grote's Journal, 1862.
[4] Willson, *Our Minerva*, p. 196.

It was, therefore, sixty-seven years after the University of London appeared in its earliest manifestation, and thirty-four years after Convocation had been established, that the latter was not led by a man born before either institution existed. Edward Henry Busk was first elected to the Annual Committee in 1868. In 1892, at the age of forty-eight, he was elected Chairman of Convocation and simultaneously nominated by it for a place on the Senate, to which he was appointed almost immediately afterwards. He was another solicitor but also had taught law for the Incorporated Law Society. He was to have a remarkable career in the University, remaining as Chairman of Convocation until 1922, as a Fellow until 1926, and serving as Vice-Chancellor from 1905 to 1907.

All four Chairmen were UCL graduates. All four, as would be expected, were immersed in University and Convocation politics. All were strong attenders at Senate – comparable to the Vice-Chancellors – and at Annual Committee. As the longest serving, Storrar is worth particular attention. After ten years as co-chairman of the Graduates' Committee, from 1858 he was also the University's representative on the General Medical Council, and he sat on innumerable Senate and Convocation committees, as well as being long a member of the Council of UCL. Indeed he must be regarded as practically a full-time academic and medical politician over a period of forty years.

The experience of those who came to represent the University in the House of Commons, and those who tried to do so but failed, will be reviewed in detail later. Here it is sufficient to note that the first Member for the University of London, who sat from 1868 to 1880; and the second, who sat from 1880 to 1900, were already Fellows when they were elected. Robert Lowe was, effectively, a controversial Minister of Education in the years prior to his election, and became Chancellor of the Exchequer within days of being chosen to represent the University. But he was far less involved in University affairs than his successor, John Lubbock, who was a major participant in the arguments which preceded the passage of the London University Act, 1898. Sir Michael Foster, who succeeded Lubbock in 1900, was a graduate of the University, but neither a member of the Senate nor an active member of Convocation.

Neither Lowe nor Lubbock was a London graduate, but almost all those who tried to become candidates, and were either not chosen or were defeated at the polls, were graduates, or Fellows, and most had been prominent in Convocation's affairs. They included Walter Bagehot, Sir Charles Locock, Charles James Foster, Richard Quain, Julian Goldsmid, William Withey Gull, Sir George Jessel, S.D. Waddy, Frederick John Wood, Arthur Charles, William Job Collins and Edward Henry Busk. The exceptions were Sir John Romilly, who had been much involved, however, in UCL's affairs; Edwin Chadwick; and Frederick Harrison, who had been an examiner for the University, and whose candidacy in 1886 was entirely focussed on the controversy over Irish Home Rule.

The Registrar was the only senior, full-time, salaried officer of the University until 1870, when he was joined by an Assistant Registrar and Librarian. The first two Registrars were scientists: Richard Wellesley Rothman was a Fellow of Trinity College, Cambridge, who retained his Fellowship and continued his studies in astronomy while at London from 1838 until his death in 1856. He was followed by William Benjamin Carpenter, a distinguished physiologist who held the Fullerian Chair at the Royal Institution in 1845 and the Chair of Medical Jurisprudence at UCL in 1849. He examined for the University of London from 1847 until, in 1856, he was elected as Registrar. Carpenter held office until 1879, and was then appointed by the Crown as a Fellow, serving on the Senate until his death in 1885.

The tendency to welcome scientists was confirmed by the appointment, in 1870, as the first Assistant Registrar, of Thomas Archer Hirst, FRS, a German educated mathematician and physicist who became Professor of Mathematical Physics at UCL in 1865, and Professor of Pure Maths two years later. Hirst left in 1873 to become Director of Studies at the Royal Naval College, Greenwich, and in 1882 was appointed to a Fellowship of the University, serving on the Senate until 1892.

After 1879 the scientific hold on the post was broken. Arthur Milman, son of a Rector of St Margaret's, Westminster and Dean of St Paul's, was a barrister who became Commissary of the Dean and Chapter of St Paul's. At the age of forty-four he followed Hirst as Assistant Registrar and Librarian of the University, and succeeded Carpenter as Registrar in 1879. But like Carpenter, on his retirement, in 1896, he was appointed by the Crown to a Fellowship. Carpenter, Hirst and Milman thus brought their knowledge and experience as senior University administrators to their service on the Senate between 1879 and 1896.

The practice of promoting the Assistant Registrar to the senior job was repeated when Milman retired. His successor, Frederick Victor Dickins, had been Assistant since 1882, and held office as Registrar until 1901. He had begun professional life as a Parisian educated doctor who served in the Navy as a Medical Officer in Chinese and Japanese waters, in the 1860s. But he retrained as a barrister and served for fourteen years as Assistant to Milman. Subsequent to his administrative work he developed his scholarship in the field of Japanese and Far Eastern literature, and at the time of his death, in 1915, was Reader in Japanese at the University of Bristol.

All three Registrars, in the period from 1858 to 1900, were no doubt in some respects increasingly significant figures in the University's world, simply because of the growth of the institution. As a Fellow, Carpenter attended 68 per cent of the Senate meetings during his five years as a member, and Milman was even more assiduous, turning out for over 89 per cent of the sessions between 1896 and 1900.

The Clerk of Convocation held a part-time post, and was paid a very small salary. Unlike the University Registrars and Assistants, of whom three became Fellows, only the first of the three Clerks of Convocation, who were in office between 1858 and 1900, became a member of the Senate. William Shaen, an early law graduate from UCL, a Unitarian, a solicitor and a controversial figure for the medical men because he practised homoeopathy, was elected, unopposed, to the Clerkship annually from 1858 until 1868. He was a persistent contender for nomination, by Convocation, for membership of the Senate. He tried first in 1864 and came third. After resigning the Clerkship he was elected to the Annual Committee, and in 1871 tried again for nomination, but failed to come in the first three. In 1876 he came second, and at last, in 1880, he won the first place and reached the Senate, where he sat for seven years. He could be regarded, fairly, therefore, as a full-blooded Convocation politician.

Shaen's immediate successor was John Robson, another early UCL graduate, a master at University College School who became a barrister and then began a career in educational administration. He served as Secretary of the College of Preceptors and, from 1867 to 1876, as Assistant Secretary and then Secretary of UCL. He was one of the original members of the Annual Committee of Convocation, and was re-elected to it every year until 1868. In that year – only months since he had become Secretary of UCL – he was unopposed in taking over the Clerkship from Shaen. He held the two posts simultaneously until his death in 1876. As we have seen, the Clerkship was then contested very closely. One candidate was Talfourd Ely, a Fellow of UCL, and a Classics master at University College School, who was to serve as an assistant examiner for the University, Principal of University Hall, Secretary of UCL, and Professor of Greek at Bedford College. At the time of the election he was in his eleventh year on the Annual Committee. He was defeated by two votes. His rival, Henry Ebenezer Allen, who had taken his degree as a student of Spring Hill College, had never served on the Annual Committee; but he was to be Clerk for thirty-five years.

Only five Fellows, who had been examiners before 1858, continued to examine after the new Charter came into effect, but all finished in or before 1861, when the eligibility of any Fellow to serve was abolished. Thereafter, examiners were still subject to annual election, but could not serve more than five years, though they could be re-appointed after a break. The normal complement was two examiners per subject, and assistant examiners were added to cope with additional numbers of candidates. In 1860–61 there were thirty-eight examiners: by 1899–1900 the numbers of subjects and candidates had grown so much that they demanded the attention of sixty examiners and a dozen assistants. Over the period the University employed 363 full examiners, twelve of whom had also served as assistants; and sixty-five assistants.

Once an examiner was appointed, it was common for him to go unchallenged at the annual elections during his spell or spells of five years. It was relatively rare for another candidate to put himself forward in such circumstances, but some did so – almost always unsuccessfully – no doubt in order to bring their names to the notice of the Senate, with future possibilities in mind. Genuine vacancies, whether after five years or less, on the other hand, were almost always occasions for real competition. The most numerous candidates applied in the most popular arts subjects – English, Classics, French and German; moderate numbers tried for Laws; while the Sciences and Medicine attracted noticeably fewer people. A list of twenty or more was normal for the popular arts, and the record number of thirty candidates put themselves forward for French in 1894. These numbers were due, in part, to the considerable recruitment of teachers from schools, particularly in French and German. Between six and twelve was a much more usual turn-out in Philosophy, Music and Political Economy. Legal examiners were often drawn from the ranks of practising barristers, and vacant places would usually attract competition from between fifteen and twenty candidates. It was very unusual for there to be as many as ten candidates for examinerships in science and medicine – the average would be about seven. And despite the increasing scale of the operation and the widening of the curriculum, competition for examinerships showed little or no increase as the century advanced.

A little more than three-quarters of the examiners were engaged for not more than one term of five years. Twenty-seven held their posts for between six and nine years; fifty-four served for two full terms of five years; and fourteen of them served for more than ten years. The record seems to be held by Thomas Stevenson of Guy's Hospital, who served four full terms – twenty years – between 1867 and 1901, as an examiner in Forensic Medicine. Thus, within a subject area, the influence of some examiners may have been considerable over a long period and may well have helped shape the character of teaching and even the nature of the discipline. That is a matter for historians of curriculum: but long service as examiners does raise the question as to whether they, as a group, were able to exercise any notable pressure on the overall direction of the University's affairs.

The answer is almost certainly very little. These were men contracted to set and mark examination papers, which entailed performing intensively for short periods, once or twice a year. They would meet only with their disciplinary colleagues, certainly at the end of the exercise and, if they were sufficiently close to each other, perhaps at the beginning. There is no evidence of any general meetings of all examiners, and there can have been little opportunity to organise any professional or even social, let alone political, association. The University chose examiners from all over the country and from quite a wide range of institutions. Professional camaraderie, the accidents of personal acquaintance, and alliances of like-minded people in geographical proximity, might well have produced a wealth of shared experience and the development of shared ideas about the whole examination system, among a few groups and over limited periods. But any notion of a cohesive 'academic staff' or 'faculty', with a continuing self-consciousness, is surely not viable.

Nonetheless, the possibility that some examiners, mainly but perhaps not entirely in their individual roles, might have helped to shape opinion about the operations of the University, is worth floating, cautiously. It is unlikely that more than about a half of the examiners and assistants were London graduates, but by the end of the period at least 143 of them – a third of the total – were enrolled in Convocation. More significantly, about sixty of those served at one time or another on the Annual Committee, and twenty-two of them were Fellows. In the absence of detailed attendance records there can be no proof, but it would be unsurprising if a majority of the examiners who were members of Convocation were based in London, and formed no small proportion of the regular band of members who turned up at Convocation's meetings. Certainly, scrutiny of the lists of examiners shows a sizeable representation of UCL graduates, and of teachers there and at other London institutions. There may well have been occasions when discussion on academic matters reflected the collective experience of those who were central to the whole business of examining.

And in a wider context, many of those examiners who worked in institutions in or near London may well have been involved in the surge of opinion in academic circles which, from the late 1870s onwards, supported moves for the establishment of a teaching university in the capital city. When an Association for Promoting a Teaching University for London was set up in 1884, it soon enrolled almost 250 members, all but a handful of whom were practising academics. Among them were seventeen Fellows of the University, and twenty-eight men who had served or were serving on Convocation's Annual Committee. But additionally, no less than sixty of the 250 were or had been examiners for the University, many of whom were influential members of Senate or Convocation.

# 5

# *The political community*

What is clear from the foregoing chapter is that the top personages, the parliamentary politicians, the few senior officials, and no small proportion of the examiners, were almost all so closely associated with either the Senate, or with the Annual Committee of Convocation, or with both, that the collective behaviour of the two bodies really embraced most of the contributions made by those special, small groups to the political life of the University community. And the Senate, whose formal membership remained unchanged throughout at thirty eight, and the Committee, whose formal size increased over the years from thirty-two to about fifty-six, were organically related.

The Convocation Senators, whether Convocation-nominated or Crown-chosen, were, after 1862, always members of both the Senate and the Annual Committee. This meant that dual membership grew from eleven in 1872 to twenty-three in 1900 – i.e., from roughly a quarter of each body in 1872, to a little over 60 per cent of the Senate and 40 per cent of the Standing Committee, at the end of the century. Many of those London graduates who became, by virtue of their Senate membership, *ex officio* members of the Annual Committee, had previously been elected members of that Committee. And, as would be expected, membership of the Annual Committee from 1858 included many men who had been active in the Graduates' Committee during the previous decade. As we have seen, forty-seven out of 119 Fellows were also members of the Annual Committee, reflecting both the early decision of Convocation to make any member who was appointed to the Senate an *ex officio* member of the Committee, and the willingness of Governments to appoint to the Senate an increasing number of London graduates.

The combined membership of the Senate and the Annual Committee of Convocation between 1858 and 1900 was 293. Of that total, 174 sat only on the Committee and were elected by the London-based members who regularly attended Convocation's annual meetings. In addition to the 293, there were about seventy-five members of Convocation who tried, but never succeeded by elective means, to enter either the Senate or the Annual Committee. But they tried, and should be included in any estimate of those who constituted the seriously competitive pool of people who took the leading parts in the politics of the University. But even allowing for them, and adding, rather generously, another twenty or thirty people who, as

parliamentarians and Ministers, officers, or examiners, exercised notable influence from time to time, the pool scarcely reached four hundred, spread across
four decades.

The figures and the characteristics of formal membership, both of Senate
and of Annual Committee, and estimates of the total political community,
are important as indicators of the attitudes of appointing or electing agencies,
and of the shifting influences of various groups. But they give no guidance as
to the behaviour of persons once appointed or elected to office. After having
seen who was entitled to be present, it is necessary to turn to the matter of
actual attendance.

We have complete statistics of attendance at the 540 Senate meetings which
were held between 14 April 1858, when the new Charter was accepted, and
10 October 1900, which saw the last session of the Senate before the
University became a teaching institution. And we have extensive though not
complete records of committee meetings. The Senate sat during each academic
session, October to July, coming together never less than ten times and, in
only three sessions, more than fifteen times. The average attendance at
meetings in each session ranged from eight to eighteen, but in slightly over
two-thirds of the sessions it was in the range twelve to fifteen. In four sessions
it fell below twelve, and in eight it exceeded fifteen. Thus the average sessional
attendance never reached nineteen – half the size of the Senate – and the most
usual turn-out, on a sessional basis, comprised only a little more than one-
third of the membership.

These figures were a notable improvement on Senate practice during
much of the first twenty years of the University. However, sessional averages
hide the fact that sixty-six meetings – one in eight – were attended by less
than ten Senators, while there were forty-seven occasions when there were
more than twenty present. Two-thirds of the thinly attended meetings were
held before 1875. Conversely, three-quarters of the larger attendances occurred
after 1875. The five biggest turn-outs were each of twenty-seven Senators –
almost three-quarters of the members. All but one of those strongly attended
meetings took place after 1875.

The generally increased attendance, particularly in the second half of
the period, coincided significantly with the more frequent appearances of the
Convocation-nominated Fellows, especially after the full complement was
appointed; and, though to a lesser extent, with the increased number of
Crown-chosen London graduates, especially from the early 1880s onwards.
The average sessional figures show that the London graduates first 'out-
attended' the non-London appointees as early as 1874–75, and were always
more numerous from 1879–80 onwards. Given the more contentious concerns
of the last quarter of the century, it is reasonable to imagine that the London
graduates were likely to be rather more passionately engaged than their
non-London colleagues.

We have almost full records of attendance at the 261 meetings of the Annual/ Standing Committee of Convocation held between 8 July 1859 and 30 March 1900; and full records of its sub-committees.

In 1860 Convocation adopted strict rules about attendance at the Annual Committee. Those elected members who fell below the minimum require-ments were ineligible for re-election in the following year. At first, it was provided that members who did not attend one half of the meetings would be ineligible. But in 1865 it was decided that, in future, the third of the membership who had attended the fewest meetings would be disqualified for the following session. However, this proved to be too punitive, and from 1865 it was decreed that the quarter of the membership who attended least would be ineligible. The introduction of the rule had a salutary effect: in the first three full sessions average attendance had varied between eleven and thirteen. From 1863 until 1900 it never fell below sixteen, and in twenty-seven of the thirty-seven sessions was twenty or more, with a high of twenty-six in 1869–70.

Most of the Fellows who were *ex officio* members of the Annual Committee were infrequent attenders at its meetings. If they are all added to the elected membership, the average attendance at the Committee, especially in the later years, was below 50 per cent. But if the calculation takes account only of the elected members, plus a small addition for the few Senators who did turn out with some frequency, then the Annual Committee could claim an average attendance of some 60 per cent, roughly twice that of the Senate; the latter, however, met much more frequently and applied no sanctions against non-attenders.

Average attendances of a third of its membership at the Senate, and of rather less than two-thirds of the eligible Convocation members at meetings of the Annual Committee, will be unsurprising to anyone aware of the tendencies of large, unpaid boards and committees, and particularly unsurprising in the context of the University of London, given its experience in this context, prior to 1858. Further detailed analysis produces a great deal of evidence which shows the same characteristic patterns of individual attendance as developed in the earlier period. It is sufficient to give a few salient facts which help to isolate those people whose consistent attendance must have been a major factor in enabling them to exercise considerable authority and influence.

Over a quarter of the Fellows and half the elected members of the Annual Committee served for less than five years, and among them were over 8 per cent of each group who never attended a meeting. These 120 largely ineffective members included ten Senators who had been appointed before 1858, and whom death or very advanced age soon removed from active service. Many of the group, however, were Annual Committee members who sat for only one or two sessions, and either found their professional commitments too onerous to permit them to give time to Convocation affairs, or were, perhaps, members who had been persuaded to stand for membership and did not find the experience to their liking.

Some 54 per cent of the Senate and 43 per cent of the Annual Committee served for between five and nineteen years. Only 39 per cent of the Senators and 47 per cent of the Annual Committee attended more than half the meetings which were held during their tenures. Only fifty-four Senators – 45 per cent – were present at fifty or more – 9 per cent – of the 540 meetings of the Senate; and only thirteen elected members of the Annual Committee attended more than a quarter of the 264 sessions of the Committee.

If three criteria – years of service, total number of meetings attended, and percentage of possible attendance, are brought together, and if committee service (always a minority activity) is also noted, it becomes clear that, over the whole period 1858 to 1900, the leadership of the University, and discussion of the affairs of the Senate and of the Annual Committee, often closely entangled, were dominated by no more than about seventy-five to a hundred men – not much more than a quarter of the membership of the Senate and the Annual Committee of Convocation. Between 1858 and the middle of the 1870s that figure reduces to just over forty, including fifteen who did not continue beyond 1875. From then onwards, thirty-three new men come into prominence who, together with the twenty-seven who served (in many cases for remarkably long spells) during both periods, made up the fifty to sixty who saw the University through the arguments over its eventual conversion into a teaching, as well an examining, institution.

It would be inaccurate and grossly unfair to suggest that all, or even most, of the more than two hundred people who were not included in the small group of dominant figures, had no influence or did nothing of particular importance in the political manoeuvrings over forty years. Nor were the members of Senate and of the Annual Committee of Convocation the only significant contributors to debate and decision in the University's affairs. There was a handful of politicians, Ministers, administrators and prominent members of the teaching profession, whose interventions were notable. But when all allowance is made for the possibility of influence being exercised, in certain circumstances, by less prominent Senators or members of the Annual Committee, or by particular people outside the University, the debates on major matters were the special concern of those who held the high offices, those who persistently attended the Senate, those who pursued and retained elective office in Convocation, and those who devoted themselves to the minutiae of committee work.

But while there was much overlapping between Senate and Convocation, each had its own quite separate functions and characteristics. The Senate continued, from 1858 until 1900, to be an executive council whose regular work was done, by and large, by little more than a third of its membership, though on the bigger issues up to another third of the Fellows might be involved. Its functions and its duties were clearly established; it was served by a small professional staff and supervised the work, over the whole period, of its several hundred examiners.

Convocation's situation cannot be so easily described. Its membership grew from a few hundred to about five thousand by the end of the century, and comprised about half the total number of eligible graduates. The whole membership had only limited opportunities to play any important role, and, for a high proportion of that membership, action was restricted to voting in the three contested elections of the MP for the University. A much smaller proportion of the membership took part in the elections of candidates who would be nominated for membership of the Senate. But the continuous work of watching over the University's progress, taking part in the close consideration of policy, and trying to exert pressure on the Senate, was effectively confined to the quite small group – at any one time almost certainly no larger than two hundred to three hundred interested members – who were overwhelmingly based in London, who could easily attend the Annual Meetings, and could compete for places on and take part in the work of the Annual Committee.

In effect, Senate and the mass membership of Convocation obviously shared common action only in the election of the University's MP, and in the filling of a quarter of the Fellowships by Convocation-nominated candidates. They shared in the discussion of policies only at a distance, through the normal channels of written communication and exchanges in the press. But the relationship between the quite small proportion of active Convocation members in London, and particularly of their leaders, and the Senate, was complex and intriguing. The governance of the University, and its development, was greatly influenced by that unique relationship.

# Part II

## *An Uneasy Beginning*

# 6

## Convocation's medical militants

Convocation met for the first time on 4 May 1858. A list of signatures of those present contains 153 names, but whether there were others at the gathering is uncertain.[1] Charles James Foster was elected Chairman, William Shaen Acting Clerk, and a committee of twelve members was set up to prepare Standing Orders and other organisational proposals to lay before a meeting to be held on 10 November. During the following months, that Committee, on its own and in co-operation with a parallel body appointed by the Senate, worked out the details within the overall provisions of the Charter, which included the responsibility of the Senate for keeping the Register, resolving problems of membership, and convening meetings. So far as the great bulk of routine arrangements were concerned, this was, apparently, an exercise carried through harmoniously, and the proposals which emanated from it were accepted by Convocation without any major opposition. But far from ushering in a new regime in a spirit of goodwill, the second and subsequent early meetings of Convocation produced some violent disagreement which reflected past, and foreshadowed future, problems in the relations between and within the University, Convocation, and the medical profession.

While the introduction of a new element – Convocation – into the University's constitutional system was celebrated as a major achievement, it was not received, by Convocation itself, with wholehearted enthusiasm. The high expectations which had been entertained, as far back as 1840,[2] by some of the Fellows, that the University should have, in a decade, a Senate wholly elected by its graduates, had been steadily eroded over the following years. The limited power conferred on Convocation by the 1858 Charter was a bitter disappointment to many of those who had fought so long for recognition. It is not surprising, therefore, that the establishment of Convocation was followed by a somewhat turbulent period in which resentment and frustration arose on a number of issues. Some short-term turbulence might be regarded as the inevitable price of re-adjustment to a new legal and political reality. Some of the major issues, however, had a long history, and were to

---

[1] UL CN 1/2.
[2] Willson, *Our Minerva*, p. 142.

remain controversial for the rest of the century. What happened in the context of those issues in the first few years after 1858 was very relevant to subsequent events.

There was argument over the respective jurisdictions of Senate and Convocation; there was suspicion, on the part of Convocation, of some of the actions of Senate; and there were problems and conflict within Convocation. Much of the noisier contention was closely related to a particular incident concerning the medical profession; but there was also a deeper sense within parts of that profession that their interests had been neglected by the University. The initial tensions were not significantly calmed until 1863.

The essential political background to an understanding of what happened in 1858 to 1863 was the fact that Convocation was the successor body – and practically the same body, in terms of its leading personnel – as the Graduates' Committee, which had for a decade conducted a long and often frustrating campaign to bring Convocation into being. The Committee had worked very largely as a coalition of two sub-committees, one composed of sixteen representatives of the Arts and Laws men, and the other made up of sixteen medical graduates. The papers of the Graduates' Committee are not available, so that details of its inner workings are exiguous. But one anonymous and admittedly angry doctor claimed that the medical side of the Committee was mostly inactive, and that 'a little knot of six', of whom only two were medicos, made all the running. The other medical members, he asserted, had 'retired, worn out by the everlasting talk to which they were compelled to listen, disgusted by the selfishness and illiberality which they heard inculcated'.[3]

If at least some of the medical faculty were unhappy with the leadership of the Graduates' Committee, a considerable proportion of the Arts and Laws people were up in arms, in 1858, because the leadership of the Committee had accepted the inclusion, in the new Charter, of the provision whereby the University's examinations for degrees in Arts and Laws were henceforward to be open to all comers, without regard to how they prepared themselves for those examinations – in other words, abandoning the previous requirement that candidates had first to attend one of the limited number of institutions approved by the Home Secretary, for two years. The proposal, by the Senate to the Home Office, had led to a long and bitter row during 1857, and there is no doubt that a majority of graduates – and all but one of the recognised Colleges – were hostile to it.[4] But Foster and his nearest colleagues realised that there was no possibility of persuading the Government to reverse it. In their final report they admitted that the Graduates' Committee,

---

[3] *Lancet*, 4 December 1858.
[4] For a summary of the arguments, see W.H. Allchin, *An account of the Reconstruction of the University of London*, Pt I (London, 1905). For the struggle in 1857, see Willson, *Our Minerva*, ch. 21.

... looking to the position of Lord Granville [Chancellor of the University] in Lord Palmerston's Ministry, and to his strong opinion adverse to the views of the Graduates, and having regard to the fact, that similar opinions were entertained by Lord John Russell and others, whose co-operation would have been almost indispensable to success, did not feel in a position to undertake a Parliamentary campaign.[5]

The idea of opening Arts and Laws degree examinations to all comers was as old as the University: it had been fought for by Henry Warburton and others at the outset and throughout the University's early years. The Senate argued its case for change soberly, in 1857, but something of the passionate feeling against the colleges, which lay behind their apparently rational case, is contained in the *Lancet's* memory of Henry Warburton's view that 'the University of London, as represented by the majority of graduates, "stinks of illiberality"'. To this the journal added its own, typically over stated denunciation:

Nurtured in petty schools, which degrade the name of Colleges, moulded in the narrow die of class interests and prejudices, the majority have hitherto evinced less zeal to make the University subservient to the advancement of learning than to use her as an instrument for the promotion of party and personal ends. Professing to be metropolitan in name and in aim, a more exclusive, a more bigoted, a more ungenerous University, until the recent Charter was imposed in open contempt of the clamour of the collegiate party, did not exist.[6]

The 'collegiate party', however, was not by any means restricted to the products of those 'petty schools' whose affiliation to the University had, indeed, caused the Senate concern. A host of graduates of UCL and King's, let alone many members of the governing bodies of those Colleges, were outraged by the abandonment of the required term of institutional study for candidates for the University's examinations. All feared that the new order would result in a drop in the status of the London degree, and that the way would be open for narrow, vocational, private study to be encouraged at the expense of the wider intellectual and cultural coverage provided in a collegiate setting. But alongside these legitimate educational doubts there was, also, almost certainly a strong element of regret that, in future, degrees could be taken by persons who had not had the social experience of enrolment in a college – an experience seen as the appropriate culmination of the education of gentlemen.

The arguments about affiliation or non-affiliation of Colleges, and about the educational advantages and disadvantages of private versus institutional

---

[5] UL RC 1/2/g, Annual Report of the Graduates Committee, April 1858.
[6] *Lancet*, 21 May 1859.

study, are not the same arguments as apply to the matter of whether a University which only examines, and does not provide teaching, is a real University. But the two separable themes are closely enough related to ensure that there could be an overlap of argument about them. Many of those who regretted the loss of the required link between colleges and the University in 1858 were to be involved in the major struggle which set in twenty years later to bring teaching institutions and the University into an organic relationship. In 1858 to 1863, the memory of the controversy over the abandonment of the required period of collegiate affiliation was quite bitterly alive.

Another factor of major political importance was the position of University College London in the affairs of both the Senate and Convocation. The College and University College Hospital provided a high proportion of the candidates for degrees; there were several members of Senate who were also members of the governing body of UCL; and the leadership of Convocation was very largely made up of UCL graduates, many of whom held teaching positions in the College. The UCL men did not always agree among themselves, but, as will be seen, they tended to dominate much of the electoral and committee life of Convocation, and that dominance aroused suspicion and some hostility in some quarters, from time to time.

Lastly, in this preliminary list of relevant political tensions at the end of the 1850s, was a feeling on the part of the medical profession that their representation on the Senate had been for too long allowed to weaken. This was felt particularly strongly because of the widely accepted view that the University owed most of the public respect which it had attracted to what its Chancellor, Granville, was to describe as its 'great glory', the 'medical school . . . [which] performed . . . the same function with regard to the medical profession which Oxford and Cambridge did with regard to the Church'.[7] The medical men's concern was understandable. In the beginning, in 1836, there were sixteen medical men among the thirty-six Fellows, but, after a few years, anxiety was expressed as to the dangers of a predominance of medical opinion, and there was also some worry over the tendency of medical Senators to have to abandon attendance because of the demands of medical emergencies.[8] As a result, the only medical appointee to the Senate after 1837 was William Withey Gull, who was chosen primarily as a leading member of the Graduates' Committee, in 1856. Deaths and retirements had ensured that at the end of 1858 the list of Senate members included just ten medical Fellows, of whom Gull was one: the other nine had all been appointed more than twenty years before, and two or three of them had become only very occasional attenders.

But however much the medical people were upset by their under-representation on Senate, they were not in a position to dictate changes in

[7] *BMJ*, 12 May 1860.
[8] Willson, *Our Minerva*, pp. 65–6.

their favour. And in Convocation, the number of medical graduates was less than half the number of BAs, MAs and LLBs; they were a tight-knit professional group, but, even working as a team, were clearly outnumbered. Events were to show that divided counsels would not impress Government and would further weaken their potential power among their fellow graduates.

One of the most significant powers given to Convocation was to choose three nominees for every other place vacated on the Senate, until a quarter of the Senate was filled by Convocation nominees, and thereafter to fill every fourth vacancy. The names of the chosen trio of nominees were to be laid before the Home Secretary, who would then recommend an appointment to the Crown. New vacancies occurred shortly after the new Charter became effective, and two of them were earmarked for filling by Convocation nominees. But late in June, 1858, the Chairman admitted that 'some months must elapse probably before [Convocation] . . . will be in a position to exercise the privilege of nomination'.[9] The first elections of Convocation nominees were to be held on 10 November. Meanwhile Convocation's interests were effectively represented in the Senate by the three London graduates who had already been appointed by the Crown – Gull and Wood in 1856, and Foster, earlier in 1858.

It was merely coincidental that in August, 1858, legislation was enacted which brought into existence the General Council of Medical Education and Registration, soon to be known, generally, as the General Medical Council (GMC).[10] That body was the result of a long struggle within the medical corporations, and in Parliament, in which the University of London, along with other universities, had been an anxious participant. The new Council, as its title suggested, was entrusted with powers to bring about a rationalisation of the qualifications which should be required of medical practitioners, and to authorise them to practise. The Council was to be representative of all the interested parties, and, on 14 October 1858, the Privy Council Office asked the University of London to nominate a member. The matter was put on the agenda of the meeting of the Senate six days later: and so, rather fatefully, was the Home Office's formal request for the nomination of six candidates by Convocation, to fill two empty seats on the Senate.

There was an average attendance at the Senate on 20 October. The Chancellor and Vice-Chancellor were there, as were five medical men and five others. There is no record of debate, but it is clear that there was uncertainty as to whether the Senate was the appropriate body to choose a representative of the University to sit on the GMC, or whether, under the terms of the new Charter, there was an obligation to consult or involve Convocation. It is quite conceivable that Foster and Gull would have raised

9 UL RO 1/2/20, Carpenter to Waddington, 26 June 1858.
10 21 & 22 Vic c. xc.

the issue, but, whether or not that was the case, the Senate agreed to ask their counsel, Thomas Tomlinson, and the up-and-coming barrister, George Jessel, who was one of the leaders of the graduates, to give their opinion on the question as to whether the Senate had a right to nominate.

The Senate met again on 3 November. They had before them the opinion of the two lawyers, dated the previous day, to the effect that the Senate did have the power to choose a person to represent the University on the GMC. And they were aware of pressure from the Privy Council Office to make the nomination quickly. The Senate had given no publicity to the fact that they had been asked to make a nomination, but the establishment of the GMC was newsworthy, and *The Times* had asserted, confidently, on 26 October, that 'The University of London will either appoint Dr Storrar or Dr Gull. No other candidates are in the field.' In fact the Senate had received a letter from Edward Smith, offering himself as a candidate for nomination as the University's representative on the GMC. Smith had taken his MD from London in 1843, and an LLB five years later: he was to be, like Storrar, a candidate in the forthcoming election for nomination as a Convocation Senator.

Neither the Chancellor nor the Vice-Chancellor was present on 3 November; Grote was in the Chair. There were five medical men present and six others, among the latter being Foster and Wood, strong Convocation lawyers. It is quite unclear how a ballot of the Fellows was arranged, who proposed the contenders, or even how many candidates there were – Gull was not present, nor is his name mentioned. Nor is there any record of the votes cast. The minutes simply state that there was a ballot, and that Dr John Storrar was elected.

While there is no way of knowing how the votes were cast, it is quite possible that there were no candidates other than Smith and Storrar, and that Storrar, who had been leading the medical side of the Graduates' Committee for ten years and was well known to the Senate, had a comfortable victory. If there was any real hostility to his appointment, and any suspicion of how it was to be received, it was well concealed, for, in the furore that followed, no medical member of the Senate who was present on 3 November admitted to having been opposed to Storrar. It is very likely that the Fellows, all seasoned University politicians, regarded Storrar as practically one of themselves, who knew his way round in the tortuous medical negotiations which had gone on for years, and was recognised as a staunch upholder of the University's positions. The closeness of all concerned is implied by the fact that the Registrar, Carpenter, had received from Wood, in mid-October, the latter's nominations of Jessel, Osler and Storrar for election as Convocation nominees for Fellowships.[11]

---

[11] UL RO/1/2/20, Carpenter to Wood, 18 October 1858.

No doubt those who intended to be active in the affairs of Convocation were looking forward to the meeting on 10 November eagerly enough. The chance of being chosen to fill seats on the Senate had stimulated political ambitions to the extent that no less than twenty-eight names had been put forward of men known to be keen to stand, or of men who it was thought would be desirable candidates. Only six – to be chosen at the meeting – would win the right to have their names sent to the Home Secretary for his final choice of two new Fellows of the University. Those who were more concerned to see Convocation tackling strictly educational issues, like the content and shape of the examinations being offered, would have been keen to see how such concern could be channelled. There were bread and butter matters of procedure to settle; and there was the question of appointing a Clerk, William Shaen only having been given Acting status in April. And there was a long-standing expectation that, Convocation having been established, every effort should be made to persuade the legislature to create a Parliamentary Constituency for the University.

But what would almost certainly have been an important, and perhaps in some respects a mildly controversial session, was dominated by some bitter conflict which exposed a number of rifts within the ranks of the new Convocation, and which arose directly out of the Senate's nomination of Dr Storrar to be the University's representative on the GMC. The argument had several strands.

The disappointment and frustration felt by many of the graduates with the very limited powers which had been given to Convocation in the new Charter was responsible for their indignation over the Senate's assumption that such actions as the appointment of Storrar did not need the participation and agreement of Convocation. This was an understandable and respectable objection, which was to be tested in the courts. But it was accompanied by a violent attack, by sections of the medical graduates and the medical establishment, on the propriety of appointing Storrar, on the ground of his personal unsuitability. It was claimed that he had no high status as a doctor, and had retired from practice: he could not be regarded, therefore, as a widely-known and respected member of the profession. Some of the senior medicos felt that because he did not move in their social circles, he could not exercise any desirable influence. These objections, however, were to a large extent a reflection of a more specific resentment.

Storrar, as a leading member of the Graduates' Committee, had long supported the University in its war with the medical corporations, and particularly with the Royal College of Physicians. In a published letter he outlined his part in previous episodes in 1848, 1854, and 1856, and encapsulated the nature of the quarrel:

> ... the great question contested by universities on the one hand, and by medical corporations on the other, was, whether medical graduates should be entitled to practise on the sole authority of their degrees; or, whether the hitherto limited

powers of the medical corporations should be extended over the whole kingdom, so as to compel graduates to join a medical corporation before they could become legal practitioners.[12]

The issue had been settled, in favour of the universities, by the Medical Act, 1858. But in the preparatory stages of that legislation, Storrar learned that a provision was being considered whereby the title of Physician was to be reserved for Fellows of the Royal College of Physicians. Together with a colleague from Edinburgh, and through the help of the Member for Ayr, E.H.J. Craufurd, Storrar ensured that the provision was dropped.[13] This infuriated a group of London graduates who had become members of the College: the University's appointment of Dr Storrar as its representative on the GMC was regarded by them as 'an act of hostility and disrespect to the Royal College of Physicians'.[14]

As is not unusual, the initial row over one issue and one man led to wider accusations and recriminations. The widening of the dispute was encouraged by the impact of the election of nominees for places on the Senate, and later by expectations of a contest for a parliamentary seat.

On 10 November 1858, 194 members turned out for a meeting which was to last for no less than six hours. There is no list extant of who attended, but judging by the number of graduates qualified for membership of Convocation, and by the record of those who attended the inaugural meeting, it is highly unlikely that as many as half were medical men.[15] And the medical contingent was divided over Dr Storrar.

All the scheduled business was put aside until motions condemning the Senate's action in making a unilateral appointment to the GMC were debated. It was moved that the representative of the University on the GMC 'should be chosen by the whole University; which consists of the Chancellor, Vice-Chancellor, Fellows and Graduates'. That motion was extended after it was announced that 'certain members of Convocation' had taken legal advice and received an opinion which was contrary to that given to the Senate by Tomlinson and Jessel. The final resolution, apparently approved unanimously, asked the Senate to submit the case to the Law Officers, and in the meanwhile to suspend confirmation of their election of Dr Storrar.

---

[12] *BMJ*, 27 November 1858. Letter from Storrar.

[13] *BMJ*, 27 November 1858. Letter from C.H.F. Routh. This action of Storrar and his colleagues may have been taken during early, drafting stages of the Bill. By the time of its Second Reading, on 2 June, Cowper-Temple, on introducing it, mentioned that the RCP and RCS had reservations, but that their wishes had not been granted. There was no attempt made to alter that during the debates on the Bill. 3s Parl. Deb., vol. 150, cols 1404–21

[14] *BMJ*, 13 November 1858.

[15] UL CN 1/2, CN 2/1.

It was a group of forty-six medical men who belonged to the Royal College of Physicians who were incensed by the appointment of Storrar. The composite resolution, including the request to suspend Storrar's appointment, was doubt-less acceptable to the whole meeting because of the widespread indignation at the Senate's assumption of power. But the personal sympathies of the majority, comprising the non-medical graduates and the medicos who opposed the Royal College of Physicians' faction, was demonstrated unequivocally by the outcome of the election for the six nominees for places on the Senate. There had been twenty-eight candidates before the meeting began, but twelve withdrew, leaving sixteen to contest six places. Of the original twenty-eight, only ten were medical men: and, of the sixteen serious competitors, only six came from the medical faculty. When it came to counting the votes, four of the places went to non-medical candidates. First place went to the lawyer, Timothy Smith Osler: Storrar came second with ninety-three, and William Allen Miller, who had qualified in medicine but had been Professor of Chemistry at King's College since 1845, came third with eighty-two. No other medical man made the group of six whose names were to be sent to the Home Secretary. And towards the end of the day, to add to the discomfort of the orthodox medical men, a shrunken meeting voted by thirty to seven to confirm William Shaen, a lawyer with a declared faith in homeopathy, as Clerk.

In brutally simple, political terms, the meeting of 10 November underlined the power and appeal of the long-established leadership of the Graduates' Committee. Most of those who had put themselves forward for nomination had been long-serving members of that Committee. Storrar had been assured of a great deal of visibility among the graduates, and had earned their respect. Miller had been a close colleague. Neither was seriously threatened within the newly constituted Convocation by the offended Royal College of Physicians' men and their allies.

But the widespread indignation over the by-passing of Convocation, combined with the more concentrated disapproval of Storrar as the Senate's choice for the GMC, was sufficiently strong to lead to the calling of a meeting of medical graduates – not sponsored by Convocation – a week later. At it, a delegation was chosen to call on the Home Secretary to present medical griev-ances, and an apparently small number of those present agreed to subscribe money to enable a legal action to be brought to prevent Storrar from taking his seat on the General Medical Council. A resolution asserting that Storrar's appointment 'is calculated in every way to alienate from the University the respect both of its Graduates in Medicine and of the Medical Profession at large', was signed by seventy-seven graduates, though whether as many as that were actually present is unclear – a figure of sixty was claimed by an unsympathetic commentator.[16] What examination of the list of seventy-seven

---

[16] The resolution was received by the Senate and recorded in the Minutes of 12 January

signatories does show, however, is that less than half of them were at that time Licentiates or Fellows of the Royal College of Physicians. The unpopularity of the Senate's action was not, therefore, wholly confined to the RCP.

The furious medicos met on the same date – 17 November – as the Senate, but earlier in the day, for the Senate was well briefed on what had transpired. On learning that legal action – an application for a writ of *quo warranto* – was being taken against Dr Storrar, the Senate authorised the Vice-Chancellor to apply to the Treasury for defence in Storrar's behalf to be undertaken by the Treasury Solicitor.

Spencer Walpole, the Home Secretary, agreed to meet the medical delegation on 19 November. What was put before him, and what was contained in a number of contemporary press reports, reveals a range of concerns felt by the medical people much wider than the immediate controversy over the Storrar appointment, and indicative of significant strains and divisions within both the University and Convocation. The delegation was instructed to start at the top, as it were, and urge

> . . . the necessity of sustaining the medical and scientific elements of the University, which had been gradually dying out, whilst the legal and political elements, which had far less appropriate means of usefulness, had been unreasonably increased in the late nominations in the Senate.[17]

As the Senate had received a report recommending the introduction of degrees in Science four months earlier, and would adopt the idea formally early in January, 1859, the instruction to the delegation was hardly relevant to the 'scientific elements'; but, as we have seen, so far as the medical side was concerned, its comment on the Senate nominations was fair.

The delegation wanted more representation of medicine on the Senate; and they objected to Storrar's appointment to the GMC. These two matters came together in the delegation's concern over the result of the election by Convocation of the six candidates from whom the Home Secretary would have to choose two as new members of the Senate. As Storrar had come second on the list, if the Minister was to select the two who had won the most votes, Storrar would become a Fellow as well as the University's representative on the GMC. The *Morning Chronicle*, highly supportive of the medical delegation, and doubtful of Storrar's appointment to the GMC being upheld by the courts, suggested that he should resign; and argued that, in the matter of the selection of new Fellows,

1859. The claim of sixty was made in a letter by Henry Savage, MD, in *LUM*, December 1858. See also UL RO 1/3/4.
[17] *Lancet*, 20 November 1858.

It was only by seeing the numbers of the Senate that the sentiment of the Senate could be rightly arrived at, and should the gentlemen who stood at the head of the list be selected, the Crown, in making that selection, would be acting purely out of compliment and deference to the wishes of the University.[18]

An even wider attack had been made during the meeting of medical graduates on 17 November, when it was claimed that

> ... the medical graduates had been excluded by the tactics of a section of the late Graduates' Committee, from all opportunity of expressing their sentiments in the late elections. The six [candidates who won most votes] were all of one College, all of one party, and *only one* medical candidate – viz Dr Storrar was included. The obvious design was to dictate to the medical faculty, to the Senate, and the Home Secretary, by sending for selection Dr Storrar and no one else.[19]

It was clear that Storrar and Miller were also not acceptable to the objectors because they were not in practice: as it was still being pressed some months later, 'workers only can fitly represent workers'.[20]

The *Lancet*, which had been very supportive of the Graduates' Committee in its campaign for recognition, now turned savagely on the leadership of Convocation:

> Was it politic [of Convocation] to set against the struggling University the sympathies – or prejudices, if it be preferred – of the educated classes, by selecting for its Chairman a gentleman prominently known as a sectarian agitator; for its Clerk, an attorney, who may be described as bristling with eccentricities; for its representative on the Medical Council ... a gentleman almost unknown to the scientific world, and who has devoted very fair abilities and perseverance to boring Members of Parliament about Medical Reform, and the dark designs of the College of Physicians?[21]

Even when Convocation, on 24 November, appointed a Committee to negotiate for parliamentary representation, exception was taken to the fact that only two medical men were included – Storrar and Miller. This was fully in line with an overall complaint that the leadership of Convocation was confined to 'one clique', made up overwhelmingly of the old Graduates' Committee.[22]

As the papers of the Graduates' Committee are apparently lost, it is impossible to probe these assertions thoroughly, though there can be little doubt

---

[18] *Morning Chronicle*, 19 & 20 November 1858.
[19] *Lancet*, 20 November 1858.
[20] *LUM*, December 1858; *Lancet*, 21 May 1859.
[21] *Lancet*, 27 November 1858.
[22] *LUM*, December 1858; *Lancet*, 4 December 1858.

that the leadership of both the Committee, and subsequently of Convocation, was indeed concentrated in a very small group, at least a high proportion of whom would have been classifiable, in terms of national politics, as Liberal or Radical. Nor is there any doubt as to the extent of UCL representation. Of the twenty-eight men who put themselves forward as prospective candidates for election to Fellowships, no less than seventeen were UCL graduates, as were eleven of the sixteen who eventually stood. Five of the six victors were from UCL, the exception being Miller, a King's man.

Three days after Walpole had received the medical deputation, he was made aware of correspondence between two leading medical men, Richard Quain and Alexander Tweedie, in which they argued that, as the new Charter allowed the Secretary of State to select each new Convocation Fellow from among the top three candidates elected, there should not be any automatic choice of the numerical winner. But Walpole brushed this aside: 'It is clearly right the two to be selected would be Mr Osler and Dr Storrar.' Two years later, Walpole's successor, Sir George Cornewall Lewis, was pressed to pass over George Jessel, who had most votes, in favour of George Johnson, then Professor of Materia Medica and Therapeutics at King's, who had come second in the third election of Convocation nominees. Foster objected strongly, in his capacity as Chairman of Convocation, and, like Walpole, Cornewall Lewis ignored the appeal.[23] It is unlikely that either Home Secretary needed to be persuaded: the precedent set by Walpole and confirmed by Lewis seems never to have been challenged, subsequently. The Home Office's acceptance that whoever won the election of candidates for nomination would be made a Fellow established majority rule in a body where the medical men would always be in a minority.

In 1858, however, Walpole was troubled over the fact that six names were sent to him for two vacancies, rather than separate lists of three for each vacancy. But his Permanent Secretary, Horatio Waddington, whose advice he followed, was confident that the 'present construction' was in conformity with the provision of the Charter, which 'says that Convocation shall appoint three times as many persons as there are vacancies, when there is more than one vacancy'.[24]

The first two Convocation Fellows, Osler and Storrar, were appointed in January, 1859. Walpole also had other vacancies to fill on the Senate, but did not take the opportunity to increase the medical presence there. Indeed it was not until the following year that the medical strength on the Senate was further increased: Richard Quain won the second Convocation place, and

[23] HO 45/6434, Lawrence to Percival, 20 November 1858: HO 45/7021, Carpenter to Lewis, 10 August 1860; Foster to Lewis, 25 October, 6 November 1860.
[24] HO 45/6434, Walpole to Waddington, 4 December 1858.

Granville recommended to George Cornewall Lewis that the Crown should appoint the leading London surgeon at Bart's, James Paget.[25]

If the protesting medical graduates were unhappy at the outcome of the first elections for membership of the Senate, many members of Convocation, irrespective of their specialisation, were doubtless disappointed at the fate of the challenge to the Senate's unilateral appointment of Storrar to the GMC. The application for the writ of *quo warranto* was upheld in January, 1859, and the case went to the High Court in June. There, the Attorney General successfully defended the Senate's right to choose who should represent the University. That decision underlined heavily the limited role which Convocation could play in the University's affairs.

The fact that, from time to time, relations between parts of the medical fraternity and the rest of the University were somewhat fraught, in large part reflected the professional separateness of medicine and some sense, among its practitioners, that their special role in society gave them the confidence to expect other interests to be readily acquiescent to their demands, even though, in the university context they became, in sheer numbers, a steadily diminishing minority.

But the potential tensions and occasional explosions have to be set against the major, continuing progress of the University. Even if the medical members of the Graduates' Committee may, on occasion, have been bored or indignant with their fellows in Arts and Laws, they had long managed to combine effectively enough with them to achieve their main aims. From the outset, the Graduates' Committee had been a loose coalition of equal sub-committees of Arts and Laws graduates, on the one hand, and medical graduates, on the other hand. The advantage – nay, the necessity – of continuing at least the same degree of co-operation, after Convocation had been set up, was recognised, with rather a bad grace, even before the row over the GMC and Dr Storrar had blown over.

That the atmosphere was still tense before the Annual Meeting due on May 10 1859 is indicated by the fact that there had been suggestions of 'some kind of separation' being made between medical and other graduates 'in respect to the nomination of persons from whom the Crown is to select members of the Senate'.[26] No such separation was made, but, on another front, two medical men had given notice of a motion for the appointment of separate committees, one for Medicine, and one for Arts and Laws, which should act conjointly to form the annually elected Standing Committee of Convocation. Each committee should be of the same size, and each of them should depute a quarter of their number to act with the other. Both the proposers of this arrangement were Fellows of the Royal College of Physicians who had been

---

[25] HO 45/7021, Granville memo and Granville to Drummond, nd [1860].
[26] *LUM*, May 1859. Letter attacking the idea from Alfred Wills, 23 April 1859.

among those who had condemned Storrar's nomination to the GMC; but their proposal was relatively moderate. It did emphasise, however, their clear wish that the medical graduates should operate to a considerable extent separately from the other faculties, and that they should be given a weight in the overall control of Convocation's day-to-day affairs, disproportionate to their numbers.

When Convocation met on 10 May, doubtless after much negotiation, a revised version of the original motion was put forward: there should be only one committee, with thirty-two members divided between two sub-committees of equal size, one for Medicine and the other for Arts and Laws. And each sub-committee would choose four of its members to sit with the other sub-committee.

But this further attempt at amelioration was insufficient either to assuage the anger of some of the medical fraternity, or to overcome the objections on the side of the Arts and Laws to the arguably privileged position of Medicine. Two amendments were proposed immediately. One, by the young Michael Foster, called for the establishment of a sixteen-strong committee to report on the 'present state of Medical affairs in relation to the University'. This has to be seen as a wrecking amendment, whose author was prepared, presumably, to see all the other business of getting Convocation off the ground delayed, in order to force attention to the alleged neglect of medical interests by the Senate. The other amendment was more directly aimed at the substance of the main motion. It was moved by Rev Albert Creak, who called for the appointment of three committees, one for each of the Faculties of Arts, Laws and Medicine, and each consisting of six members. Thus was the special claim of Medicine challenged by the assertion that each Faculty should have the same representation. But if the argument shifted to the numbers of graduates involved, then Creak's motion, if carried, would have given gross over-representation to Laws.

This amount of detailed narrative is included to demonstrate the knife-edged nature of this short era in the early life of Convocation. There was, obviously, a protracted and in all probability a bad-tempered argument, which the Minutes describe, economically, disappointingly, and flatly, as a 'long debate'. At its end, the two amendments were withdrawn, and the original motion was carried on a count of heads by thirty-two to thirty-one, resulting in an immediate demand for a division, which produced a confirmation of the first count by a majority of forty-one to thirty-six. There is no division list, nor any list of who attended the meeting. It is conceivable that either the medics were present in sufficient force to carry the day; or that some members of Arts and Laws felt it wiser to mollify their medical colleagues in order to hasten a settlement which would allow Convocation to make progress.

Thus the principle of the old arrangement of the Graduates' Committee was accepted as the basis for day-to-day operation of the new Annual Committee, which became, in effect, the working nucleus of Convocation. And, as was described in an earlier chapter, the method of selecting the Annual Committee developed into an orderly election at every Annual General Meeting. But for the first year or two the selection was in accordance with a simpler procedure.

Dr Sibson was the originator of the successful motion. It having been carried, he was immediately charged with the nomination of its members. This implies a good deal of previous – and perhaps some last-minute – manoeuvring, made perhaps easier by the strong likelihood that those who wished to serve were not numerous. That Sibson's list of thirty-two names was readily accepted must be seen as a sign that there was a widely shared conviction among those present that compromise between factions was essential. Sibson's diplomatic bargaining doubtless helped to sooth the ire of those medics who had been among the pro-RCP and anti-Storrar faction at the special protest meeting of medical graduates held in November, 1858. Ten of them, including Sibson, were among the sixteen medical graduates appointed.

The arrangement of having four Arts and Laws members sitting with the Medical Sub-Committee, and four medical men serving on the Arts and Laws Sub-Committee, took effect in July, 1859. The medical group chose Storrar and Henry Thompson, both UCL men, together with Richard Quain and Sibson, both Fellows of RCP – perhaps another step back to normal relations between previously opposed groups. But though the size of each group was increased from four to five in 1863, the whole provision for sub-committees was dropped at the end of the following year. From 1865 onwards the medical graduates had to share their sixteen places on the Annual Committee with graduates in science.

By 1865, however, the fiery divisions of 1858–59 had cooled, and not only – perhaps, not even mainly – because of the pressures for compromise within Convocation. The principal cause of the establishment of a calmer and more co-operative relationship between Senate and Convocation was the steady recognition of the complementary interests of the two in furthering the progress of the University. There were still a few misunderstandings and resentments, but they were much reduced by several developments. First was the fact that the Senate involved its Convocation-nominated Fellows fully in its work, and that they were very attendant to their duties. Second was Convocation's decision, in 1862, to make those Fellows of the University who were members of Convocation, but were directly Crown-chosen, *ex officio* members of the Annual Committee: this was a gesture no doubt welcomed, but, in practice, attendance by such Fellows – who were not numerous in the early years – was rarely significant. And third was the tendency for committees of both bodies to have some members who belonged to both Senate and Convocation.

But there was also significant widening of the University's offerings, which produced a little friction on occasion, but, overall, closer co-operation and discussion between Senate and Convocation. The two biggest events were the introduction of Science Degrees in 1859, and the granting of a new Charter, in 1863, which authorised the granting of degrees in Surgery and made a few desirable changes to details of the arrangements for Convocation.

The Senate had appointed a committee to advise it on the possible introduction of degrees in Science, just before the 1858 Charter took effect, in March of that year. Not without some internal protests by some veteran Fellows, in July they received the committee's recommendation that such degrees should be introduced. But it was not until January, 1859, that the recommendation was adopted in principle, and consideration of ways and means began. And it was August, 1859, before the draft regulations for the new degrees were approved and sent to the Home Secretary, who accepted them readily. Examinations in Science, and the award of degrees, began in 1860.

There is very little documentation of the progress of the introduction of the Science degrees in 1858–1860, but it appears that the whole business was brought to a conclusion without any reference being made to Convocation. Given the fact that the early stages occurred while Convocation was putting its own house in order, and that the decision in principle to introduce the degrees was taken well before the long and momentous Annual Meeting of Convocation in May, 1859, it is perhaps unsurprising that the Senate did not refer the matter formally. The generally tense atmosphere of the period was reflected in the Annual Committee's complaint, in 1860, that Convocation had been given no opportunity to comment: but their parent body took no further action.

A much happier note was struck by the negotiation of the introduction of degrees in Surgery. The Senate agreed in November, 1859, to seek legal advice as to whether the University's present powers would cover the introduction of a degree of Master in Surgery. In the following March, the Law Officers advised that the University's degree in Medicine could not be recognised as a legal qualification in surgery, nor did the Charter allow the Senate to create the proposed Master's degree. Meanwhile, Convocation's Annual Committee had been discussing the University's medical offerings and reported to the Annual Meeting in May, 1860, when Convocation accepted its advice and recommended the Senate that the degree of Master in Surgery be instituted. A further request for legal opinions as to the powers of the General Medical Council to interfere with courses of study and examinations prescribed by the University's regulations was made by the Senate in July 1860.

During the winter of 1860–61 the issue became more complicated, perhaps, in part at least, because of the apprehensions of the Royal College of Surgeons. On 17 April 1861, a Committee on Degrees in Surgery was appointed by the Senate. It met only once, when eight of the eleven members attended, including Foster, Osler and Storrar, and considered how to go about ensuring that the University could 'confer on graduates in Medicine a legal qualification to practice Surgery and also to confer the degree of Master in Surgery'. The outcome was another request for legal advice, especially in the light of a recent decision on a case before the Privy Council. That request produced, in July, the opinions of the University's counsel, Tomlinson, and of the Law Officers, which repeated the earlier advice that the University had no power under the present Charter to give degrees in Surgery. A new Charter could give such power, but 'whether the Crown ought to be advised to grant such a Charter, regard being had to the rights and privileges formerly granted to the College of Surgeons, is a question which admits of very considerable doubt'.

But the desirability of providing for Surgery was not the only matter on the constitutional agenda of Senate and Convocation. Convocation was pressing for certain additional powers, and the University had been approached by Henry Cole, at the Committee of Council on Education, to consider the establishment of a degree in Mining, primarily for students of the Government School of Mines.[27] This last request was turned down by November, 1861, after being studied by a committee including Foster and Storrar, on the grounds that the candidates would be insufficiently qualified to be deserving of a degree. But on the Surgery front, the major breakthrough came in August, 1861, when the Government intimated that it was prepared to grant the University a Supplementary Charter for a Master in Surgery.[28]

At the beginning of the session 1861–62, the shape and content of a possible new Charter must have been well advanced, and must have resulted to no small extent from consultation with Convocation. In October, Tomlinson advised the Senate that as well as providing power to offer degrees in Surgery, a new Charter would be needed to enable graduates outside Arts, Laws and Medicine – i.e. Science – to become members of Convocation. The Senate resolved to have a new Charter drafted: it was approved on 7 May 1862, when an amendment to make women admissible to degrees was defeated, after an exciting debate – of which more, later. The proposed Charter was subsequently agreed with Convocation, which provided, through George Jessel, a draft of one important section which was incorporated in the final version, before it was sent to the Home Office on 4 June.[29]

Unfortunately, the file on the new Charter is missing from its appointed place in the Home Office papers. The proposal was challenged by the Royal College of Surgeons in the autumn of 1862, but the objection was withdrawn in November, though the College retained a *caveat*. The new Charter was finally granted in January, 1863, to general satisfaction, Convocation putting on record its gratitude to the Senate for the latter's acceptance of Convocation's wishes. Clearly, the relationship of the two bodies had greatly improved. The new Charter gave the Senate authority to introduce new degrees in any subject save Theology, and awarded several new powers to Convocation – to recognise any degree as qualification for admission

[27] UL RO 1/3/6, Cole to Carpenter, 18 July 1861.
[28] UL RO 1/3/6, Home Office to Vice-Chancellor, 2 August 1861.
[29] UL RC 17/5 & 6.

to Convocation; to accept and surrender any 'supplemental' as well as any new Charter; and to introduce postal voting for the election of candidates from among whom the Home Secretary would recommend appointment as Fellows.

# 7

# *The ambitions of Charles James Foster*

By the autumn of 1863, Convocation had been in existence for four and a half years, and, by then, its activists had accommodated themselves – if not without some resentment – to the legal and practical limits of their involvement in the University's affairs, and had survived a period of difficult internal relations between some of their medical members and the majority. There was still one early constitutional adjustment to be made, within the Annual Committee, which would involve the medical graduates sharing their sixteen places with graduates in Science: but that seems to have been accepted without controversy. The framework thus established by 1865 would remain virtually unaltered for more than thirty years, until each of the four faculties of Arts, Laws, Medicine and Science were given nine members on the Annual Committee, renamed the Standing Committee, in May 1897.

Though there were to be no significant alterations to the formal scheme within which Senate and Convocation co-existed between 1865 and 1900, there was no shortage of controversy. It was accepted, essentially, that action in the context of University affairs would be conducted within the parameters settled by the end of the first five years of Convocation's existence; and to no small extent the early era of confrontation gave place to a future apparently dominated by the notion of mutual accommodation, by both Senate and Convocation. But this relative calm was accompanied by a series of attempts to strengthen the position of Convocation, which were reflections of the discontents over the limited role allotted to it by the Charter of 1858. And those attempts were the precursors of the rancorous episodes which marked the arguments over the future of the University in the 1880s and 1890s, though those arguments were complex and, in reality, a conflict of many factions rather than a straightforward confrontation between the two principal institutions.

If one searches for a turning point in the transition from an atmosphere of touchiness and unease in the relations of Senate and Convocation to one of relatively relaxed co-operation, one is driven to point to the disappearance from the scene of the first Chairman of Convocation, Charles James Foster. Foster was a political activist of the first order. He was a leader who had a clear idea of what Convocation's role – and his role – should be. But though some of what he envisaged came about many years after his time, the full extent of his ambition for Convocation simply proved to be unviable. He resigned in

November, 1863, and emigrated to New Zealand. It is time to consider his career as the first Chairman.

There can be no doubt as to the strength of Foster's influence, from his original attempt, at Lincoln's Inn, as far back as 1840, with Frederick John Wood and Jacob Waley, to have men with London degrees given the same terms of entry as those enjoyed by the graduates of Oxford and Cambridge. He was a leading member of the small group who, in 1848, set up the Graduates' Committee. He published a book arguing for the establishment of a parliamentary seat for London University, in 1851,[1] and throughout the 1850s he used his skill and energy as a parliamentary lobbyist to push Governments of any hue to recognise the claims of the University and of its graduates.

It has to be emphasised, however, that the University of London was not the primary focus of Foster's loyalty. He was a Baptist, fiercely committed to the abolition of Church rates and to the eventual disestablishment of the Anglican Church. Moreover, since the mid-1850s he had been the salaried Chairman of the Parliamentary Committee of the Liberation Society and had been a leading broker in parliamentary dealing over all matters concerning the causes of the Dissenters. His devotion to those causes was not weakened by his efforts on behalf of the Graduates' Committee, nor by his election to the Senate and then to the Chairmanship of Convocation, in 1858. Indeed, he was ungrudgingly energetic in the cause of Convocation, and it is clear that he was a determined and a courageously self-reliant leader: one of his closest colleagues admired 'the readiness with which he accepted responsibility in those not infrequent crises in which it was necessary either to take an important decision without authority or not at all'.[2]

Foster had no independent means, and he gave up the Chair of Jurisprudence at UCL on his appointment to the Senate. He cannot have had much time to devote to a private law practice, and his hope of appointment to a legal post in government was disappointed.[3] The financial pressure which he was put under, as a result, must have been clear to some of his closest colleagues, and it is not surprising that an attempt was made, after Convocation had been in existence for twelve months, to raise the question of some remuneration of the Chairmanship.

The Charter of 1858 made no mention of remuneration of Convocation's officers. At the Annual Meeting of May, 1859 – the same meeting which saw the struggle over the establishment of the Annual Committee – the Rev. Albert Creak had given notice, and duly moved, 'That, in view of the important duties devolving upon the office of Chairman of Convocation, the Senate be requested to attach such a salary to it as shall be commensurate

---

[1] C.J. Foster, *The University of London – A Parliamentary Constituency* (London, 1851).
[2] UL RC 1/2/i/ii. Draft by T.S. Osler.
[3] UCL College Corresp., Foster to Atkinson, 4 December 1860.

with the dignity of the representation of the Incorporated Graduates.' But after debate in a thinning house, this motion was withdrawn. Another motion was substituted, in the names of two lawyers – T.S. Osler and Henry Matthews – and carried. It made no mention of the Senate and authorised the setting up of a committee 'to consider and report . . . upon the duties of the Chairman and the amount of the salary appropriate to his office'. A later motion added consideration of a salary for the Clerk of Convocation to the Committee's duties.

The minutes of almost all of Convocation's committee meetings were normally printed and published, but in the very earliest years that did not always happen. Perhaps understandably, in view of its subject matter, there is no record of this particular committee's proceedings, other than its report, signed by Storrar, as Chairman, on 26 April 1860. There is no way, therefore, of telling how many times the committee met, who attended, and what divisions of opinion were expressed, if any. But we do have two documents which reveal very different attitudes, not merely to the question of remuneration, but to wider issues which go to the heart of the contemporary relationship between Senate and Convocation.

Foster's view of the matter was written in answer to a request from Convocation's committee when Osler was its Chairman, in December, 1859. His letter to Osler is reproduced in full.[4]

> I readily give my views on the subject of Creak's motion. As I have said, it did not originate with me; tho' I felt it no part of my duty to interfere to prevent it. I think the present position of Chairman of Convocation an unjust one – both to Convocation and to whomsoever it may be by whom the post is occupied. I do not think [it can be put] perfectly right but by a new Charter, but as I think a Supplementary Charter will be felt to be desirable both by the Senate and by Convocation on other grounds, I may as well state my own views. How far, supposing them to be right abstractedly, they can at present be carried out is another question.
>
> I think that the office should bear an academic title – have attached to it a salary measured both by the absorption of time that it requires and by the dignity of the office itself – and be of a practically permanent tenure: and I think it very desirable that the chairman should be *ex officio* a member of the Senate during his term of office.
>
> The object of course is that the choice of Convocation should as far as possible not be limited beyond the consideration of fitness for the post. At present, among many who are certainly fit, I am sure there would be more difficulty than there ought to be in finding candidates for this office.

---

[4] The final letter from Foster to Osler is in the Granville Mss, PRO 30/29/23/6 fols 415–24, nd. There is a copy of an earlier draft in the University's archives, dated December 1859, which is different only in unimportant ways, though it does include the suggestion that the academic title proposed might be Dean, Provost or Master. UL RC 1/2/h.

It must practically be part – and a most important part – of the duty of Chairman to attend on committees appointed either by Convocation or by the Senate. Independently of his personal views upon any subject referred, he will naturally be able to give effective official or semi-official assistance to the Convocation committees in the arrangements necessary for their meeting – their communications with the Senate – printing documents etc. Unless the Chairman is looked to in these matters the Committees of Convocation will be subject to a degree of dependence upon the Registrar which will hardly be desirable. Of committees appointed by the Senate on matters on which University graduates have any probable interest, the Chairman of Convocation is almost an inevitable member.

Thus upon him falls an extent of duty attaching to no other member of the University, and involving an absorption of time such as to render the assumption of the office a serious matter to any professional man having the ordinary professional engagements of law or medicine. This is certainly no theory in my case. I believe I may say that I have been at Burlington House three days a week and five hours in a day.

In these engagements the personal convenience of the Chairman cannot be more consulted than that of other members of University Committees. Indeed, unless he is prepared to make somewhat greater sacrifices than others, it will be likely to interfere appreciably with the prosecution of their enquiries.

I have no hesitation in saying – looking to the class of men from whom it is desirable that our Chairman should be taken – that the probable loss of income due to the time thus required from him is not less than £300 a year. Looking to the dignity of the office I entertain great doubt whether a less sum than £500 a year ought to be proposed as a salary.

I think it decidedly objectionable that an office placed upon such a basis as I have sketched should be open to scramble every three years. On the other hand the real importance of its duties requires virtual superannuation to be guarded against. The Chairman's probable age on his first assumption of office would perhaps be not much under forty. Probably a term of ten years with capability of re-election would nearly hit the practical convenience of the case.

I am aware that the sum I have named will involve a considerable addition to our present demands upon the public purse. But remembering the facility with which double our present increased grant has lately been given to the Scotch universities and more than five times the amount to the Queen's Colleges in Ireland, I am personally of the opinion that the University barely performs its duty to the public in not seeking for much greater means to be placed at its disposal.

Foster's letter to Osler rests among Lord Granville's papers. How and why it reached the Chancellor, and whether with or without Foster's knowledge and consent, is uncertain. Perhaps Osler, who was just on the point of becoming a Fellow, sent it to him directly. But perhaps the most likely route for the letter to have taken was for Osler to have handed it to the Vice-Chancellor, Shaw Lefevre, because Shaw Lefevre's undated memorandum on it, marked 'Private and Confidential', is also in the Granville Mss. On the other hand, Granville may have received it from Osler, and then invited

Shaw Lefevre's comments. Whatever happened, there is about the event some suspicion that nothing of any likely significance that came out of Convocation failed to reach the University's leading officials.

The Vice-Chancellor, who had been closely involved throughout the Graduates' Committee's campaign for Convocation, respected Foster but took a profoundly different view of the proper role of Convocation and its Chairman:

> It is impossible to read the new Charter . . . without seeing that it was clearly intended that the Convocation should only meet rarely and should not sit continuously – and if this body were to keep within its intended limits in that respect the proper duty of the Chairman would be anything but onerous and would certainly not require remuneration.
>
> His labours as a member of the various Committees of Convocation may undoubtedly be considerable, but I entertain the strongest objection to the existence and proceedings of these Committees. They seem to me to be inconsistent with [the] intention of the Charter and to have the effect of making the Convocation a continuously acting body. Their recent report on the curricula for our degrees affords a sufficient proof of the tendency to usurp and encroach on the functions of the Senate – and if the Chairman were paid he would infallibly multiply and increase the number and activity of these committees and they would inevitably come into collision with the Senate.
>
> With regard to the labours of the Chairman of the Convocation as a Member of the Senate and of its committees – to remunerate him for these would place him in a different and indeed an invidious position with reference to his unpaid colleagues and would be felt as an injustice by those who make personal sacrifices in order to attend to the business of the University.
>
> Moreover he would become, as it were, the delegate and mouthpiece of the Convocation at the Senate instead of being a colleague. This would be further aggravated if he were to be made an *Ex Officio* member. His desire for an academic title is a further indication of the disposition to encroach and to claim for the Convocation a share in the management of the University.
>
> Although I am satisfied of the inexpediency of Mr Foster's proposal, I am bound to say that he has devoted much more time and labour to the affairs of the University than is consistent with his private interest and his professional avocations – that his view as to the amount of remuneration and as to the period of office is fair and moderate, and that I should be glad to see him employed in the public service, believing him to he an honest, intelligent and laborious person . . . [5]

It is unlikely that Foster's vision of a highly active Chairman, paid to help drive a highly interventionist Convocation, would have appealed to most members of Senate. But it is obvious enough that there were also considerable

[5] PRO 30/29/23/14 fol. 143.

reservations within Convocation itself about Foster's ambitions. There must have been many graduates who had doubts as to how much the quite restricted powers of Convocation would allow an aggressive policy to be pursued. Even so thrustful an operator as Fowler, who was prepared to use the Senate as a way into Conservative politics, and who became quite prominent in Convocation affairs, had written in his diary, after the inaugural meeting of 4 May 1858, that he found it 'interesting, though I fear Convocation will not amount to much'.[6] And as will be seen, later, during the very time when the payment of the Chairman was being considered in committee, Foster pushed his candidacy for the University's parliamentary seat – which then seemed likely to be established, but in fact was long delayed. Even among some of his closest Convocation colleagues, the reaction was hostile to his radicalism and especially to his salaried position as a Dis-establishment lobbyist. There was, in all likelihood, some shrinking away from any prospect of creating a paid Chairmanship which would be held, in all probability for many years, by a professional political activist.

The Committee's report dealt with the case for paying the Clerk of Convocation a small salary, and agreed fully with the idea. But they were unconvinced of the desirability of having a long-term, salaried Chairman. How much they may have been made aware of the Vice-Chancellor's reaction, and what they knew of grass-roots Convocation opinion, is unknown, but they built their negative attitude on the uncertainty of the connection between the Chairman and membership of Senate, which had loomed so large in Shaw Lefevre's memorandum. They recognised the heavy load which Foster carried by his attendance to the work of the committees of both Convocation and Senate, and noted that the Senate 'has followed the practice of putting the Chairman . . . upon all its Committees'. This made the Chairman's 'functions there . . . incompatible with the active duties of professional life'. But they also stressed that the Chairman's close involvement in the affairs of Senate 'operates favourably in making the influence of Convocation continuously felt, and in securing a general harmony between the proceedings of the Senate and of Convocation'.

In effect, the Committee made a case and then left it hanging:

> . . . the amount of duties performed by the Chairman, which could alone justify a salary . . . 'commensurate with the dignity of the Representative of the Incorporated Graduates' are dependent upon the circumstance of the Chairman happening to be a member of Senate. Supposing that by a new Charter the Chairman . . . were made *ex officio* a Member of the Senate, then, inasmuch as the nature of his functions would interfere seriously with professional avocations, Convocation could not have any large power of selection among its members, unless it could offer such a salary as would induce its Chairman to give up the regular exercise of a profession.

[6] J.S. Flynn, *Sir Robert N. Fowler, Bart., MP, A Memoir* (London, 1893), p. 134.

This, again, would . . . be ineffectual unless the office were tenable for life, inasmuch as no person could be expected to sacrifice professional prospects for a mere temporary office.

The Committee have felt that . . . they will best discharge their duty by doing no more at present than placing the facts of the subject before Convocation, and indicating the conditions under which the question submitted to them has to be discussed; inasmuch as they think it impossible to deal with the question of attaching a considerable salary to the office, except in connexion with large constitutional changes in the tenure and incidents of the office. The expediency of making or attempting any such changes has not as yet been considered by Convocation, and the Committee have not deemed it within their province to entertain the subject.[7]

At the Annual Meeting on 8 May 1860, despite the Committee's report, Creak moved that a salary of £500 be attached to the Chairmanship. But an amendment proposed by Henry Mason Bompas, a lawyer, to adjourn discussion until the next meeting, was carried. No division was demanded, so that support for the amendment must have been clear-cut. There is no indication that the subject was ever raised again. It does not even seem to have appeared as a subject for possible inclusion in the Supplementary Charter which was negotiated in 1862 and came into effect early in 1863.

While the arguments against a paid Chairmanship, as expressed in the Committee's report, were not unreasonable, the whole episode – and the subsequent silence – leaves some sense of embarrassment on the part of Foster's colleagues on the Senate and in the small group of Convocation's leaders. All of them, unlike Foster, were able to rely either on high professional earnings, or private wealth, or both, to allow them to give unpaid time and effort to the University's affairs. There may well have been an unspoken feeling that only a gentleman of independent means was really acceptable in such positions as Foster was holding, however much he, personally, was respected for his abilities and his contribution. It is as though he was regarded, in this context, as an exception to a general rule, and that further exceptions should not be encouraged.

Foster may well have been disappointed by the lack of sympathy for his proposal, and he may well have been similarly crestfallen over the collapse of the legislation, in July, 1860, which – as we shall see later – would have provided the University with a seat in the House of Commons, for which Foster would have been a strong contender. He was too good a judge of the machinations at Westminster in 1861 to make any effort to put himself forward again as a potential candidate for what he saw was not yet to come the

---

[7] The report, dated 26 April 1860, is printed with the Minutes of the Annual Cmte of Convocation held on 8 May 1860.

University's way. For two more years he continued to be an energetic and obviously respected Chairman of Convocation, but in 1863 he came up against troubles which led him to give up his work in England and to emigrate to New Zealand. The main cause of his difficulties lay in his relations with the leadership of the Liberation Society. He had worked closely with Rev. Edward Miall, the founder of the Society, for many years, but in the early 1860s there developed severe differences over political tactics between the Society at large and the Parliamentary Committee of which Foster was Chairman.

> Foster had a basically different approach to the work of Liberation from that of the forceful and relentless Miall. Sooner or later one of these contrasting styles of leadership had to give way, and it was eventually that of Foster, who resigned on 26 June 1863 . . .[8]

His resignation from the Liberation Society deprived Foster of probably the bulk of his income. It seems likely that his personal difficulties and his forthcoming resignation from the Liberation Society post may have become known to his close collegues in Convocation a little earlier. On 6 May 1863, a *Testimonial to Dr Foster, Chairman of Convocation* was circulated to graduates by twenty-one leading members of Convocation, including several who were strongly opposed to his political stances. The *Testimonial* called for subscriptions to raise 'at least £1000' as a fund 'of which Dr Foster's acceptance should be requested, and which would prove to him that his labours in behalf of his fellow Graduates have earned for him their warmest esteem and gratitude'. Those who signed had already contributed £260.[9]

Whether Foster's friends were aware that he was contemplating emigration, or only resignation from the Liberation Society, they scrupulously avoided mentioning any such possibility in their appeal. But they pointed out that he was 'not possessed of an independent fortune', and that as a result of his devotion to the cause of the graduates, he had 'undoubtedly neglected to a considerable extent his own professional interests, and that too at a period of his career at the bar when such neglect must have been particularly detrimental'. But perhaps the most interesting observation concerned the failure of the proposal to make the Chairmanship a salaried position: the friends of Foster seemed willing to blame the Senate, and to have forgotten the somewhat evasive report of the committee which reported to Convocation:

> For some time past it has been felt by a large number of Graduates that the University ought no longer to allow Dr Foster's services to remain unrequited . . .

[8] W.H. Mackintosh, *Disestablishment and Liberation: The Movement for the Separation of the Anglican Church from State Control* (London, 1972), p. 59.
[9] UL RC 1/2/i/i.

three years ago this feeling led to a proposal in Convocation, that the Senate should be requested to attach a salary of £500 a year to the office of chairman. It appeared, however, that the peculiar financial circumstances of the University would present insuperable obstacles to such a measure, and hence it was reluctantly abandoned.

There is no evidence as to whether Foster accepted whatever was raised by this appeal. But he continued as Chairman of Convocation for another six months, resigning in November. In retrospect, he can be seen as a Chairman very different from his successors: indeed, he was unique. It was not merely that he was a paid lobbyist – he was intimately concerned with Parliament, and was instrumental in shaping the tactics of the small but growing group of Dissenting MPs. Political manipulation in Westminster and Whitehall, and in the often intricate and highly charged manoeuvres of the Nonconformist churches, was his forte, but he gave his time and his ability to the University, generously though not exclusively. It is probable that his successor, John Storrar – a non-practising medical man, apparently of modest, independent fortune – who served as Chairman for twenty-one years, gave to the University more of his time, proportionately, than did Foster. But Storrar and those who followed him were essentially academic politicians, seeking the attention and the favours of Government and Parliament from without: Foster, in that context, was an insider and a professional. His departure in 1863 must, to some extent, have weakened Convocation's effectiveness in a parliamentary context, but perhaps cleared the way for less aggressive and more accommodating relations between it and Senate.

No time was lost, when Foster's departure was confirmed, in starting the race to succeed him. A pamphlet was issued in November, 1863, by a group of six UCL men, in support of James Walter Smith.[10] Smith was an Oxford graduate who had taken his London LLB and LLD from St Mary Hall, in 1853 and 1856 respectively. Four of his backers were lawyers, one – Joseph Sharpe – being a successor to Foster as Professor of Jurisprudence at UCL. One of the other two, John Robson, was also qualified as a barrister, though he had taught at University College School, and later become Secretary of the College of Preceptors. He was to succeed Shaen as Secretary of Convocation. The sixth supporter was John Hall Davis, a physician who had just become a Fellow of the Royal College, and who had protested against Storrar's appointment to the GMC in 1858. Smith was described by his backers as

> . . . a gentleman of . . . knowledge and experience, who has taken such a constant and active part in the affairs of the University, and has devoted so much attention

[10] UL RC 1/2/j.

to the conduct of public business, [that he] would discharge the duties of the office in a manner beneficial to the interest of Convocation.

Unfortunately, this pamphlet is the only document about the subsequent election, except for some partial statistics, which seems to have survived. The contest between Smith and John Storrar, the only other candidate to stand, went unreported in the daily press and in the medical journals which might have been expected to comment. Nor can we do anything but speculate on why there were only two contestants. It may be that the voting members of Convocation had taken to heart the message of their committee, that whoever was Chairman would do a better job for Convocation if he was a Fellow, and that, even if he did not belong to the Senate, he would have to expend a great deal of time and unpaid effort. In other words, Foster would be a hard act to follow. There were, by February, 1864, no less than eight Fellows who were members of Convocation – Gull, Wood, Osler, Storrar, Richard Quain, Jessel, George Johnson, and Fowler. All were doctors or lawyers, save Fowler who was a banker pursuing political advancement: all save Storrar were strongly devoted to what became distinguished professional careers. None, save Storrar, seems to have been attracted to the prospect of chairing Convocation.

There is no evidence of how Storrar's campaign was conducted, but he would have had the advantage of long standing at the top of the medical side of the Graduates' Committee, followed by five years on the Senate and on the General Medical Council. He was well known, but the interesting aspect of his candidacy is that it must have presented some of the medical graduates with a dilemma. As the only medico standing, Storrar must have appealed to the strong notion that the medical fraternity deserved more recognition within the University; and that it was Medicine's turn, Foster having been a lawyer. But how strong were the memories, and the lack of forgiveness, among those medical men who had resented so deeply Storrar's antagonism to the Royal College of Physicians, and to his appointment to the GMC, given his relative lack of medical prestige? On this point, there are some partial figures available worth examination.[11]

Storrar won the election, beating Smith easily, by 121 votes to seventy-nine, at the General Meeting of Convocation on 10 May 1864. There is no other record of the actual voting, but there are lists of those who had nominated each of the candidates, and they were much more numerous than those who turned out to vote. Storrar was nominated by 204 graduates: 108 nominated Smith. Each set of figures represents roughly a two-to-one majority, so that a breakdown of the nominations should give a strong indication of the breakdown of actual voting, and in any case gives interesting data on the nature of the support for Storrar.

[11] UL RC 1/2/h. Nominations for the Chairmanship of Convocation, 10 May 1864.

Of the thirty-nine law graduates among the nominators, nineteen supported Smith and twenty preferred Storrar. The arts graduates went strongly for Storrar over Smith by 118 to sixty-one nominations. Similarly, the medical men put Storrar first by sixty-six to twenty-eight. Of the twenty-eight doctors who supported Smith, at least twelve were Fellows, Members or Licentiates of the Royal College of Physicians, nine of whom had opposed Storrar in 1858. But no less than thirteen of those medical men who had condemned Storrar's appointment in 1858 nominated him for Chairman in 1864, and Storrar's list included about a dozen who belonged to the RCP.

Storrar's victory underlines the strength of the Arts graduates, and the respect felt for the old guard of the Graduates' Committee. It also seems to imply a considerable weakening of the objections taken to him by senior members of the medical profession, and particularly by the Royal College of Physicians, in 1858. Not that his opposition to them disappeared: in an obituary, a quarter of a century later, it was remarked that

> On the General Medical Council his knowledge of detail and his strong affection for University influence were often of great value in combating propositions which seemed to aim especially at the predominance of the interests of corporations.[12]

No doubt his success in 1864 is to some extent explainable in terms of the keeness of the medical graduates to have a doctor as Chairman, and to the fact that the profession was probably more approving of the University since the introduction of degrees in Surgery and the presence of more medical men on the Senate. Moreover, after five years, it would seem that he had come to be accepted as a capable representative of the University's interests on the General Medical Council.

In a wider perspective, Storrar's election can be seen as marking Convocation's adjustment from a somewhat resentful and aggressive role to a more relaxed and collaborative relationship with the Senate; and a considerable easing of tensions between disciplinary divisions and internal medical factions. He was to have two decades as unchallenged Chairman, and while there were certainly controversies during his long term of office, there were also indications that concensus came to be regarded as a most desirable characteristic of Convocation's life, that factions had to have their turns, and that national political alignments were rather unwelcome, though their existence could not be wholly ignored. He died just before the controversy over the future of the University intensified, and one might speculate on whether his continued presence might have moderated the extent of the disagreements.

[12] *Times*, 12 March 1886.

The somewhat tortuous manoeuvring which Storrar's aspirations for concensus produced were perfectly illustrated within a year of his taking the Chair. The occasion was the election of the Senatorial List of three candidates to be nominated for a vacant seat in the Senate. By the end of 1864 there were seven Convocation-nominated Fellows. Osler and Storrar had been on the Senate since 1859: after them had come, in order, Richard Quain, Jessel, Johnson, Fowler, and William Allen Miller. The call to nominate the next slate of nominees came in the Spring of 1865, and four candidates came forward: Francis Sibson, long prominent in graduate affairs; Richard Holt Hutton, editor of the *Spectator* and a Professor at Bedford College; Henry Matthews, barrister and coming Conservative politician; and Thomas Harrison, a graduate of King's, who came in last with only twelve votes. Harrison was ignored in the following notice, on University of London headed paper, which was sent out on 4 May 1865, from three lawyers at Lincoln's Inn – Osler, Ebenezer Charles and Herbert Hardy Cozens-Hardy, all mainstream Liberals. The last two would become Fellows later.

> You will have already received the List of Nominations for the vacancy in the Senate. It is necessary, as you are aware, that three names should be submitted to the Crown.
>
> It is generally hoped that the Medical Candidate (Dr Sibson) will be returned at the head of the list. We believe it to be understood that this is a medical turn.
>
> May we ask your help in placing Mr Hutton in the second place. His well-known position in the literary world will, we trust, justify us in thus bringing his name before your notice.
>
> It must not be supposed that we are desirous of introducing a political element into these elections, but as it is beyond a doubt that any success obtained by Mr Matthews will be considered as a triumph of a Conservative organization, we think it would be undesirable that he should occupy the second place now as a stepping stone to further political successes hereafter. We may add that Mr Hutton is a Liberal of moderate opinions.[13]

The electorate duly obliged, giving Sibson 280 votes to Hutton's 124 and Matthews's forty-five. However, three points in the notice deserve attention. First, the idea of 'Buggins's turn', was clearly well established. But, second, it is not clear how it worked, because the medical representation was already in the lead before the 1865 election – Storrar, Quain, Johnson and Miller, against Osler, Jessel, and Fowler. Perhaps Miller was not regarded as a 'real' medico, and all that mattered was the balance between Medicine and everything else. If so, it may be that the lawyers gave Fowler honorary legal status.

[13] UL RC 2/6.

Third, the support for Conservatives within Convocation, weak enough when Locock was considered as a potential parliamentary candidate in 1860, had clearly not improved markedly by 1865, when Matthews received just less than 10 per cent of the vote.

# Part III

*Degrees for Women*

# 8

# *The campaign and defeat of Elizabeth Garrett*

Two major political issues had arisen before 1865 and continued to be highly significant after that year. The first – the question of attaining a place in the House of Commons for a representative of the graduates of the University of London – had been on the agenda of the Graduates' Committee since at least 1851, and had received the blessing of the leadership of both main political parties, in principle, in the early 1850s. The Senate took up the case after Convocation was established, and, as will be seen in Part IV, the seat was at last obtained in the Reform Bill of 1867, its first occupant being elected in the following year. The achievement of this objective could be celebrated by both Senate and Convocation as the desired result of their close collaboration.

The second issue – whether women should be admitted as candidates for the University's examinations and degrees – was only fully resolved, by contrast, over a period of twenty-six years, which saw some bitter controversy. The initial stage of the story, concerning the attempts by two young women to obtain medical training, has been covered many times. The first attempt – by Jessie Meriton White – was made in 1856 and summarily dismissed. The second attempt, by Elizabeth Garrett, in 1862, was also unsuccessful but raised the temperature very considerably. The remainder of the struggle has been less fully narrated: it included the admission of women, from 1869, to a special examination similar to Matriculation.

For seven years after that, intensive argument and negotiation continued before there was a breakthrough. Passage of important legislation relating to medical registration of women, in 1876, led to a new argument as to whether women should be admitted first to medical degrees, or whether admission was only acceptable if it was offered for all the University's offerings. The second view prevailed, but involved Senate and Convocation in some strained relations over constitutional proprieties. A new Supplemental Charter was approved in 1878, providing authority to open all the examinations of the University to women. The first women graduates took their degrees in 1880, and were admitted to Convocation in 1882.

No attempt is made in what follows to repeat or to extend what is already known of the wider social pressures for the advancement of educational and other opportunities for women, which were, of course, vital to the prospects of women wishing to enter universities. And the remarkable, sustained hostility which was shown in many quarters to the attempted social change is taken as read. What is essayed here is as detailed a story as can be put together of the sheer politics of the processes involved within (and to a limited extent without) the community of the University of London, over the question of admitting women, during its particular and protracted struggle with the matter.

Jessie Meriton White did not persist in her efforts to gain acceptance to the University's examinations, and abandoned her intention of becoming a doctor. There is no evidence that, in 1856, she had behind her any organised group, and none which implies that she was able to involve influential people to support her application or to appeal against its rejection. The Senate took Counsel's advice and, on 9 July 1856, rejected Miss White's application because they did not consider themselves 'empowered to admit Females as candidates for Degrees'. If there was any discussion among the fourteen Senators present, of whom nine were medical men, it was not recorded: nor was there any division on their resolution.

But before the Senate took their final decision, they had indicated to the Home Secretary that they would like to know the Government's attitude, in view of the fact that while, in the opinion of the Vice-Chancellor, Shaw Lefevre, the Charter did not limit the University's examinations to males, the founders of the University had not had any extension to females in mind. There is, apparently, no piece of paper extant on which any ministerial views were made available. What have survived, however, are Shaw Lefevre's own comments: he was sympathetic to the idea of having 'a certain number of female practitioners well instructed as to the diseases of women and children', but felt 'that there are very grave objections to their pursuing the course of education prescribed for male practitioners'. His concern was one which would be expressed time and time again in the years ahead – how to protect female delicacy and decorum, if women were taught the same curriculum as men, and especially if they were taught in mixed classes or in classes given by male lecturers.[1]

Jessie Meriton White received no sympathy from the graduates who were at the time still fighting for the creation of Convocation. The *London University Magazine* remarked, in paranoid fashion, on her application having caused Senate to ask for Counsel's opinion, that

> We only hope the opinion . . . will prevent the Senate committing the folly that their own common sense ought to have forbidden them to dream of . . . Are they, finding that they cannot defeat the claims of the Graduates by fair means,

---

[1] Shaw Lefevre to Grey, 30 June 1856. An extract from the letter is reproduced in Willson, *Our Minerva*, p. 291.

adopting the plan of rendering the degrees so worthless that no-one will think them worth disputing about?[2]

There is no sign that the subject of admitting women to the University was raised again, either in the Senate, or in Convocation after its establishment, until 1862. But one event which was significant for the future, in this context, was the creation, in 1858, of the General Medical Council, with responsibility for enforcing a minimum standard of medical training and instituting a register of qualified doctors. The enabling legislation did not exclude women, 'since it imposed no restrictions on candidates for registration other than having received a proper training'.[3] And the Council, using a special power relating to doctors trained abroad who had been practising in Britain before 1858, did admit to the register, in 1859, Elizabeth Blackwell, after being satisfied with the appropriateness of the medical degree she had obtained in the United States. But the Medical Act, 1858, did not require universities or medical schools to admit women or to permit them to take qualifying examinations. The struggle which ensued was not between aspiring women and Government: it was between, on the one hand, such women and their supporters, in and out of the medical profession; and, on the other hand, the governing bodies of the professional corporations, the medical schools and the universities.

But there had been other developments in the years between 1856 and 1862 which ensured that Elizabeth Garrett's unsuccessful campaign to gain entry to the University's examinations was very different in its conduct and its long-term effects from Jessie Meriton White's apparently limited attempt. What has long been known as the Women's Movement was given a considerable boost in those years, drawing upon the intellectual and political resources of new organisations devoted to social advancement, including the education of middle and upper class women, the nature of their employment, and the amelioration of the lack of property rights for those of them who were married. The full range of these related tendencies has been much researched in recent years, and need not be rehearsed here, except to mention those developments which were particularly supportive, such as the foundation of the National Association for the Promotion of Social Science, in 1857, and the appearance of the *English Woman's Journal*, in 1859.

---

[2] *LUM*, September 1856, quoted in Dunsheath and Miller, *Convocation*, p. 53.
[3] Jo Manton, *Elizabeth Garrett Anderson* (London, 1965), ch. 3. Much of the following account is based on Manton's book, on Louisa Garrett Anderson, *Elizabeth Garrett Anderson, 1836–1917* (London, 1929), and on two biographies of Emily Davies – Barbara Stephen, *Emily Davies and Girton College* (London, 1927), and Daphne Bennett, *Emily Davies and the Liberation of Women, 1830–1921* (London, 1990). The detailed chronology has been established, as far as possible, by reference to the Elizabeth Garrett Anderson Mss in The Women's Library at London Metropolitan University.

The existence of this feminist activity explains to no small extent the wide impact, in 1862, of what was to be a planned campaign by a spirited and remarkably determined young woman, who could count on considerable help from influential relatives, friends and the few sympathetic medical people; and a growing, if still limited, interest in and sympathy for the cause of women within the University community. In the latter context, particularly, it is interesting that the front runners, as it were, in the cause of the admission of women, were both potential medical students. For whereas, in 1856, there does not seem to have been much if any serious mention of the possibility that women might wish to take degrees in subjects other than medicine, in 1862 significant arguments were expressed in favour of women being admitted to degrees in all subjects. And those campaigning primarily for Elizabeth Garrett pressed the potential advantages to education of having women with degrees in other fields, because they recognised that the wider approach was, tactically, more likely to weaken opposition to the enrolment of women as medical students.

Elizabeth Garrett was the daughter of a successful and aggressive East Anglian entrepreneur. She decided in 1860, when she was twenty-four, that she would become a doctor, and persuaded her father to give her his full support. She was much influenced and guided by her friend Emily Davies, the future founder of Girton College, who was six years her elder, through whom she came to know Elizabeth Blackwell, Barbara Bodichon, Mrs Russell Gurney, and others, all of whom were at the forefront of contemporary feminist activities. Emily Davies's elder brother, the Rev. John Lewellyn Davies, Rector of Christ Church, Marylebone, was a member of The National Association for the Promotion of Social Science. In short, Elizabeth Garrett was, in 1862, though young, a prominent member of the small but growing group of politically aware supporters and leaders who formed the core of the Womens' Movement.

Elizabeth wanted to be a doctor, and especially wanted to qualify as an MD. But no medical school would accept her as a student. With the advantage of her father's willingness to spend money, and with the advice of knowledgeable and sympathetic friends, she was able to persuade the Middlesex Hospital to take her on as a surgical nurse, in August, 1860. She spent a full year in a strange, undefined position, partly nurse, partly student, taking tuition from some of the junior doctors. How she managed to persuade the hospital to give her these opportunities is partly explainable as the triumph of her own ability and determination, and partly by the willingness of the hospital to accept a donation from her, while denying that she could pay fees which would involve their recognising her as a student. What was remarkable was her capacity to move in an almost entirely masculine world, the great majority of whose members demonstrated anything from contemptuous amusement to brutally expressed resentment towards her presence. And it was the hostility to her among a majority of the male students, who petitioned the authorities to remove her, which led to her being refused any continuance for a second year. Even the offer of the endowment of a woman's scholarship by her father did not persuade the hospital to defy their own male students, whom they feared would desert the institution.

During the second half of 1861 Elizabeth Garrett continued her studies privately. Her previous experience at the Middlesex did not seem to have greatly advanced her cause, and she needed more basic theoretical knowledge. She tried a number of medical schools and universities, and the Royal College of Surgeons, to no avail. She was always refused entry on the grounds that 'no medical examining body would admit women candidates for degrees and the schools would therefore be educating illegal practitioners'.[4] But she did succeed, in August, 1861, in having an application to be registered as a student accepted by the Council of the Society of Apothecaries, though only after the Society had taken the advice of their Counsel, James Hannen, QC, that 'they could not refuse to admit a woman to the examination imposed on candidates for their licence'. Such a licence provided a 'minimum qualification for the family doctor'.[5] But in addition to passing the Society's examinations, three years of hospital attendance was required. There were still major obstacles to be overcome, therefore, but the chance of taking the Apothecaries' examination was welcome and something tangible to keep in reserve.

If Elizabeth's sojourn at the Middlesex had not always been comfortable, it had also become rather notorious, and not unnaturally had come to the attention of the medical press. Unfriendly comment in the *Lancet* ended with an editorial which 'maintained the uselessness of educating women in medicine when they could not obtain a valid diploma of qualification' and dismissed Elizabeth's efforts as 'a restless, morbid agitation in which no worthwhile principle was involved'.[6] No doubt this did reflect majority opinion within the medical profession, but such publicity may well have strengthened the resolve of those who favoured the admission of women, and must certainly have promoted Elizabeth Garrett as a name to be recognised. What all the experience of the past two years had done was to have made this young woman into a shrewd and resilient political operator: but perhaps not a little abrasive – Carpenter, the Registrar of the University, who was himself equivocal about the admission of women, recalled her being, in 1862, a 'bumptious self asserting girl'.[7]

In September, 1861, Elizabeth insisted that

[4] Manton, *Elizabeth Garrett Anderson*, p. 115.
[5] Manton, *Elizabeth Garrett Anderson*, pp. 116–18. Lord Hannen was a Fellow of the University from 1892 to 1894.
[6] *Lancet*, 6 & 27 July, 3 August 1861.
[7] UL RC19/7, Carpenter to Granville, 8 May 1868. D.P. O'Brien, *The Correspondence of Lord Overstone* (London, 1971), iii, 1307–8, Carpenter to Overstone, 26 January 1878.

> I really do not feel very anxious about entering a school this winter; the plan
> would be to be able to matriculate next summer at the London University or at
> St. Andrews, and begin the medical school work this time next year.[8]

She spent much of the winter studying for such matriculation, and helping
with the work of the existing women's organizations. It is possible that the
timing of the approach to London was influenced by the well-connected
Lewellyn Davies's awareness of the negotiations going on for a Supplemental
Charter to allow the University to award degrees in Surgery, and by his
optimism about the the Senate, whose members he believed were 'all advanced
Liberals'.[9]

Elizabeth Garrett's application to London was acknowledged by the Registrar
on 8 April, and was reported to the Senate on 9 April 1862.[10] But for some
weeks before, Elizabeth and her supporters had carried on a campaign cleverly
directed from the outset in favour of the admission of women to all the
examinations of the University, making no specific mention of medicine.
There is no absolute proof of contact or co-operation between the Garrett
camp and the classicist and lexicographer William Smith, who had been
a master at University College School, was currently an examiner for the
University, and, after becoming editor of the *Quarterly Review* in 1867, would
join the Senate. But the earliest evidence of support in the press came from
him, on 15 March, 1862, when the *Morning Star* published a letter in which
he argued that

> An examination for a degree acts both as a stimulus and as a test; and there seems
> no sufficient reason for witholding these advantages from women, if they can be
> secured without risk of collateral evils.

As will be seen, his closing phrase was reproduced in a manifesto circulated
by Emily Davies and Elizabeth Garrett. The *Morning Star*'s leading article, on
15 March, was very sympathetic to Smith's views, and trusted that 'the Council
of the London University may be induced to take the good work in hand
without delay'.

The drumming up of support for Elizabeth's application included the
printing and circulation of a statement of which the essential points were that

> A strong desire has for some time past been felt by many women, of the upper and
> middle classes, for some test of proficiency in the more solid branches of education,
> such as our Universities offer to young men . . . The prospect of passing a thorough

---

[8] Garrett to Davies, 11 September 1861, quoted in Manton, *Elizabeth Garrett Anderson*,
p. 87.
[9] Stephen, *Emily Davies*, p. 72.
[10] UL RO1/2A/3, Carpenter to Garrett, 8 April 1862.

Elizabeth Garrett. In 1866, aged 30.

examination would . . . operate as a most useful stimulus to exertion, and the possession of a Degree would be a guarantee of well-directed mental energy . . . a certificate of ability would be especially valuable. It is believed that this privilege might be accorded by the University of London without risk of collateral evils. . . . It is, therefore, hoped that the Senate may be willing to give the widest interpretation to the words of their Charter, and to 'hold forth to all classes and denominations' of Her Majesty's subjects, not excluding women, 'an encouragement for pursuing a regular and liberal course of education.'

Emily Davies's first biographer tells us that this statement was sent to all members of the Senate, and apparently to several papers, though few included any notice of it in their pages.[11] It was given prominence in the 1 April edition of the *English Woman's Journal*, with a strongly supportive introduction stressing the potential advantages for education:

> If, as would probably at first be the case, the candidates were chiefly ladies intending to be governesses, the benefit would not be confined to themselves, but would be indirectly felt throughout society. Teaching would no longer be looked upon as the one profession which all women, however uneducated and unfit, may take up as a means of support. Governesses holding a Degree would find themselves in a position somewhat akin to that of schoolmasters and private tutors, who can give similarly undeniable proof of preparation for their work, and the unqualified members of the profession would naturally sink to their proper level.

On 5 April, the *Spectator*, one of whose joint editors, R.H. Hutton, was active in Convocation and became a Convocation-nominated Fellow in 1866, included an article on 'Girl Graduates', which was supportive of the admission of women to degrees, but insistent that they would need a curriculum different from that offered to males – a view which was to be voiced increasingly in future years. Neither the *English Woman's Journal* nor the *Spectator* mentioned medicine.

In addition to hoping for some publicity in the press, the two women, with Emily Davies acting as Secretary, and Elizabeth Garrett and her father paying all the expenses, also approached many prominent people directly. But it is not entirely clear how much of that exercise took place before the first rejection of her application. She certainly had considered and abandoned the idea of asking Florence Nightingale for help, because she envisaged that famous lady's 'indifference or dislike to the scheme', in the middle of March.[12] But she may well have also embarked on a round of visits before 9 April, for calls on such people as her legal adviser, James Hannen, on the Vice-Chancellor and the formidable Mrs Grote, and on 'several members of Senate', are mentioned by biographers, though without dates attached.

The exact extent to which, and how, interest had been aroused by the time of the Senate meeting on 9 April 1862 is, therefore, somewhat doubtful, but attendance was certainly above average, with nineteen members present. There is no report of the debate, simply a record of the resolution, which was moved by Lord Overstone, and the result of the vote. The Senate, by seven to six, found 'no reason to doubt the validity of Counsel's opinion given in the

---

[11] Stephen, *Emily Davies*, p. 72. The other journals listed by Stephen were the *Star*, *Telegraph*, *Daily News*, *Globe*, *Athenaeum*, and *Medical Times*. None of these appear to have given the matter space before the Senate's deliberation except the *Star*, which also printed a letter from Newson Garrett on 31 March, 1862.

[12] Manton, *Elizabeth Garrett Anderson*, p. 124.

case of Miss Jessie Meriton White in 1856.' Elizabeth was informed of this on the following day.[13]

One can only admire Overstone's acuteness: by framing the resolution that the Senate 'saw no reason to doubt the validity of Counsel's opinion', he made the issue a narrowly legal one. Those who were sympathetic to allowing women to take the University's examinations would have to take exception to Tomlinson's interpretation of the Charter, and this may have given the lawyers present pause. The outcome was very close.

Only thirteen of those who are listed as having been at the meeting voted. Of the six who either abstained, or were not present when the vote was taken, no less than five were medical men. The other non-voter was Foster, a lawyer. The seven who carried the motion were made up of three medicos – Thomas Hodgkin, Gull and Storrar; and two lawyers – Jessel and Osler – together with Lord Overstone and Michael Faraday. But there were six who were prepared to express themselves, either as doubtful about the validity of Tomlinson's 1856 opinion, or simply to express their general support for at least having the admission of women considered. The six were the Chancellor and Vice-Chancellor; James Heywood MP, the Mancunian Unitarian who fought long and hard for the reform of entry to Oxford and Cambridge; Ryan, E.T.B. Twisleton and Lord Wodehouse (the future Earl of Kimberley). None was a medical man. Ryan and Twisleton were both lawyers long involved in governmental administration. Ryan, an ex-Indian judge, had been a Railway Commissioner and Assistant Controller of the Exchequer, and had just become a Civil Service Commissioner: Twistleton had been a Poor Law Commissioner, had contested the Cambridge seat in 1859, and had only just joined the Senate.

Of those who attended, whether voting or not, three lawyers and eight doctors did not oppose the legal *status quo*, while three senior parliamentarians, two distinguished public servants and the scholarly Grote were apparently sympathetic to the cause of women. Perhaps, within the Senate, at least on that occasion, the doubts and the outright opposition to the admission of women were concentrated mainly in the professional ranks of medicine and law. It is also worth noting that the Convocation-nominated Fellows – Foster, Osler, Storrar, Quain, Jessel and Johnson – and Gull, the London graduate appointed by the Crown in 1856, were all either lawyers or doctors and either voted for the resolution or did not vote. Whether this reflected their estimate of the majority opinion in Convocation, and their self-imposed duty to support it; or whether it was another piece of evidence of professional antagonism to the prospect of admitting women to examinations, is unlikely ever to be established. It is only fair, however, to point out that the positions taken by the three lawyers, Jessel and Osler, who voted, and Foster, who did not, can be defended as legally correct – Tomlinson's interpretation of the Charter was

---

[13] UL RO1/2A/3, Carpenter to Garrett, 10 April 1862.

never successfully challenged. A new Charter would be needed to give the University power to make women eligible to take its examinations.

The narrow vote was a disappointment but at the same time a stimulus to immediate further effort by the Garrett camp. Again, it is difficult to be absolutely sure of the sequence of events, but they comprised an intensive lobbying exercise concentrated into less than four weeks. The formal move was made by Elizabeth's father, Newson Garrett: he consulted the Attorney General, who advised him that the only way forward would be to ask for a new clause to be included in the draft Charter then about to be presented to the Senate. Garrett *père* drafted an appropriate memorial, which was sent to the University on 28 April. But well before then, Emily Davies, with some help from the Committee of the Society for the Employment of Women, had organised the printing and distribution of fifteen hundred copies of 'a letter asking for an expression of opinion, with a statement of the question, a form of adhesion for signatures, and a stamped addressed envelope', which was sent to 'persons of distinction and members of the University of London'.[14]

No full copy of the original document seems to have survived, but it must have been attached to a statement sent to the University listing ninety-four signatories. A single printed sheet of it, numbered '5', is available: it is headed:

> The following ladies and gentlemen have by signing the annexed form, or by personal communication, given their sanction to the proposal
>     'I hereby express my opinion that it is desirable to obtain the admission of ladies to the Examinations of the University of London.'[15]

Among the ninety-four signatories were thirteen peers; forty-four MPs (thirty-three Liberals, seven Conservatives and four who described themselves as Liberal-Conservatives); the Master of the Rolls, Lord Romilly; and many people prominent in professional, intellectual and educational circles; but few academics, though there were a couple of professors from UCL and KCL. Not included in that list, perhaps only for reasons of timing, were the names of some whom the biographers specifically claim as having written in support, such as Gladstone, Cobden, F.D. Maurice and Mrs Somerville. It was Mrs Somerville's contribution which made the greatest impression on the Vice-Chancellor, George Grote, who subjected the whole list of supporters to detailed scrutiny, in Emily Davies's presence, to ensure that they were valid.[16]

By the beginning of May, there can have been few people involved with the Women's Movement or with the University of London who were unaware

[14] Stephen, *Emily Davies*, p. 73.
[15] UL RC19/25.
[16] Stephen, *Emily Davies*, pp. 73–4.

of the challenge likely to be made at the forthcoming meeting of the Senate. Elizabeth Garrett and Emily Davies had probably made their best impression on a key figure, the Vice-Chancellor, George Grote – and on his spouse. Harriet Grote, writing as 'A Fortunate Wife', to the *Times* on 3 May, began a closely argued statement with the words: 'I am decidedly favourable to the endeavour now being made to procure for female students the privilege of being admitted to examinations in the London University.' Whether by accident or design, the paper published it in the issue of 8 May, the day following the Senate's crucial meeting. That meeting attracted twenty-four Senators – a substantial attendance.

On 7 May, Grote moved that the draft Charter, which had been prepared, primarily, to allow the Univerity to give degrees in Surgery, should include provision for the admission of women to degrees but not to membership of Convocation. There was a long debate, apparently unreported, and at 7.30 p.m. the house divided. Of those who are recorded as attending, three had apparently left the meeting: of the twenty-one present at the time of the vote, one abstained.[17] The twenty who voted were evenly divided. Granville had voted against, and was left to cast the Chairman's vote, which he did, traditionally, in favour of maintaining the *status quo*. The decision effectively ended Elizabeth Garrett's campaign to enrol in the University of London.[18]

The four Fellows who were at the meeting but had either left it or abstained were Hodgkin and Locock, medicos; Wood, a lawyer and a major figure in Convocation; and Wodehouse, the future Earl Kimberley. Which of them was present and abstained cannot be established. Of the twenty who voted, two medicos – Kiernan and Roget, together with Lowe, Nassau Senior and Stanley, had not been present on 9 April. Two doctors – Johnson and Quain – who had been present then, did not appear on 7 May. One can calculate and speculate interminably on how a slightly different pattern of attendance might have altered the outcome.

There was no legal ambiguity about Grote's motion: the decision called for was quite straightforward. Immediate controversy about female member-ship of Convocation was avoided. Voting, therefore, was clearly revelatory of members' convictions about the desirability of admitting women to the University's examinations. Of the ten who were in favour, perhaps the most notable was Robert Lowe, then in the middle of his controversial years as Vice-President of the Committee of Council for Education. Only one of the ten was a working doctor, but a very significant one – James Paget, the leading London surgeon, who had been on the Senate since 1860. He was joined by

---

[17] Manton, *Elizabeth Garrett Anderson*, p. 126.

[18] Elizabeth Garrett subsequently studied at St Andrews, took the qualifying examinations of the Society of Apothecaries, and went to Paris to achieve her MD. She married J.G.S. Anderson in 1871.

Peter Mark Roget, one of the leading medical men on the original Senate, but now eighty-three years of age and long retired from a public life which had embraced much more than medicine, and had included a spell as Secretary of the Royal Society. Of the other seven, Foster was a lawyer and Chairman of Convocation, but, as we have seen, essentially a radical political activist. And though a few of the rest had legal qualifications, none could be thought of as being in normal legal practice. Two parliamentarians – Heywood and Lord Stanley – were joined by Grote, Ryan, and Twisleton, who had all taken the same position on 9 April; and by Nassau Senior, thinker and teacher of law and economics and a senior adviser to Governments.

Granville, Overstone and Faraday were joined in opposition by five medical men and two lawyers. Jessel and Osler were both in mid-careers as lawyers, but of the doctors only Archibald Billing, Gull and Francis Kiernan were still practising. Neil Arnott was seventy-four, and had given up his London practice in 1855; Storrar was a medical and a Convocation politician, rather than a practising physician. If the opposition came largely from the medical and legal professionals, it is also clear that the Convocation-nominated Fellows and Gull, who may be regarded for this purpose as one of them, were divided from their Chairman. It is likely that Foster's radicalism overruled in his mind any obligation to represent what he may have known would be majority feeling in Convocation.

Overstone was a determined opponent of the admission of women. Granville, as befitted a good politician, was far more flexible, and was sufficiently troubled in his mind about his voting on 7 May to ask Shaw Lefevre, who had given up the Vice-Chancellorship in the previous year, how he would have voted on 'the great Feminine question'. Shaw Lefevre, a rather timid and cautious man, responded comfortingly, but sympathetically to the cause of women, and his reading of the current state of public and graduate opinion was in all probability correct. 'I should have voted as your Lordship did – but perhaps on narrower grounds', he wrote, and went on:

> I think that the present mode of educating women is objectionable and that it would conduce to their own welfare and that of their husbands and families if their minds were to be trained in the subjects which we have considered requisite for the due general education of young men. I think too that the examination of female candidates for matriculation and degrees might be conducted without serious difficulty or expense and in a manner which would not infringe any feeling of decorum or delicacy, care begin taken that they should be examined apart from male candidates and that they should only compete with each other.
>
> Nevertheless I conceive that there is no public opinion favourable to this novel measure and that on the contrary it would create surprise and excite ridicule and perhaps obloquy (whether just or not is not the question). These latter consequences I should not mind as regards myself but I should be sorry if they attacked either the University or the graduates and I believe that the graduates would complain and very justly if contrary to their opinions, or to the opinions of

a considerable part of them we were to go beyond our province and to recommend the Government to make the desired important modification in our Charter.[19]

The Clerk to Convocation, William Shaen, offered an interesting analysis of the voting some weeks later. Shaen was a successful solicitor who 'could not bear to see the advantages of higher education limited by the accident of sex'. He had helped to found Bedford College, would be a benefactor of Girton and Newnham, and solicitor to the Girls' Public Day School Trust. He pointed out that 'The motion was lost by the [London] graduate element; for, excluding the graduate element, there would be a majority of three in favour of the motion.' It would seem that Shaen was probably considering only the Convocation-nominated Fellows, and excluded Gull, also a London graduate. Shaen also commented, ironically, that from the vote, 'It appeared that the Convocation was the most conservative element in the constitution of the university, though the fear of its radical tendencies had led to a struggle [for its establishment] of ten years' duration.'[20]

So far as the Senate was concerned, the matter was closed. But the impact of two such narrow votes ensured that those who embraced the cause of gaining admission of women to the University's examinations were strengthened in their resolve. And in the first instance this led to a recognition that the prime need would be to win the support of Convocation.

---

[19] PRO 30/29/19/4 fol. 54, Shaw Lefevre to Granville, 9 May 1862.
[20] *TNAPSS*, London Meeting, 1862 (London, 1863), p. 340. M.J. Shaen, *William Shaen A Brief Sketch* (London, 1912), pp. 8–9. Pauline Adams, *Somerville for Women. An Oxford College 1879–1993* (Oxford, 1996), p. 21.

# 9

## *The General Examination for Women*

The National Association for the Promotion of Social Science held its first London meeting in June, 1862, and devoted one of its sessions to a discussion of the expediency of granting degrees at the universities to women. William Shaen moved that the Council of the Association

> ... should represent to the Senate of the University of London the desirableness of their undertaking the duty of affording women an opportunity of testing their attainments in the more solid branches of learning.[1]

Shaen added to his analysis of the recent voting in Senate. He and Foster focussed on the importance of Convocation for the future of the question. Shaen declared that

> ... though the Senate, and not the Convocation, is the governing body, still the Senate would not force female graduates upon the others, in opposition to the wishes of Convocation; and, on the other hand, there could be no doubt, that when Convocation made up its mind that degrees shall be thrown open to women, the Senate would be of the same opinion.

Foster had no doubt as to where pressure had to be exerted: 'the most advantageous mode would be to attack the Convocation, and leave the Senate till the Convocation was won'.

But the discussion underlined what had become a widespread uncertainty, among those sympathetic to the cause of female enrolment, as to whether or not 'the same training and discipline should be applied to men and to women'. Foster himself claimed that

> The ladies who desired to be admitted to the universities did not want to take the same degrees as were given to men, but they wanted some competent authority to say, that they have acquirements equal to those for which the degrees were given: that the degree of proficiency was the same, whether by the same mark or by any other.

---

[1] *TNAPSS*, London Meeting, 1862, pp. 339–42, from which this and subsequent extracts are taken.

Another speaker interpreted the Senate's debate as having taken this aspect of the matter into account:

> The issue presented to the Senate was the identity of a long protracted scheme of education for men and for women. They had long been endeavouring to improve the continuous course of education for young men, and now they were called on to say that the same course of education, with the same severity of examinations, and the same intervals betwen periods of study which would suit young men, would also be the best calculated to suit young women. They did not feel that they were in a position to say anything of the kind. They thought it right that the attainments of women should be tested and attested, and if so, it ought to be performed by a body of weight and dignity; but they thought that the examinations and the whole course ought to be such as was adapted to the wants of women.

This view of what should take priority in consideration of future developments became very influential, and it certainly led to modification of Shaen's motion at the NAPSS meeting: the final resolution expressed the opinion that

> . . . means ought to be provided for testing and attesting the education of women of the middle and higher classes, and requests the Council of the Association to take such measures as they may deem expedient for the attainment of this object.

Throughout the NAPSS meeting, the question of whether women should be admitted to medical schools does not seem to have been raised: perhaps there was a widely shared feeling, at least among those most closely involved, that avoidance of the issue, for the present, was the most sensible political attitude. In the years immediately ahead, it is noticeable that admission of women to medical degrees was not high on the agenda of the reformers. On the other hand, the controversy was by no means forgotten. The *Educational Times*, which had published a full report of the Senate's decision in its June issue, sat on the fence in a leader about Female Education the following month. But at the end of the year, in its December issue, the journal argued strongly for a separate medical school for women, regarding mixed teaching of medicine as unimaginable. And even the *Lancet*, on 24 October 1862, while declaiming that 'there is no avocation for the practice of which women are more unsuitable' than that of medicine and surgery, went on, a little ambiguously,

> We desire to see this question settled. If women wish so earnestly for academic distinction, let them organize a college to which they alone would be admitted.

Whether the Department of Education of the NAPSS was able to do any significant thinking or lobbying about the admission of women to higher education during the remainder of 1862 is undisclosed. The next move within the University of London came from the Annual Committee of Convocation, and there is nothing to indicate whether, and, if so, how much credit for it may have been due to efforts by Foster and Shaen. But on 26 March 1863, John Robson, then Secretary of the College of Preceptors, moved, and the Rev. Creak seconded:

> That this Committee, recognizing the desirability of elevating the standard of Female Education, recommend Convocation to represent to the Senate the propriety of considering whether it might not forward the objects of the University, as declared in the Charter, to make provision for the examination and certification of Women.

There were only nine men at the meeting, including four doctors and two lawyers. The other three, including Creak and Robson, were MAs. On this motion, only eight voted and they were equally divided. James Walter Smith, one of the legal men, was in the Chair, and gave his casting vote in favour. There is no division list. In the light of the apparent shift in emphasis from medical to general aspects of the admission of women, and because the motion made no specific reference to degrees, it may be tempting, but would certainly be risky, to believe that this was a case of the medicos against the rest.

Shaen, as Clerk to Convocation, was present at the Annual Committee, and it was his draft of their report to Convocation which was considered by the Committee on 16 and 21 April. Shaen, perhaps mischievously, had recorded the resolution about women as beginning, 'Heartily recognizing the desirability . . .', but this was deleted when 'The preliminary paragraphs were adopted with verbal amendments', on 21 April. At that session there were twenty present, with Foster in the Chair, and the proposed recommendation on women was again attacked. A motion to omit it from the report to Convocation was moved and seconded by two medical men and was lost by one vote – nine to ten. There were ten doctors present, and the others included at least six lawyers. Again, there is no division list, and no indication of an absentee or abstainer: but a predominantly medical/non-medical vote was certainly quite possible.

The Annual Committee's recommendation went to the meeting of Convocation on 12 May 1863, and was moved by Robson. But an amendment was moved which would have added the words 'that the interests of Female Education would not be promoted by the admission of Women to Examinations for the ordinary Degrees'. Neither of the movers of the motion were members of the Annual Committee: neither of them was medical. It would seem likely that the argument about the appropriateness of the existing content and structure of the degree requirements had divided the pro-women group, and that neither faction would yield. There seems to be no report of the debate, and no record of voting, but both the amendment and the original motion were lost. Fowler noted in his diary that Robson's resolution

> . . . was opposed by [Alfred] Wills [a lawyer], several medical men, and myself; and supported by [William Taylor] Malleson, Foster and Bompas. Wills made an admirable speech, setting forth the objections to it. It was thrown out by a large majority after a good debate.[2]

It was to be two years before the subject was re-opened in Convocation. In the interim, much educational attention was focussed on an experiment at Cambridge, in which girls were allowed to sit for the Local Examinations which had been introduced by the University, and on the prospects of the girls' schools and colleges such as Cheltenham Ladies and Queen's. No little hostility was expressed generally, and towards female professional employment in particular, at the meeting of the NAPSS in Edinburgh, in 1863, at which two London Fellows, Heywood and Lowe, gave qualified support to the women's cause. At the York meeting in 1864, the local examination experiment in Cambridge was a leading topic: the Education Department reported that,

> The proposal to admit girls to Oxford and Cambridge Local Examinations and, under certain conditions, to the degrees of the University of London, has more than once been discussed in this Department.[3]

Whether and how much those discussions, in themselves, were in any way responsible for what happened at the Annual Meeting of Convocation in 1865 cannot be known. But given Fowler's note of the 'large majority' against a motion sympathetic to the acceptance of women as candidates in the London examinations two years earlier, it is clear that there must have been a considerable change of mood subsequently.

On 9 May 1865, Convocation accepted, without division – and without recorded debate – a resolution moved by Ebenezer Charles, a barrister, and Joshua Girling Fitch, an enthusiast for teacher training who was just becoming Assistant Commissioner for Schools in Yorkshire, 'That it be referred to the Annual Committee to consider and report whether any, and, if any, what steps should be taken to establish Examinations for Women in this University.' Within a month, at Sheffield, Elizabeth Wolstenholme's remarks to the NAPSS indicate that the debate was being steadily extended:

---

[2] Flynn, *Sir Robert Fowler*, pp. 183–4.
[3] *TNAPSS*, Edinburgh Meeting, 1863 (1864), York Meeting, 1864 (1865).

The working range of our present Ladies' Colleges should be widened, and their numbers increased, whilst, if possible, some means should be attached to them of teaching how to teach. In the last place, we would offer to women as well as girls, the opportunity of real study, and the means of satisfactorily testing their acquirements. It is hoped that ere long, the University of London will lend a helping hand in this matter. If so, it is much to be desired that the examinations for women may be not less searching and comprehensive than those of men.[4]

As was quite normal, the Annual Committee did not get down to the subject which had been referred to them, until early in the following year. A sub-committee was appointed on 9 February 1866. There are no minutes extant of the three meetings of the sub-committee, but its members, and their attendances, were listed. An important five-page report was compiled, and its recommendations were put first to the Annual Committee and then, on 8 May, to Convocation. The Chairman of Convocation, John Storrar, was a member of the sub-committee, and it is quite likely that he took the chair; the report was, apparently, agreed unanimously.

The sub-committee's membership is worth a look. There were four medical men – F.E. Anstie, Matthew Baines, Henry Maudsley and John Storrar; three practising lawyers – Bompas, Ebenezer Charles, and H.H. Cozens-Hardy; Robson had recently moved from the College of Preceptors to be Assistant Secretary at UCL; Talfourd Ely and A.D. Sprange were teachers. In terms of their professional careers and their service to Convocation, this was quite a formidable group: the core of them, who attended all three meetings, were Baines, Charles, Ely and Robson. Anstie and Baines were KCL graduates: all the rest were UCL men.

The report was concise, careful, moderate, diplomatic, but quite firm. It rehearsed the 'remarkable movement in the direction of the Education of Women', in the last fifteen years, which it suggested was 'the natural expression of a subsisting under-current of feeling, and not the temporary or spasmodic utterance of a few enthusiastic persons'. It listed the establishment of the Ladies' Colleges, the examinations opened to women by the Society of Arts and the College of Preceptors, and the very recent introduction of girls to the Local Examinations of the Universities of Cambridge and Edinburgh. And it made a particular point of the testimony given to the current Royal Commission on Middle Class Education by its Assistant Commissioners (of whom Fitch was one), which was 'strongly in favour of the establishment of some examination which may give a high general standard to the teaching in the Girls' Schools and Ladies' Colleges . . .'

But, having declared that it would be 'desirable that Examinations for Women should be established in this University', the report then made clear that the Committee was only discussing the possibility in the context of

[4] *TNAPSS*, Sheffield Meeting, 1865 (1866).

what would now be called secondary education, at the school leaving stage. Any attempt to rescue the proposals for degree examinations was scrupulously avoided:

> It was generally felt that it would be unsuitable to admit Women as Candidates for the Degrees of the University, or to any of the existing Examinations. At the same time, the present Matriculation Examination, which is in point of difficulty greatly in advance of the Examinations for Girls which have been hitherto held in connexion with the Universities of Cambridge and Edinburgh, seemed . . . to furnish a good standard by which a Special Examination for Women in this University might be regulated, with a view to the preservation of the cardinal principle involved in all the Examinations of the University – viz. that the Candidate shall show a thoroughly good general education.

The report then dealt, gracefully and astutely, with the need to take account of anxieties about 'the social and intellectual requirements of Women'. They recognised that

> . . . fear has been expressed by many persons that the opening of University Examinations to Women would have the effect of removing, to some extent, the modesty which is the chief ornament of the sex, and also of creating an unnatural excitement and an unhealthy spirit of emulation. Your Committee believe that, proper precautions being observed, none of these results are likely to follow . . . from information received from several quarters, your Committee think it improbable that any Women will apply for admission . . . at any rate for some time to come, before the age of nineteen . . . inasmuch as a greater amount of preparation must be contemplated as a necessary preliminary to the proposed University Examination than is necessary for the Cambridge Local Examinations, it would be desirable to provide expressly against any strain being placed upon the constitution at too early an age. Your Committee, availing themselves upon this point of the advice of their Medical colleagues, therefore recommend that no Woman be permitted to be a candidate for Examination in the University until after she shall have attained the age of Seventeen years.

While the sub-committee examined at some length the wording of the Charter and the advice given to the Senate by their Counsel in 1856, they shrewdly denied that it was 'their province to pronounce an opinion whether in point of law . . . Examinations in the University may be extended to Women'. But they declared that 'it does not appear . . . to be inconsistent with the spirit of the Charter that Examinations for Women should be established'.

Politically, this moderate and conciliatory statement met with almost immediate success. Gone was the drama of the White and Garrett cases, which had pushed the issue to the top of the agenda, but in doing so had outraged most professional and no doubt a high proportion of general upper and middle class opinion. The switch from degrees, especially medical degrees, as the immediate aim, to a matriculation level examination, reduced professional anxieties and pleased the growing number of educated men who were sympathetic to the improvement of school education for girls. Those who were still determined to pursue the aim of entry to degree courses could at least see more light at the end of the tunnel if the Committee's report was accepted.

There is a disappointing lack of reportage of the debate at the Annual Meeting of Convocation on 8 May 1866, when Charles and Maudsley moved the resolutions in favour of establishing an examination which 'should not, on the whole, be less difficult than the existing Matriculation Examination', for women over the age of seventeen. A single, hostile amendment, expressing the view that 'It is not desirable for Convocation at the present time to consider the question of Examinations for Women', was moved by Hammond Chubb, and seconded by Henry Matthews, then two and a half years from beginning his career as a Conservative MP. It was lost, and the recommendations accepted – but there are no details of the voting.

Shaen and Foster had forecast, in mid-1862, that, once Convocation had approved of the enrolment of women, the Senate would soon fall into line; and in what might be thought of as the first instalment, in 1866–67, that proved to be true, though not without some late manifestations of medical concern. Storrar took Convocation's recommendations to Senate on 20 June 1866. His motion called for the establishment of an Examination for Women, 'special in its nature', and proposed that the Committee on Examinations in Arts Science and Laws should prepare a scheme. Those who, presumably, would have been happier to see a step taken to bring closer the entry of women to the existing examinations of the University, then took their places alongside the Vice-Chancellor, George Grote, when he moved that the words 'special in its nature', be omitted. The vote was close, and the amendment was only lost by eight to ten. Grote was supported by Billing, Shaw Lefevre, Lowe, Ryan, William Sharpey, William Spottiswoode and Stanley; Billing and Sharpey were medicos.

Those who opposed the amendment clearly included two groups – the genuine supporters of a special examination, and those who were apparently unreconciled to any concession to the candidacy of women, and voted for a special examination as the lesser of two evils. When the original motion was put, it was carried by fourteen to three: the irreconcilable trio were Fowler, Miller and Overstone. All the eight who had failed to carry the amendment were among the fourteen, and they were joined by six of the ten who had defeated it – Acton, Hutton, Johnson, Osler, Sibson and Storrar. Wood, who had voted against the amendment, was either absent or abstained on the original motion.

Having thus agreed in principle on the desirability of having a special examination for women, the Senate then decided, without division, that it was first essential to ask the Law Officers of the Crown whether they had the power, under the Charter, to introduce such an examination and to award Certificates of Proficiency to those who passed it. The power to grant Certificates of Proficiency was in the Charter, but had never been used, hitherto. And as the long vacation was just about to begin, it was obvious that nothing could be done until the new session. In the interim, it is worth noting that Fitch sent a long letter to Grote in support of the idea of extending the existing examinations to girls, and against the notion of a special examination.[5]

The Law Officers, however, issued their opinion, on 27 August, that 'The same reasons and arguments which would prevent Examination for, and the conferring of Degrees upon, Women seem to us to apply equally to Examinations for and the granting of Certificates for Women . . . the Examination of, and granting Certificates to, Women is not within the scope of, or authorized by, the present Charter . . .' This was reported, formally, to Senate on 24 October, and that body, as a result, felt themselves to be 'precluded from giving effect to the wish of Convocation' on the matter. But not for long.

Doubtless there had been much discussion, in Senate and Convocation circles, between the end of August and the end of October, and it is regrettable that there seems to be no record of it. However, on 19 December, Storrar moved, in the Senate, that they should seek a Supplementary Charter 'to enable the University to establish Special Examinations for Women'. Attendance that day was an average thirteen, and the resolution was carried by nine to three. The objectors were Fowler and Miller, whose opposition was consistent; and Wood, who had not wanted to delete the words 'special in nature', but had not voted on the main question in June. Those in favour included earlier supporters, together with G.J. Goschen and Sir John Lubbock, who had only joined the Senate in the previous year. Goschen was Liberal MP for the City of London and had begun his career in the Cabinet, as Chancellor of the Duchy of Lancaster, in January, 1866. Only three of those present were medicos, Johnson and Storrar among the Ayes, and Miller on the other side. The Convocation-nominated Fellows were clearly split: Hutton, Johnson, Osler, and Storrar being for; Fowler, Miller and Wood, against.

Having won approval in principle, Storrar then moved for 'the necessary steps' to be taken to approach the Home Secretary and ensure the granting of a new Supplemental Charter. Fowler and Miller held out against the majority; Wood joined it, presumably feeling that he had expressed his opposition to a special examination, but in the last resort preferred such an examination to none at all.

The Home Office was obviously sympathetic, and early in January told the Registrar that a petition for a Supplementary Charter would be received and sent to the Privy Council Office. The subsequent and final developments

[5] UL RC19/2, Fitch to Grote, 23 July 1866.

revealed the extent of anxieties which had not surfaced in the earlier stages of the pursuit of the new examination.

Tomlinson, the University's Counsel, was set to work on the preparation of a draft Charter, which he must have completed before the end of the month, because Storrar was able to lay a copy of it before the Annual Committee of Convocation on 1 February 1867. That Committee resolved to thank the Senate for their co-operation, but to ask for an opportunity to consider the draft before the Senate adopted it, in order to clear up 'a question which has been raised as to whether the proposed Supplemental Charter will enable Certificates to be granted to Women in Medicine and Surgery'. Storrar took the request to Senate on 6 February, where it was received favourably. Two days later the Annual Committee set up a sub-committee to consider the language of the draft and to alter or modify it 'in accordance with the resolutions adopted by Convocation in reference to the subject'. The sub-committee had five members – two medical men and three lawyers. They produced a report within two weeks.

The University Counsel's draft had kept the new provisions to a minimum. The essential new authority was defined as being 'to enlarge the powers of the . . . Chancellor, Vice-Chancellor, and Fellows, so as to enable them to examine Women and grant Certificates . . .' Power was given to hold 'a Special Examination of Women, being Candidates for . . . Certificates of Proficiency . . . and Women shall be admitted as Candidates to every such Examination on such conditions, and shall be examined in such subjects in Literature, Science, and Art', as might be determined by regulations.

The sub-committee felt that the draft had 'been prepared under some misconception of the nature of the recommendations of Convocation'. What Convocation had contemplated, they claimed, was 'the establishment of Examinations for women of such a character as to test the *general* knowledge of the Candidates'. Certificates of Proficiency should not be given to women in *separate* branches of knowledge except where it was desirable to award Honours after a general examination. And quite specifically, 'It was not contemplated by Convocation that the Examinations for Women should embrace any subject coming under the headings of Medicine or Surgery.' The recommendation that women candidates should not be less than seventeen years of age was not in Tomlinson's draft, and the sub-committe hoped that if it was not to be included in the Charter, it should be made clear in regulations.

The sub-committee submitted an amended draft, incorporating the new and altered wording they deemed necessary, to the Annual Committee on 22 February. A few verbal changes were made there, and then the draft was approved for presentation to Convocation. However, without waiting for Convocation's approval, though no doubt with the agreement of the Annual Committee, Storrar presented the amended draft to Senate on 13 March, when its consideration was postponed for two weeks.

By this time it would appear that Tomlinson's draft had become fairly easily available, for the *British Medical Journal* criticised it on 23 March. Their editorial of that issue declared that the draft had been

> . . . drawn with so much width of expression, that it seems to authorise more than Convocation demanded, and might admit of the institution not only of examinations such as those of the Universities of Oxford and Cambridge, which would be useful to governesses and others, and test general education, but also of special examinations for degrees. This would, of course, be opposed, under present circumstances, although we believe that, if the legal members of the University are willing formally to admit ladies to examinations and diplomas in law, the medical members would not oppose their admission to degrees in medicine. We understand that many more ladies are desirous of admission to the bar than seek an entrance into medical practice.

Whether the journal's editor had good reason for his suggestions about women wishing to practise law, or whether he was simply challenging lawyers on the Senate rather mischievously, is not easy to judge. But there were other, more definitely serious opponents. On the day of the next meeting of Senate, 27 March, the Convocation-nominated Fellow, William Allen Miller, Professor of Chemistry at KCL and Treasurer of the Royal Society, presented a protest against the University's 'undertaking the duty of instituting examinations for women'. The Senate allowed the protest to be read, but refused to receive it, as being contrary to usual practice. They also postponed, once again, consideration of the proposal to a specially summoned meeting on 3 April. But Miller's objections no doubt represented the contemporary views of a sizeable section of the University community, and are worth recording.

Miller was in favour of the improvement of the intellectual education of women, but opposed competitive examinations because they 'are calculated to excite a spirit of rivalry and contention . . . which are exactly opposed to the dispositions which most cultivated men desire to see fostered in the female character'. But in addition, he cited three practical objections: that the proposed examinations were 'foreign to the object with which this University was founded'; that the University 'has already in the examination of men, duties sufficiently ample, onerous, and complicated, to demand its undivided attention'; and that 'the examination of women will be more suitably performed by a body specially constituted for that purpose'.[6]

When the Senate eventually addressed the main question at a specially called meeting on 3 April, debate turned on how much the Senate should be willing to impose any restriction on its operations. Both Tomlinson's draft

[6] UL RC37/6.

and the amended draft recommended by Convocation were on the table, and the Vice-Chancellor moved that the Senate should accept Convocation's amendments, subject to reference to a Special Committee to deal with certain legal objections raised by Jessel. Grote's long motion went on to assert that the amended draft would enable the Senate 'to provide that every Candidate receiving a Certificate shall have given evidence of a good general education, according to the wish expressed by Convocation'. However, the sting was in the tail. The motion ended:

> But the Senate desire that . . . acceptance of the Amendments recommended . . . may not be understood as implying any opinion respecting the propriety or impropriety of excluding women from Examinations in Medicine and Surgery.

This was too weak for those who rejected the idea of any restrictions on the academic discretion of the Senate. Robert Lowe moved that the two drafts be referred to a Committee

> . . . with an instruction that the Senate do not desire to limit the powers proposed to be conferred upon the Senate with respect to the subjects to which the Examinations shall extend.

Lowe's motion was lost, six to eleven, but he was supported by three powerful ex-Ministers – Granville, Cardwell, and the 1st Earl Kimberley (previously Lord Wodehouse) – who were joined by Lord Overstone, and by only one academic, Dr Billing. They were defeated by the Vice-Chancellor; by seven Convocation-nominated Fellows – Fowler, Hutton, Jessel, Osler, Sharpey, Sibson and Storrar; and by Gull, Lubbock and Ryan. When it came to Grote's original motion, all but four voted in favour. Cardwell, Fowler, Kimberley and Overstone opposed. Jessel voted against the amendment but abstained or was absent for the vote on the main motion. Richard Quain was listed as present, but did not vote on either issue.

There was no further controversy. The small sub-committee appointed at the Senate meeting of 3 April made some technical amendments suggested by Jessel to the draft submitted by Convocation, which was then sent to the Home Office with a petition signed by the Vice-Chancellor and the Chairman of Convocation. The Supplementary Charter was authorised on 27 August 1867, accepted by the Senate on 23 October, and by Convocation on 20 November.

There is insufficient archival material available to make a definite judgement as to how much of this last episode could be fairly described as revolving around seriously debateable issues relevant to the education of women, and how much it had more of the nature of a constitutional confrontation between Senate and Convocation. But a year later the Registrar wrote to Granville:

You will probably recollect that the Charter as drawn by Mr Tomlinson gave larger powers to the Senate than was thought prudent by the representatives of Convocation; and that the form now adopted was the result of a great deal of discussion. Lord Overstone and the Vice-Chancellor were a good deal discomposed at the spirit shown by some of the Convocation members of the Senate; but the Vice-Chancellor thought it best to yield.[7]

Carpenter's comments help to explain the combination of the Conservatives, Overstone and Fowler, with the Liberals, Cardwell and Kimberley, on the main motion – and with Granville and Lowe on the latter's amendment. Fowler's and Overstone's fundamental objection to the candidacies of women was probably irrelevant. They were objecting, as were Cardwell and Kimberley, to an attack on what they saw as the constitutional authority and desirable flexibility of the Senate. Grote – and presumably, in the last resort, Granville – backed away from a test of strength with Convocation. And as far as the exclusion of women from medical examinations was concerned, Grote no doubt argued that a specific resolution on the neutrality of the Senate would be acceptable to the majority as a recognition that an armed truce was, for the time being, inescapable.

As will become apparent later, this first emergence of an argument over constitutional issues within the argument about the admission of women to the University's examinations can be seen, in retrospect, as the beginning of a process which was to be increasingly significant in the remaining stages of the controversy.

During the rest of the session 1867–68, the form and content of the Special Examination was debated and finalised, and the Regulations were approved by the Home Office in July, 1868. The first women candidates would take their examinations in May, 1869. Progress had been slow, difficult and limited from the beginnings of Elizabeth Garrett's campaign early in 1862, through the agreement to introduce only a Special Examination for Women, similar in standard to Matriculation, in 1867, to the holding of the first of those examinations in May, 1869. And it was to be another five years before the next significant moves were made to take the process further. But during those five years opinion and attitudes shifted noticeably.

The basic reason for the changes in attitude was, no doubt, the sheer extension of the demand for the better education of upper and middle class girls. That was responsible for the appearance of more schools and the formation of associations devoted to the cause. Those associations were willing to exert pressure, and the movement also gained strength from the hearings and the report of the Schools Inquiry Commission in the mid- and late 1860s.[8]

---

[7] UL RC19/7, Carpenter to Granville, 8 May 1868.
[8] PP 1867–68, xxviii.

Sympathy towards the extension of degree examinations to women increased, and of a sudden, in the mid-1870s, the action of Parliament gave the Senate the opportunity to admit women to degree examinations in Medicine and Surgery. With eventual support from Convocation, the Senate extended the exercise to all the University's degrees.

The first, direct contribution which the University of London made towards meeting the new demands – the 'General Examination' – lasted for nine years, from 1869 to 1878. The regulations which the Senate designed for female candidates called for a General Examination in a group of subjects, and examinations for Higher Proficiency Certificates in individual subjects, the two exercises corresponding, roughly, to the Matriculation and Intermediate BA examinations. The numbers involved over the nine years were not large: 139 passed the General Examination, and all are listed by name. But there were 264 candidates, and those who did not pass are not listed. As it is possible that some of those who failed took the examinations at a later date, the figure of 264 candidacies probably overstates the number of persons who tried. Of the 139 who passed, fifty-five were also awarded Certificates of Higher Proficiency in one or more subjects. One student, Alice Gardner, passed the General Examination in 1874, and in that and the four following years obtained Certificates in seven additional subjects.

Forty of the 139 young women who passed the General Examination prepared themselves for it by private tuition, or private study, or both. Forty-four were pupils at Cheltenham Ladies' College, and twenty-eight at the North London Collegiate School. Of the remaining twenty-seven, one was a student at UCL, where women students were welcomed from 1869 in courses 'at times deliberately chosen to avoid the possibility of meetings with male students';[9] one was enrolled at Newnham Hall, Cambridge; and the others were spread among only twelve schools. Queen's College, Harley Street; Kendal Ladies' College; and Bedford College put forward candidates, along with Cheltenham Ladies' and the North London Collegiate, throughout the period. But they were only joined after 1875 by Heath Brow, Priory House, Bradford Girls Grammar School, Bath High School, Notting Hill High School; Waterloo School, Liverpool; Dallington Hall; Clergy Dan School; and the Mount School at York. The minimum age prescribed for candidates was seventeen, but the actual average age of those who passed was just over twenty-one.

The General Examination was a modest contribution to the cause of offering women an entry to higher education. Its demise was due to its producing evidence which was very influential in discrediting the argument that it was desirable to have differently designed examinations for men and women. Over the years, it was discovered that 'the women who did enter for the

---

[9] Harte, The University of London, p. 132.

examinations excelled, not in the special subjects considered (by men) to be suited to their sex, but in Classics, Mathematics and Science'[10] – the staple fare of the education of men.

It would have been normal for the first hint of this unexpected proof of feminine capacity to have come to the notice of the Senate's Committee on Examinations in Arts, Science and Laws. In 1873 and the following few years, which were critical for the question of examinations for women, that Committee's most active members were the Vice-Chancellor (Lubbock), Heywood, Hutton, Osler, William Smith and Storrar. To them should be added, in 1876 and 1877, Fitch, Alexander William Williamson, and Wood. It was Hutton, who had incurred the wrath of a disappointed Emily Davies by supporting the introduction of the Special Examination,[11] who must have come to feel that a new situation had arisen which required attention. He moved, on 26 March 1873, that the Senate should direct the Committee on Examinations in Arts, Science and Laws, 'to consider what changes, if any, shall be made in the Examinations for Women'.

The Senate Committee may well have put their minds to the question, but there is no record of their discussions, and no report by them to Senate about it. Hutton, however, was involved again when the subject of women was raised in a much more aggressive manner, in Convocation, on 20 January 1874. The aggression may well have been introduced by Alfred Peach Hensman, a barrister who was to have a controversial legal and political career as Attorney General of Western Australia. He was a fervent supporter of women's causes in both countries, but this was the first occasion when his name appeared in the records of Convocation. Hensman had given notice of a motion asking Convocation to declare the view that 'it is desirable that women should be permitted to take degrees in the University of London'. Another motion was put down in the names of Henry Arthur Nesbitt of UCL, who had taught at Cheltenham College in the early 1860s, and George Serrell, a barrister: they wanted Convocation to say that 'the Degrees in Arts of the University of London ought to be open to women'.

The Order of Business for the meeting listed Hensman's motion as Item VIII, and that of Nesbitt and Serrell as Item IX. However, when the meeting got under way, A.W. Bennett, a Lecturer in Botany and Geology who became a Fellow of the Linnaean Society, succeeded in having Hensman's motion brought forward on the agenda. The second motion – that of Nesbitt and Serrell – was never reached. There followed 'a lengthened discussion', which must have seemed to Hutton and Sibson unlikely to produce a meaningful result. They moved the adjournment of the debate until the Annual Meeting due in May, with the proviso that Hensman's motion should be placed first on the agenda of that meeting. No division was recorded, and the house

---

[10] Dunsheath and Miller, *Convocation*, p. 57.
[11] Bennett, *Emily Davies*, pp. 71–2.

adjourned. It is possible that Hutton and Sibson, both Fellows, were aware of relevant developments which might be handled by Senate before Convocation met again. Whether this was so or not, the whole subject of women's education was much to the fore in the business of both bodies in the next few months.

Between February and July, 1874, the Senate was targetted by several new bodies – the National Union for Improving the Education of Women of all Classes; The Birmingham Ladies' Educational Association; the Queen's Institute of Female Professional Schools, Dublin; the Leeds Association of Schoolmistresses; the Rugby Council for Promoting the Education of Women; the Ladies' Educational Association, London; the London Association of Schoolmistresses; and by twenty-nine of the women who had passed one or more of the University's examinations. The National Union for Improving the Education of Women of all Classes started the ball rolling by offering a Scholarship worth £25 to the best candidate, at the next General Examination for Women, who was engaged in or preparing for the profession of teaching. The offer, made in February, was referred to the Committee on Examinations in Arts, Science and Laws, and refused, rather ungraciously, in April, on the grounds that it could not be awarded 'without departure from existing regulations'.

There are clear signs that much of the content of the memorials presented to the Senate was the result of co-operation between the various groups involved. All of the organisations mentioned above called for the University to open its examinations for degrees to women, and denied that there was any danger that women would be over-strained by the effort involved in higher study. This concern about stress was underlined by Henry Maudsley, a specialist on mental health, who sat on the Annual Committee of Convocation, in the first of a projected set of six articles in the *Saturday Review*, in May, which 'took for its theme that "study is the cause of ill-health in women"'. Maudsley's view was immediately challenged by Elizabeth Garrett Anderson, now well established as a doctor. She and Emily Davies, who had started her College in 1869, and had moved it to Girton only in the autumn of 1873, put together a 'bristling reply' to Maudsley. It was readily published by the *Saturday Review*, which also discontinued Maudsley's series of articles.[12]

It was Convocation which first declared themselves unequivocally on the desirability of women being permitted to take degrees. They did so on 12 May 1874, in the midst of all the lobbying of the Senate which was going on. The motion by Hensman, seconded by Serrell, in January, duly appeared as the opening item at the annual meeting. Whether or not there had been a significant change of heart on Serrell's part, in January, or whether

[12] Bennett, *Emily Davies*, pp. 155–7.

he had simply made himself available to both Hensman and Nesbitt in order to facilitate the launching of debate, in May he remained with Hensman, while Nesbitt stuck to his motion in favour of a degree in Arts only, which was still low on the agenda. But Nesbitt did not need to fear that his idea would not be put forward at the May meeting, for as soon as Hensman's motion was introduced, an amendment was put forward by Creak, which read:

> That . . . it is desirable that Women should be permitted to present themselves for the Examinations in Arts, and that the successful candidates should receive not Degrees but Certificates of having passed.

The Minutes record only that 'After discussion' the amendment was defeated by eighty-three to sixty-five. There is no division list. The original motion was then passed, apparently without a division. Convocation had declared their opinion that 'it is desirable that Women should be permitted to take degrees in the University of London'. This historic affirmation was greeted in the *Times*, two days later, with a supercilious and dismissive leader in which the Women's Movement's 'own frank memorials' were preferred to 'the political and apologetical speeches of their friends in Convocation'.

The confident assertion of William Shaen, twelve years previously, that, once Convocation had embraced the idea that women should take degree examinations, the Senate would accept it readily, was not borne out in 1874. Osler gave notice, at the Senate meeting of 17 June, that he would bring Convocation's opinion forward at the following session. But at the 17 June meeting, the Report of the Committee on Examinations in Arts, Science and Laws (at which Osler was a conscientious attender) recommended that from the beginning of 1876 the Regulations for the General Examination for Women should be the same as those for Matriculation. The two examinations should be held at the same time, and the same papers should be set at both. Whether or not this implied abandonment of the title, 'General Examination for Women', it clearly marked acceptance of the ability of women to take all the subjects required in the Matriculation Examination.

No action was taken by the Senate, on 17 June, on the recommendation, and, when Senate met again on 1 July, consideration of the Committee's report was postponed 'until after decisions of the Senate shall have been taken' on the major motion of which Osler had given notice. In accordance with Convocation's expressed opinion, Osler moved 'That in the opinion of the Senate it is desirable that the University of London should be empowered to admit Women to its degrees.'

But before Senate, on that day, was a letter from the Association for Promoting the Higher Education of Women, Bristol. Unlike all the other letters which had been received, it was hostile to the idea of treating men and women as the same, educationally. It called for advance, but through a different curriculum from that appropriate for men. The present General Examination for Women was only for 'very few women of exceptional powers and opportunities'. What was wanted was a proposal for the average woman. 'The experiment of giving an identical education to men and women is as yet very incomplete, and needs to be conducted in a cautious and tentative manner.'

It is very unlikely that the letter, in itself, heavily influenced the debate, but it neatly expressed a point of view which was clearly widespread, and which was directly opposed to the recommendations of the Senate's own powerful Committee on Examinations. The approach of those who were unwilling to snub their own Committee, but were averse to movement on the major issue, was expressed by the newly Crown-chosen Fellow, Williamson, Professor of Practical Chemistry at UCL since 1849, and fresh from a year as President of the British Association. He proposed an amendment, stating that the Senate was 'desirous to extend the scope of the educational advantages now offered by the University to Women, but is not prepared to apply for a New Charter giving power to admit Women to its degrees'. It was carried by seventeen to ten.

There were twenty-eight present on 1 July, one of the largest turn-outs recorded between 1836 and 1900. The only non-voter among the listed attenders, whether from absence when the vote was taken, or from abstention, was Sir William Stirling-Maxwell, Bt., MP. The issue split the other twenty-seven in such a way as to make it extremely difficult to suggest that any groupings were significant. Convocation-nominated Fellows voted five to three for the amendment: London graduates went the same way by seven to three; medical men supported the amendment eight to two: eight parliamentarians divided equally. It is probable that this was an issue on which personal conviction was exercised to a high degree, and perhaps the only firm conclusion to be reached is that those who were defeated must be regarded as the hard-core supporters of opening the University's examinations to women; while those who went with Williamson's amendment were a mixture of a small number of determined opponents, together with a larger element of the genuinely uncommitted, who wanted to wait on further developments.

The Vice-Chancellor, Sir John Lubbock, was on the losing side, and he was joined by Billing, Goschen, Heywood, Hutton, Kimberley, Lowe, Osler, Edmund Alexander Parkes, and Ryan. The Chancellor voted for the amendment, along with Lord Acton; Sir George Burrows, President of the Royal College of Physicians; Cardwell; Fowler; Sir Philip Grey-Egerton, MP; Gull; Johnson; Overstone; Paget; Richard Quain; Sharpey; Spottiswoode; Sibson; Storrar; Williamson; and Wood.

During the rest of 1874, the Senate twice agreed to postpone discussion of their Committee's recommendation about the General Examination for Women, but declared on 21 October that a decision should be reached at their first meeting in the following February.

Convocation was no more active in the balance of 1874, but at a meeting on 19 January, 1875, Hensman and Serrell reopened the major question by moving that it was desirable that women should be permitted to take degrees in Arts. Given that Convocation had accepted, only eight months earlier, their motion that it was desirable that women be permitted to take degrees, and in the process had defeated the proposal that women should only be permitted to take examinations in Arts for the award of certificates, their tactics in January, 1875, are puzzling. It may be that they regarded the Senate's unwillingness to seek new powers as being due primarily to medical fears, and were willing to push for degrees in Arts as the most practicable way of removing those fears. In all probability they were desperately anxious to see graduate – not merely certificated – women teaching in schools, and were willing to see the hopes of potential women doctors postponed. Or they may have wished to focus attention on the Senate's coming decision about the General Examination, with the hope that they could influence the voting in favour of at least opening the Matriculation Examination to women.

Whatever their motives, Hensman's and Serrell's motion may well have caused confusion. Seemingly at an early stage of the debate, Nesbitt and Osler moved for adjournment, and 'After discussion, the original motion was, with the consent of the House, withdrawn by its mover and seconder.' Perhaps Osler had been able to offer persuasive advice to Convocation, and to promise some action in Senate. Three weeks later, on 10 February, he moved in the Senate

> That there is no sufficient reason for perpetuating the slight differences which at present exist between the curricula of the Women's General Examination and the Matriculation Examination: and that in and after the year 1876 the curriculum of the Women's General Examination be the same as the curriculum for the time being of the Matriculation Examination, except that in the year 1876 women shall have the option of being examined according to the present instead of the altered curriculum.

An amendment by Richard Quain, to refer the matter back to the Committee on Examinations in Arts, Science and Laws, 'to consider and report on a course of study and examination calculated to improve the education of women', was defeated by seven to three. Quain was supported by Sibson and Williamson. Osler's backers were the Chancellor and Vice-Chancellor, Hutton, Parkes, Ryan and Sharpey. The original motion was carried by seven to five: on that occasion Quain, Sibson and Williamson were joined by Storrar and Wood. Thus the medical men were divided – Quain, Sibson and Storrar against Parkes and Sharpey: as were the leading Convocation men – Quain, Sibson, Storrar and Wood against Hutton, Osler and Parkes. Acton and Gull made up the fourteen who were listed as present at the meeting, but they did not vote.

The changes to the Regulations which were to govern the remaining years of the General Examination for Women were treated as a matter of some urgency, and were approved by the Home Secretary on 19 March 1875. The substance of Osler's motion was accepted, but the timing of the change was extended, no doubt to take account of the possible difficulties for schools and candidates. The last General Examinations for Women were held in 1878. Subsequently, all those who had passed since 1869 were regarded as having passed Matriculation.

# 10

# *The consequences of Gurney's Act*

In January, 1876, Convocation reiterated its desire to see the degree examinations of the University extended to women. But this only happened after another debate which revolved around whether or not the University should offer, to women, degrees in Arts alone. And as before, it would seem that the apparent repetition of a proposal to seek entry to degrees in Arts only was due to a conviction that there was a real chance that pressure from the schools lobby would be enough to swing Senate behind it, and an equal conviction that progress could not be made if any desire for medical degrees was expressed.

Hensman's motion, on 18 January 1876, raised the idea of a new Charter. This may have indicated eagerness for a wider constitutional revision of the relationship between Senate and Convocation. But the debate it sparked was kept strictly to the issue of women's entry to examinations. The motion read:

> That it is desirable that a new Charter should be granted to the University; and that no such Charter will be acceptable to Convocation which does not enable the University to grant degrees in Arts to Women.

The first amendment offered was a lengthy declaration devoted to the concept of not rocking the boat. The essential support for the admission of women to degrees was combined with appreciation of the moves made so far by Senate; and Convocation was invited to be 'earnestly desirous to see the extension of these advantages to women further carried out'. This cautious advice was rejected, but only by thirty-three votes to twenty-six. The next amendment was also intended to soften Hensman's approach, but did not remove its essence; it aimed to take out any reference to Convocation, and simply to ask that 'such Charter should contain provisions enabling the University to grant Degrees in Arts to Women'. This was readily accepted by Hensman: it became the main motion, and may well have seemed to the movers highly likely to carry the day.

But a final amendment was moved by Osler, to remove the words 'in Arts'. By 'a large majority on a show of hands' it was carried, so that Convocation was on record as wishing for a new Charter which 'should contain provisions enabling the University to grant degrees to women'. Thus by the middle of

January, 1876, Convocation had twice expressed itself firmly in favour of opening up the examinations of the University to women, across the board. The Senate had shown themselves to be 'desirous to extend the scope of the educational advantages now offered by the University to women', by recognising that women were fully capable of taking the Matriculation Examination. But they had stopped short of showing keenness to seek new powers to enable the University to offer women examinations leading to degrees.

It may well be that the progress within the community of the University of London towards winning entry for women to examinations had been due mainly, since 1862, to the growing awareness of the desirability of improving school education for girls, and of the corresponding need for graduate women to strengthen the teaching profession. The medical possibilities had never been abandoned by those in search of equal opportunity for women, but the opposition of orthodox medical opinion had shown itself to be so great, and the public distaste for any notion of mixed teaching so tangible, that it is not surprising that the pressure for women to be allowed to pursue studies for medical degrees alongside men had been relatively muted, and hopes of success in all probability concentrated on a future generation. Nor, apparently, were the lawyers overkeen to welcome women into their ranks. When Robert Barnes, a founder medical member of the Graduates' Committee, was standing for election to the Senatorial List from whom the Home Secretary would choose the next Convocation-nominated Fellow, in June, 1876, he revealed the bias of the professions when he declared that 'Women have a just claim for admission to degrees in Arts, but it is not expedient nor practicable to admit them to degrees in Laws or Medicine.'[1]

It is ironic, therefore, that the attainment of entry by women to all degree examinations in London University was brought about, rather suddenly, as a result of developments in the legislation governing the registration of doctors. And it is even more ironic that the chances of women entering degree courses in Medicine seemed likely to be given priority over the acceptance of women in other Faculties. To understand those developments it is necessary to turn to happenings elsewhere than those which had been occurring in Burlington Gardens.

As we saw earlier, a small loophole had existed in the constitution of the Apothecaries' Society. It had been exploited by Elizabeth Garrett and had enabled her to become, in 1865, only the second woman registered as a medical practitioner in the country, joining Elizabeth Blackwell, who had been on the register since 1859. But in the wave of antagonism which seemed to have swept through the majority of the leadership cadres of the profession in the mid-1860s, the loophole was closed, and the Society joined all the other universities and medical corporations in refusing to accept women as medical

---

[1] *Lancet*, 10 June 1876.

students. By depriving them of the chance of graduating, they effectively barred them from being registered as practitioners by the General Medical Council. Even those few women who took degrees in Medicine at established universities abroad could not be registered, as the GMC had no power to recognise such degrees for men, let alone for women.

The details of how a group of determined women and their allies continued the struggle for recognition during the next decade have been given in many accounts, and here it is only intended to outline those episodes which had a direct influence on what happened in the University of London. The first of those episodes happened at the University of Edinburgh during the years from 1869 to 1872. In 1869 the Faculty of Medicine there had agreed to matriculate six women as students. When the women, having survived much hostility, were within a year or two of graduating, divisions within the Faculty led to an appeal to the courts, which resulted in the refusal of the University to allow the women to receive degrees. It was this episode which led one of them, Sophia Jex-Blake, to abandon Edinburgh and set about organising the establishment of the London School of Medicine for Women, which opened in 1874.

At Westminster, the Liberals had been ousted by the Conservatives in February, 1874. Disraeli's new Administration included the Duke of Richmond as Lord President of the Council, with Viscount Sandon as Vice-President, in the House of Commons, and Richard Assheton Cross at the Home Office. The change of Government did not deter the campaigners, however. The bitterness aroused by the Edinburgh saga led to the early introduction, in the new Parliament, of a Bill to 'remove doubts as to the Powers of the Universities of Scotland to admit Women as students and to grant degrees to Women'. The Bill was put forward by William Francis Cowper-Temple (later Baron Mount Temple), a prominent Whig who, as Vice-President of the Council and President of the Board of Health, had played the major part in the passage of the Medical Act of 1858; he was joined by three other MPs, Russell Gurney, Orr Ewing, and Dr Cameron.

Problems in the way of the Bill's passage forced its early abandonment – it was introduced on 14 April 1874, and withdrawn, without having been debated, on 11 May. But Cowper-Temple was able to introduce a short debate in the House of Commons on 12 June 1874, the Hansard report of which is headed 'University Female Education'.[2] It is unlikely that there was any direct link between the Bill, the debate, and the vote of Convocation, exactly a month earlier, in favour of admitting women to degree examinations in London. But the parliamentary discussion ranged over the whole controversy about women being enabled to enter the universities, and included contributions from three London University men – one Fellow, Stirling-Maxwell,

---

[2] 3s Parl. Deb., vol. 219, cols 1526–60.

and two graduates, Francis Goldsmid and James Stansfeld. The only immediate public response was a hostile leader in the *Times* of the following day, deploring any notion that women should try to pursue careers traditionally regarded as the preserves of men.

Cowper-Temple and his allies were now determined to keep the whole matter of women in medicine before Parliament, and in March, 1875, adopted a new tactic. They produced another Bill – the Medical Act Amendment (Foreign Universities) Bill – which provided for women who held foreign degrees in medicine to be registered by the GMC. This brought the matter to the attention of the Privy Council Office, whose official head was the powerful advocate of improved public health, Dr John Simon. No doubt on Simon's advice, the Lord President, on 8 June, referred the Bill to the GMC, but in addition asked that body to let him have their observations on the whole question of women in medicine. It was this reference which was to produce a turning point, not only for medicine, but for the whole dispute over the admission of women to the University of London.

A week after the reference to the GMC, James Stansfeld asked in the Commons for 'the views of the Government on the right of women to study and practise medicine in this country'. Stansfeld was no doubt reminding the Government of the existence of Cowper-Temple's Bill; but it is quite possible that he knew by then of the reference to the GMC and wanted to bring it out into the open. Viscount Sandon was extremely cautious: he admitted later that Stansfeld and Cowper-Temple had raised the issue at the beginning of the session[3] but on 15 June he replied that the matter 'had only very lately been submitted to the attention of the Government, and they could pronounce no opinion on it'. However, he promised careful consideration during the recess and hoped to be able 'to express an opinion next year as to whether legislation was desirable or not'.[4]

In fact, the GMC debated the matter on 24 to 26 June, 1875, and the Lord President had their response by the end of the month. Their minutes reveal that, like almost every other body concerned with medical education and the medical profession, they were, on the basic issue, deeply divided. They admitted, at the outset, that the matter of Cowper-Temple's Bill should not be considered in isolation: and they agreed that any introduction of medical education for women raised difficult problems. But their report included the vital statement, agreed by a clear majority, that 'the Council are not prepared to say that women ought to be excluded from the profession'.[5]

The Council had twenty-four members. The crucial vote for including the words reproduced at the end of the previous paragraph was fourteen to seven, with two abstentions and one man absent. One of the abstainers was

[3] 3s Parl. Deb., vol. 226, cols 267–70, 30 July 1875.
[4] 3s Parl. Deb., vol. 224, col. 1937, 15 June 1875.
[5] PP 1875 lviii, 301. Correspondence on the Medical Registration of Women.

John Storrar, the representative of the University of London; at an earlier stage he had tried, unsuccessfully, to argue that the Council was not empowered 'to represent to the Government any authorised opinion on the large social question of the expediency or otherwise of admitting women to practise medicine'. There were four other Fellows on the Council, as appointees of the Crown. Three of them – Gull, Parkes and Sharpey – voted to include the words: Richard Quain voted against. Thus the two Convocation-nominated Fellows were divided – Parkes for, Quain against; the Chairman of Convocation, Storrar, abstained. The two Crown-chosen Fellows, Gull and Sharpey, were on the winning side.

But despite their refusal to endorse the idea of excluding women from the profession, the GMC had no hesitation in condemning Cowper-Temple's Bill. They argued that, as they were precluded, by the Medical Act, 1858, from registering men who held foreign degrees, and had no way of assessing the worth of such degrees, it would be wholly improper to have separate jurisdiction for women only. And they were also agreed on the necessity, if women were to be trained as doctors, of their being trained and examined separately from men. More constructively, they put forward a practical and diplomatic scheme whereby the right of women to be registered could be advanced.

Cowper-Temple's Bill was withdrawn, without any debate, on 28 July, and two days later its sponsor, obviously fully aware of the GMC report, called on Sandon for action, while Lyon Playfair asked that the minutes and correspondence of the GMC be laid on the table. Sandon agreed to Playfair's request, but would only promise that next session the Government would let it be known whether they would take action themselves, or would rely on a private Member to introduce legislation.[6] There the matter rested until early in 1876, by which time it must have become apparent that the Government were not, themselves, willing to introduce any Bill. As we saw earlier, in mid-January, Convocation had voted in favour of a new Charter for the University which should enable it to admit women to degrees. No doubt cheered by that development, Cowper-Temple re-introduced his Bill in February, probably only as a tactical move: some time later Russell Gurney and John Bright brought in another Bill, intended 'To remove Restrictions on the granting of Qualifications for Registration under the Medical Act on the ground of sex.' This latter was to be known as Gurney's Bill.

It was not until 25 May, 1876, that Gurney's proposal had its first reading, and not until 5 July that the House of Commons debated Cowper-Temple's Bill. In that debate, the Government indicated that it was giving its tacit backing to Gurney's Bill, and, in the light of that, Cowper-Temple happily withdrew his own piece of legislation.[7] Thereafter, within five weeks, Gurney's

---

[6] 3s Parl. Deb., vol. 226, cols 267–70, 30 July 1875.
[7] 3s Parl. Deb., vol. 230, cols 996–1020.

Bill went through all its processes in Commons and Lords, without debate, and received the Royal Assent on 11 August.[8] Its smooth passage, and the apparently total absence of opposition, implied that Government and Parliament were very happy with its brief formulation of the solution proposed by the GMC.

The majority of the GMC had been willing to conceive of the possibility of women being permitted to enter the medical profession and to be registered. But the Council also wanted to protect the freedom of the universities and medical corporations to award or not to award the necessary qualifications, and to avoid the issue of whether women who did receive such qualifications should become eligible to exercise any constitutional powers within the universities and corporations. Registration would become possible if the Council was simply given power to recognise such examinations, for women, as were given by the universities and corporations listed in the Medical Act, which the Council deemed sufficient for the purpose – a power they already had for men. And the Council felt that examinations of female candidates should be equivalent to those of male candidates.

Gurney's Act encapsulated these notions in its single paragraph:

> The powers of every body entitled under the Medical Act to grant qualifications for registration shall extend to the granting of any qualification for registration granted by such body to all persons without distinction of sex. Provided always, that nothing herein contained shall render compulsory the exercise of such powers, and that no person who but for this Act would not have been entitled to be registered shall, by reason of such registration, be entitled to take any part in the government, management, or proceedings of the universities or corporations mentioned in the said Medical Act.

In short, henceforward, so far as the University of London was concerned, if it wished to admit women to its degrees in Medicine, those women who graduated could be registered by the GMC, but they would not become entitled to participate in the governance of the University. Parliament had expressed its approval of the idea that women should be permitted to practise medicine. But the decision to allow them the opportunity to be trained and graduated was left to the University.

Once Gurney's Bill had received the Royal Assent, not much time passed before a formal challenge was made to the University to take advantage of it. An application was laid before the Senate on 8 November 1876, from Edith Shove, asking for admission to examinations for degrees in Medicine under the Act. Whatever may have been said at the meeting, there was no division on the proposal to ask for the Law Officers' opinion to be taken, on the 'nature and extent' of the new powers conferred on the University, and

[8] 39 & 40 Vic c. 41.

on whether women, if admitted to degrees in Medicine, would 'be entitled thereby to become Members of Convocation'. The Treasury was approached on 9 November, and the Law Officers gave their opinion on 5 December.[9] It was reported to Senate on 20 December. Thus, by the end of 1876, the Senate knew what use they could make of the new powers.

The Law Officers' opinion covered several points which had worried the Senate. It was quite clear that while Gurney's Act gave the Senate the authority to admit women to medical degrees, it did not affect their power to regulate the examinations for such degrees. Regulations, so long as they were agreed by the Home Secretary, need not be the same for women as for men. And as passing the Matriculation Examination was a condition of a man being allowed to study for a medical degree, the Law Officers felt that unless the regulations were altered, 'Women desirous of entering upon the study of Medicine may subject themselves to this Examination but . . . the Senate has power to substitute any other examination for it.'

The Senate, seemingly recognising the paranoid suspicions of some of its members, had enquired about the possibility of a woman being able to claim that if she passed the Preliminary Scientific Examination for the MB, she should be recognised as having passed the First Examination for the BSc. The Law Officers assured them that 'If a Woman was not before the passing of 39/40 Vic c 41 [Gurney's Act] capable of entering herself for those examinations, there is nothing in that statute to make her capable.'

In a constitutional context, the Senate was told that women with medical degrees would become members of Convocation in the same way as men, but that Gurney's Act would prevent them from taking any part in the 'government management or proceeding of the University'. This reading of the Act was to cause serious problems.

Thus at the beginning of 1877 the Senate found itself empowered, if it wished, to permit women to take examinations for degrees in Medicine, but was left without power to admit women to examinations for any of its other degrees. And female medical graduates, apparently, would not automatically become fully effective members of Convocation. Supporters of the women's cause, in Senate and Convocation, were faced, therefore, with the problem of whether the opportunity which was now offered, to enrol women for medical degrees, should be seized at once, or whether any action should be delayed until the struggle to obtain entry to all degrees had been won. Those opposed to the idea of women being permitted to take examinations for medical degrees may have felt that they were beginning to lose the argument in principle, and would have to think in terms of raising constitutional objections to any Senate action, and of using Convocation's power to block acceptance of any new Charter.

---

[9] UL RC 19/14.

Convocation was first to have an opportunity to debate the dilemma. But at a meeting on 16 January 1877, the attendance was not large – an early motion attracted votes by seventy-two members – and few medical men were present. Towards the end of the session, in a small house, it was decided, by a vote of twenty-two to sixteen, to ask the Annual Committee to 'consider and report on the best means of carrying into effect the desire of Convocation that the degrees of the University should be open to Women'. There is no list of voters, but the resolution was 'strenuously opposed' by two doctors.[10]

What amount and character of lobbying and plotting went on in January and February has to be imagined, in the apparent absence of any documentary evidence. But what was to transpire was the success of those members of Senate who took the hawkish view that the medical possibilities offered to women by the new legislation should be grasped, immediately. On 28 February, with twenty-three members present, Granville directed the Senate's attention to the opinion of the Law Officers, and Osler moved that the University should exercise the new powers conferred on it. Goldsmid moved an amendment designed to set up a committee

> . . . to consider on what terms, if any, and under what regulations, it is expedient that Women should be admitted to any of the Degrees of the University.

In the light of the previous caution with which Senate had handled the whole question of enrolling women, the ease with which Osler's motion was carried is rather surprising. No doubt there had been a few genuine changes of view over the recent years, but perhaps more likely was the growth of a sense that the trend in favour of women was beginning to seem irreversible, and that the University of London might as well take the opportunity to go along with it. Some of those who had been broadly sympathetic, but unwilling to make haste in the face of strong opposition, may suddenly have felt both more comfortable about progressing, with a new Act of Parliament to point to, and rather impatient with opponents whom they were coming to see as pursuing mere delaying tactics.

All twenty-three Senators present voted on Goldsmid's amendment, which was defeated by fifteen to eight. Osler's motion was then carried by fourteen to seven. Those who voted against the amendment and in favour of the main motion included many of those who had consistently backed the idea of admitting women. But the biggest convert to the cause was the Chancellor, Lord Granville. He joined the Vice-Chancellor (Lubbock), Billing, Fitch, Gull, Heywood, Hutton, Jessel, Lowe, Osler, Paget, Lord Arthur Russell, and William Smith. The seven who supported Goldsmid were Joseph Williams Blakesley, the Dean of Lincoln; Cardwell; Sir William Jenner; Quain, Sharpey, Storrar and Williamson. Williamson and Fowler did not vote on the main

10 *Lancet*, 20 January 1877.

motion; and Fowler, consistent in his opposition to any move towards the admission of women, voted against Goldsmid's amendment. When the voting was detailed in the *Lancet*, Fowler felt impelled to explain that he had not voted against Osler's motion only because he wished to have time to consider whether Gurney's Act left the Senate with no option.[11]

On Osler's motion the medical men divided: Billing, Gull and Paget in favour; Jenner, Quain, Sharpey and Storrar, against. The Convocation-nominated Fellows split, and that split emphasised the medical–non-medical division: Jenner, Quain, Sharpey and Storrar, anti; Fitch, Hutton, Jessel and Osler, pro. Of the parliamentarians, only Cardwell and Goldsmid were opposed, while Granville, Heywood, Kimberley, Lowe, Lubbock, and Russell were on the winning side.

Exactly how many, of those who had wanted more consideration to be given to the next step, were utterly hostile to the entry of women to degree examinations, and how many genuinely thought that an immediate decision on entry to medical qualifications was unwise on other grounds, could only be ascertained if we had a verbatim report of the debate. As will be seen later, Jenner was certainly an outspoken opponent of women in medicine, and according to Fitch's biographer, Richard Quain was the 'main opposer' of women in the University of London.[12] But Storrar's vote, as so often in these and other episodes, may well simply illustrate the difficulty of a Chairman of Convocation aware of his own political vulnerability, rather than reveal his personal and professional conviction on the merits of admitting women as medical students.

The Senate immediately appointed a committee chosen from those present, in close approximation to the strengths of the groups opposed on the question just decided, to recommend ways and means of giving effect to their decision.

For a few weeks, Convocation's response to the Senate's decision to use the powers given by Gurney's Act was deceptively mild. At the meeting of the Annual Committee on 2 March, Nesbitt gave Notice of a composite Motion to thank the Senate for their resolution to admit women to medical degrees; to ask the Senate to take the Law Officers' opinion as to their power to admit women to degrees under the existing Charter, and if necessary, to apply for a new Charter giving them power to grant degrees to women in Arts, Science and Laws; and to ask that the subject of the admission of women to degrees be referred by Convocation to the Annual Committee with power to confer with Senate.

A week later, Nesbitt first moved that section of the motion which asked that Convocation should be recommended to thank the Senate for their

---

[11] *Lancet*, 30 June 1877.
[12] A.L. Lilley, *Sir Joshua Fitch* (London, 1906), p. 145.

resolution to admit women to degrees in medicine. There were twenty-three present, but the motion was passed only by a vote of nine to one. There is no division list, and therefore no way of knowing exactly how many members were present when the vote was taken. But there were no less than twelve medical men among the twenty-three, and it is not unlikely, given the hostility of at least eight of them in future voting, that most of the doctors preferred to abstain. Good manners, and perhaps a recognition of the need for diplomacy, may have prevented a deliberate snub to the Senate. The recommendations to ask for the Law Officers' opinion, and to request that the Committee be directed to confer with Senate, were accepted without division.

When Senate met again on 28 March 1877, they were presented with the Report of their Committee on the Admission of Women to Degrees, but the Report is not to be found in the printed records. Also before the Senate was another strand of pressure from without – an application from the London School of Medicine for Women, where Edith Shove was a student, for recognition as an institution qualified to prepare students for the examinations of the University. It was referred to the Committee on Examinations in Medicine.

The inevitably hostile but somewhat delayed reaction to the Senate's decision to make use of their new powers to introduce the right of women to enter for medical degrees surfaced at the Senate's meeting on 18 April. A memorial was presented, signed by 230 medical graduates, including three members of Senate – Jenner, Johnson and Quain. It stated that the exercise of powers by the Senate under Gurney's Act 'will be detrimental to the interests of the University'. Sir William Jenner moved that whenever the memorial was taken into consideration, 'the Resolution of the Senate with regard to the admission of Women to Degrees in Medicine be rescinded'.

As the signatories to this memorial comprised the largest group to give written expression of disapproval of the Senate's intention, it is worth examining who they were and whence they came. It is highly probable that the memorial was the work of a Medical Graduates' Committee, apparently set up in the early summer of 1876, when concern increased over the progress of the move to allow women to become candidates for medical degrees. The issue had produced something of a revolution in the level of interest which medical graduates had hitherto taken in Convocation's affairs. According to the *Lancet*, before 1876,

At the meetings of Convocation medical graduates could be counted on one's fingers, and serious votes were arrived at in meetings so small that the Senate very justly took not the slightest heed of them.[13]

[13] *Lancet*, 11 August 1877.

There does not appear to be any record of who constituted the Committee and held office in it, but for the memorial it must have done considerable canvassing, presumably by post outside London. And perhaps the most noteworthy aspect is the size of the provincial participation – some 45 per cent of those who signed worked sufficiently far away from London to make it highly unlikely that more than a small handful of them would be likely to attend Convocation's meetings, and practically impossible for any of them to serve on the Annual Committee. The main, potential threat at meetings of Convocation was therefore composed of the 126 signatories who lived and worked in or within easy reach of the centre of London, together with other London-based medical graduates who were sympathetic but who had not been reached in time to sign the memorial.

But even within the London area, the consistency of medical support for opposition to the admission of women was not impressive. In May and July 1877, and January, 1878, there were, respectively, two, four and one crucially important votes in Convocation on the matter. Only eighty-two of the 126 London-based doctors who signed the memorial of April, 1877, voted in any of those seven divisions, and only just over thirty of them voted in all of them. But the turn-outs were improved by the attendance of doctors who had not signed the memorial, and by the votes of a very few members who were clearly willing to travel considerable distances to vote. About fifty of them participated at one stage or another, but the largest turn out was twenty-nine in May, 1877. Only forty-seven doctors turned up at all three vital meetings: even so, they did better than the non-medicals, for whom the figure was only thirty-nine. So much inconsistency in attendance must have been a nightmare for those organising the votes.

In the seven divisions the hostile medical vote was highest soon after the memorial was presented: it reached 106 and 108 at the May meeting; in July the votes were eighty-seven, seventy, sixty-nine, forty-nine; and in January, 1878, it was eighty-three. Those pressing for action in favour of women, therefore, may well have calculated, as the second half of 1877 progressed, that the maximum medical vote against them in Convocation would be unlikely to exceed a hundred. Such calculation, however, could not have taken into account the rise of new factors which complicated the issue and aroused opposition from non-medical sources to proposed changes.

# 11

## *Constitutional complications: Parliament or Charter?*

The Senate did not have the question of degrees for women on its agenda at its meetings on 25 April and 9 May, 1877. But on 8 May the Annual Meeting of Convocation saw the whole debate over the entry of women to medical degrees widened by the raising of sophisticated issues of timing and by the introduction of constitutional controversy. Not at first, however, because Nesbitt and Bennett began by moving the resolution previously adopted by the rather grudgingly small vote in the Annual Committee, recommending Convocation to thank the Senate for deciding to admit women to degrees in Medicine. An amendment was immediately proposed by two doctors, quoting the memorial signed by 230 medical graduates which had been put before the Senate, and proposing that Convocation should recommend that no resolution in Senate to admit women to medical degrees should be adopted.

It must have become apparent, after a while, that neither of these formulations would be accepted. The house was, clearly, nicely balanced. Obviously enough, there were present representatives of both pro- and anti-women camps. But the pro camp included those who were unwilling to see medical degrees introduced for women before other degrees; and no doubt those opposed to the entry of women could see the possibility of exploiting that unwillingness to force abandonment of the whole venture.

The original motion and amendment were quickly found to be inappropriate, and were withdrawn. Nesbitt and Bennett, building on Convocation's previous commitment, then came up with a new proposition:

> . . . Convocation desiring that Women should be admitted to Degrees in all Faculties, thanks Senate for their resolution to admit Women to degrees in Medicine.

This, if passed, might well have been taken as giving Senate a green light to go ahead with the acceptance of women as candidates for medical degrees, leaving the question of entrance to other degree examinations to be pursued later.

But two medical men, William Scovell Savory and Robert Barnes, saw a splendid opportunity to combine the supporters of those who genuinely wanted to ensure an early entry for women to all degrees, with those who wanted, by any means, to delay and perhaps upset the decision to admit women to medicine. They moved that

> . . . it is inadvisable for this University to admit Women to the Degrees in Medicine before it shall have considered the general question of their admission to the Degrees of all Faculties.

There followed two divisions. Those who wanted to retain the original wording of the motion by Nesbitt and Bennett were defeated by 140 to 129. Then those who wanted to insert the new wording proposed by Savory and Barnes carried the day by 141 to 114. As a result, Nesbitt and Barnes then withdrew the motion carried at the Annual Committee about asking for a new Charter.

This declaration by Convocation, that Senate should consider the entry of women to all degree examinations before it opened the doors only to those women who wished to study medicine, was the beginning of a constitutional confrontation which raised matters well beyond the entry of women to the University. It is important, therefore, to emphasise that while, on this occasion, the medical men opposed to the entry of women to degrees were riding high, the voting on 8 May was not a victory for an overwhelming majority of medical graduates. Of the 269 who voted in the first division, only 114 were doctors, and they divided 106 to eight. The majority was composed of 106 medicos and thirty-four non-medical graduates: the medical men could not have won alone. On the second division only 255 votes were cast, but, again, there were not 128 medical votes – the majority was made up of 108 doctors and thirty-three non-medical graduates. Only three men changed sides from one division to the other, though more than a dozen abstained or left the meeting before the second vote was taken.

Thus the outcome of the 8 May voting was as much the result of objections taken by non-medical graduates to the Senate's intentions, as it was to the disapproval of a very large majority of the medical men who were present. It is worth noting, in passing, that no less than forty-three of the medical men in the majority were teachers at the London medical schools: only one medical teacher, H.C. Bastian, of University College Hospital, was among the few doctors in the minority.

That a historically important vote in the Senate was expected, following the extent of the controversy which had developed, was clear from another heavy attendance – twenty-eight – on 20 June 1877. Before that meeting the University had received letters praising the Senate's resolution that they should exercise the new powers available to admit women to degrees in Medicine, and expressing the hope that effective action would be taken on that resolution. Letters, not surprisingly, came from the Governors of the London School of Medicine for Women, from the Society for Promoting the Employment of Women, from Elizabeth Garrett Anderson, and from sixty women who had passed the General Examination for Women since 1869. But some measure of the wider support for the cause was indicated by a letter signed by A.W. Bennett and 677 others, including seventy-three medicos, fifty-nine clergymen, eight Heads of Oxbridge Colleges and Headmasters of Public Schools, thirty-three Fellows of the Royal Society, thirty-seven MPs and Peers, fourteen members of the London School Board, representatives of the Governing Bodies of Girton, Newnham, Bedford and Queen's Colleges, and a long list of professors, examiners and teachers.

Sir William Jenner did not press the motion of which he had given notice in May, and gave way to Storrar to move that the Senate concur in the opinion expressed by Convocation on 8 May, namely:

> That it is inadvisable for this University to admit Women to the Degrees in Medicine before it shall have considered the general question of their admission to the Degrees of all Faculties.

Of all the twenty-eight present, only Frederick John Wood did not vote – either abstaining or being absent when the division was taken. The motion was lost, eleven to sixteen.

The most likely explanation of the vote is that the majority had taken to heart the old adage of a bird-in-the-hand being worth two in the bush, and felt, more formally, that to risk losing an opportunity to bring women into the Faculty which had been most opposed to receiving them would have been a dereliction of duty. And it is surely not impossible that the majority may have felt that the Senate, a Crown-chosen body governing an institution financially dependent on the support of Parliament, should not fail to take advantage of recent legislation – implicity blessed by the Government – designed to facilitate the entry of women to the medical profession. There may also have been, on the part of some of the majority, some resentment at what they regarded as an attempt by Convocation to dictate how the Senate should proceed. The voting followed the pattern already established, in not producing any undivided expression of group opinions. Six doctors, five Convocation-nominated Fellows, and three parliamentarians, were among the losers: three doctors, four Convocation-nominated Fellows, and five parliamentarians were among the majority.

So clear-cut a decision was followed quite quickly by further refinements of the respective positions of those pursuing a complete acceptance of women as candidates for all degrees, and of those defensive of Convocation's constitutional rights. On 4 July, the Senate considered the Report of its Committee on the Admission of Women to Degrees in Medicine, which had been set up in the previous February. It was then resolved that they should seek the Law Officers' opinion as to whether, if the Senate wanted to use the power conferred on it to admit women to medical degrees, they were competent, legally and constitutionally, to do so under the Charter without the concurrence of Convocation. Such a reference had not been discussed or recommended in the Report of the Committee, which was restricted to important but mainly procedural matters. It is almost certain, therefore, that the agreement to seek the Law Officer's advice must have been a result of pressure from Convocation since the previous meeting.

However, the 4 July meeting was also to take further the campaign for an extension of the admission of women to all degree examinations. Osler had voted in favour of not delaying the exercise of the new powers to enable women to take examinations in medicine at the 20 June meeting, but now he returned to the wider matter he had raised successfully in Convocation on 18 January 1876, and moved

> That it is desirable that a New Charter should be obtained, extending the power of granting Degrees to Women, already possessed by the University of London in the Faculty of Medicine, to the case of Degrees in all other Faculties.

There was an attendance of nineteen, but Osler's motion was voted on by only fourteen, and carried by ten to four. Nine of those in favour had already declared themselves as supporters of the entry of women to the University: the Chancellor and Vice-Chancellor were joined by Kimberley, Fitch. Hutton, Lowe, Osler, Paget and Spottiswoode. The rather surprising addition to their ranks was Sir George Burrows, who had been previously in the other camp. The opponents were Fowler, Goldsmid, Grey-Egerton, and Wood. Thus the only medical men who voted – Paget and Burrows – were in favour. Three other doctors – Gull, Quain, and Sharpey – together with Cardwell and Williamson, were either absent at the time of the vote, or abstained.

On 6 July, the Annual Committee met and took a position which moved the argument further towards the constitutional relations between Senate and Convocation. Two medical men, John Curnow and Tilbury Fox, carried by fifteen votes to seven a motion asking for an Extraordinary Meeting of Convocation to consider

> . . . how far the constitutional privileges of Convocation have been superseded by the Senate in adopting a permissive Act of Parliament by which the constitution of the University will be materially altered, without consultation with Convocation.

There is no division list. Of twenty-six members listed as present, thirteen were medical graduates, so that there is a great probability that a high proportion of the fifteen who carried the motion were drawn from them.

A few days afterwards, there was an exchange of letters between the Registrar, W.B. Carpenter, and the Master of the Rolls, Sir George Jessel. It is worth quoting from it at some length, because it is one of the rare items in the archives which illustrates the inter-relationship of Senate and Convocation and the divisions of opinion which ran through both bodies. Here was Carpenter writing to Jessel, a Convocation-nominated Fellow, about Sir Julian

Goldsmid's motion (Goldsmid was a Crown-chosen Fellow) on 4 July, to ask the Law Officers of the Crown for an opinion on

> ... the legality of the action of the Senate in the admission of women to Medical Degrees. [Quain raised] the *constitutional right* of the Senate to act alone in this matter ... and this seems to the Vice-Chancellor [Lubbock] ... as to myself, to deserve very grave consideration, more especially as a meeting of Convocation is to be forthwith called to consider it, at the instance of the Annual Committee.

Could Jessel give him a *judicial* opinion? And Carpenter went on to spell out what he saw as the essence of the situation.

> While giving to the Senate the uncontrolled power (subject only to the *veto* of the Home Secretary) of directing the affairs of the University within the limits prescribed by the Charter, that Charter explicity provides that no new Charter shall take effect nor any old one be suspended, without the *joint assent* of the Senate and Convocation. And it is contended that this is *morally* tantamount to providing that no fundamental change in the constitution of the University, such as would (unless by Act of Parliament) require a new Charter to effect it, should be made without such joint assent.
>
> This provision would of course be overridden by any *positive* enactment of Parliament. But, it is urged, a merely *permissive* Act ought not to be applied by the Senate, without the concurrence of Convocation, in any way which *fundamentally changes the Constitution* of the University; the *spirit*, if not the *letter* of the Charter requiring that in such a matter the University should act as a *whole*.

And Carpenter added a postscript which revealed his own reservations about at least some elements of Convocation:

> It seems to me much to be regretted that this constitutional question was not raised and disposed of in the first instance, before the *odicum medicum* was excited. And I cannot see that Convocation would *now* be justified in passing a vote of censure on the Senate (which is the real meaning of the Resolution to be proposed), when its own organs in the Senate have only urged it at the last moment, and this by the mouth of one of its Medical – not Legal – Representatives.

The Master of the Rolls, though himself, in Carpenter's definition, one of the Senate's Legal Convocation Representatives, had no time for the arguments of Goldsmid and Quain, constitutional or moral:

> The powers given to the Senate by the Charter are enlarged by the Act of Parliament and that is all. According to the Charter the Senate could not have accepted similar powers from the Crown without the assent of Convocation – all the Crown could do by Charter would be permissive – i.e. the conferring of the power to grant these degrees. Parliament has conferred this power for the public benefit, and it seems to me to be the plain duty of the Senate to exercise it, if

thought beneficial, without regard to any arrangement with Convocation not to apply for or accept such power from the Crown . . . this is not a contract between individuals, but the terms of a Crown Charter which everyone knows was liable to be altered by Parliament as had been done already in the case of the older universities. Indeed it is not a contract at all, the Crown granted the Charter on such terms as it chose as regarded the government of the affairs of the University and Parliament has altered the terms.[1]

Whether or not the Law Officers accepted the same reasoning, they came to the same conclusion. On 17 July, the Treasury sent to the University the Law Officers' opinion, which supported the Senate's competence under the Charter to grant degrees to women without the concurrence of Convocation. The Senate decided, the next day, to send the opinion to the Chairman of Convocation. The stage was set for another major debate, at an Extraordinary Meeting of Convocation, scheduled for 27 July.

But, *pace* Jessel, Convocation's constitutional concern had an interesting history. To understand how, from this point onwards, the pressure for accepting women as examinees, though still not met and being strongly supported, was seriously affected and became, for many, almost a secondary matter, by comparison with the importance of a constitutional issue, we must go back to 1873. In that year, negotiations were taking place over the introduction of the Conjoint Scheme which required the co-operation of the medical corporations and the universities. In order to take part, the Senate discovered that they would need certain new powers. The Vice-Chancellor, Sir John Lubbock, who had taken office in June, 1872, and had been Liberal MP for Maidstone since 1870, offered to introduce a Bill to give the University the required authority. He, along with three other Fellows in the Commons – Fowler, Grey-Egerton, and Lowe – brought in the Medical Act Amendment (University of London) Bill, which went through the Lower House, and was piloted through the Lords by Granville, apparently without any debate. It received the Royal Assent on 28 July, 1873.[2]

The object of the exercise met with the full, informal approval of Convocation, but the method by which the Senate had achieved it gave offence. Whether, in what was probably seen as a small matter needing urgent attention, anyone in the University demurred at the time of Lubbock's offer to obtain new powers from Parliament quickly is very doubtful. But the Senate was choosing only one of the two alternative ways of increasing the powers of the University – to go directly to Parliament. The other way was to ask for a Supplementary Charter, which would have required the formal consent of Convocation, and which would undoubtedly have taken far longer. Whether,

---

[1] UL RC37/12, Carpenter to Jessel, 10 July; Jessel to Carpenter, 11 July 1877.
[2] 36 & 37 Vic c. 55.

in the late summer of 1873, anyone had doubts as to which route should be taken, they could hardly have included Fowler, a Conservative who was normally very protective of Convocation's rights. But at some point between then and the spring of 1874, William Shaen, the Clerk of Convocation, expressed concern over the Senate's action to the Annual Committee.

Shaen argued that the Senate, by going directly to Parliament for new powers, had by-passed Convocation's right to be consulted and to agree to any constitutional change. The Annual Committee agreed and reported the matter to Convocation which, at its meeting on 12 May 1874, resolved unanimously, on the motion of Cozens-Hardy, a lawyer, and C.H. Fagge, who taught at Guy's Hospital,

> That, while cordially concurring in the object of the Medical Act Amendment (University of London) Act, Convocation request the Chairman to express to the Senate their hope that for the future no similar action may be taken without the previous consent of Convocation.

It is not surprising, therefore, that this episode was recalled very sharply, and used very effectively, three years later, when the Senate proposed to take advantage of Russell Gurney's Act. And as will be seen, despite Jessel and the Law Officers, the Senate chose not to use the new statutory power.

The requisitions which resulted in the calling of an Extraordinary Meeting of Convocation on 27 July 1877 were signed by thirty-three medical men and eight others. When they met, members had before them the Law Officers' opinion supporting the Senate's competence to grant degrees to women without the concurrence of Convocation. Notice had been given of three motions, but precedence was given to one put forward by Curnow and Fox, regretting

> ... that the Senate has, by adopting a permissive Act of Parliament ... without reference to or consultation with Convocation, materially altered the constitution of the University, and has thus practically superseded the privileges of Convocation.

There were two challenges to the motion, the first of which, from Hensman, asked the house to accept that

> The Senate, by adopting the Act which permits it to grant Degrees in Medicine to Women, has promoted the best interests of the University.

That was lost by eighty-two to 142. The second challenge was based on doubts as to whether, in the event of the Senate admitting women to degrees, they would be eligible to become members of Convocation. Delay and consultation should be requested in any application for a new Charter. That was lost seventy-six to 113.

The main motion of Curnow and Fox was then carried by 114 to seventy-one. It was, in effect, an expression of indignation and anger, but it did not point to any specific action. Curnow moved

> That it be referred to Annual Committee to confer with Senate with reference to the foregoing Resolution and to ask them not to take any further action under the Act.

By this stage of the proceedings the drift of members away was increasing, and an attempt was made to adjourn. But the debate continued and the motion was at last carried by eighty-eight to fifty-two.

The largest contribution to the majorities in all the four divisions were certainly made by medical graduates, but the size of the contribution by non-medical men was considerable. The medical figures in each division were eighty-seven, seventy, sixty-nine and forty-nine, but the non-medical votes numbered fifty-five, forty-three, forty-five and thirty-eight. The introduction of constitutional controversy had clearly aroused, in the consciousness of many non-medical members, a basic concern for Convocation's rights. Those on the losing side, who either felt that the constitutional issue was relatively insignificant, or who believed that priority should be given to the women's cause, were overwhelmingly non-medical.

There was no likelihood of further meetings during the summer recess, and doubtless all concerned welcomed an opportunity to review the controversy of the past few months and to prepare for more negotiation in the autumn.

The Annual Committee met on 12 October 1877, and appointed a sub-committee to draw up a memorandum to present to Senate. Those entrusted with the task were three lawyers, James Anstie, E.H. Busk, and J. Horne Payne; and two medical men, John Curnow and Tilbury Fox. Five days later the Senate met and were presented by Storrar with the Minutes of Convocation's Extraordinary Meeting of 27 July. The briefness of the record and the absence of divison during the meeting implies that a good deal of diplomatic negotiation had been going on. Senate simply resolved to accede to the wish of Convocation for a Conference to be held between Senate and the Annual Committee. That conference was held a month later, but in the interim, on 2 November, the Annual Committee accepted that a meeting of Convocation should be convened for 15 January 1878. There was also a long process of amending and approving the memorandum which would go to Senate, and a deputation to take it there was chosen.

When Senate met on 14 November, they were presented by the deputation from Convocation with a Memorandum with Appendices, and the Resolution of the Extraordinary Meeting of 27 July. Convocation made it clear that the problem, for them, was 'not that of the admission of women . . . but one affecting the privileges of Convocation only'. Nor did they challenge the

Senate's legal right to adopt Gurney's Act, 'in accordance with the opinion of the Law Officers of the Crown'. What they claimed was that

> ... having regard to the permissive character of the Act, and the circumstances under which it was adopted, the Senate ought not to have exercised the powers conferred upon it by that Act.

Advice had been sought from two QCs, Farrer Herschell, MP, and Montague Cookson. In Herschell's view, while the Senate had unquestioned executive authority to exercise the power given by Gurney's Act, the intention of the 1858 Charter,

> ... in depriving the Senate of the power of accepting a new charter without the consent of Convocation, was to prevent any fundamental change in the nature of the University, or in its operation, being made without the concurrence of the latter body.

While Convocation was not denying the legal right of the Senate to admit women, both their advisers did claim that one impropriety of the Senate's proposal to adopt Gurney's Act rested on a misreading of that section of the Act which affected the status of any medical women graduates. Both lawyers challenged the notion that membership of Convocation depended on registration as a medical practitioner: membership of Convocation resulted from the award of the degree. Thus a woman holding a medical degree would be a Member of Convocation and as such would have a say in the governance of the University. Herschell felt that it was 'to say the least, very doubtful whether the courts would not hold that the female graduates became members of Convocation'. Such a change in the constitution would be

> ... fundamental. It is wholly beyond the powers of the existing charter, and, but for [Gurney's] Act, could only have been done by virtue of a new charter; and I think the Act, being permissive only, should only have been adopted by the same authority which could accept a new charter – viz., the Senate and Convocation combined.

Although there are no relevant papers extant, it is clear that much discussion must have taken place, among at least the leading members of Senate, before the meeting on 14 November. The Vice-Chancellor had been present on 17 October, but then went abroad and did not attend Senate again until February, 1878. No doubt he had conferred with the Chancellor before he left, and, fortunately for the Senate, Granville was out of office, for otherwise he might well have found it impossible to devote so much time to the affairs of the University. As it was, he oversaw a fundamental shift of position. In simple terms, the Senate accepted Convocation's wishes without debating their arguments.

The new intention of the Senate was announced to the Convocation deputation verbally by Granville on 14 November. The admission of women to medical degrees by using the powers available under Gurney's Act was to be abandoned. Instead, admission of women to all degrees should be sought through a new Supplemental Charter which would also limit the admission of women to Convocation. A draft of such a Charter would be submitted to Convocation. The Convocation case, was, in effect, conceded, but arguments of the immediate past were pushed aside quite brusquely:

> It would answer no practical purpose to raise a debate at the present moment on the arguments used in the Memorandum which has just been presented, or on those in justification of the course which the Senate has pursued.

When the deputation reported back to the Annual Committee two days later, Tilbury Fox moved that, while accepting with satisfaction the abandonment of further action by the Senate under Gurney's Act, the Annual Committee should not recommend Convocation to discuss the proposed Supplemental Charter 'except upon the understanding that no one Faculty of the University is to be dealt with in an exceptional manner'. There is nothing in the minutes of the Committee to explain the exact nature of whatever apprehensions this motion expressed, but an amendment by Pye-Smith and Shaen, carried by seventeen votes to ten, gave thanks to the Senate for abandoning Gurney and for agreeing to submit to Convocation a new Charter 'which will apply to all the Faculties'. Two medical men, Jenner and George Vivian Poore, Professor of Medicine at UCL, wanted to do no more than thank the Senate, but their amendment was defeated by seventeen to twelve. The final version, by Pye-Smith and Shaen, was carried by sixteen to ten.

There are no voting lists, but this was a very large turn-out for the Annual Committee, and included four medical Fellows. Storrar attended as Chairman of Convocation, but the other three – George Busk, Jenner and Quain – were exercising their right of *ex officio* membership. Altogether there were eighteen medicos present, and eleven others. There must have been a considerable split within the medical contingent: even if the non-medical group voted almost solidly in one direction, they would have needed half a dozen medical votes to carry the main motion.

The Senate had, in fact, bought off the constitutional objections raised by Convocation, and that must, undoubtedly, have weakened the position of those principally unhappy about the admission of women to degrees. Indeed, as will be seen in a later chapter, the concerns of those within Convocation who were keen to address other constitutional changes were pursued at the Annual Committee henceforward with the tacit understanding that the question of the admission of women was a separate and isolated issue. But that only followed the refusal of John Storrar, as Chairman of Convocation, on 16 November, to call an Extraordinary General meeting which had been asked for by seventy-two members to consider various constitutional resolutions. However, only a quarter of the seventy-two petitioners were medical, and those most concerned to concentrate on the 'women in medicine' question were impatient with and unsympathetic towards the constitutional reformers.[3]

It is probable that Storrar must have known of the favourable deal which was being made over the abandonment of Gurney's Act, and have felt strong enough to assert his authority as Chairman in order to avoid any renewal of hostilities with the Senate. He was not seriously challenged, but the spokesman for the seventy-two petitioners, Thomas Tyler, gave a frank explanation of his attempt to requisition a meeting – an explanation which no doubt would have rung bells in the minds and memories of many members whose previous efforts to raise issues had been frustrated:

> . . . long experience of the meetings of Convocation has shown that it would have been inexpedient, not to say useless, to place the questions with which the requisition is concerned on the Agenda of an ordinary meeting of Convocation, at which, other business taking precedence, their consideration would probably have been deferred through accident or strategem till a late hour of the evening when, on account of the thinness of the House, no satisfactory decision would have been possible.

The Annual Committee, however, recognised the strength of feeling in Convocation about the desirability of seeking further constitutional changes, and set up a sub-committee which recommended 'several measures of great importance'. But the sub-committee also expressed the opinion, with which the Annual Committee concurred, that, at the present time, 'it would be undesirable to complicate the simple question now at issue, with regard to the admission of Women'. The non-medical reformers turned their energies elsewhere, and in January, 1878, set up a London University Reform Association, whose short career will be examined in a later chapter.[4]

The Senate, on 7 December, expressed their pleasure at the outcome of the conference with Convocation, and trusted that

> . . . the objects desired in common by the Senate and by Convocation may be obtained in a manner to which neither party objects, by a new Supplementary Charter . . . for the admission of Women to all Degrees, with the requisite limitation in regard to the admission of Women to Convocation.

The Senate reminded Convocation that no resolution as to the future had yet been taken, but they did order the preparation of a draft Charter which should empower the University 'to grant all its Degrees to Women with a

---

[3] *Lancet*, 3 & 10 November 1877.
[4] *Lancet*, 5 January 1878.

proviso that Female Graduates be not admissible to Convocation without the concurrence of that body'.

It took less than two weeks for a draft Charter to be finished, and it was presented to Senate on 19 December. It was approved, but not before Quain challenged the proviso that female graduates should not become members of Convocation unless and until Convocation so resolved. He declared that there was 'no reason why they should be deprived of any of the privileges to which the holders of . . . Degrees are legally entitled'. Quain would have known very well that such a change would make acceptance of the Charter by Convocation unlikely; and given his consistent opposition to the admission of women hitherto, his proposal, at the last moment, can only be seen as a wrecking amendment. He was supported by Burrows, Heywood and Johnson, but was defeated by ten Fellows, of whom four were doctors. Granville and Storrar were present but did not vote.

The draft Charter went to the Annual Committee on 21 December, and was passed on to Convocation with the recommendation that it should be taken into consideration at the forthcoming meeting on 15 January 1878.

# 12

## *The final hurdle*

A reading of the formal documents of the meetings in the autumn of 1877, however sparse and clinical they are, nonetheless gives a strong impression that all concerned had come to realise that a resolution of the long argument over the admission of women to the University's examinations was overdue. After the final settlement of the issue early in 1878, the Registrar, W.B. Carpenter, told the Home Secretary that

> There seems a very general feeling that the higher Education of Women should be encouraged by Academical Honours; and that the University of London should take the lead in such recognition, as it can accept Candidates from any Educational Institution.[1]

But at the end of 1877 there were still anxieties about the final stages of what Lord Granville himself had called, in 1862, 'the great Feminine question'.

The Chancellor was not happy about the situation, and clearly felt the strength of medical opposition. On 30 December 1877, he wrote to the Vice-Chancellor, Lubbock, from Walmer Castle:

> I am very glad to hear that you are in England. I am afraid that the prospect of success in Convocation is doubtful, and if our compromise is rejected, the position will be difficult, and bad for the University.
>
> I have writen a letter to the Chairman of Convocation, and I have asked Carpenter to correct the historical part of it. It may be thought *infra dig* for the Chancellor to descend into the arena, but I believe something of the sort is necessary. I shall beg you to look at the draft with your most powerful micro-scope, and to suggest every possible amendment of faults, either of commission or omission.
>
> I have asked Henry James [later Lord James of Hereford] to explain matters to Herschell, and I have written privately to Newman Hall [an eminent Congre-gationalist]. Is there anybody you can *quietly* influence to take an active part. The medical organization is good, and I have no doubt their whipping will be complete. I do not know whether the other side has any wirepullers, and whether

---

[1] HO45/9453/70698, Carpenter to Cross, 18 January 1878.

any practical attempts are being made to secure a majority. Of course, you and I could not put ourselves forward in this work.[2]

Lubbock and Carpenter would have made some comments on the draft, but the long letter which Granville sent to the Chairman of Convocation was a comprehensive and masterly statement, rehearsing the whole history of the controversy and arguing the case for the acceptance of the new Charter. It was marked by his own disarming frankness and polished diplomacy. He admitted that he had changed his own mind on the issue, and believed that he was, in the context of medical degrees, 'acting in accordance with the views of Convocation'. He was firm in defence of the Senate's action in proposing that a Supplementary Charter be sought, and in defence of the Senate's refusal to look further until the issue of the admission of women to degrees was settled one way or the other. And he leaned heavily on Convocation:

The Senate purposely abstained from taking any decision as to the future, in any direction whatever, in the event of this proposal being rejected; as its members could not bind themselves or their successors in regard to their action in all contingencies.

It is contrary to all custom, that, when differences arise between two parties (especially in the case of bodies closely connected, and animated by friendly feelings towards each other), and one is willing to make a compromise, it should at once abandon all freedom of action for the future, whether the proposed compromise be or be not accepted.

It is more uncalled for in the present case, as, in the proposal now made by the Senate, all the concessions come from it, none being asked for from Convocation.

Nor did Granville miss the importance of the feeling of a sizeable group drawn from all quarters of Convocation that the opportunity of making desirable changes in the constitution of the University was being missed in the present proposal for a limited Supplementary Charter. He argued that constitutional change

. . . has not yet been sufficiently discussed in Convocation for any definite agreement to be arrived at on the subject. When such an agreement is matured, the Senate will be bound to give any recommendation of Convocation the most careful and respectful attention; and the granting of the proposed Supplemental Charter could not with any reason be used to prejudice the claims of Convocation to a new Charter reforming the Constitution of the University. It is clearly desirable that both bodies should enter upon the consideration of a subject which may powerfully affect the future prospects of the University for good or evil, with calmness, and undisturbed by any existing differences bearing upon a separate point.

---

[2] BL Add Mss 49644, Granville to Lubbock, 30 December 1877.

The question, however, of delay in order to attempt the amendment of the present Constitution of the University, is one which is beyond the scope of this letter; the only object of which is to correct a misapprehension that the Senate has been or is actuated, in any degree, by want of respect for, or of confidence in, Convocation. It is written in the hope that an agreement will be arrived at acceptable to Convocation as well as to the Senate.[3]

The meeting of Convocation on 15 January 1878 was believed to be 'the fullest . . . ever held' up to that time. There were at least 374 members present, for the vote in favour of accepting the draft Supplemental Charter was 242 to 132. It was a convincing victory, despite the fact that, as Carpenter claimed, 'every effort was made by the opponents of the Admission of Women to Degrees, to defeat the Draft Charter'.[4] The resolution to accept the Charter was moved by two lawyers – Bompas and Hensman – and the debate provided some high drama, of which the most famous episode was perhaps described most sensitively by the psychologist James Sully. Sully admitted that, doubtless like many others present on 15 January, he had hitherto taken 'for the most part but a lukewarm share in the doings of the Convocation'. However, 'Being in favour of extending the whole curriculum of studies to women, I gave my vote accordingly.' And

> . . . when Sir William Jenner made his stirring appeal against the proposed change, I was sitting high up near one of the doors, and Sir William was almost opposite me on the other side of the passage. As his fine head, with its silky white hair, appeared above the sitters, one could see that he was agitated. There was a discernible tremor of the voice, and I thought I saw the gleam of a tear in his eye as he urged his passionate personal argument. 'Gentlemen,' he said, 'I have only one dearly beloved daughter, and rather than see her on the benches of a dissecting room I would follow her to the grave.' As his voice ceased there was a long hush: university disputes seemed for a long moment cold and almost unreal by the side of this baring of a father's breast. It was the most moving bit of oratory that I ever listened to, and the very futility of the protest added to the pathos of it.[5]

The publicity and the lobbying which preceded the vote must have been most effective in arousing the interest and pressing for the attendance of pro-women members. By contrast, the medical turn-out – and the vote against – was less impressive than on previous occasions. Only 28 per cent of all who voted were doctors – 105 of them – and for the first time more than a token number were in favour of the admission of women. While eighty-three medicos

[3] HO45/9453/70698, Granville to Storrar, 11 January 1878.
[4] HO45/9453/70698, Carpenter to Cross, 18 January 1878.
[5] James Sully, My Life and Friends (London, 1918), pp. 203–4.

William Benjamin Carpenter. Physiologist. Fullerian Professor at the Royal Institution. Registrar 1856–1879. Crown-chosen Member of Senate 1880–1885.

voted against, twenty-two made up part of the majority. The vote against was boosted by forty-nine non-medical men who must either have been opposed to the admission of women on principle, or were dissatisfied with the decision of the Senate not to consider including any other constitutional changes. The 197 Arts, Laws and Science graduates who voted for the admission of women were sufficiently numerous to have carried the day more than comfortably, even if the twenty-two medical graduates who voted with them had been of a different view.

Convocation was quickly engaged in internal considerations of further constitutional change, and the new Supplemental Charter, dated 4 March, which was submitted to them formally on 14 May 1878, was approved without division. The Senate accepted it on the following day, but they had lost Lord Overstone, who had resigned, being unwilling 'that the last acts of my life, should be an effort to promote the assimilation in all respects, of the education of women to that of men'. His letter of resignation moved the Registrar to admit that his own utmost efforts had been 'to prevent a collision between the Senate and Convocation, which would have been (I am strongly persuaded) far more injurious to the University, than the Admission of Women to its Degrees can be'.[6]

In October the necessary new regulations for the medical degrees were approved: more notably, the London School of Medicine for Women and its newly acquired partner, the Royal Free Hospital, were recognised by the Senate as appropriate institutions for the training of medical students.

The first four women BAs graduated in 1880, the first two BScs in 1881, and the first two MBs in 1882. Edith Shove, who had asked the Senate to use the powers of Gurney's Act so that she could be accepted as a candidate, was one of the new Bachelors of Medicine. In 1882, the first women to graduate became Bachelors of two years standing, thus reaching the stage at which, had they been male, membership of Convocation would have been open to them. The question of whether Convocation should agree to admit women graduates had been raised, and consideration of it postponed, in May, 1881. On 17 January 1882, two motions were before the house. Hensman and Nesbitt wanted to include women in Convocation and to enable them to vote at elections: but their colleagues preferred to accept, without division, a straightforward motion of McDowall and Bennett, 'That female graduates be admitted to Convocation.'

---

[6] For the resignation of Overstone, see his letter to Granville, 18 December 1877; Granville's reply, 21 December 1877; and Carpenter to Overstone, 4 & 26 January 1878, in O'Brien, *Correspondence of Lord Overstone*, iii, pp. 1304–8.

# Part IV

## *The Parliamentary Seat to 1886*

# 13

# A trial run

The University's case for parliamentary representation had been looked on favourably in the early 1850s, and supported in principle by both major parties. Derby and Disraeli had approved the notion when in office in 1852, but had made it clear that the new University, whose graduates were not yet legally recognised as an integral part of the institution, was too immature.[1] Subsequently, the Crimean War, a decade of shifting parliamentary opinion, and a long spell of Palmerstonian indifference, delayed further change to the representative system until the Second Reform Act of 1867. But the second Derby/Disraeli Government, coming into power at the beginning of 1858, removed one of the legal obstacles to the University's enfranchisement by approving the Charter which brought Convocation into existence. There was, henceforward, a potential constituency.

Convocation, from the beginning, kept their eyes on the possibility of the University's obtaining a seat in the House of Commons. At the end of November, 1858, they set up a committee, which included Foster and Storrar, to prepare a case to be put forward; and in January, 1859, they announced that William Nathaniel Massey, MP for Salford, who had been Under Secretary at the Home Office in 'the late Administration', had 'undertaken the case of the interests of the University during the coming session of Parliament'.[2] A month later, a Representation of the People Bill was introduced which, among Disraeli's 'fancy franchises', provided that, henceforward, graduates of any University of the United Kingdom would be entitled to vote. However, the Government was defeated on another provision of the Bill, and fell in June.

The new Palmerston Administration, which took over, was prepared to go much further. On 1 March 1860, they introduced a Bill which contained specific provisions whereby 'In all future Parliaments the University of London shall return one Member to serve in Parliament.' As soon as the Bill was launched, the Senate moved quickly to produce a memorial to Government and to Parliament, using a committee which included all its parliamentary members – Devonshire, Monteagle, Macaulay, Overstone, Wodehouse and

[1] Willson, *Our Minerva*, ch. 17.
[2] *LUM*, February 1859.

the Bishop of St Davids (Connop Thirlwall), in the Lords; Baines, Heywood, Sir James Graham, Cornewall Lewis, and Stanley in the Commons – and also Foster, Osler and Storrar, the last two having only just become Fellows. Foster tried to get the Senate 'to act in accordance with Convocation's committee', but his motion was not carried 'in consequence of the objection on the part of some members of the Senate, that this would pledge the Senate to a course upon the advisability of which they were not unanimous'.[3] But when the Senate's memorial was announced, Convocation's committee blessed it and the Senate's intention that Lord Granville should present the memorial in the Lords, and Sir James Graham in the Commons. However, the combined efforts of Senate and Convocation in 1860 were of no avail, as the Bill was an early casualty of the complex manoeuvres over franchise reform, and was withdrawn on 11 June.

In 1861 there was, briefly, another chance for the University, when four seats in the Commons were vacated by the disfranchisement of the constituencies of Sudbury and St Albans. The University was only one of several claimants to be considered for the award of one of those seats, and was prepared to fight particularly hard against the claims of the Scotch Universities. But there was clearly little enthusiasm in Government circles, where political considerations dictated the desirability of strengthened representation of centres of heavy population, like the West Riding of Yorkshire. Granville, the Chancellor, was Lord President of the Council, and Sir George Cornewall Lewis, a Fellow, was Home Secretary: neither would press the University's case. The elder statesman, Sir James Graham, was prepared at one stage to move an amendment in favour of London, but later was unwilling.[4]

In the circumstances, both Senate and Convocation felt it advisable to withdraw their claim. Foster had told Granville in confidence that he did not think enfranchisement was feasible 'this session', though as Chairman it was 'impossible . . . to appear even indifferent on the matter'. He advised Convocation that it

> . . . would not be wise to press . . . claims to representation in a sense hostile to the arrangement brought forward by a Government, so many of whose members have shown themselves to be its active and zealous supporters.[5]

Granville was frankly pessimistic: he told new graduates that parliamentary representation was

> . . . just now a thing to be looked forward to rather with hope than confidence. Last year, we believe, confidence predominated. Reform now looms in the distance

---

[3] *LUM*, February 1859.
[4] *Lancet*, 8 June 1861; *BMJ*, 6 July 1861.
[5] PRO/29/19/5, Foster to Granville, 16 June 1861.

more like a headland we are leaving in our wake, than a haven we are approaching. The University must bide its time.[6]

There was to be no MP for London University for another seven years. But the possibility that a seat was in the making in 1859–61 produced the first candidates, giving some indication of the ideas and interests involved. The significant activity was concentrated in the short life of the Representation of the People Bill, from March to July, 1860, with a minor flurry in the following year during the few weeks when it seemed possible that the University might secure one of the four seats previously allocated to the constituencies of Sudbury and St Albans.

In 1860, and for quarter of a century thereafter, there was an ambivalence in the situation of both those who contested the University's parliamentary seat, and their supporters. Partly because of genuine conviction, and partly, perhaps, because the London seat was being debated at a time when the party-political scene in the country was very confused, there was present, on the one hand, a belief that the representative of the University should be distinguished – preferably as an intellectual – and non-partisan. On the other hand, however, there was no doubt that the whole process of choosing a man to send to Westminster was still noticeably influenced by orthodox party loyalties and, not least, by special interests in the University context.

Charles James Foster, the acknowledged leader of the drive for Convocation, and its first Chairman, who was also a Fellow of the University and a Professor at UCL, might be regarded as the candidate who most saw himself as a spokesman, primarily, for the University in whose interests he had been and was so passionately engaged. But as we have seen, he was at the same time a Radical, a prominent Dissenter, and the salaried lobbyist of the Society for the Liberation of Religion from State Patronage and Control, deeply involved in the struggle to abolish church rates. Much though his work for Convocation was respected and praised, it is unlikely that he would have triumphed over a majority of graduates who would have held more orthodox political views. He was strongly backed by Frederick John Wood, another Dissenter who had been his colleague in the cause of the graduates since as long ago as 1840, by many of his fellow Nonconformists, and doubtless by a large group of grateful members of Convocation.

Sir Charles Locock, *accoucheur* to Queen Victoria, one of the original medical appointees to the Senate, was undoubtedly a Conservative, but the ambivalence just discussed was clearly revealed by the support which he received from the *British Medical Journal*. Its leader writer, after arguing that, as the medical profession had 'done immeasurably more than either of its sister

---

[6] *Lancet*, 25 May 1861.

professions [law and the church] to build up and promulgate [the University's] renown', it would be 'but a natural act to select a medical representative'. Locock had 'a magnificent fortune' and would devote all his time to Parliament. However,

> It has been urged against him . . . that his conservative tendencies unfit him as a candidate for the representation of the most liberal of universities; and some expressions in his address would seem to favour this conclusion, but we have reason to believe that those expressions were put in his mouth by his purely conservative supporters, and was not intended by him to imply any party leaning whatever. Indeed, it is well known that Sir Charles would enter Parliament as an entirely independent member, whose policy it would be to hold himself aloof from all political parties. Such a man would advocate the interests of this young university with far more effect than a mere party man with well marked hereditary tendencies . . .[7]

Locock's committee was strongly backed by Robert Nicholas Fowler who, as we have seen, was himself tenaciously preparing for what developed into a major career as a Conservative in Convocation, in the Senate, in the City of London, and in Parliament.

When the shadow boxing was at its height, a pamphlet appeared, attributed to Edward Smith, MD. Smith had put himself forward to the Senate, in 1858, as an appropriate person to represent the University on the GMC. Now he wrote as the chairman of an unidentified group calling for a non-partisan candidate with scientific aims. The pamphlet hinted at the willingness of the 'most powerful scientific man of the present day', to stand. Smith's view was that the successful candidate should 'avoid intimate alliances with any political party', because

> . . . the object in granting the franchise to a University is not that the political views of the members of the University may thereby find expression, but that the claims of learning may be advocated in the legislature. Members of a University have the opportunity of voting on political principles in another capacity.

Smith's scientific candidate for Parliament was not named, but was almost certainly Sir Roderick Murchison, who had toyed with the idea of standing, but had insisted to Huxley that he was in favour of 'any improvement which our advanced state of Society demands, provided they do not carry us into Democracy'.[8]

Given the generally liberal stance of the University, hitherto, it was always likely that its graduates would favour some figure from the left of centre

---

[7] *BMJ*, 12 May 1860
[8] UL RC 1/7/d, 8 May 1860. Adrian Desmond, *Huxley* (London, 1994), p. 287.

– though to define with any precision what that location implied was, in 1860, no easy task. But among the younger men in the graduate elite was Walter Bagehot, who

> By the time he joined *The Economist* in 1859 . . . was convinced that if he was to wear a party label, he must call himself a Liberal. He was too convinced a Free Trader to acccept membership of the Conservative Party, too much a realist to be a Whig, too sceptical to be a Radical.[9]

Bagehot was the first choice of a committee chaired by Timothy Smith Osler, now a Fellow, and Richard Holt Hutton, who would become a Convocation-nominated Senator in 1866: both had been prominent members of the Graduates' Committee. Hutton was Bagehot's colleague on the *Spectator* and on the *Economist*: Osler was a distant cousin of Bagehot and was related to Hutton by marriage. Bagehot was doubtful of his chances, and at a meeting on 31 March 1860 he proposed Sir John Romilly, but was himself adopted by those present. What transpired in the next days or very few weeks is not recorded, but the committee must have been subjected to increasing pressure in favour of Romilly, and perhaps was disturbed by Bagehot's own doubts. At a subsequent meeting, at Freemasons' Tavern, the date of which is unknown, another vote was taken in which Romilly was the winner by four votes, an outcome foreseen by Bagehot, who had told his sister that 'The tide is setting in favour of Romilly as I always said it would.'[10]

Romilly, who had played a significant role in the early years of UCL and of the University, had served in the House of Commons for two terms, had been Solicitor and Attorney General in Lord John Russell's Administration, and had been Master of the Rolls since 1851. The *Times* declared, in 1861, that

> . . . the metropolitan University justly prided itself on the near probability of possessing a representative of so illustrious a descent and so illustrious in his own person.[11]

Not surprisingly, Romilly was defensive of his situation, and it was rumoured that he made his acceptance of nomination, in April–May, 1860, dependent on being assured that he had a majority of the promises made by intending voters. After some delay, he did accept, on the basis of an invitation signed by 231 graduates, but whether this was a figure clearly larger than what was being promised to Foster is uncertain.

---

[9] Alastair Buchan, *The Spare Chancellor* (London, 1959), pp. 146–7.
[10] Mrs Russell Barrington, *Life of Walter Bagehot* (London, 1914), pp. 112, 291; Norman St John Stevas (ed.), *The Collected Works of Walter Bagehot* (London, 1986), vol. 13, p. 561.
[11] *Times*, 28 May 1861.

The invitation to Romilly was the result of the prospect of a contest between Foster and Locock. Those who might be thought of as the orthodox Liberals, or even the Liberal Establishment, did not take the possibility of a Locock victory seriously. But they did not want Foster. As Romilly's committee explained, in a letter probably composed by J.R. Quain:

> Many of us object to [Foster's] connexion with extreme parties in public life; others think that the first Member for the University should be one whose name is illustrated by achieved distinction; and almost all of us consider that his avowed position as the salaried agent of a political Society, employed as such to conduct private negotiations among Members of Parliament, is wholly incompatible with the high and independent station in the House of Commons which we desire that the Member for our University should maintain . . .[12]

The Romilly Committee's main concern, therefore, was to lure medical voters away from Locock:

> . . . the candidateship of Sir C. Locock calls for one short remark: namely, that, if persevered in, it will ensure the election of Dr Foster . . . Sir C. Locock['s] . . . position as the nominee of a Conservative Committee, who brought him forward as a Candidate pledged to a general support of the Conservative party in the House, is fatal to any hope of representing the University which he may entertain. His friends must not suppose that by weakening the Committee in whose name we speak, they will prepare the way for a transference to him, in any event whatever, of any adequate portion of the support now given, or likely to be given, to Sir John Romilly. Whatever objections may be entertained to the political attitude of Dr Foster, or to his position with reference to the Liberation Society . . . a contest between him and Sir C. Locock would at once raise the broad issue between Liberal and Conservative, and the result could not be doubtful in the University of London.[13]

Evidence of the confusion of thinking about the role of the Member for the University, and the consciousness of general political divisions of opinion, is readily available. Those who sponsored Locock very likely included those who had been outraged by what they had seen as the apparent lack of concern for medicine within the Senate and Convocation. They declared that medical graduates who supported Romilly would 'prove themselves forgetful of their own position and of the best interests of the whole Medical Profession'. They simply wanted a medical man. At the same time, the Romilly people were desperate to emphasise the gap between the safe constitutional attitudes of their candidate and the dangerous radicalism of the Foster camp:

[12] UL RC 1/7/n. Copy of letter to Romilly from his Committee, enclosed with a letter to supporters, 24 May 1860.
[13] UL RC 1/7/l. Letter to Romilly's supporters, 17 May 1860.

As to Sir John Romilly being 'a very advanced liberal', if it is intended to imply that he holds democratic opinion, the assertion is simply unfounded and untrue. He has always belonged to the class of politicians who revere and value the historical institutions of the country, and no Graduate need fear that support given to him will be given to the advocate of democracy, whether of the American or of the Gallican type. We are satisfied that in his own opinion . . . a vote for the Ballot implies no adhesion to extreme views, and this conviction unites many in his support who strongly disapprove of the Ballot.[14]

The only contemporary press comment on the course of the aborted selection was given in the *British Medical Journal*: by the middle of May it reported that

Every moment is adding to the interest of the coming contest for the proposed seat for the University . . . The constituency . . . is about 900, and it is believed that each candidate has secured the promise of 250 votes or thereabouts. As . . . Romilly made it a condition of his contesting the seat, that a majority of promises should be insured to him, we trust that the evenly divided state of the canvass will lead to his withdrawal from the candidature, in which case Sir Charles Locock would probably be returned.[15]

A week later, the journal assumed that Romilly had declined to stand because of insufficient support, and announced, with some jubilation, that

This . . . will set free the pledges of a number of medical graduates . . . who will now, it is trusted, give their united support to the candidate of their own profession.[16]

But the assumption was invalid: all three candidates were still *in situ* when the Bill was withdrawn. The few surviving lists of supporters which were published from time to time are insufficiently full to indicate how the graduates stood in the early summer of 1860.

It would seem that only the Romilly camp was seriously exercised by the prospect of a University seat resulting from the relevant, brief parliamentary manoeuvring of May and June, 1861. There is no sign of a renewal of interest by Foster or Locock, but it was reported that Romilly's supporters were 'organizing again'; they received the warm support of both the *Times* and the *Lancet*.[17] Five months later, long after the prospect of a seat had receded, Percy Greg, a member of Locock's committee in 1860, told Bagehot's sister that the University's Conservatives would join the Liberals to return her brother, but not Romilly. Whether this was written as retrospective comment,

---

[14] UL RC 1/7/n.
[15] *BMJ*, 19 May 1860.
[16] *BMJ*, 26 May 1860.
[17] *Times*, 28 May 1861; *Lancet*, 1 June 1861.

or was intended to influence thinking about a possible future alliance, must remain matter for mere speculation.[18] As it happened, Romilly was lost to the University as a prospective representative in the Commons when he was ennobled in 1865. Locock stood, unsuccessfully, as a Conservative candidate in the Isle of Wight, in 1865, but did not appear subsequently on the University's political scene.

The experience of 1860 and 1861 in the electoral context underlines the enormous significance of UCL in the politics of Convocation. Three of the four candidates belonged to the College. Foster held the Chair of Jurisprudence, and he and Bagehot had been students. Romilly had long membership of the College's governing councils. After Bagehot dropped out, the leaders of the three committees sponsoring the other candidates were all UCL graduates – Frederick John Wood for Foster, Timothy Smith Osler for Romilly, and Robert Nicholas Fowler for Locock. Indeed, the only four names we have of Locock's team were all of former UCL students. Five of the nine members of Romilly's Committee were College men. The initial group who backed Foster consisted of sixteen UCL graduates, one from King's, and nine from several Nonconformist Colleges, all but one in the London area. There are two lists of Romilly's supporters which contain 183 names: of those, ninety-two were UCL graduates.[19] There can be little doubt that Gower Street was the focal point for the ambition and the manipulation of those who wished to represent the University of London in Parliament.

---

[18] St John Stevas, *Bagehot*, vol. 13, p. 561.
[19] UL RC 1/7/d, l, n.

# 14

## *Choosing Robert Lowe*

After the hope that a seat in the House of Commons would be given to the University of London was disappointed, in 1859–61, it was to be five years before the mood in Parliament shifted decisively, again, towards further reform of the representation of the people. After Palmerston's death in October, 1865, Russell's short-lived Government tried to introduce legislation, but its members were divided, and took the opportunity of defeat by the Opposition on an amendment to resign. Lord Derby formed an Administration, with Disraeli leading in the Commons, in June, 1866, and fourteen months later the Royal Assent was given to the Second Reform Bill. The Liberal proposals on redistribution, in 1866, and the Conservative Bill of 1867, both provided a seat for the University of London, but the settling of its details was not without drama.

The University was not backward in demanding attention to its claim. A special meeting of Convocation was requested of the Chairman in February, and held on 21 March 1866, when a petition was called for, to be presented to Parliament, asking for two seats, which would have given London the same representation as Oxford, Cambridge and Dublin. Senate met a week later, and set up a committee to prepare a memorial in consultation with the Annual Committee of Convocation. This was done at high speed; a memorial was sent to the Prime Minister, and petitions were despatched to both Houses of Parliament, in the first week of April. They rehearsed at length the history of the University and of the earlier agreements in principle by Governments to grant representation. And they packed the paragraphs with statistics of matriculation, of graduation, and rate of growth, in support of its comparability with the older universities and its entitlement to two seats. The Petitions to Parliament were presented by Granville in the Lords and by Lord Stanley in the House of Commons.

But when Gladstone introduced the proposals for redistribution, on 7 May 1866, they provided only one seat for the University. As would have been expected, there was an immediate demand in Convocation for pressure to be brought by a deputation to Russell and Gladstone for the addition of a second seat; but in the Annual Committee, on 11 May, Storrar suggested that the joint comitee of Senate and Convocation ought also to settle some other important issues. These were whether the franchise should be conferred on all graduates who were entitled to be members of Convocation, or only on

155

actual, paid-up Members of Convocation; and whether there should be proxy voting for the far-flung constituency.

In the ensuing debate, the Annual Committee decided to recommend that the franchise should extend to all paid-up Members of Convocation, to all Senators who were not graduates of London, and to the Registrar. The Register of Members of Convocation should be made up annually, and, because of the nature of the constituency, some lengthening of the period between the issue and return of the writ might be desirable. Proxy voting was recommended. However, the Committee thought it 'inexpedient' to press for more than one Member and, for the moment, was cool towards sending any deputation to the Prime Minister. In all this, James Anstie, Matthew Baines, and Julian Goldsmid (who had been MP for Honiton since the previous year) were prominent in debate.

Ebenezer Charles, Goldsmid, Maudsley, Robson and Storrar met with the Senate Committee on 14 May. All the amendments proposed by the Annual Committee were accepted, except the inclusion of the Registrar in the franchise. The Senators urged Convocation to reduce the Convocation fee, 'in order to induce all Graduates . . . to qualify', and on 8 June Sibson and Robson carried in Annual Committee a reduction of the annual fee from ten shillings and sixpence, to five shillings, and of the Composition Fee from three guineas to one pound.

Ten days later the Liberal Government resigned, and it was nine months later, in March, 1867, before the Conservatives, after much intra-party wrangling, produced what proved to be a nearly-final draft Bill. An Appendix contained the definitive provision that

> Every person whose name is for the time being on the Register of Graduates constituting the Convocation of the University of London shall, if of full age and not subject to any legal incapacity, be entitled to vote . . .

But it also included much of what had been seen by the University as needing amendment in the previous year's Bill, and a new idea – the enfranchisement of those men who had passed a 'Senior Middle Class Examination' of any University of the United Kingdom.

Senate and Convocation continued to co-operate fully. The Annual Committee seized on the lack of inclusion of the London Matriculation in the 'Senior Middle Class examinations'. Maudsley carried a resolution that Undergraduates of London should have the vote. Convocation backed the notion, and the Senate set up a Committee to watch the progress of the Bill, on 27 March. This became a non-issue when the Government subsequently dropped the whole idea of an extra educational qualification. But before it did so, the prospect of a seat exclusively for London was seriously endangered by another development.

On 13 June 1867, in Committee, Disraeli proposed that the seat originally intended for London should also provide for the representation of the

University of Durham. It was claimed that Disraeli himself did not like the idea, but was prevailed upon by the Judge Advocate General, John Robert Mowbray, one of the MPs for Durham, backed by a number of Northern Members, including H.G. Liddell, the Member for Northumberland South.[1] To join the small, Anglican University of Durham to the far larger, non-sectarian University of London was quickly seen by the London men as an unnatural act, and, in the Commons, Goldsmid immediately objected. In an interval in the Committee debate, the Annual Committee was called together urgently and approved a strong, condemnatory motion. The matter was settled in the continuation of the debate at Westminster on 17 and 18 June, when a great deal of heat was generated. There were four closely fought divisions. Four Fellows – Cardwell, Goldsmid, Grant Duff and Lowe – argued London's case.

On 17 June there were two procedural votes which went against London, by 183 to 169, and by 196 to 114; but a final resolution was postponed to the next day by the persistent arguments of Lowe and Grant Duff. Before debate was resumed, a petition by the Vice-Chancellor and the Chairman of Convocation, stressing the incongruity of the proposal, was laid before the House:

> . . . the University of London receives into its body, on a footing of perfect equality, all persons, whether educated in general or in denominational colleges or schools, or elsewhere . . . to modify its political expression by compelling it to share the franchise with a University which represents the predominance of one Church, would interfere with the principles of religious equality on which the University of London is established.

A more colourful indication of how strong a reaction the proposal excited was given, retrospectively, in the *Lancet*, which declared that

> To bind [the University of London] in the same electoral union with the little, languishing, and *bornée* University of Durham would be almost as absurd and disastrous as to yoke the ox with the ass.[2]

Whether or not the University's petition carried much extra weight, the two final divisions, on 18 June, were excitingly close. The first, on the motion to alter the word 'University' to 'Universities', was carried by 226 against 225. But the second, on the motion 'to insert after "London" the words "and Durham"', was defeated by 234 to 226. The Government accepted defeat. Comparison of the two later division lists shows that the voting was over-whelmingly partisan: regional loyalties only overrode party lines in a few cases.

---

[1] 3s Parl. Deb., vol. 188, col. 29.
[2] *Lancet*, 22 June 1867.

Of 244 MPs who voted for the linking of Durham and London, 193 were Conservatives, twenty-eight were Liberal-Conservatives, and twenty-three were Liberals, Whigs or Radicals. But of those twenty-three, only thirteen represented constituencies in or near the North-East. Of the 246 who supported London, 230 were Liberals, Whigs or Radicals, ten were Liberal Conservatives, and six were Conservatives. There were no changes of loyalties between the two divisions. The issue was settled either by some last-minute whipping on the London side, or, more likely, simply by the luck of how many Members were present after the first division. Eighteen of those who favoured the link between the two Universities on the first count, and twelve of those supporting a London seat, were absent for the second vote; and among the thirty-nine who turned up for the second vote only, London prevailed by twenty-one to eighteen.[3]

The House refused to accept an amendment moved by Goldsmid to enfranchise those members of Senate who were not London graduates [4], but did extend to London the proxy system of 'voting papers' granted to Oxford, Cambridge and Dublin in 1861. When the Bill became law on 15 August 1867, London University was guaranteed a seat in the House of Commons, some sixteen years after Charles James Foster had published his book calling for such representation.[5] The electorate was restricted to paid-up members of Convocation: but graduates had to pay much less than before for the privilege of joining and thereby having a vote. The first General Election which would afford them the opportunity to send an MP to Westminster would be called in fifteen months' time. But the campaigns to choose candidates were already well advanced.

It would have been remarkable if the University of London had been represented, at least before 1886, by anyone without notable sympathy for moderate, reformist, liberal causes. The great majority of members of Convocation were the products of an institution created and supported to offer opportunities to those who could not hope to graduate at the ancient Universities on account of religious barriers, and in the late 1860s the Whig/Liberal Party was still the champion of that cause. But there was 'a growing Conservative element; in fact, a distinct and active Conservative Party, which was not without influence in the final selection', in 1868.[6] Moreover, the orthodox Liberals had shown in 1860 that they were unhappy with a Radical candidate like Foster, and had stressed that Romilly, their

---

[3] 3s Parl. Deb., vol. 188, cols 44–8.
[4] 3s Parl. Deb., vol. 188, col. 1460.
[5] Representation of the People Act, 30 & 31 Vic c. 102. Foster, *The University of London. A Parliamentary Constituency* (London, 1851).
[6] A. Patchett Martin, *Life and Letters of Rt. Hon. Robert Lowe, Viscount Sherbrooke* (London, 1893), vol. ii, p. 350.

favoured choice at that time, had 'no adhesion to extreme views', and would not support any advocacy of democracy. Leaders of the two orthodox Parties in Convocation, as in the country generally, had to find moderates: but, in that context, the Liberals had a far wider choice.

While the sponsors of Convocation candidates urged the importance and relevance of personal, intellectual qualities, none seemed to feel that the University's MP would, or should, need to spend much of his time in direct support of the University. Most of the sponsors, and in all probability the mass of the graduates, thought a University MP should be independently-minded, though not necessarily non-partisan, and certainly as active as any partisan Member in parliamentary business. But one of the most interesting aspects of the search for a potential representative in 1867–68 was the further development of the non-partisan approach, which had been advocated in 1860.

On 13 May 1867, there appeared a pamphlet signed by forty-three graduates. Seemingly they were called together by Graily Hewitt, Professor of Midwifery at UCL, and John Horne Payne, and argued the case for choosing

> . . . a Graduate who has distinguished himself in the University, and has subsequently done honour to the body to which he belongs . . . a Representative of extreme views of whatever kind . . . would be most unsatisfactory to the general body of Graduates, and detrimental to the welfare of the University.

But the text then went on to deplore the lack of MPs with 'adequate and special scientific knowledge' and supported the idea of having

> . . . a Medical Graduate of distinguished ability and position, and of high scientific qualifications [who was] willing to make the professional sacrifices which the position of Representative in Parliament of the University of London might entail.[7]

The forty three signatories were almost exactly divided between the medical and the other faculties. The twenty-two doctors included no less than five Fellows, as well as several men already prominent in Convocation. There was only one BSc, but the score of Arts and Laws graduates included some who were firm Conservatives. Indeed, the whole operation had a strong hint of Conservatism about it, and raises the suspicion that the Conservative Party, conscious of their weakness in the University community, were attracted to the notion of a non-partisan candidate as the best hope they had of some sympathetic representation of their views. The group here described soon adopted the title 'Liberal-Conservatives', and the candidature for the 1868 election was settled by a long process of elimination, involving them and the

---

[7] UL RC 1/7/r.

orthodox Liberals. There was no sign of an orthodox Conservative challenger, but it was a Conservative graduate who initiated the final choice.

The Liberal Committee – Ebenezer Charles, a barrister who had just become a Convocation-nominated Fellow; William Farrer, Secretary and Librarian of New College, London; Timothy Smith Osler, a Convocation-nominated Fellow since 1859; and Jacob Waley, until the previous year Professor of Political Economy at UCL – met on 15 May 1867, when they decided to ask for the names of candidates to be submitted by 24 June. But a potential struggle of a rather delicate nature between two powerful Liberal candidates had begun earlier, and was interestingly linked with the concern to find a representative with high scientific credentials.

It is not clear when Hutton set up a committee to push the claims of Walter Bagehot; but before the end of May he was aware of the possibility of facing strong competition. Sir John Lubbock, Liberal MP for West Kent and a Crown-chosen Fellow of the University since 1865, was a well-respected banker and scientist. On 10 May he had been approached by Thomas Archer Hirst, then Professor of Mathematics at UCL, and William Odling, soon to be Professor of Chemistry at the Royal Institution, who wanted to suggest his name to a Liberal Party meeting at the Freemasons' Tavern on 14 May.[8] Though Lubbock does not appear to have agreed, the approach to him must have become known, and Hutton tried hard to dissuade him from standing:

> . . . though there will be a very warm feeling for you personally, everywhere, and possibly among the scientific and medical graduates a *preference* for you over my friend Mr Bagehot, the popular University feeling will be strongly in favour of one of our own men.

Lubbock's position on the Senate would help, but Hutton still feared

> . . . that on the whole the Oxford and Cambridge men on the Senate are looked upon by the mass of the graduates as external to the University.[9]

Hutton had overstated his case, as Lubbock had attended no university. And Hutton had understated Lubbock's connection with London, which rested not only on current membership of the Senate, but on the fact that Lubbock's father had been the founding Vice-Chancellor. Lubbock, however, was very well able to keep his options open: he replied that

[8] BL Add Mss 49642, Hirst to Lubbock, 10 May 1867. For another account of this episode, *see* St John-Stevas, *Works of Bagehot*, vol. 13, p. 616, fn 1.
[9] BL Add Mss 49642, Hutton to Lubbock, 24 May 1867.

. . . it would be uncandid for me to deny that I feel greatly honoured at being thought of.

It is . . . natural perhaps that there should be a feeling in favour of electing a graduate, just as a County always prefers one of its own landowners. I looked through the list of graduates the other day and saw no one whom so far as I know I should prefer to Bagehot, and I say this not only from friendship but because there are few men with whose opinions I more thoroughly agree, or for whose judgement I have a greater respect. Our family having become intimately connected with the University from its very commencement, I naturally feel much interest in the election, and if the choice of the Committee falls on Mr Bagehot he will have no warmer supporter than [myself].[10]

Having thus rather smoothly put Hutton in his place, Lubbock did not make any decision until the middle of June, but after talking with Odling and George Carey Foster, Professor of Physics at UCL,[11] he let his name be added to the list of Liberal candidates. The others were Walter Bagehot; John Richard Quain, QC; Frederick John Wood; and George Charles Brodrick, second son of the 7th Viscount Middleton, who had graduated at Oxford and then taken an LLB at London.

Formal letters addressed to the graduates, enclosing lists of declared supporters, were sent out by Bagehot, Lubbock, Quain and Wood in late June and early July.[12] Quain described himself as 'a decided supporter of Liberal politics' who did 'not hold what are commonly called extreme views'. Wood played rather heavily on his past services in getting Convocation started, but stressed that he was against universal suffrage, and had never been a 'hot politician or a violent party man'. Both wrote politely, but hardly compellingly, of their support for Liberal policies. By contrast, Bagehot, editor of the *Economist*, a long-practised political journalist, with *The English Constitution* just published, wrote with unreserved partisan enthusiasm, making it clear that the first duty was 'to restore Mr Gladstone to power', and declaring, unwisely, that 'Mr Disraeli . . . believes that by influence and corruption the mass of the new voters may be made to aid him.'

Lubbock's challenge was spelled out in an open letter to him by Carey Foster and Odling: his other listed supporters were mostly drawn from the front rank of scientists and medical men, and included Airy, Darwin, Lyell, Max Muller, Paget, Hooker, Huxley, Tyndall, Herbert Spencer, Wallace and Wheatstone. The letter declared that the University of London

. . . has already rendered the greatest services to scientific education in general and especially to the Profession of Medicine. How better can it maintain its well-earned

---

[10] BL Add Mss 49642, Lubbock to Hutton, 28 May 1867.
[11] BL Add Mss 49642, Odling to Lubbock, 13 June, Lubbock to Odling, 14 June 1867.
[12] UL RC 1/7/s–u, x, y.

reputation and still further influence the country for good than by returning as its first Member one so well qualified to advocate its principles?[13]

Brodrick, a journalist with the *Times* who had straightforward parliamentary ambitions, was sponsored by Grant Duff. He admitted, candidly, many years later, that at the time he was 'more or less in negotiation with a larger number of constituencies than I care to specify, with a view to coming forward as a decided, though moderate, Liberal', and felt that 'Most of the openings proposed to me . . . were very unpromising . . .'[14] He withdrew, early in July, 1867, seemingly very conscious that the seat was more suitable for 'one more closely identified than myself with the past history and struggles of the University', and because he saw no point in 'needlessly dividing the Party'.[15] He went on to stand for Parliament, three times, unsuccessfully, before retiring to academic life as Warden of Merton. But he was linked to London once more, through his very brief membership of the Royal Commission which enquired into the future of the University at the end of the 1880s.[16]

In the orthodox Liberal context, Bagehot seemed the man to beat. By early July, his letters to graduates listed seventy-nine supporters, among them three MPs – Goschen, Stansfeld, and Myles O'Reilly – and many men deeply involved in University and Convocation affairs. But only six medicos appended their names. And though Bagehot had made a favourable impression five years earlier, he had not moved into the top echelons of Convocation. Twice he had stood for election to the list from which the Home Secretary would choose to fill a vacant place on Senate. In March, 1862, the result was George Johnson ninety-seven, Bagehot forty-six, Fowler twenty-six: but in January, 1864, he was soundly beaten by Fowler, an active and popular graduate and Member of Council of UCL, 'notwithstanding his Tory principles',[17] by 256 to sixty-one. On this occasion, too, Fowler – now well established as a Fellow of the University – was to be his nemesis.

Fowler had signed the call for a non-partisan candidate issued by the Liberal-Conservative group in May, but on 24 June, the deadline for submission of names of prospective Liberal candidates, he recorded in his diary his attendance at 'a large meeting at [Graily] Hewitt's . . . where a good deal of contrariety of opinion seemed to prevail'. The same night he wrote to Robert Lowe, whom he knew only through their mutual membership of Senate, asking 'whether, under any circumstances, you would consent to be placed in

---

[13] Horace G. Hutchinson, *Life of Sir John Lubbock, Lord Avebury* (London, 1914), vol. 1, pp. 94–5: UL RC 1/7/z.

[14] G.C. Brodrick, *Memories and Impressions, 1831–1900* (London, 1900), ch. 8.

[15] *Times*, 5 July 1867.

[16] Brodrick, *Memories*, pp. 171–4.

[17] Flynn, *Fowler*, p. 162.

nomination'. Fowler was careful to make clear that he was writing 'merely in [his] own name', but admitted that he had to be 'guided by the opinions of those with whom I act'. At least some of those have been identified:

> As early as June, 1867, certain influential members of the University, among whom were Dr George Buchanan, Mr J.F.Rotton, and Sir Richard Quain, initiated a movement for the nomination and return of Robert Lowe . . .[18]

Whether or not Fowler was the acknowledged agent of a group, Lowe replied within three days. He could not imagine a 'higher honour to a public man than to represent . . . the University of London . . . [but it was] . . . probably nearly two years from the time when the election will take place . . . [and he was] . . . entirely ignorant of the views of the constituency'. He hoped, however, that Fowler would 'be content with this general expression of my feeling . . . and not expect from me any more definite answer'.[19]

Lowe was not to give any formal acceptance for several months, but the idea of his standing was immediately publicised by the issue of a circular, of which an unsigned version appeared in the *Times* on 3 July. Fowler and his associates had made a very shrewd move. Lowe was at the height of his fame as a parliamentary performer: he was an outstanding intellectual; as the Minister responsible for education, he had been a vigorous proponent of the highly controversial system of payment by results; and in 1866 had outraged the bulk of his Party by taking an elitist position, refusing to support Russell's Reform Bill, and retreating with a few others into the Cave of Adullam. While he was, in fact, at the moment somewhere in the political wilderness, his recent attitudes made him far more attractive to orthodox Conservative opinion than Walter Bagehot. And ominously for the orthodox Liberals of the University, many medical men were attracted to Lowe because of the support he had been giving to the improvement of public health.[20] By the middle of July the *Lancet* was reporting an increasing desire by medical graduates to support him.[21] Even Lubbock's appeal to the scientific community was threatened – Sir Roderick Murchison declined to join his Committee because he was 'unwilling to do anything in opposition to Lowe'.[22]

As the long vacation approached in the summer of 1867, and as the Reform Bill was going through its final stages, the Liberal Party, with the choice of Bagehot, Lubbock, John Richard Quain and Wood before them, 'decided

[18] Martin, *Robert Lowe*, vol. 2, p. 350.
[19] Flynn, *Fowler*, pp. 163–4.
[20] James Winter, *Robert Lowe* (Toronto, 1976), p. 157.
[21] *Lancet*, 13 July 1867.
[22] BL Add Mss 49642, Foster to Lubbock, 27 July 1867.

to cease all agitation until next spring'.[23] Many of the potential Liberal-
Conservative voters must have been pinning their hopes on Lowe, but he was
a heavyweight politician, and hardly fitted their original ideal of a non-partisan
London graduate. However, their search for such a candidate had been
disappointing. Their first favourite, William Withey Gull, was unwilling to
stand. There was talk of running William Allen Miller, Professor of Chemistry
at KCL, a Fellow of the University, Treasurer of the Royal Society, and a very
prominent member of Convocation, but it came to nothing.[24]

In August another non-partisan candidate appeared, in the person of one
of the most famous – and famously controversial – administrative reformers
of the age. Edwin Chadwick had been the driving force behind many of the
Poor Law and Public Health campaigns of the century. In the context of the
London University seat, he responded to the call of two men – Arthur Hill
Hassall, a London MD trained at the Royal College of Surgeons of Ireland,
working at the Royal Free Hospital, and William Tanner Imerson, a graduate
of UCL. Chadwick put out a sizeable pamphlet, listing his administrative
achievements at length, and stressing his special concern for Public Health,
Police, and National Education. He told graduates that

> It will be for the members of the University to judge whether these large organic
> questions are more worthy to be promoted by them, through their representative,
> than those usually brought before common constituencies. These questions
> involved advanced application of the sciences more or less specially cultivated by
> various sections of the members of the University.

John Stuart Mill was warmly supportive, stressing that Chadwick's administrative, educational and sanitary expertise were 'well entitled to recognition
from a scientific body like the University', which Mill regarded as

> . . . one of the few bodies which, being emancipated from all local influences, are
> peculiarly called on to guide their choice exclusively by the capability of a candidate
> to render important public service.[25]

But Chadwick seems to have made little or no impression on the London
University electorate. There is no evidence of any active committee sponsoring him, and no reports, other than the pamphlet, of any efforts which he
may have made. By mid-October, William Odling, in search of support for
Lubbock, was telling Lyon Playfair that 'Chadwick has not the remotest chance

---

[23] *Lancet*, 13 July 1867.
[24] *Lancet*, 13 July 1867.
[25] *Address to the Members of Convocation by Edwin Chadwick Esq CB and A Letter from John
Stuart Mill Esq MP* (London 1867).

with the University of London'.[26] Chadwick's biographer thought that he had not 'much hope of being returned', and that 'During the entire period he was feverishly seeking a seat elsewhere.'[27] He withdrew well before the poll.

If graduates were unenthusiastic about Chadwick, the country's leading scientists produced, in September, a boost for Lubbock. At the meeting of the British Association, a group with Tyndall in the Chair expressed strong support for Lubbock, seeing his election as 'an opportunity . . . of obtaining for science a representative in the House of Commons'. The *Lancet* disapproved of using the meeting of the British Association 'in this way', but listed several senior men among those associating themselves with Tyndall's view.[28]

Lubbock had taken on the physician, Philip Henry Pye-Smith, as his secretary. Odling approved, and passed on to Lubbock much advice on the intricacies of academic politics:

I think you will find Pye-Smith a very good secretary. He belongs to the evangelical dissent party, and though a very Liberal member of it would not I suppose like to go too far. He was at first disposed to support Wood, the nominee of that party. Seeing that we have a fair proportion of the sceptically inclined on our committee it is well to balance those with some of the other way of thinking and the name of Pye-Smith is much respected by dissenters in general. Moreover we wanted a representative of Guy's. I hope however that Michael Foster will continue to sit prominently with us . . . my only reason for not proposing him as Secretary was that I thought it preferable to get another name from another school and party, rather than a second irreverent Foster from University College.[29]

The competition was clarified and intensified between late January and mid-March, 1868, thus coinciding with the retirement, in February, of Lord Derby as Prime Minister, and his replacement by Disraeli. The first University move was Wood's withdrawal as a Liberal candidate in favour of Robert Lowe, because he approved of the latter's views on National Education and the Irish Church. On 4 February, Bagehot responded with a long letter, which readers 'would have recognised . . . [as an attack on] . . . Lowe's campaign for universal primary and utilitarian middle class education'; and as questioning the likelihood that Lowe would be willing to have the Irish Church revenues 'used to endow the Roman Catholic clergy'. And on the very same day, Henry Bompas, an outspoken supporter of Lubbock, accused Bagehot

[26] Playfair Mss 508, Odling to Playfair, 11 October 1867.
[27] S.E. Finer, *The Life and Times of Sir Edwin Chadwick* (London, 1952), p. 494.
[28] *Lancet*, 21 September 1867.
[29] BL Add Mss 49642, Odling to Lubbock, 21 October 1867.

of failing to work for the University, and denounced Lowe's educational ideas.[30] Lubbock had been uncomfortable about the proposed attack on Bagehot, partly because he felt it might backfire, but partly because of friendship with his opponent and his concern that 'the contest should be free from any trace of bitterness'.[31]

Despite these signs of potential intra-party conflict, on 10 February, Lowe, who had indicated that he needed the support of at least 250 voters to persuade him to stand – and had quickly received it – addressed a letter to Julian Goldsmid and 250 Graduates of the University of London, making a clear pitch for selection. While still arguing about the merits and demerits of any extension of the franchise, Lowe had been moving back into the Liberal fold. On the following day he received an invitation to stand from the three Honorary Secretaries of the University's Liberal Party – James Anstie, George Buchanan, and J.F. Rotton.[32]

Lowe was doubtless very relieved: his own seat at Calne had been abolished by the Reform Act, and no orthodox Liberal constituency was sympathetic to a man who had deserted Russell in 1866. It was Lowe's appeal as a major political figure, as an intellectual, as an educational and medical reformer, and as an elitist who shared the distrust of democracy felt by many of the graduates, which combined to attract Conservatives as well as the conservatively inclined Liberals. But even so, though now standing as a Liberal, he still faced competition from Bagehot, Lubbock and Quain.

The leaders of the Liberal-Conservatives who had invited Lowe to come forward cannot have felt too pleased by his willingness to transfer to the orthodox Liberals; but at least they had more sympathy for his views than for those of his immediate rivals for the seat. But the real sufferers from Lowe's adherence to the Liberals were those in the Liberal-Conservative group who had been so strongly averse to a partisan candidate. These were mainly scientists. Odling was scornful of them and told Lubbock that

> . . . the Liberal-Conservatives have at last resolved not to start a candidate of their own and that as they are not returning a man they like they will content themselves with preventing the return of the two men they most dislike namely Bagehot and Lowe. This tallies with some overtures that were made to George [Carey] Foster and with some remarks of Dr. Sibson – a great Liberal Conservative – made to me a day or two ago – to the effect that he preferred you and would vote for you rather than for either of the other two candidates if Dr Miller did not come forward. I think something ought to be done with this section of the graduates. They professed to want a man of science and of stationary views in politics. As they

[30] UL RC 1/7/cc: St John-Stevas, *Works of Bagehot*, vol. 13, pp. 623–4.
[31] BL Add Mss 49642, Lubbock to Pye-Smith, 10 February 1868.
[32] UL RC 1/7/ee, ff, gg, hh: *Lancet*, 22 February 1868.

cannot get a stationary politician they must put up with a man of science. On this ground we down them.[33]

By the middle of March, the Liberal-Conservatives had decided, at a meeting at the home of Dr Meadows, that they would 'not bring forward a Conservative [sic] candidate', but would advise Liberal-Conservatives to hold on. The *Lancet*, reporting this, thought it probable that Lowe would get their support.[34] The graduates were left, therefore, with four Liberal candidates – Bagehot, Lowe, Lubbock and J.R. Quain. The Liberal Party committee, headed by Osler, felt obliged to say, in the middle of May, that there was no sign of a Conservative candidate, and, until there was, it was not necessary to make any choice.[35]

The choice was not made by the Committee, however. Towards the end of June, Lubbock withdrew. He may have seen clearly that his chance of election for the University was far less likely than it would be for West Kent, where he was well known and supported. Indeed, at the outset of his campaign for London, his rivals had been quick to spread a report that

> . . . your connection with the Liberal Party in West Kent is such as to make you by no means specially desirous of being elected for the University.[36]

His biographer claimed that his 'old friends in West Kent . . . were very anxious that he should again fight their battle, and that this finally he felt to be his duty'.[37] He wished Bagehot and Lowe well and, like Brodrick at an earlier stage, dutifully declared that he did not wish to divide the University's Liberal Party.[38]

With Lubbock gone, and a straight fight most likely between himself and Lowe – for J.R. Quain was hardly a match for either – Bagehot saw the writing on the wall. He gave up a month later, explaining very succinctly his own view of Lowe's recently changed situation and renewed strength:

> It is a great honour to receive so much more support than any other graduate of the University, and to be pitted against a statesman selected on account of his eminence. And if Mr Lowe still stood where he stood last year, I should not fear the event. He was them, as now, able and eminent, but he was an able and eminent 'nondescript'. It was not settled whether he would co-operate with Mr Gladstone, whom he helped to turn out, or with Mr Disraeli, whom he helped to bring in.

[33] BL Add Mss 49642, Odling to Lubbock, 16 February 1868.
[34] *Lancet*, 14 March 1868.
[35] *Lancet*, 16 May 1868.
[36] BL Add Mss 49642, G.C. Foster to Lubbock, 20 July 1867.
[37] Hutchinson, *Lubbock*, vol. 1, p. 95.
[38] *Times*, 25 June 1868.

So long as his political place was thus dubious, the prospects of his candidature could not have deterred a well supported opponent. But now Mr Lowe has defined his course. He supports Mr Gladstone, he acts as a Liberal, it is said he will be in the next Liberal Cabinet. This has given him in our University a curious coalescence of force. Many Conservatives vote for him relying on the history of 1866, and many Liberals vote relying on the hopes of 1869, and it is hard to meet the two. The Tories think he is the most like a Tory who can possibly be chosen; the Liberals think him the only Liberal Cabinet Minister who is likely to be chosen, and the combination is irresistible.[39]

Julian Goldsmid, Chairman of Lowe's Committee, lost no time. On 3 August, in a letter to the *Times*, he thanked Bagehot for withdrawing, asked J.R. Quain to follow suit, and spurned any notion of non-partisanship – he wanted the unopposed return of 'one of the foremost advocates of that Liberal policy towards Ireland of which Mr Gladstone has been the great exponent'. And Goldsmid had his wish, for Quain dropped out later, leaving Lowe to be formally returned as the Member for the University of London on 17 November, when the Indenture of Election was signed by Grote, Storrar, Goldsmid, Hutton, Osler, Richard Quain and Sibson.[40] Lowe had been lucky to survive politically by finding a peculiar, new constituency which was prepared to take him on at a rather desperate stage of his career. He was also fortunate that the expenses of his – and his successors – elections were fully met by his graduate constituents.[41]

Members of Convocation never had a chance to cast a vote for the University seat in 1868. And within three weeks of Lowe's election he was chosen by Gladstone to be Chancellor of the Exchequer. As was the constitutional requirement, Lowe had then to submit himself again to his constituents, but, as on the first occasion, there were no other candidates. In Gladstone's Cabinet he joined four other members of the Senate – Cardwell, Goschen, Granville and Kimberley – all, as the *Lancet* declared, 'deeply interested' in the University's 'welfare and progress'.[42]

---

[39] St John-Stevas, *Works of Bagehot*, vol. 13, p. 630, Bagehot to Hutton, 30 July 1868.
[40] UL RO 1/16/1.
[41] UL RO 1/16/2: Martin, *Lowe*, pp. 354–5.
[42] *Lancet*, 12 December 1868.

# 15

# *Sir John Lubbock: Liberal into Liberal Unionist*

Although the Liberals were defeated at the General Election in February, 1874, Robert Lowe was not opposed, and continued to represent the University until 1880. He must have retained the support of so many of the graduates as to make the prospect of unseating him seem remote, in 1874, even though he had lost popularity in the country and had been moved from the Treasury to the Home Office following 'financial irregularities' at the Post Office, for which he had a shared ministerial responsibility. There are no University records of the 1874 election, and there was very little press comment. Gladstone's decision to dissolve Parliament, on 24 January, seems to have caught the Convocation politicians of all parties unprepared. Certainly it was true of the Liberals. Lowe put out an election address on 27 January 1874, and it was only on the following day that his Committee met to make preparations in case any opposition appeared. But it was reported on 2 February that he would not be opposed; he was duly proposed by Goldsmid and Richard Quain, and declared elected.[1]

The story was very different in 1880. By then the London University Conservative Club was better established, and doubtless more self-confident as a result of there having been a Conservative Government in power for six years. The Club met on 13 June 1879, and decided to set up a Conservative Election Committee of the University of London. Robert Norman Fowler, who had been MP for Penryn and Falmouth in the 1868–74 Parliament, and who was to be elected for the City of London in 1880, was Chairman, and the four other officers were W.M. Ord, Dean of St Thomas's Hospital Medical School; Albert Kaye Rollit, an Honorary Fellow of King's College, who would be knighted in 1885 and join the Senate in 1890; Henry Stevens, MD; and R.V. Tidman of New College. At that stage there were altogether fifty-five members of the Committee, of whom twenty-four were medical men.

The Conservative candidate was Arthur Charles, QC, Recorder of Bath, who agreed to stand on being supported by 250 potential voters. Charles was a UCL graduate and Member of the College Council, as well as being a current University Examiner in Common Law. He accepted nomination in a letter to Fowler, dated 22 December 1879, and published early in the New

---

[1] *Times*, 27, 29 January, 2, 3, 4 February 1874.

Year, in which he attacked Lowes's alleged virulence against the Disraeli Government.[2] By that time Dr W.H. Allchin, Dean of Westminster Hospital Medical School, had replaced Henry Stevens on his Committee.

But the decision to run a Conservative candidate was not welcomed by some traditional Conservative opinion. As must have been widely expected, Charles was defeated. The *Standard*, five weeks later, published a statement which reflects a belief that University representation should be governed, if not wholly on a non-partisan basis, certainly on an idea well removed from the normal canons of competitive politics:

> When Mr Charles came forward some weeks since to contest Mr Lowe's seat, we were unable to express any sympathy with his attempt, for the simple reason that it was contrary to a well established usage in Academic politics. If a University has once made a public declaration of its political confidence it is not in the habit of withdrawing its trust, unless there has been some decided change of front executed by the member of Parliament in whom that trust is reposed . . . Mr Lowe dwelt upon this circumstance, and showed conclusively the utility of its recognition.[3]

If this doctrine, clearly claimed as being based on the practice of the electors of Members for the Universities of Oxford, Cambridge and Dublin, was widely accepted, then London's Conservative graduates were simply demonstrating the radicalism which the very creation of their University represented.

Attitudes towards the election may have been affected to some extent by uncertainty as to Lowe's continuation as the University's representative. It was widely understood that he was likely to be raised to the peerage. But whatever the extent of knowledge of that possibility, it did not prevent participation in his contest with Charles from being impressively high – a fraction below 80 per cent of all the qualified voters. Voting began on 31 March and closed on 5 April. When the result was announced on 6 April, the *Standard* remarked that

> Mr Charles had against him all the traditions of the University in favour of Liberalism. It was not to be expected that he would fight a successful battle against a competitor recommended by so many qualifications.

But Charles was by no means disgraced: he collected 535 votes against 1014. The list of those who voted is given in full,[4] and some analysis of it offers significant pointers to the contemporary and future character of political

---

[2] *Times*, 2 January 1880.
[3] *Standard*, 17 May 1880.
[4] University of London, *List of Voters March 1880*.

leanings within Convocation. But it is worth quoting, first, the admirably succinct description of the poll given in the *Times* on 6 April 1880:

> There are over 1900 voters on the Register of Convocation, but allowing for members abroad or deceased, the voting power probably does not exceed 1750, and it will be noticed that 1549, or 88.5 per cent recorded their vote. Of the whole number recorded, 899 or 58 per cent were given by proxy and 650, or 41.9% by voters in person. The proportion in which the proxy and personal votes were distributed between the two candidates differed considerably. Approximately the proxy voters for Mr Lowe were to those personally given to him as sixty one to forty, while in the case of Mr Charles the proportion was as twenty eight to twenty four. The exact numbers were for Mr Lowe 612 proxy and 402 personal votes, and for Mr Charles 287 proxy and 248 personal . . .
>
> the University Calendar . . . shows that of the graduates in Arts nearly five hundred have come from one or other of the various Dissenting Colleges throughout the country (excluding University College London which, though attended by many Dissenters, is non-sectarian) and that there are upwards of two hundred dissenting Ministers on the present list of voters.

While the importance of the dissenting vote was considerable, it was hardly surprising. In terms of the future, what was more significant was the extent of medical support for the Conservatives – only 16 per cent of Lowe's votes came from medical graduates, as opposed to 42 per cent of Charles's total. And had the sitting candidate been any but Lowe, the medical Liberal vote may well have been even smaller. Richard Quain, a highly respected medical member of Convocation, had been pressed to stand as a Conservative, but 'personal considerations of allegiance to Mr Lowe . . . prevented him from accepting'.[5]

Law graduates formed 12 per cent of Lowe's support and 10 per cent of Charles's, but that is highly unlikely to be the truth about the attitude of the legal profession, because most of Convocation's lawyers did not take the London LLB and are thus hidden in the much larger figures for Arts graduates. Three quarters of the Arts graduates voted for Lowe, but it is probable that many of the 229 who supported Charles were lawyers.

The inference is that the medical and legal professions were turning against the Liberals, and this was to be marked even more strongly six years later. A smaller margin between the parties, in terms of personal and proxy voting, might also be seen as a pointer to a tendency by the professions in London to move away from the Liberals. If it is assumed that the personal turn-out included, overwhelmingly, the core of Convocation membership in the London area, which had a high proportion of doctors and lawyers, then

[5] *BMJ*, 24 January 1880.

Charles's share was 38 per cent; but in the proxy vote, presumably mainly from outside the London area, it was only 32 per cent.

The Liberals had been sufficiently relaxed about the challenge to Lowe not to call a meeting of his Committee until mid-January, and it was not until a month later that Lowe offered himself for re-election in a letter to Goldsmid which contained strong denunciation of the Conservatives and all their works.[6] There was no question of any challenge to his candidacy within the Liberal group, and he had a relatively easy victory over Charles. But within three weeks of the poll his forthcoming ennoblement was announced, and the suspicion that it was about to happen was enough to initiate considerable speculation and manoeuvre as to who should succeed him. In what followed, the most prominent person was the Vice-Chancellor, Sir John Lubbock.

Lubbock had held the seat for Maidstone since before he became Vice-Chancellor in 1872, but in 1880 he lost it, the result being made known on 31 March. It was as Vice-Chancellor and Returning Officer, but not as an MP, therefore, that he announced the result of the University's poll on 6 April. But by then, Lowe's move to the Lords was so much taken for granted that, three days before, Julian Goldsmid had told Lord Reay of his keenness to stand for the seat, and asked Reay to find out whether Lubbock was intending to run.[7] After the declaration of the poll, Lubbock wrote in his diary that E.H. Busk had come to him 'and said that if as was probable Lowe was made a Peer then there was a strong wish I should come in for the University'.[8]

Lubbock had been invited to stand in four county constituencies within a day of losing Maidstone, but they cannot have appealed as much as the prospect of representing the University.[9] He held back, therefore, until after the formal announcement that Robert Lowe was to become Viscount Sherbrooke was made, on 24 April. On that day the *Standard* 'expected that Sir John Lubbock will be invited to stand for the University'. But it was not until 27 and 29 April that Lubbock gave his newly appointed Secretary, Busk, the go-ahead to send out a circular, and acknowledged that he would have Goldsmid, Jessel and Gull as rivals. On 29 April he also offered his resignation as Vice-Chancellor to Granville.[10]

Preparations for a new election went on quickly. On May 1, the Conservatives asked that

---

6 *Times*, 17 January, 13 March 1880.
7 BL Add Mss 49645, Reay to Lubbock, 3 April 1880.
8 BL Add Mss 62680, Lubbock's Diary, 6 March 1880.
9 BL Add Mss 62682, Lubbock's Diary, 1 April 1880.
10 BL Add Mss 49645, Lubbock to Granville, 29 April 1880; 62680, 62682, Lubbock's Diary, 27 & 29 April 1880.

... graduates should not commit themselves by promising to support any of the present candidates until the names of all candidates were definitely brought before the constituency.[11]

If this was issued in the hope that a Conservative candidate would come forward, it was issued in vain: no such candidate appeared. All the action was to be Liberal-centred.

The Liberal Committee called a meeting for 3 May, which produced five candidates. Alfred Carpenter, who held high office in the British Medical Association, had himself been reported as a candidate, but joined Richard Quain in proposing Gull.[12] Serjeant Simon proposed Goldsmid; Jessel, Master of the Rolls, was put forward by Osler; Carey Foster and J.G. Fitch proposed Lubbock; and the fifth candidate was a barrister, Samuel Danks Waddy, QC, who had been MP for Barnstaple and then for Sheffield from 1874 to 1880, and was nominated by Sidney Pocock. The Committee then decided that each member of Convocation who had voted for Lowe on 6 April should be ballotted, and asked to list the candidates in his order of preference. Before this could be done, Waddy withdrew, so that only four names appeared on the cards which were despatched on 10 May.

As will be seen, Lubbock won this contest overwhelmingly. Neither Goldsmid nor Gull proved to be strong candidates: Jessel was Lubbock's main opponent, but some mystery surrounds his position. Jessel had been Gladstone's Solicitor General; he had been deeply involved in the formulation of the Judicature Act of 1873, which brought about a major reorganisation of the courts, and provided a specific ban on judges sitting in the House of Commons. Jessel had been appointed Master of the Rolls in 1873, and had immediately resigned his seat, though, because the Judicature Act did not take effect until two years later, he was not legally required to do so. It is inconceivable that he was not aware, seven years later, that, as Master of the Rolls, he could not sit in the House of Commons. But not only did he allow his name to go forward as a potential Liberal candidate for the Liberals of the University of London, but neither he nor his sponsors appear to have made any reference to the constitutional significance of his position as a judge.

Jessel's Committee was first in the field with a printed address, and in a personal letter to Lubbock, dated 1 May, Jessel gave no hint of being aware of any problem with his candidacy.[13] Lubbock, however, had his doubts, for he entered in his diary, a couple of days later, 'Jessel is a very formidable opponent, but the general opinion of the lawyers seems to be that he cannot stand'. That opinion had already been expressed in anonymous letters to the *Standard*; and at the Liberal Committee on 3 May, Fitch, who was proposing

---

[11] *Standard*, 1 May 1880.
[12] *BMJ*, 1 May 1880.
[13] BL Add Mss 49645, Jessel to Lubbock, 1 May 1880.

Sir George Jessel. Solicitor General 1871–1873. Master of the Rolls 1873–1883. Convocation-nominated Member of Senate 1861–1883. Vice-Chancellor 1880–1883.

Lubbock, argued that it would be contrary to the intention of the 1873 legislation if Jessel's candidacy of the Master of the Rolls was approved.[14] But the candidacy was accepted, and even after the poll was held and Jessel was

[14] BL Add Mss 62682, Lubbock's Diary, 3 May 1880. *Standard*, 30 April, 4 May 1880.

decisively defeated by Lubbock, he was still reported as being prepared to stand if he was wanted.[15]

It is possible, but unlikely, that Jessel, who was only fifty-six years of age and was at the height of his powers as an eminent judge, was prepared to resign the Mastership of the Rolls in order to represent the University in Parliament. If he was so prepared, then his electoral appeal would surely have been stronger if he had made an announcement to that effect. If he was not so prepared, is it believable that he was convinced that some legal way could be found to circumvent the requirement of the Judicature Act? Or was he merely being mischievous? If we assume that he knew perfectly well that only resignation would permit him to sit in the Commons; and if we assume that, in the last resort, he was unwilling to relinquish the Mastership of the Rolls; then perhaps the only reasonable explanation of his insistence on standing in the private poll of the University Liberals was that he wished to impress on the party, by making a grand, personal gesture, the desirability of nominating a London graduate.

The question of whether the University's MP should be a London graduate was one of the two issues which provoked controversy. Goldsmid, in pressing his own candidacy, felt that 'the University would like to have him as a representative of their own graduates'.[16] Jessel told Lubbock that

> Although nothing would give me greater pleasure than to see you in Parliament again, candour compels me to add that I think the time has arrived when the University of London should be represented by one of its own Graduates.[17]

When the Liberal Committee met on 3 May, two lawyers moved that candidates should be London graduates, and only withdrew the motion after strong objection led by Anstie and Herschell.[18] The Conservatives, on announcing that they would not run a candidate, expressed their strong support for the nomination of a London graduate.[19] Even after Lubbock's convincing victory, the strength of sentiment within Convocation towards following precedents set elsewhere was reflected, if a little sourly, by the *Standard*:

> London University may fairly content itself with the distinguished financier and the tolerably independent politician in whom she is apparently willing to place her confidence. But the time will certainly come when – if Academic Constituencies continue to exist – London University will no more think of sending

---

[15] *Standard*, 15 May 1880.
[16] BL Add Mss 49645, Reay to Lubbock, 3 April 1880.
[17] BL Add Mss 49645, Jessel to Lubbock, 1 May 1880.
[18] *Standard*, 4 May 1880.
[19] UL RC1/7/ss.

to Parliament one who is not her *alumnus* than would Oxford, Cambridge, or Dublin.[20]

But, as we have seen, Lubbock, who had not attended any university, had a special position. His father had been the first Vice-Chancellor of London, and had stayed on the Senate until 1865, when his son succeeded him. And the younger Lubbock had been Vice-Chancellor since 1872, and was still in office; for his offer of resignation to Granville on 29 April does not seem to have been made public, and was not accepted by the Senate, until well after the internal poll. In addition, his supporters could point to the fact that Lowe, not a graduate of London, had sat for the University as its first MP.

The other issue which excited many graduates, as it had done in 1868, was whether the University's seat should be filled by a spokesman for science and/or medicine. The *Lancet* was realistic about the poor chance of success for a medical man, because the medical graduates were 'barely one third of the constituency'.[21] But although the medical journals paid lip service to the idea that the University should be represented by one of its own graduates, there appeared in their columns correspondence which argued for Lubbock as a scientist as against Jessel, who was seen as the legal candidate. This was not only the message from Liberals: many doctors normally loyal to the Conservatives supported Lubbock because 'there are lawyers enough; whilst the members fitted to represent science might be counted on one's fingers'.[22]

Lubbock was also helped by the fact that Gull, an eminent medico, cannot have gained much support from fellow doctors, and was not pushed by the *Lancet*, probably because it was seen as likely that he would switch support to Jessel; indeed he tried to withdraw from the poll but was prevailed upon to leave his hat in the ring.[23]

The result of the Liberals' poll – 'a great surprise', according to Lubbock's biographer – demonstrated his dominance:[24]

| Preferences | 1st | 2nd | 3rd | 4th |
| --- | --- | --- | --- | --- |
| Lubbock | 769 | 132 | 53 | 39 |
| Jessel | 192 | 354 | 203 | 125 |
| Gull | 49 | 130 | 201 | 419 |
| Goldsmid | 33 | 241 | 358 | 191 |

[20] *Standard*, 17 May 1880.
[21] *Lancet*, 1 May 1880.
[22] *Lancet*, 8 May 1880.
[23] UL RC1/7/ss. *Times*, 10 May 1880.
[24] Hutchinson, *Life of Lubbock*, I, 168–73.

Goldsmid, no doubt disillusioned by early returns, gave up before the end of the polling and became candidate for Deal, where he lost: Gull withdrew as soon as the result was known;[25] and there was no attempt to persuade Jessel to think of running. There were no last minute nominations of other contenders, and no poll: Lubbock was declared elected on 2 June.

Given the doubts about the validity of Jessel's candidature, and the weakness of the appeals of Gull and Goldsmid, the result is not surprising. But it also reflected the success of a vigorous campaign which was conducted for Lubbock: that campaign, however, attracted accusations of dubious practices. Jessel's Committee complained that Lubbock's Committee was organised and actively pushing his candidacy 'before there was even time to ascertain the names of any eminent Graduates of our University who would, if elected, be willing to represent it'.[26] And in a letter to the *Times*, it was claimed that there was a significant element of the Liberal Party Committee supportive of Lubbock, and that they had 'canvassed almost the whole constituency in his behalf before calling in their old capacity a meeting to consider the question of the future representation of the University'.[27] However, the size of the gap between Lubbock and all his opponents was such as to make it highly unlikely that a little sharp electoral practice added greatly to his victory.

The details of the poll were not published at the time, at the request of the defeated candidates.[28] And it would seem that Lubbock's preferred resignation of the Vice-Chancellorship may not have been made public until after the poll closed.[29] But his sense of the propriety of giving up the post was justified by events. At a Senate meeting on 19 May – more than two weeks before the election – it was taken for granted that Lubbock would be the new MP. Lubbock was certainly in an odd situation, being, as Vice-Chancellor, the Returning Officer for the constituency: and it was felt that he could not return himself. But there were wider arguments, and, on 26 May, 'Lowe, Sir P. Egerton and two or three others spoke strongly about the "incompatibility of the two offices"' of Vice-Chancellor and Parliamentary Representative of the University. Granville and Derby suggested making a temporary appointment of F.J. Wood as Vice-Chancellor, but they found 'opinions so greatly divided' that they did not pursue the idea. The Chancellor told Senate that Lubbock was willing to help, but was 'rather inclined to agree on the technical inconvenience' of a temporary arrangement. Lowe then proposed that Jessel become Vice-Chancellor, and he was elected 'with three "No's"'.[30] There were twenty-two Senators present.

[25] BL Add Mss 62682, Lubbock's Diary, 15 May 1880. *Standard*, 15 May 1880.
[26] UL RC1/7/ss.
[27] *Times*, 8 May 1880.
[28] BL Add Mss 62682, Lubbock's Diary, 15 May 1880.
[29] His resignation was noted in *BMJ*, 22 May 1880.
[30] BL Add Mss 49645, Granville to Lubbock, 26 May 1880.

Sir John Lubbock was to be the University's Member of Parliament for twenty years. But Sir George Jessel, who continued as a judge, died after less than three years in office as Vice-Chancellor.

There was little interest, and apparently no serious intention, among the University community in the election of November, 1885, in trying to unseat Lubbock. He was, after all, a Liberal, and had by then had five years as the representative of graduates, a comfortable majority of whom were still strongly in favour of the rule of a Liberal Government. He does not seem to have upset any significant faction in Convocation, though he was realistic enough to record, with some self-satisfaction, after his re-election, that 'behind my back I understand some attacks were made on me, without notice and of which of course I knew nothing . . .'[31] By 9 November the Registrar, Milman, had heard 'no whispers of any opposition', and on the following day a meeting of the London University Conservative Association accepted the suggestion drafted by their Honorary Secretaries,

> That having fully considered the existing state of political parties in the University . . . and having regard to the fact that no other Candidate has been brought forward, the Committee of the . . . Association feel it to be undesirable on the present occasion to offer any opposition to the re-election of Sir John Lubbock.[32]

Lubbock's was one of only fifteen uncontested seats.

Hitherto, therefore, in only one of the four General Elections since the University seat was established had there been a normal contest. In all four elections the strength of the appeal of the Liberal Party to the majority of the graduates had been such that even, on the one occasion that it was challenged, by the Conservative, Arthur Charles, in April, 1880, the Liberals prevailed easily. On that occasion, though, it was clear that when there was a real contest, what mattered most to the voters was their allegiance to the national policies offered by the major political parties. The significance of narrow University issues, and even of professional arguments in the educational context, were not entirely absent in the one contested election. But it was only in the internal choice of candidates in 1868–69 and in 1880 that discussion, negotiation and, in Lubbock's case, voting, tended to be centred on whether the candidate should be a graduate of London, and whether it was desirable to choose a man who would be an advocate for medicine and science.

[31] BL Add Mss 62683, Lubbock's Diary, 24 November 1885.
[32] BL Add Mss 49648, Milman to Lubbock, 9 November; Fowler to Lubbock, 13 November, enclosing printed Notice of London University Conservative Association, 2 November 1885.

But in 1886 the graduates of the University of London put aside all academic, educational, and internal constitutional concerns. When the second reading of Gladstone's Irish Home Rule Bill was thrown out in the House of Commons, on 8 June, and a dissolution followed, the struggle for the University seat became simply the same as that which engaged the whole country. John Lubbock declared himself a Liberal Unionist; Michael Foster acted as his Chairman, and E.H. Busk continued as his secretary. The University's Conservatives saw no reason to do anything but support Lubbock again.[33]

Lubbock recognised the possibility of strong opposition in the traditionally Liberal majority in Convocation.[34]. But that previous majority was utterly split. The pro-Home Rule group in Convocation was given some leadership by J. Allanson Picton, MP for Leicester, and William Job Collins, a young medical man from Barts, destined for a major career in politics and the University. A Committee was set up, chaired by Picton and with Collins as Secretary. The intial appeal to graduates, sent out on 25 June 1886, was approved by a group of thirty-one: only four of them were medical men, and only six more had science degrees. They called a meeting at Freemasons' Tavern for 30 June, and told their prospective supporters that

> Neither the personal regard which we all have for Sir John Lubbock, nor our respect for his high scientific attainments, can exonerate us from our first duty as citizens, to look on such an occasion as this, to principles rather than to men.

And they were 'not without hope of winning for our University a place amongst the strongholds of sturdy Liberalism'.[35] According to Collins, it was he, together with Sophie Bryant and R.D.Roberts, who 'resolved to bring out a Home Rule candidate'.[36] But, pressed for time and apparently unable to find any London graduate who might carry weight against Lubbock, the Gladstonian Liberals invited the influential humanist Frederic Harrison to stand – which he agreed to do, only three days before nominations closed.

Both candidates paid only minimal courtesies to the special interests of London graduates. Harrison, in accepting his candidacy, stated, simply,

> I have not touched upon questions other than that of Ireland. I have for many years worked heartily in the great cause of freeing religion from the fetters of an Establishment, in the Reform of the Laws relating to Land, in the cause of the Education of the People, and the social elevation of the Working Classes.[37]

---

[33] BL Add Mss 49649, M. Foster to Lubbock, 11 June; Allchin to Lubbock, 25 June 1886.
[34] Hutchinson, *Life of Lubbock*, I, 168–73.
[35] UL RC1/7/tt.
[36] W.J. Collins, in *Sophie Bryant D.Sc. Litt.D. 1850–1922* (London, 1922).
[37] Frederic Harrison, *Autobiographic Memoirs* (London, 1911), II, 219–23.

But on Ireland, as Harrison found to his cost,

The whole of the Conservative and Unionist voters and most of the scientific and professional men were pledged to Lubbock, and the chances of defeating them were small indeed.[38]

The electorate was 2579 strong. Of them, 71 per cent voted, and, of those who cast their votes, 71.8 per cent – 1314 – supported Lubbock, while only 28.2 per cent – 516 – supported Harrison. Of the 1830 who cast votes, 538 – 29.4 per cent – were medical men. Only forty-three of them chose Harrison, while 495 chose Lubbock – 92 per cent. Unfortunately, there do not seem to be any figures extant which would give an accurate indication of the extent to which the lawyers followed the doctors in condemning Home Rule. But the number of science graduates was still comparatively small, so that Harrison's claim that 'most of the scientific and professional men' supported Lubbock implies that a large group of lawyers took the same position as the medicos.[39] Lubbock claimed, fairly enough, that, as the maximum Conservative vote would only have been five hundred to six hundred, he had won 'even on the Liberal vote', and celebrated after the poll with a 'a Scientific and Liberal Unionist party'.[40]

Sir John Lubbock was not opposed at either the election of 1892, or that of 1895, and served in the House of Commons until his elevation to the Lords in 1900. Between 1886 and 1892 the bitter controversy over the future of the University ran half its course: in 1895 the struggle to have a new constitution adopted was at its height. And throughout the decade from 1886 onwards, the Liberal split over Ireland continued to divide Convocation. While there is little evidence of the impact of either controversy on Lubbock's electoral situation in 1892, the arguments over the University's future was clearly an important background to his re-election in 1895. It is, therefore, desirable to postpone consideration of the later elections for the University seat – in 1892, 1895 and 1900 – until they can be placed in the relevant contexts – contexts very different from those prevailing in 1868, 1874, 1880 and 1885–86.

[38] Harrison, *Memoirs*, II, 219–23.
[39] Hutchinson, *Life of Lubbock*, I, 168–73.
[40] BL Add Mss 62683, Lubbock's Diary, 7 & 15 July 1886.

# Part V

## *The University and Secondary Education*

# 16

# *The schools lobby*

Three Royal Commissions and a Select Committee of the House of Commons produced significant reports on Education during the 1860s. Two of the Royal Commissions dealt, respectively, with the two ends of the school spectrum: the provision of elementary education was made the business of a Commission on Popular Education, while there was a separate Commission to deal with the condition of the handful of Public Schools which served the upper classes. The Select Committee broke new ground by probing the need for Technical Education. Secondary education, other than that offered in the Public Schools, was the remit of the third Royal Commission, whose terms of reference covered all schools not being discussed by the other two Commissions, and was soon known, simply, as the Schools Inquiry Commission.[1] It was chaired by Lord Taunton, signed on 2 December 1867, and surveyed the patchy, complicated world of hundreds of endowed schools, grammar schools and proprietary and private schools. The Taunton Commissioners found a great need of reform of this sector, which they recognised as the natural provider of education for the increasingly numerous and demanding middle classes.

In following the course of the struggle to allow women to be candidates for University examinations in London, we saw that the cause was helped by the wider and more immediate concern for the improvement and extension of secondary education for girls. But that concern was itself narrower than the perceived need to understand, analyse and offer a better way forward for the secondary education of all the children of the middle class. From the mid-1860s to the early 1880s, the University of London, responding to internal and external pressure, and to the examples set by older universities and other institutions,[2] worked out its own contribution, which included pioneering the inspection of secondary schools, and introducing post-graduate qualifications for teachers.

---

[1] R. Comm. on Popular Education, PP 1861, xxi; R. Comm. on the Public Schools, PP1862, xliii; Sel. Cmte on Technical Education, PP 1867–68, xv; Schools Inquiry Commission, PP 1867–68, xxviii.

[2] For a masterly survey, see M.E. Bryant, *The London Experience of Secondary Education* (London, 1986), chs 5 & 6.

In addition, the University was drawn into the arguments about school examinations. Examinations held locally for pupils in secondary schools, the greater number of whom would leave at the age of fifteen or sixteen, had been introduced in some areas in the late 1850s, and had been taken up by the Universities of Oxford and Cambridge. The notion of developing a system or systems of school-leaving examinations, for fifteen- or sixteen-year-olds, became entangled with the use of more advanced examinations designed for pupils wishing to enter university. The Matriculation Examination of the University of London was being used, increasingly, as a school-leaving qualification. The possibility of re-shaping it and equivalent examinations, and even of replacing them, on a national scale, with a two-tier examination, was canvassed heavily. Despite the efforts of enthusiasts, however, Matriculation was to remain the only examination which London offered at school level. But Matriculation itself underwent important, and controversial, changes as a result of a demand for a greater inclusion of modern languages and the natural sciences, which challenged the place of the classics in the compulsory curriculum.

The arguments about and the innovations made in the three areas of Matriculation, inspection and examination of schools, and the training of teachers, did not follow a tidy chronology. Progress in each overlapped, and sometimes seem to have been almost unrelated to each other. Broadly speaking, the controversy about Matriculation began first, the introduction of inspection of schools came second, and the offering of qualifications for teachers, last. But having made that point, one can find an attempt to engage the Annual Committee of Convocation in promoting the training of teachers as early as 14 February 1862, and echoes of the arguments over local examinations were heard until 1884. While some cross-referencing, and occasional repetition, is inevitable, therefore, the following narrative concentrates first on Matriculation, then on inspection of schools, and finally on the introduction of qualifications for teachers. Before beginning those separate sections, however, it is important to say a little about who, within the University community, were particularly involved.

While there was a very small group in Senate and Convocation who made it their business to play a part in almost every aspect of the University's life, beyond them there tended to develop, inevitably, groups of members particularly concerned to pursue specialised interests. The representatives of the medical fraternity, and to a lesser extent of the legal profession, had from the outset acted on occasion as pressure groups. The same was to be true of the teachers in secondary schools, who were becoming steadily more evident in Convocation, as demand for the employment of graduate teachers grew – a growth much further increased after women were admitted to degrees.

The campaign for the admission of women to the degree examinations of the University had drawn support from a wide spectrum of interests. Similarly, there was certainly enthusiasm and support for reform of secondary education from many quarters in the University community. But the lead was given and the campaigns dominated by a group of men, more numerous in Convocation than in the Senate, who were professionally engaged in school teaching or in the administration of education – and who were, by no means, necessarily in agreement with each other. The movement was fortunate to have the sympathy and support of William Benjamin Carpenter, the University's Registrar until 1879, and Fellow thereafter until his death in 1885. Until 1880 he could only operate in his administrative role, backed by his considerable reputation as a scientist, but he then joined those Fellows and members of Convocation who were enthusiasts for extending and improving the scope of secondary education. Two of the most influential were graduates who became Convocation-nominated Fellows. They came from very different backgrounds, and were men of very different temperaments.

Joshua Girling Fitch, born in 1824, was an Anglican from a poor family who began to teach at the Borough Road School in Southwark – 'the original and central school of the whole Lancasterian system'[3] – at the age of fourteen. He returned to the Training College at Borough Road as its Vice-Principal in 1852, and became Principal from 1856 until 1863 when, probably on the advice of Matthew Arnold, Granville appointed him Inspector of Schools. He was posted to York, and did not return to live in London until 1870. His career as an inspector, which ended in 1894, after almost a decade as Inspector of Training Colleges for Women, was much interrupted, earlier, by spells as an Assistant Commissioner for Lord Taunton's inquiry, and under the Endowed Schools Act. Fitch had taken his BA and MA at UCL in 1850 and 1852, and was a founder member of Convocation. He served for two periods, each of five years, as University Examiner in English. His absence from London did not prevent him from standing, in 1867, for nomination by Convocation as a Fellow: he came third, collecting only forty votes. After returning to London, he withdrew from nomination for the Annual Committee in 1870, but joined it in 1873, and two years later won nomination for Fellow by a convincing 336 votes against prominent medical and legal rivals – Jenner, who polled 185, and Herschell, who polled 111. Fitch remained an important member of Senate for the rest of the century, and was also made a Life Governor of UCL.

Philip Magnus, eighteen years younger than Fitch, came from a moderately properous Jewish family, attended University College School and College, took degrees in Arts and in Science in the mid-60s, then spent some years at the University of Berlin. In 1866 he was appointed third minister of the West London Synagogue, the Reform Synagogue among whose founders and supporters were the Goldsmid family, who played so large a part in the history of University College and the University of London. Magnus remained at the Synagogue until 1880, but increasingly concentrated his interests

---

[3] A.L. Lilley, *Sir Joshua Fitch. An Account of his Life and Work* (London, 1906), p. 9.

Sir Joshua Girling Fitch. Principal, Borough Road Training College 1856–1863. Inspector of Schools 1863–1894. Convocation-nominated Member of Senate 1875–1900.

on the development of technical education. In 1879 he applied, unsucessfully, for the post of Assistant Registrar at the University, but in the following year became Secretary and Organising Director of the City and Guilds of London Institute, a post he would hold until 1913. He had joined Convocation in his twenty-sixth year, 1868, and in 1872 was elected to the Annual Committee, on which he sat, as an elected or an *ex officio* member, throughout the rest of our period. He was to become a Convocation-nominated Fellow in 1890, was to retain his place on the Senate until 1931, and was to represent the University in Parliament, as a Unionist, from 1906 to 1922.

These very different but powerful men were supported in the pursuit of an improved secondary school system by a group in Convocation, some of whom were closely involved in the College of Preceptors. Among them were John Robson, who moved from the Secretaryship of the College to the Assistant Secretaryship of UCL while the Taunton Commission was sitting, and was Clerk of Convocation from 1868 to 1876; and A.K. Isbister, Secretary and later Dean of the College; while two of the College's Vice-Presidents were Rev. Albert Creak – from 1858 a keen member of Convocation, who ran a school in Brighton; and R.F. Weymouth, Headmaster of Mill Hill and a prominent member of the Annual Committee for two decades. Others who took a regular part in the numerous committees which struggled with the problems were Talfourd Ely, A.W. Bennett of St Thomas's Hospital, Andrew McDowall, and H.A. Nesbitt.

In addition, however, there were also a number of men not involved as administrators or teachers in secondary schools, who none the less played important roles in the protracted discussions of the period. Among the lawyers were three UCL graduates: Benjamin Kisch; William Shaen, a founder of the Girls Public Day Schools Trust; and Joseph Maurice Solomon, who examined for the University. There was relatively little interest shown by the medical men, but Alfred Meadows and Philip Henry Pye-Smith pulled their weight in several relevant committees. On the Senate it is less easy to underline the names of Fellows who were heavily committed, especially in the initiation of action, because Senate was, in this context, in the main responding to pressure. But in the early years, Hutton was keen to keep the Matriculation issue before his Senate colleagues, and occasionally turned up at Convocation and at Annual Committee to have his say.

It would be quite false to claim that the people listed were always in perfect harmony, or to suggest that they worked in a close-knit unit. But they, and perhaps as many as another dozen in Senate and Convocation, or in both, were at the heart of what the University thought about and acted upon in the context of middle class education during the two decades from 1865.

The Chancellor, Lord Granville, was Lord President of the Council when the Schools Inquiry Commission was set up in 1864, and was much involved in settling its membership. His correspondence with various ministerial colleagues shows that several London University Fellows and examiners were considered. Heywood wanted to be included; William Smith, Grote, and

Overstone were all thought possible as representatives of the University; Grote did not want to serve, nor did Lowe; Overstone declined on health grounds, and recommended Wodehouse (later Lord Kimberley); Stafford Northcote felt that Shaw Lefevre should be excused because he was carrying too large a load, while Northcote and H.A. Bruce both suggested Carpenter, the Registrar, as 'a well educated Dissenter'. Lingen, Secretary of the Education Department of the Privy Council, wanted Ryan, and Bruce thought of Twisleton. But in the end the only London men chosen were Lord Stanley, who, as a member of Derby's Government when the Commission reported, abstained from signing; and John Storrar, who was pressed on Granville by Shaw Lefevre, on the grounds that 'from his position in reference to our University [he] may be considered as representing a large class of persons interested in the improvement of School Education'.[4]

But though only two members of the Senate sat on the Commission, several Fellows and prominent members of Convocation gave evidence to it. Among the Fellows were Robert Lowe, James Paget and William Withey Gull; among the very active members of Convocation were John Robson, William Smith, a long-established examiner and classical scholar; and the Rev. Albert Creak. In our context, however, the most significant witness was Carpenter, the Registrar, who suggested at an early stage of the inquiry a course of action which the Commission backed strongly in its Report.

The Commission heard a great deal about the effect of the local examinations which had been introduced by the ancient universities less than a decade earlier, and declared that they

> . . . have already succeeded so far, as to mark out the Universities as the fittest bodies that can be found, for testing and in some degree guiding school work. These examinations have their faults, but they are the best examinations of their kind, and appear to have secured to a great extent the confidence of the country. To the same effect it may be observed that the matriculation examinations of the University of London to a great degree perform a similar office for a large number of proprietary and private schools.

But this recommendation, published in 1867, came in the middle of a prolonged battle, within the University of London, which had begun in 1862 and would continue for a decade, over what should be included in the Matriculation Examination.

---

[4] PRO 30/29/19/4, 30/29/18/12, and 30/29/25 – letters to Granville from Grey, Bruce, Lowe, Overstone, Lyttelton, Lingen, Shaw Lefevre, Grote, Stanley and Storrar, between 9 August and 26 November 1864.

# 17

# Matriculation: Greek or Chemistry?

Before the inspection and examination of schools became prominent as a potential task, Convocation and Senate were embroiled in a controversy which excited academic passions among Fellows and graduates alike. In contention was the compulsory inclusion of Greek as a subject, and the level of achievement required in the Matriculation Examination as a whole. On the one side were the supporters of a classical education; on the other, proponents of more modern studies, especially modern languages and subjects appropriate to preparation for further work in natural science. Behind the arguments over curriculum and stringency were the social divisons and different employment prospects of those who attended the Public Schools, and those who constituted the bulk of those most likely to take the London Matriculation – the middle class children who attended the far more numerous endowed and proprietary schools.

There had been concern about the content and alleged severity of the Matriculation Examination since changes were made subsequent to the 1858 Charter. Early in 1862 a memorial was sent to the Senate by almost a hundred senior teachers and heads of institutions, including the Principals of KCL and of Owens College, and several Professors from both UCL and KCL, arguing that while the standard required for passing the Matriculation was appropriate, the number of subjects included was too great. The memorialists asked that either Chemistry should be dropped, save for intending medical students, or that candidates should be permitted to choose between Chemistry and Natural Philosophy. At about the same time, a number of individual educators wrote letters on the matter to the Senate.

It was Convocation which made the first move to consider what the memorialists were proposing. On 12 March 1862, the specific propositions were raised and debated at some length. The proposal to allow an option of Natural Philosophy or Chemistry was defeated. But Hutton, seconded by A.D. Sprange, who taught at the Military Establishment in Bayswater, carried a motion 'That . . . it is not expedient that candidates for Matriculation should be required to pass in Chemistry.'

Senate received the memorial and the various letters on 14 March and referred them to the Committee on Examinations. That Committee was totally unsympathetic to any proposals for change, and at a well-attended meeting of Senate, on 7 May, three votes settled the issue for a decade. Osler's attempt to have Chemistry dropped was lost by seventeen to five; the Chairman of Convocation, Foster, tried to introduce an option of 'one Greek *or* one Latin subject', but that was defeated by sixteen to five: and the Vice-Chancellor's original motion to accept the Committee's report was carried by eighteen to four. It was quite correct for another committee of Convocation, seven years later, to admit that the proposed changes had been defeated 'by considerable majorities'.

The last suggestion, in this early episode, was forthcoming in March, 1863, when Creak and Robson carried a motion in the Annual Committee to simplify the Matriculation examination in English History. But a month afterwards the proposal was struck out of the Committee's Report to Convocation by a vote of eleven to two. Clearly, there was insufficient force behind any impetus to alter the shape of Matriculation. Minor procedural adjustments were made, but after 1864 the essential scope seemed firmly settled: the examination was of twenty-eight hours duration, and the subjects included were Mathematics, Natural Philosophy, Chemistry, Greek, Latin, English Language, English History, French or German.

Any change in the range of subjects had been soundly rejected. But the next attack was focussed on the standard set by the examiners. On 11 February 1870, two lawyers, Cozens-Hardy and E.C. Dunn, alarmed at a 19 per cent increase in the number of rejected candidates between 1858 and 1870, moved in the Annual Committee that 'it is desirable that Senate should consider the propriety of diminishing the extent and lessening the severity of the Matriculation Examination'. After debate the motion was withdrawn and the subject referred to a sub-committee composed of three medicos, two lawyers, and two Arts men. All the members save one were very regular attenders at the six meetings of the sub-committee, whose report to the Annual Committee was only slightly amended and passed on to the Senate, in April, 1870. It was supportive of the essence of Cozens-Hardy's original motion.

The Registrar had worked closely with the sub-committee, making available to them the statistical information available. All the possible factors which might have influenced the increase in the failure rate were examined carefully, and all but one were felt to be relatively insignificant. The sub-committee were

> . . . convinced that the Examination is far more severe than formerly, and that the increased percentage of rejections is mainly due to the gradual but steady raising of the standard in almost all subjects, either by more difficult papers being set, or by more thorough and exact answers being required. . . . There is no ground for supposing that the education given in Colleges and Schools has deteriorated . . . even Candidates of the highest class and from the best Colleges and Schools find the Examination more difficult than it was a few years ago. . . . The real difficulty . . . appears to lie in the natural tendency of each Examiner to overrate the importance of his own subject, and to draw his paper as if it were the only one in which Candidates would have to be examined. He never sees the papers proposed

to be set by the other Examiners. A very slight increase in the severity of each of nine or ten papers makes a very serious increase in the severity of the Examination as a whole.

Convocation had the report before them on 10 May, when Cozens-Hardy moved 'That in the opinion of Convocation it is desirable that the Senate should consider the propriety of lessening the severity of the Matriculation Examination.' That motion survived votes on three amendments, none of which contained serious criticism of the sub-committee's findings, and was approved by sixty to forty-eight. Unfortunately, there is no list of voters.

As in 1862, the Senate was less worried than Convocation, but was now much more respectful of the latter's advice. The Committee on Examinations received Convocation's report in June, 1870, and reported to Senate in November. Senate formally adopted the report and Convocation's resolution that they should consider 'lessening the severity' of the Matriculation Examinations. In admitting that the examinations had become harder, they argued, somewhat complacently, perhaps, that it was necessary to guard against any lowering of standards which would otherwise follow from 'that increased influx of imperfectly prepared candidates which the growing celebrity of the University was sure to attract'. This may not have been an unfair comment on the poor level of teaching in some schools, and on the likelihood that a percentage of the wider range of persons enrolling themselves for examination may have lacked sufficient preparation. But, given the seriousness with which the Registrar had treated the inquiry, it is highly probable that some discreet advice, based on the findings of the careful report, was passed on to examiners. In any event, the Annual Committee, in its report to Convocation in May, 1871, had good reason to feel satisfied that the Senate had accepted and acted upon their findings and recommendations.

The relative success of raising pertinent questions about the standards being set by the examiners must have re-invigorated those whose prime interest in Matriculation was still focussed on the desirability of making changes in what subjects should be compulsory, and whether some should be made optional. Only a month after the Senate had adopted the resolution of Convocation on the consideration of the severity of the whole examination, Hutton gave notice of a motion to introduce an option between Greek and English. On 14 December 1870, his motion was lost by five to seven in a division which saw members of various disciplines, and of differing routes to the Senate, on both sides.

With Senate still unwilling to make any concessions, Convocation was silent on the matter throughout most of 1871. Shaen and Ely tried to persuade the Annual Committee, on 24 February, to set up a committee 'to consider and report upon the subject of enabling candidates to matriculate . . . without undergoing any examination in Greek', but withdrew the motion, no doubt finding insufficient support. Three months later, at the Annual Meeting,

Francis T. Bond and A.W. Bennett tried to gain support for the encouragement of engineering students by making changes in the curriculum of the BSc
degree. This was tied to another motion by Bond, 'that it is not expedient
to retain Greek as a compulsory subject at the Matriculation Examination'.
Ely and Shaen attempted to have the latter sent to the Annual Committee,
but debate on all the topics raised was stopped by a vote of forty-three to thirty-
one on a motion to move to the next item on the agenda.

Real progress by those seeking change was not made until November,
1871, when Herschell and Shaen, at Annual Committee, were able to secure
the appointment of a sub-committee to report on compulsory Greek at
Matriculation. An attempt by James Anstie and Pye-Smith to add 'And
Latin or either of them', was lost five to twelve. By the same margin the
Sub-committee on Greek was approved, and given power to enquire widely
of relevant persons, by thirteen to four. This important sub-committee was
made up of four lawyers – Arthur Charles, Cozens-Hardy, Herschell, and
Shaen; two scientists – Bennett and Frederick George Finch; three medical
men – Tilbury Fox, Meadows, and Pye-Smith; and two educationists – Talfourd
Ely and Weymouth.

They met six times, and produced a significant report for the Annual
Committee, after having made enquiries of ninety-nine school heads and
several foreign universities. These enquiries revealed

> ... that in the majority of the grammar schools, and in a good number of the older
> as well as the more recently established public schools, a 'modern' side had been
> established in which Greek had no part.

School heads considered that Greek was being abandoned because of

> ... the parents' opinion that Greek was useless for a professional or business career;
> the time could be more profitably spent in studying modern languages or science.
> One headmaster summed up the reasons laconically as 'caprice of parents, idleness
> of boys'.

Four British and ten foreign universities offered degrees in science, medicine
or engineering without requiring any previous examination in Greek. And
at Cambridge 'a proposal to allow modern languages as an alternative to
Greek had recently been rejected but was likely to be revived'.[1]

A majority of the sub-committee felt, in the light of these findings, that
'a movement so extensive surely indicates a widespread conviction amongst
education authorities that a knowledge of Greek should not be made a
condition precedent to every description of University career'. Their first
recommendation, 'that such a modification should be made in Matriculation

---

[1] Dunsheath and Miller, *Convocation*, pp. 44–5.

. . . as would open a University career to students without requiring any examination in Greek', was moved by Shaen and Meadows and carried by six votes to two. The second recommendation, moved by Bennett and Ely, the voting on which is unrecorded, was that 'it is desirable to give an option . . . between Greek and Chemistry or Natural Philosophy'.

But when the Annual Committee met on 26 April 1872, with twenty-six members present, and Herschell presented the sub-committee's report, James Anstie and Julian Goldsmid tried to have the whole subject considered further. Eventually Herschell and Shaen managed to carry, by fifteen to five, a compromise whereby the report would be submitted to Convocation by the Annual Committee, but only as the report of a sub-committee, not blessed by its parent body. And when Convocation met on 14 May, the motion 'that in the opinion of Convocation such a modification should be made in Matriculation . . . as would open a University career to students without requiring any examination in Greek', was withdrawn when an amendment to leave out the words 'in the opinion of Convocation', was carried by forty-nine votes to forty-two. The report was referred back to the Annual Committee. The opposition to change may have weakened, but it was still enough to bar the way to any relaxation of the requirements.

There followed some eighteen months of intensive in-fighting in Convocation, which was paralleled by a far less controversial progress in the Senate towards what, in retrospect, may seem to have been an inevitable loosening of the previously rigid requirements of Matriculation. Hutton, doubtless drawing heavily on the report of the Annual Committee's sub-committee, showed much political prescience by giving notice to Senate, as early as 19 June 1872, that he would ask for consideration of the following, in February, 1873:

> That considering the large number of good first-grade Schools now existing, which do not include any provision for instruction in Greek – and considering that our University already confers Degrees in Science, Medicine and Law, which imply no more study of Greek than is requisite to qualify the student for passing the Matriculation Examination – it is desirable to give Candidates for that Examination an option between Greek and a second modern language.

However this move by Hutton was regarded by the embattled factions in Convocation, the conflict between them raged all through the interval between May, 1872, and February, 1873, and indeed continued beyond that. It was carried on in four sessions of the Annual Committee, three in June and one in November, and culminated in a meeting of Convocation in January, 1873. These Annual Committee meetings were very well attended – of thirty-one members who turned out, twelve came to all four meetings and another thirteen were present at three of them. The proceedings were marked by numerous divisions and motions to adjourn, which it would be enormously tedious to record in detail, though verbatim reportage would doubtless reveal some colourful disagreements. The struggles involved those who, basically, resented any contemplation of change; those who simply wanted to see one or more subjects dropped altogether; and those who sought to create options between existing subjects and make room for new subjects. The outcome, by the end of 1872, was a complete failure to approve any initiative.

The basic problem was the fierce unwillingness of the classicists to lose Greek, and the bitter unhappiness of the scientists at the prospect of losing either of the compulsory papers in Chemistry and Natural Philosophy. There was much jockeying for position, and the leading members of the Annual Committee in favour of change in one degree or other – Julian Goldsmid, J.H. Payne, Philip Magnus, James Anstie, Bennett, Shaen and Herschell – tried a series of compromise motions. But all failed and allowed the defenders of the *status quo* – seemingly led by L.M. Aspland, a barrister and member of the Council of UCL, and W.H. Holman, a London Hospital man practising in Hampstead – to carry the day, effectively on 28 June 1872, by twelve to seven. Subsequently the thwarted reformers tried to ensure that a statement of the reasons for not making any change was produced, but this was refused on 8 November by a margin of twelve to five.

The failure of the reformers to gain support in the Annual Committee was rubbed in when Convocation met on 21 January 1873, and threw out any support for modification of the Matriculation Examination by forty-three votes to twenty-four. But in a development not very different, in essence, from what happened in some stages of the later negotiations over the admission of women to degree examinations, Convocation's position was ignored by the Senate.

The Notice of Motion given by Hutton in June, 1872, calling for the Senate to allow an option of Greek and a second modern language, was put before Senate on 12 February 1873, in the following form:

> That Greek be no longer compulsory . . . at the Matriculation Examination but be ranked as optional with French or German; so that it shall be sufficient for any Candidate to pass in any one of these three languages.

Storrar reported Convocation's wish to retain Greek, and Sibson attempted to have the matter sent to a committee, but was defeated seven to ten. Hutton's motion was then carried by ten to eight. Storrar abstained, but Wood, the other Convocation-nominated Fellow present, took the majority view expressed by Convocation on the matter, and voted against the change.

The Senate wished to make the new provisions operative for the June examination, and, after consultation between the Chancellor, Vice-Chancellor and Registrar, it was decided to follow established precedent – that when change would be to the advantage of candidates the Senate's Resolution should be published immediately. But the change had to be ratified by the Home Secretary: application for his formal approval was made simultaneously, and was received within a few days. There was, therefore, an interval between publication of the Resolution, and formal approval of that Resolution by the Home Secretary. This was seized upon by those in the Annual Committee who were piqued by the Senate's indifference to their advice about Matriculation, and by those specially watchful of constitutional routines, who suspected that there had been an apparent willingness to cut legal corners.

By the time the Annual Committee came together, on 21 February, the indignation was channelled into a motion by Arthur Charles and Weymouth. They regretted Senate's having taken action without any consultation with Convocation, and so soon after Convocation had decided 'by a large majority' that it was inadvisable to alter the Matriculation regulations. Shaen and Ely carried an amendment to adjourn discussion of that motion for a week. But then attention was focussed on the Senate's alleged premature publication of the decision to drop compulsory Greek. It is notable that Shaen, a supporter of that change but also the founding Clerk of Convocation, and a stout defender of its prerogatives, took a lead in challenging the Senate's behaviour. Seconded by Magnus, he successfully moved that the Chairman of Convocation should ask the Chancellor or Vice-Chancellor whether the Senate had authorised the publication of the Senate's resolution before it had been sanctioned by the Secretary of State.

Storrar duly wrote to the Vice-Chancellor (Lubbock), who did not reply until 12 March 1873. Without that reply, when the Annual Committee met again on 28 February, they devoted the whole session to further debate on the Matriculation controversy, and approved the critical motion of Charles and Weymouth, regretting the Senate's action, by nineteen to nine. But that was only after an attempt by Aspland to force an adjournment, presumably because he hoped for some stronger denunciation, was defeated by eighteen votes to ten.

In March, Senate was conciliatory. William Smith, who had voted against dropping Greek as a compulsory language, persuaded them that candidates who chose French or German should also be allowed to receive credit for taking Greek in the Matriculation Examinations in June, 1873, and January, 1874. And another opponent of the change, Twisleton, gave notice of a proposal that the principle of making Greek optional must be admitted, but that the Committee on Examinations should consider what other changes in the subjects for Matriculation might be desirable.

At the same time, the Vice-Chancellor sent a long letter to the Chairman of Convocation, explaining and justifying the action of the Senate in publishing the intention to change the rules before formal governmental authority had been received. Lubbock also took the opportunity to praise and thank the Annual Committee for its work. Pragmatism and diplomacy were thus restoring harmony. This episode, however, demonstrated the touchiness of Convocation about its prerogatives, and foreshadowed the much more serious row which followed the later decisions of the Senate about the admission of women.

Convocation, moreover, had by no means yet come to terms with the new Matriculation situation. At the Annual Meeting on 13 May 1873, there were attempts by J. Horne Payne and Ely, and by Rev. Philip Smith and Creak, to stress, in one form or another, disappointment and regret at the Senate's action and failure to consult; but these were pushed aside by Herschell, who gained support for simply thanking the Annual Committee for their efforts, and for passing to the next item. A more forward-looking resolution, proposed by Magnus and J.M. Solomon, was then approved, instructing the Annual Committee to consider, quickly, the alteration made by the Senate in the Matriculation regulations; and calling on the Senate to defer final decisions on the remodelling of the examinations until after Convocation had discussed its Committee's report.

The Annual Committee appointed a sub-committee on 16 May. Magnus took the chair and drafted the report, which was threshed out in three meetings on 20, 26 and 29 May. They presented the draft to the Annual Committee on 6 June and it was accepted with only one amendment; several attempts to make changes failed. The amended version was put before Convocation on 2 July, and emerged from it further amended, after much debate and argument over subject options and examination content. Magnus and Bennett led almost all the successful proposals, which seem to have been settled clearly by show of hands, but they lost two divisions over the content of the paper in Natural Philosophy by fifteen to seventeen and fourteen to seventeen. All but one of the proposed amendments accepted the introduction of options, but Rev. Philip Smith tried in vain, at this last moment, to persuade his colleagues that compulsory Greek should be restored.

Convocation's proposals were presented to Senate on 23 July, when 'The whole subject of the Matriculation Examination' was referred to the Examinations Committee, who were instructed to take into account the Minutes of the last meeting of Convocation and the report of the sub-committee of the Annual Committee. The Examinations Committee deliberated during the early part of the following session, and they reported to Senate in January, 1874, when a special meeting to discuss the Regulations for Matriculation was arranged for 18 February.

At that meeting there were twenty-two present, and the major division, over a motion that 'it is not desirable to diminish the number of subjects required . . . below the number required previously to February, 1873', was carried by twelve to eight. It is difficult to see any pattern of opposing organised groups in that vote, and perhaps the only realistic explanation is that the majority accepted some moderate, limited change, whereas those against were either opposed entirely to change, or wanted some further relaxation of the requirements. But there were Crown-chosen and Convocation-nominated Fellows, and representatives of different disciplines, on both sides.

In any event, there was no division on the further motion, which called for confirmation that Greek would no longer be compulsory, but that those who did not take Greek must take German; and that the examination in Heat be transferred from the Chemistry paper to the paper in Natural Philosphy. These changes meant that the new regulations called for candidates to be examined in Latin; in any two of Greek, French or German; in English Language, English History and Modern Geography; in Mathematics; in Natural Philosophy; and in Chemistry.

Convocation was gratified by the outcome. They welcomed the fact that the Senate had accepted some of their recommendations and had framed 'other Regulations substantially in accord' with their views. They pointed out that Matriculation had been 'carefully considered for several years past, both by Convocation and Senate', and hoped that there would be no need of further change 'for a considerable period'. In fact, there was another round of enquiry and discussion of change in the mid-1880s, initiated by Convocation, turning largely on continuing demand for a greater recognition of the mathematical and scientific subjects. Resulting changes, made in 1888, remained in force until the end of the century.

Debate on the content and standard of Matriculation would have broken out within the London commmunity, whether or not there had been any contemporary moves to introduce new, school leaving examinations, which should either be designed and administered by the University of London on its own or, on a wider scale, in co-operation with other universities. And it is unlikely that such negotiations as developed about those possibilities had much influence on the limited changes which were made to the 'London Matric'. The idea of new, school leaving examinations on a national scale was always overshadowed by consideration, still to be discussed, of the introduction of inspection of schools. But, for the record, it is worth describing, briefly, the exchanges which took place.

The first, extremely short-lived, attempt to raise the matter came five months after the Taunton Commission's Report was signed. On 2 June 1868, R.P.B. Taaffe, a Bart's man, moved in Convocation that it was desirable that London institute 'Middle Class Examinations similar to those of Oxford and Cambridge', which would have been quite separate from matriculation. But immediately the issue of priorities came up, in the form of an amendment to delay any such move 'until such time as an efficient system of inspection [of schools] has been devised'. The hour was late, there were insistent calls for adjournment, and the movers of the motion, and of the amendment, withdrew them. There is no record of further discussion of such ideas, by Convocation, for six years.

The idea of introducing inspection of schools, which will be detailed in the following chapter, had been developed strongly during the years of the Gladstone Government. In January, 1874, Convocation recommended the Senate to accept proposals of a Report on Secondary Education, which had been put together by Shaen, Magnus, Nesbitt, and Meadows. The main thrust of the proposals was to extend a first experiment in inspection of schools. But, perhaps because the same people who wrote it were still preoccupied with the attempts to change the Matriculation regulations, the report also pressed strongly the establishment, 'for all schools', of a 'Leaving-Examination'.

The case for such an examination was laid out succinctly:

> At the present time great difficulty is felt by schoolmasters in preparing small classes of boys for various examinations which are required previously to entrance upon professional life; as, for instance, the preliminary examinations for the Medical, Legal, and Military professions; and it is hoped that the new Leaving-Examinations will in course of time be accepted instead of such of these as are not competitive, so that Candidates could be prepared for them without any interference with the regular work of the schools.

The Committee, however, was firmly opposed to the new tests having any 'University value', though they accepted that many schools used Matriculation as a Leaving-Examination. They saw, clearly, the problem posed by the existence of two different school traditions:

> The chief difficulty in the way of our uniting in these Examinations with the Universities of Oxford and Cambridge appears to be that, although throughout the country an approach has of late years been made to what may be called the London system, by encouraging at schools the teaching of Natural Science and of Modern Languages, it still remains true that, as a general rule, those schools which prepare their pupils for Oxford and Cambridge give a much larger share of their attention to Classics, and a much smaller share to other subjects than those schools whose scholars proceed to graduation in London.

Optimistically, the report assumed that it would not be too difficult 'to frame a fairly uniform standard for these two classes of Schools', and then outlined what they felt should be the main features of a common system. The greater number of those features were straightforward provisions of an administrative nature. But they did include the fundamental proposal that 'The examinations should be divided into two branches; one adapted to pupils under sixteen, and the other adapted to pupils under eighteen years of age.'

The Senate's Examinations Committee went to work with a will to establish contact with Oxford and Cambridge: but the search for a workable agreement was to be in vain. Lubbock wrote to the Vice-Chancellor of Oxford, who was Chairman of the Oxford and Cambridge Schools Examination Board, on 26 March 1874. He asked if Oxford and Cambridge would be 'disposed to accept the co-operation of the University of London' in the preparation of a scheme whereby London 'should institute a System of Examination of Schools' which 'should eventually be open to the acceptance of all Schools throughout the kingdom, other than Primary'.

The response came at the end of November, 1874. The technical difficulty was seen by Oxford and Cambridge to be the provision whereby their examinations gave exemptions, to those who passed them and received Certificates, from the first examinations in the University courses at Oxford and Cambridge.

> These certificates, if granted with the concurrence of the University of London, would naturally be expected to confer a similar privilege in that University. But a comparison of the examinations in the three Universities as they are now arranged, seems to show that the certificates could hardly be made both to serve their present purpose at Oxford and Cambridge, and also to give exemption from the Matriculation Examination in the University of London.

But the major problems were, clearly, administrative and political. London was seen as envisaging a scheme on a scale which would threaten the relative autonomy of existing units. The Oxford and Cambridge Board had only limited jurisdiction, and had

> . . . not been empowered to enter so large a scheme as that which the University of London appears to have in view. A system of examinations extending to all schools throughout the kingdom, other than primary, would cover ground which has been occupied in part by the Oxford and Cambridge Local Examinations. The bodies which superintend these examinations are distinct from one another, and from the Board, and the Board could not interfere with them.

Moreover,

> The experiment of co-operation on the part of the Universities of Oxford and Cambridge is as yet in an early stage, and the Board hesitates to increase the practical difficulties which they encounter in carrying it out by adding a third centre of action to Oxford and Cambridge.

Senate had the disappointing correspondence with Oxford and Cambridge before them on 7 April 1875. They turned away from further consideration of new school-leaving examinations, and concentrated on finding a solution to the remaining problems in the way of introducing inspection of schools. The Annual Committee, however, refused to give up. Yet another sub-committee, with much the same membership as the previous one, worked throughout the summer and autumn of 1875. Driven by Magnus and Nesbitt, they produced a thirty-seven page report which spelt out a much more detailed set of proposals than those which they had produced in 1873. The Report covered both inspection of schools and new school-leaving examinations. But it took no account of the Senate's declared disapproval of any notion of giving University credit to candidates who passed a new examination, and ignored the fact that Oxford and Cambridge had refused to co-operate in part over the same problem.

A majority of the sub-committee must have pushed through a re-iteration and embellishment of a connection betweeen the projected school-leaving examination, and credit towards university degree requirements. But when the Report reached the Annual Committee on 26 November and 3 December 1875, it did not receive unanimous support. The Annual Committee must have recognised the difficulty which Senate would have in accepting a repetition of a theme they had already rejected: they therefore sent the report forward to Convocation, explaining diplomatically that

> Owing to the full and necessarily elaborate character of this Report your Committee have refrained from adopting it as a whole, and have limited themselves to approving the general principles embodied in it, and to accepting it as the basis of conference with the Senate.

What followed were decisions and discussions by and between Convocation and Senate which were to lead, by early 1877, to authorisation of a scheme for inspection of schools. But no progress was made on the introduction of any new school-leaving examinations. The report of Convocation's sub-committee had recommended a system of Junior and Senior Certificates, 'for those who do not propose, or who do not necessarily propose, to proceed to a Degree', and which, in the case of the Senior Certificates, would have involved a complex relationship with Matriculation. Senate was simply unwilling to entertain the proposal, but this did not deter those who had put it forward.

On 23 July 1879, the Senate also had before them another letter from Magnus to the Vice-Chancellor, pressing the expediency of the University introducing a system of Local Examinations similar to those already on offer by Oxford and Cambridge. This letter, like Magnus's earlier one of 1873, was referred to the Committee on Examinations: and as in 1873 that Committee reported unsympathetically to Senate a week later.

No more was heard on this score until January, 1882, when W.J. Spratling carried a resolution in Convocation 'That . . . the establishment of London University Local Examinations, similar to those conducted by the older Universities, is desirable.' Exactly a year later, Spratling persuaded Convocation to set up a Special Committee of six to consider the introduction of Local Examinations. The committee was chaired by Bompas, and included in its membership Richard Wormell – the last-named being Headmaster of the London Middle Class School which, as will be seen, had been inspected by London University from 1869 to 1877. They met five times between February and April, 1883, and produced a long report which was considered by Convocation on 8 May, and sent to the Annual Committee with an instruction that the Special Committee should continue their discussion of the proposals.

The Special Committee's report was the product of an enthusiasm for participation in the examination of pupils at an age well before any of them would be facing University entrance, and for the great majority who would not aspire to higher education. But by 1883 it must have been clear that this was an enthusiasm not shared by mainstream opinion in Senate or Convocation, which saw Matriculation as the lowest level at which the University should operate. The Special Committee had itself gone through arguments about introducing examinations at two levels, but had finally agreed to recommend a single examination for pupils under sixteen.

The Annual Committee handed the proposals to a sub-committee of seven, which included only Spratling from the Special Committee. They held nine meetings between June, 1883, and April, 1884, at several of which they dutifully consulted with other members of the Special Committee. But the sub-committee was seriously divided, and, on 5 March 1884, four of the seven declared, in an appendix to the draft report, that in their view 'the proposal is undesirable in the interests of the pupils, the Schoolmasters and the University'. Thus the final report was, in effect, a minority report which recommended a simplification of the original scheme, drew attention to potential problems of financing a programme of examinations, and agreed that candidates should be under sixteen years of age.

It is hardly surprising that there was little prospect of further progress. The Annual Committee's report to Convocation was received on 13 May 1884, when motions concerning the character of the examination and on some details of requirements were approved. But the suggestions on financing a programme were challenged and withdrawn. The most contentious matter was still the age of candidates. Magnus pressed for under sixteen: Nesbitt wanted the limit for boys to be seventeen and, for girls, eighteen. But the day was won, by a margin of twenty to thirteen, by a proposal that there should be no age limit.

No more was heard about Local Examinations until 1889, when Convocation sent a letter to Senate urging them, should a new Charter be in prospect, to ensure that power be sought to enable the University to introduce such examinations. But Senate seems not to have given the subject any consideration.

Despite the unshaken intention that the Matriculation Examination should remain a test of the abilities of those intending to study for degrees, it continued to attract increasing numbers of candidates who regarded it as a school-leaving qualification. In 1857, there were 266 candidates: in 1880 there were fourteen hundred: in 1900, 4341 sat the examination. In the same three years, the numbers of degrees awarded were 120, 189 and 472 – or 45 per cent, 13 per cent, and 11 per cent, respectively, of those sitting Matriculation. Clearly, in simplistic numerical terms, the biggest contribution to secondary education made by the University was the 'London Matric.'

# 18

# *Inspection of schools*

In the discussions which went on in the mid-nineteenth century about the advisability of introducing what came to be referred to, simply, as the inspection of schools, the process was frequently described as 'the examination and inspection of schools'. In some of the quotations which follow in this chapter, that phrase is reproduced. But elsewhere in the text, wherever possible, in order to avoid any confusion with the parallel arguments which were going on about the examination of school leavers, 'examination and inspection of schools' has been reduced to 'inspection'.

The earliest sign of the University's interest in the idea of inspecting schools came in the evidence of Carpenter, the Registrar, to the Taunton Commission, on 14 March 1865. He spoke as Registrar, though occasionally he admittted that he was expressing a personal opinion. But he gave such strong support, for both the routine inspection of schools and the examination of candidates for the profession of teaching, that he may well have had the blessing of senior members of the Senate. Carpenter was in favour of Government attestation, and stressed that the University of London was a Government institution. But he felt, along with most of the other witnesses, that the new work would best be done by the universities acting together.

The Commission agreed – 'The Universities, as being themselves institutions for education, are considered by the schoolmasters to be their natural centres.' And they recommended the establishment of a Council of Examinations, with twelve members, two from each of Oxford, Cambridge and London, together with six appointees of the Crown, 'to draw up rules and appoint examiners for examination of schools and for examination of candidates for the office of teacher'. But while the Commissioners were willing to propose action on testing the competence of those wishing to teach, they were not willing to recommend any scheme for the training of teachers.

The Taunton Commission did not report until the end of 1867. In the succeeding twelve months both Convocation and Senate gave their support to its recommendations, but such internal discussion as was reported centred mostly on the demands for the training and certification of teachers, rather than on concern for the inspection of schools. But Convocation did prepare a petition calling on Parliament to introduce early legislation for the improvement of secondary education. A draft of the petition was put before the Annual Committee on 4 December 1868. But on that very day, Gladstone was in the midst of constructing his first Cabinet, and within a few weeks the terms of the petition were substantially changed.

The new Liberal Government had a heavy programme of reforming legislation, entrusted in education to W.E. Forster, who found room in 1869 to introduce an Endowed Schools Bill which included clauses establishing the Educational Council recommended by the Schools Inquiry Commission, and authorising it to inspect schools and certify teachers. Publication of the Bill meant that the draft Petition of Convocation, which was approved by the Annual Committee's sub-committee on 19 February 1869, rubber-stamped by the Annual Committee a week later, and then routed to the Senate was, by then, already in some respects out-of-date. Senate met on 3 March and agreed to a joint meeting of the Committee on Examinations in Arts, Science and Laws, with the sub-committee of the Annual Committee. The inter-locking of memberships, and of views, was reflected in the group which met on 5 March – Grote, Osler and Ryan from the Senate; Storrar, Fagge and Shaen from Convocation. They were happy to amend the Petition 'into one in favour of the Endowed Schools Bill which Government had introduced in the House of Commons'. Senate approved the draft on 10 March; it was signed by Grote and Storrar and presented to Parliament on 15 March. Convocation blessed the Endowed Schools Bill at its meeting on 11 May, and instructed the Annual Committee to continue monitoring the situation.

But the hopes raised by the new Administration's legislative initiative were soon to be dashed. The early and major clauses of the Endowed Schools Bill dealt with the need to provide for a systematic review and re-casting of the constitutional and financial conditions of hundreds of schools. And the Bill itself had to compete for parliamentary time: it was sent to a Select Committee, and by the early summer had run into such difficulties that the last section, which dealt with the inspection of schools and the certification of teachers, was dropped, with the intention that it would be incorporated into a separate measure. The shortened Endowed Schools Bill reached the Statute Book: inspection of schools and certification of teachers simply faded from the parliamentary scene. At the end of 1872, Storrar gave notice of reminding the Senate that the Endowed Schools Act, 1869, would soon have to be renewed. He wanted the Senate to 'press on the attention of Government' the need to re-introduce the clauses of the original Bill which had been dropped. But no more was heard of his attempt.

The failure of Parliament to produce the necessary legislation meant that, if any action was to be taken to meet an apparently desirable development of inspection of secondary schools and certification of their teachers, it would have to come from non-governmental initiatives. So far as the University of London was concerned, its first relevant initiative came while the Endowed Schools Bill was still being debated. An approach was made by a body called the Corporation for Middle Class Education in the Metropolis and Suburbs, which had been founded 'with the co-operation and very liberal financial help of bankers and merchants of the City'.[1] It had been set up largely because of the initiative of the entreprenurial Rev. William Rogers, Rector of St Botolph's – known as 'Hang-Theology Rogers', because of his off-the-cuff impatience at denominational interference with his plans. The Corporation, operating under a Royal Charter of 1866, had established the London Middle Class School, as one of a group of institutions, in Bath Street – though about to move to Cowper Street – in Finsbury, and in the Spring of 1869 its Head-master, Rev William Jowitt, wrote to the Registrar.

Doubtless this approach must have been preceded by much informal discussion and by recommendations from members of the University community sympathetic to what the school was attempting. John Lubbock (whose father, incidentally, had been a Vice-Patron of the College of Preceptors) and G.J. Goschen, who had both joined the Senate in 1865, had been members of the committee headed by the Lord Mayor which had set up the school. And it is possible that Richard Wormell, a young London graduate who was teaching mathematics at the school, may already have been active in Convocation, though he only became a member of the Annual Committee in 1896. Wormell succeeded Jowitt as Headmaster in 1874, had a distinguished career there until 1900, and became President of the College of Preceptors. Certainly Rogers felt that the success of the school was 'pre-eminently due' to Jowitt and Wormell.[2]

Carpenter found both the Chancellor and Vice-Chancellor favourably inclined, and gave an encouraging reply. Jowitt was delighted 'that the University of London might be willing to throw its aegis over us', and spelt out his wishes:

> The scheme I should like to see carried out is that you should send (at our expense of course) some gentleman of experience in school work, of sympathy for our 'non-classical' system and for our unique position and difficulties, who would not only conduct by superintendence an Examination – bringing his own Assistants if desirable – but would also help by his judgement and advice in perfecting or establishing our present tentative arrangements.[3]

Jowitt's request was put before the Senate's Committee on Examinations, on 7 June 1869, and they commended the idea to the Senate. On the motion of Lords Kimberley and Stanley, the exercise was approved by Senate, on

[1] J. Avery, *Bishopsgate Schools 1702–1889* (London, 1932), p. 16.
[2] W. Rogers, *Reminiscences*, compiled by R.H. Hadden (London, 1888). For a brief account of the work of the Corporation for Middle Class Education, see Bryant, *The London Experience*, pp. 238–47.
[3] UL RO 1/2A/7 & 8, Carpenter to Jowitt, 27 May & 3 June 1869; UL ST 3/2/7, Jowitt to Carpenter, 26 May 1869.

condition that it would be regarded as experimental and renewable yearly, and that the Corporation should pay the University £50.[4] In fact, it became a regular event, and the only inspection undertaken by London, for eight years. The first visitation was carried out by Carpenter; Fitch (presumably in a private capacity, as he was by then an HMI); Charles Cassal, Professor of French at UCL; Dr E.J. Mills, a chemist who had tutored at the University of Glasgow and had just joined the Annual Committee; and a founder member of Convocation, John Purdue Bidlake.

In the years from 1870 to 1877 another seven examiners inspected the school, three of whom were University examiners and one, Rev. Philip Smith, another founder member of Convocation, had been Headmaster of Mill Hill School from 1853 to 1860. The experience gained over those eight years must have been influential when a wider scheme of inspection and examination came to be considered. That was not to happen until four years after 1869. But it is worth recording that, in 1869, there was established the Headmasters' Conference, a body with an important future as a representative group. At their Annual meetings, the Headmasters would develop and press for the acceptance of their ideas for inspection of schools and the establishment of nationally recognised leaving examinations for their pupils.

The Headmasters' ideas were picked up by sympathetic but critical enthusiasts in Convocation. But the first indication of interest did not appear in the records until 21 January 1873, when there was an inconclusive debate on a motion which declared

> ... that this University should take a more active part in Secondary Education, and that to this end it would be preferable to inaugurate a system of inspection of Private Schools rather than an Examination of Pupils.

This reference to a choice of alternative possibilities no doubt reflected argument going on, perhaps within the Annual Committee, which had been charged with promoting the University's concern for the improvement of secondary education. Doubtless there would have been different views about what should have priority, but the motion certainly shows an awareness of inspection as a significant exercise.

Within a month of that debate, Magnus wrote to the Senate, suggesting that the University should take up inspection. Whether Magnus's letter, and sketch of his general scheme, was sent with the knowledge and informal blessing of the Annual Committee must remain a matter for conjecture. Senate received it on 12 February and referred it to the Committee on Examinations.

---

[4] Minute Book of the Corporation, 16 June 1869. I am obliged to Penny Herterich, Clerk to the Governors and Trustees of the Central Foundation Schools of London, for making this available.

But only a couple of days afterwards, on 14 March 1873, Shaen and Weymouth persuaded the Annual Committee to set up a sub-committee to follow 'the recent and pending action of the [Headmasters'] Conference'. That sub-committee was to sit during the rest of the year, and had a conscientious membership. As early as 27 March, on the initiatives of Magnus, Meadows, Nesbitt and Fagge, they recommended to the Annual Committee that the University should 'unite with other Universities in undertaking the Examination and Inspection of Schools', and that the University should frame a draft scheme 'which might serve as a basis of negotiation with other Universities'.

With the more intensive discussion of the content of Matriculation taking most of the attention of both Senate and Convocation, it is not surprising that there was no further reference to inspection until 26 May, when the Committee on Examinations met to discuss Magnus's letter. Those attending included three who had served in June, 1869, when hopes of a governmentally inspired programme of inspection were disappointed. The new Vice-Chancellor, Lubbock, was joined by Heywood, Hutton, Osler, Smith and Storrar: they appreciated

> ... the importance of the subject, and would be disposed to recommend the Senate to entertain favourably any request for inspection, [but] they are not as yet prepared to recommend any general scheme of the kind proposed by Mr Magnus.

Undeterred, the Annual Committee's sub-committee produced, as we have seen earlier, a report on Secondary Education which was accepted by Convocation on 20 January 1874, when Convocation resolved, unanimously,

> ... that the University of London should without delay, and if possible in conjunction with the Universities of Oxford and Cambridge, frame a scheme for the Inspection and Examination of Schools for both sexes and offer such Scheme to the acceptance of all schools ... other than Primary.

Storrar presented this resolution and the report to Senate. On 18 February the Senate referred both to the Examinations Committee who were directed to report on the 'desirability, and if desirable with the best mode, of carrying out the views of Convocation'. This warm endorsement reflected not only the quality of Convocation's report, but the continuing general concern for the future of secondary education, and in particular the need, as the report put it,

> ... to facilitate co-operation with Oxford and Cambridge, which have already proceeded some way in preparing a scheme and expressed their readiness to work it jointly with other Universities.

The leading members of the team which put together the Convocation report were Shaen, Magnus, Nesbitt and Meadows. The report took account of the fact that the University of London 'has already, on several occasions, examined one important London school', and felt that 'the time has now arrived for this University to take a fair share in what appears likely to become a great national movement'.

But the negotiations with Oxford and Cambridge were no more successful in the context of inspection than they were in the context of school-leaving examinations, and almost a year passed before their failure was admitted. Once that happened, in April, 1875, Senate was still unwilling to do more than declare that Convocation's proposals on inspection were still under consideration. Another sub-committee of the Annual Committee then produced a second report, as recorded in the previous chapter: but it was not fully acceptable to its parent body, mainly because of doubts about the proposals on school-leaving examinations. As we have seen, at the end of 1875, the Annual Committee sent the report to Convocation, cautiously approving its general principles and 'accepting it as the basis of conference with the Senate'.

Storrar felt able, as a result of this action by the Annual Committee, to give notice in Senate on 15 December 1875 that he would move to request a conference between the Examinations Committee and the Annual Committee, using the report of the sub-committee as the basis for discussion. The conference was authorised on 26 January 1876, and there followed four meetings between deputations from the Annual Committee and the Examinations Committee of the Senate. The outcome was a report by the Examinations Committee to the Senate on 26 April, which was adopted, and which committed the University to establishing its own system of inspection.

The Examinations Committee paid tribute to 'the singular thoroughness and ability of the Report of the Sub-Committee' of Convocation's Annual Committee. They 'generally concur[red]' in its recommendation

> ... that the University should undertake the Examination and Inspection from time to time of any schools, other than primary, which may apply for such Examination or Inspection, provided that the cost to be incurred be paid when the application is made ... There is a large and daily increasing number of schools, either bound by their legal constitution, or impelled by their teachers' desire of standing well with the public, to undergo annually the examination and criticism of some external authority, but unable at present to obtain the assistance of this kind which they require, and which the University if well fitted to supply; and your Committee would be extremely reluctant that the University of London should renounce the influence over the course of education which the exercise of such functions involves.

But as earlier, the Senate was unwilling to adopt the more far-reaching commitments and the more complicated proposals of the Convocation men. They were not prepared

> ... to adopt the suggestion ... that the University should take the responsibility of stamping particular schools with its approval, or of giving them a peculiar *status* as 'in connexion with the University.' The difficulties first of fixing a standard and then of ascertaining that the standard has been attained, and still more that a school once recognized has kept up to the standard, appear ... to be too serious to encounter, at all events with any means now at the disposal of the University.

And Senate refused to accept the idea of appointing a Board to carry out the new work, 'comprising Members of Convocation not having seats on the Senate,' because they did not think any new machinery was needed to undertake the limited system of inspection which they were ready to support.

Having made their decision, Senate directed the Examinations Committee to produce a relevant scheme of 'conditions and regulations', which were in due course approved on 28 February 1877.

The inspection of schools introduced in 1877, however significant qualitatively, developed only on a very moderate scale. Under the regulations, the reports of the inspectors and examiners were to be made to the schools and copies filed in the Registrar's office. There is, today, no sign of them in the University's archives, though the Central Foundation School for Boys, which is the successor to the London Middle Class School, has some of the reports, and it is likely that some other schools may have saved them.

The London Middle Class School in Cowper Street had been accepted for inspection in 1869, and was overseen by the University each year until 1876. The only other school to request similar attention before 1877 was the North London Collegiate, which applied in 1876. Neither school made application after 1876. Between 1877 and 1900 some fifty schools were inspected, but the ideal of annual visitation was very rarely achieved for more than short periods. Altogether, between 1877 and 1900, there were nearly two hundred visitations – an average of a little less than ten per year, with a maximum of twelve in each of five years, four of them in the 1890s. Only two schools in Bedford – the Crescent House School and the Bedford Modern School (which was singled out for much praise by the Royal Commission on Technical Education in 1884) – were inspected in twenty-two and twenty years, respectively, between 1878 and 1900. The Caterham Valley School, the Stroud Green High School for Girls, and the Lewisham Grammar School for Girls, each applied a dozen times. But most schools only asked for inspection over periods of about five to seven years, and no less than seventeen were visited on three occasions or less.

The University appointed no less than twelve inspectors for the London Middle Class School alone, between 1869 and 1876. But from the introduction of the new regulations in 1877, until 1900, only twenty-two were appointed. By far the most active was E.E. Pinches, who conducted twenty-seven visits: R.H. Belcher and T. Randell made seventeen each; J. Lawrence and W.K. Hill each were employed for twelve; Philip Magnus and G.T. Moody each inspected on ten occasions. Four of the twenty-two were University examiners.

The Registrar took on the administration of the scheme as part of his general duties, and answered to a Committee on the Examination and Inspection of Schools, which was re-appointed each session, and rarely met more than once a year. It began as, and was for most years, a committee of five, but it doubled in size for a short time in the early 1880s. Over the twenty-two years, some score of Fellows served, but attendance by most of them was minimal: the working core of the committee was made up of Fitch, who was a member throughout, Hutton, William Smith and Storrar. Three of those were Convocation-nominated Fellows. Lubbock was a member for many years, but rarely attended: the two ex-Registrars, Carpenter and Milman, no doubt added strength, and Magnus was a member in the late 1890s.

Inspection brought the University into close contact with schools, but it never became as widespread as a quite different kind of participation in secondary education – the practice of appointing members of the governing bodies of schools. As a kind of coda to this chapter, it is worth recording some of the early instances of the practice, and some episodes which illustrate how much there continued to be a need to re-assert the non-discriminatory character of the University and to insist on recognition of its independence.

The first episode developed from a suggestion by the Special Commissioners who had been appointed under the Public Schools Act, 1868, to re-draft the instruments of governance of the major public schools. As John Shaw Lefevre was one of those Commissioners, it may be that he had helped to persuade his colleagues that the University of London should be authorised to appoint one member of the governing body of each of Winchester, Rugby, Harrow and Charterhouse.

This proposal must have reached the University late in 1869, and there is no indication that Convocation were immediately aware of it. But the Senate took a firm position at their meeting on 1 December. The proposal provided that whoever the University appointed must be a member of the Church of England. The Senate resolved that 'it would be contrary to the principles and practice of the University to make any inquiry into the religious opinions of persons whom they appoint to any office'. And they felt sufficiently strongly as to authorise and send to the Privy Council, in March 1870, a memorial protesting the form of the proposed statute of the Commissioners. At their annual meeting on 10 May, Convocation thanked and supported the Senate for their action.

The University's stand was followed, later in the year, by negotiations which led to a withdrawal of the original proposal. New statutes for Charterhouse and Rugby provided for London appointees without reference to religious affiliation. Winchester and Harrow were apparently unwilling to accept any non-Anglicans, and London appointees were not included in their governing bodies.

Another development, perhaps closer to the hearts of the London community, came in the autumn of 1870, when there was a proposal, dependent on the attitude of the Endowed Schools Commissioners, that London should appoint a member of the new governing body of the Bedford Charity. This moved the Annual Committee to express their pleasure that 'a beginning has been made in bringing the influence of the University to bear upon Secondary Education'. As we have seen, two Bedford Schools were later to be inspected by the University. But there were still obstacles in London's way. Two years afterwards the Senate felt it was necessary to ask the Vice-President of the Council to ensure that new legislation would ensure that London graduates were eligible for the headmasterships of Public and endowed schools.

But while the Senate was alert to the need to protect the University and its graduates from any hint of undue religious influence or discrimination, they showed themselves to be open-minded in their choice of school governors – their first appointee to Rugby was a future Archbishop of Canterbury – Frederick Temple. John Storrar, Chairman of Convocation, became the University's appointee to Bedford School. The practice of nominating members of school governing bodies spread rapidly.

# 19

# Training the teachers: qualifications and registration

With the achievement of a modified Matriculation syllabus, the introduction of inspection of secondary schools, and the admission of women as candidates for degrees, those pushing for an improved education system could concentrate on two last major demands – the acceptance of Education as a subject of University study, and the award, to those who undertook it, of formal qualifications for teaching: and the registration of teachers, which had been promised in Forster's Bill of 1869, but not achieved a decade later.

The first shot in the campaign (other than the futile attempt by John Robson to have the notion raised in Annual Committee, fifteen years earlier) was aimed directly at the Senate, on 22 May 1877, and was fired by the Heads of the North London Collegiate School and of Cheltenham Ladies' College – Frances Mary Buss and Dorothea Beale. They, writing for themselves and for fourteen other Head Mistresses of Endowed and Proprietary Schools which shared almost five thousand pupils, memorialised the Senate,

> . . . in favour of the establishment by the University of an Examination of Teachers above the grade of Elementary School Teachers, with the view of certifying their professional competency.

The memorial expressed succinctly the argument which was eventually to carry the day:

> We believe that, under the present conditions of higher education in England, the offer of any means of professional training will prove quite inadequate to induce those preparing to become higher-grade Teachers, unless they have a prospect of obtaining, through examination by a competent authority, certificates of qualification of sufficient value to ensure to the holders of them a compensating advantage in the competition for educational employment. This can only be done either by the Government or by the Universities. We believe the Universities . . . to be the fittest authority to test the qualification of Teachers intending to give such instruction; and we are of opinion that a Certificate or Diploma given by them would alone command the confidence requisite for currency.

The Senate referred the memorial to the Examinations Committee, but there is no record of any action by the Committee in that or the following session. Ten months later, a letter expressing similar sentiments was sent by the College of Preceptors, and was also referred to the Examinations Committee by the Vice-Chancellor. Again, there was no early response. Senate must also have been aware of the desire expressed by the Headmasters' Conference for the introduction of training schemes, and of the submission of such a scheme to the Universities of Oxford and Cambridge, both of which, by 1878, had made arrangements to introduce relevant examinations and award certificates of proficiency. Moreover, the Universities of Edinburgh and St Andrews had recently established Professorships of Education.

Nor was there formal recognition of any approaches made to Convocation in 1877 and 1878. But at a meeting of that body in January, 1879, Magnus and Nesbitt moved 'That it is desirable that the Senate should institute examinations in the Theory and Practice of Education, open to graduates of the University.' It was defeated on a show of hands, but an amendment by Shaen and Weymouth, calling for the Annual Committee 'to consider and report on the subject of examinations in the Theory and Practice of Education', was approved. When the Annual Committee met, ten days later, Magnus, with the support of Andrew McDowall and John Curnow, carried the setting up of a sub-committee.

Magnus's sub-committee was well attended, and organised the gathering of evidence from a variety of educational sources, including Training Colleges. They agreed, as early as the middle of February, that if practical difficulties could be overcome, it was desirable that examinations in Education be instituted; that candidates should have had some recent teaching experience in a recognised school or Training College; that they should be graduates in Arts and Science of the University of London – thus disfranchising graduates in Law, Medicine and Music who had not taken a BA; and that a Special Certificate should be awarded to those who passed. McDowall was entrusted with the drawing up of a scheme, which he undertook with the help of Ely.

The sub-committee's proposals came before the Annual Committee on 21 April 1879, and were only slightly amended before acceptance. Their report argued, at some length, the desirability of introducing 'the examination of Teachers in the Theory, History and Practice of Education'. They hoped that the new examinations 'may possibly pave the way for the establishment of some generally recognised qualifying test of efficiency', and stressed the importance of that in the context of the hoped-for legislation to introduce registration.

Early in 1879, Lyon Playfair, with the support of John Lubbock and two other MPs, had brought in a Private Member's Bill to provide for the Organisation and Registration of Teachers engaged in Intermediate Education in England and Wales, containing arrangements which were similar to what had been originally included in the Endowed Schools Bill of 1869. W.E. Forster was reported as having the same sort of interest, and there was some confidence that Playfair would 'meet with the support of the leading members on [Forster's] side of the House'. But as Playfair had not 'obtained a day for the second reading' by April, it was seen as unlikely that the Bill would gain 'even a full discussion in the present session'. That forecast was borne out by events, for the Bill was withdrawn on 30 July, having been 'ousted . . . by the Sunday Liquor Traffic Bill'. But it was clear that the proposal had received a mixed reception, and Forster later expressed his disagreement on several aspects of Playfair's scheme.[1]

While Playfair's Bill was making no progress, the Annual Committee modified the submission of its sub-committee. There is no evidence of wide divisions of opinion, but, at the Annual Committee, Kisch and Weymouth moved successfully for further consideration of that section of the first draft which read:

> The Certificates granted on the result of such examination will carry with them a value, as evidence of efficiency and culture in education, of the kind which the MB and the LLB degrees connote with regard to Medicine and Law; and the general recognition of this fact will tend to raise the social and professional status of teachers by placing their calling on the same footing with other professions.

Whether or not this seemed either unrealistic, or misleading, or too threatening to the established sense of legal and medical superiority, the result of further consultation was the excision of any mention of Law and Medicine. The introduction of examinations was seen, in the final version, as

> . . . the means of creating a class of teachers of higher intelligence, and of superior culture, and better qualified to discharge the several duties of their profession . . . The certificates . . . would tend to raise the social and professional status of Teachers by placing their calling on the same footing with other professions.

The detailed scheme of examination followed, but it was the last suggestion of the Report which was to cause discord when it reached Convocation. There is no record of whether the sub-committee was divided, nor was there any division in Annual Committee, on the matter, which was described with admirable clarity in the Report:

> Your Committee further considered the question, whether it would be advisable to recommend the Senate to confer a new educational degree . . . or merely to grant a certificate. The analogy of the medical, legal, and music degrees, and the urgent memorial on this subject, presented by the College of Preceptors, were considered . . . as arguments in favour of an educational degree. But on the other hand it was urged that the multiplication of degrees is in itself undesirable, that a great part of the qualifications for this Degree is included in the B.A. and B.Sc. Degrees, one of which the Candidate would be required previously to obtain; that such a course

---

[1] *Jnl of Education*, March, April, August, September 1879.

might lead to a demand for Degrees in other departments of knowledge; and lastly, that the measure is in itself tentative, and that if found advisable a special degree could later on be instituted.

The adoption of the following resolution is, therefore, recommended to Convocation:

That candidates who pass the examination in Education
shall be arranged alphabetically in two classes, and
shall receive a special certificate.

When Convocation met on 13 May 1879, Magnus and McDowall were able to carry, easily, motions endorsing the desirability of the University's introducing examinations of teachers in the Theory, History and Practice of Education; and also the notion that only London graduates in Arts and Science should be eligible to take the examinations. But when they moved for support of the idea of Special Certificates in two classes, they lost by one vote. It is uncertain how many members were present, but the division was twenty-six to twenty-five, and the victory went to those who either felt that a degree was preferable to a certificate, or who wanted no examination in Education to be introduced. Of the fifty-one voters, forty-two had BAs, of whom four had also taken LLBs; two had become DScs; and four were medical graduates. Of the remaining nine, four were lawyers and five were doctors. But the distribution of qualifications on both sides was not dissimilar, with the 'straight' BAs divided seventeen to eighteen, the lawyers three to five, the medicos five to one, in favour of the certificates; while the two DScs were opposed.

This close vote was followed, immediately, by a compromise which was, apparently, carried without division. It was proposed by Weymouth and Nesbitt and called for the offer of a degree or the addition of 'a fourth branch in which the MA may be taken, co-ordinate with the three existing branches Classics, Mathematics and Philosophy'.[2]

Convocation's recommmendation was not before the Senate on the following day, 14 May 1879, but on the table was a second memorial from Miss Buss and her colleagues, very similar to the first, but now claiming that the schools represented by the Association of Headmistresses had eight thousand pupils, as opposed to five thousand in 1877. This memorial was also passed to the Examinations Committee, and may well have been considered when that Committee met only five days later. It reported to Senate on 18 June, but the findings were not printed.

Given the voting record of several members of the Examinations Committee on the issue, before and after, it is highly likely that a majority

[2] J.V. Chapman, *Professional Roots. The College of Preceptors in British Society* (London, 1985), pp. 114–16.

were sympathetic, in principle, to the position taken by Convocation and by Miss Buss and her colleagues. But that position would not be readily conceded by its opponents. On 18 June, two conflicting Notices of Motion were announced: Fitch would ask Senate to authorise the Examinations Committee to report on the practicability of introducing an Examination in the Theory and Practice of Education, and to produce a Draft Scheme of such Examination; Blakesley, the Dean of Lincoln, would move against such introduction. When those motions were put before the Senate on 23 July, Fitch carried the day by thirteen to five.

So distinct a step as appeared to have been taken in July, 1879, raises expectation that further progress would have been made relatively quickly. But in fact the Examinations Committee decided to delay for more consideration, and the delay extended for no less than eighteen months. The Committee, which met ten times between July, 1879 and February, 1881, was concerned 'in particular to observe the working of the experiment . . . tried at Cambridge, in which University the first Examination in the History, Theory and Practice of Teaching took place', in July, 1880. There is no indication of how much time was spent, and how much division of opinion there was, within the Committee, on the question of the introduction of an Examination in Education. A score of Senators attended those meetings, but only nine of them were present on five or more occasions; of them, Fitch and Hutton appeared nine times, Osler seven, and Storrar six.

But after so long a delay, there was almost certainly a clear majority of attending members of the Examinations Committee sympathetic to the idea of a new Examination, by the beginning of 1881, when they produced a report whose recommendations were very close to those made by Convocation on 13 May 1879. It was presented to Senate on 16 February 1881, and was debated on 30 March. During the whole period since the Convocation meeting of May, 1879, there is no record of any comment by the Annual Committee or by Convocation in full session, on the progress – or lack of progress – of the Senate's consideration of the issue. A possible explanation of this silence is offered later.

The Examinations Committee were of opinion that the establishment of an Examination in the History, Theory and Practice of Teaching was practicable. They sketched its desirable content, and recommended that candidates who passed a written and practical test should not receive degrees but should be awarded Special Certificates to be called Teachers' Diplomas. They felt that the Examination should be open to any London graduates, which was less restrictive than Convocation's wish to limit candidacy to BAs and BScs: but they widened the field of entry by suggesting that, in addition to graduates, any one who had passed the First Examination for BA or BSc, or who had passed in Honours at Matriculation, should be accepted as candidates.

There were twenty present at Senate on 30 March 1881, and there is no record of the discussion of the Examination Committee's report. Nor is there any sign of a division. The Senate resolved to accept the basic idea of instituting a Special Certificate called a Teacher's Diploma, but ruled that only London graduates could be candidates. And they sent the matter back to the Examinations Committee for the preparation of detailed regulations. Such regulations were drafted, approved and sent to the Home Secretary for his authorisation by the end of November, 1881, when it was decided that the first Examination for the Diploma would be held in 1883.

The Registrar's letter to the Home Office spelt out at some length the history of the Senate's conversion to the view that a Teacher's Diploma was desirable, amd emphasised the support of Convocation and the pressure which had been brought to bear by the College of Preceptors, the Association of Headmasters of Endowed and Proprietary Schools, the Headmasters' Conference, 'and many other bodies or persons having a general and professional interest in obtaining a proper guarantee for the qualifications of Teachers'. And in commenting on the Senate's decision to wait on the experience of the Cambridge examination in July, 1880, before coming to their final conclusion, the Registrar reveals a good deal about the inherent caution, the exclusivity and the confidence of the University:

> It is true that the examination at Cambridge was by no means confined to Graduates or Members of that University, and that the Senate, in conformity with its invariable rule, proposes to limit the examinations of this University to its own members, in this case to its Graduates. But on the other hand probably a far larger proportion of the Graduates of the University of London in the Faculties of Arts and Science are engaged in teaching than of those of the older Universities; and an increasing number of Headmasterships in the Schools reorganized under the Endowed Schools Act, especially of Science Masterships, are year by year obtained by London Graduates.[3]

If there was any worry about the reaction of the Home Secretary, it was soon laid to rest. The Office file bears no comment other than a direction to approve, which was implemented in the following month. The Annual Committee reported what the Senate had done, in the simplest of terms and without comment, to the Annual Meeting of Convocation, on 9 May 1882.

From 1883 until 1899, the Teacher's Diploma attracted, on average, each year, only six candidates, of whom five passed. The biggest entry was in 1893, when there were ten candidates, all but one of whom were successful. Altogether, there were ninety-five candidates, of whom seventy-seven passed the examination. Almost two-thirds of those who obtained the Diploma were women, and roughly the same proportion were graduates who were either enrolled as students of, or teachers at Training Colleges, or University Colleges.

---

[3] HO 45/9614/A10970, Milman to Harcourt, 28 November 1881.

We can now look back to the long silence of Convocation on the subject, after May, 1879. It may be that Convocation was convinced that the institution of a special qualification for teachers had been accepted by the Senate, in effect, at that time; or that they recognised the wisdom of waiting to see how the pioneering examination turned out at Cambridge in July, 1880; and that thereafter they were made happy by their informal understanding of how the Senate's Examination Committee was likely to frame their recommendations. And it is possible that, as a result of one or more of these factors, Convocation felt that there was no further need to apply pressure. This could be the main reason for the absence of debate, though it has been claimed that after the Senate's refusal to consider the award of an MA in Education, 'The steam went out of the movement.'[4]

But it is also arguable that Convocation simply put the teachers' qualification aside while they turned their attention to further attempts to re-open the issues of Local Examinations and the registration of teachers. Their discussion of those issues came to nothing, but the concern for registration is worth recording.

There is no sign that when Lubbock, then Vice-Chancellor, joined Playfair in the attempt to launch a Bill to introduce registration of teachers, he had either informed or consulted Senate, officially, or had responded to Senate concern for registration. A few months later, at the General Election of 1880, Lubbock lost his West Kent seat in April, resigned the Vice-Chancellorship in May (though retaining his Fellowship), and was then elected, as the University's representative, in June. Within a few weeks of his re-election, he had taken over the sponsorship of the Bill, now providing for the Registration and Organisation of Teachers, and submitted it in the names of himself, Playfair and Arthur Balfour, on 3 August. But the Bill's second reading was dropped when the session ended in September. It became known that Lubbock would try to re-introduce the Bill in the following session.

It was only at this point that Convocation showed interest. On 12 November 1880, Nesbitt and Weymouth persuaded the Annual Committee to set up a sub-committee to consider Lubbock's Bill. They reported on 3 December, when their report was received, considered, amended and adopted by Annual Committee. Nesbitt and Magnus then carried a motion recommending Convocation to approve the general principles of Lubbock's Bill and asking that the Annual Committee should confer with Senate if the Bill was re-introduced into Parliament.

Senate never broke its silence on the matter, but Convocation met and considered the report from Annual Committee, on 18 January 1881. Debate was cut short by a motion to adjourn. It was becoming clear that Lubbock's Bill was hotly opposed in some quarters. The Headmasters' Conference did not want the inclusion of powers to inspect schools, and criticised the method

---

[4] Chapman, *Professional Roots*, p. 117.

of financing the operation by the imposition of fees. And the inclusion of Elementary Teachers in the scheme of registration was widely unwelcome – Lubbock's strategy was later criticised for not having been concentrated on Secondary Teachers only.[5]

The Bill was scheduled for a second reading on 11 May. On the previous day, at the Annual Meeting of Convocation, when Nesbitt and Magnus moved 'That it is desirable that there should be an Act providing for the registration of teachers', they were unable to hold the interest of members, and the House moved to the next item. As it happened, the House of Commons were no more sympathetic: there was no Second Reading, and the Bill was withdrawn on 19 July, without ever having been debated. The University was not involved in any further discussion of registration during the rest of the century.

While Convocation made more dramatic excursions into some other aspects of the University's development between 1858 and 1900, it might fairly be argued that their efforts in connection with secondary education showed their capacity to work with the Senate at its best. Philip Magnus claimed that 'At that time the reforming body in the university was Convocation',[6] and, insofar as secondary education was concerned, he and his colleagues led – though not without some intensive argument among themselves first – while Senate tended to follow their lead, admittedly exercising considerable restraint on the more radical proposals. It was a constructive partnership, without the more difficult confrontations which occurred in some other areas of the University's life.

[5] *Jnl of Education*, January, February, April, July 1881.
[6] Sir Philip Magnus, *Educational Aims and Efforts 1880–1910* (London, 1910), p. 53.

# Part VI

*Examining and Teaching – the Long and Crooked Road to Compromise*

# 20

# The case for change

Despite the growing numbers of candidates for its examinations, and its extension of offerings, by the mid-1870s serious questions were being raised about the long-term future of the University of London. This questioning was preliminary to what developed into a major struggle, which began in earnest in 1884, after the Senate's apparent disinclination to contemplate any significant degree of change, and was to continue until practically the end of the century. Before attempting any narrative and analysis of that struggle, it is as well to offer a brief overview of the major issues and the parties involved.

In a strictly academic context, the overwhelming question which hung over the University of London was whether it really could justify being called a university at all. It was an examining board, whose matriculation examination was widely used at secondary level as a school-leaving qualification. And to those who matriculated and passed its more advanced examinations successfully, it awarded degrees. It did not teach, and since 1858, save for candidates for medical degrees, who had to attend recognised medical schools, its examinations were open to anyone over defined age limits, irrespective of how they prepared themselves – whether by attending courses at institutions, or by purely private study, or by a mixture of the two. The sole research activity of the University began only in 1871, at the Brown Animal Sanatory Institution, and had little or no connection with the examining function.

The arguments about the merits of open examinations as a means of encouraging candidates whose social and personal circumstances preclude them from attendance at orthodox teaching establishments are not peculiar to the nineteenth century. But in the case of the University of London, the abandonment of the pre-1858 practice, which had required all candidates, not only those taking medical examinations, to have attended recognised educational institutions, exacerbated the controversy about the quality of the achievement of those who received the rounded education claimed for collegiate study, as compared with that of those unattached examinees who, allegedly, had experienced only narrow 'cramming' in order to pass specific tests. The political overtones of that debate were obvious enough in an era of persistent demand for a broader franchise, for non-discrimination on religious grounds, and for social and educational improvement, all set against a background of enormous population growth.

But the principal grumble of those who wanted change in the examinations context was the absence of any organised liaison between the Senate, which authorised and approved the syllabuses, the examiners who set and marked the papers, and the teachers who prepared candidates for degrees. The University employed examiners on relatively short-term contracts, and the great majority of them were teachers and scholars, the best and brightest of whom were operating at the forefront of knowledge. Increasingly it was felt by the latter that the Senate had too few members with experience as teachers; that too few of those Fellows who were, or had been teachers, had practical and up-to-date knowledge of subject matter; and that at least some examiners were not sufficiently in touch with current intellectual developments. But for a high proportion of the Fellows and the graduates, the separation of examining from teaching, in order to prevent collusion and to guarantee standards, was regarded as essential. There was a widespread suspicion of teachers, in the words of a Scottish peer, 'branding their own herrings'.

Leaders in the medical profession generally agreed with their colleagues in other faculties about the need to bring teachers and examiners into closer co-operation. But they had additional and quite specific criticisms of the University. Its output of medical graduates was a mere fraction of those who were entering practice; partly because the Senate's policy had been to produce a scientific medical elite by keeping the standard of the degrees very high; and partly because of the introduction of stiff preliminary science examinations which a high proportion of candidates failed. There was also a widely held view in the profession that all medical practitioners should be called Doctors, but that the London MD was reserved for only a highly trained minority. There was great pressure, therefore, to widen the recruitment of candidates, to relax the perceived obstacles to entry, and to find a way of accommodating the desire of practitioners to have a qualification which would entitle them, formally, to be known by the title which they were given, informally, by the general public. And if the University of London could not or would not oblige, then other institutions should be permitted to provide alternative and additional medical qualifications.

What might be called the academic arguments for change were thus concentrated on the weakness of an examination system brought about by the virtual separation of examining from teaching. And the basic solution was seen as the combination of the two functions within a single institutional framework which would give much more influence to teachers. This indicates the growth and increasing self-confidence of the teachers, both at university and school level. The whole controversy over the future of London University reflected the sheer increase in teaching as an occupation, and the advance of a more aggressive academic professionalism. Among these teachers, there was an accompanying distrust of traditional lay elements:

. . . not even examiners in the constitution of the University are entrusted with control over the examinations. The administration lies with the Senate, a body appointed partly by the Government, partly by – of all people in the world – the body of graduates. It consists chiefly of eminent men who are, in all that concerns the educational profession, amateurs. The examiners, many of them also eminent, not only have no voice in the administration, but have no official standpoint even from which to tender advice in concert.[1]

The teachers' case was strengthened by the rise of demand for instruction and research in the natural sciences. By the end of the century, the number of candidates graduating in science exceeded the number taking the traditional BA. Those who led the scientific advance were particularly aware of the need for larger scale laboratory facilities, both for teaching and research, and saw the likelihood that such demands would be more likely to be provided in larger, inclusive university institutions.

To the ambitions of teachers, doctors and scientists, must be added the resentment of Londoners – or, to be more precise, London teaching institutions, professional organisations, and many of those specially concerned about educational provision for the capital. The existing University served not only the whole country; its examinations were being used, increasingly, in the colonies. It had become, in fact, a National and an Imperial institution. But London, which housed numerous colleges and medical schools, had no degree-granting institution to call its own. And metropolitan educational pride was especially hurt from 1880 onwards, when the Victoria University was set up, bringing Owens College in Manchester, and its equivalents in Leeds and Liverpool, into a federal relationship. As all three were teaching institutions, the University of London's isolation as a narrow examining board was felt more keenly. The City of London showed some sporadic concern for various educational institutions and, as will be seen, came near close involvement with the University in the mid-1890s. But when the London County Council was established in 1889, civic pride, combined with the urge to improve educational along with other social provision, moved many of its members to add pressure to, and to offer financial support for, a genuinely metropolitan university.

By the middle 1880s there was clear evidence of the existence of dissatisfaction with the role of the University, and of wide agreement that there should be change which would accommodate the desire to have teaching, examining, the award of degrees, and the encouragement of research brought together in an institution which would, primarily or even exclusively, serve London. Inevitably, this raised a fundamental issue: should that university be the existing University of London, suitably modified? Or should it be a

---

[1] Sir George Young, President of the Senate of UCL, in a paper given to a Conference on Education at South Kensington in August, 1884, reproduced in Allchin I, fn to pp. 66–7.

totally separate venture, operating alongside the existing University, which would be left to carry on its present operation, as the provider of examinations and degrees, to candidates who were either prepared for them in institutions outside London, or by studying privately?

The first alternative – a combined institution – raised what was to be seen as perhaps the most difficult question of all – was it possible to achieve equality of standards of assessment for 'internal' students attending orthodox courses of instruction, and for 'external' students who prepared for examination by a variety of methods and in a variety of places, at home and abroad. It was, to some extent, another round of the controversy of the late 1850s – collegiate preparation or open entry. It focussed attention on what should be the relationship of colleges offering higher education in London, particularly University and King's Colleges, to the existing University. And it should be remembered, in that context, that the old, pre-1858 colleges who had been formally 'affiliated' to the University had stayed 'on the books' for years, though they no longer enjoyed any special privileges.

The subsequent long drawn-out debate and manoeuvre, and the eventual outcome, involved Parliament, Government, and two Royal Commissions. In the often impassioned arguments of the contemporary educationists, it sometimes seems that they tended to forget that the University was itself a small Government department, and to take too little account of the fact that Governments rarely fail to look after their own. The University's affairs came within the ambits of the Home Office, the Treasury and the Privy Council. Ministers and ex-Ministers were always to be found on the Senate, and, as will be seen, the future of the University on occasion reached the Prime Minister and the Cabinet.

This book is primarily concerned with the relations between the Senate and Convocation of the University of London, but it is impossible to write meaningfully about that relationship, in this context, without taking account of the fact that, within the world of education itself, the future of the University was a matter of persistent controversy. Numerous institutions were involved, some with quite specific and uncomplicated intentions; others at best ambivalent and at worst utterly split over their objectives. The whole scenario was made no easier to describe or understand by the fact that many of the leading people were members, simultaneously, of several of the concerned institutions, which were on no small number of occasions at loggerheads.

Senate was sometimes divided on the issues which arose. But it was a small body with defined, executive powers which it was left to exercise by Government, subject to largely formal approval. Moreover, it was a body which, even if on occasion divided on major policies, was still possessed of substantial authority and, broadly speaking, was not desirous of more than marginal extensions of it. Convocation, on the other hand, had in its active membership, not only representatives of almost every possible point of view about the future of the University, but a core of members who were and had

224

always been desirous of increasing Convocation's own powers, and were determined to repel any moves to reduce them.

Because that attitude was to lead to major controversy in the 1890s, it is necessary to go back, in the following chapter, to record the attempts which had been made, and which were largely unsuccessful, to boost the power of Convocation, in the period before the main struggle over the University's future began in the mid-1880s. For in addition to those trying, in vain, to augment Convocation's constitutional power and status, were those who shared a vision of a different kind of university. In the late 1870s, they took a lead in sketching what needed to be done. Much of the argument which went on in Convocation, and which is reported in the next chapter, may seem tiresomely petty, inasmuch as it involved conflict between small groups of activists who seemed, often, to have little chance of bringing about real change. But it is worth recording those arguments, because it is to the credit of the more far-seeing members of Convocation that their sketch of what was desirable for the University was a remarkably accurate forecast of what was only achieved twenty years afterwards.

Parts of what transpired between 1884 and 1900 have been covered, from different viewpoints, in one very large and four smaller studies.

Between 1905 and 1912, Sir William Allchin, an influential figure who, first as Assistant Registrar of the College of Physicians, and later as Dean of the Westminster Hospital Medical School, had been deeply involved in the whole controversy, produced a three-volume account of what happened between 1884 and 1892.[2] It is an intensely detailed narrative, based almost exclusively on his own private knowledge and on such official records and journal articles and press reports as were then readily available. It reproduces many important documents in full, and contains extensive extracts from others. Allchin's own insights and judgements are valuable, and, understandably, he gives close attention to the medical side of the story. It is, altogether, a remarkable piece of work, and it would be an insult to its author to suggest that anyone trying to deal with those years afresh could avoid drawing heavily from his 1028 pages of narrative, and his 260 pages of Appendices. Readers who need to examine the formal and public events between 1884 and 1892 in basic chronological and microscopic detail must be recommended to refer to the relevant parts of Allchin's huge saga.

In the third volume of A History of the Royal College of Physicians of London (Oxford 1972), A.M. Cooke gives an admirable account, from the medical standpoint, of relations between the University of London, the Royal Colleges, and the city's Medical Schools, from 1878 until well into the twentieth century. A slightly earlier work, by Zachary Cope, The Royal College of Surgeons

---

[2] W.H. Allchin, An Account of the Reconstruction of the University of London (London, 1905–12), 3 vols.

*of England* (London, 1959), covers the ground more briefly. The official histories of UCL and KCL contain relatively short accounts; Hearnshaw's work on King's contains a close study of the special problems which the College had to surmount because of its strong Anglican connection.

By the beginning of the twenty-first century, relevant Public Records and private archives, memoirs of some of the leading figures, and other previously confidential material, have become available for study. Even in a much shortened version, therefore, the story can be augmented in some of its particulars, and can be presented with greater concentration on personal involvement, on governmental and parliamentary interventions, and on the political experience of Senate and Convocation.

# 21

# Convocation's pursuit of power and reconstruction

As long ago as 1840, a powerful group in the Senate had agreed on the desirability of creating a convocation, and had envisaged that by about 1850 the Senate would in effect be elected by that convocation.[1] That possibility had been accepted as dead, long before Convocation was established in 1858, but there was resentment and disappointment among many of the graduates about the very limited powers which the new body was given. In the following quarter-century, much of that resentment was doubtless modified by the developing partnership between Senate and Convocation and by the success of Convocation in initiating and seeing accepted a number of important University policies. But there remained an ambition among many members of Convocation to see its constitutional position *vis-a-vis* the Senate strengthened. In part this desire was expressed, and to a minor extent achieved, by successive changes to the internal procedures of Convocation, incorporated in the Standing Orders. And it might be argued that the establishment of the University's seat in the House of Commons, whose filling was effectively a Convocation affair, might be regarded as giving some extra edge to Convocation's status *vis-a-vis* Senate – though electoral manoeuvring and later experience was to show that the incumbent of the seat could be involved in University affairs without necessarily supporting Convocation positions. But in any event, a more fundamental shift of authority to Convocation could only be brought about by altering the Charter and by the award of specific new powers.

Efforts to bring about any major shift were unsuccessful. In the 1863 Charter, Convocation's fundamentally important existing power to accept or surrender any new Charter was extended to cover any Supplemental Charter: Convocation was given power, if they wished, to introduce postal voting for electing nominees to be appointed to the Senate: and Convocation could decide whether holders of new degrees were qualified to become members. There were no other changes until the legislation which re-arranged the constitution of the University for the twentieth century. But there were attempts to acquire new powers which are worth attention because of the contexts in which they were made, and because of the people who led them.

---

[1] Willson, *Our Minerva*, p. 142.

Alongside the resentment which was felt about the relatively limited powers granted to Convocation was the very specific objection taken by the great majority of pre-1858 graduates, to the abandonment of the requirement that admission to the degree examinations of the University be restricted to those who had studied in affiliated colleges. The desire of many graduates to see the re-introduction of a real, as opposed to a merely ceremonial link, between the University and the London teaching institutions which prepared their candidates for examination, was almost certainly more significant in the overall arguments about the future of the University in the 1880s and 1890s than was concern for increasing the constitutional powers of Convocation. Indeed, during those later years, Convocation was more concerned to use and defend its existing powers than to increase them. But between 1858 and the early 1880s, the issue of re-establishing a practical link between the University and the 'affiliated' colleges often went in tandem, as it were, with the notion of achieving a noticeable augmentation of Convocation's constitutional position.

As early as January, 1862, when the need to introduce postal voting for the elections of Convocation nominees for the Senate was raised in the Annual Committee, the desirability of having the Chancellor elected 'by the University', was proposed as an extra item. The idea was approved, but no more was heard of it for many years. The first substantial discussion of desirable change came in May, 1867, when, at the Annual Meeting of Convocation – and apparently without any previous debate in Annual Committee – R.P.B. Taaffe raised two issues. He moved, first, that

> ... the representation of the Graduates on the Senate is inadequate, and that it be an instruction to Annual Committee to consider and report on the subject to the next meeting.

Secondly, he moved that

> ... no person ought to be admitted to any Degree unless he has previously studied at a College affiliated to the University.

Taaffe was seconded for the first motion by Thomas Tyler and for the second by Wale Hicks. None of the three was a member of the Annual Committee, and they may well have been seen by the leading people in Convocation as acting inadvisedly. Two old hands, Osler and Robson, tried to have the first motion pushed aside, but failed on a vote – losing twenty-four to thirty-four. On the second, Osler and Robson again tried to move to the next item, and this apparently led to a stalemate, broken by the agreement of both Taaffe and Osler to withdraw their motions.

It is highly probable that Taaffe was indignant over the fact that the quota of nine places on Senate for Convocation-nominated Fellows had now been reached, and that there was therefore little likelihood of any further increase of influence being exercised for the benefit of Convocation. He must have found some support for his concern, because when the matter came up in Annual Committee in November, 1867, a resolution was carried, 'That the right conferred by the Charter on Convocation of nominating for every fourth vacancy on Senate cannot be accepted by the University as a permanent arrangement.' Even so moderate a statement, however, was too much for the majority, who felt it was 'premature to take steps to obtain any alteration in the Charter in this behalf'. And when an attempt was made to have a sub-committee appointed 'to consider what immediate steps should be taken with reference to representation of Graduates on the Senate', it was defeated by fourteen to two.

The sequel was surprising. By the middle of February, 1868, there had been some apparent reversals of opinion. The relevant minutes of the previous Annual Committee meeting were referred to a sub-committee charged with the preparation of an appropriate paragraph for inclusion in the Annual Committee's report to Convocation. The sub-committee met on 27 March, when it was left to Cozens-Hardy to prepare a draft. Exploration of the realities of the situation led both sub-committee and Annual Committee to agree that, though in the future some increase in the number of Convocation-nominated Fellows would be desirable, the time was not yet ripe to press for it. And unlike the pioneers of 1840, they had no ambition to see a Senate fully elected by Convocation. They reported that:

> . . . a Senate consisting solely, or with few exceptions, of Graduates nominated by Convocation would . . . be far less adapted to promote the interests of the University than one in which Crown nominees form a large proportion . . .
>
> . . . having regard to the relations of the Senate, both to the general public and to the very eminent staff of Examiners, many of whom are Members of other Universities, it would be a serious loss to the University to be deprived of the services of Senators of high social position, great Parliamentary eminence, and literary and scientific reputation, but who are not Graduates of the University.

Even any modest, immediate increase in Convocation-nominated Fellows seemed impracticable:

> The absence of any numerous class of Graduates in London, corresponding to the resident Tutors and Fellows at the older Universities, and the fact that the active Members of Convocation are generally persons engrossed by the duties of London professional life, would alone render it difficult to choose from amongst ourselves a sufficient number of competent Senators having adequate leisure for the performance of their duties . . . there is a great deal of business to be transacted by Committees of the Senate, and . . . it would be exceedingly difficult to secure the attendance requisite for the purpose without relying to a great extent upon the Crown nominees.

The Report concluded with a reminder that the full quota of one-quarter of the Senate had only been filled by Convocation-nominees for one year, and that the University was 'now making considerable demands upon the Treasury', – a reference to the provision of the new building at Burlington Gardens, which opened in 1870. It seemed to the sub-committee and the Annual Committee that now was not the time to begin 'a movement the object of which is to diminish the influence of the Government' in the University's affairs. Convocation felt the same, and, on 12 May 1868, accepted what Solomon and Cozens-Hardy had carried in Annual Committee the previous November, namely:

> That although . . . the right conferred by the Charter upon Convocation of nominating for every fourth vacancy on the Senate cannot be accepted by the University as a permanent arrangement, yet it is not expedient at present to take any steps to obtain an alteration in the Charter in this behalf.

The 12 May meeting thus closed the file, for six years, as it turned out, on any prospect of an increased proportion of Convocation-nominated Fellows. But the meeting was adjourned until 2 June, 1868, when the persistent Taaffe, seconded by W.T. Lynn, introduced for a second time his motion providing that only those who had attended affiliated Colleges should be admitted to any degree. On this occasion, the discussion survived an attempt to adjourn the House, but the motion was lost.

When the constitutional issue was raised again, it is highly likely that it then reflected some of the contemporary disagreements, at their height within Convocation, over the admission of women to degrees and over matriculation requirements. Certainly the motion which began another round of constitutional questioning bears the marks of disapproval of the conduct of some Convocation-nominated Fellows, and a wish to see them replaced. Hensman, who was a prominent supporter of the admission of women, and Thomas Tyler, gave notice that, at the Convocation meeting on 12 May 1874, they would move:

> That the mode in which Convocation is represented in the Senate, namely, by senators whose tenure of office is not limited to a prescribed term of years, is unsatisfactory and that it is desirable to consider how the representation may be improved.

The meeting on 12 May 1874, as we have already seen, was particularly memorable because Convocation, on Hensman's motion, voted in favour of the admission of women to degrees, a subject which must have dominated the session. But the motion of Hensman and Tyler about Convocation representation on the Senate was reached, and must have been regarded as too critical of what might have become describable as the Establishment of

Convocation. It was challenged and in effect replaced by an alternative offered by Cozens-Hardy and Weymouth, who simply reiterated the decision which had been reached in 1868, that 'the present representation of the Graduates on the Senate cannot be accepted by Convocation as a permanent arrangement'. But, perhaps reflecting the higher temperature of the debate which was raging within the University, they did agree – apparently without any division – to a reference of the matter to the Annual Committee, who were charged with considering 'what changes should be introduced in the event of any Supplemental Charter being applied for'. It was six months before the Annual Committee had it on their agenda.

In November, 1874, Annual Committee handed the problem to a sub-committee chaired by Goldsmid, which agreed to recommend that Senate should apply for a Supplemental Charter which would provide for a larger number of Convocation-nominated Fellows. They wanted all members of Senate to continue to be appointed for life, but they wanted appointments to be made to the thirty-six Fellowships, in turn, by the Crown, by nomination of the Senate, and by nomination of Convocation; and they wanted to see the principle of co-optation introduced for the filling of vacancies. This was a moderate proposal which, if put into practice, would have given Convocation a third rather than a quarter of the seats in Senate. But the report had a mixed reception in both Annual Committee and in Convocation.

At Annual Committee, on 4 December 1874, Bennet and Charles wanted to drop co-optation, but were defeated by a 'large majority'. So, too were attempts to emphasise the need to have men on the Senate who had educational experience. But Goldsmid and Charles did manage to have included a new proposal, that any Chairman of Convocation who, when elected, was not already a Fellow, should be made a Member of Senate *ex officio*. That proposal was extended at the next meeting, when Horne Payne carried a motion that any Chairman who became an *ex officio* Senator should be additional to the ordinary Convocation-nominated members.

When the proposals reached Convocation on 11 May 1875, the desirability of increasing the number of Convocation-nominated Fellows, and the desirability of continuing to have Crown appointees, were propositions easily accepted. Co-optation was accepted after a division, by forty-five to thirty-six, and after the defeat of an attempt to make co-optation valid only 'until such time as all of the vacancies in the Senate can be supplied by candidates nominated by Convocation', – an interesting re-assertion of a sentiment which had apparently been long abandoned by the moderate leadership. But the major upset of the Annual Committee's recommendations was the refusal to agree to a Senate of one-third appointed by the Crown, one-third by Senate and one-third by Convocation. Albert Creak carried an alternative proposal calling for Convocation to nominate half of the Fellowships, and for the Crown and Senate to nominate a quarter each. And Osler carried the idea of having the Chairman of Convocation made an *ex officio* Member of Senate if he was not already a Fellow.

But when it was moved that Fellows should continue to be appointed for life, and when Nesbitt tried to carry a motion that Senate should apply for a Supplemental Charter to carry into effect the agreed recommendations, they were defeated by motions to move to the next items. The session ended, therefore, in some confusion, seemingly due to the rather sudden appearance of a more radical presence in Convocation which was challenging the willingness of the usual leadership to accept the present balance of power within the University. It was, in fact, the beginning of a wider debate on the University's future, in which the main emphasis tended to shift from concern for the powers and status of Convocation towards the need to consider the idea of converting the University from an examining to a teaching and examining institution.

When discussion began again on 18 January 1876, the initial emphasis was still on the matter of the desirable tenure of Convocation-nominated members of Senate. A resolution calling for a new Charter which 'should provide for the nomination by Convocation of a larger number of Senators than hitherto, and for their tenure of office being limited to a Term of Years', was passed, in a poorly attended meeting, by sixteen to eight, after two attempts to amend the motion to leave the question of tenure aside. At the Annual Meeting of Convocation on 9 May, a more conservative attitude prevailed. Nesbitt gave notice that he would raise the matter of limiting the tenure of Senators, 'especially considering the small number of votes by which the motion [of 18 January] was carried', and expressed the view that 'it would not be conducive to the interests of the University that the tenure of office of a Senator should in any case be limited to a term of years'. He had to wait until 20 June to have his motion debated, but then accepted a shortened version, which was carried by 'a large majority'.

More significantly, for the longer term, was that, on 18 January, Hensman called for the appointment of a Special Committee of fifteen Members 'for the purpose of considering what changes in the constitution of the University are desirable, and the best means of obtaining such changes'. Nesbitt lost a motion to adjourn, but the House was later counted out, Hensman declaring that he would raise the matter again. He did so at the Annual Meeting on 9 May 1876, when his motion was not only carried, but strengthened by Bompas, who persuaded the House that the inquiry should also cover 'whether any, and if any, what changes in the mode of electing the Annual Committee of Convocation is desirable'. It may well be, in the light of what happened subsequently, that this addition was another expession of concern on the part of the younger and more radical elements about the concentration of power in the hands of an 'old guard'.

But Hensman and his small band of reformers were to be disappointed. Procedural rules provided that the mover of a motion to set up a committee should nominate its members, and it was over the choice of names that Hensman ran into trouble. He put forward a list which, presumably, included the names of many of his supporters. The debate on this list was brought to a close by Nesbitt, who successfully moved an adjournment to 20 June. On that day, the tide turned against Hensman. He produced a new list, which included only ten of the original fifteen, to whom were added Henry Greenway Howse, Herschell, Hutton, Pye-Smith and Walter Rivington. But almost at once, three of the original ten – Cozens-Hardy, Russell Martineau, and Weymouth – and Hutton, declared that they wished to withdraw. Anstie and Bennett then moved to proceed to the next item, and carried the day without division.

Undaunted, Hensman tried again on 16 January 1877, when he moved the appointment of a Special Committee. But his proposal was immediately rejected by fifty-seven to fifteen. This was at a hectic stage of the campaign to admit women to degrees, and Hensman seems to have misread the extent to which the community was still preoccupied with that proposal and unwilling to shift their attention from it to the wider constitutional reforms he sought. However, the Senate's decision, just a month later, to take advantage of Gurney's Act, and to propose admitting women to medical degrees without waiting until they could be admitted to all the other degrees, gave a boost to the case for wider constitutional change.

Those totally opposed to degrees for women – mainly the medical fraternity – were joined by those who were bitterly unhappy that only women intending to study medicine should be admitted, and by those who wanted wider constitutional reform. As we have seen, towards the end of 1877, the Senate decided not to use Gurney's Act, and to seek a new Charter, after consultation with Convocation, to secure powers to admit women to all the examinations of the University. The constitutional reformers then tried to have these moves extended to include their desire to see some fundamental changes brought about. Again, they underestimated the wish of the majority to have the question of women's admittance settled first. But their support had undoubtedly grown.

On 12 November, Thomas Tyler presented to the Chairman of Convocation a requisition, signed by seventy-two members, to call an Extraordinary Meeting to consider a number of proposals to increase the powers of Convocation and to make other changes in the constitution of the University. Of the seventy-two signatories, thirty-seven were Arts men, eleven had Law degrees, six were scientists, and eighteen were medical graduates. The latter were treated unsympathetically by the Lancet, which wanted everyone to concentrate on the 'women in medicine' question.[2] The Chairman, John Storrar, simply refused to accept the requisition, almost certainly because he felt confident that a great majority would not wish, at this stage of settling the admission of women, to allow the delicate balance of forces in Senate and Convocation to be upset. Nonetheless, the petitioners must have impressed

---

[2] *Lancet*, 3 & 10 November 1877, 5 & 12 January 1878.

upon the more senior members of Convocation the need to recognise that a growing concern within the ranks would have to be appeased, and quickly.

The requisition for an Extraordinary Meeting had listed the following proposals:

(i)    An enlargement of the powers directly exercised by Convocation.

(ii)   An increase in the proportion of Senators to be nominated or elected by Convocation, and the limitation of the tenure of office, in the case of all Senators, to a term of years.

(iii)  The encouragement of mature study and original research among the members of the University, by the establishment of University Lectureships, of limited tenure, in different departments of learning and science.

(iv)  The introduction into the constitution of the University of such modifications as may remove all reasonable ground of complaint, on the part of any of the affiliated Colleges, with respect to the absence of means for expressing opinion and giving advice to the Senate on the examination regulations, and on the changes proposed to be made therein from time to time.

This statement was perhaps the first which brought together the specific powers relating to the number and tenure of Fellows, pressed by Hensman for some years, on the one hand; and the academic aspirations of a growing band of scholars and teachers, especially at UCL, KCL and the London Medical Schools, which were shared by a few members of Senate, and had been voiced, to no avail, on a number of occasions over the previous decade.

Storrar had refused the requisition, probably for good tactical reasons, but was no doubt instrumental in helping to find an acceptable way forward. He and his allies ignored the request for discussion of additional powers for Convocation, but, on 16 November, in the Annual Committee, Pye-Smith and Anstie, neither of whom had signed the requisition, moved to invite the Senate

> . . . to consider by what measures the connexion of the affiliated Colleges with the University may be strengthened, and, generally, how the objectives of the University in the promotion of sound learning and liberal education may be more efficiently attained.

Debate was adjourned for a week. On 23 November, no doubt after due deliberation among the leaders, Pye-Smith and Anstie substituted a motion that the matter should be referred to a sub-committee. Shaen and Magnus then carried an additional requirement, that the sub-committee should 'consider and report whether the opportunity of the contemplated Supplemental Charter should or should not be sought, in order to introduce any, and what constitutional changes, in addition to the admission of women to all degrees'.

The sub-committee chose Pye-Smith as Chairman, and its other members were A.R. Abbott, Anstie, E.B. Baxter, Busk, Charles, Ely, Fagge, McDowall, Magnus, Shaen and Weymouth. None of them was of Hensman's persuasion, and only Magnus had signed the requisition. The group held five meetings in November and December, 1877, and was to be re-appointed in February 1878, after which it met three more times. Abbott never attended, but none of the others was present at less than five of the meetings, and no less than seven of them turned out on seven or eight occasions. They produced a document of some historical importance. The first version was presented to Annual Committee on 21 December 1877.

When the sub-committee met for the first time on 28 November 1877, the Chairman, Pye-Smith, 'indicated the outline of a Draft Report'. Whether or not this was a modest way of saying that Pye-Smith was the draftsman, the draft, though discussed over five meetings, was very largely a readily agreed document, with only one item exciting a formally recorded division. The completed version, of about four thousand words, reads like a well-polished argument, developed over quite some time, in extended discussion, by a group of committed academics. And it covered well cultivated ground.

After a potted history of the University and an expression of pride in its achievements, the Report focusses, first, on the exclusive concentration on examinations.

> . . . there has of late years appeared growing doubt of the superlative value of even the best examinations, which strongly contrasts with the enthusiastic belief in their efficacy which was common among the most enlightened statesmen and friends of education twenty or thirty years ago . . .
> . . . it is assuredly desirable that the advantages of strict and competitive examinations should not be jeopardised by too rigid a forcing of the process, and also that the public usefulness and estimation of a University should not rest too exclusively upon this single basis.

This scepticism about examinations is then smoothly connected to the need for a closer link with teaching institutions:

> The original exclusive connexion of the affiliated Colleges with the University cannot be revived, nor is it desirable that it should. But it is desirable that there should be stronger and mutually advantageous influence of the University upon its Colleges and Schools, and of these educational bodies upon the University. Few of the members of Convocation who take an active interest in University affairs have ever acquiesced in the exclusive character so often assigned it of a Government examining board.

The sub-committee then quoted the

... lamentable want of interest in and loyalty to the University among many of its graduates, and the complete absence of any pretence of attachment to it on the part of the educational bodies which supply its graduates.

And they recorded recent public criticism; a request for a Royal Commission; the requisition for an Extraordinary Meeting of Convocation; and 'the efforts made by one of our most important Colleges to throw off all connexion with the central body'. The remedy was described in the first of their firm recommendations,

... that, with the view of creating and preserving a harmony between the requirements of the University and the course of study pursued in . . . the institutions where the candidates for degrees are chiefly educated . . . it is expedient that those bodies should be brought into closer connexion with the Senate . . .

. . . it is desirable for the Senate to revise the list of affiliated Colleges, and from time to time to admit or exclude from this list according to the position taken by these Colleges at the University examinations for degrees, and on such other grounds as the Senate may in each case determine.

The possibility of adding representatives of the 'principal Colleges' to the Senate was put aside, but the Report suggested that those institutions which prepared candidates for degrees should have the opportunity to communicate and deliberate with Senate, especially about examinations. And the Report admits the sub-committee's internal disagreement over the idea

That it is desirable for the examiners of the University, either in faculties or collectively, to form a board, one of whose functions would be to consider and report upon any subject connected with the examinations which they might deem of importance to the University.

That recommendation had only been carried by Pye-Smith's casting vote in favour of a motion by Fagge and Shaen. How the others present voted is not indicated in the minutes.

But while the Report pressed the case for a closer connection with Colleges and Schools, it also struck out in a very different direction, by arguing strongly, and at some length, for the 'cultivation of such higher or less usual branches of study as can be more conveniently, or more efficiently, taught by a central body', and called for the institution of University Chairs in such areas. And they also recommended the inclusion of a requirement for independent research in the examinations for the higher degrees.

In conclusion, the Report took account of the political realities of the time. The sub-committee 'have ascertained unofficially that a strong view is entertained in the Senate that the question of the admission of women should be settled on its own merits, and by itself'. In the light of that, they felt that 'questions of all other constitutional changes be adjourned until after the next meeting of Convocation'.

The Annual Committee, on 21 December 1877, regarded the Report as 'of such value as to justify its general circulation as an Appendix', but agreed with the sub-committee in recommending that 'it would be undesirable to complicate the simple question now at issue, with regard to the admission of Women to all degrees, with any other questions affecting the constitution of the University'. Discussion of such changes should be delayed until after the next meeting of Convocation, which meant the meeting after that due on 15 January 1878, when the new Supplemental Charter was to be accepted or rejected. But 'the subject of such changes' should be referred back to the Annual Committee.

The contents of the Annual Committee's Report to Convocation must have become generally known almost immediately after 21 December. They were very unwelcome to those who had organised the requisition for an Extraordinary Meeting, and had been so brusquely turned down. Although there was only a three-week gap between the meetings of Annual Committee and of Convocation, Hensman and Tyler were determined to have maximum attention devoted to the desirability of more constitutional changes than the admission of women. Hensman, as Chairman, and Tyler as Hon. Secretary, set up what they called the London University Reform Committee, and called a meeting at King's College on 9 January 1878, 'To discuss reform based on proposals of the recent requisition.' Press reports imply that there was a modest attendance and that the occasion was more concerned to express dissatisfaction than to make any firm decision about any future activity.[3]

Tyler gave notice that he would raise the issue of the requisition at the meeting of Convocation on 15 January, and published the correspondence about it with the Chairman of Convocation. But Convocation was overwhelmingly interested in the Supplemental Charter and its provision for the admission of women. After the memorable debate and vote on that issue was finished, the attempt to have the correspondence about the requisition debated was swept aside, and the question of any additional constitutional change was adjourned and referred back to the Annual Committee, on the motion of Pye-Smith. On 25 January, Annual Committee re-appointed the sub-committee.

From February to April, 1878, the sub-committee, and then the Annual Committee, went over the first Report of the former and fought some of the same battles again. The outcome was a document only slightly changed in content. The basic arguments for bringing the University closer to the schools and colleges which taught its examination candidates, for the creation of an

---

[3] *Times*, 10 January 1878. In addition to Hensman and Tyler, there were listed among those present H. Chaplin BA, Alex Muirhead DSc, S. Elliot BA, Tilbury Fox MD, B. Reynolds MA, Josiah Miller MA, A.H. Barford BA, James Stevens BA LLB.

Examiners' Board, for the establishment of Chairs, and for the recognition of original research as part of the requirements for higher degrees, were almost untouched. And to these broadly academic concerns was added the proposal that the University should ask for specific power to examine and inspect schools. The new Report gave added weight to the importance of additional finance, and hoped that 'the practically boundless resources of this City would not be entirely refused to the Metropolitan University', – almost certainly the first public statement reflecting anxiety about the continuance and adequacy of the annual parliamentary grant.

Differences of approach to the narrower questions about the composition and powers of the Senate were again apparent, however. Agreed were the need to increase the representation of the graduates, the desirability of life membership of the Senate for all who were appointed, and provision that the Chairman of Convocation would be *ex officio* a member of the Senate. But co-optation was still unwelcome, as was the motion to make non-London graduates, who were Senators, *ex officio* members of Convocation. And the notion that the Chancellor should be elected by Convocation was withdrawn. But hardest fought was the idea that there should be direct representation of the affiliated colleges on the Senate. Anstie and Magnus were defeated on this in the sub-committee, and Weymouth and Curnow failed to introduce it in the Annual Committee. The items listed against such representation foreshadowed some of the problems which were to haunt the University in the coming decade:

> ... the difficulty of so apportioning the right of election as to ensure fair representation to even the more important Colleges and Medical Schools; the objection to entrusting this franchise either to the official 'heads of houses' who might have no intimate knowledge of or interest in the system of our University, or to the graduate members who would thus have a double voting power; the danger of exciting ecclesiastical or other jealousies between our Colleges; and lastly the serious objection to these delegated members of the Senate being of necessity removable at the will of their constituent bodies, and therefore occupying a different position from that of senators for life.

The majority of the sub-committee clearly had doubts as to whether they had done enough to provide a way forward which would attract general support, while keeping their more radically inclined colleagues, let alone the outspoken members of the London University Reform Committee, on side. The final paragraph of their Report says:

> It may be thought that the measures which your Committee submit to the judgement of Convocation are too moderate and tentative to be of service towards the objects in view. But if the wants which they have described be acknowledged, and the methods indicated be in principle approved, they believe that an important step will have been taken.

Convocation, on 14 May, accepted the great bulk of what had been recomended to them. Creak and Hensman tried, in vain, to upset the proposal to revise the list of affiliated colleges and to institute a system of admitting or excluding them. The most serious opposition was made to the idea of instituting Chairs – another aspect of the distaste, felt by many, for any centralising tendency which might weaken the independence of the teaching institutions. Cozens-Hardy moved to pass to the next item when this proposal was debated, but was defeated in a division by thirty-nine to twenty-three; the proposal for Chairs was then carried. But the idea of making the Chairman of Convocation *ex officio* a member of the Senate was lost because Hensman and Magnus succeeded in moving the adjournment of the House. One may well wonder whether it was felt by them that a major principle was involved; or whether this was a way of protesting at the moderation of all the proposals; or whether there was a hint of revenge over the treatment of the requisition for an Extraordinary Meeting, six months ago.

But having endorsed most of the Annual Committee's proposals – which, it must be said, were to be accepted twenty years and innumerable struggles later, and put into practice at the beginning of the twentieth century – both Convocation and Senate left them hanging, in limbo as it were, for eighteen months. To no small extent, this may well have reflected an exhaustion, among all concerned, following the culmination of the long battle over the admission of women.

Even after eighteen months, however, Convocation showed it had little stomach for renewing the fight. Pye-Smith, who begins to look increasingly like one of the major, continuing and persistent forces behind reform, moved in Annual Committee, with George Carey Foster seconding, on 12 November 1880,

> That the Senate be requested to consider the advantage of constituting Boards of Studies, one for each Faculty, to advise the Senate on matters connected with the detail of Examinations, and to form a medium of communication between the Senate, the Teachers and the Examiners of the University, the members to be chosen by the Senate from their own body (either in addition to, or including the present Committees of the Senate), from Professors and Teachers in the Affiliated Colleges and Medical Schools, and from present or past Examiners.

McDowall wanted to substitute for this motion all the Resolutions which had been passed on 14 May 1878, except for the Resolution which favoured the institution of Chairs. But the amendment was lost by ten to four, and Pye-Smith's motion was carried. There were twenty-six members of the Committee listed as present, so the extent of apparent indifference to the wider claim was ominous for the more full-blooded reformers. However, Pye-Smith won the right, in the following week, to have the Resolution submitted to the next meeting of Convocation. But on 18 January 1881, Convocation adjourned without giving any consideration to the Report of the Annual Committee. Yet another full year was to pass before Pye-Smith was to try again.

On 17 January 1882, Pye-Smith and Magnus returned to the fray, and, after some negotiation of the exact terms of a motion, carried in Convocation another plea to Senate to set up Boards of Studies. A month later, Storrar took the reference of Convocation's request to Senate, and persuaded that body to set up a Special Committee, six of whose thirteen members were Convocation-nominated Fellows, while two of the others were Gull and Wood, the original London graduates appointed to Senate before Convocation was established. They met three times, but their report was not considered until 26 July. In the meantime, Convocation continued to debate its position on other aspects of reform.

In addition to trying to re-start the argument about introducing Boards of Studies, Convocation, in January, 1882, referred back to Annual Committee the desired proportion of Convocation-nominated Fellows, and the *ex officio* membership of Senate for any future Chairman of Convocation. These items, which had been left undecided on earlier occasions, were put to a sub-committee. In the course of four meetings in March, McDowall and Baxter carried the desirability of having *ex officio* status for the Chairman; Pye-Smith and Busk won approval of a three-way split of Senate membership – equal numbers nominated by the Crown, by the Senate and by Convocation; and Kisch and Baxter persuaded their colleagues to support life membership for Senators.

When these suggestions were reported to Convocation on 9 May 1882, there was still clear evidence of the presence of people with more radical views than those of the majority of the Annual Committee. Convocation accepted the idea of a future Chairman having *ex officio* membership of the Senate. But though the proposal that the Senate should have its member-ship divided into three equal groups, nominated respectively by the Crown, by the Senate and by Convocation, was also approved, it was only after a challenge which tried to substitute a fifty-fifty split between Crown and Convocation. And the implied discontent with the existing immovability of the Convocation nominees on the Senate must have been quite strongly shared, for Hensman and Lynn succeeded in having the House pass to the next item when Nesbitt and Curnow moved that membership of the Senate should be for life. Another refinement of the nominating process for Convocation representatives on Senate was moved successfully by John Hennell and Nesbitt, who thought it desirable that the nominations should be made, 'as a general rule, alternately, from the Faculties of Arts and Laws, and the Faculties of Medicine and Science'.

One other issue was raised in the sub-committee in March, 1882, and was supported by Convocation in May. Weymouth had brought up the desir-ability of exploring the possibility of the University's finding financial support from the City of London. As we have seen, the idea was first pursued in the important Convocation Report of 1878. Since then a Royal Commission had been appointed to review the activities of the City Companies.[4] Weymouth wanted Convocation to urge the Senate to lobby the Commission and argue that the University had some claim on the funds and facilities of the Trustees of the ancient City foundation, Gresham College. The Annual Committee's Report to Convocation included a short paper on the subject, and it was, in due course, approved, but not sent on to Senate until after the meeting of 16 January 1883. At that meeting, there was an attempt to have the motion to approve and send to Senate ignored; but by a vote of thirty-two to fourteen the debate was allowed to continue. Unfortunately, no division list survives.

In late July, 1882, Senate simply rejected most of Convocation's recommendations. They resolved that there should be no permanent Boards of Examiners, and that it was neither practicable nor expedient to form a representative Board elected by Colleges and Schools. The most that Senate would approve was the desirability of having meetings of examiners convened by the Examination Committees of Senate, and chaired by the Registrar, to which past examiners might be invited; and that the Committees of Examiners should be formally authorised to communicate directly with Colleges and Schools and to confer with them on questions relating to the examinations.

As for suggestions of changes to the constitution of the University, Senate ignored them. Indeed, according to Joshua Fitch, the Vice-Chancellor, Sir George Jessel, who Fitch regarded as 'decisive and masterful', and 'whose reputation as one of the strongest judges on the Equity Bench has never been questioned', simply ruled that 'the creation of representative Boards of Studies . . . would be *ultra vires* and inconsistent with the terms of the Charter'.[5] And when the idea of pursuing the idea of making a claim on the funds of Gresham College came under consideration in February, 1883, Senate felt that, as a State-supported institution, it would be undesirable for the University to make any approach.

Convocation's attempts, described in this chapter, to have its own constitutional position *vis-à-vis* the Senate strengthened, and to persuade the Senate to make some substantial move towards a widening of the University's activities, had seemingly failed by the winter of 1882–83. Its contribution hitherto to the major reforms and developments – the admission of women to examinations, and the recognition of the pressing needs of secondary education – had been outstanding. And the scheme of constitutional change

---

[4] R. Comm. to inquire into the Livery Companies of the City of London, PP xxxix, C4073, 1884. Unlike the University, UCL made representations to the Commission and offered evidence.

[5] Stephen Paget (ed.), *Memoirs and Letters of Sir James Paget* (London, 1901), p. 332.

which it had sketched in 1878 was eventually to be achieved. But although Convocation was to continue to play a leading – and at times a highly controversial – role in the events which dominated the next fifteen years of the University's life, the main initiative for reform passed, in the early 1880s, to others – and not to the London University Reform Committee, of which there seems to be no record after the beginning of 1878. It is possible that the chance of building on its first meeting was lost when its leading figure, Arthur Peach Hensman, sailed for Western Australia to become Attorney General there. It is interesting that Convocation lost two radical spokesmen – Charles James Foster and Hensman – to the Antipodes, each of them at a particularly vital point in the history of the University.

# 22

# One, two, or three universities?

A major attempt to bring about changes in London which would inevitably involve the existing University was three-pronged, and began in the mid-1880s. An attack on all fronts, as it were, was made by a body established in 1884, called the Association for the Promotion of a Teaching University for London – hereinafter the Association. Membership of it was wide, but its basic support was concentrated in UCL and KCL. Those two Colleges were to adopt the main propositions in the Association's scheme and then to make a determined effort to have themselves recognised as the nucleus of a new Teaching University, quite separate from the existing University of London.

An equally comprehensive campaign was launched from within the existing University community by Convocation. But from the outset that campaign, though it caused deep trauma within Convocation, took for granted the desirability of there being only one institution for the city – a modified version of the existing University of London.

Despite their disagreements, the Association, UCL and KCL, and Convocation, all regarded it as natural and desirable that a university should be a multi-faculty organisation. However, either from conviction or from impatience with an unsatisfactory *status quo*, there were powerful people in the medical profession – primarily the controlling majority of the Royal Colleges of Physicians and of Surgeons, with encouragement from the Metropolitan Branch of the BMA – who professed indifference to the argument that there were overriding advantages in having the study of medicine carried on alongside other disciplines, within a normal, multi-faculty university. They were not only uninterested in reform within the existing University of London: they were also uninterested in joining with other non-medical institutions in forming a new university, separate altogether from the University of London. They were prepared to consider the creation of a one-faculty university, by empowering a combination of the existing Colleges of Physicians and Surgeons to confer degrees in Medicine and Surgery.

At the same time, in addition to the arguments about which institutions should exist, and in what forms, a group of senior academics at UCL, joined at a later stage by colleagues from elsewhere, began to press for the acceptance of the principle of professorial control of any teaching university – a move which provoked considerable controversy during the following decade, when it developed into a demand for a centralised, rather than a federal or quasi-federal institution.

This and the next chapter cover the period from 1884 to the early part of 1888, by which time there were applications before the Privy Council, which, if granted, could have given London three universities – the existing University, left basically untouched as an examining board with a national and imperial catchment area: a new multi-faculty teaching university for the metropolis, called the Albert University, based on UCL, KCL, and such of the London medical schools as wished to join: and a medical university called the Senate of Physicians and Surgeons – though the title University of Westminster had been considered by its sponsors.

It was the medical men who made the first move. At the Royal College of Physicians, Wilson Fox, a UCL graduate, raised the idea of the Royal Colleges granting MD degrees, as early as November, 1883. He was strongly supported by the President, Sir William Jenner. The Royal College of Surgeons followed suit in March, 1884, and the subject was taken on board by the Metropolitan Branch of the BMA in June and July. By contrast, the Association was only constituted in May, 1884, and did not begin to operate seriously until the autumn of that year. Convocation's first consideration of the future of the University, following the publication of the Association's recommendations, came in January, 1885. The Senate did not react, formally, to any of the discussions of the medical bodies, the Association, or Convocation, until April, 1885.

Being first in the field, however, was hardly of any significant benefit for the medical parties, though, as will be seen, the Senate was more quickly embroiled in the medical manoeuvres than in dealing with the Association and Convocation, and eventually took an equivocal position on the notion of a separate medical degree-giving authority.

It is as well to stress at this point how limited was the support – even though it was support from very influential quarters – for the one-faculty university. It was clear from quite early in the negotiations that there was no sympathy for the idea among those who wished to reform the existing University, or from those who contemplated a new teaching university based on existing colleges. And it is also clear that many, if not most, of those who taught medicine in London preferred the orthodoxy of a multi-faculty university. Membership of the Association was 250 in 1886, and almost exactly half of them were medical people, reflecting 'the larger actual numbers of teachers in the numerous separate branches of Medical, Surgical, and Obstetrical Teaching', including 'A very large number of Junior Men [who] joined the Association . . . in 1885.'[1]

---

[1] Selborne Commission, PP 1889, xxxix, C5709, Appendix 28.

The enthusiasts for a separate Medical University were concentrated in the Royal Colleges and in some sections of the non-teaching ranks of the profession. As will be seen, this made difficult the position of some at least of the sizeable group of senior doctors, who were members of one or more of the Senate of the University, the Royal Colleges, Convocation, the Association, UCL, KCL, and other medical schools, and who were much involved in all the negotiations about the future arrangement of higher education in London. Conflicting loyalties sometimes produced attitudes and decisions which were neither smooth nor clear. But we must postpone discussion of that, and turn to the wider issues raised by the actions of the Association and Convocation.

Credit for the establishment of the Association for the Promotion of a Teaching University for London is given to Sir George Young, 3rd Bt., who, after Eton, Trinity College, Cambridge, and Lincoln's Inn, had unsuccessfully fought three parliamentary elections and had been employed for some years on various Government Commissions. In 1875 he had joined the governing body of UCL, its Council. Three years later he also became Vice-President of the College's academic authority, its Senate, and subsequently served as President of the Senate from 1880 to 1886. Meanwhile, in 1882, he had become a Commissioner under the Endowed Schools Act: he was based at the Charity Commission, and ended his official career as Chief Charity Commissioner. Though not himself a teacher, Young became, in effect, a leading spokesman for the UCL professors.

There is no evidence on which to build a narrative of the discussion and negotiations which must have preceded the inauguration of the Association. But there can be little doubt that Young had found a strong colleague in Donald James Mackay, 11th Baron Reay, who was born in Holland and worked in Government there until inheriting the Scottish title and coming to live in England, in 1875. His interest in education accounted for his election to the Council of UCL in 1881, and to his becoming Rector of St Andrews in 1884.

It is probably fair to assume that the shape and intention of the Association had already been agreed between a rather smaller group than the twelve who met, privately, in Reay's house at the beginning of May, 1884. Indeed, the meeting may well have been planned in part to put the heads of three dominant institutions on formal notice of the launching of the new body. Two of them – John Eric Erichsen, President of UCL, a surgeon, and Rev. Henry Wace, Principal of KCL, a divine, may well have been involved in prior discussions, and can be regarded as supporters who became members of the Association. However, the Vice-Chancellor of the University, Paget, another medical man, attended the meeting but kept his distance once the Association was established. The dominance of UCL, and to a lesser extent of KCL, was obvious. Of the other nine present, seven had UCL credentials: in addition to Reay and Young, Pye-Smith was a Life Governor; Sir Joseph Lister was a

Fellow of the College; G. Croom Robertson was Grote Professor of Philosophy; Alexander William Williamson was a Governor and Professor of Chemistry; Farrer Herschell, then Solicitor General, was a graduate. G.C.W. Warr was Professor of Classical Literature at KCL. Lord Justice Bowen represented the Council of Legal Education.

At the same time, it should be noted that Erichsen and Lister were also on the Council of the Royal College of Surgeons, and Lister worked at King's College Hospital; Pye-Smith was a Fellow of the Royal College of Physicians and taught at Guy's Hospital; Herschell and Williamson were University Senators. Even so, it would be naive to deny that the Association was, in its origins, an offshoot of UCL. And throughout its active existence, UCL and KCL were heavily represented. When the Association established an Executive Committee, in February, 1885, its members included most of the group which had met in the previous year. Reay had since been made Governor of Bombay, and served in India for the next five years. He relinquished the Presidency, but returned to UCL in 1892 as Vice-President of the College, became its President in 1897, and served in that and an equivalent capacity until his death in 1921.

On Reay's departure, the leadership of the Association was offered to Lord Rosebery, who had joined; but he declined, having just been appointed to the Cabinet. Young then tried to persuade the new Bishop of London, Frederick Temple, to preside, explaining that there was a lull in the Association's affairs but that

> ... when we meet ... at large once more, neither Mr Marshall nor myself nor any other of our committee will be fitted to fill the place, which requires more weight, and the position of a public man. If we might hope that you would consent to take the chair, of course after communication, and explanation, to your satisfaction, of what we propose to submit, I should feel that the first man in England for the purpose had come to us at the critical moment.[2]

Temple was apparently not moved by this flattery, but subsequently played no small part in the controversy, partly as a strong supporter of King's College. The leadership of the Association fell to 'Mr Marshall' – John Marshall, who had been Professor of Surgery at UCL since 1866, had serious interests in art, and was regarded as 'a scientific man with good business capacity', whose services were in 'great demand.'[3] Of nine additional appointments to the Executive during the succeeding two years, seven were of UCL and KCL men, the other two being doctors from Barts.

The dominant position of the two Colleges was also reflected in the overall membership. Of 163 members in December, 1884, at least sixty-three

---

[2] Lambeth Palace, Fulham Pps F. Temple, vol. 50, Young to Temple, 6 May 1885.
[3] Hale Bellot, *University College London*, p. 348.

belonged to one or other of them; and the same was true of a hundred of the total membership of 250 a year later. As we have seen, half of the total membership was medical. Roughly half of the non-medical, and over a third of the medical members in December, 1885, belonged to UCL or KCL. Numerous other institutions were represented, either by their heads or by small groups of teachers or members; they included the Hospital Medical Schools, the Inns of Court, the British Museum, Nonconformist Colleges, the South Kensington scientific foundations, the Royal Academy of Music, Women's Colleges, the City and Guilds Institute, several important schools, and the London Society for the Extension of University Teaching. But it is hard to believe that any or all of them were in a position to do more than modify the overriding wishes of the UCL and KCL contingents.

Young and Reay followed up the meeting in early May, 1884, by circulating an invitation to join the new Association to the members of all those institutions listed in the previous paragraph. The appeal was narrowly focussed on the basic theme of the desirability of having a teaching university for London, based on the 'existing institutions in London of University rank', which would be 'partially or completely incorporated, with the minimum of internal change'. Teaching and examining would both be directed 'by the same authorities'. Those 'engaged in the work of University Teaching and Examining' would have 'a substantive voice in the government of the University', which would have Faculties of Arts, Science, Medicine and Laws.[4]

For the clientele which they addressed, thirsty for change, this was rather like asking support for the proposition that motherhood was a good thing. The response was generally enthusiastic, but among the letters of acceptance there were hints of apprehension that there would be deep controversy over constitutional issues. A significant reply, for instance, came from Philip Magnus, by then Director of the City and Guilds Institute, who declared

> I am distinctly opposed to the establishment of any new University in London, but
> . . . I have been for some years in favour of widening the influence of the present
> University of London by making it a teaching as well as an examining body.[5]

The leaders of the Association found that they had to accept that theirs was a very broad church. At the end of the list of members who had joined by the end of December, 1885, there was added:

> . . . it must not, however, be considered that all those whose names appear on the
> list are in entire accordance with the proposals of the Executive Committee, as
> sanctioned by the General Meetings of the Association.[6]

---

[4] UL RC23/1/a.
[5] UL RC41/6, Magnus to Young, 12 December 1884.
[6] Selborne Commission, Appendix 4, p. 223.

It was November, 1884, before the Association was in a position to begin framing a proposal. A small committee was set up, six of whose nine members – Reay, Young, Marshall, Pye-Smith, Warr and Williamson – were UCL or KCL men. They were joined by Ord from St Thomas's Hospital, Frederick Pollock from the Council of Legal Education, and R.S. Poole from the British Museum. Their draft was put before the Association on 15 December, and a final version approved. The proposal was immediately made available, and achieved what, in the longer term, can be seen as the Association's major contribution – it compelled the attention of the interested parties, particularly Senate and Convocation.

The Association's original scheme, which was in many respects loosely and diplomatically drafted to allow room for manoeuvre when the reactions of all the potentially interested parties were known, was the first of many which were submitted during the following years by Convocation, Senate, Teachers and Royal Commissions. Whether they were pressing the case for one or more institutions, all of them, except the short-lived proposal of the Royal Colleges of Physicians and Surgeons, accepted a similar, fundamental, university structure, even if they used different names for some of the organisational units. That structure included a Governing Body, Constituent Colleges, Faculties, and Boards of Studies. Much of the accompanying argument was focussed on the composition and representative strengths of special interests in those units, and it is not intended to rehearse here in detail the endless succession of moves and countermoves to secure or to shift the balance of advantage, except when such manoeuvres illustrate particularly significant political activity. The texts of all the schemes are included in Allchin's work.

Emphasis is laid here on the political processes, particularly within and between Senate and Convocation, whereby the larger issues were resolved. Those major issues included whether there should be one or more universities; whether constituent colleges should be confined to the London area; whether constituent status should only be conferred on colleges offering instruction at university level; whether it was possible to combine internal and external teaching and examining within a single institution; and what, within a university, should be the degree of influence and authority given to lay governors, professional teachers, and the organisations representing graduates.

The scheme put forward by the Association in December, 1884, was revised but never formally recast. It had been produced by a group well before the Association itself had recruited almost half its final membership, and before there was an Executive Committee. When the latter was set up in February, 1885, Young appointed the young Francis Charles Montague, later to be a distinguished constitutional historian at UCL, as part-time Secretary. Surviving letters to him reveal the dominant roles of Young and Marshall, and also illustrate some of the difficulties involved in arranging meetings and recruiting to a range of faculty panels which the Association established to consider its scheme. Thus Frederick Pollock challenged the number of theologians in the Arts group, but supposed that 'they are there *qua* principals of colleges'. He thought that Edward John Poynter, the head of the Royal Academy, was 'a good name as names go, but [was] . . . profoundly sceptical as to any good coming out of the RA as at present constituted'. Nor did he feel that the Association would 'get much work out of either Bryce or Dicey, but they will be good for occasional consultation'. As for approaching the Council of Legal Education, they

> . . . would only say they were incompetent, and we must go to the Inns of Court: so we had better go there in the first instance as best we may – but this requires fresh consideration and feeling our way.

The problem of overlapping membership of interested parties is illustrated by Thiselton-Dyer's refusal to join the Association's Science panel because he was already actively engaged, representing Science on a Convocation Sub-Committee 'to ascertain how far the existing University can be adapted'. He thought

> . . . it would . . . be embarrassssing to be a member of two bodies whose aims are not exactly identical, although the object aimed at is practically the same.

And William Ord warned Montague not to try to hire a room at the Royal College of Physicians – 'the President of the College being supposed to hold somewhat hostile views.'[7]

The panels were all constituted by the end of May, 1885, and were largely constituted of members of UCL, KCL and the twelve London medical schools, including eleven members of the Association's Executive, of whom Young, Carey Foster and Pye-Smith served on each of the Arts, Science and Medicine panels. The panels worked throughout June and July, and no doubt their thinking was passed on to meetings which took place later between the Association's Executive, UCL and KCL, Convocation, and the Senate. No overall review of the panels' advice seems to have been produced, and though the Association must have been quietly active, there is no sign that its representatives took part in formal discussion with the Senate until May, 1886. By that time, however, there had been much turmoil within Convocation.

At the meeting in Reay's house on 3 May 1884, Pye-Smith had given a resumé of the suggestions, largely framed by himself and James Anstie – a colleague of Young's on the Charity Commission – which had been adopted

---

[7] For Montague's correspondence, see UL RC41/10–12.

by Convocation as long ago as 1878. After the Association's proposal was released, it was Pye-Smith and Anstie who successfully moved in Convocation, on 9 February 1885, for the setting up of a Special Committee of forty members to consider it. Anstie took the Chair on 9 February, when thirty-three of the forty met and agreed to report that Convocation should give general support to the Association's ideas. But at an Extraordinary Meeting of Convocation on 24 February, when that suggestion was discussed and carried overwhelmingly, the first formal sign of dissension appeared. It may well have been an early expression of hostility to the fact that the Association's scheme allowed for the possibility that a Teaching University might well be an institution quite separate from the existing University of London: any hint of such separation was anathema to fervently loyal members of Convocation, on this occasion represented by three Fellows of the University – Hutton, Osler, and Shaen. They moved an amendment to the effect that Convocation was 'not in a position to affirm the expediency of the adoption by the University of the diversified and indefinite objects of the Association'. But at this point in time, the enthusiasm of the reformers swept any opposition aside, and the Special Committee was re-appointed to continue to promote the acceptance of the Association's scheme.

When twenty-six of the Special Committee resumed their task, on 25 March, the Chair was taken by Sir Edward Fry, then usually known by his judicial title of Lord Justice, which will be used here. Lord Justice Fry, then Vice-President of the Council of UCL, was to be a leading figure in what followed. A sub-committee representative of the several proposed Faculties was set up. Fry took the chair; Andrew McDowall spoke for Arts, Thiselton-Dyer for Science, Savory for Medicine, and Anstie for Laws. A discussion with Senate, if the latter thought it desirable, was suggested, and Senate agreed, on 1 April, that they would be 'happy to receive and consider any definite plan for the promotion of objects which may be proposed by the Committee of Convocation'. It is unclear whether, and seems unlikely, that any such discussions took place; but the Convocation sub-committee certainly met a representative group from the Association six times between 30 April and 16 June. The Association's men were Young; J.W. Cunningham, Secretary of KCL; Marshall; Ord; Pollock; Pye-Smith and Wace – of whom Ord and Pye-Smith were also members of Convocation's Special Committee.

Only twenty-two of Convocation's Special Committee were present on 26 June, when Fry presented the recommended scheme of his sub-committee, which was accepted and in turn offered to Convocation at another Extra-ordinary Meeting on 28 July. It was then that serious disagreement within Convocation became apparent. Up to that point the proposals had not excited unusual attention among the high proportion of graduates who lived in the London area. Attendance at meetings was not noticeably larger, and it would seem highly probable that those members who were regular attenders included a clear majority in the Annual Committee, that they comprised most of the Special Committee of forty, and were predominantly reform-minded. They

Sir Edward Fry. Lord Justice of Appeal 1883–1892. Crown-chosen Member of Senate 1885–1900.

certainly included many practising teachers at UCL, KCL and the medical schools.

But there was a large element of the membership which was tribally defensive, and highly suspicious of any change which might weaken, rather than extend, the influence of Convocation. Though Fry's scheme did not envisage any possibility of establishing a separate university, it excited anxiety about the proposal to create Faculties, whose members would necessarily include non-London graduates, and whose representatives on the governing body would outnumber those of Convocation. Not far below the surface, too, was disapproval of any predominance of teachers as opposed to laymen in the governing councils of the University – a fear which would blossom later. Defence of the provincial and imperial connections; worry over which colleges and other institutions should be recognised as of university rank; and concern about whether the standard of the degrees could be maintained were other issues which threatened easy acceptance of Fry's suggestions.

There were 184 present on 28 July. Fry moved the receipt and adoption of the draft scheme. John William Bone moved not to adopt. After much debate, a motion to adjourn the meeting was carried by a vote of seventy-eight to forty-four. While too much should not be read into the figures of such a vote, taken in a clearly reducing House, it is interesting that no member of the Association was in the minority, and only fifteen Association members were among the victorious seventy-eight. Indeed, the Association had not attracted many members of Convocation.

During the long summer vacation of 1885, and the first weeks of the new session, disagreement over what was acceptable to Convocation in the way of support for a scheme of reform was stimulated by the opposing factions. Magnus made the running. He told his ally, William Job Collins, that he would be calling a private meeting of graduates 'to consider the objections to the proposed scheme and the course of action to be adopted'. The meeting was duly held on 21 October, and a circular listing objections was distributed after the meeting.[8] Those objections were the central points at issue in a rowdy and bitterly contested session of Convocation, convened for 3 November, and adjourned until 8 December. Attendance was 239 in November and 238 in December. The outcome was a rejection of parts of the Fry scheme, but more notably the rejection of Fry and many of his erstwhile colleagues. Magnus and a largely new team took over the leading role in Convocation's deliberations.

At the beginning of the meeting, Fry accepted that his Committee's Report should be received, not adopted. He asked that the House consider what amendments might be made to the scheme, and that instructions be given to a committee of revision. But this was defeated by 122 to seventy-eight. Magnus and Collins then proposed an amendment which indicated their main concerns:

> Convocation, whilst affirming the general principles of the desirableness of bringing the Teachers and the Examiners of the University into closer relationship with one another and with the Senate, and of modifying the constitution of the Senate in accordance with the previous recommendations of Convocation, and without giving to the Teachers an undue share of representation on the governing body of

---

[8] UL Ms812/41, Magnus to Collins, 4 October 1885. UL23/3/c.

the University, refers back the scheme to the Special Committee for further consideration . . .

Magnus and Collins also wanted to increase the size of the Special Committee by half – to sixty – but were prevailed upon to reduce the number to fifty. Their motion was carried on a show of hands, and Magnus was then asked to nominate a list of Committee members. But this he failed to do, because Fry and 'several other members of the former Special Committee', declared that they were unwilling to serve on any new body.[9] After several attempts to adjourn were defeated, it was proposed by Nesbitt and Weymouth that the new proposal be referred to the Annual Committee. At that stage, and without having voted on the Nesbitt/Weymouth motion, the debate was adjourned for five weeks.

Given the heat generated, it is perhaps unlikely that there was much chance of the long interval, before the second session, producing a compromise. But any such hope may have been dashed, finally, by a development which must have exacerbated the internal situation in Convocation. Towards the end of October, Sir Henry Maine resigned his seat on the Senate. On the very last day of the month, Lord Granville wrote to the Home Secretary, Richard Assheton Cross, telling him that

> The Vice-Chancellor, Sir James Paget, Sir John Lubbock his predecessor, and several of the leading members of the Senate have talked on the subject with me and we are all agreed as to the person whom it would be advisable to appoint.[10]

However, relations between the Liberals, now in opposition, and the Salisbury Government, were strained, and Granville was extremely cautious in his approach to Cross. As he explained in his letter to the Home Secretary, he had 'got "scalded" the other day in another quarter' and therefore did 'not like without encouragement from you to mention the name for your consideration, but will do so if you will send me one word of approval'.

Inevitably there was a delay of some days before Cross replied, and it was not until a week after the first of Convocation's two stormy sessions that Granville's recommendation was written. His letter shows that he, and presumably his close colleagues on the Senate, were very well aware of the situation:

> The person we recommend for your consideration as a succesor to Sir Henry Maine, is Lord Justice Fry, who has taken a great interest in the question of converting the University of London into a teaching institution. The feeling of the Senate seems to be adverse to the idea (although they have not committed themselves in any

---

[9]  Allchin, I, p. 107.
[10]  BL Add Mss 51275, Granville to Cross, 31 October 1885.

way) and it would make the discussion more harmonious and more efficient if we had so good an exponent of the views of a portion of the Graduates on the Senate. The appointment would be popular, as Lord Justice Fry is a very much respected graduate.[11]

Cross was very respectful of Salisbury. In 1878, when Salisbury was Secretary of State for India, Cross – then in his first spell as Home Secretary – had consulted him about filling places on the Senate, and accepted Salisbury's advice to appoint Rev. Alfred Barry, then Principal of KCL, rather than any of a short list which included Fry.[12] Seven years later Cross sought advice again:

It has been the invariable practice of the Home Office to consult with the Chancellor of the University on these vacancies, but I always as invariably consult with the Prime Minister also. Sir James Paget spoke to me the other day strongly about the Lord Justice Fry on the ground of the part which he had taken on the subject of a teaching university of London. Perhaps you would be good enough to let your secretary send me back Lord Granville's letter with your own observations.[13]

Lord Salisbury replied, on 17 November:

Lord Justice Fry is an excellent man – somewhat fanatical about some things – but I should think perfectly fitted for the proposed appointment.[14]

To what extent would it be fair to portray the appointment of Fry as a Senatorial *coup*? It is a little hard to believe that Granville's concern for 'more harmonious and more efficient discussion' in the Senate did not imply some sympathy for Fry's approach to the arguments about the University's future. Fry himself believed that it was Paget who wanted him on the Senate – 'with special reference to the contemplated changes in its constitution',[15] – a belief backed by Cross's letter to Salisbury quoted above. Paget may have alerted Granville, Lubbock and their colleagues to the controversy in Convocation – sparked in July and stoked by the meeting of Magnus and his supporters on 21 October – and persuaded them that, in a potentially difficult developing situation, Fry should not be lost to the Senate by being sidelined in Convocation.

Fry's appointment to the Senate was made on 2 December, less than a week before Convocation's adjourned meeting was resumed. Whether or

---

[11] BL Add Mss 51275, Granville to Cross, 10 November 1885.
[12] Hatfield House, 3M/E Cross to Salisbury, 2 March 1878.
[13] Hatfield House, 3M/E Cross to Salisbury, 16 November 1885.
[14] BL Add Mss 51263, Salisbury to Cross, 17 November 1885.
[15] Paget, *Sir James Paget* (London, 1901), p. 326.

not there had been any political calculation by Paget, Granville and others behind the appointment, it is quite likely that, by those in Convocation unhappy with Fry's scheme, his addition to the Senate, at that particular time, could have been seen as an indication of the support of the University's 'Establishment' for his ideas.

When Convocation resumed on 8 December, Nesbitt and Weymouth wanted to withdraw their suggestion that the matter be referred to the Annual Committee. They seem to have recognised that the Annual Committee was not regarded by the majority on the issue as any more properly representative than the original Special Committee. However, there were enough supporters of the Annual Committee present to prevent permission being given to withdraw the motion. But they did not have enough to force it through, and the motion was defeated on a show of hands. Then William Cawthorne Unwin, himself a member of the Annual Committee, and W.A. Tilden, moved for the setting up of a quite new committee of twenty-five. This, which offered the prospect of a more accurate representation of apparent majority opinion, was readily accepted, and Unwin presented his list of twenty-five members, no doubt previously negotiated. Unwin had just relinquished a Chair at the Royal Indian College of Engineering at Coopers Hill, in favour of the Central Technical College of the City and Guilds Institute, of which Magnus was Director. Tilden was Professor of Chemistry at Mason College, Birmingham.

But this did not settle the issue, for there was an immediate demonstration of the existence of at least one more organised group in opposition to the Fry scheme. Spratling, who sat on the Annual Committee, and was a graduate of UCL and the Royal School of Chemistry, put forward a further thirteen names. This provoked an argument over whether or not to suspend a Standing Order which governed the nominating procedure, only settled by a vote of seventy to forty-two. After that, the Chairman moved that the new Committee should consist of the twenty-five members proposed by Unwin: but the motion was lost. Then all thirty-eight names suggested – twenty-five by Unwin and thirteen by Spratling – were put to the meeting *seriatim*, and voted on by show of hands. Of the twenty-five members thus chosen, Anstie received eighty-eight votes, and the last five nominees each received forty-two votes. Even at the latest stage there was argument, when W.H.Broadbent and Spratling (only five of whose nominees, and not himself, were voted on to the committee) tried but failed to call for the adjournment, before the committee of twenty-five was formally appointed.

The extent of the change, within Convocation, between January and December, 1885, in who was to negotiate their proposal to alter the nature of the University, was considerable. Of the thirty-six members of the Special Committee of forty, set up in January, who had attended any of its meetings, only ten were elected in December to the new committee, and they included Magnus and four others who were sympathetic to his point of view. Of the sub-committee of five who had drawn up Fry's plan, only three joined and one of them, Thiselton-Dyer, attended only one meeting – in 1888. Altogether, thirteen of the twenty-five had voted for a new approach in November.

Magnus was to chair this committee until its demise in 1891. It was a group which hung together well. Twenty of its members kept up a high level of attendance, and in the crucial period up to May, 1886, there was an average turn-out of fourteen. But what is striking is that they were mostly persons from outside the formal hierarchies of the University, UCL and KCL. Nor were there more than a very few members of the Annual Committee. And though five of them were listed as members of the Association, it is clear that most of them were unsympathetic to some major aspects of the proposals of that body.

There is little doubt that the great majority of Magnus's Committee shared a dominant concern that there should only be one University in London, that it should be the existing University suitably modified, and that the present power and privileges of Convocation should be protected and enhanced. But it is also clear that they represented interests which were very conscious of being outside the 'magic circle' of University and King's Colleges. Thus Magnus, Silvanus Thompson, Unwin, and Wormell were all heavily involved in Technical Education and the City and Guilds Institute; while Sophie Bryant – the only woman – was teaching at the North London Collegiate School. Andrew McDowall was Secretary of the Girls Public Day School Trust. Of the five doctors, at least two were close allies of Magnus, and only two were from the medical schools of University and King's Colleges' Hospitals. The two barristers and two solicitors included only one – E.H. Busk – who taught law, and he did so for the Law Society. The only member long and closely associated with UCL was Talfourd Ely.

Despite the changes in personnel and the clear move away from some of the basic notions of the earlier exercise, the scheme which the Magnus Committee eventually produced, though it permitted the affiliation of Provincial Colleges and strengthened the defences of Convocation against overmuch teacher representation, was less radically different from that of the Fry Committee than might have appeared probable in December, 1885. In large part this was due to the influence of James Anstie and Philip Pye-Smith, those veterans of Convocation's plans of 1878 which the Senate had turned down. Pye-Smith carried his arguments to the press, presenting Magnus with a very plain challenge, that it was one thing to reject a scheme, but not so easy to put an acceptable one in its place.[16] As a result, the bargaining within the committee, which met seven times before submitting a report in May and June, 1886, was hard hitting and tended to be crisply focussed on a few major points.

---

[16] See his letter to the *Lancet*, November/December 1885, quoted in Allchin I, pp. 110–11.

Sir Philip Magnus, 1st Bt. Secretary and Organising Director of the City and Guilds of London Institute 1880–1913. Convocation-nominated Member of Senate 1890–1900; elected Member 1900–1931. Unionist MP for the University 1906–1922.

The more extreme proposals would have left the University as a nationwide institution, free to associate with any colleges except those affiliated to other universities. But the main thrust of those proposals was aimed at keeping the representation of Convocation high on all University bodies from the Senate downwards. The details need not detain us here, but it is worth stressing the strong desire to keep Convocation members within the University as a single body for voting purposes, rather than having them distributed – and their strength therefore diluted – among the Faculties, which would be mixed groups of members and non-London graduates. And when the Committee's proposals were debated by Convocation, there was at least one clear streak of opposition to any growth of the influence of teachers – a proposal from the floor provided 'That of the eight Members [of the Senate] to be elected by Convocation, not more than two shall be directly interested in Teaching.' That particular motion was defeated by forty-two to one, but, as will be seen, a degree of suspicion of, and hostility to, teachers re-surfaced later.

The minutes of Magnus's Committee reveal a good deal of complex, tactical voting, which makes recognition of many individual positions difficult. But it is clear that the main proponents of a hardline approach by Convocation were Collins, Napier and Rollit: Magnus was doubtless very sympathetic to their views, but as Chairman must have been fully aware that he would have to compromise with the more moderate element, whose chief spokesmen were Anstie, Pye-Smith and McDowall. The balance within the Committee was delicate. Only two divisions were recorded, and no lists of voting were printed, but in one case a split of six to six was decided by the casting vote of the Chairman: and in the other the voting was seven to six.

Drafting was delegated to Anstie, Magnus and Napier, approved by the Committee and debated by Convocation in two Extraordinary General Meetings on 25 May and 29 June, 1886. Interest in the outcome by the bulk of the London contingent of Convocation had waned severely since the previous winter. Only 126 attended on 25 May, and 113 on 29 June. There were a few amendments offered, and some attempts to close discussion by motions to adjourn. But the Committee's scheme, presented by Anstie and Magnus, suffered only very minor alteration, and was approved for discussion with Senate.

# 23

# *Things falling apart*

Convocation was the first interested party to subject the Association's original proposals to detailed scrutiny. During the eighteen months of that scrutiny, in 1885–86, just reviewed, the Association had acquired an Executive Committee, had established faculty panels to consider its proposals in detail, and had held conferences with representatives of most of the institutions who had responded to invitations to become members. As a result, by early in 1886, the Association's original scheme had been refined, and was deemed to be sufficiently developed for a fully documented version to be presented formally, for their consideration, to the University, UCL, KCL, the Royal Colleges of Physicians and Surgeons, the Medical Schools and the Council of Legal Education.[1]

The Senate responded first, on 14 April, by establishing – on the motion of its new member, Fry – a committee empowered to confer with a committee of the Association, with a committee of Convocation, and with anyone else whom they might think fit to consult. The experience of this Senate committee is best dealt with a little later. But it is worth noting now that it became, in effect, the parallel body to the Convocation committee of twenty-five, headed by Magnus, though much smaller. From 1886 until mid 1888 it met seventeen times: the average turn-out was eight. Sir Henry Paget, the Vice-Chancellor, and Fry, were never absent, while Pye-Smith (only appointed by the Crown to a Fellowship in the previous month), Quain, Hutton, Fitch, George Carey Foster, and the mathematician, E.J. Routh, were very regular in attendance. Of these, Pye-Smith was the only one who was, simultaneously, on the Magnus Committee, and it must be some indication of the difficulties of dual membership that he attended only one of the Convocation committee's meetings between May, 1886, when the Senate committee first met, and mid-1889.

Senate may have acted first in appointing a committee, but therefter the governing bodies of KCL, UCL and the Royal Colleges of Physicians and Surgeons moved more quickly. Both UCL and KCL met the Association's representatives in May, 1886, and subsequently recorded a general approval of the Association's proposals, without committing themselves in detail.

---

[1] For the data sent to the Senate, see UL RC23/1/j.

However, the reception of the proposals by UCL was made particularly memorable by the attitude of the College's academic Senate, which had been invited to comment by the College Council.

Eighteen Professors of UCL met on 15 June, and declared that the College should only approve the scheme if the Association accepted that the proposed University should be 'a local teaching, examining and degree-granting body', and that 'purely academical matters' should be 'under the control and management of its teachers'. Moreover, they recommended that 'No power in the proposed University be given to graduates as such.' All this clearly reflected the influence of Ray Lankester and Karl Pearson, who had been arguing the case for adopting the German or Scottish pattern of university government since at least 3 January 1885, when the former had raised the matter in a letter to the *Times*.

Professors Croom Robertson and Carey Foster would have preferred supporting general approval for the Association's ideas, together with an emphatic claim that, so far as the Arts and Sciences were concerned, KCL and UCL would be the 'proper constituents of a Teaching University'. But this was lost on a tied vote five-five. Professors A.J. Church and Charles Graham moved an amendment to omit the proposed ban on graduate participation, but lost by seven to four. The original motion was carried eight to one. No names were listed in the Minutes, and there is no way of knowing whether the low votes were an indication of indifference by almost half the members who attended, or whether those members had drifted away as the meeting progressed. It would be understandable if Carey Foster voted against or abstained, for he was a long-standing member of Convocation's Annual Committee and was within three weeks of being a convincing winner of the contest for nomination as the next Convocation-chosen Fellow – he defeated Weymouth and Philip Magnus, and took his seat in Senate on 5 August.

The UCL Council had entrusted consideration of the Association's proposals to a committee headed by Fry and including Arthur Charles – the Conservative candidate for the University seat, who had been defeated by Lowe six years previously – Cozens-Hardy, Professors Erichsen and Graham, Lord Hobhouse, John Rotton and Sir George Young. When Council met on 10 July 1886, there were fourteen members present, and they had before them Fry's committee report and the opinion of the College's professorial Senate. The outcome was a division in favour of giving general approval to the objects of the Association, by eight to four. There was no record of either the discussion or of the voting. The more radical professors had made their point, but for the moment their reservations were put aside. Of the fourteen present, Lord Kimberley was in the Chair; he, Fry and Buchanan were members of the University's Senate.[2]

---

[2] For a more detailed narrative of the UCL debate, see Allchin I, pp. 74–7.

Thus with the long vacation of 1886 in sight, UCL and KCL had, in effect, blessed and adopted the Association's proposals, but had taken no decision on how, whether and when to try to have them implemented. Such a decision would be taken in principle at the end of January, 1887, by UCL, and the final determination by UCL and KCL to seek the grant of a new Charter by the Crown to a teaching university, of which they would form the nucleus, would be made in the following May. At almost the same time, the Royal Colleges of Physicians and of Surgeons agreed to make their bid for a separate medical university. It is as well to look briefly at the medical developments before recording how the Senate reacted to them and to all the other proposals, after Fry joined their ranks in December, 1885.

While the importance of the interests of the Royal Colleges and the Medical Schools to the future of university organisation in London can scarcely be exaggerated, the debate in 1886–87, as to how those interests should best be met, was overwhelmingly conducted within the medical world. The efforts of the Association, UCL and KCL to attract the Royal Colleges and the medical schools into their camp were rebuffed. Convocation as a body took no formal part in the relevant negotiations, though several of the doctors most closely involved in the controversy were active members. The Senate was much exercised over the matter but, in the last resort, was also rebuffed. But while UCL and KCL were almost certainly disappointed, and while Convocation and the Association openly expressed disapproval of the policy of the medical institutions, the Senate was internally divided and took a neutral stand.

The Royal College of Surgeons was the first medical body to call, publicly, in March, 1884, to be granted the power to award degrees. Almost exactly a year later the Metropolitan Branch of the British Medical Association were prepared to throw their weight behind the idea if it proved impossible to extract 'adequate concessions from the University of London'. In Allchin's judgement, those concessions reflected a

> ... strictly utilitarian view ... The guiding principle throughout was not aimed at an improvement in education, whether general or professional, and thereby raising the status of the medical man, but rather on the contrary a lowering of the standard, for although this was not admitted it is what the proposals, so far as they had taken coherent shape, amounted to.[3]

A deputation from the BMA met the Senate on 29 April, 1885, when they were told by Paget that, while there was no 'direct opposition' to their views, the University had a primary duty to raise the level of medical education and to ensure that its degree

---

[3] Allchin I, pp. 52–3.

... shall indicate an attainment higher than that which commonly exists, not only in the practical subjects, but in the whole of that education which goes to make a well-educated gentleman as well as a practical physician.

Nonetheless, a couple of weeks later, Julian Goldsmid persuaded the Senate to consider the whole matter further: a familiar group of Fellows were named to constitute a committee – Carpenter, Fitch, Goldsmid, Gull, Huxley, Lubbock, Quain, Shaen, Storrar and Wood. They met another BMA deputation on 1 July, but thereafter contact between the Senate and the BMA in this context seems to have lapsed. Attention shifted decisively to the actions of the two Royal Colleges.

Between May, 1885, and December, 1886, the Physicians and Surgeons debated the practicability and the desirability of trying to obtain powers whereby the two Royal Colleges, acting together, could grant medical degrees. The detailed story is told in the books by Allchin, Cook and Cope listed earlier. The fundamental argument was between the majority, who had no confidence that the University of London could or would meet what they saw as the real need – to attract more people into the profession and to ensure that they were adequately, if narrowly, trained: and the rather small minority, who defended the liberal education of doctors, the protection of existing standards, and the raising of those standards, through the provision of medical studies within a university – whether it be the University of London or another.

The outcome was the agreement of both the Royal Colleges, just before Christmas, 1886, that they should petition the Crown for the grant of a Charter to enable them to offer degrees and to become, in effect, a one-faculty university. Plainly stated objections by the Association and by Convocation, and pleas to deter the Colleges from pursuing a separate path, had been ignored. The Report of the Association's Executive Committee, dated 20 July 1885, had commented on the

... proposal which is understood to be now under discussion among members of the medical profession, that the Colleges of Physicians and Surgeons should be independently empowered to grant medical degrees ... Your Committee would regret any severance of the machinery for granting degrees in London from academic influences.[4]

The same sentiment was built-in to the scheme for a reformed University of London which had been endorsed by Convocation at the end of June, 1886, and which became 'a strong competitor to the course so warmly advocated in many quarters, that the Royal Colleges should seek to obtain powers to confer a degree in medicine'.[5]

[4] UL RC23/1/c, reproduced in Allchin I, 73.
[5] Allchin I, p. 121.

The actions of the Royal Colleges in this period illustrate vividly the conflicting pressures bearing on several of the leading participants. The negotiating body set up by the two Colleges was called the Committee of Delegates. It was chaired by Sir William Jenner, President of the Physicians but also a Fellow of the University. Of the other members, no less than seventeen of the twenty were listed as belonging to the Association, and John Marshall was its President; Richard Quain was a long-standing Convocation-nominated Fellow; Pye-Smith, appointed to the Senate by the Crown in March, 1886, was a leading proponent of Convocation's scheme for the University; John Curnow had been elected to the Annual Committee every year since 1875, and was also an active member of the Association's Executive. Perhaps most notably, Sir James Paget was simultaneously Vice-Chancellor and a member of the ruling Council of the Royal College of Surgeons.

Inevitably there were some agonising personal decisions and no small number of inconsistencies in behaviour. Pye-Smith found it impossible to reconcile the University's and the Colleges' plans, and resigned from the Committee of Delegates. (As we have seen, he also refrained from attending the meetings of the parallel committee of Convocation, though retaining his membership.) But on the day after the Association had approved its Executive's report, including its hostility towards any move by the Colleges to seek degree-granting powers, the Council of the Royal College of Surgeons, with Marshall and Paget present and approving, accepted the proposals of the Committee of Delegates without demur. And in the final debates of the Royal College of Physicians it was revealed that a third of the Committee of Delegates had supported the Association's position. Allchin, who was then Assistant Registrar at the Royal College of Physicians, moved an amendment to provide 'for the conferring of degrees by some University body outside the Colleges', but it was defeated seventy to nine.

Allchin resigned his office, and commented, many years later, that he found 'the action of certain individuals who were members of the Executive Committee of the Association and also of the Joint Committee of the Royal Colleges inconsistent and indeed inexplicable'.[6] He may well also have felt that his much earlier view, expressed in March, 1885, was now even more justified:

> . . . in view of the inability of the University [of London] to adapt itself to the proposals of the [Association] and of other bodies it would be advisable that a Royal Commission should be appointed to inquire into the working of the University.[7]

[6] Allchin I, p. 79.
[7] *Lancet*, 28 March 1885.

Sir James Paget, 1st Bt. Surgeon, St Bartholomew's Hospital. Crown-chosen Member of Senate 1860–1899. Vice-Chancellor 1883–1895.

Fry attended his first Senate meeting on 23 December 1885, the day after Magnus presided over the opening session of the Convocation committee of twenty-five, which had effectively replaced Fry's earlier committee of forty. A week or so earlier, the Government added another Crown-chosen Fellow. Cross had told Salisbury:

There is now another vacancy and Lord Granville recommends Lord Lingen. I have written to him privately to say that though I have never looked upon the post as a political one yet if I were to recommend two such strong liberals . . . it would look as if there was *no* conservative Graduate in that University fit for the appointment and suggested such a man as Matthews QC who had been named to me by Sir Robert Fowler.[8]

Salisbury clearly had no scruples about treating the appointment as political: he wrote to the Home Secretary, brusquely, 'I certainly would *not* appoint Lingen. It is too much Radicalism all at once'[9]. He thought well of the Conservative, Roman Catholic, barrister and politician, Henry Matthews, who was duly given the Fellowship.

But if Fowler, Cross and Salisbury had hopes of Matthews making a Conservative mark on the University, they must have been disappointed. Matthews had been an examiner for the University in the 1870s: he was to be Home Secretary throughout Salisbury's Government of August 1886 to 1892, and to be a member of Senate until 1900; but he attended no meeting, either of Senate or any Senate committee, until 1896. Unlike his Cabinet colleague, Lord Cranbrook, the Lord President of the Council, therefore, he is unlikely to have had much if any impact on the University's controversies of the late 1880s.

But with the return of Gladstone as Prime Minister in February, 1886, Granville was back in the Cabinet, as were two other prominent Fellows – Kimberley and Herschell. Thus when John Storrar died, early in 1886, Paget must have been confident of sympathy from Granville when he instructed the Registrar to tell the Chancellor that it was

. . . of great importance, especially having regard to the last appointment [i.e. Matthews] that the Senate should secure some accession of strength on the scientific side, particularly in relation to the Medical Schools.[10]

But before this plea reached Granville, the Home Secretary, Hugh Childers, had already been lobbied by Julian Goldsmid, who had suggested Philip Magnus. Childers then asked Granville for his opinion.[11] The documentary evidence then dries up, but the outcome was the appointment of Philip Pye-Smith.

If Granville and Paget were searching, primarily, for a strengthening of support in Senate for a balanced and sympathetic approach to constitutional change, they must have welcomed Pye-Smith and, in the following August,

[8] Hatfield House, 3M/E Cross to Salisbury, 7 December 1885.
[9] BL Add Mss 51263, Salisbury to Cross, 11 December 1885.
[10] PRO 30/29/213, Milman to Granville, 11 March 1886.
[11] PRO 30/29/213, Ruggles Brise to Antrobus, 15 March 1886.

the nomination by Convocation of another doctor, Samuel Wilks of Guy's Hospital. But Paget may have had some regrets about Pye-Smith, who did not support the Vice-Chancellor's tolerance, later, of the possibility of a separate medical university. Pye-Smith was consistent in his belief in a reformed University of London:

> I want to make the London MB more accessible, more manageable, more flexible, but to keep the examinations as difficult or rather say as thorough and high as now. But here we want a Board of Studies where the teachers and examiners could meet and settle their points and report to the Senate. And I feel sure we shall get that and other reforms nearly as much needed if we unite in urging them.[12]

Both Fry and Pye-Smith were included in the committee set up in April, which met first on 24 May, and four additional times before the end of July. By then, though there is no record of internal dissension, they had not made sufficient progress to feel able to meet either the Association or Convocation. But it is clear that, though the Vice-Chancellor always took the chair, Fry was the driving force within the committee.

During the Long Vacation of 1886 there took place the seismic split within the Liberal Party, the defeat of Gladstone over Home Rule for Ireland, and the establishment of the Conservative-Liberal Unionist Administration led by Salisbury, which would be in power for the next six years. It was in a new, national political climate, therefore, that the Senate committee, on 23 November, met Marshall, Young, Henry Morley and Montague from the Association; and in the following week talked with Anstie, Collins, McDowall and Tilden from Convocation. By late December they would be fully aware of the resolve of the Royal Colleges of Physicians and Surgeons to prepare a case to take to Government in search of a new Charter; and they knew that UCL and KCL had been waiting to decide on a similar possible move since the end of the previous summer. At New Year, 1887, therefore, the Senate committee had to consider what they could come up with, which might divert the other parties from pursuing separatist courses.

Reasonable scepticism about the future, in this period, must have assailed many of those who shared responsibility. Kimberley had written to Reay in the summer of 1886 that 'The "teaching" University controversy still rages in London, with apparently not much prospect of a practical solution.'[13] Six months later, Joshua Fitch – himself a member of the Senate's committee – commenting on a recent article in the *Quarterly*, asked whether it did

---

[12] Archives and Mss Section of the Wellcome Library, Papers of Sir Edward Sharpey-Schafer, PP/ESS/B.53/6, Pye-Smith to Schafer, 19 February 1885.
[13] Bod Mss Eng c4231, Kimberley to Reay, 16 July 1886.

. . . not, after all, indicate the limits beyond which the present institution, at any rate, is unable to go . . . ? A great federation of all the colleges and agencies for higher teaching in London would undoubtedly be a good thing. But the impulse in favour of such a project, and the means and resources for giving effect to it must come from without. It is difficult to see how either can come from the present University. And the 'Association' though very much in earnest, is not strong in numbers or in influence, and has during its two or three years of life made very little way. It certainly does not represent either money, or any very weighty public opinion; and its demand that the University should *first* change its constitution, and then set about organizing the higher education in London, seems to me an unreasonable one. But the matter will soon come before the Senate, in a formal way, on the consideration of Fry's report.[14]

Fry's draft was put before the committee at the beginning of February, 1887, but it was early March before a version was agreed for report to Senate, which included the exhortation that 'it is expedient to introduce changes' into the constitution of the University. An open letter from Fry to the Vice-Chancellor, dated 4 March, laid out what, from the Senate's point of view, was fairly described as involving 'very radical changes'. This was, in fact, the turning point in the University's attitude. After years of casting an indifferent eye on all efforts to bring about change, the Senate were about to be persuaded by Fry and his colleagues to accept many of the major themes proposed by the Association and already adopted by Convocation. What was now envisaged was a scheme of Associated Colleges across the country whose teachers would form Faculties; 'an enlargement of the objects and purposes of the University', to include 'the foundation of professorships and the further-ance of original research'; and some important alterations to the composition of the Senate.

There were some significant differences between Fry's Scheme and the other proposals, but at least they all incorporated a broadly similar institu-tional framework – the devil, as always, lay in the detail. And Fry himself was clearly somewhat daunted by the complexity of the overall situation: he accepted that there were 'at the present moment . . . very numerous and various schemes in relation to the higher education in London', and admitted his own belief that the whole subject deserved the attention of a Royal Commission.

The Senate, with eighteen present – an above average turn-out, but not a specially large one – gave their committee's scheme general approval on 16 March. There would appear to have been no major opposition, and this suggests that until Granville and Paget had managed to get Fry on to the Senate, there had really been nobody who had the grasp and persuasiveness

---

[14] BL Add Mss 49650, Fitch to Lubbock, 17 January 1867. *Quarterly Review*, vol. 164, January 1887.

to force attention to the claims of the various reformers and to call for concensus on the necessity of a more flexible approach. Be that as it may, there was only one division on 16 March, before the whole plan was referred back for further consideration. The contentious item was a proposal by Pye-Smith that the committee should consider whether, in a new Senate, all or any of UCL, KCL, the two Royal Colleges, the Council of Legal Education and the Incorporated Law Society should be represented. This was only approved by a vote of ten to nine, and was no doubt one of the issues discussed when the committee met another deputation from Convocation, on 18 May.

But, by then, pressures on the other parties to act independently had been intensifying. The Royal Colleges were petitioned by students and teachers in several of the metropolitan medical schools, and by the Association of General Practitioners, all supportive of the Colleges' proposals. At UCL the professorial Senate, on 28 January 1887, after considerable debate, resolved, unanimously, to back the College's Council decision of the previous July, to organise 'a teaching University in and for London, with Faculties of Arts, Science, Medicine and Law', but only after it had been made clear that many of the professors were still pushing hard for control of any new university by its teachers. The Annual General Meeting of the Members of UCL, on 23 February, gave a blessing to the Council's resolution of 10 July 1886 – but not the scheme of the professors – that the College, in conjunction with KCL, should petition the Crown for a Charter.

Subsequently, UCL and KCL approached the two Royal Colleges, suggesting that a conference of all four be held to prepare a combined application to the Privy Council. The Royal Colleges referred this to their Committee of Delegates, but the latter recommended against, on 2 April, arguing that it was desirable for the medical bodies to proceed,

> . . . conjointly and independently of other Bodies, with their endeavour to obtain the right to confer Degrees in Medicine and Surgery; and that, therefore, it is at present inexpedient to hold a conference with the University and King's Colleges for the purpose of procuring further powers to grant Degrees in Arts and Sciences.[15]

So far, only the Royal Colleges had shown themselves to be quite adamant in their desire to obtain separate degree-giving status. Despite the vigorous dispute within Convocation, there was still a lot of debate within and between UCL, KCL, Convocation – and now Senate. But in May, 1887, hopes of any agreed solution between the Senate and Convocation, on one side, and the Association, UCL and KCL, on the other side, disappeared. The crisis arose through the determination of the UCL professors, and their allies in the

---

[15] Allchin I, p. 159.

governing Council of the College, to press for the incorporation of ideas of teacher control in any petition for a new Charter.

Whether the professors feared that they were losing momentum; or whether, simply, they lost patience, the matter was brought to a head on 25 March when Young, seconded by Croom Robertson, carried a motion through the College Council providing that, in the new university to be sought, candidates for degrees should be required to attend approved courses of study. This, like the notion of teachers controlling their own examinations, so offended Fry and Wood, the Chairman of Convocation, that they resigned. Fry was persuaded to stay for the moment, but Wood was unrepentant. However, on 21 May, at a Special Meeting of the Council, Erichsen and Rotton moved to approve the submission of a petition to the Crown for a Charter to make UCL and KCL the cornerstones of a new University. Cozens-Hardy and Goldsmid put forward an amendment designed to delay until the University's Senate had made a firm decision on the proposals of its committee, which had been discussed again with a delegation from Convocation only three days before. But the amendment failed by eleven to seven, and the original motion was carried by the same margin.

This was a step too far for the seven defeated members. Lord Kimberley, the President of the College, Fry, Buchanan and Goldsmid, all Fellows of the University, resigned, as did Cozens-Hardy, Blake Odgers, and Augustus Prevost. Thus, together with Wood, the UCL Council lost eight members and moved decisively away from association with Senate and with Convocation. Privately, Kimberley condemned the Council's action as 'This foolish move', which he saw as having arisen 'from jealousy of the new Victoria University and the desire of the Professors to get the examinations into their own hands, the worst possible system'.[16]

In a rather more restrained, formal statement, the seven who resigned after the 21 May decision argued that what was now proposed went far beyond the general welcome which the Council had given to the Association's ideas in July, 1886. Their declaration did not conceal a strong bias against control by teachers:

> In the first place, we object to the proposal that the professors and teachers should confer degrees upon their own students. The petition, which has been adopted . . . affirms this principle in the strongest terms. In the second place, we object to making attendance on a regular course of instruction in the College a condition of obtaining a degree. It is contrary to the best tradition of the College to prescribe attendance at the lectures of a professor, however eminent he may be, and the experience of the College shows that it is impossible to secure the same high standard of efficiency in every chair. The welfare of students, without reference to the professional or pecuniary interests of the teachers, should be the aim of a great

[16] Bod Mss Eng e2793, Kimberley's Diary, 7 June 1887.

teaching institution. In the third place, we are convinced that the only prudent course for the College in this crisis is to endeavour to maintain cordial relations with the University of London, and to seek for even a more intimate union with it.[17]

And in a slightly different statement, dated 16 June, Kimberley and his colleagues made clear that they found it difficult to take 'any part in a movement for the creation of a second University in London'.[18]

Thereafter, matters moved more swiftly. The Senate's committee agreed its further consideration of Fry's scheme and made some concessions to the views of Convocation. The scheme, thus amended on 22 June, never seems to have been formally adopted by Senate, but it was practically so regarded, and used in future negotiations. However, further debate on it on the floor of the Senate was simply avoided.

By mid-July, UCL and KCL had submitted a petition calling for the establishment by Charter of a new institution to be called the Albert University of London. The draft Charter included provisions which were inserted in the hope that the Royal Colleges would join them, but the latter had already decided to accept the advice of their Committee of Delegates, and thereafter showed no interest in changing that decision. The Association presented a petition in favour of a new teaching university which would include a medical faculty: the petition specifically disapproved of the proposal of the Royal Colleges. In effect, the Association's petition was supportive of the scheme sought by UCL and KCL.

The Senate, thus forced into a defensive position, was quick to respond to the scheme of UCL and KCL. Their objections were forwarded to the Privy Council at the beginning of August. And though Convocation had not persuaded the Senate to meet all its demands for constitutional change, the challenge of UCL and KCL encouraged Convocation and the Senate to close ranks. Convocation formally expressed its approval of the Senate's stand against the creation of the Albert University on 17 January, 1888. But the responses by the Senate and Convocation to the demand for a Senate of Physicians and Surgeons were very different.

Despite their earlier decision, the Royal Colleges were slower to present their petition than were UCL and KCL: the Privy Council Office did not receive it, and the draft Charter, until November, 1887. As soon as that happened, the Senate referred the matter to its committee, which had not met for five months, since drafting the Senate's statement to the Privy Council opposing the UCL/KCL petition. But the minutes of the meeting of the committee on 14 December read, bleakly, that 'There being a difference of

---

[17] Allchin I, p. 179.
[18] Bod Mss Eng c4466.

opinion . . . it was resolved to postpone taking any action . . . until after the next meeting of Senate.'

What followed must have been tense and embarrassing. Paget, the Vice-Chancellor, in his role as a member of the Council of the Royal College of Surgeons, had voted in favour of seeking separate degree-granting status for the Royal Colleges. At least two eminent Fellows – Richard Quain, and Huxley – were supporters. But all three must have been very well aware of the strength of feeling against any division or diversion of the existing University's authority and coverage. Indeed, only a few months earlier, Quain had harangued the Registrar about the Government's duty to 'guard the interests of our University' and had written:

> There can be no doubt that a second University in London would seriously damage the interests of the State University. For this there is no justification – very much the reverse in many respects.[19]

On medical matters, however, he felt differently.

At the last meeting of Senate in 1887, the issue of how the University should respond to the submission of the petition for a Charter by the Royal Colleges was discussed, and it was agreed that statements in support of and against the petition should be prepared – by Huxley for, and by Fry, against. Those statements were circulated to Fellows, and, on 11 January 1888, Quain proposed that the Senate should not oppose the Royal Colleges, but would want guarantees that their degrees should not be 'in any way confounded with' the degrees of the University of London; that 'the preliminary education' of those who received degrees from the Colleges should be 'not inferior to the like education of those who receive University degrees'; and that no degrees of the Colleges should be conferred on those who have 'already passed the professional examination'.

To this somewhat tortuous proposal Fry offered an amendment which was, effectively, a substitute motion. He called for an approach to be made to the Crown, asking that the petitions of UCL and KCL, and of the Royal Colleges, and 'the whole subject of the higher education in London', be considered by a Royal Commission. The voting was dramatic. There were fourteen present. On the amendment the result was a tie, six-six: for the Ayes, Fry was joined by two medicos, Buchanan and Pye-Smith, and by Thiselton Dyer, Joshua Fitch and Hutton. For the Noes, three doctors – Paget, Quain and George Johnson, Professor of Clinical Medicine at KCL, were together with Huxley, Osler and Bradley, the Dean of Westminster. Fowler and Wood, the Chairman of Convocation, either abstained or had left the meeting.

The Vice-Chancellor, Paget, gave his casting vote to the Noes. Quain's motion was carried six to five, Pye-Smith, Fowler and Wood not casting

---

[19] UL RC23/9, Quain to Milman, 31 August 1887.

any vote. Thus no formal objection was made to the Privy Council by the University against the petition of the Royal Colleges. Convocation expressed strong disapproval of the Senate's decision, early in March. Meanwhile the Senate had agreed to ask the Home Secretary and the Treasury to give attention to the Petition of UCL and KCL; had requested that nothing be done before the University had been allowed to state its case; and had set up a committee to watch over the petition proceedings, whose members should be Fitch, Fry, Goldsmid, Herschell, Hutton, Lubbock, Quain and Wood. On 22 February 1888, they learned that the Privy Council hearings would not take place before 16 April. And at the same time, with a much fuller house of twenty-two members present, Fry regained some ground by proposing and carrying – without a division – a motion calling on the Chancellor, who was in the Chair, to request a Royal Commission.

# 24

# *The Selborne Commission*

By the time the petition of UCL and KCL arrived at the Privy Council Office in the summer of 1887, some observers of the higher educational scene were confident that a far more wide-ranging inquiry than hearings of petitions by Privy Council Committees was inevitable. 'Of course,' wrote the *Journal of Education*, on 1 July, 'there will be a Royal Commission to consider them and the cognate petitions from the Doctors and Surgeons', and did not doubt 'that the upshot will be a Teaching University for London'. But despite a steady stream of letters to the *Times*, and articles in the medical press, it is unlikely that even the few Ministers who were aware of the argument going on in and between the institutions mainly concerned were prepared for what developed in the following six or eight months. They may well have been taken aback to discover how the proposals for the Albert University and for awarding degree-giving powers to the Royal Colleges of Physicians and Surgeons were to be challenged by provincial Britain and within the medical profession. In the months after July, 1887, petitions filling thirty files in the records of the Privy Council were received, mostly from Universities and Medical Schools, all but three either opposing the proposals outright, or asking that institutions should be recognised and their places ensured in any settlement.[1]

The Senate excited some scorn for rejecting the idea of the Albert University while not offering direct opposition to the proposals of the Royal Colleges. But what is particularly striking was the opposition within medical circles to the scheme of those Colleges. The *Lancet* felt that

> To object in *toto* to the formation of a real Teaching University in London, which would at any rate secure an adequate knowledge of arts and science in candidates for its degrees, and passively support a movement which is admittedly for a purely professional object, without any relation to academic education, is a policy which can hardly fail of being characterised as eminently selfish. The University, by this false move, has been placed in an isolated position as the supporter of the Royal Colleges, and in virtual antagonism to every other University in the kingdom which are unanimous in their opposition to a degree-granting power being bestowed upon the Corporations.[2]

[1] PC8/384/60553.
[2] *Lancet*, 10 March 1888.

But whatever the Lord President of the Council may have thought of the Senate's different views on the two main petitions, he was obliged to take some note of their formal request that he refer the whole matter to a Royal Commission; and it was reported that Lords Granville, Derby, Kimberley and Herschell would urge the Government to initiate such an inquiry.[3] In any event, the prospect of several Privy Council committees having to cope with a host of hostile petitions covering so complex and extensive a subject matter made normal procedure impossible. When exactly the decision was made is unclear, but on 12 March 1888, in the House of Lords, Lord Cranbrook told Lord Herschell, standing in for the Chancellor, Lord Granville, that

> . . . he had come to the determination to recommend the issue of a Royal Commission to inquire into the subject, which was one dealing with a large number of interests. He thought the Commission need not be a large one, and then they would get through the work more speedily, and perhaps in time to report this Session.[4]

This first of two Royal Commissions set up to consider the future of higher education in London was often called the Albert Commission; and the second was often called the Gresham Commission. Those titles reflected the proposed names of a university whose establishment was sought, and they will be found here in several quotations from relevant contemporary documents. But in the present text the conventional practice of calling Royal Commissions by the names of their Chairmen, is followed: hence, Selborne and Cowper.

There is remarkably little material in the papers of the Lord President of the Council, Gathorne Hardy, Viscount Cranbrook – he became an Earl in 1892 – about the setting-up of the Royal Commission. It is difficult to believe that such a move could be made without the Prime Minister being consulted, but Salisbury's papers do not yield any comment. There was a much larger and more potentially explosive debate raging about school education, and it may be that Cranbrook was simply given a free hand to deal with what was probably seen, politically, as a knotty but relatively minor matter. He did talk with Goschen, the Chancellor of the Exchequer, about the new Commission, but they 'did not come to a conclusion'.[5] Goschen was the founder and presently the President of the London Society for the Extension of University Teaching, whose relationship to university institutions in London would be scrutinised in the inquiry; but whether this caused any problem for Cranbrook can only be matter for speculation. In view of what was to happen, it is

---

[3] *BMJ*, 25 February 1888.
[4] Parl. Deb. 3s, vol. 323, col. 817, 12 March 1888.
[5] Nancy E. Johnson (ed.), *The Diary of Gathorne Hardy, later Lord Cranbrook, 1866–1892: Political Selections* (Oxford, 1981), p. 699, 12 April 1888.

Gathorne Hardy, 1st Earl Cranbrook. Lord President of the Council 1886–1892.

reasonable to suggest that, overall, the Lord President, in hoping for a quick and definitive solution, may have seriously underestimated the tenacity with which the institutions and the controversialists of higher education would defend their entrenched positions.

Cranbrook's selection of Commissioners was an interesting combination of Establishment thinking, Conservative instinct, and, seemingly, some anti-medical bias. He appointed no representative of the medical profession. Perhaps he could find no one who he felt was genuinely neutral about the idea of a separate medical university. Perhaps he was himself convinced that the idea was unacceptable and did not deserve serious consideration. Three years later he commented, at a more advanced stage of the continuing controversy over university education, that 'The Doctors have been obstinate and unreasonable which is not uncommon'.[6]

Cranbrook put his trust in seven men, one of whom dropped out very quickly. Of the six who signed the Report, three were lawyers, two were scientists and one was a headmaster. The Chairman was the high churchman, Lord Selborne, who had been Gladstone's Lord Chancellor but had become a Liberal Unionist in 1886. The first of his legal colleagues was J.T. Ball, who had been Solicitor General, Attorney General and Lord Chancellor of Ireland in Disraeli's Governments and had represented Dublin University as a Conservative: he was currently Vice-Chancellor of Dublin. The third lawyer was the highly respected judge, Sir James Hannen, in earlier days an adviser to Elizabeth Garrett. He had stood, unsuccessfully, as a Liberal candidate for Shoreham in 1865. In September, 1888, while the Commission was still sitting, he was made President of the inquiry into the forgery of Parnell's letters to the *Times*.

The first of the two scientists, the future Lord Kelvin – Professor William Thomson of Glasgow – was an 'ardent unionist', according to the DNB; his colleague was George Stokes of Cambridge, President of the Royal Society since 1885, and Conservative MP for Cambridge University since 1887. They and their legal companions were all in their sixties or early seventies. By contrast, the Rev. J.E.C. Welldon, Headmaster of Harrow, was only thirty-four.

The joker in Cranbrook's pack was G.C. Brodrick, who was Warden of Merton College, Oxford, and had been briefly a contender for the London University seat in Parliament, in 1867. Late in March, 1888, whether by invitation or at his own request, he called on Cranbrook, who recorded in his diary: '. . . yesterday George Brodrick called about the Royal Commission on Universities. He thinks a good deal of himself'.[7] It may be that this episode followed Cranbrook's invitation to Brodrick to join the Commission: if not, it did not deter the Minister from appointing him. The Commission was

[6] Johnson, *Diary of Gathorne Hardy*, p. 804, 14 July 1891.
[7] Johnson, *Diary of Gathorne Hardy*, p. 698, 20 March 1888.

announced on 2 May, 1888, 'to inquire whether any and what kind of new university or powers is or are required for the advancement of higher education in London'. The first meeting was held on 2 June; it was the only meeting which Brodrick attended, and he resigned very soon afterwards.

Brodrick defended his action a dozen years later in a volume of memoirs.

> In my opinion, a Royal Commission should retain absolute control over the reception of evidence, selecting expert witnesses at its own discretion, inviting representative witnesses from bodies interested in the subject of inquiry, receiving offers from individuals desirous of being examined, but exercising a strict discrimination in the acceptance of such offers, and rigorously limiting both the scope and the duration of the proceedings. Unhappily, the contrary policy too often prevails, the consequence being that inquiries which might be completed in a few months are too often protracted over years, resulting in a halting report, with one or two memorandums of dissent, followed by piles of evidence so voluminous that hardly any one reads them, and published so late as to be almost obsolete for purposes of legislation. . . . Finding the London University Commission disposed to adopt a like course by welcoming evidence from all comers, and having failed to carry a motion in a contrary sense, I declined to be responsible for the sacrifice of time which I thought would ensue. In the end, this proved less than I had anticipated; but the recommendations of the Commission did not meet with general acceptance.[8]

It is possible that the touchy Brodrick may have clashed particularly with Selborne. Though, in his memoirs, he expressed gratitude for the Chairman's friendship, Brodrick also wrote of Selborne that

> He was said to be rather supercilious in his consultations with juniors, and his bearing on two Commissions of which I was a member enables me to understand this complaint.[9]

And it may be that Brodrick persuaded William Anson, the Warden of All Souls, against taking his place on the Commission: Anson told Cranbrook that he wished 'to discuss with Brodrick before replying to the invitation'.[10] After Anson's refusal, Cranbrook must have decided to leave the membership of the Commission at six.

This petty and regrettable incident may have set the mood for what was, in most respects, a disappointing exercise. Some of Brodrick's criticisms of procedure were certainly valid in this case. The Commission took oral evidence from forty-five witnesses – twenty of them medical – representing nineteen institutions, and received written submissions from fourteen

---

[8] Brodrick, *Memories*, pp. 172–4.
[9] Brodrick, *Memories*, p. 235.
[10] Suffolk RO, Ipswich, HA43/T501/63, Anson to Cranbrook, 13 June 1888.

organisations, of whom ten did not send representatives to appear before the Commissioners. All the interviews were held between the beginning of June and the beginning of August, 1888, but the Report was not signed until the end of April, 1889. Selborne, late in 1888, 'had a serious attack of illness, partly in consequence of acting as Chairman of a Royal Commission on University Education for London, the duties of which proved harder than I had expected'. And when a second Commission was in prospect in 1892, he refused to serve, claiming that 'it nearly killed him before', and that 'Jealousies and prejudices have combined to uproot a sound foundation.'[11]

The greater part of the Report of the Selborne Commission left the whole issue of the future of university education in London unresolved. But in one respect the Commissioners cleared the air decisively. They simply dismissed the idea of a separate medical university.

> ... a great demand exists for medical degrees attainable in London more easily than at present, and ... it may be desirable to provide for that want in some proper manner. But a careful consideration of the whole evidence has led us unanimously to the conclusion, that the establishment of such a body as the Senate of Physicians and Surgeons proposed by the Royal Colleges would not be the best means by which that end could be attained; and that a remedy may be found for any practical grievance under which the medical students of London, the licentiates or members of the Royal Colleges, or the licentiaties of the Society of Apothecaries, may now labour in respect of access to medical degrees, without either conferring the power of giving such degrees upon colleges which have no academical character, or creating a new examining and degree-giving university in a single faculty: neither of which innovations appears to us in itself desirable ... the charter asked for by the Royal College of Physicians of London and the Royal College of Surgeons of England ought not to be granted ...[12]

After April, 1889, there was no early possibility of three universities in London.

The Selborne Commission's dismissal of the case for a separate medical university was their most dramatic and effective recommendation. But, in the widest context, the Commissioners gave their full support to the desirability of providing London with a Teaching University. However, in their Report, signed by all six members, they were reluctant to recommend the creation of a new institution separate from the existing University of London. They stressed that neither of the two schemes put forward by Convocation, nor the single scheme produced by the Senate committee, to give the University of London a more inclusive character, had been 'either finally approved or

[11] Selborne, *Memorials* (London 1896–98), Pt 2, vol. 2, pp. 297–8. Johnson, *Diary of Gathorne Hardy*, p. 820, 11 March 1892.
[12] PP 1889, xxxix, C5709.

absolutely rejected' by their parent bodies. And they argued that within UCL, the main promoter of separation, there were divisions of opinion on the matter. In short, the Report favoured the continuation of a single University, stretching out to include all legitimate higher educational ventures, in a London confederation; and recommended that the whole question should be referred back to the Senate and Convocation, which should be given reasonable time to come up with a scheme agreed by all parties.

It is interesting to speculate on whether, had this advice from the Commissioners been unequivocal, as its main Report implied, and had Government been willing to give unqualified support to the desirability of having a single University for London, the sought-after agreement would have been reached and the University re-shaped within a year or two. Certainly the confidence of the Association, and of UCL and KCL, would have been shaken, and the Physicians and Surgeons might have felt even more deterred from any further attempt at separation.

But the chance of the future being heavily influenced by an unequivocal Report was undermined by the bizarre behaviour of half of the Commissioners themselves. Having put their names to the main Report, the three educationists – Stokes, Thomson and Welldon – added a Note stating that

> . . . considering the very large number of candidates who present themselves for the various examinations leading up to a degree [of the existing University], we doubt the possibility of effectually combining the functions of an examining, and of a teaching as well as examining, university in the University of London, and on this account we should have preferred the establishment of a new teaching university for London, leaving it to the London University to continue to discharge its present functions. At the same time we feel that there are objections which may be urged against the plan of having two distinct universities in London discharging totally different functions, though we are not disposed to attribute so much importance to these objections as some of our colleagues. If it is assumed that there is to be but one university for London, we think that the change in the constitution of the London University recommended in the Report is as good as could be desired, and we acquiesce in the recommendation that an attempt should be made to unite the teaching and examining functions in a single university.

In the light of such a statement, the main Report could scarcely be regarded as convincing, and the whole exercise was received with a good deal of scepticism. There is no account of how the Commissioners came to adopt the formula of a short Note of fundamental disagreement with aspects of an apparently agreed draft, rather than to present fully argued majority and minority reports. A few years later, there were differently remembered views of the positions taken by two of the educationists, Thomson and Welldon.[13] But we

---

[13] Allchin II, p. 150n.

have seen that Selborne was a sick man, and was certainly unhappy with the task of chairing the inquiry. And Lord Hannen, who attended all the hearings of the Commission, and signed the Report, was almost certainly prevented, by the calls of the Parnell case on his time, from giving much attention to the final consideration of evidence and drafting of the recommendations. Perhaps, if Selborne had been well, and Hannen present throughout, the differences of view might have been at least presented less equivocally.

Be that as it may, the doubts so oddly expressed by the educationists ensured that few, if any, opponents of all or parts of the Commission's main recommendations were likely to accept those recommendations. As for the Government, the view of Ministers about the Report may well have been accurately summed up by Goschen, the Chancellor of the Exchequer, who was a Fellow of the University and a strong supporter of University Extension. He remarked, dryly, that

> . . . all the members of the legal profession taking one view, and all the members of the educational profession the other [was] a circumstance which somewhat impaired the authority of the conclusions to which [the Commission] had come.[14]

In the circumstances, the Government apparently felt that the only way ahead was to accept the suggestion of the main Report, that Senate and Convocation be given the chance to try again to come up with an agreed scheme to convert the University of London into both a teaching and an examining institution. The Report, and its acceptance by Government, meant that the Senate had to take, and sustain, a new initiative. On 19 June 1889, they formally received the Commissioners' recommendations. On that day they set up a committee to report on 'the expediency of a Re-constitution of the University' as indicated by the Report, and to base their consideration on the Scheme which had been submitted to the Senate in March, 1887, and amended on 22 June of that year. It was the Scheme drafted by Fry, which incorporated some – but by no means all – of the ideas contained in the earlier Convocation exercise headed by Philip Magnus.

The committee to which Senate entrusted the negotiations in the new situation was the same as that which had considered the earlier schemes since April, 1886, with the addition of Lord Herschell, James Anstie, and the Chairman of Convocation, Wood. Anstie would become a major force in

---

[14] BL Add Mss 49706 fol. 119–1233, 17 February 1892, Draft of 'Answers to Objections of a Committee appointed at a meeting of the Society for the Liberation of Religion from State Patronage and Control.'

the whole of this and later exercises. The committee was unchanged until October, 1890, when Sir Albert Rollit and Philip Magnus, both prominent in Convocation's affairs, who had become Fellows, respectively, in the previous February and July, were added. The great majority of the group may perhaps be reasonably thought of as representative of the University's 'Establishment' in this context. They met every two weeks in each of the sessions 1889–90 and 1890–91. Attendance was high: the Vice-Chancellor (Paget), Anstie, Fry, Pye-Smith, Wood, and Quain, were rarely absent, while Lubbock, Osler and Carey Foster turned out for four-fifths of the meetings. Magnus and Rollit were present at almost every meeting in the session 1890–91. Fitch, Herschell, Hutton and Routh were less in evidence, but nonetheless attended about half the sessions.

We have seen that the committee of Convocation, set up at the end of 1885, with Magnus as Chairman, continued to function until April, 1891. It had not met for almost a year when it came together again in June, 1889: thereafter it met fifteen times. Most of those who served on it were also members of the Annual Committee during the period. The most regular attenders were Magnus, Baines, Collins, McDowall, Napier, Ely, Anstie and Wood, while Rollit, Silvanus Thompson and Johnson were present at more than half the meetings. Four of the five members who were also Fellows – Anstie, Magnus, Rollit and Wood – also attended almost all the parallel Senate committee meetings. All this cross-membership, however, did not prevent the leadership group in Convocation from becoming badly split.

The cast of characters at University College and King's College remained much the same as in previous years. Young was the driving force at UCL, but that College was less united than was King's, which was perhaps more confident because the Conservative Government in office was naturally sympathetic to an Anglican institution. Dr Wace was an aggressive leader, and had the support, on the Council of KCL, of the Prime Minister, the First Lord of the Treasury and Leader of the House of Commmons (W.H. Smith), the Home Secretary (Matthews), the Attorney General (Sir Richard Webster), and the formidable Bishop Temple. Rollit was also a member.

In the two years from May, 1889, to May, 1891, there took place some of the most stressful and difficult negotiations of the whole long controversy over the future of the University of London. And the bitter reality is that all those negotiations came to nothing. The demands of the various parties were so tenaciously pursued that they proved to be quite incompatible: agreement was brutally rejected. The *coup de grâce* would be administered by Convocation – though, in truth, it was the result of the unyielding opposition of several particular interests, and also reflected legitimate doubt as to the viability of a proposed final scheme characterised by unsatisfactory compromises.

The Selborne Commissioners had recommended a number of detailed changes to the membership of the Senate, and elective procedures for Faculties and Boards of Studies, which were certainly not readily accepted. But the suggestions which aroused the most concern, and which were the principal causes of the political rejection of any compromise, related to which Colleges should belong to the University; to the delegation of control and conduct of some examinations to Colleges; to the employment by the University of its own professors; to the reduction in standard of the medical qualifications; and to the introduction of different designations for existing medical graduates and for those who would take the new degrees.

The decisive disagreement was over the very concept of a University of London which should serve only London, as opposed to a continuation of the existing University as a national and imperial institution. The Royal Commission gave strong support to the idea that component teaching institutions of the University should be situated in or near London, and expressed the strong opinion that

> It is not reasonable that county colleges should have a negative voice upon the enlargement of the present University for teaching purposes, especially concerning the metropolis.

There was no case, in the Commissioners' view, for any constitutional link between the University and any teaching institutions outside the London area which prepared candidates for the University's examinations. Within the London area, the major, multi-faculty Colleges, primarily UCL and KCL, should become 'Constituent Colleges', and the single-faculty institutions, like the London Hospital Medical schools, should be 'Associated Colleges' of the University.

The Commissioners' views of the powers which the London Colleges should have over examinations contrasted starkly with the sole control which the Senate had so far enjoyed. While the Commissioners had supported strongly the practice whereby the final examination for degrees should 'be the same for all candidates, whether taught in constituent or associated colleges or institutions . . . or elsewhere', they introduced a much more explosive idea for other examinations.

> A matriculation examination is necessary, and intermediate examinations may be desirable, for students who have not gone through the curriculum of arts and science in any constituent or associated college or institution of sufficient rank. But in the case of students who have done this, for some adequate period or periods of time, and who can produce from the college or institution satisfactory evidence of proficiency in the general subjects of the matriculation examinations, as tested by examination within that college, it would seem reasonable that there should be power to matriculate without any examination by the University; the certificates of the college or institution being acccepted in lieu of examination. And the same principle seems also to be applicable to intermediate examinations, which ought not to be made so severe or difficult as to divert the attention of students from

the regular courses of instruction given in constituent or associated colleges or institutions to other lines of study.

The Commissioners denied the need for a medical university, but were sympathetic to the notion that medical education should be more readily available:

... if men cannot obtain the Doctorate of Medicine without much difficulty in London, but can obtain it elsewhere, many of them will leave London for other places. ... The degrees of Doctor of Medicine which have been conferred by the University of London are strangely few ... The great majority of London medical students, if they take a degree at all, take it elsewhere than in London, and that is a fact which the highest representatives of the medical profession view with regret. It is injurious, not to the men themselves only, but to the public.

And they had gone on to recommend that

... the University should have power to dispense with the preliminary scientific examination now required from candidates for medical degrees, in favour of candidates who have passed the examinations of the Royal Colleges of Physicians and Surgeons in London. ... As to medical degrees, we think that a standard of attainment appropriate for honours ought no longer to be required by the University for an ordinary or 'pass' degree.

These recommendations were followed by a proposal which would be particularly controversial:

To prevent confusion between the present graduates of the University of London, whose degrees (though not so designated) may be equivalent to what would for the future be recognised as honour degrees (in the lowest class of honours), and those who may hereafter pass without honours in the same faculty, some honourable mark of distinction might properly be conferred upon the present graduates; we would suggest, by raising them into an honour class ranking next to the honours already recognised.

These proposals ensured that there would be no relaxation of the intensity of argument within the London medical community over what should be the most appropriate way forward.

An additional, complicating factor, in the debate aroused over what should be the relationship between the University and its Constituent Colleges, was the complaint of many professors, who at a later stage formed themselves into an Association for the Promotion of a Professorial University. They did not want to remain as College teachers, preferring the authority and status of being professors in a university modelled on those of Germany or Scotland.

There were strong pointers, therefore, in the Report of the Commissioners, to the Senate's being pressed hard to give ground. In effect, for two years, the Senate tried to meet their own and the Commissioners' desire to maintain a single university, extended into teaching and research. But in their increasing desperation, they accepted modifications of their scheme, which eventually was so messy that it was rejected by many of the interests it was aimed at satisfying.

# 25

# *Confusion worse confounded*

The long vacations of 1889 and 1890 must have been welcome breaks for the participants in the tortuous negotiations which went on relentlessly during the two academic sessions which followed each of them. No attempt is made here to describe and analyse every move: Allchin, who was, throughout this and later periods, Secretary of the Committee of the Royal College of Physicians which took part in the negotiations, gives a detailed account. What follows illustrates the experience of Senate and Convocation in a period of particularly significant shifts of attitude, notable decisions, and signs of hardening opposition to a general settlement.

The immediate reaction of UCL and KCL to the Commissioners' Report, and to the Government's decision that the University should have another try to find an acceptable way of turning itself into both a teaching and an examining institution, was bitter disappointment. But that was followed, almost at once, by a determination to try to persuade Ministers to abandon their acceptance of the Report and to proceed with the granting of a new Charter for the Albert University. They sent a deputation to Lord Cranbrook to argue their case, led by a particularly indignant Bishop of London, whose petition to the Commissioners had apparently been ignored. But, on 25 July 1889, the Lord President indicated firmly that he thought a year was a reasonable time to allow for the further exercise in search of a compromise, and insisted that he was in no position to take any earlier position on the outcome.[1] However, though Cranbrook was scrupulous in his firm treatment of the deputation, on the following day he wrote in his diary, of their plea for a separate Teaching University, that 'I am rather favourably inclined and doubt the London University meeting the need.'[2]

But Cranbrook's 'reasonable expectation' that a year would be enough for the Senate and Convocation to produce a new Scheme was not fulfilled. The Senate committee's first draft, approved for discussion with other parties, was produced in November, 1889, and two revised versions were put forward in June, 1890. But, at least before the revisions, there were misgivings at the

---

[1] For the joint statement by KCL/UCL, and a report of the interview with Cranbrook, see Allchin II, 166–72.
[2] Johnson, *Diary of Gathorne Hardy*, p. 743, 26 July 1889.

highest levels. Granville admitted to Lubbock that he was 'not sure of the success of the new plan . . . but we are bound to give it every chance'.[3] The Chancellor had not enough time left in which to try to lead the Senate on to safer ground. He presided for the last time over Senate on 25 June 1890, and died in the following January, having been Chancellor for thirty-four years. One may wonder whether, had he lived a little longer, his political and diplomatic *flair* might have ensured the Senate's Scheme a better fate.

Cranbrook had sent a reminder to the Senate of their need to make progress, in April, 1890, but it elicited only an explanation that delay was due to the complexity of negotiations. On 25 November, perhaps under some pressure from KCL and UCL, he threatened that petitions from other parties would be considered if he did not receive, 'at once', notice of the Senate's intention to petition for a new Charter. Under such pressure, the Senate adopted, nine weeks later, on 28 January 1891, a Scheme which must have seemed to many of its members, let alone to the rest of the academic community, to have only a very modest chance of wide acceptance.

The Senate's Scheme of January, 1891, was the outcome of bargaining between their own committee and the small teams of all the interested parties, over a period of nearly eighteen months. No doubt all of those teams were, from time to time, involved in arguments within their own parent bodies, just as the Senate itself was not without internal differences, while disagreements within Convocation were to become torrid. The major, continuing discussions, which dominated the whole process, were held between the Senate and Convocation, KCL and UCL, the Royal Colleges of Physicians and Surgeons, the London Medical Schools, and the representatives of the Provincial University Colleges. But in addition, there were interventions by the Metropolitan Branch of the British Medical Association, and by the particularly aggrieved Society of Apothecaries.

In retrospect, what all the small, specialised groups of negotiators seem to have failed to understand was the impact of the ideas being canvassed between them on the consciousness of the graduates of the University, medical and non-medical, enrolled in Convocation. For purposes of exposition, it is best to relate, first, the objections taken by interests and institutions outside the University of London; and then to describe the accompanying and resulting struggles within and between Senate and Convocation.

Though the contest of wills between the two London Colleges, on the one hand, and the Senate and Convocation, on the other hand, was by now long established and pervasive; and though the relationship between the University and the medical profession was always highly significant; the most crucial and ultimately the most compelling pressure was brought to bear by the provincial University Colleges of England and Wales, led by Mason's and

---

[3] BL Add Mss 49654, Granville to Lubbock, 5 May 1890.

Queen's Colleges, Birmingham. Their basic argument was that, under existing arrangements, the University of London's examinations were

> . . . open to all comers without regard to place of education, and the syllabuses of the subjects of examination are drawn up without reference to the curriculum of any particular College or Colleges. If the proposals of the Commission be adopted, this impartiality will be destroyed, to the detriment of places of education outside London, and especially of the Provincial University Colleges and Schools of Medicine of England and Wales.

Unless the provincial Colleges were granted appropriate involvement in the control of curricula, etc., and enjoyed proper representation on the University's Boards and Faculties,

> . . . the standard and character of the whole of the examinations will be practically in the hands of the London Colleges and Medical Schools, and will naturally . . . be made to suit the London curricula, without reference to the needs of other parts of the country.

The provincial Colleges made their first announcement of opposition on 17 October 1889, and thereafter kept up steady pressure. They sent a deputation to Cranbrook, who received them sympathetically, in February, 1890, and one of their leaders, William Tilden, Professor of Chemistry at Mason's College, wrote soon afterwards, underlining their resolve:

> What our next step might be I am not very clear. But I think we should put up some one in Parliament to draw attention to the question and if the Senate perseveres in its course of disregarding the country we shall see if there are points of law which might be made the ground of an action to stop the new Charter if obtained. I do not know about that – but we have not given up hope of stopping the scheme.[4]

By June, 1890, the provincial campaign was in full flow, and its sponsors flexed their political muscles: they wrote to the Home Secretary, Matthews, and to Lord Randolph Churchill – but, most significantly for the future, they enlisted the help of Joseph Chamberlain, who suggested an addition to the draft Scheme.[5] As a result of this prolonged assault, the Senate, over time, was forced to abandon the Royal Commission's recommendation and to propose retention of the provincials as Constituent Colleges, but with significantly less influence than would be granted to the London Colleges.

---

[4] UL Ms 812/45, Tilden to Collins, 26 March 1890.
[5] Allchin II, pp. 371–2.

In the medical context, negotiations between the Royal Colleges, KCL and UCL, were difficult and at times threatened the prospect of any accommodation with the Senate. But the Senate, which had been very divided over the proposal that the Royal Colleges should be allowed to establish a separate medical university, were eventually able to reach agreement with them, and also with the twelve London Medical Schools, on most of the relevant suggestions of the Commissioners.

By contrast, the Senate's negotiations with KCL and UCL were strained throughout, reflecting the lukewarm attitude which the Colleges had towards a continuation of the single University. The rather sparse correspondence which has survived shows Wace and Young as the most combative of the College men. Wace was pressed towards compromise by Rollit, who sat on the Council of KCL as well as on the Senate, while Young resisted the conciliatory approach of Carey Foster at UCL.[6] Negotiations were particularly intense in the late summer of 1890, when the two Colleges reserved their right to withdraw their co-operation and to ask for re-instatement of their petition for a separate Teaching University. But while that threat remained, the two Colleges had not taken it further when the Senate finalised its Scheme at the end of January, 1891.

Cranbrook was by then very wary. His own inclination may have been towards the idea of the Albert University, but when he had received copies of statements and reservations by KCL and UCL about the Senate's efforts, sent with a personal letter by Dr Wace, in September, 1890, he commented to Frederick Peel, Clerk to the Privy Council, that the Colleges' declarations were 'by no means satisfactory as regards the negotiations and it must be remembered that the Convocation of the London University has yet to speak'. And he added 'I think an official and not personal answer to Dr Wace would be best.'[7]. He retained this coolness late in November, when after meeting Wace and Erichsen he recorded that the 'interview . . . was I think satisfactory to them and my course is left quite open'.[8] There is a note prepared for the interview, either by Erichsen or Wace, as a reminder to press Cranbrook, that should the Royal Commission be re-appointed the Colleges' interests ought to be more strongly represented. It ends: 'Effective support may be counted on in both Houses: Temple, Reay, Playfair, Shuttleworth, Bryce, Courtney, etc., (I name only Liberals).'[9] One wonders what so staunch a Conservative as Cranbrook would have made of such a suggestion, if indeed his visitors were so tactless as to make it.

But though Cranbrook had been willing to meet the heads of KCL and UCL, he refused to meet members of the Senate's committee, who wanted to

[6] KCL, KAS/GC2/F3, Rollit to Wace, 21 & 24 March 1890; Young to Wace, 14 February 1891.
[7] PC8/510/65784, Cranbrook to Peel, 9 September 1890.
[8] Johnson, *Diary of Gathorne Hardy*, p. 782, 24 November 1890.
[9] KCL, KAS/GC2/F3.

discuss the main points of their Scheme before they took it to Senate for endorsement. Cranbrook argued that he would have to sit in judgement on any scheme which was put to him, and could therefore express no opinion on its merits before it was presented to him formally.[10] But the outline of the Scheme reached him, as the result of a copy being leaked to Peel early in December, by Richard Quain, with or without the approval of either the Chancellor or the Vice-Chancellor, or of both. Peel immediately sent Cranbrook the following letter, which illustrates rather vividly the conspiratorial atmosphere in which so much of the negotiations were conducted.

> . . . Quain arrived to show me *confidentially* a letter which is coming asking you to receive a deputation from the London University to explain a fresh scheme by which they hope to meet all reasonable objections. The scheme itself has not been finally approved by the Council, but the Committee are in favour of it, and he tells me that Lord Justice Fry prefers it to his own scheme. It has been drawn up on the advice of Mr Anstie QC who is in the Charity Commission. The letter asking for a deputation contains a kind of summary of this scheme, but the Scheme itself will not be sent to us officially at present. Quain however gave me a copy of it, and he authorized me to send it to you in confidence. It admits, as you will see, the Provincial as well as the London Colleges, and Quain thinks it will fairly satisfy the Provincials, and the Medical Colleges, but not perhaps the two London Colleges who will object to the admission of the Provincials. It is clear however that no scheme which leaves the latter Bodies out in the cold, would be satisfactory. We shall probably receive the letter asking you to receive a deputation in a few days, and although it may be slightly altered it will be very much in the terms of the letter now enclosed. I thought you might like to know what was in store for you! The deputation will be a small one consisting of Sir James Paget, and a few of his colleagues – Quain seems to think that they will not bring the Scheme itself with them, but that if you ask them for further details, they will then finally settle and submit the Scheme very much in the form of Mr Anstie's draft.[11]

No meeting took place, and the Scheme was adopted by the Senate on 29 January 1891. Cranbrook must have come to feel increasingly cynical about the whole exercise, for, only a week after that, he wrote in his diary that 'The Bishop of London spoke to me of the London University plan as quite novel and unsuitable to the London Colleges. Of course I must wait for petition for the Charter and have my doubts about it coming at all.'[12]

The Senate's compromise plan, which was thus attracting so much criticism, even before its official flotation, provided, against the recommendations of the Selborne Commissioners, that the University would continue to be a national

---

[10]  PC8/510/66222, 12/13 December 1890.
[11]  Suffolk RO, Ipswich, HA43/T501/33, Peel to Cranbrook, 11 December 1890.
[12]  Johnson, *Diary of Gathorne Hardy*, p. 789, 7 February 1891.

and imperial, rather than a strictly London institution. Its Constituent Colleges were to be of two kinds – London and Provincial – whose teachers would form similarly separate Faculties, which in turn would elect separate Boards of Studies. There would be separate Standing Committees of Senate, in Arts and Science, for each of the two sets of Colleges, and for the Faculties of Medicine and Laws. The Senate would be enabled to arrange for Matriculation Examinations and Pass Examinations for the BA and BSc degrees to be conducted by College teachers acting together with Senate-appointed examiners, and for the Colleges to confer those degrees. A separate Standing Committee would look after those candidates for matriculation and degree examinations who were not enrolled in Colleges.

In medicine, despite the controversy about its allegedly over-rigorous standards, the existing MD degree would remain unchanged; but examinations for a Pass MB degree would be conducted by a Board consisting of appointees of the University and of the Royal Colleges of Physicians and Surgeons, and the examinations could, by agreement, 'be conducted in combination with Examinations for the Royal Colleges'. The University would be able to establish Professorships and Lectureships, 'whether attached or not to any particular College'. On all the Standing Committees and on the Senate itself, there would be direct representation of the Colleges, but the London institutions would enjoy a noticeably larger membership than the Provincial Colleges.

But, before passing to the reception given to the Senate's Scheme of January, 1891, it is as well to look at the behaviour of Senate and Convocation during its difficult development over the previous year and a half.

Despite the tension of the situation and the intensity of the meetings, in the development of the Scheme by the Senate's committee and the Senate itself, it was only rarely that either body resorted to formal divisions. But opposition to the conciliatory approach which was to predominate began early. The committee produced its first revised Scheme in the autumn of 1889, after some discussions with Convocation: it provided for the delegation of some examinations to Colleges, for the restriction of Constituent Colleges to the London area, and for the introduction of a less rigorous MD degree. On 20 November, the veteran, Convocation-nominated Fellow, Timothy Smith Osler, moved that 'the acceptance of the Examinations of Constituent Colleges in lieu of University Examinations is inconsistent with the general principles and aims of this University'. His motion to that effect was lost by six to thirteen. Attempts by William Smith to stop the fundamental proposal to limit the Constituent Colleges to the London area, and by Buchanan to omit the provision for a special MD degree, failed even to provoke a division. Of the nineteen Fellows who voted on Osler's motion, no less than eleven were members of the committee: of those eleven, eight were in the majority, and the Convocation-nominated members were split, four to four.

A subsequent revision of the Scheme, reflecting consultation with KCL and UCL, and consideration of suggestions by Carey Foster, came before Senate on 12 March 1890. By then, considerable further delegation of examining powers was included, and attempts by Osler, Pye-Smith and Carey Foster to strengthen the authority of the University, particularly in relation to Matriculation Examinations, were defeated without going to divisions. But on the addition of certain clauses to consolidate the proposed extension of collegiate powers, the House did divide, thirteen to five. On that occasion the opposition consisted of Derby, Rev. Hubert Ashton Holden, Kimberley, Thiselton-Dyer, and Wood. The majority was mainly composed of the same group who had carried the day four months before, but, of the Convocation-nominated Fellows, this time Fitch and Osler went along with the majority, while Wood opposed.

Perhaps more significant than the votes on 12 March was the departure of Thiselton-Dyer, which followed within weeks. An eminent botanist and Assistant Director of Kew, Thiselton-Dyer was deeply antagonistic to the idea that control of Honours in BA and BSc degrees, and of the superior degrees in Arts and Science, should be delegated to the Colleges. But when he so proposed, on 26 March, Fry moved that 'this Motion be not now put', which was carried, by ten to two. Dyer resigned, understandably angered by this pretty brutal treatment. He protested that the adoption of the Senate's policy

> . . . completely paralyses my interest in the science faculty or my power of being useful in developing it. I could no more remain a member of the Senate after its mistaken action than I could remain a follower of Mr Gladstone after the introduction of his Home Rule Bill. I discussed the matter with Sir Joseph Hooker and Michael Foster and they both agreed that my proper course was to resign. The Senate would not listen to me but embarked on a foolish course which it did not even take the trouble to ascertain would be rewarded by success. I confess I am sorry to see an institution which has done work of such immense utility abandon the definite policy which has made it what it is, and drift aimlessly from its moorings . . .[13]

But Thiselton-Dyer at least had the satisfaction of seeing his wishes adopted only a few weeks later. By the time a third revision was adopted on 4 June, the proposal to delegate powers over superior degrees to colleges had been dropped; and when Fry moved the delegation of power over the award of Honours in the BA and BSc degrees he was defeated eleven to five. On the same occasion – 4 June – hostility towards the big London Colleges was shown by Hutton, who tried to prevent the inclusion in the new Senate, in addition to the heads of UCL and KCL, of two Fellows who would be elected by each

---

[13]  BL Add Mss 49654, Thiselton-Dyer to Lubbock, 24 May 1890.

of the Colleges. Hutton was supported by Buchanan, Hopkinson and Pye-Smith, but they were overridden.

The limited extent to which the proposals of the committee were subjected to motions leading to divisions in the Senate can be seen, on the one hand, as a manifestation of the confidence which a clear majority of Fellows had in the possibility of achieving a workable compromise. On the other hand, such limited objections can be interpreted as the somewhat despairing protests of a minority, made for the record, rather than in any hope of reversing the line of policy being pursued. Such voting as did take place showed that there was always a group large enough to put the acceptance of a compromise firmly in first place, by rejecting any diversions. But the hard core of that group was quite small – it was formed by the Vice-Chancellor, Anstie, Fry, Herschell, Lubbock and Quain, all members of the committee: the additional six or eight who supported them and gave consistency to their policy were drawn from a longer list of those who were by no means regular in their attendance.

Professor Thomas Edward Thorpe, from the Royal College of Science, who had been a Fellow since 1889, felt that the Senate was 'not strong enough to enforce' their ideas of a University, and claimed in 1892 that 'in consequence of their failure . . . a certain number of the members actually seceded from that body'.[14] It is unclear what time span Thorpe had in mind, but in 1889–91 the only recorded resignation seems to have been that of Thiselton-Dyer.

It is difficult, therefore, to build a case for the existence of a clear-cut opposition party within the Senate, though on certain matters it is obvious that a few of the older Convocation-nominated Fellows were particularly unhappy. However, it seems very probable that several quite prominent members of the Senate were unwilling to express doubts on many of the details of the Scheme, but were watching with a good deal of reluctance where negotiations were leading. It has to be said, however, that if attendance at meetings is a guide, a sizeable portion of the Senate showed relatively little interest in the proceedings. There were seventeen meetings between 23 October 1889 and the end of 1890. While thirty of the thirty-eight members turned out during the period, seventeen of them were members of the committee, all but four of whom were present at more than half the sessions. Of the thirteen Fellows who came, but were not members of the committee, only four attended more than half. Only four of the seventeen meetings attracted an attendance of more than half the membership, and the largest turn-out was twenty-one.

Thiselton-Dyer had been a Crown-chosen Fellow, but the vacancy he caused fell to be filled by a Convocation-nominated successor. By then, there

---

[14] Evid. to Cowper Commission, 308.

were many strands of concern, widely publicised, about the future, which could have influenced the subsequent election. Victory went to Magnus, who polled just under 48 per cent of the 2070 votes cast, and was several hundred votes ahead of his nearest rivals. John Syer Bristowe, then Medical Officer of Health for Camberwell, who had been the first man to call for an easing of the standard of the medical degrees, as far back as 1879, attracted 626 votes. A.W. Bennett, and M.F. O'Reilly, both scientists, drew support from 274 and 180 graduates, respectively. Insofar as one assumes that the reconstitution of the University was the major focus of interest of the voters – an assumption which can only be made tentatively – the result might be seen as underwriting the policy of co-operation with the Senate, which Convocation's representatives had been pursuing. But the sizeable vote for Bristowe might well be seen as traditional support for a medical candidate, rather than as any indication of enthusiasm by London graduates for any future lowering of the existing standards of their degrees.

The election, held in July, 1890, though significant in its outcome, was not the only notable action of Convocation, in the context of the debate on the future of the University. Convocation had necessarily had to wait, after the Royal Commission's Report, until the Senate took an initiative to renew discussion. Such discussion, between the Committee of Senate and a delegation from Convocation's Special Committee, took place in July and November, 1889. Convocation's deputation was led by Magnus, and he was accompanied by Baines, Sophie Bryant, Busk, Collins, McDowall, Napier and Tilden. The Scheme put forward by Senate in November – for further consideration by other parties – had the blessing of Convocation's Committee. But when Convocation met on 21 January 1890, the Senate was still waiting for the result of a conference about the draft Scheme, to be held with KCL and UCL: and the Magnus Committee had still not produced their Report on their recent discussions with their Senate counterparts. Convocation's meeting, therefore, was being held at a difficult moment, and, as Allchin reported, 'was a good deal perplexed by opposing counsels'.[15] Some of those counsels carried intimations of serious opposition.

There were no formal divisions, reflecting a rough concensus among the 128 members present that there was not yet any definite plan to which to react. But on a show of hands, Tyler and Lynn – against the wish of Magnus – carried a motion condemning the proposal to limit the University to institutions in the London area and to give them special privileges, as being

... incompatible with the fair and just treatment of the provincial colleges ... [and] ... detrimental alike to the interests of the provincial colleges and to those of the University itself.

[15] Allchin II, p. 199.

Sophie Bryant. Headmistress, North London Collegiate School 1895–1918. First woman to be awarded DSc by the University. First woman member of the Annual Committee of Convocation. First woman Member of Senate 1900–1917.

Tyler and Lynn were strongly opposed to teachers being examiners, and, though Allchin doubted the extent of support for such an extreme position, he believed that the acceptance of the motion made it clear

> ... that Convocation was determined to prevent any real authority in the University of London being exercised by the teachers of the London Colleges and Medical Schools.[16]

By the time Convocation held its Annual General Meeting in May, 1890, there was still no sign of a revised Senate Scheme. The Report of the Magnus Committee to Convocation laid out the history of negotiation so far, and claimed a degree of success as a result of their discussion with the Senate committee. But they were under no illusions:

> It is not, of course, contended that any one of the Schemes which the Senate or their Committee have provisionally adopted is exactly the kind of Scheme which Convocation would have recommended. But it must be remembered that the Senate have advisedly attached great weight to the suggestions of the Royal Commissioners, and have been desirous not only of meeting the views of Convocation, but also of arriving at some terms of agreement with the London Colleges. To what extent they have succeeded in this latter endeavour is not yet ascertained.

And, as they commented, rather pointedly, 'In the negotiations that have taken place between the Senate and University and King's Colleges, your Committee have had no share.'

In the circumstances, the committee simply asked for acceptance of their Report, and for their re-appointment with authority to continue to confer with Senate. This was agreed, on motions by Magnus and Collins, but there were hostile noises made by Tyler and by Napier – the latter expressing a widespread and basic anti-teacher bias, and grave suspicion of UCL and KCL – while two medicos carried a resolution disapproving of any move to reduce the standard for medical degrees. Allchin, admittedly not a sympathetic observer, felt that

> ... the tone and temper of the discussion ... sufficed to show that Convocation was largely possessed with the spirit of hostility to any change in the University in the direction wished for by teachers and by those whose position and knowledge of the subject rendered them most capable of forming an opinion ... [17]

---

[16] Allchin II, p. 200.
[17] Allchin II, p. 397.

When Convocation met on 24 June, primarily to vote for a successor to Thiselton-Dyer, there was a further attack by Tyler and Lynn, reacting to the latest revision of the Senate's proposals. Incensed by the introduction of collegiate examinations, they tried to persuade Convocation to resolve that

> ... the proposal to confer London degrees after two, or possibly many, differing examinations, would impair or even destroy the value of these degrees, and would cause such division and disintegration as would render the very name of 'University' no longer suitable.

This was put aside by the acceptance of a substitute motion of Silvanus Thompson and H.A. Nesbitt, calling strongly for further consultation with the Senate. Thompson represented, on this occasion, those who, while disapproving of the latest suggestions, did not wish to embarrass the Senate in the negotiations, and who argued that Senate would surely not risk refusing consultation before drafting a new Charter. Tyler had openly stated his willingness to see Convocation reject a Charter – perhaps the first occasion on which the possibility was publicly voiced – though all concerned were well aware of Convocation's constitutional power.

But in a poorly attended meeting, with a mere eighty present, Thompson's amendment was forced to a division and only carried by thirty-three to sixteen. Such limited participation did not enhance Convocation's reputation.[18] In any event, the vote had no practical significance, and it marked the last expression of any kind of opinion during the rest of 1890. By then, the active leadership of Convocation was still putting on a good show of holding together. But such relative harmony has to be attributed mainly to two factors: the failure of the Senate to produce a definitive Scheme; and Convocation's quiet confidence in their own crucial importance as the body whose agreement was necessary for the adoption of any change in the University's Charter. However, there had been signs of some generalised unease about the future within the ranks of Convocation, especially, though not exclusively, among the medical contingent; and the existence of that unease was almost certainly more significant than the few recorded small bursts of extreme opposition to any proposed change.

Despite some last-minute grumbles from Colleges both metropolitan and provincial, the Senate decided – doutless mindful of Cranbrook's displeasure – to resist making further changes, and approved the latest version of their Scheme at the end of January, 1891. During the next five weeks, it was blessed by the Royal Colleges of Physicians and Surgeons, by the London Medical Schools, other than those of the Hospitals of UCL and KCL, and by Magnus's

---

[18] *The Lancet*, on 28 June 1890, commented that the vote enabled the Senate to know 'the opinion of forty nine out of its 3000 graduates'.

Convocation Committee. But there were formal objections from some of the Provincial Colleges, who told the Senate that if their representation on the Senate was not improved, 'the door to any further consideration of the scheme on their part' would be closed. Worse was to come: early in March, UCL and KCL withdrew their support, and spelt out in long letters to the Lord President, at the end of April, a comprehensive list of their objections. In the first days of May, the British Medical Association condemned the Scheme because it did not afford what they regarded as required facilites for graduation to London medical students; the Society of Apothecaries protested their exclusion from any part in the Scheme; and the Inns of Court declined a seat on the Senate for the Chairman of their Council of Legal Education – though the Law Society was happy to accept membership for their President.

Almost simultaneously with the rejection of the Scheme by UCL and KCL, Cranbrook wanted to know when it would be submitted to Convocation, and expressed the hope that the whole business would be completed before the end of the session. Thus forced into a corner, the Senate instructed their committee to draw up a draft Charter, and announced that it would be presented to Convocation at its Annual Meeting on 12 May. The Special Committee entrusted the drafting to James Anstie. While he worked on it, campaigns developed, for and against.

# 26

# A Charter rejected

Whatever was felt about the very existence of the power which Convocation held to accept or reject a new Charter, none of the parties would have been in any doubt about the crucial significance of the decision which would be taken on 12 May 1891. Defeat for the Senate would mean that UCL and KCL would see their chance of creating the Albert University revived; the Provincial Colleges would face the likelihood of losing their place in a Teaching University, but would retain their influence within the continuing, existing University of London; and the Medical Colleges and Schools would have to begin yet another attempt to modify the rigours of the London degrees. Thus the contest in Convocation would be fundamental to the interests of all those parties: it would reflect their followings in Convocation, but, in addition, it would demonstrate the extent of concern among members about the future of Convocation – for a defeat of the proposed Charter might well imply the division of the existing University and a consequent reduction in their power and influence. Indeed, the more far-seeing might even have envisaged a negative attack on the Senate's policy as leading, in the longer run, to a removal of Convocation's most important power altogether.

University and King's Colleges, as we have seen, came out against the Scheme in March, 1891. It is clear that the decisions owed not a little to the persistence of Sir George Young and Dr Wace. Young seems to have had the blessing of the *Times*, to which he almost certainly contributed, on 17 February, a long condemnation of the Scheme, 'illustrating [its] cardinal and inherent vices', and preferring the idea of a separate Teaching University. Since he received the final version of the Senate's Scheme, earlier in the month, Young had written twice, privately, to Wace, on the tactics to be pursued by the two Colleges. He was contemptuous of the Senate's proposals, and felt sure that

> If we fail to defeat this, still it can never pass: if it could pass, it would not work; if it could be worked for a time, it would soon have to be abandoned, or modified profoundly. But except we defeat it now, we shall hardly get a good scheme in its place.[1]

[1] KCL, KAS/GC2/F3, Young to Wace, 6 February 1891.

Young saw a need to raise the temperature. Apparently Sir Alfred Rollit, the only member of the KCL Council who pleaded the Senate's case, had suggested to Wace that he might threaten 'a motion in the two Houses'. Rollit, who later described himself in *Who's Who* as 'a progressive and independent Conservative', had been MP for South Islington since 1886. It is just possible, therefore, that he was threatening a parliamentary manoeuvre, but much more probable that he contemplated action in Senate and in Convocation, which were, in that period, occasionally referred to as Houses. In any event, Young felt that

> If Rollit threatens a motion in the two Houses, my idea is that he should be offered every possible provocation to fulfil his threat. It is privacy that has driven us into a corner. The publicity of a *notice of motion* will of itself go far to raise a storm against this scheme. I think he is probably right in considering that Convocation will accept it. Convocation has been contemptuously let alone by the older University Senators, till it has got restive to their guidance. But this scheme is the work of the very men who have during later years given it all its importance – Fry, Rollit, Anstie, Magnus & Co. If some of them descend into the arena, and the London medicals are whipped up (as they will be) in support, I do not think the *old Groucher* party will have a majority.[2]

Young's letters – which, in retrospect, show his own and Rollit's rather poor judgement of the immediate future – look forward correctly to an unhappier outcome for KCL and UCL in the longer term when he refers to the provincial situation.

> I don't think the 'University Teaching of the Country', even outside all the *real* Universities, will in any case come to be handed over to this Senate – but the scheme is open to condemnation for what it contemplates, as well as for what it is calculated to effect. Anstie no doubt hopes to stop the Country Colleges from getting made separate universities, and even from entering the Victoria University. But this is absurd. Meantime *we* shall be held bound, not by anything expressed in this Scheme, but by the memories of our failure to get 'a second University' established in London.

Finally, it is worth quoting Young's respect for and fear of his legal colleague, James Anstie.

> In driving wedges into this scheme we shall be told, you by Rollit, we by Carey Foster, that 'something else was meant, and if not clear, it can be made clear,' and so forth. We very fairly may (and we absolutely must, for safety's sake) insist on a deaf ear being turned to this. The present draft has been cleared of all the popular language, bad grammar and slipshods which, coming from so good a draftsman as

[2] KCL, KAS/GC2/F3, Young to Wace, 14 February 1891.

Fry, showed that it was intended as proposals for a scheme, and not as a draft scheme. This is a very ably drawn scheme, the work of a man who has drawn all the schemes in his department of the Charity Commission with his own hand, and betraying quite as much in its ambiguities and apparent incongruities the intent of a man who knows what he is about, as in the more accurate drafting by which the absolute power reserved to his own friends is guarded. He is the most pertinacious of negotiators, the most determined of argufyers, the most impracticable of antagonists. We should not get any glory by trying to improve his draft, or profit by trying to alter it. Everything must now be taken as it stands, and interpreted for the worst.

Wace may have been helped by this advice, but he had more compliant colleagues to deal with than had Young. The decision to withdraw support for the draft Charter was fully backed by the staff at King's, and unchallenged in its Council, except by Rollit. But at UCL, Young had anxieties about the extent of support the Professors would give him in the UCL Senate, though in fact they were unanimously against the Scheme. However, when the issue did come before UCL Council, Young proposed an amendment to a strong but moderately worded resolution against the Charter, moved by Erichsen and the Vice-President, Ughtred Kay-Shuttleworth. Young wanted a shorter and more direct repudiation, and he lost only after a tie – ten to ten – when Erichsen used his casting vote. The original motion, which effectively led to the College joining with King's to reject the draft Scheme, was carried by ten to seven.[3]

There were several other published expressions of views, in the press and in pamphlet form, which must have helped to inform members of Convocation about the forthcoming meeting and its importance – and doubtless much informal contact, especially in the teaching institutions, and in medical and legal circles in London. But the most notable public statements made, at the last minute, were letters to the *Times*, one from Lord Justice Fry, which appeared on 8 May, setting out the case for the new Charter; and a short response, published the following day, by the heads of UCL and KCL, claiming that the Scheme was unjust to their Colleges and would not establish a Teaching University 'in the proper sense of the words'.

Fry was aiming directly at Convocation, and admitted that the new Scheme was a compromise, because anything else was impossible.

> The Senate, assisted as it has been, by Committees of Convocation, has had to deal with the London Colleges (not even yet quite satisfied), with the two Royal Medical Colleges (which did not always see eye to eye), with the medical schools (which thought their interests more or less distinct from those of the Royal Colleges), with the provincial colleges (full of youth and hope), and with the claims of Convocation itself.

[3] UCL Minutes of Senate and Council: KCL Minutes of Council.

If the reference to the 'provincial colleges' – interestingly not dignified with capital letters! – reads somewhat patronisingly, Fry's final warning to Convocation was more than a shade hectoring:

> If Convocation refuse to join with the Senate, we must expect to see a new University constituted in London and smaller Universities springing up over the country, and by their competition for graduates degrading the value of a University degree, and we shall still see the medical students of our great London hospitals quitting them at the earliest moment to get degrees in some northern or foreign University. Let there be no mistake; if the Convocation go wrong now the University will be a very Esau and will find no place for repentance.

On 11 May, the day before the vote in Convocation was to be taken, the *Times* printed another long article comprehensively hostile to the proposed Charter, again almost certainly written by Sir George Young. On this occasion, while attacking Fry and Magnus because, *inter alia*, they feared a multiplication of small universities, which he regarded as inevitable, Young argued that, in any case, a separate, new London Teaching University would not be small.

The minutes of the committee of Senate record no formal divisions during the long run-up to the finalisation of the Scheme in late January, 1891. But at almost the last meeting before that decision was taken, Magnus and Fitch – both Convocation-nominated Fellows – separately proposed motions designed to ensure a uniform standard of examinations in each Faculty and across London and Provincial Boards of Studies. One motion was withdrawn, the other negatived, but doubtless they reflected disapproval expressed in the parallel Special Committee of Convocation, to which the movers belonged. However, having made the gestures, they accepted the decisions of the other Fellows, and remained loyal to the Senate scheme to the bitter end. But in the counterpart Special Committee of Convocation, they came up against much harder opposition than they had shown in the Senate.

There was more serious hostility to the Scheme within the ranks of Convocation than was indicated by the rather wild motions put forward regularly by Messrs Tyler and Lynn. Within the Special Committee, Magnus, the rebel of 1885, who had ousted Fry and taken over the chairmanship, had by now moved into support of the Senate's proposals, and had majority backing from his colleagues. There was almost certainly opposition within the closed meetings, but those who felt most hostile to the emerging Scheme waited until the Senate made their final decision. When McDowall and Silvanus Thompson moved that the Special Committee should recommend the Scheme to Convocation, on 9 February 1891, they only carried the day by six to two, with four abstentions. No names, just the figures of the vote, were recorded. Five weeks later, when the Committee's draft Report to Convocation, which included the recommendation, was on the table, there were thirteen present, with Magnus in the Chair. On this occasion the

Committee divided, and the vote was recorded in full: the Report was adopted by ten to two, the opposing members being Collins and Napier. Wood, the Chairman of Convocation, did not vote. Those in favour were Anstie, Ely, Johnson, McDowall, Magnus, Martineau, Pye-Smith, Rollit, Thompson, and Wormell.

It was agreed that the minority should be permitted to present a Report to lay before Convocation on 12 May. When it was ready, it had six signatories – Matthew Baines, Sophie Bryant, Busk, M.P.M. Collier, Collins and Napier. Bryant, Busk and Collier had not attended any meeting of the Committee since 1889, perhaps feeling that their minority position made their contribution worthless. But they joined in signing the Minority Report, which ended with a concise statement of their objections:

> We regard the opportunities afforded for varying the character of the degree, the devolution of large powers to outside bodies, the restriction of the rights of Convocation, the inadequate consideration of the private student, as cardinal defects in this Scheme; we feel that it contains concessions not required by the Royal Commission, fraught with danger to the University, and opposed to the resolutions of this House. We are, therefore, unable to concur in the recommendation to Convocation to adopt it.

But opposition was by no means limited to the committee rooms. It was, in the last resort, lodged in the consciousness of many graduates, who felt that Convocation had a very special role – expressed, perhaps too strongly, but not inaccurately, by the *St James' Gazette*, admittedly promoting a pro-provincial and anti-KCL/UCL view, on 23 July 1890:

> Convocation's function is to prevent any pernicious and unfair tinkering with the constitution of their University. If the Charter finally presented to the Convocation ... for acceptance be equitable, by all means let them accept it; if not, at any cost it should be rejected.

The press commentaries already quoted, to which could be added many references in provincial papers, reveal the quite widespread concerns disturbing the minds of interested graduates.

The Senate took the lead in circulating a comprehensive explanatory memorandum about the Scheme, after its meeting on 25 February. This no doubt stimulated a co-ordinated effort to produce a hostile majority on 12 May. There was published, on 17 March, a pamphlet entitled *The Proposed Reconstruction of the University of London* and addressed 'To the Members of Convocation', to whom it was circulated.[4] There was no indication of who

---

[4] BL 8304D2c(2).

were the leaders, or under what, if any, group title they were operating. There were fifty-six signatories, all but two of them London-based. Holburt Jacob Waring, a medico, and J.G. Joseph, a lawyer, were listed as Hon. Secs, though in Allchin's version two more Hon Secs were mentioned – J.W. Carr, a doctor, and A.L. Morris, another lawyer.[5] Waring and Morris later became important members of the Annual Committee. Twenty-nine of those listed had medical degrees, and among the fifty-six there were some who had already established themselves, or would in the near future reveal themselves, as leaders of the opposition .to the proposed new Charter – Baines, Bompas, Collins, Napier and O'Reilly.

This pamphlet, whose appearance coincided with the withdrawal of support for the Scheme by KCL and UCL, was particularly critical of what was seen as the under-representation of Convocation on the proposed Senate and Boards of Studies. According to Allchin, it produced a petition against the planned reconstruction, signed by over eleven hundred graduates. It was a protest not authorised by Convocation, but organised by

> . . . certain members . . . who felt strongly upon the subject. They sent out cards for signature and return which included the sentence: 'I hereby beg to express my dissent from the proposed reconstitution of the University of London upon the lines of the Senate's scheme.'[6]

This brought a response, pointing out that the committee of Convocation was recommending the acceptance of the Charter, and urging attendance on 12 May. That response came from a group of thirty-five senior, politically active members of Convocation, half of whom were either members of Senate (twelve Fellows), or members of one or other of the negotiating committees, or of the Annual Committee, or who fell into more than one of those categories.[7] Among them were Anstie, Magnus, Pye-Smith and Rollit, who were enrolled, simultaneously, in all five bodies.

By the time the meeting of Convocation was held, therefore, there had been substantial attempts on both sides to inform and to influence those who would attend. Certainly, the publicity and the lobbying produced a record result. Out of a membership of some 3200, spread across the British Isles and overseas, 733 graduates – 23 per cent of the total – turned up at Burlington Gardens on 12 May. The previous highest attendance had been in 1885, when 239 members were present.

Convocation threw out the recommendation that they should approve the draft Charter by the convincing margin of 447 to 197 – 69.4 per cent to

---

[5] Allchin II, p. 412.
[6] Evid. to Cowper Comm., 549–53.
[7] Allchin II, pp. 412–13.

30.6 per cent. What happened at the meeting, whose energy and temper Allchin felt was 'considerably strained', and which the *Times* described as 'occasionally somewhat stormy',[8] was to no small extent dictated by a procedural factor. The Standing Orders of Convocation provided that 'Any business which the Senate may think it expedient for Convocation to entertain', should precede 'The Reports (if any) of Committees of Convocation and motions thereon'. Senate had asked Convocation to consider the draft Charter, and had given normal notice. The Clerk of Convocation had circularised members, in the usual fashion, a week before the meeting, listing the business and the terms of resolutions which would be proposed. The order of proceedings was declared to be, first, the election of the Chairman and the appointment of the Clerk, followed by tributes to Lord Granville, the Chancellor, who had died on 31 March. Then the new draft Charter would be laid on the table, and Herschell and Quain would move and second its acceptance. Only after that would come the Report of the Annual Committee, followed by a motion of Magnus to receive the Report of his Committee on the Reconstruction of the University.

It is difficult to believe that capable Convocation politicians would not have realised that under the normal routine the vitally significant Reports – Majority and Minority – of Magnus's Committee would not be aired and discussed before a vote was taken on the acceptability of the proposed Charter. The Standing Orders included provision for the order of business to be altered by a special vote – a device not infrequently used. But there is no sign that, on this occasion, any such alteration was contemplated or attempted. Perhaps those promoting the new Charter were so confident of its acceptance that they felt it unnecessary, and unwise, to facilitate long, drawn-out arguments arising out of the Magnus Committee Reports. And perhaps, even if, at the last moment, it was realised that a rearrangement of the order of business would be appropriate, there was a practical appreciation that the unexpectedly large gathering, including hundreds of graduates who had never attended before, would be impatient to bring matters to a head, and would have been quite unsympathetic to a technical motion to alter the programme.

Whether prior discussion of the Reconstruction Committee's Reports would have made any difference to the eventual outcome is very doubtful. But the initial debate on Herschell's motion, and the decisive vote which followed, meant that Magnus, who would have had a leading role if his Committee's Reports had been discussed first, was practically squeezed out. His biographer claims that he 'had allowed himself to be outflanked by a skilful move of his opponents'.[9] If that is a reference to the prior publicity which the opposition had given to their views, and the collection of eleven hundred

---

[8] *Times*, 13 May 1891; Allchin II, p. 428.
[9] F. Foden, *Philip Magnus, Victorian Educational Pioneer* (London, 1970), p. 117.

signatories to their complaint, then perhaps 'outflanked' is the right word. But there is no evidence that those who led opposition to the draft Charter had any influence over the procedure followed on 12 May. Whether or not Magnus had failed, tactically, he was embittered by the incident. He had effectively ousted Fry from the leadership of Convocation's Special Committee five years earlier. But unlike Fry in the aftermath of that *coup*, Magnus refused to take any further part in the reconstruction exercise, though he long continued to be prominent in the University's affairs.

Herschell moved, and Quain seconded, the recommendation to approve the draft Charter, and were the only speakers in favour. Opposition was spearheaded by Bompas, followed by Hutton (the only one of the twelve Fellows present who voted against the Senate's Scheme), and three doctors – A.E. Sansom, Mrs Scharlieb, and Collins. A few less than 650 members participated in the vote, meaning that some eighty-odd members either abstained or had left the meeting. Immediately after the vote, a very large proportion of the attenders drifted away, so that Magnus's presentation of his Committee's Report, which was simply received, was a dismal anti-climax.

Analysis of the voting shows that roughly three-quarters of those present were London-based: it is notable that some 140 members were prepared to make journeys from provincial places to cast their votes. Both metropolitan and provincial groups were divided roughly two-thirds against the Charter, one-third in favour. Just under a third of those who voted were medical graduates, and they also divided almost exactly two-thirds against and one-third in favour. A rather higher proportion of the non-medicals were hostile – some 72 per cent, as against 28 per cent in favour. The London medicos were rather more inclined to vote 'Yes' than were their counterparts in the provinces, because there was a sizeable contingent of metropolitan Medical School doctors, other than those attached to the Hospitals of KCL and UCL, in favour of the new Charter: but the ratios were not markedly different.[10]

The particular objections taken to the draft Charter, all of which must have influenced the voting in one degree or other, have all been mentioned at one time or another in the foregoing narrative. The inclusion of the Provincial Colleges offended, especially, those members of KCL and UCL, who were yearning for a separate Teaching University, of which they would form the nucleus. But while just over a third of those who voted were graduates of UCL and KCL, they divided in almost exactly the same way as did the other groupings – two to one against the Charter. It is clear, though, that whatever the opinions of the voting graduates of those Colleges, their Professors were hostile to the Scheme, even if some of them were by no means enthusiastic about the proposed structure of the Albert University.

[10] Figures compiled from the Division List and the Membership List published in 1894, UL CN2/3/3. See also Allchin II, p. 445.

There are few contemporary, personal comments available, but one heavily sceptical view, some at least of which must have been quite widely shared, was expressed only nine days before the vote, by E.H. Busk, who was to become very prominent in the University's affairs:

> The hope I entertained when the Commissioners' Report appeared that our University, while maintaining its special characteristics, could be so modified as to meet the desires of the Teachers and the Medical Profession have died out. The proposed scheme is extremely ingenious; but the necessity for so much ingenuity confirms my opinion that the result arrived at will prove unattainable in practice. My objections to the Scheme would not have prevailed in my mind, if I had thought it would lead to the more friendly action with the Colleges which all must desire. But how can we expect that result even if the scheme were carried, seeing that the London and the Provincial Colleges alike oppose the scheme warmly? Apart from the action taken by the Council of University College I am told by a good authority that every one of the Professors there, without one single exception, is dead against the scheme.[11]

Those who supported the existing University were unhappy with the delegation of examining and degree-giving powers to Colleges. There were those who believed it to be impossible to combine successfully the imperial and external examination work with the teaching and research functions of a university dedicated primarily to London interests. There were very differing views as to whether the reconstruction of the existing University would or should prevent a multiplication of universities across the country. And, perhaps above all, as the historians of Convocation have pointed out, 'the non-collegiate graduates feared that the colleges would acquire undue influence and all considered that the standard of their degrees was being imperilled'.[12] In 1892 it was claimed that 'in recent lists' three-quarters of the candidates who passed degree examinations in Arts and Laws had prepared themselves by private tuition and/or private study.[13] Examination of the division list reveals that four-fifths of graduates who had achieved their degrees by private study voted against the Senate's proposal.

Allchin may have been overstating his case somewhat, when he claimed that, 'The thorough-going supporters of the scheme were in reality but few, and were to be found chiefly among a section of the Senate who were responsible for it and some of the metropolitan teachers – chiefly in the medical schools . . .' But he was surely correct in believing that

> . . . it is doubtful . . . if any scheme of reconstruction would have passed Convocation as this body would have equally opposed the setting up of a second

[11] BL Add Mss 49656, Busk to Lubbock, 3 May 1891.
[12] Dunsheath and Miller, *Convocation*, p. 91.
[13] Evid. to Cowper Comm., 543–4.

university in London; a majority could have been whipped up to negative any and every proposal, and it was this which made the situation alike hopeless and impossible.[14]

Thus, while Convocation was the instrument through which the Charter was defeated, the defeat accurately reflected the disapproval of many of the parties involved. The fear that acceptance of the Charter would inevitably mean a reduction of Convocation's power and influence, though of primary concern to a minority, almost certainly carried less weight than the objections of the Colleges and the doubts about the alleged likelihood of a fall in the status of a London degree. Nonetheless, it was in Convocation that the matter was decided, and the heavy defeat of the Senate's plan was a political achievement which did credit to the leaders and organisers who had publicised and manipulated the protests which ensured it. They would play an increasingly leading part in subsequent stages of the long conflict.

[14] Allchin II, pp. 439–40.

# 27

## One or two universities?

The adverse vote in Convocation gave Cranbrook the opportunity to do what normal procedure, and probably his own private preference, dictated. He could have referred the whole matter back to the Selborne Commissioners, who had suggested such a move if the Senate could not produce an acceptable new Scheme. But given all that had ensued since 1888, and the fact that the Commission's Report had been not a little equivocal, it was no surprise when the Lord President decided that the Privy Council should now consider the original petition of KCL and UCL for the grant of a new Charter to establish the Albert University.

No time was lost: the official announcement was made exactly two weeks after the Convocation vote; cases to be heard were to be delivered by 22 June; and the first hearings of counsel would take place on 29 June. Cranbrook was to chair the Committee himself, and appointed Lords Selborne, Monk Bretton, Basing and Sandford to sit with him. Selborne, as the Chairman of the previous Royal Commission, was clearly the most influential member, taking a dominant part in the questioning of counsel throughout the hearings, and in subsequent discussions, held in July. 'Selborne is a great help', wrote Cranbrook in the middle of the hearings, and of the penultimate session he commented that 'We practically ended our work on the Teaching University and concurred in Selborne's views almost entirely.'[1]

By the beginning of August, 1891, the Privy Council Committee had blessed what it thought would be the final version of a new Charter for the Albert University. The only major difficulties which had faced the Committee concerned the Royal Colleges of Physicians and of Surgeons and the Medical Schools, which had been the greatest losers – save for the Senate – from the defeat of the draft Charter in May. The Royal Colleges made a strong bid to form the Faculty of Medicine, but after intensive negotiations between them, the Medical Schools, KCL and UCL, it appeared to Lord Selborne and his colleagues that there was 'no prospect of any arrangement being come to between them'. The Privy Council Committee therefore imposed its own terms, denying any place in the new University to the Royal Colleges but offering the Medical Schools membership as Constituent Colleges of the

---

[1] Johnson, *Diary of Gathorne Hardy*, pp. 802, 804, 25 June & 14 July 1891.

Faculty of Medicine. Cranbrook grumbled that 'The Doctors have been obstinate and unreasonable', but, the Medical Schools having accepted the proposals, he expected that 'the University will start in force'.[2]

Disagreement with certain provisions of the draft Charter, and anxieties over a possible loss of students, were put before the Committee by counsel for the Society of Apothecaries, and for the Medical Corporations of Scotland and Ireland. Both the General Medical Council, whose President was Sir Richard Quain, and the British Medical Association, raised objections which were made known to the Committee either verbally or in writing. Counsel appeared for the Incorporated Law Society and for Bedford College for Women. None of the objections or pleas made by any of these parties appear to have moved the Privy Council to make any alterations in the draft. One matter to which attention was drawn on several occasions was the need to consider the confusion which was foreseen through there being two Universities in London, and the desirability of having a title for the new University which was fully appropriate. The Committee declared that the area to be covered by the new University should be that of the newly defined administrative county of London, and that the name 'London' should not be included in the title of the University. Selborne noted, privately, that he hoped the new institution could operate 'under some more meaning name than "Albert" but there are difficulties'. Whether he had, at the time, any inkling of the possible adoption of the name 'Gresham', which came up only a few months later, is unknown.[3]

In our context, the principal interest in the hearings before the Committee must focus on the positions taken up by Senate and Convocation. The Senate, humiliated on 12 May, soon afterwards delegated to its committee the task of considering whether a case should be put to the Committee of the Privy Council, and to investigate whether any accommodation could be reached with the Royal Colleges and the Medical Schools. The latter move, though discussion continued during the next few months, came to nothing. As for the former, counsel was briefed not to oppose the proposed Charter, but to try to ensure that the new University's degrees were only awarded to students who had 'pursued their entire academic curriculum within the Colleges'. They also objected to the inclusion of the words 'of London' in the title of the new University. The Privy Council agreed to the second, but not to the first, request. Apart from these mostly abortive manoeuvres, Senate as a body was

---

[2] Johnson, *Diary of Gathorne Hardy*, p. 807, 29 July 1891. For the conflict within the medical profession over the roles of the Royal Colleges, the Medical Schools in London and the Provinces, see Allchin III, pp. 58–110. Allchin covers the hearings before the Privy Council Committee in considerable detail in his third volume: a copy of the verbatim proceedings before the Committee is in UL RC/24/13.

[3] Johnson, *Diary of Gathorne Hardy*, p. 807, 29 July 1891.

effectively sidelined until March, 1892, though individual members were active in other capacities.

Far more significant developments occurred in Convocation. Rollit, who was a member of the Annual Committee, suggested in Senate, on 27 May, that its committee should invite the Annual Committee to make a joint approach to the Privy Council. Not surprisingly, he failed to get support. Convocation's own Special Committee had not been re-appointed, so that the Annual Committee was the natural body to initiate any action. Convocation had voted down the Senate's proposed Charter, for all the reasons already discussed; but Convocation had never been anything but unhappy with the prospect of a second university in London. Even if the majority vote on May 12 had been augmented by many members who had no particular interest in its wider constitutional implications, those who had led the protests could count on considerable sympathy for any attempt to wreck the plans of KCL and UCL. But the more senior leadership of Convocation was cautious and unhappy about any display of aggression.

When the Annual Committee met on 22 June, Collins and Baines carried, by eleven to seven, a motion in favour of making the Committee's and Convocation's views known at the hearings of the Privy Council, and of setting up a sub-committee to make the necessary preparations. There is no division list, but Rollit did not vote and asked that his abstention be recorded. Napier, Busk and Sophie Bryant were present and would certainly have voted in favour. Three other members abstained. The sub-committee was composed of Baines, Busk, Collins, Richard William Hinton, Napier, Nesbitt, Unwin and William Hale White, but when they came together the next day Hinton had already written a letter of resignation, and Hale White resigned as well.

It is clear that this challenge was very unwelcome to the Chairman of Convocation, Frederick Wood, who was one of the two graduates who were made Fellows by the Crown, in 1856, before the establishment of Convocation. He wrote to Milman, the Registrar:

> I did all I could, to prevent the Annual Committee from taking the course they have, but, in vain, for by a small majority they appointed a sub-committee to prepare a case, and take steps to be heard. They have been fully warned, that they must be prepared to bear their own expenses, and that the minority refuse to be answerable pecuniarily, for what they may do. I went further, and told them I did not consider that they had my authority to represent Convocation in this matter. Probably not much harm will come of it. The Privy Council may decline to hear them. If otherwise they state that their intention is to back up the Senate, that will not do much harm, even if it does no good. One of themselves is preparing their case, and I should say the fees to counsel will not cost them much. Collins, Baines and Napier are the prime movers, helped, in legal matters, by Busk.[4]

---

[4] UL RC/24/12, Wood to Milman, 25 June 1891.

The sub-committee made application to appear before the Privy Council Committee on 29 June, and arranged to be represented by Bompas, with J.G. Joseph, who had prepared for his degrees by private study, as his junior. Their petition was presented in the names of Baines, Busk, Collins, Napier, Nesbitt and Unwin. But as Wood had predicted, they failed to convince the Privy Council Committee of their legitimacy, and were ruled to have no *locus standi*. Undeterred, the group then pressed for more action from the Annual Committee, and one result was the decision to invite Lubbock 'to meet this Committee on the position of the University and proposals affecting the interest of its Members'. Busk, who had been keeping Lubbock posted, sent him a statement which had been prepared, apparently suggesting that an attempt should be made to have the whole business referred back to the Selborne Commissioners, as those Commissioners had proposed in their Report.[5] Lubbock immediately sent the statement to the new Chancellor, Lord Derby, who agreed that there probably might have been a case for a review of the situation, but that

> . . . the petition for a new charter to be given to a new university is before the Privy Council and we (London University) have not opposed it as a whole but only objected to certain provisions which we shall probably succeed in striking out. It seems therefore too late to refer back to the Commissioners.[6]

Lubbock met the Annual Committee on 22 July, by which time it must have been clear that the Privy Council would soon settle the terms of the Charter for the Albert University. There is no indication of what Lubbock told the Committee, but he may well have influenced the decision to set up another sub-committee to report on the new Charter when the full text was available. While there is no record of debate over the composition of the new sub-committee, it is interesting that, while all but one of its members had voted 'No' on 12 May, the most combative opponents – Busk, Napier and Collins – were not included. Some relatively new names appeared among the seven members: Baines, Curnow and N.I.C. Tirard were all King's medical men, the last two being Professors; William Paice and William George Lemon were lawyers; Spratling and Thompson were scientists from the School of Mines. Appointed, as they were, at the end of the session, they would not report back before the autumn.

By July, 1891, however, there were signs from others than the hostile members of the Annual Committee that a Charter for the Albert University would not be accepted easily. Thiselton-Dyer, who could not have had kind memories of the Senate, told Lubbock that

---

[5] BL Add Mss 49657, Busk to Lubbock, 10 July 1891.
[6] BL Add Mss 49657, Derby to Lubbock, 11 July 1891.

... the Government ought not to be allowed to rush the thing till public opinion is a little more matured. The more one reflects on the matter the more undesirable it seems to have two examining Universities working side by side in London.

He also reported, somewhat tartly, Karl Pearson's claim

... that some of the leading Professors at University College are dissatisfied with the scheme. I cannot say that I feel much sympathy with them. Their manoeuvres all through have not been altogether disinterested and now they have burnt their fingers.[7]

As will be seen, Pearson and his colleagues would persist in their disapproval.

Lord Justice Fry was eager to see the final form of the proposed Charter, and would not have been alone among the legal fraternity in recognising the existence of a channel for potentially hostile action:

I find that there is a statute ... which requires that the draft charter of any proposed new university shall lie on the table of the house for thirty days, before a report is submitted to HM. This will no doubt ... put us in possession of the draft and give us an opportunity for consideration and if needful for remonstrance.[8]

But perhaps the most ominous event of the summer was a trio of Questions in the House of Commons. Sir Henry Roscoe, Liberal MP for South Manchester, a distinguished chemist who had been Professor at Owens College until 1885, asked the initial one on 10 July. He enquired of the First Lord of the Treasury, W.H. Smith, who, as we have seen, was a prominent supporter of KCL, whether the Government intended to grant a Charter to establish a University formed by University and King's Colleges,

... in the latter of which a religious test is imposed upon all teachers with the exception of the Professors of Modern and Oriental Languages; and whether, in the event of such a University being founded, all such restrictions upon the teaching staff will be abolished?

Smith had no information to offer – except that the Privy Council was still considering the petition. Ten days later, and again a week after that, the MP for Huddersfield, William Summers, demanded to know of the Chancellor of the Exchequer, Goschen, whether the proposed Charter would 'abolish the religious tests at present imposed in King's College'. Goschen's replies underlined the importance of what Fry had told Lubbock – that the draft

---

[7]  BL Add Mss 49657, Thiselton-Dyer to Lubbock, 8 July 1891.
[8]  BL Add Mss 49657, Fry to Lubbock, 16 July 1891.

Charter would be open to discussion in Parliament and that the issue would be settled by Parliament, not by the Government.[9]

Thus was launched a controversy which would run for several years: in the immediate future it raised doubt as to the acceptability of the Charter in the minds of those who had strong libertarian consciences, especially Nonconformists, in whom the tradition of antipathy to religious tests was ingrained.

Had the Privy Council's Report been available six weeks earlier, it could have been laid on the table of the House of Commons and its future decided, one way or other, by the end of July, 1891. There were to be many retrospective criticisms of the apparent hurry in which the hearings had been arranged and conducted, and some at least of Cranbrook's impatience with the delays caused by the medical negotiations must have reflected his anxiety to see the whole business tidied up by the end of the session, when Parliament would be five years old. But the Report on the Charter was not lodged at the Privy Council Office until 1 August, and Parliament had by then gone into a recess which would not end until 9 February, 1892.

Just as it is possible that, had the Selborne Commissioners been unequivocal in their recommendations in 1889, the outcome of further enquiry might have produced an agreed solution; so it is not unlikely that, had the Privy Council Report been available to Parliament by late June, 1891, the Albert University would have come into being. Though there might well have been some opposition, whether it would have been sufficiently developed to withstand some firm support from Ministers is doubtful. As it turned out, the six months which elapsed before the Charter eventually reached the Commons saw a steady growth of opposition which became quite intense in the early weeks of 1892. The contribution of the Senate to that opposition was minimal, and that of Convocation, though substantial, was not the most crucial. But Convocation had been first in the field, and its subsequent behaviour justifies giving it priority, especially because of its significance for the longer term.

At some point in the late summer or early autumn, two members of the sub-committee to which the Annual Committee had delegated the job of examining and commenting on the new Charter – Curnow and Thompson – resigned, for reasons unknown. The sub-committee, reduced to five in number, produced a unanimously agreed and surprisingly submissive recommendation. The chairman, Lemon, and his colleagues, Baines, Paice, Spratling and Tirard, declared that the provisions of the Albert Charter

> . . . do not appear to be in any way antagonistic to the interests of the University of London, and that, under the circumstances . . . [we] . . . do not recommend the Annual Committee to take any action in the matter, beyond instructing the

[9] 3s Parl. Deb. vol., 355, cols 872–3, 1765; vol. 356, cols 410–11, 10 & 27 July 1891.

Clerk of Convocation to draw the attention of the Member for the University to Clauses 11 and 24, with special reference to the possibility of Colleges outside the area of the Administrative Council of London being admitted as Constituent Colleges of the Albert University.

Given the existence of a more radically inclined group on the Annual Committee, the sub-committee's report did not get an easy reception. Napier and Busk argued strongly, on 18 December, that the Charter would enable the Albert University to confer degrees on many candidates who would only have studied briefly at one of its Colleges; this would enable the new University

> . . . to confer degrees upon persons not to be distinguished, so far as their course of education was concerned, from those known in the existing University as 'private students', and would thus encroach upon the province of the London University, and would depart widely from the intentions expressed by the supporters of the new charter before the Royal Commission and the Privy Council.[10]

Napier and Busk could not raise enough support to force any re-statement, but the Annual Committee were very divided and eventually agreed that, as yet, they were unable to make a final report on the matter to Convocation. When Convocation met on 19 January 1892, Wood was terminally ill, and Busk was asked to take the Chair. The session, attended by a mere ninety-five members, was dominated by the leaders of those most opposed to the Albert Charter – Busk himself, Collins, Napier and O'Reilly. What emerged, after some argument over the strengthening of the sentiments to be conveyed, was the firm view expressed in a motion by Collins and Busk, that

> This House is of opinion that the Albert University Charter if granted would neither supply a Teaching University for London as recommended by the Royal Commission, nor tend to promote the interests of higher education, while it might interfere with the work of the University of London.

Lubbock was to be asked to bring the resolution to the notice of Parliament. And the Annual Committee was authorised to act as they thought expedient, in conjunction with Senate, to represent and guard the interests of Convocation.

If serious discomfort was felt by many members of Convocation about the hostile stance being taken, by its spokesmen, towards the Albert Charter, there is little evidence of it. And before the Annual Committee met again on 1 February, there were plans being laid to ensure that the more aggressive

---

[10]  Allchin III, p. 143.

leadership would further consolidate its position. Within days of Wood's death, on 25 January 1892, there was an interesting correspondence between Busk and Collins which not only reveals their own and others' personal ambitions, but also clarifies their attitudes towards the future of the University. The letters were written five weeks after the death of the 7th Duke of Devonshire, previously the Earl of Burlington, the first Chancellor of the University, who had remained a member of the Senate after giving up that post in 1856. His and Wood's deaths meant that there were two vacancies on the Senate, one of which would be filled by a Crown nominee, and the other by the winner of an election by Convocation.

Busk declared his interest first:

> The vacancy on the Senate occasioned by Dr Wood's death is to be filled by a Graduate in Arts or Laws on the nomination of Convocation; and some of my friends have already written and spoken to me on the subject. They propose to send a Circular next week with nomination post cards for signature and are very sanguine of success. They have entrusted the business part to J.B. Benson, LLD . . . I need hardly say that election by my fellow Graduates would be far preferable to me than a Crown nomination.[11]

Collins was a little put out:

> I was hoping that you had been or would be nominated to the Crown vacancy and that Napier would come forward for the Convocation vacancy. I trust that your joint action with Napier and myself which I believe has been of value to the University in the past will pave the way for promoting a party on the Senate in general sympathy with those objects which . . . we have agreed upon – viz., the increase of Convocation Fellows; the abolition of life tenure of office by Senators; the maintenance of standards of the independent nature of our examinations and a more liberal consultation of Convocation generally. I have been hoping that we might utilise the present opportunity of election of a Fellow and of a Chairman of Convocation for these purposes. Should Napier decide not to stand for the Senate vacancy I should certainly support you if I may conclude (as I believe I may) that you would continue to work for those objects which I have summarised above and for which we have co-operated in the past.[12]

Busk explained that there was no chance of his being nominated by the Crown, 'owing to my opposition to the action of the Senate'. But he assured Collins that

> It has . . . long been, and is, my opinion that there ought to be an increase in the number of Convocation Fellows in proportion to the Crown Fellows, that

---

[11] UL Ms 812/64, Busk to Collins, 29 January 1892.
[12] UL Ms 812/67, Collins to Busk, 30 January 1892.

all Senators should be appointed for a term of years only, that the Senate should consult with Convocation more liberally and that the standards of our Examinations should be maintained and independent. I wish to see the Senate so constituted that it will agree in these views and concur in carrying them into effect – and I think we certainly now have an opportunity of forwarding them.[13]

This exchange is a corrective to any notion that the attack on the Albert Charter was completely dominant in the calculation of the future prospects of Convocation. And the complexity of relationships within the small circle of leading people was apparent from another move. Collins was pressed by a member to support Rollit as a candidate for the Chair of Convocation, and must have enquired of Rollit as to his intentions. Rollit, a faithful supporter of the Senate's draft Charter, avoided mention of the Chairmanship, but told Collins that he supported the nomination of Busk for membership of the Senate by Convocation.[14]

But these electoral manoeuvres, despite their longer term significance, were definitely subordinated to the controversy over the Albert Charter in the early weeks of 1892, when the various strands of opposition to the Charter came together strongly.

Most of the objections to the Albert Charter were much the same as those made against the Senate's Scheme. Some sections of the medical profession were hotly opposed to what they saw as a strong possibility that degrees of the new institution would be awarded on easier terms than had applied so far in the University of London. And the provision that medical students would have to spend at least the last two years of their course of study in London, in order to qualify for the award of the new degrees, was seen as a major threat to the Provincial Medical Schools, who were sure that they would lose many of their students to London, half-way through their training. This was the major issue for the Provincial Colleges.

The hope of the Selborne Commissioners, that a new Teaching University would be inclusive of all the London-based institutions of higher learning, was dashed by the new Charter. It was, therefore, opposed by Bedford College, which had been excluded from the Senate's Scheme, but also more strongly by the London Society for the Extension of University Teaching, within which there was an extensive debate. The Society had on its Council Sir George Young and Dr Wace, representing UCL and KCL, but also representatives of Bedford, Birkbeck, the Working Men's College, and several other metropolitan bodies; while in his individual character, Sir James Paget, the Vice-Chancellor of the University, was also a member. The Society's President was the Chancellor of the Exchequer, Goschen. The debate on what position

[13] UL Ms 812/66, Busk to Collins, 30 January 1892.
[14] UL Ms 812/65 & 68, Roberts to Collins, 29 January; Rollit to Collins, 3 February 1892.

the Society should take was extensive, but those who disapproved of the new Charter prevailed. A petition to Parliament was agreed on 9 February, praying that assent to the Charter should be delayed until it was amended to take account of the special interests of evening students, and arguing that, in the Charter as it stood,

> . . . no attempt is made to give practical effect to . . . [the] . . . wide conception of a University, by welding together the various educational agencies engaged in work of a University character in the Metropolis.[15]

The concern expressed in Parliament in the summer of 1891, about the restriction of all but two offices in KCL to members of the Church of England, was the more important of two issues raised about the Albert University which had either not been discussed, or had not loomed large, in the debate on the Senate's scheme, and the hearings before the Privy Council. Early in January, 1892, a group called a conference to protest against the granting of the Charter, because 'the scheme violates the spirit of the Universities' Test Act, 1871; while it is also objectionable on educational grounds'. The conference was held on 18 January: resolutions were passed which contained criticism of several aspects of the proposed University – some shared with others – and stressed particularly what those attending saw as the contradictory situation of KCL which, by its sectarian provisions, was in conflict with the prohibition in the Charter of any tests of religious belief in the University. A Committee for opposing the Albert University Charter was set up, and the sectarian issue was to be pursued not by it alone, but by some of the other objectors as well.

The second issue which, though it had been aired quite often in the recent past, had not been very prominent in the formal debates on the Senate's proposals or in the Privy Council hearings, came much more to the fore at the beginnning of 1892. This was the campaign, pressed by a group at UCL, led by Karl Pearson and Ray Lankester, for having a German or Scottish type of university. Pearson contributed several colourful and somewhat abrasive articles on the theme, which were collected and published in book form.[16] Lankester moved from UCL to Oxford, but continued his concern for London. He told Arthur Balfour that

> When I was at UCL most of the professors did not approve the details of Young's draft charter. But we thought it a good proposal for the [Selborne] Commissioners to look at and improve upon. I myself – and many others there as well as all the

---

[15] Quoted in Allchin III, p. 170. Allchin gives a full account of the Society's internal debate – see pp. 153–79.

[16] K. Pearson, *The New University for London: a guide to its history and a criticism of its defects* (London, 1892).

men I know who take an interest in University questions – are horrified at the prospect of this Charter being granted. The problem of establishing a University in London which can grow and become a really satisfactory institution is *not* solved by Young's charter . . . The objection . . . is that it does not contemplate the existence of 'University' Professors – but only of College teachers elected by the Colleges and medical schools. A plan is needed which while giving a status to the Colleges and medical schools shall make the creation of a strong well paid professoriate an essential part of the University . . .[17]

The organisation of opposition to the Senate's draft Charter, which culminated in the heavy defeat inflicted by Convocation on 12 May, 1891, had been the work, in large measure, of the small group which, since that date, had become increasingly prominent in Convocation's affairs. Its most prominent member was William Job Collins, who was at the beginning of his political career. While the crisis over the Charter was going on, he was also standing, in West St Pancras, as a Progressive candidate for election to the London County Council. The poll, in which he was successful, was held on 5 March 1892, the day when, as will be seen, the Charter crisis reached a climax. Collins went on to bigger things: he became Chairman of the LCC in 1897; he stood for Parliament in West St Pancras in 1895, for the University of London in 1900, and entered the House of Commons in 1906, as a Liberal, sitting until 1910, and again in 1917–18. He found time to be a Fellow of the University from 1893 until 1927, and to serve as Vice-Chancellor twice – in 1907–09 and in 1911–12.

Collins's close Convocation colleague, T.B. Napier, won his way on to the LCC in 1893, contested North Islington in 1895, and sat as Liberal MP for Faversham from 1906 to 1910. These two men were, in 1892, in their thirties, and though joined by able academic politicians like Busk it is unlikely that, by themselves, they would have had the political weight to produce the extent of opposition to the Albert Charter which developed – though they and their lieutenants made no small contribution. But the protests against the Charter were given heavyweight status by the participation of veteran politicians who were brought into the controversy, in the main, by the sectarian problem at KCL, the indignation of some sections of the University Extension movement, and the anxieties of the Provincial Medical Schools.

Though Collins, Napier and Busk were among them, the signatories to the call for the conference which led to the establishment of the Committee for Opposing the Albert Charter were brought together mainly by J. Spencer Hill, and included Charles Roundell, Allanson Picton, Lyulph Stanley, J. Carvell Williams, the elderly James Heywood, and others, mostly Nonconformists, many of whom had long parliamentary experience and were

---

[17] BL Add Mss 49850, Lankester to Balfour, 25 February 1892.

fiercely antagonistic to any hint of religious tests in education. The call went out early in January, and the conference on 19th appointed the Committee, with Roundell as Chairman and Spencer Hill as Secretary. Most of those involved were Gladstonian Liberals, but Joseph Chamberlain championed the Provincial Medical Schools, and some of the Government's supporters were hostile to the Charter. Notable among the latter was G.T.C. Bartley, long associated with the Department of Science and Art, founder of the Penny Bank, and at one time Conservative Central Agent: over time he had offended and subsequently had rather awkward relations with the Marquis of Salisbury.[18] In short, the opposition could now depend on a group of hardened campaigners, who had wide contacts in Parliament and were in a position to rally support against the draft Charter, which reached the table of the House of Commons on 19 February.

Again unlike the situation before the Convocation vote of May, 1891, there was much greater public discussion of the issues. Newspapers and journals carried articles and letters – notably an exchange of correspondence between Roundell and the Bishop of London on the status of denominational colleges and the particular situation of KCL. The opposition viewpoint was widely publicised and supported, but the proponents of the Charter were by no means silenced. There were public meetings, at one of which, presided over by Lubbock at the Birkbeck Institute and convened by various educational bodies, a resolution was passed recommending petitions to Parliament to withold approval from the Charter, and calling on Lubbock to oppose it in the House of Commons.[19] But at another meeting, this one at Toynbee Hall, a group hotly opposed to the pleas of Lankester and Pearson showed their animus against teachers:

> . . . no teaching University for London can be satisfactory in which the teaching staff has a preponderating influence in its government; and further, that it cannot be satisfactory when its teaching staff is not controlled, directly or indirectly, either by its governing body or by the Crown.[20]

The Annual Committee of Convocation had been given authority, on 18 January, 'to confer and to take action with the Senate, and should act otherwise as should seem expedient'. Senate was informed of this, but made no response. When the Annual Committee met on 1 February, Napier and Nesbitt tried but failed to initiate a petition against the Charter. However, both of them were included in a new sub-committee which was given power to confer with Senate on the most appropriate action to take. The other

[18] A. Roberts, *Salisbury, Victorian Titan* (London, 1999), pp. 290, 312, 319, 789.
[19] BL Add Mss 49657, Mure to Lubbock, 16 January 1892.
[20] Allchin III, p. 217. The volume contains a comprehensive survey of the press coverage.

members were Busk, Collins and O'Reilly. The actions they took were reported to Senate, who were also asked whether consultation over joint action was desired. But Convocation had given too much offence: Senate did not reply.

The sub-committee then took the matter into their own hands. They met five times in the next month. On 3 February they agreed to prepare a Petition to Parliament, which would be sent to all members of Senate and Convocation, for signature. They must have set their helpers to repeat the kind of canvass which had preceded the May, 1891, vote in Convocation. On that occasion they had produced eleven hundred signatures, though only 644 votes were cast at the May meeting, and, of those, only 447 voted against the Senate's proposals. Early in 1892, the petition which, for technical reasons, had to be replaced by a memorial to the Prime Minister, attracted 1228 signatures. Some probing of the list reveals the shifting and inconsistent pattern of support, which must have made any appeal for Convocation votes something of a nightmare.

Of the 1228 who signed the memorial, only 288 – just under a quarter – had attended and voted on 12 May, 1891. Less than half those who voted against the Senate's proposals then, signed the memorial eight months later. On the other hand, it was doubtless very gratifying for the organisers of the memorial to find that seventy-eight of those who did attach their names had voted in favour of the Senate's draft Charter. Unfortunately, we do not have a list of the eleven hundred members of Convocation who signed the petition early in 1891, but it is quite likely that, a year later, no less than three-quarters of those who signed the Memorial were either newcomers to Convocation, or were older members, many of whom had not been sufficiently interested to participate in earlier exercises.

No doubt many UCL and KCL graduates would have found it difficult to oppose a scheme which promised independent status to the Colleges within a Teaching University. But no small part of the reduction in support for the new Charter reflected ambivalence in the medical camp. The doctors, of whom 229 signed the memorial, included only sixty-two who had been at the memorable meeting in the previous May. And several of them, at least, must have found opposition to the Charter very hard to contemplate, because, under it, the London Medical Schools were given a major place in the new University. But the possible lowering of standards of the medical degree was much resented, and Collins must have been delighted to receive the following letter from Mathew Baines, who had been a staunch ally against the Senate's scheme. Baines's struggle with himself, while heavily biased by purely medical considerations, may well have been repeated in the minds of not a few medical graduates, and perhaps of many non-medical graduates as well.

'Never too late to mend' you may say but I have now, after serious consideration of the matter, determined to join the opposition of our graduates to the new proposed Charter. . . . I had intended to have remained entirely neutral, for I confess until lately my sympathies have been in favour of the Charter, but late events have changed my mind so completely that I gladly join your ranks. I think, however, that some of your objections and many of those advanced by Victoria University and the Provincial Schools to be trivial and far beside the mark. Yet the idea of allowing the conjoint examination (or rather the possibility) to take the place of MB and so to lead directly to the MD is so monstrous that human nature stands aghast at the very thought.

I find and know that though the Senate is equally opposed as we are to the scheme, yet it will not work with us and why? Because that body cannot get over the snub we gave it last year. Even now it says that their scheme could have been altered to our wishes had we expressed them and that so a satisfactory charter could have been propounded. Need I tell you the answer I made to the senator thus speaking to me.

It is not for us to make a Charter but we must watch those who do and if in the future all the Colleges and Teaching Centres could be bound together in subjection to our University, such could be the degree giving source in London – but it must be free from all Royal Colleges and all the existing Colleges and Institutions which must be guided in their programmes of study, etc., by our Senate and it must not be ruled by them. I shall be very pleased if even yet our University can be worked into such general scheme tho' I fear the impossibility – we had better remain as we are and retain our prestige than be swamped by the cry for easy medical degrees.[21]

The sub-committee did much more than organise a collection of signatures, however. Despite Senate's silence – and it is worth noting that no Fellow signed the memorial to Lord Salisbury – the Chancellor, Lord Derby, agreed to meet the sub-committee, on 9 February, when he advised them to ascertain the views of Joseph Chamberlain 'as representing the Provincial Colleges'. Derby's personal sympathies were clear from the fact that on 22 February, in the House of Lords, he had presented a Petition against the Charter from the Victoria University and its Constituent Colleges.[22] Subsequently the sub-committee met Chamberlain and Lubbock, separately, and as a result of all these interviews they decided to ask the Prime Minister to receive a deputation, which would lay before him the memorial: Derby had promised that he would introduce them. Chamberlain, meanwhile, had presented a Petition on behalf of the Provincial Medical Schools. Lord Stanley of Alderley had been lobbying Lord Derby, the Duke of Devonshire, Chamberlain and Sir Henry James, on behalf of the University Extension group, but thought if Lubbock would 'say a few words of explanation to them particularly the Peers it may help our work in defeating this Charter'.[23]

---

[21] UL Ms 812/69, Baines to Collins, 27 February 1892.
[22] H of L Journal, 22 February 1892.
[23] BL Add Mss 49657, Stanley of Alderley to Lubbock, 14 February 1892.

But the deputation which was received by Salisbury at the Foreign Office, on 3 March, was by no means restricted to the Convocation sub-committee. Indeed, it was a large gathering of all the groups opposing the Charter. It is not absolutely clear who should be given the credit for organising so widely representative an attendance, but it would seem likely that Bartley, as an influential member of the Committee for Opposing the Charter, played a major role. Only hours before the meeting, the *Times* had reported that

> Mr Bartley has undertaken to move for an address to the Crown. . . . he will be supported by Mr Mundella, Mr Chamberlain and other Gladstonian, Liberal Unionist and Conservative Members.

Not only were all the educational interests represented, but three peers – Spencer, Derby and Ripon – and no less than twenty-one MPs were present, including Chamberlain and Herbert Gladstone. Among the MPs were eight Conservatives, two Liberal Unionists, nine Gladstonian Liberals, a Radical and an Irish Nationalist. Overwhelmingly, they represented constituencies in Lancashire, Yorkshire, Birmingham and Wales. Bartley was the only London MP, and only two others came from southern constituencies – North Bristol and Cricklade in Wiltshire. The deputation was heavy with Northerners and Nonconformists.

However, before the narrative of events can be taken further, it is essential to describe the last major move made by the promoters of the Charter – the change of name of the projected new University from 'Albert' to 'Gresham'.

# 28

# *Neither Albert nor Gresham*

Gresham College, and its seven lecturers in the liberal arts, which is sometimes thought of as the very first London University, was established by the will of Sir Thomas Gresham, who died in 1579. By the middle of the nineteenthth century it had a relatively small endowment, and a modest building in the City, which was the venue for popular lectures, rather in the fashion of University Extension exercises. They were delivered by what one of the 'Gresham Professors' described – rather too sweepingly – as 'the best men that could be got for the money', who would 'make no pretence to being men of light and leading in science and literature'.[1]

In the course of the great wave of concern over the condition of Charities, and a few years after the creation of the Charity Commission in 1853, one of its Inspectors, Francis Offley Martin, produced *Notes, Evidences and Suggestions relating to Gresham College*. He wrote:

> It is by no means improbable, were the Trustees required to furnish a Plan for re-modelling the College, that a Committee of practical men might be found possessing the confidence of the City, and that the friends of education there would then come forward, and, by judicious changes and additions, raise the Institution to the rank of an affiliated Member of the University of London.

The then Gresham lecturer in Law, William Palmer, responded:

> I hardly know what he means when he talks of raising it to the '*rank* of an *affiliated* Member of the University of London'. But if, without detriment to the old foundation or prejudice to the present Professors, it can be erected into a College like King's College, forming an integral part of the University, I think that a Scheme with such object would be well worth consideration.

Another lecturer took this further, and suggested that the College should have a Charter of incorporation, authorising the 'President and Fellows of Gresham College in the University of London',

---

[1] *Pall Mall Gazette*, 13 February 1892, quoted in Allchin III, p. 267.

... to open Classes, deliver Lectures, and generally prepare the Undergraduate Members of the College, who were matriculated Members of the University for the Examinations for Degrees in Arts and other Faculties.[2]

It is clear that neither Martin nor the professors were particularly well informed as to the actual legal and constitutional positions of the University and the Colleges, but, in any event, no move seems to have been made to consider the possibilities further, until 1882. In that year the Government set up a Royal Commission to enquire into the City of London Livery Companies. It seems probable that an initiative was then taken by Edmund Symes Thompson, a well-known Professor of Medicine at KCL, who had become the Gresham College Professor of Physic in 1867, and had many connections in the City. Symes Thompson had been a member of the Annual Committee from 1862 to 1873, and he may have impressed some of the current members with his idea. Andrew McDowall, whom we have met as a champion of teacher training and Secretary of the Girls Public Day School Trust, carried a resolution in Convocation urging the claims of the University to be put before the Commission, 'with special reference to Gresham College'. That was at the Annual Meeting of Convocation in May, 1882, and at the subsequent meeting in January, 1883, it was proposed that Senate should be urged to pursue the matter. But Senate decided that, as a Government-financed institution, it would be inappropriate to seek additional financial support from charitable funds. UCL and KCL, however, did make submissions to the Royal Commission.[3]

In the following decade, the Joint Grand Gresham Committee, composed of equal numbers representing the City of London and the Mercers' Company, considered schemes for improving the programme of lectures, and at the beginning of the 1890s were also being wooed by people interested in the establishment of a Technical University. But suddenly, with no prior publicity, the Committee was presented, late in January, 1892, with a suggestion that they should co-operate with UCL, KCL and the London Hospital Medical Schools, 'in the establishment of the proposed University in and for London'. On 29 January, the Joint Grand Committee agreed in principle, on the understanding that the University should be called the Gresham University. This proposal was then taken to the Privy Council Committee, which agreed to alter the draft Charter by changing the University's name. What was laid on the tables of both Houses of Parliament on 19 February, therefore, was a draft Charter, not for an Albert, but for a Gresham University.

[2] Corporation of London RO, PD 87.5, 11 July 1857.
[3] BMJ, 6 February & 6 May 1892. The Royal Commission reported in 1884, PP xxxix. An earlier attempt by UCL to raise funds through the Gresham Trustees had been violently opposed by Ray Lankester. See Times, 7 July, and Nature, 8 July 1880.

There is extraordinarily little written material on which to build any account of how this move came about.[4] From the point of view of the sponsors of the new University, a major objective must have been to boost the financial base on which the new University could operate, to forge a continuing link with the City of London, and thus to present a stronger case for the acceptance of the Charter by Parliament. KCL and UCL had been seeking financial support for years, and the formal letter from their Principals – Wace and Erichsen – to the Lord Mayor, in his capacity as Chairman of the Gresham Grand Committee, on 23 January, could be seen as one more effort in a long and continuing search for backing. But the letter, while suggesting that Gresham College might 'be made the centre of the University', scrupulously avoided any mention of money, concentrating on the desirability of the University being 'connected as closely as possible with the City of London'.[5]

Allchin asserts that the proceedings had begun with 'an informal conversation' between the then Master of the Mercers' Company, Ralph Charlton Palmer, and Dr Wace.[6] Palmer, a barrister, had been Secretary to the Public Schools Commission in 1868, and Principal Secretary to Selborne when the latter was Lord Chancellor in Gladstone's second Administration, before rising to senior legal positions. Clearly he had experience, interest, and relevant connections in education which enabled him, in later years, to become important in the City and Guilds Institute, and to serve on the Senate of the University of London from 1912 to 1920. It would seem quite likely that the Gresham Trustees, who had been exploring ways of promoting and extending the work of Gresham College, may have been persuaded by Palmer to take the initiative which brought the Gresham University proposal forward. But whoever started the ball rolling, he was certainly heavily involved. In the middle of January, Frederick Peel, the Clerk to the Privy Council, wrote to Cranbrook:

> I met Ralph Palmer . . . he told me that he and others have been quietly canvassing amongst the City and Metropolitan Members to secure their support of the Albert University Charter in the interest of Gresham College which is desirous of joining the University. I should think it would be a very good thing if they did, as they are a much older, much richer, and much more thriving body than either University or King's College. (I am not sure that they might not furnish a better *name* than the present one and one which has been for so long connected with the City of London) . . .[7]

---

[4] The archives of the Mercers' Company include the Minute Books of the Grand Committee, and formal documents, but no relevant private correspondence about the proposed link with the University.
[5] Reproduced in Allchin III, p. 261–2.
[6] Allchin III, p. 263.
[7] Suffolk RO, Ipswich, HA43/T501/33, Peel to Cranbrook, 19 January 1892.

Whoever should be credited with bringing about the proposed connection and change of name, the move was given a warm reception in some quarters, especially by the medical press. There was some speculation that the Gresham College building would become the University's headquarters, and that, in the near future, there would be a notable increase in the extent of funds available to the new institution. But within weeks, Palmer was insisting that the Gresham Grand Committee had made no financial commitment.[8] Whether the shift from Albert to Gresham affected significantly the fate of the proposed University is somewhat doubtful. Certainly it did nothing to meet the main objections raised against the Charter, though it may have given confidence to those of its potential supporters who had doubts as to the proposed University's capacity to survive and thrive as a free-standing institution.

It is very unlikely that the future of university arrangements in London was of much concern to Ministers, other than Cranbrook, until the early weeks of 1892. Larger questions dominated the political scene, particularly the fact that the Government would have to face a General Election within months. Cranbrook was probably still confident of seeing the Charter, blessed by the Privy Council's Committee, through Parliament either without challenge, or with sufficient support to defeat any move against it. But such confidence must have been weakened considerably by the beginning of March. A number of factors contributed to this: one was the death of W.H. Smith, First Lord of the Treasury, and his replacement by Arthur Balfour, late in 1891.

Smith had been a strong supporter of King's College. The first sign of concern came from Dr Wace, who wrote to Balfour, towards the end of January, 1892, asking for an interview because the Charter was due to lie on the table of the House of Commons and 'some opposition is threatened'. Smith, said Wace, 'took a deep interest in the promotion of the Charter, and was always kind enough to see me in any emergency in the course of its progress'.[9] Only a few days later, as we have seen, Balfour received a letter from Ray Lankester, in Oxford, arguing strongly against the Charter, and another from Henry Sidgwick, in Cambridge, who simply wanted to know where the matter stood. Balfour, who had been thoroughly immersed in Irish affairs for some years, clearly had little awareness of the matter, though he had recently made a speech in Glasgow in which, while not referring directly to London, he insisted that a university must be a teaching and not an examining body.[10] He promised Sidgwick that 'I will try and find out whether the Home Secretary knows more than I do; and if so, what are his views.'[11] The Private Secretaries

---

[8] *Times*, 26 April 1892.
[9] BL Add Mss 49850, Wace to Balfour, 21 January 1892.
[10] *Educational Times*, 1 January 1892.
[11] BL Add Mss 49850, Lankester to Balfour, 25 February 1892; 49877, Balfour to Sidgwick, 27 January 1892.

were set to work, but all Balfour learned was that, 'unless there are special circumstances charters are dealt with by the Council Office and the Vice-President – Hart Dyke – would appear to be the Minister responsible in the House of Commons'.[12] This would seem to confirm that the Home Secretary, Matthews, was certainly not heavily involved.

Balfour was cordial to Wace but suggested he should see Hart-Dyke, 'in whose department the matter is, and who will have charge in the House of Commons'.[13] In fact, Hart-Dyke seems to have had little or no part in any of the discussions on the Charter, and Wace may well have known that this was the case. In any event, he directed his next letter to the Prime Minister, who had long been a Life Governor of King's, asking for an interview.[14] It is unclear whether he got his wish on that occasion, but a few months later he remarked that Salisbury had seen him once 'for ten minutes, but he seems to take no real interest in the fate of the College'.[15]

It is probable that the whole business had been handled, hitherto, within Government, almost exclusively by Cranbrook. However, not long afterwards, when the future of the Charter was within a week of being settled, Balfour was seemingly inclined to support its approval, and told Lankester that

> . . . the general impression left upon my mind by the papers that have come before me is that although the scheme is far from perfect yet if it be now rejected the inherent difficulties of the question are so great that in all probability they will defer to an indefinite period the institution of a Teaching University in London. This, you will agree with me, would be a misfortune. I will endeavour to look more closely in to the case.[16]

This might well have been the general view of the few in Government who took an interest in the matter, at the end of February. The growing strength of opposition to the acceptance of the Charter was probably not known widely among Ministers, or much discussed between them, before the Prime Minister met the deputation on 3 March.

It is difficult to believe that the request for a deputation to be received by Salisbury would not have been the subject of some contact between him and the Lord President, but Cranbrook's diary entry for the following day gives the impression that he might not have been consulted, and that he himself was, until then, not fully aware of the extent of the forces ranged against the Charter.

---

[12] BL Add Mss 49760, Sandars to Browning, 28 January 1892.
[13] BL Add Mss 49850, Balfour to Wace, 1 February 1892.
[14] Hatfield House 3M/E, Wace to Salisbury, 12 February 1892; Benson Mss, vol. 111, fols 285–7, Wace to Benson, 30 October 1892.
[15] Benson Mss, vol. 111, Wace to Benson, 30 October 1892.
[16] BL Add Mss 49878, Balfour to Lankester, 1 March 1892.

I was sent for by Salisbury to meet a deputation on the Gresham Charter. Conflicting interests joining in a common assault. All nominally in favour of a Teaching University but not *this*, jealousy desire to be important etc., on the ground of some appearances. Still there is a formidable combination as I told the Bishop of London. Chamberlain was reasonable but warned me of the probable fate of the motion in the House of Commons.[17]

At the meeting, Earl Spencer spoke first, as the Chancellor of the Victoria University; Chamberlain represented the Provincial Medical Schools; Ripon put the case for the Society for the Extension of University Teaching; Derby made clear that he was not speaking for the Senate, but 'could not ignore the fact that the great body of members of the University, as represented by Convocation, were entirely hostile' to the Charter; Busk followed him; M.H.N. Story Maskelyne spoke for Bedford College; Prebendary Richard Whittington for the Birkbeck Institute, the City of London College and the Working Men's College; Bartley and Roundell rounded off the speeches, as leaders of the London Committee which had organised the opposition.[18]

Salisbury made a brief and inevitably non-committal reply, but doubted that the Government was in any position 'to withdraw or revoke' the Charter, whose fate was entirely in the hands of Parliament. This provoked an immediate legal argument between Napier, who took the view that the Government could, and R.S. Mure, who argued that the Government could not, withdraw a Charter submitted by the Committee of the Privy Council.[19] The point was not resolved by what happened thereafter; but the deputation had done its work well. Only three days later the *Observer* reported that the Cabinet, on Saturday 5 March, had 'gravely considered' the subject. The paper claimed that Bartley and Lubbock were poised to move the rejection of the Charter in the Commons.

Assuming that such a threat was known to be valid, the primary reaction of the Cabinet may well have turned on an assessment of whether such a motion would or could be defeated, and on whether it was politically wise to risk a damaging row at this stage of the session. The strength of the opposition, reaching across the normal party divisions, and reflecting, in no small part, old, denominational suspicions and bitternesses, may have been crucial. Balfour, for example, sat for a Manchester constituency, where the strength of provincial pride, indignation and Nonconformity may well have given him pause on the issue.[20] At the same time, it is not impossible that Salisbury and some others in the Cabinet – Goschen, for instance, who had

---

[17] Johnson, *Diary of Gathorne Hardy*, 4 March 1892, p. 819.

[18] The proceedings were fully reported in the *Times*, 4 March 1892, and the report is reproduced in Allchin III, pp. 298–304.

[19] Letters to the *Times*, 4 & 5 March 1892.

[20] H.E.J. Bevan, in E.G. Sandford (eds), *Memoirs of Archbishop Temple*, (London, 1906), ch. iv, p. 77.

loyalties to the Extension movement[21] – were genuinely impressed by the objections raised and, as a result, were uncomfortable about pushing what was clearly a divisive scheme. And no doubt the lack of any great urgency weakened the case for trying to impose an apparently flawed solution.

The main decision, therefore, seems to have been not to oppose any motion to reject the Charter, and to have the matter re-assessed. But the question of how and by whom that re-assessment should be tackled was, perhaps, not one which the Cabinet was willing to spend time discussing. It seems likely that the business of future arrangements and of coping with the parliamentary proceedings was delegated to Balfour and Cranbrook. On the very next day, in response to Bartley, who asked when the Charter would be discussed, Balfour in effect announced that the rejection of the Charter would not be opposed.

> I hope it will not be necessary to cut short the ordinary business in order to carry out that discussion. . . . I believe we can go a great way to meet the views of Honourable Members in regard to the propriety of remitting the draft charter for reconsideration. I think we shall be able to make a statement on the subject on Thursday.[22]

What had to be decided was whether to return the Charter for further consideration, either by the Privy Council Committee, or by the Selborne Commissioners, or by a new body; and whether to restrict the consideration to the Gresham proposals, or to widen it. Speculation began immediately, and the Registrar of the University put the prospects very clearly in a letter to Lubbock:

> I see that the 'Gresham University' draft Charter is to be referred back to the Privy Council or to the Commissioners it does not appear quite certain which. In any case it would seem to be of the utmost importance that the terms of the references should be wide enough to re-open the whole question of University reorganization in London so as to give one more chance – probably the last chance – of a settlement on a broader foundation than that provided by the scheme of the two Colleges. I hope that you will consider this for I imagine that it is by no means unlikely that the reference back may limit the area of inquiry to London colleges and schools claiming an interest in the new University only: though how any scheme for re-organization which does not embrace this University can be otherwise than unsatisfactory it is hard to conceive. I am afraid that, whether referred to the previous small Committee of the Privy Council: or to the Commission, there is not much hope that new views will prevail. A Royal Commission considerably enlarged

---

[21] On the rather hostile relations of Goschen and Wace, see Stuart Marriott, *A Backstairs to a Degree, Demands for an open university in late Victorian England* (London, 1981), pp. 31 & 32.

[22] 4s Parl. Deb., vol. 2, col. 168.

or a Parliamentary Commission would be more likely to come fresh to the matter and to over-ride special interests but I suppose it is too late to hope that such a course may be taken. The Senate did not feel at liberty, their scheme having failed to secure the consent of Convocation, to take an active part in the case before the Privy Council last summer, but this reference back must surely restore its full freedom of action and its right to urge its own views in the interest of education.[23]

Milman's pessimism was to be proved unjustified. There is no evidence to show whether Lubbock made representations to the Ministers, but Balfour and Cranbrook must have come to feel that only a new approach was appropriate. Cranbrook certainly consulted Selborne, who had presided over the first Commission and had taken the leading part in the Privy Council hearings. Selborne felt that a new Royal Commission was prudent in the circumstances, but he would not serve on such a body.[24] Cranbrook was also supported in the decision by the Duke of Devonshire.[25] In the House of Commons, pressure was kept up on Balfour[26], and on Thursday, 10 March, when Bartley asked him, directly, 'whether, in the event of the Draft Charter . . . being referred back to the Privy Council, it is understood that it will be brought before a Royal Commission,' Balfour replied, 'Yes, there would be a new Commission.'[27]

Later in the day, Bartley moved that the Queen should be asked to withold her assent to the proposed Charter until there had been further consideration of the matter. There was a short debate in which Lubbock and Rollit took part, along with A.H.D. Acland and H.J. Roby, Liberals, and Bartley and F.S. Powell, Conservatives; they made short statements, practically all in favour of what was being proposed. There was no opposition, and, though the terms of reference of the new Royal Commission had still to be drafted, Balfour assured the House

> . . . that he had no intention of limiting the inquiry by prohibiting the consideration of a scheme which would include a teaching University and the existing London University in one combined body.

And he added that

> . . . if it should be possible to frame a scheme which should associate with the existing examining body a new teaching body it would be . . . a good thing.[28]

---

[23] BL Add Mss 49658, Milman to Lubbock, 8 March 1892.
[24] Johnson, *Diary of Gathorne Hardy*, p. 820, 11 March 1892.
[25] Suffolk RO, Ipswich, HA43/T501/105, Devonshire to Cranbrook, 10 March 1892.
[26] 4s Parl. Deb., vol. 2, col. 443, 9 March 1892.
[27] 4s Parl. Deb., vol. 2, col. 543, 10 March 1892.
[28] 4s Parl. Deb., vol. 2, cols 594–9, 10 March 1892.

Her Majesty witheld her consent to the Charter on 21 March 1892.

The arguments in favour of establishing a new university, additional to the existing University of London, were not suddenly silenced. But in effect, the hopes of University and King's Colleges for Gresham University had been killed, by a combination of forces whose real political power came mainly from the supporters of Provincial Colleges and Medical Schools, helped by the antagonism of those MPs who were highly suspicious of the sectarian exclusiveness of KCL. The Senate of the University of London had been a non-player in this phase of a long struggle. Convocation, having brought down the Senate's proposals, thus allowing the plans of the Colleges to come within close reach of success, then helped in no small measure to defeat the Gresham advocates, though they could not have done it by themselves. For almost six more years, however, they were to be at the heart of continuing constitutional conflict.

# 29

# *The Cowper Commission*

The Government lost no time in setting up a new Commission. Cranbrook sent off letters of invitation on 29 March, and, though there were clearly one or two changes in his original list, the membership was completed, handed to the Home Office for drafting by 9 April, and announced three weeks later. There are only a few letters which throw light on the choice of Commissioners. Cranbrook had consulted the Archbishop of Canterbury and Lord Spencer, who had both pushed the claims of Sir Henry Roscoe, as a scientist and as a spokesman for higher education in the North of England: the Duke of Devonshire passed on the opinion of C.D. Liveing of Cambridge that Professor George Forrest Browne, Canon of St Paul's, should be appointed, and Devonshire himself felt that Browne would be a better representative of Cambridge than Sidgwick. As it turned out, both Browne and Sidgwick were included, but not Roscoe. J.L. Goddard, who had been Secretary to the Selborne Commission, was appointed Secretary, on the recommendation of Lord Selborne himself.[1]

The 7th Earl Cowper agreed to be Chairman of the new Commission. As Gladstone's Lord Lieutenant of Ireland, in 1880–82, he had been strongly opposed to the conciliatory policies of the Liberal Government, and in 1886 had taken a prominent role as a Liberal Unionist. He was, therefore, similarly placed, politically, as Lord Selborne, who had presided over the previous inquiry. Unlike Selborne, however, he was not to report to the same Government as that which appointed him. Within a few weeks of that appointment, there were significant political developments.

The Commissioners' first spell of asking questions coincided with the last weeks of Conservative/Unionist Government. The General Election of July, 1892, returned a majority of Liberals and Irish Home Rulers, and Salisbury resigned early in August, to make room for the octogenarian Gladstone. Lord Herschell and the Earl of Kimberley, Fellows of the University of London, became Lord Chancellor and Lord President respectively.

---

[1] Suffolk RO, Ipswich, HA43/T501/91, Spencer to Cranbrook, nd; T501/44, Ed. Cantuar to Cranbrook, 22 March 1892; T501/105, Devonshire to Cranbrook, 1 April 1892; T501/100, Goddard to Cranbrook, 11 March & 5 April 1892. Johnson, *Diary of Gathorne Hardy*, 29 March & 9 April 1892, p. 822.

Kimberley simultaneously held the Secretaryship of State for India, which took much of his attention. H.H. Asquith was Home Secretary, and for the first time, the Vice-Presidency of the Council, whose holders had for many years been the Ministers principally involved in the Governments' concern for school education, was included in the Cabinet. The new Vice-President was A.H.D. Acland.

The election saw no change in the parliamentary representation of the University of London. E.H. Busk had begun to prepare the ground for Lubbock's re-election at the end of 1890, as a Liberal Unionist. At that time he saw little danger from the University's Liberal Association, and was most concerned to see that Lubbock got an appropriate Chairman for his election committee. Busk thought Fitch 'would do most admirably if he would allow himself to be nominated', though reminding Lubbock that Fitch and Wilks, his previous Vice-Presidents, 'were both Home Rulers.'[2] But more than a year later the matter was still unsettled, though Busk and John Curnow, Dean of Medicine at KCL, were working hard on the organisation of local lists of sympathetic voters.[3] There was no great sense of urgency, however, and Lubbock's willingness to take part in opposing the Gresham Charter probably removed any likelihood of his being challenged in the context of University affairs. It was not until June, 1892, that there was any sign of a committee at work, with Busk clearly involved and with J.B. Benson, a solicitor and a Fellow of UCL, acting as Lubbock's Secretary. Lubbock, who had 'hopes of not being opposed', found those hopes justified: he was re-elected, unopposed, on 2 July.[4]

Cowper and his twelve colleagues formed a far more academically based team than the small group who had served with Lord Selborne in 1888–89. There were two Liberal politicians, both of whom had impeccable university interests. Lyon Playfair, a former Professor of Chemistry at Edinburgh, had been in two of Gladstone's Administrations – the second time, briefly, in 1886, he was Vice-President of the Council. He joined the new Liberal Government as a peer, holding the junior office of Lord-in-Waiting, which entailed acting as a Government spokesman for several Departments in the House of Lords. Lord Reay, back from his spell in India, we have already met as one of the promoters of the now defunct Association for the Promotion of a Teaching University; he became Vice-President of UCL in 1892, and would join the Government, as Under Secretary of State for India, when Lord Rosebery took over from Gladstone in 1894. Thus there were two members of the Commission closely linked with the Liberal political establishment at ministerial level.

---

[2] BL Add Mss 49655, Busk to Lubbock, 16 December 1890.
[3] BL Add Mss 49656, Busk to Lubbock, 26 February, 3 May 1891.
[4] BL Add Mss 62682, Lubbock's Diary, 13 & 18 June, 2 July 1892.

If Reay would have been seen as having an association with UCL, then Bishop Alfred Barry, now Canon of Windsor, must have been regarded as a KCL man, having been Principal of the College from 1868 to 1883, but, additionally, a Fellow of the University of London from 1878 to 1884. The other Churchman was Forrest Browne, who combined being Canon of St Paul's with holding the Chair of Archaeology at Cambridge. The medical world filled three places. Sir William Scovell Savory, Bt., a graduate of Bart's, taught and practised surgery, and was an eminent member of the Royal College of Surgeons. Sir George Murray Humphry was Professor of Surgery at Cambridge. John Scott Burdon Sanderson held the Chair of Physiology at Oxford. There were only two lawyers: James Anstie, Charity Commissioner and Fellow of the University of London, and Ralph Charlton Palmer – the enthusiast for the Gresham College connection – who was listed as 'Barrister-at-Law and one of the Lord Chancellor's Visitors in Lunacy'.

The membership of the Commission was completed by Henry Sidgwick, Professor of Moral Philosophy at Cambridge; and two nominees from much further North. Gerald Henry Rendall, a classicist, was Vice-Chancellor of the Victoria University; George Gilbert Ramsay was Professor of Humanities at Glasgow.

Cowper and his colleagues carried out a very different and far more extensive exercise than had Selborne and his smaller group in 1888–89. They heard evidence on sixty-eight days – between 25 May and 29 July; between 13 October and 23 December 1892; and betweeen 12 January and 27 March 1893. Almost fifty institutions and associations put forward their views, and 150 witnesses appeared before the Commissioners, who asked them 25,594 questions. Among the institutions represented which had not appeared on the scene in 1888–89 were six Nonconformist Colleges, three of the four London Music Schools, the Royal Institute of British Architects, the Royal Agricultural Society, and the Surveyors' Institute. It would have been difficult to find any organisation seriously involved in higher education in the metropolis which failed to have its say. And after they had all expressed themselves, it was almost nine months before the Commissioners' Report was signed, on 24 January 1894.

The evidence, and the issues, therefore, were well considered, by what was clearly a hard-working group whose membership was unchanged by the new Liberal Government. Six of the Commissioners – Anstie, Cowper, Reay, Humphry, Sidgwick and Palmer – were present on fifty-two or more of the sixty-eight occasions when evidence was taken: Anstie missed only three sessions. Six of the remainder turned up at between a third and a half of those meetings. Bishop Barry did not appear after October, 1892, having attended seventeen of the first twenty-five hearings. But he was obviously very much involved in the preparation of the Report.

When it was issued, Playfair thought the membership strong, and Cranbrook doubted whether 'it will be cavilled at by anyone but Irish with whose indignation Ashbourne [Lord Chancellor of Ireland] threatens me'.[5] It was not the Irish, however, but Convocation, who objected to what they saw as their exclusion from the Commission.

Woods's death, on 25 January 1892, had left Convocation without a Chairman. The election of his successor would not take place until the Annual Meeting early in May, but, as we have already seen, canvassing for the Chair and for the other vacancy on the Senate, left by the death of the 7th Duke of Devonshire, began before the end of January. Even without the controversy over the Gresham scheme, there was concern that Wood had been appointed to the Senate before Convocation existed, and there was no constitutional provision for the new Chairman to sit on the Senate *ex officio*.

That the constitutional position was not widely understood was revealed within days of the withdrawal of the Gresham Charter, when Weymouth, a member of the Annual Committee, urged Collins to stand for Chairman 'and *ex officio* member of the Senate'. Weymouth argued that Busk and another lawyer, William George Lemon, were the only candidates so far, and that Collins and Napier would be welcome as representing a younger generation: he also felt that Collins's recent election to the London County Council would strengthen his candidacy.[6] But Collins was already committed to Busk, and to the need to have the Chairman on the Senate:

> . . . inasmuch as it is the unwritten rule for Convocation vacancies on Senate to be filled alternatively from Medicine and Science and from Arts and Laws graduates, and inasmuch as Magnus, the last Convocation nominee, was regarded as a Science representative, this vacancy [i.e., that caused by the death of the Duke of Devonshire] should be filled by an Arts and Laws man, and as Napier deferred to Busk I agreed to support the latter. Since the Chairmanship of Convocation currently is <u>not</u> *ex officio* a Senator, it is obviously desirable . . . that he should be made so by election. Therefore I support Busk for the double event. I am desirous of running for the Senate for the next vacancy – which will probably soon arise. I shall esteem your support for *that* very highly. I am desirous of continuing to work for Convocation as I have done in the past, believing in the University and loyal to its policy. I think as Chairman I should be less well able to serve it. If it is thought wise to merely formally nominate me for this vacancy not with any serious intention but merely to show I mean to go for the next, I am willing. Napier fully agrees with me in the above policy and will act for me.[7]

Busk was obviously well thought of by the core, London-based members of Convocation, not least as a leader of the campaign against the Gresham Charter. Moreover, the number of people able, financially and professionally, to devote the amount of time demanded by the Chairmanship, was almost

---

[5] Johnson, *Diary of Gathorne Hardy*, 9 April 1892, p. 822.
[6] UL Ms 812/70, Weymouth to Collins, 19 March 1892.
[7] UL Ms 812/70, Collins to Weymouth, draft of letter, 21 March 1892.

certainly very limited. Busk's popularity and willingness, therefore, ensured that Lemon and any other potential candidates simply faded from the scene. Busk was returned as Chairman unopposed. But Collins's argument that it was desirable for the Chairman to be on the Senate, and that the best way to make that happen was to elect Busk to be nominated for appointment to the seat vacated by the Duke of Devonshire, was not acceptable to all members of Convocation. Whereas the Chairman had to be chosen by those present at a meeting, voting for candidates for the Senate seat could be done by post. Lemon and Talfourd Ely, both established members of the Annual Committee, stood but received between them only a quarter of the votes cast – 143 and 136 respectively. Busk's tally was 781.

Convocation had entrusted the negotiations over the Charter to the Annual Committee. Recognition of the importance of the issues, and differences of views as to how Convocation should respond to those negotiations, were no doubt the main reasons why the annual elections for membership of the Annual Committee began, in May, 1892, to attract more serious competition than had been usual for many years. In practice, there had been only one or two applications in excess of the sixteen places in each of the two groups, one of which represented Arts and Laws graduates, while the other represented Medicine and Science graduates. In 1892 there were forty-two candidates for the thirty-two places, and in the three following years the numbers increased to forty-seven, sixty-two and sixty-six. And as we shall see, the later elections became intensely partisan.

The Annual Committee set up a sub-committee to 'represent the views and guard the interests of Convocation in all matters connected with the proposed Charter' on 1 February 1892, and, by 18 March, its membership was all drawn from what might be thought of as the Busk camp. Busk himself was joined on it by Baines, Collins, Napier, Nesbitt and O'Reilly. On 8 April, a month after the decision to appoint another Royal Commission, that sub-committee, on the initiative of Nesbitt and O'Reilly, suggested to the Annual Committee that they should be replaced by a Special Committee of fifteen, which should be authorised to monitor the work of the Royal Commission and confer and take joint action with the Senate. The Annual Committee elected on 10 May, at the General Meeting of Convocation, must have felt that fifteen was too large a group, but re-appointed the sub-committtee, with its previous six members plus Sophie Bryant, Lemon, A.L. Morris, and A.E. Sansom of the London Hospital, a Fellow of KCL.

By 26 April the sub-committee was aware of the membership of the new Royal Commission. None of the members was appointed as the formal representative of any particular institution, and the only one who belonged to Convocation was James Anstie. Anstie had graduated from King's in 1856, had been for many years an elected member of the Annual Committee, and became an *ex officio* member, as a Convocation-nominated Fellow, in 1888. But a majority of the current Annual Committee regarded Anstie as hostile to their view of Convocation's present concerns. On 20 May, Lemon and

Spratling carried a resolution which stated that Anstie had been 'closely identified' with the Senate's scheme, which had been thrown out by Convocation in May, 1891, and that 'Convocation is by no means in sympathy with his views'.

The Annual Committee had deplored the non-representation of Convocation on the Royal Commission on 26 April, and a week later resolved to petition the Privy Council and to send letters of protest to Balfour, Cranbrook, Chamberlain, Lubbock and Bartley. At the Annual Meeting of Convocation on 10 May, O'Reilly and Collins moved a resolution, readily accepted, regretting the absence of any representative of Convocation on the Commission; and, at its first meeting, the newly elected Annual Committee urged a further attempt to secure direct representation of Convocation by its Chairman.

All of this was to no avail. The Government made no move to add any members to the Royal Commission; and it is perhaps not unreasonable to feel that the special pleading of Convocation at this point in time may not have helped to facilitate sympathetic consideration of their viewpoints later. It is clear, however, that Busk, Collins and their supporters appeared to be in firm control of the Annual Committee as the Royal Commissioners began their work. And Collins was able to pursue his ambition for a place on Senate within a few months, while the Commission was still sitting. He replaced the late Lord Sherbrooke, after winning the Convocation election with 855 votes, against another medico, H.G. Howse, of Guy's, who received 642. A.W. Bennett was third with 218 votes. Bennett was the choice of those professors, the most prominent of whom were at UCL, who were keen to promote a German or Scottish type of university – which meant a non-collegiate institution. His heavy defeat no doubt reflected in part what was described as the 'strong prejudice' which the 'majority' of Convocation had against 'teachers of University College and King's College in particular'.[8]

The protests against the Gresham proposals, which had mushroomed in the months preceding the withdrawal of the scheme, can be seen as a watershed in the campaign by University and King's Colleges to break away from the University of London and to become the nucleus of a new institution, federal in character and restricted to the teaching of students in the London area. In the hearings before the Selborne Commission and the Privy Council, those Colleges and their allies were clearly on the offensive, and the opposition to their proposals in some disarray. But perusal of the evidence given to the Cowper Commission reveals a reversal of that position. UCL and KCL were on the defensive, while Senate was revitalised and fully in agreement with Convocation in wishing to see the Gresham proposals rejected. To no small extent, the change of emphasis reflected both the character of the new

---

[8] Cowper Comm., Evid. 13827.

Commission and the emergence of a vigorous body of the academic profession – usually spoken of at that time as 'the teachers', – in which scientists predominated.

The Cowper Commission's membership was at least half composed of working academics, and almost all the others were heavily involved in the governance of universities. This, in itself, distinguished the Cowper from the Selborne Commission, and ensured a fuller and more informed consideration of the complex range of topics. It may also have ensured a more sympathetic attitude towards the claims of the teachers, who appeared before them in a new guise. Karl Pearson and Ray Lankester had pursued the idea that the German or Scottish university model should be adopted in London, and this had made them lukewarm about the proposals of UCL and KCL. Their persistence was rewarded by the establishment, just as the new Royal Commissioners began to take evidence, of an Association for Promoting a Professorial University for London – hereinafter the Professorial Association. This group, in June, 1892, had some eighty members drawn from university institutions across the country, of whom a large proportion were teachers of science and technology. T.H. Huxley, himself a Fellow of London University, was its President, and Karl Pearson its Secretary: two other members of the Senate – Thorpe and Carey Foster – sat on its Executive Committee, and a fourth Fellow – Philip Magnus – was a member. F.V. Dickins, then Assistant Registrar of the University, was also on the Executive, whose membership was almost entirely scientific. No less than fifteen members of the Association gave evidence to the Commission – by far the largest contingent from any institution or representative body.

The Professorial Association put forward, quite aggressively, their objections to what they saw in the Gresham proposal as a university in the form of 'a federation of certain colleges for examination purposes'. They were, essentially, centralisers, who wanted a policy of absorption of the independent institutions in London which operated at university standard into a single university. They were particularly concerned with the need to provide 'central, fully-equipped laboratories' for teaching and research in science, instead of a 'perpetuation of the present system of second-rate competing laboratories'. But overall, they wanted a university whose governing body would be composed, primarily, of the professors, though they accepted that there should also be a minority of Crown-chosen lay members.

The major constitutional questions which the Professorial Association posed to the Commission were, therefore, that of choosing between a unified or a federal university, and that of preferring academic to lay governance. They raised other complaints against the Gresham proposals, not least, in the context of the Medical Schools, the suspicion that some of them wanted 'to cheapen degrees, and so to attract students'. And they dealt a shrewd blow to UCL, the principal sponsor of the Gresham scheme, by reproducing for the Commission the statement circulated to all MPs just before the scheme was withdrawn, signed by 120 'governors, life governors, fellows and members of the teaching staff of University College', expressing dissatisfaction with the scheme and pleading for its suspension and modification. No doubt somewhat embarrassingly for him, the list included J.S.B. Sanderson, now a member of the Royal Commission.

But the wishes of the teachers did not necessarily help to solve, automatically, the question which had divided the Selborne Commissioners so disastrously – could a single university combine, practically and equitably, the teaching and examining of 'internal' students with the examining of students taught or self-prepared elsewhere? Without a clear opinion on this matter, the choice between one and two universities could not be resolved. On this absolutely basic question, the Cowper Commissioners received plenty of contradictory advice from all quarters.

There were many other issues of academic and educational importance which faced the Commissioners, and the discussions of them make interesting reading in the voluminous evidence and appendices to their Report. But for the purposes of this book, which is focussed on the relations between Senate and Convocation, it is not necessary to deal with them in any detail. What was fundamental to the future of that relationship, however, was the resolution of the apparent problem of how any recommendations should be implemented.

The Cowper Commission had been authorised

> To consider, and if we should think fit, alter, amend and extend the proposed Charter for the Gresham University . . . so as to form and report . . . a scheme for the establishment under Charter of an efficient teaching University for London . . .

The Commission's terms of reference thus implied that any change recommended should be effected by Charter. But Convocation's exercise of its power to refuse consent to a Charter, little more than a year previously, had clearly dismayed and, indeed, outraged many people, who felt instinctively that the use, and even the sheer existence, of such a power was constitutionally inappropriate. The Senate was, naturally enough, unforgiving, but they at least had been fully aware of Convocation's privilege. Some other interested parties were amazed to find that Convocation had such a power. By the time the Commission began to take evidence, it was clear that the likelihood of Convocation repeating its opposition to a Charter was a factor which could not be ignored.

Lord Cowper and his colleagues did not hesitate to invite witnesses to comment on how Convocation might react to various proposals, and on how they regarded its power to thwart change. The responses they received did not bode well for Convocation. There was sympathy for the notion that the graduates had an appropriate organisation which had done much in support of the University, and should have the ability to initiate questions and discussions of University policy. But there was widespread criticism of the unpredictable and unsatisfactory nature of some of its actions, which was blamed on fluctuation of attendance, and the fact that, as there was no differentiation by Faculty, many important issues were simply not understood by many members present and voting at general meetings. For such a body to have a veto over proposals for constitutional change was seen by many as unacceptable.

It is worth quoting a few of the statements of witnesses in this context. Joshua Fitch, himself a quite conscientious member of Convocation, thought that

> It is not a very satisfactory legislative body. The people who attend it, attend it rather casually; they happen to be just those out of the three or four thousand graduates who live near London; they have no representative character, and from their very constitution they have little sense of responsibility. I for one have always regretted that the present constitution of the University gives them a veto upon the reception of a new Charter.[9]

Thiselton-Dyer was more impatient:

> We have reasoned with and talked to Convocation long enough, and why such an extraordinary body was ever called into existence I cannot conceive . . . we must not allow Convocation to have the mischievous power of simply obstructing everything.[10]

And Fry thought that

> . . . there is very great difficulty in any scheme passing through Convocation . . . a very large number of members . . . are interested in one way or another in opposing every scheme, and the opponents will always be the more active in coming to vote.[11]

From outside the University of London the same view was taken by Sir William Anson, and by James Bryce.[12]

When Lord Cowper asked Busk how he felt about the matter, the Chairman replied, only briefly – which was probably very wise – that Convocation had no wish to exercise executive powers, but that the 'working Members' would want to cling to their right to veto an alteration to a Charter.[13] Cowper asked

---

[9] Cowper Comm., Evid. 2984.
[10] Cowper Comm., Evid. 14645–6.
[11] Cowper Comm., Evid. 6452–3.
[12] Cowper Comm., Evid. 20542, 16779–80.
[13] Cowper Comm., Evid. 20785.

many witnesses how they thought that Convocation's veto could be abolished. All agreed that only an Act of Parliament would achieve that end.[14]

During the deliberations of the Royal Commission, both Senate and Convocation were involved in internal, tactical discussions, in responding to what they knew was being said before the Commission, and in rather wary negotiations with each other. Each operated through a committee. We have seen the membership of the sub-committee set up by Convocation's Annual Committee. The Senate, on 30 March 1892, appointed their Special Committee, composed of Anstie, Fitch, Fry, Herschell, Holden, Hutton, Kimberley, Lubbock, Magnus, Osler, Pye-Smith, Quain, Rollit and Wilks.

But there were significant movements of Senate personnel in the following months. Busk became a Fellow on 23 May 1892, and at the end of November he was added to the Special Committee. He was joined there by Collins, shortly after the latter took his seat in Senate in February, 1893. Thus the two leading members of the Convocation sub-committee were installed on the Senate's Special Committee for a year before the Commission reported. There were moves, too, which ensured that the increasing strength of the teachers was also recognised. Thorpe was joined by a colleague at the Royal College of Science, Arthur Rucker, Professor of Physics, who was appointed to the Senate by the Crown on 1 June 1892. Both men were strong supporters of the Professorial Association, and, on 29 June, both were added to the Special Committee.

In June, 1893, Lord Herschell became Chancellor; his place as a Fellow was taken by Sir William Scovell Savory, Bt., a member of the Cowper Commission. And on 25 January 1894 – the day after the Cowper Commission's Report was signed – Sir Henry Roscoe, another strong member of the Professorial Association, who had given evidence to the Commission, joined the Senate. Both Savory and Roscoe were Crown appointees.

Fellows who were London graduates were members of the Annual Committee, *ex officio*, and in 1892–93 there were twenty-two of them, including all save two members of the Senate's Special Committee. But it was only rarely that any of them attended the meetings of the Annual Committee. During the year from April, 1892 to March, 1893, only Goldsmid was present, twice, while Fitch and Magnus turned out for one meeting each. Busk and Collins were only appointed to the Senate's Special Committee in November, 1892, and February, 1893, respectively: Busk attended two, and Collins, one of its few remaining meetings. The fact that there was a small overlap of membership of the negotiating committees may have helped to ensure that the two groups understood what each was doing. But the apparent lack of enthusiasm for joint meetings implies, in all probability, simply a recognition

---

[14] Cowper Comm., Evid. of, *inter alia*, Bryce, 16780; Sir Charles Clark, Bt., 7019–22; Fry, 6452; Milman, 10248–51; Pye-Smith, 13780; Roscoe, 17858; Thiselton-Dyer, 14645.

of differing concerns and, possibly, a sense, on most of the Fellows' parts, that it was better to keep Convocation at arm's length. Certainly, while both Senate and Convocation were keen to see the Gresham proposals denied, each had its own agenda and clientele to consider.

Convocation tried to build on the ambitions of institutions other than UCL, KCL, the Medical Schools and the legal societies. Collins, Napier and Baines carried a resolution that approaches should be made to the London County Council's Technical Instruction Committee, the Department of Science and Art, the City and Guilds Institute, the City of London College, the Working Men's College, the Birkbeck Literary and Scientific Institute, the London Society for the Extension of University Teaching, Bedford College and Queens College. Those institutions were asked if they would support a Teaching University as an extension of the University of London; as most if not all of them were keen to join an expanded university, their replies were generally supportive of Convocation's approach.

But Convocation was anxious, from an early stage in the hearings. Their leaders quickly recognised the hostility being expressed before the Commission about their power of veto over changes to the Charter. On 17 June 1892, with a General Election due in the following month, Collins and Sansom carried a resolution that a letter be sent to all members of Convocation stressing the importance of endeavouring 'to obtain from [Parliamentary] candidates promises that they will oppose any attempt to diminish the powers and privileges at present possessed by Convocation'. This was the first, defensive strike in what would become a war of attrition.

By contrast, the teachers on Senate had an early success. When, on 29 June 1892, the Special Committee put before Senate a draft letter on policy, addressed to the Secretary of the Cowper Commission, Thorpe carried a motion expressing agreement to 'add to present functions . . . teaching by means of a Professoriate appointed by the University . . . to which an adequate share of the government of the University should be accorded'. In November, the Committee agreed a comprehensive proposal for the establishment of Faculties and Boards of Studies, for the creation and maintenance of Professorships and Lecturerships, for the acceptance and administration of fees of every description, for 'adequate representation' of the Professoriate on the Senate, and for incorporation within the University of 'Teaching Institutions of the higher rank'.

The only serious disagreement came over the opening paragraph of that proposal, and almost certainly reflected the concern of those protective of London College interests. The controversial sentence, as originally drafted, declared willingness to consider changes 'in order to promote the efficiency of the University, and with a view to its reorganization as a Teaching University in and for London'. Fry moved that this should be replaced by the words 'in order to promote higher education in the Metropolis and to increase the efficiency of the University'. On a division, the Special Committee was equally divided, and the original statement was retained by the casting vote of the Vice-Chancellor. The division list was not published, but those present were the Vice-Chancellor, Anstie, Fry, Holden, Magnus, Osler, Pye-Smith, Rollit, Rucker and Thorpe. It is easy to believe that Magnus, Rucker and Thorpe would have voted for the exclusivity of London; but much more difficult to pick the crucial fourth and fifth men who must have supported them. In any event, the agreed draft was approved by Senate with only minor changes, though Fry again tried but failed to have it defeated.

Meanwhile, Convocation's committees had numerous discussions in pursuit of an agreed scheme to put before the Commission. There were few indications of discord within the sub-committee, but in the Annual Committee two doctors, Sansom and Curnow, tried but failed to carry important suggestions. They lost the proposal that the University should have two Departments, Imperial and Metropolitan, ruled by one Senate; and they could not persuade their colleagues to accept a scheme to guarantee the introduction of easier medical degrees. The divisions for those two motions were settled, ten to five, and ten to six, respectively, but there are no lists of voters. Napier was defeated, nine to two, on an attempt to propose allowing certificates of attendance to be accepted in lieu of intermediate and preliminary science examinations. The draft scheme approved by the Annual Committee was accepted by Convocation, as a basis for discussion with Senate and with the Royal Commission, in January, 1893. There was only one major division, when Silvanus Thompson moved the rejection of the proposal to introduce Divinity as a subject of study in the University: his motion was lost by 101 to thirty-five.

The Professorial Association had completed their plan in June, 1892, and in December their Executive Committee met the Senate's Special Committee. The Association's delegation included Huxley, Carey Foster, Rucker and Thorpe, all Fellows of the University. On that occasion the Vice-Chancellor thought that the Special Committee's own proposals were wide enough to cover the Association's scheme, and Huxley expressed himself happy with the way things were going. In mid-February, 1893, a Deputation from the Annual Committee, comprising Busk, Sophie Bryant, Collins, Lemon, and Napier, met the Special Committee and presented Convocation's plan. There seems to have been an inconclusive discussion, leading to no more than a sense that further action was best postponed until after the Commissioners had reported.

But only three weeks later, the Special Committee considered, amended and approved a draft prepared by Huxley – presumably wearing his Senate hat – which called for action on basically agreed lines, while leaving details to be settled by a Statutory Commission. This was followed, on 29 March, by a formal letter from the Senate to the Commission, which implied that there were three main points on which the Senate, Convocation and the Professorial Association were all agreed:

1. That the present University of London and the various Teaching Institutions of higher rank which may desire connection with it shall constitute one organic whole, with common, and equitably adjusted, financial arrangements.

2. That the Professoriate shall be adequately represented on the Senate.

3. That proper provision shall be made for higher learning and research.

It is unlikely, however, that Convocation, in particular, would have been pleased with the additional paragraph:

> Senate conceive that no difficulty will arise in adjusting matters of detail; for example, by a Statutory Commission, before which the University and the Teaching Institutions in question would place their views respecting matters which lie outside these fundamental conditions, and are of relatively minor importance. In fact, the Senate believe that, in view of the rapid change of opinion which is in progress, it is not desirable that the freedom of action of the University in the future should be unduly restricted by Charter.

This coincided with the end of the direct submission of evidence to the Commission. The committees of Senate and Convocation, which had laboured over the last months, simply stopped meeting, and all parties had to compose themselves for almost ten months, until the Royal Commissioners reported. Their internal debates have remained strictly confidential, and there is nothing which reveals details of their progress. Doubtless hints or rumours of shifting attitudes may have reached the ears of the Commission. When Lubbock was preparing a speech, late in May, he was briefed by Dickins, the Assistant Registrar, though it is unclear whether the latter was writing in that capacity or as a member of the Professorial Association, for which he had appeared as a forceful witness. Dickins warned Lubbock that re-organisation was 'ticklish . . . owing to the considerable differences of opinion that exist', but he stressed the wide extent of agreement on some basic principles, and suggested that the Association would like the University to have authority

> . . . to guide the colleges to a sense of being parts of a great whole rather than distinct perhaps clashing units and thus pave the way at all events for a real voluntary union so far as academic work is concerned – of course such colleges as University College and King's College would always retain what constitutes a major part of their work their school special general and evening classes etc.[15]

Whatever the Commissioners were thinking, we have seen that the leaders of Convocation were very apprehensive, from early days, about the prospects

---

[15] BL Add Mss 49659, Dickins to Lubbock, 8 May 1893.

of losing their veto power. But they were not the only people to be disturbed by the progress of what the Senate had shrewdly observed was a 'rapid change of opinion'. Four months before the Commission stopped taking evidence, Dr Wace was quite pessimistic about the prospect for KCL:

> The Gresham Charter, the result of five years hard work and some £1500, would have given the College a secure position, and would have entrenched Church principles in the heart of a London University. That was the reason why Mr W.H. Smith was so anxious to promote it . . . We are now confronted by a Commission which is evidently hostile to the Church principles of the College, and the best we can hope for is that they may make no Report in time for the present Government to act upon it.[16]

Though the Cowper Commissioners signed their Report on 24 January 1894, it was another month before it was published. An accurate summary appeared in the *Times* on 6 February: two weeks later Gladstone admitted that the Government was unaware how the Report had been obtained.[17] The official release came on 27 February, but the Evidence and the Appendices, whose printing was described as a 'big task', were not available until the summer.[18]

The recommendations of the Royal Commission, much argued over and changed in detail, nonetheless provided the basis on which the University of London, despite enormous growth, was to operate throughout the twentieth century. The long-term educational and structural changes which they proposed, and which were, in time, essentially achieved, are best treated ahead of the procedures which they recommended should be followed in order to implement their proposals.

The Commissioners' most fundamental recommendation was that there should only be one University, based on the existing University of London, which they believed could combine the two functions of 'teaching with examining and examining without teaching', and could do so 'without injury to either class of student, and with benefit to both classes'.

Having plumped for a single University, the Commissioners felt that the only way forward was to retain the independence of existing institutions: absorption into a centralised organisation was ruled out. The teaching function should be limited to London and its neighbourhood, and should be carried out by existing institutions, each of which would be admitted 'either as a whole or in certain departments, as a School of the University, that is

---

[16] Benson Mss, vol. 111, fols 285–7, Wace to Benson, 30 October 1892.
[17] 4s Parl. Deb., vol. 21, cols 849–50, 20 February 1894.
[18] 4s Parl. Deb., vol. 23, cols 1575–6, 27 April, & vol. 24, col. 1003, 22 May 1894.

as a School at which University courses of instruction are to be pursued; and that all such Schools shall be open to the visitation of the University'. The existing system of 'external' examination should continue unchanged, with some necessary administrative adjustments.

The professors were not offered a unified University, but they were given the status of University teachers, and it was proposed that they should elect a third of the Senate, which should be almost doubled in size, to sixty-five members. There were to be six Faculties – of Arts, Laws, Science, Medicine, Music and Theological Science. The initial, component Schools were listed as UCL and KCL, the Medical Schools, the Royal College of Science, four Colleges of Music and six Theological Colleges. No institution, as such, was to be listed or represented as part of the governing body, but the make-up of the Senate provided for appointees of the Crown, of Convocation, of the Faculties and of other professional bodies.

At least initially, Convocation could take pleasure in the Commission's judgement that the Gresham University should not be established, and that the University of London's existing functions should be retained. But in important respects, Convocation was somewhat cold-shouldered by the Commission. Cowper and his colleagues did not favour the inclusion of several of the institutions approached by Convocation, because they were not offering instruction at university level. Worse still, while the Commissioners were unanimous in recommending that Convocation should, in future, have the right to appeal against constitutional proposals, they also provided the necessary mechanism for removing their existing veto, by proposing that all suggested changes should

> . . . be effected not by Charter but by legislative authority and by the appointment of a Commission with statutory powers to settle . . . arrangements and regulations in general conformity with the recommendations which we are about to submit.

The use of a Statutory Commission was in accordance with precedents followed in other cases of university reform, at Oxford and Cambridge and in Scotland.

There was a formidable degree of agreement among the Commissioners, though Barry and Sidgwick recorded serious doubts as to the compatibility of internal and external degrees; Reay wanted to press for more resources; Anstie thought the examination problem had been overestimated and should be left to the University to disentangle, and quibbled over the status of the MA degrees. But the most divisive disagreement was about the majority's recommendation that no grants of money should be given 'for any purpose, in respect of which any privilege is granted or disability imposed on account of religious belief'. The Commissioners were split almost evenly: Barry, Humphry, Palmer, Rendall and Savory opposed the recommendation outright, and Forrest Browne was prepared to support them 'if the Report goes beyond the principle of the University Tests Act'. This disagreement, which was particularly relevant to King's College, would prove to be a major obstacle to future developments.

Neither King's – nor Convocation – was to concede defeat meekly.

# 30

# *Anxiety and division in Convocation*

The early reactions to the report of the Cowper Commission were, from most quarters, generally favourable. But the reaction of those presently dominant in the councils of Convocation was hostile. Convocation's effective executive, the Annual Committee, was, however, subject to election at the General Meeting held at the beginning of May. The sequence of events between early March and early May, 1894, has to be read, therefore, with the forthcoming choice of a new Annual Committee in mind.

On 28 February – the day after the Report of the Cowper Commissioners was released – the Senate met and appointed a Special Committee to consider and advise on it, and to confer with the Annual Committee of Convocation. The new Committee's membership, in addition to the Chancellor and Vice-Chancellor, was larger than its predecessor, but contained twenty-four familiar names. Seventeen of them met on 14 March, when Anstie's proposal of a general acceptance of the Commission's Report was put aside, to make room for an agreement to invite the Annual Committee to meet with them in a week's time. It is not unlikely that Busk, who was present, would have reported the hostility to some aspects of the Report felt by the sub-committee of the Annual Committee, which had met the previous evening.

The sub-committee had worked on a draft Report to the Annual Committee at three meetings, on 2nd, 7th and 13 March. Three new members had been added, and at their third meeting a crucial motion by Napier was carried, recommending Convocation to adopt the view that, while being

> . . . favourable to the inclusion of provision for Higher Teaching and Original Research . . . [it was] of opinion that such reconstitution of the University as the Gresham Commission proposes is incompatible with the system of graduation successfully conducted by the University of London in all parts of the Empire, and must interfere with the high standard and equality of the Degrees, which are its distinctive features.

This was not only accepted, but Busk and Napier were authorised to strengthen the draft further.

The sub-committee's Report was finalised at the first of three significant meetings which took place, one after another, on 20 March. The sub-committee was followed by the Annual Committee, to which it presented its

Report. That Report protested against the proposed withdrawal of the Charter of the University, without consultation with Convocation; reaffirmed a desire to see teaching and research introduced; felt that the proposals of the Commission were insufficiently definite to increase efficient teaching, would tend to destroy the present work of the University, and would be injurious to higher education throughout the Empire.

All these expressions of concern were agreed to, without division, by the Annual Committee. However, there was opposition to the suggested inclusion of a sweeping proposition which advised Convocation to confirm that, while they would regret a second University in London, they would feel that 'it would be less disastrous to establish such a University with a distinctive title than to carry into effect the Scheme of the Gresham Commissioners'. This was a step too far for six members, but they were overridden by Baines, Curnow, Ely, Joseph, S.P. Moore, Nesbitt, Rev. Jacob Stephenson, Taaffe and Unwin. The vote was surprisingly limited, inasmuch as there were twenty-nine members present. No less than twenty-six of the twenty-nine stayed on for the conference with the Senate's Special Committee, so the abstention of fourteen members, including the Chairman, must have been quite deliberate.

The conference with the Senate Special Committee which followed – still on 20 March – was a gathering of forty people: twenty-six from the Annual Committee, and fourteen Senators. The event seems to have been an occasion, essentially, for members of Convocation to address the Senate. Speeches were made by Napier, Sidney Webb, Silvanus Thompson, Lemon, Bennett, Moore, Nesbitt and Morris. The Senate team seems to have kept silent, and the summing up was left to the Chancellor, Lord Herschell, whose diplomacy was exemplary and left the issues to be explored further and settled later.

A couple of days afterwards – on 22 March – the Home Secretary was asked in the Commons, by Carvell Williams, whether the Government would bring in a Bill or take other steps to give effect to the Report of the Cowper Commission. It was not an unreasonable request, inasmuch as the Government had learned the substance of the Report two months ago. Asquith declared that Government was giving the matter 'careful attention', but that the question of giving effect to the recommendations 'must depend to a certain extent upon the unanimity shown by the different bodies interested in accepting' them.[1] But by then, at least one significant approach had been made to Government.

It is not surprising that Sidney Webb was among those who abstained from voting in the Annual Committee's meeting on 20 March. On only the previous day, in his capacity as Chairman of the London County Council's Technical Education Board, he had signed a *Memorandum on the relation of a Teaching University in London to the work of the Board*. The Memorandum

[1] 4s Parl. Deb., vol. 22, col. 867, 22 March 1894.

was on its way to the Prime Minister.[2] It expressed general approval of the Commission's Report, but wanted students who had passed through training provided by the Board, at technical and secondary schools and in evening classes, to be able to go on to study for degrees without having to study subjects new to them, and in which they had no previous instruction – specifically, no Latin or Greek to be necessary in the Faculty of Science. The Board also wanted to see University laboratories presided over by University Professors who would be distinct from Professors of Schools, and which would be available for postgraduate study and original work.

But the Board was not merely supportive of the ideas of the Commission:

> If satisfactory assurances could be given as to the adoption of the policy here indicated, the Board might properly make a substantial annual grant towards the cost of the special items named, and establish a system of higher scholarships to enable scholars to continue their education up to the age of twenty-one or twenty-two in the Schools of the University.

And in a covering letter to Lord Rosebery, William Garnett, the Secretary of the Technical Education Board, referred to the LCC's notion, reflecting the influence of a Report by H. Llewellyn Smith on Technical Education, that an annual grant of £10,000 should be made to a Teaching University. Garnett, naturally, repeated the sort of changes which would be required to be made to the Cowper Commission's suggestions to ensure LCC approval, and recommmended that any Bill for the constitution of a Statutory Commission should empower the Commissioners to modify the original Scheme.[3]

This approach must have been one of the first made, directly, to the Prime Minister, and may well have been initiated by Webb on the basis of Rosebery's sympathetic understanding of the LCC, of which he had been the first Chairman. But Rosebery felt unable to do more than scribble on the papers, 'Still under consideration. No possibility of legislation this session', and, a few days later, the Chancellor of the Exchequer, Harcourt, told Rollit that it would be impossible to introduce relevant legislation in the current session.[4] On the following day, Rollit claimed that, in view of Harcourt's reply, he would 'draw attention to the Report, and move a resolution', on Friday, 20 April – but he did not do so.[5]

Whether or not Asquith's hint of a desirable unanimity was a factor, the Theological Colleges announced, on 3 April, their general acceptance of the Cowper Commission Report; and three days later Sir George Young claimed

[2] NLS Ms 10149, fol. 3.
[3] NLS Ms 10149, fol. 7, Garnett to Rosebery, 21 March 1894.
[4] 4s Parl. Deb., vol. 22, col. 905, 29 March 1894.
[5] 4s Parl. Deb., vol. 22, col. 1009, 30 March 1894.

that UCL, 'and some others,' had accepted the Commissioners' Scheme as a compromise.[6] Meanwhile, twenty-five members of the Annual Committee, perhaps believing that it was tactically wise to try and secure backing, quickly, for their hostile stance, had requisitioned an Extraordinary Meeting of Convocation, for 10 April. But a week before that meeting, with a session of the Senate's Special Committee due, Busk was afraid that he and Collins would

> . . . not be able to do anything which will prevent a report from being drawn up recommending the Senate to approve the Scheme of the Gresham Commissioners' Report. It is clear that the matter is being rushed by the Chancellor at the instigation of Anstie . . . there is . . . no reason for such indecent haste, especially as the Government do not propose to bring forward a Bill . . . this Session. The real object must be to anticipate the vote of Convocation next Tuesday evening.[7]

Matters were not made any easier for those opposing the Cowper Commissioners' Scheme when, whether with the connivance and agreement of either Senate or Convocation, or not, the *Times* published the most crucial parts of the Annual Committee's report to Convocation, on 5 April. This sparked anxious concern on the part of Busk and Collins. Busk had private conversations with Rollit and Silvanus Thompson, called a meeting of his main allies, and suggested approaching Lubbock – all with the intention of finding common ground with Senate, and exploring a notion of Rollit, to convene a Joint Consultative Committee of the two bodies.[8] There was no time, however, to publicise any such suggestion before Convocation met on 10 April.

The Extraordinary Meeting was attended by 399 members, and the division of opinion, which had been made evident in the last meeting of the Annual Committee, re-appeared. The strategy which those hostile to the Commission's Report seem to have adopted was to avoid for as long as possible any vote on the general issue of the Report's acceptability. No such motion was put before Convocation, and the first business was the opening draft resolution contained in the Annual Committee's report, protesting against the Commission's recommendation to withdraw the Charter of the University. It was moved by by Napier and Hart.

A year later, a different Annual Committee gave the following explanation of what passage of the resolution would have implied, and an account of what transpired:

> . . . if it had been carried it would have placed Convocation in an irreconcilable attitude with respect to the entire Scheme of the Royal Commission. Convocation

---

[6] *Times*, 3 & 6 April 1894.
[7] UL Ms 812/76, Busk to Collins, 3 April 1894.
[8] UL Ms 812/77–9, Busk to Collins, 5, 6 & 9 April 1894.

rightly prizes the privileges it possesses under the present Charter; but few of its Members were prepared to go as far as to use its present right of veto on any new Charter to prevent the widening of the usefulness of the University as a whole; the greater number believed that in the new Scheme might be discerned the outlines of a really great and important extension of its influence and of its functions as an educational power. This larger view prevailed over the view presented by the hostile first Resolution, and by an almost unanimous vote Convocation passed on to the next business on the Agenda.

This account almost certainly dignifies what seems to have been a confused and difficult session. As soon as Napier and Hart had presented their motion, Silvanus Thompson moved a wrecking resolution of doubtful procedural legitimacy, substituting the following:

> Convocation re-affirms its desire that power should be conferred on the University of London to make extended provision for teaching and for the advancement of learning and for original research in London, and therefore is prepared to give a general support to the Scheme of the Royal Commission.

The Chairman, surely correctly, ruled Thompson's motion out of order, as referring to another motion on the Agenda. Magnus and Osler then carried, without a division, the motion to pass to the next business. But this allowed Napier and Spratling to find another way to avoid any blessing being given to the Commission's Scheme. They took Thompson's amendment, and changed the words after 'research in London', to read 'according to the Schemes of 1886 and 1893 adopted by Convocation, or with modifications thereof'. Dickins and Carey Foster immediately moved an amendment expressing general approval of the Commission's Scheme, and a desire that conciliatory arrangements should be made by the proposed Statutory Commission.

At this point in what may well have become a dangerously tense exchange, the desirability of referring the whole business for joint discussion with the Senate was mooted. This doubtless reflected the liaison between Busk and Rollit in the week immediately preceding the meeting. The debate was brought to a close when Rollit persuaded Napier and Dickins to withdraw their motions. Then, seconded by Collins, Rollit carried a motion that the 'whole question of the constitution of this University' be referred to the Annual Committee, 'with power to nominate members of a Joint Consultative Committee of the Senate and Convocation'. It was implied that all sections of opinion in Convocation should be represented, and that Convocation's representatives should not be confined to members of the Annual Committee. The meeting was then adjourned to the close of the Ordinary Meeting due on 8 May.

Rollit, Busk and Collins were all present the next day, 11 April, at the Senate's Special Committee, when Rollit moved the establishment of a Joint Consultative Committee, in terms which expressed appreciation of 'the desire of Convocation for co-operation with the Senate'. Huxley proposed an alternative motion – 'that, while generally agreeing with the recommendations of the Gresham University Commission, the Senate is willing to join with the Convocation in appointing a Consultative Committee'. But the majority, probably recognising the desirability of negotiating an agreed approach with Convocation, were willing to delay a definite expression of support for the Commission's Report. They defeated the amendment by nine to six. Huxley was joined by the Vice-Chancellor, Quain, Savory, Thorpe and Wilks – all, it may be noted, being scientists and medicos. They were outvoted on the amendment, and on the original proposal, by Anstie, Busk, Collins, Carey Foster, Fitch, Lubbock, Osler, Rollit and Rucker.

When Senate met on 18 April, there was a repetition of the proceedings in the Special Committee. Rollit moved for the appointment of a Joint Consultative Committee, and for the Special Committee to make the selection of Senate representatives on it. But Quain tried to have included in the resolution a phrase stating that the Senate agreed 'generally with the recommendations of the Gresham University Commission'. The amendment was forced to a division, and lost by five to fifteen. Quain had the support only of the Vice-Chancellor, Roscoe, Savory and Thorpe. Anstie, however, was particularly distrustful of any Joint Committee, and moved that another Special Committee should meet with Convocation representatives to discuss the Commission's proposals, but that such a Committee should have no power to frame any resolutions. This motion was lost, without any formal division.

Both Senate and Convocation agreed that the Chancellor and the Chairman of Convocation would attend the Joint Consultative Committee's meetings. Senate's Special Committee chose their other nine members on 28 April, and certainly ensured that Fellows on both sides of the preceding argument were included. Those chosen were Anstie, Collins, Fitch, Carey Foster, Lubbock, Rollit, Roscoe, Rucker and Savory.

The Annual Committee did not meet until 4 May, only four days before the General Meeting of Convocation, at which a new Annual Committee would be elected. Given the growing sense of controversy which had developed, it is not surprising that there was 'some discussion on the question of postponing the election [of Convocation's representatives on the Joint Consultative Committee] till after the appointment of the new' Annual Committee for 1894–95. But it was agreed to go ahead, and eighteen names were put forward for the nine places, of which five were of non-members of the current Annual Committee – Cave, Cozens-Hardy, R.D. Roberts, Mary Scharlieb, and Thiselton-Dyer. However, when the voting was finished, only Cave, Principal of Hackney College, had been chosen from among the non-members. The other places went to Baines, Lemon, Napier, Nesbitt, Sansom, Spratling, Stephenson and Silvanus Thompson. A clear majority of the delegation was opposed to some important aspects of the Cowper proposals.

But as it happened, the Joint Consultative Committee was not fated to meet.

What had occurred on 10 April was enough to spur into action those prominent in Convocation who were alarmed by the position being taken by the majority in the Annual Committee. Among the most active were Carey Foster, Professor of Physics at UCL, and Dickins, the Assistant Registrar. They plotted to undermine the opponents of the proposals of the Cowper Commission by ensuring that the new Annual Committee, to be elected on 8 May, would have a majority in favour of the proposals. They worked closely with Thomas Gregory Foster, Quain Student in the English Department of UCL, at the beginning of his distinguished career; and Holburt Jacob Waring of Bart's Hospital. Their intention was to write to all members of Convocation, and they were well aware of the need for secrecy:

> . . . it will be wise . . . not to allow any statement to be made as regards the proposed circular . . . so that the Napier Collins group may not get wind of the affair, and send out a counterblast.[9]

Early responses to their approaches seem to have been encouraging, and by 24 April, Dickins could 'almost scent victory at worst we shall greatly diminish forces against us'. But there were bargains to be struck: Gregory Foster had one correspondent who was supportive, but wanted representatives of the Theological Colleges on the Annual Committee.[10] And when another theologian, Dr Cave, seemed to raise the possibility that the Statutory Commission envisaged by the Cowper Commission might not be necessary, there was a hint of panic:

> It will be a disastrous thing if any move is permitted in the direction of doing away with the Statutory Commission. That would be to remove all means of establishing any university scheme and is the very thing . . . the other side *chiefly aim* at. Hence my anxiety to convince Cave of the impolicy of any move in that direction. We might gain some votes but at a ruinous price.[11]

Gregory Foster produced the first draft of the proposed circular, and an agenda for a meeting of interested graduates was approved on 26 April.[12] On the same day, Dickins learned that Cozens-Hardy would be willing to take the Chair of a committee, but could not promise to do any additional

---

[9] UCL College Corresp. 2A/10, Waring to T.G. Foster, nd [April 1894].

[10] UCL College Corresp. 2A/10, Whitehouse to T.G. Foster, 24 April 1894.

[11] UCL College Corresp. 2A/10, Dickins's memo to T.G. Foster, 27 April, on back of Wynne to Dickins, 26 April 1894.

[12] UCL College Corresp. 2A/10.

work.[13] Dickins suggested Cozens-Hardy for the Chair to Gregory Foster, and at the same time asked

> Do you know Sidney Webb – I should much like to have a talk with him to see whether he and through him the LCC could not be brought to a general approval of the Scheme. The Report of the LCC Committee as far as the *Times* gave it did not appear to me hostile save on one point which is really though an important one a point of detail quite within the powers of a Statutory Commission.[14]

As we have seen, Sidney Webb had approached the Prime Minister five weeks earlier. It is perhaps a little surprising that no hint of such a move had reached Dickins, a fact which indicates the rather fragmented and uncoordinated nature of the progress of the argument.

The secrecy recommended by Waring may be the reason why there seems to be no record of a first meeting of graduates sympathetic to the Commission's ideas. But at the beginning of May the committee was formed, chaired by Cozens-Hardy. It will be referred to, subsequently, as the Cozens-Hardy Committee. Its officers were Thiselton-Dyer, Allchin, Gregory Foster, Waring and W. Palmer Wynne. A statement drafted by Gregory Foster was approved and circulated to Convocation on 5 May, with a list of the Committee and early supporters, by then numbering 112.[15] The statement complained that, while 'several of the most important bodies other than the University, concerned with the higher general or professional education in London', had given a general approval to the recommendations of the Cowper Commission, there had not yet been an opportunity to enable the graduates favourable to demonstrate their support. The Committee enclosed a postcard to be returned 'in order that a memorial from graduates in agreement with the general provisions of the Report may be forwarded to the Senate', and pressed members to attend on 8 May to vote for a motion by Thiselton-Dyer, expressing 'general approval of the Report of the Royal Commission'.

But the new Committee also pursued their original intention. They challenged the opposition to the Report by sending out a list of members who were their favoured candidates for places on the Annual Committee, which would be elected on 8 May. There were fifteen names on the list for Arts and Laws, and fourteen on the list for Medicine and Science. They had a spectacular success: every one was elected, leaving only one of the sixteen places from Arts and Laws, and two from Medicine and Science, to be filled by other candidates. And of the three who did fill them, one – V.A.H. Horsley – had signed up as a member of the Cozens-Hardy Committee. Only Talfourd

---

[13] UCL College Corresp. 2A/10, Christie to Dickins, 26 April 1894.
[14] UCL College Corresp. 2A/10, Dickins to T.G. Foster, 29 April 1894; *Times*, 19 April 1894.
[15] UL RC25/4a.

Ely and Sansom remained on the Annual Committee to represent those who opposed the proposed settlement. The effect of this on the prospects of the Joint Consultative Committee was to be dramatic – but so were other aspects of the meeting of Convocation on 8 May.

There were 374 members at the Ordinary Meeting of Convocation on 8 May, 1894. The Chairman, Busk, reported the establishment of the Joint Consultative Committee by Senate and Convocation. Then Thiselton-Dyer introduced his motion, reserving the right of Convocation to represent its views before the proposed Statutory Committee, but expressing general approval of the Report of the Cowper Commission. At this point, J.B. Benson raised a point of order, claiming that, as the Royal Commission's Report had been referred to a committee, it could not be debated. The Chairman upheld Benson's view, and ruled Thiselton-Dyer's motion out of order – a ruling which was, immediately and subsequently, the subject of much controversy.[16] At the meeting, 'the great majority of those present' walked out, sat in another room and, under the Chairmanship of Henry Roscoe, adopted 'an equivalent resolution' to Thiselton-Dyer's.[17] The formal session of Convocation was adjourned for a short spell, on the motion of Silvanus Thompson, seconded by Collins, until the results of the elections to the Annual Committee were known. After the announcement of the result of the election, which clearly indicated a heavy defeat for the opposition to the Cowper Commmission, the Ordinary Meeting was adjourned. Nor was any business brought before the reconvened Extraordinary Meeting, which had been adjourned to 8 May from 10 April; so it, too, was adjourned a second time.

The active participants in Convocation were no doubt in something of a state of shock and confusion, which is perhaps well illustrated by an exchange of letters between Lubbock and Benson, which took place immediately following the meeting. Benson, as we have seen, was Lubbock's election manager, and he chose, on 9 May, to tell the MP that the present count of those who wanted to secure his continued representation of the University in Parliament was 1012. But Benson was doubtful of the wisdom of trying to increase that number at the present time:

> It would certainly give rise to much correspondence respecting your views on the University question with the certainty of displeasing some. And on general grounds I find that both Professor [Michael] Foster . . . and Mr Busk are decidedly averse to the issue of any general circular at present.

---

[16] See letters to the *Times* from Benson, S.G. Thompson and Allchin, 15, 16 & 17 May 1894; also BL Add Mss 49660, Busk to Lubbock, and Busk to S.P. Thompson, 11 May 1894.
[17] UL RC25/4b.

But Benson had a personal problem, about the propriety of his continuing to act as Secretary of Lubbock's Committee:

> I cannot at present see any practicable alternative to making the Scheme of the Gresham Commissioners the basis of the new arrangements but I do not agree that this involves a general approval of the Scheme because I think Senate and Convocation should combine to secure more adequate provision for the continuance of the work the University has hitherto done, and the independence of the old work of the new, which also I am anxious to see provided for. I want the whole matter threshed out by the Joint Committee (of which I am not a member because Napier who practically nominated the representatives of Convocation upon it was afraid I should strengthen the party of compromise whom he thought sufficiently represented by Professor Silvanus Thompson) and not debated in Convocation on party lines during an agreed truce. My point of order, the success of which raised an undignified storm, was strongly supported by Sir Julian Goldsmid who sat below me.[18]

Lubbock would not hear of Benson giving up the Secretaryship. But his comment on the controversy over the future of the University can be seen as indicative of a tendency to avoid taking a personal position, which would weaken his reputation in some quarters at a later stage:

> Like you I think we must take the Scheme of the Commissioners as a basis, and this is all I believe that is meant by those, or most of those, who express a general approval; at least several of them have expressed themselves to me very much in the sense of your letter.[19]

Senate met on the day following Convocation's meeting, and the Vice-Chancellor reported the recommended list of Fellows to form the Senate side of the proposed Consultative Committee. Senate took no immediate action, but Anstie gave Notice of a Motion which may well have reflected the attitude of many present. The proposed motion called for the Special Committee

> . . . to communicate with the Annual Committee . . . on the question of the constitution of the University; and that until such communication has taken place no further action be taken by the Members nominated by the Committee to act upon the Joint Consultative Committee . . .
>
> [And] That it be an instruction to the Senatorial Members of the Joint Consultative Committee to proceed generally upon the basis of the Report of the Gresham University Commission, with which the Senate hereby declares its general concurrence.

---

[18] BL Add Mss 49660, Benson to Lubbock, 9 May 1894.
[19] BL Add Mss 49660, Lubbock to Benson, 9 May 1894.

It was two weeks later, on 25 May 1894 that the new Annual Committee showed the extent of the change brought about by their election victory. They received, first, the resignations of five previous members of the Committee from their positions as nominated members of the Joint Consultative Committee – Baines, Lemon, Napier, Nesbitt and Stephenson. Then three of the remaining nominees, Cave, Sansom and Silvanus Thompson, also resigned, no doubt feeling that a completely new start had to be made. Sansom had been associated with the Collins/Napier group, but Cave and Silvanus Thompson were supporters of Cozens-Hardy's Committee. Only Spratling, who had been in the Collins/Napier camp, did not offer his resignation.

But, having almost cleared the ground, as it were, the new Committee was put in doubt as to whether they could legitimately nominate a new group to the proposed Joint Consultative Committee. In their Report to Convocation in January, 1895, they recorded that

> The Chairman of Convocation, while of opinion that, under Standing Order[s] . . . the Annual Committee was not a continuing body, but one needing renewal of powers from year to year, nevertheless left it open to the Annual Committee to elect members to fill the vacancies, as probably such action would be ratified by Convocation.

On this unsatisfactory basis, the new Committee then demonstrated that they were as competitive as their predecessors when it came to choosing representatives. Spratling's inclusion was not disputed, nor was the listing of the Chancellor and the Chairman of Convocation. This meant that there were eight vacancies to be filled, and seventeen names were put forward, of whom eight were not members of the Annual Committee. From the Committee itself, the candidates were Bennett, Benson, J.S.N. Boyd, Cave, A. Bassett Hopkins, Howse, Sansom, H. Spicer and Silvanus Thompson. There were six candidates who were either clearly opposed to, or had serious doubts about, the acceptability of the Commission's Scheme – Benson, Lemon, Napier, Roberts, Sansom and Mary Scharlieb.

On a show of hands, four candidates received what were considered to be unbeatable votes, and were declared elected – Allchin, Cave, Cozens-Hardy and Silvanus Thompson. But it took no less than three further ballots to eliminate those with the smallest number of votes. Thiselton-Dyer, M.J.M. Hill, Hopkins and Howse survived the test. Of Convocation's nine elected representatives on the Joint Consultative Committee, therefore, only W.J. Spratling had so far been on the side of the opposition to the Cowper Commission's major recommendations.

The next step in what, in retrospect, can be seen as the continuing development of a deep split within Convocation, was the sending of a memorial to the Senate by the Cozens-Hardy Committee, outlining the recent developments in Convocation. They claimed that the canvass of membership, which they had carried out by postcards, had produced 856 supporters, of whom they enclosed a list. In their view, the Annual Committee of 1893–94, 'did not represent the feeling of Convocation in this University question'. And they went on:

> We understand that exception has been taken to the election by the newly appointed Annual Committee of Members to fill the vacancies on the Consultative Committee caused by resignation of certain delegates, and therefore would respectfully urge that in view of the extensive approval of the Report and the urgent need there is for a settlement of this question, the Senate should at once express its general concurrence with the Scheme, and use all its influence to induce the Government to appoint a Statutory Commission forthwith.[20]

Senate was thus faced with the impossibility of continuing with the idea of a Joint Consultative Committee, and were thoroughly apprised of the divisions within Convocation. On 13 June, they adopted a motion of Goldsmid, which gave general approval to the proposals of the Cowper Commission, but also left open the door for consultation with both parties in Convocation, thus deftly avoiding any embarrassing debate over the legitimacy of appointments made by the new Annual Committee. Goldsmid's motion was carried by twenty-one to three, and, by the same margin, Busk, Collins and Routh were defeated on an amendment which called for a further delay in making a decision as to giving general approval to the Commissioners' Scheme. The Senate entrusted negotiation to its Special Committee, which was instructed 'to consider what modification of such proposals should be suggested, and especially to consider what suggestions should be made as to the terms of reference of the "Statutory Commission"'.

It is unlikely that much attention was paid to the University's affairs, within Government, for some weeks after Harcourt had announced, on 29 March 1894, that nothing in the way of legislation would be forthcoming in the current session. But towards the end of May, Cozens-Hardy, despite having warned his colleagues that he could not do more than be, in effect, a figurehead, took command to the extent of writing, apparently at some length, to Acland to press the concerns of those graduates keen to see action in accord with the Cowper Commission's proposals. Acland sent his letter to Rosebery:

> I think it tends to show that a real opportunity has arisen for introducing or considering the introduction of a Bill on the London University matter. Could we have a small Committee Herschell Bryce and myself or whoever you think right to draft a Bill for consideration. It may be that if we do not act now the opportunity will be lost. I think a good Bill would easily pass the Lords.[21]

---

[20] UL RC25/4b.
[21] NLS Ms 10149, fol. 28, Acland to Rosebery, 29 May 1894.

It is quite probable that such a Committee was appointed, but there are no papers to prove its existence – or at least no such papers have yet surfaced in the public archives. It was claimed by the official biographer of R.B. Haldane, who was just beginning his notable participation in the affairs of the University, that as soon as the Cowper Report was issued Haldane and Webb 'set to work to draft a Bill which would have some chance of acceptance', but there is nothing to show whether or not such a draft ever reached Acland.[22] A Bill was produced, but Acland's optimism was misplaced, and his worry about the effects of inaction was thoroughly justified.

Outside Government circles, however, the pressure to find a way forward was now growing apace. Most of the institutions which had been mentioned in the Report of the Cowper Commission – the two Royal Colleges, UCL and KCL, Bedford College, the Medical Schools, and the Theological Colleges, as well as the Annual Committee, Trinity College of Music, and the Society for the Extension of University Teaching – were called together for a meeting at the Royal College of Physicians, on 30 June. It is unclear who organised this gathering, but the Annual Committee, which met on 28 June, received an invitation to attend from Professor William Ramsay of UCL, and they nominated Anstie (now clearly back in favour), H.M. Murray, Silvanus Thompson and Waring as their delegates. That majority opinion was running strongly in the direction of acceptance of the Commission's proposals, was implied by the resolution to be presented to the meeting, which would approve those proposals and 'urge on the Government that a Statutory Commission be appointed at an early date in order to carry them into effect'.

At the same meeting, on 28 June, the Annual Committee responded to the Senate's invitation to meet with the Special Committee on the following day, and nominated nine delegates to accompany the Chairman. On the motion of Silvanus Thompson, they also expressed their view,

> That it is desirable to memorialize Government to take immediate steps for the appointment of a Statutory Commission to frame Statutes in general accordance with the Report of the Gresham Commission, with full power to make such modifications as they may see fit, after conference with Convocation and other Bodies affected.

Between the Annual Committee's meeting on 28 June, and the conference of interested parties on 30th, the Senate's Special Committee received, separately, both the formal Annual Committee delegation, augmented by thirteen invited members of Convocation, and a group who had been nominated to the proposed Joint Consultative Committee by the Annual Committee of the previous year – Baines, Lemon, Napier, Sansom and Stephenson. By the end of the day, as almost all the known participants in the

[22] Sir Frederick Maurice, *Haldane 1856–1915* (London, 1937), pp. 77–8.

arguments over the future of the University were present, the concerns of those who were unhappy about the proposals of the Commission had been spelled out.

Napier was the main spokesman for the opposition, and concentrated on the need to protect the interests of external students. He put aside, for the present, objections to the establishment of a Statutory Commission, but urged that 'previous to its appointment the University should form an opinion as to what modifications in the Scheme were necessary'. He felt that there was a bias in the evidence of many witnesses before the Commission towards 'the higher and more progressive departments of study, rather than the conditions to be imposed upon Pass Students'. And he threatened that, if amendments were not secured, he and his collegues would advise Convocation 'to refuse to be a party to the abrogation of the subsisting Charter'.

The detailed changes which Napier and his colleagues wanted to see made were to provide that 'all Pass Examinations up to and including the Final Examination for the Pass or Bachelor's Degree in each Faculty shall be the same for all students'. In addition, there were calls for an increased representation of Convocation on the Senate, and on the Academic Council; and the substitution of a Graduation Council for the proposed Board for external students, with powers not only regarding External Students, but also 'the duty of regulating all Pass Examinations up to and including the Final Examination for the First or Bachelor's Degree in each Faculty'.

In reply to these representations, Goldsmid claimed that Senate shared the sympathy expressed for external students, but insisted that, as the Government was 'disposed to bring in a Bill', priority should be given to determining the constitution of the Statutory Commission. The Bill would be very short, and it would not be possible to include detailed modifications of the Scheme in it. Goldsmid was a Liberal Unionist, but it may be that he had been made aware of Acland's intentions: whatever the explanation, his statement seems to have been among the first public intimations of the Government's intentions, which were apparently very different from the assertion of Harcourt on 29 March that there would be no Bill in the present Session.

The much larger delegation, comprising the Annual Committee's delegates and the other invited members of Convocation, was much more focussed on the desirability of getting a Statutory Commission appointed, and of giving it sufficient flexibility to make appropriate modifications. But when they met the Senate's Special Committee, no details of any such modifications seem to have been raised.

A similar approach dominated the conference of interested parties at the Royal College of Physicians, on 30 June, when there was a great unwillingness to attempt to deal with detail. The President of UCL moved the resolution to be adopted, and after debate and amendment which involved contributions by Allchin, Young, Anstie, Rollit, and Silvanus Thompson, the meeting agreed 'to express, generally, its approval of the proposals contained in the Report of the Royal Commission' and to urge the early appointment of a Statutory

Commission which should have power to frame Statutes and Ordinances in 'general conformity' with the Cowper Commission Report. The only abstentions were those of Dr Wace and Sir William Priestley, the delegates from KCL, who were not authorised by the College Council to express any opinion. The resolution was to be forwarded to the Government.

Senate's Special Committee met on 4th, and reported to the meeting of Senate on 11 July, which saw a last attempt to delay approval of the course so clearly defined and supported by the majority of the Annual Committee and by the conference of interested parties. Goldsmid moved for the adoption of a resolution drafted in almost identical terms to those put forward, successfully, by Silvanus Thompson, to the Annual Committee. It supported the general approval of the Cowper Commission Report but specified that the Statutory Commission's powers to make 'such modifications as may seem to them expedient' should only be exercised 'after considering any representations made to them by the Senate, Convocation, or any other Bodies affected'. This was still too much for Busk and Collins, who insisted on the desirability of co-operation between Senate and Convocation, but proposed that

> ... in view of the abandonment of a Joint Consultative Committee of the Senate and Convocation which had been agreed upon, the Senate is not prepared to memorialize the Government to take immediate action upon the Report of the Gresham Commission until Convocation shall have had an opportunity of discussing the proposed changes which must seriously affect its power and privileges.

Busk and Collins were alone in their opposition. Their amendment was defeated, and the main motion carried, by votes of fourteen to two.

Senate's decision to go ahead and memorialise the Government was relayed to Annual Committee on 13 July, along with reports of the meetings of Convocation delegates with Senate's Special Committee, and with the conference of interested parties. So far as committees of Senate and Convocation were concerned, this was the end of activity until well after the long summer break. But there had been new signs of opposition to the Cowper proposals before July, and there were to be significant moves within Government in August.

It will be recalled that, on 20 March 1894, the 1893–94 Annual Committee had approved a clause in the draft Report of their sub-committee which expressed regret at the possibility of there being a second university in London, but felt that 'it would be less disastrous to establish such a University with a distinctive title than to carry into effect the Scheme of the Gresham Commissioners'. The inclusion of the clause was carried by nine votes to six, and there could have been as many as fourteen abstainers, among them Collins. A new organisation, the Gresham Scheme (1894) Amendment Association, led by Collins and Napier, accepted the desirability of there being one University of London, but was determined to seek changes within the Commissioners' Scheme. The Association published a thirty-two page pamphlet, entitled *Objections to the Gresham Commissioners' Scheme*, which is undated but probably appeared during the summer of 1894.

But those prepared to envisage the possible desirability of a separate University were equally determined to press their point of view. Led by Bompas, they set up the London University Defence Committee, in June, 1894, with Bompas as Chairman, and another lawyer, Heber Hart, as Secretary. However, of the nine members of the 1893–94 Annual Committee who had carried the inclusion of the controversial clause, only two – Baines and Joseph – were among the fifty-one signatories to a letter which the new Defence Committee sent to all members of Convocation, on 15 June 1894. The letter was accompanied by a succinct synopsis of their opposition to the Gresham University Commissioners' proposals, and a postcard, to be signed and returned to Hart, which stated that 'I am of opinion that, if a Local Teaching University for London be desirable, it ought to be constituted apart from the existing University of London.'[23]

By mid-July the Defence Committee were able to list 895 names of members of Convocation who had signed and returned their postcards. This was about forty more than had signed the Cozens-Hardy canvass. And the Defence Committee also claimed that among their signatories were eighty who had previously signed the statement in favour of the Cowper Commissioners' Report.[24] It is not a little strange that even the existence of the Defence Committee, let alone its operations, did not seem to come to the notice of Ministers until the end of 1894. Perhaps Bompas and his collegues decided that it was better to stay on the sidelines until the Government's intentions were clearer.

The Gresham Scheme Amendment Association, on the other hand, had already put their complaint to the Prime Minister. Collins wrote to Rosebery on 5 July, interestingly linking University and LCC politics, in which Collins was presently, and the Prime Minister had been, deeply involved, by raising a matter of 'urgent importance and one on which many London University men and Progressives feel strongly'. He pressed the Government not to renege on their pledge, given by Harcourt on 29 March, not to introduce legislation to appoint a Statutory Commission in the present session. He went on:

> The evidence taken by the [Cowper] Commission has not yet been published – the Commission exceeded their reference in suggesting a scheme not *under charter* – and many of the proposals contained in their report are in the opinion of many graduates, calculated to lower the standard of degrees, especially in medicine, to

---

[23] NLS Ms 10149, fols 22, 25 & 27.
[24] NLS Ms 10149, fol. 24.

operate unfairly towards the non-collegiate students, and give undue control to the professoriate element in the manner so forcibly condemned by your countryman Sir William Hamilton in his essays on University Constitution and Reform. I beg, my Lord, that if you purpose receiving a deputation from those in favour of the Commission's Scheme you will also be so good as to grant an audience to those who desire to lay other considerations before you.[25]

Rosebery was briefed by Acland, within the next two days, that the evidence was just about to be circulated. At the same time, Acland was dismissive about any serious opposition, and revealed that, despite earlier denials, legislation was indeed in preparation:

> Mr Collins belongs to a very small group of opponents I believe. I think we may wisely introduce a Bill in a fortnight – not seeing any deputations – Huxley writes strongly in favour.[26]

On the strength of this and other information, Rosebery told Collins that he had not been asked to receive any deputation, but thought that the Lord Chancellor, Herschell, as Chancellor of the University, had been asked, and that the matter 'will therefore probably be left with him'.[27] But the persistent Collins had spoken to Herschell and had learned from him that the Prime Minister would be asked to receive a deputation. And Collins was angered by Harcourt's answer to a Question in the House, on 12 July, that there was 'still a chance of a bill being brought in this session to appoint a Statutory Commission'. Harcourt had said, in fact, that 'the chances of that Bill will depend whether it is opposed or not'.[28] Collins warned Rosebery that 'The graduates of London University would keenly resent such a bill.'[29]

What seems likely to have happened is that Rosebery must have given Acland a free hand to make what progress he could on framing a Bill, probably helped by Herschell and Bryce, and that drafting was well developed by mid-July. Bryce, either at Acland's pressing, or in response to a direct request by Rosebery, was seemingly as sanguine as Acland:

> . . . from all I can learn there is very little opposition to the Scheme of the Report, and that we could probably carry without difficulty a bill establishing an Executive Commission to carry out the report. There will, I think, be much disappointment

---

[25] NLS Ms 10149, fol. 32, Collins to Rosebery, 5 July 1894.
[26] NLS Ms 10149, fol. 30, Pencil note by Acland, nd but clearly 6 or 7 July 1894.
[27] NLS Ms 10130, Rosebery to Collins, 8 July 1894.
[28] The question was asked by another LCC colleague of Collins, John Benn. It does not appear in Hansard, but the text of the Question, printed in the House of Commons' Order Paper, with a pencil copy of Harcourt's answer, is enclosed in Benn to Collins, 12 July 1894, UL Ms 812/83.
[29] NLS Ms 10149, fol. 34, Collins to Rosebery, 14 July 1894.

if some attempt is not made this session to deal with the matter. Of course if it encounters opposition we could not persevere. But there is a very fair chance that no opposition would be made.[30]

Also in mid-July, Rosebery received advice from James Stuart, MP for Hackney, a member of the LCC, and a former Professor of Mechanism at Cambridge, where he had founded the University Extension system. Stuart pushed for early action, warning – all too accurately – that 'If it is not done now . . . combinations will have time to be formed against it.' He knew that the Technical Education Board was 'decidedly in favour' and was sure of similar support from the LCC. He was aware that Collins

> . . . takes a view in opposition to the Scheme; but he does not in this, I think, represent the Progressive Party or the London County Council. The difficulty I understand him to feel would be met, I think, by a clause in the bill obliging the Commissioners whom it appointed to provide for the maintenance of the present non-resident degree system unimpaired.[31]

Sidney Webb returned to his earlier theme, apparently stung by suggestions he had heard that the LCC was opposed to the Report of the Cowper Commission:

> This is not the case. It is true that one or two members of the Council strongly hold the view of the late Annual Committee of Convocation and object to the main principles of the Gresham report, but no countenance has ever been given to these views by the London County Council or the Technical Education Board. On the contrary the . . . Board has formally welcomed the Gresham proposals.

But Webb reminded the Prime Minister of his earlier contention that the Council 'should be represented on the Statutory Commission, which will have the framing up of a body towards the funds of which the Council is expected to be the largest donor'.[32]

Rosebery and his colleagues could hardly be blamed, therefore, for looking forward with confidence to the likelihood of having the Statutory Commission in place quickly. And in early August they received more encouragement in the form of a memorial from the Association for the Promotion of a Professorial University, with 233 signatories, blessing the Cowper proposals and 'respectfully' urging the Government to appoint a Statutory Commission to implement them.[33]

---

[30] NLS Ms 10149, fol. 38, Bryce to Rosebery, 17 July 1894.
[31] NLS Ms 10149, fol. 36, Stuart to Rosebery, 16 July 1894.
[32] NLS Ms 10149, fol. 40, Webb to Rosebery, 17 July 1894.
[33] NLS Ms 10149, fol. 46, Roscoe to Acland, 9 August 1894.

But on the very same day that Acland sent this last memorial to the Prime Minister, he had to tell the House of Commons that there would be no Bill in the current session. The sudden withdrawal was in no way due to the objections and threats of either the Gresham Scheme Amendment Association or the London University Defence Committee. It was due to the discontents of the leaders of King's College and the intervention on their behalf of the Marquess of Salisbury.

# 31

# *Lions, beaters, and the fall of the Rosebery Government*

Both King's College. and its School, on which it had been heavily reliant, financially, had been losing money and students for several years. In March, 1894, the College's Council had exhausted its borrowing powers. Appeals to the Church of England and elsewhere had failed to produce sufficient support, and

> Nothing remained except the painful alternatives of either the closing of the college altogether or the acceptance of grants from the public authorities – Her Majesty's Treasury and London County Council – on such terms as they should dictate.[1]

Such grants from the Treasury, for university colleges, had been introduced in 1889, for five years, and KCL had been receiving £1700 per year. But in March, 1892, while the Salisbury Government was still in power, Roscoe and Bryce, as members of the small committee which advised the Treasury on the grants, drew attention to the fact that King's was a 'strictly denominational institution'. In September, 1893, after Gladstone had been back in office for over a year, and when the extension of the grants for a further five years was being considered, the withholding of the grant to KCL was demanded in the House of Commons, by Carvell Williams.[2]

Sir Albert Rollit, who had stood alone in the Council of KCL in defence of the interests of the University's Senate, tried, without success, in November, 1893, to persuade the Council 'to modify [the College's] present constitution in relation to theological requirements made upon its students, professors, and governing body'. But in July, 1894, the College was told, bluntly, that unless they altered the clause in their constitution which imposed a religious test on staff other than the Professors of Oriental Literature and Modern Languages, before 31 March 1895, they would lose the grant. Meanwhile, the LCC voted

---

[1] Hearnshaw, *The Centenary History of King's College London*, p. 357. The following account is drawn from Hearnshaw's excellent narrative.
[2] 4s Parl. Deb., vol. 17, cols 1415–20, 16 September 1893. For the comments of Bryce and Roscoe, see Rpt of Cmte on Grants to University Colleges in Great Britain, 21 March 1892, PP 1892, lx, HC121.

£1000 for each of 1894 and 1895 to UCL, in aid of technical instruction, but refused the same to King's because it was a denominational institution.

Dr Wace, the Principal of King's, had tried to enlist Salisbury's support and intervention since April, 1894.[3] The threat to stop the grant was made on 17 July, only days after the evidence before the Cowper Commissioners was made available, and when the intention of Government to proceed with a Bill to set up a Statutory Commission seems to have been confirmed. Salisbury must immediately have linked the threat to the grant with the division of opinion among the Commissioners over the majority's recommendation that no University money should be used for 'any purpose in respect of which any privilege is conferred or any disability is imposed on account of religious belief'. He must have written to the Lord Chancellor, implying that there would be objections taken if the Bill proceeded. As the Conservatives had an overwhelming majority in the Lords, such a declaration was tantamount to a veto.

Acland wrote to Rosebery early in August:

> I am to say in the House to-morrow that the Bill is dropped for this year. Salisbury's letter to Herschell about the proposed Bill (with allusions to King's College) makes this necessary for this year. But I think we should go on early next session.[4]

Acland duly told Rollit, who asked him whether there would be legislation introduced along the general lines of the Cowper Commission Report, that the Government were 'really anxious to proceed with the matter', but that it was 'too late now to do anything this Session'.[5]

Given their serious financial anxieties, it is unsurprising that the Council of King's College met early in the autumn, on 25 October, when Rollit again moved for a modification of the College's constitutional arrangements in relation to theological requirements, though on this occasion he called only for changes in respect of students and professors, not of the governing body. There followed a major debate, during which the Principal, Dr Wace, had to read a letter from eleven professors of the College, and the headmaster of the School, 'expressing their desire that all tests should be removed'. But an amendment to Rollit's motion, stating that 'it is not expedient to entertain a proposal for such an alteration in [the College's] constitution as the government require', was supported by Lord Salisbury (a Life Governor), the Bishop of London, Bishop Barry, and Dr Wace, and carried by fifteen to eight. Rollit and three other members of Council resigned. Sir George Johnson, a Fellow of the University, and Sir Joseph Lister, who would become a member of the Senate in 1896, and who had favoured abolition of the tests when giving

---

[3] Hatfield House 3M/E, Wace to Salisbury, 20, 23, 26 April; 5, 7 May; 3 July 1894.
[4] NLS Ms 10149, fol. 44, Acland to Rosebery, 8 August 1894.
[5] 4s Parl. Deb., vol. 28, cols 474–5, 9 August 1894.

evidence to the Cowper Commission, voted against the amendment, but did not resign their Council seats.

There is no evidence as to how the decision by KCL was received immediately, in Government circles. But whatever apprehensions Acland may have had in August about possible opposition to legislation about the Statutory Commission, he had put them aside by early December, perhaps because of a hint to Rosebery's Private Secretary – from Lord Reay – of disagreement in the Conservative/Unionist camp.

> I have been informed yesterday that Arthur Balfour disapproves of the opposition of King's College, and, as Chamberlain wants a London University to obtain his own for the Midlands, there will be no material opposition in the Commons and Government will not have much difficulty in passing the Bill next Session.[6]

At this time, the trouble at King's did not loom large in the discussions of the Annual Committee. In mid-November, they set up a sub-committee to draft a report on recent and current developments, to be presented to the Extraordinary Meeting of Convocation, which had been twice adjourned since 10 April, and which was due to meet on 22 January 1895. Boyd, Cave, Hopkins, Thompson, Waring and Wynne were appointed, and Cave was chosen to take the Chair at the first of three meetings which were held in late November and early December. The report which they produced ran to seventeen pages, and simply mentioned KCL in passing, as the only institution which was hostile to the Scheme.

When the report was put to Annual Committee on 14 December, there was an interesting division of opinion, which showed that even within a group so heavily supportive of an acceptance of the Cowper Commission proposals, when elected only six months earlier, some doubts had crept in. Of three major resolutions recommended by the sub-committee, one was a straightforward version of the earlier motions of Silvanus Thompson in Annual Committee and of Goldsmid in Senate, approving general acceptance of the Commissioners' Scheme, while insisting that the Statutory Commission should confer with Senate and Convocation before making any modifications. But on 14 December, Thomas Lambert Mears and Sansom tried to have the expression of general approval, within this resolution, dropped. They were defeated, eight to three, their sole supporter being Hopkins. Sansom was a long-term opponent, but Mears and Hopkins were among those whose election had been sponsored by the Cozens-Hardy Committee.

The sub-committee's other recommendations were the desirability of retaining and enlarging the existing University to embrace teaching and research: it should be the only University in London, and it should retain 'its

---

[6] NLS Ms 10149, fol. 48, Reay to Murray, 3 December 1894.

existing powers and privileges' to be an examining body 'for students from all parts of the British Empire'. In addition, the sub-committee suggested the appointment of a Special Committee of nine members, including the Chairman of Convocation, to prepare a memorandum of points in the Cowper Commissioners' Scheme which needed to be modified, and to be empowered to confer with a Statutory Committee and with Senate.

The tone of the sub-committee's report was conciliatory, recognising that a violent swing of the pendulum had resulted in the return of an Annual Committee in which 'the various sections of opinion in Convocation are not by any means proportionally represented'. The Annual Committee 'is quite alive to the importance of the views of the under-represented minority in Convocation, and has no desire to ignore those views or to prevent their being fully heard and considered'. And they advised that the Special Committee which they suggested should be established should be 'chosen to represent the minority . . . as well as the majority', and that no Member of Senate, other than the Chairman of Convocation, should be a member. The report, approved by Annual Committee, would not be put before Convocation until 22 January 1895.

In the interim, pressures were exerted on the Government from elsewhere. The Professorial Association had organised a deputation to call on Rosebery in July or August, 1894, but had been told, 'privately', that to urge their case at that time was 'undesirable'. At the beginning of December, however, they made a formal approach to George Herbert Murray, Rosebery's Private Secretary. Huxley wanted to lead a delegation which would represent the Royal Colleges of Physicians and Surgeons, the Society of Apothecaries, UCL, Bedford College, four Theological Colleges, ten Medical Schools, the Society for the Extension of University Teaching, the Annual Committee, and a number of 'interested gentlemen'.[7]

The delegation wanted to urge on the Prime Minister 'the desirability of giving effect to the Report of [the Cowper Commission] by appointing a Statutory Commission'. Huxley, in a personal letter, claimed that 'all the leading men of science and especially teachers, in the country' were anxious to see the University of London reorganised. He went on:

> It is rumoured that there are lions in the path. But even lions are occasionally induced to retreat by the night and a large body of beaters – and some of us think that such a deputation as would willingly wait on you, might hasten the desired movement.[8]

[7] NLS Ms 10149, fol. 48, Reay to Murray, and fol. 50, Ramsay to Murray, 3 December 1894.
[8] NLS Ms 10149, fol. 52, Huxley to Rosebery, 4 December 1894.

Two weeks later the Senate joined in. At their meeting on 19 December, Rollit carried a resolution that representations be made to HM Government strongly urging legislation next Session on the general lines of the Report of the Cowper Commission. Collins wanted to see no move made until after Convocation had considered the report of the Annual Committee, but could not find a seconder. Thorpe then carried a motion for the Senate to send representatives to join the deputation which had been asked for by the professors, and the Vice-Chancellor, Anstie, Fitch, Goldsmid, Pye-Smith, Rollit and Savory were chosen.

The news that Rosebery was going to receive a deputation in favour of the Cowper Commission proposals reached Bompas in mid-December, and he at once wrote asking that the Prime Minister also receive a deputation representing

> . . . a body of graduates nearly nine hundred in number who believe that if a local teaching university for London is desirable it ought to be constituted apart from the existing University of London.

Rosebery, no doubt puzzled as to who Bompas was representing, minuted 'Ask Acland as to this.'[9] Acland, however, had departed northwards, to be followed by a letter from Murray, to which he responded just before Christmas:

> I suppose it will not be easy for Lord Rosebery to refuse the opponents of Gresham University scheme. But as they are not really strong so I am told, it would be a pity to receive them on the same day as the other which ought to contain a good many very distinguished men. It would be making too much of them. But of course it is a great nuisance to give part of two days to such a matter. The Lord Chancellor may have a view but as he is Chancellor of the University he is in rather an awkward position.[10]

Acland's confidence – or overconfidence – seems to have been shared by Rosebery, but the latter could see nothing worrying about Herschell's dual roles. 'I think the Chancellor would be the proper person to introduce the University Bill', he told Acland, 'as he is also Chancellor of the University.'[11]

Acland's letter does seem to imply that he believed there was only one group of opponents of the Gresham Scheme, and it was not until mid- January, 1895, that the existence of two groups was recognised in the Prime Minister's office. Murray began negotiations with Ramsay about the size of the delegation from

[9] NLS Ms 10149, fol. 54, Bompas to Rosebery, 17 December 1894.
[10] NLS Ms 10149, fol. 56, Acland to Murray, 27 December 1894.
[11] NLS Ms 10130, Ramsay to Acland, 23 December 1894.

the group in favour of the Cowper Commission's proposals at the beginning of the New Year. Rosebery did not want a large group, but Ramsay described the difficulties of allocating places to twenty-seven institutions and

> . . . a large number of members of staff of King's College [who] have declared their intention to be present, not as representing their College, which is (as regards the Council and Principal) opposed to our recommendation, but in their individual capacity, as protesting against the attitude of their Governing Body.

But by the middle of the month Ramsay had managed to reduce the number to below forty, with only 'five or six speakers who *say* they won't speak at length'.[12]

Confusion still reigned over who constituted the opposition. A document outlining the case being presented by the Gresham Scheme (1894) Amendment Association, dated 16 January, bears a pencil query, either by Rosebery or Murray, 'Is this a *third* deputation?' On the same day, Heber Hart wrote to Acland, enclosing the statement which had accompanied the postcards returned by 'about nine hundred' members of Convocation, who wanted a 'separate local Teaching University', and begging Acland

> . . . to consider that . . . an easy solution of the difficulty lies in the issue of a new charter to an entirely new body by which the necessity for the co-operation of the existing University, as well as of Parliament, would be obviated.[13]

By this time Murray had arranged for the pro and anti delegations to meet Rosebery on 22 January, at 12 noon and 3 p.m., respectively. But it would seem that the Bompas group had been recognised as representing the opposition, because, on 17 January, Bompas told Murray that 'the small deputation which Lord Rosebery has agreed to meet on 22 January . . . will be introduced by Fletcher Moulton, QC'. It soon became clear, however, that there had been an approach made to Bompas by the Collins' camp which had not been successful. The situation was at last clarified for the Ministers by Collins on 18 January:

> . . . with a view to saving the time of Lord Rosebery, we had already applied to Mr Bompas, QC and those who will accompany him as a deputation at 3 on Tuesday but they have replied that their opposition to legislation on the lines of the Gresham Report is based on a desire for a second University in London and consequently quite different from the views of the Gresham Commission Amendment Committee which I have the honour to represent and which prefers *one* University but different in some important particulars from that suggested by the last

[12] NLS Ms 10149, fols 59–63, Ramsay to Murray, 1, 4 & 13 January 1895.
[13] NLS Ms 10149, fols 69 & 67, *The Teaching University for London Question*; Heber Hart to Acland, 16 January 1895.

Commission. It is therefore the wish of both Mr Bompas's Committee and mine that their grounds of opposition should not be confused.

And on the same day, Collins wrote a second letter, saying that the Bompas group 'decline to go on a joint deputation with us as they consider their opposition totally distinct from ours'.[14]

On receiving these notifications of disagreement between the two groups, Rosebery must have said, in effect, that either they formed one delegation or they did not come at all. Whatever difficulties had to be overcome, overcome they were, and 22 January dawned with a remarkably concentrated agenda – at noon the prestigious delegation in favour of the Cowper Commission's proposals would meet the Prime Minister; at 3 p.m. he would see a delegation of opponents of the Scheme; and at 4 p.m. Convocation would convene to decide their attitude. The way was prepared by long letters to the *Times* – on 21 January from Collins and Napier, and on 22 January by Silvanus Thompson – and by a leader on 22nd which was strongly in favour of the Commission's proposals, and showed scant sympathy for the opposition.

At the end of that day, the opposition must have felt that they were at the nadir of their fortunes. The deputation supporting the Commission's proposals was led by Huxley, who had been assured of the backing of UCL, and was regarded as being able to speak 'on behalf of the University as well as for the [Professorial] Association'.[15] Institutional support was unanimous – even King's College came into line, however unhappy they were about their financial situation and the attack on their religious exclusiveness. The cause of reform was well received by Rosebery, whose basic sympathy with it dated back at least to 1884, when he had been offered the leadership of the Association for the Promotion of a Teaching University for London, and had only refused because he was just entering the Cabinet. When he met the combined delegation from the two opposition groups, a couple of hours later, he expressed the opinion that the concerns of the Collins/Napier party could be taken care of by a Statutory Commission; and he brushed aside the more tempestuous suggestions of the London University Defence Committee by twitting Bompas 'with intending to enforce his views by every means short of barricades in the streets'.[16]

When 421 members of Convocation met, at 4 p.m., for the continuation of the Extraordinary General Meeting, adjourned twice since 10 April 1894, amendments moved by Bompas, Napier, Moulton and Collins to the resolutions proposed by the majority of the Annual Committee were defeated by 206–174, and by 157–133. A Special Committee, representative of all sides

---

[14] NLS Ms 10149, fol. 74, Letters of Collins, 18 January 1895. The addressees are not clearly defined, though almost certainly either Murray or Acland.
[15] Imperial College, Huxley Ms 25.307, Rucker to Huxley, 10 January 1895.
[16] Marquess of Crewe, *Lord Rosebery* (London, 1931) II, p. 499.

of the argument, to continue negotiation and monitor developments, was then agreed without division: its members were Busk, Allchin, Bompas, Boyd, Cave, Cozens-Hardy, Thiselton-Dyer, Napier, and Silvanus Thompson. The result of the voting was clear enough, though the majorities were not large. But the *Times*, which reported the hearings of the deputations, and the debate in Convocation at length, on 23 January, expressed a fairly widely held view that there was now no reason to delay legislation establishing a Statutory Commission.

Just as the slow progress of the Privy Council hearings had thwarted Cranbrook's hopes of having a new Charter in place in 1891, so two unexpected factors influenced and delayed the introduction and reception of a new Bill in 1895. The first was that, a month after the excitements of 22 January, the Prime Minister, harrassed by strained relations within his disintegrating Government, and weakened by acute sleeplessness, 'suffered what was nearly a complete breakdown in health, a serious attack of influenza being the final factor'.[17] He was not fully recovered by June, and it is possible that, had be been fully fit, quicker progress might have been made with the production and launching of a Bill. But the delay may also have been due to concern about who should comprise the Statutory Commission; enquiries were being made from February onwards, producing many names. A typical response was received from Reay:

> Haldane and Gerald Balfour are very good. I should like Haldane to be Chairman if possible which would cut out Courtney, whose views on educational matters are unknown to me. Very important it is to give the *dissenters* a representative or the Jews and if you want a Unionist I should prefer to Courtney Sir Julian Goldsmid, who is a member of the Senate of the University of London and who has a complete mastery of the subject as he is a graduate. The St Thomas's Hospital man would not be acceptable to the profession, but Thomas Smith of St Bartholomew's would. On this point, however, I am collecting further information . . .[18]

There was also a suggestion that the Chairman should be Lord Davey, a distinguished Appeal Court judge, who had been a Liberal MP until 1892 and, briefly, Solicitor General in 1886. He was reputed to be an 'advanced Liberal' and a Home Ruler. But, at that stage, the possibility of his appointment seems to have been dismissed on account of illness.[19]

The second chance event, which was to produce another threat to the passage of the Bill, was the death, on 5 March, after a short illness, of Sir William Savory, who had only joined the Senate in 1893. This created a

[17] R.R. James, *Rosebery* (London 1963), p. 370.
[18] NLS Ms 10149, fol. 111, Reay to Murray, 1 March 1895.
[19] NLS Ms 10149, fol. 115, Note on Downing St paper, nd.

vacancy which, because of the rotation of appointments, fell due to be filled by a nominee of Convocation, not by direct appointment by the Crown. This meant an election to choose three candidates to be reported to the Home Secretary, who would automatically accept the candidate who had received the highest number of votes. Nominations closed on 1 April, and the result would be made known at the Annual Meeting on 14 May.

It is an astonishing fact that those leading the campaign for the implementation of the Cowper Commission's proposals were apparently so unaware of the potential strength and the real determination of the opponents of those proposals, that they took the virtual election of a supportive new Fellow of the University for granted. Allchin and Rotton initiated the nomination of Cozens-Hardy, and chose four Secretaries, but as Allchin admitted, he and one of them did all the work. 'The Secretaries were selected to represent the Faculties but there was never any meeting, nor any actual committee.' The short address which they circulated, calling for Cozens-Hardy's election, made no mention at all of the controversy over the reconstruction of the University, or of any matter of policy, and declared that 'Mr Cozens-Hardy is so well known that we think it unnecessary for us to recommend him further.'[20] It was a narrowly metropolitan, arrogant and naive approach, which played into the hands of a far more politically competent opponent.

Within a week of Savory's death, Napier made his bid, circulating an address, signed by seventy-seven members. It detailed his career, especially his work for Convocation, his membership of the London County Council, his concern for Technical Education, and his current involvement with the Special Committee considering the Cowper Commissioners' Scheme. He was careful to avoid any direct expression of opinion about that Scheme, but claimed that he had 'always upheld the policy of maintaining the high standard and impartial character of our University Examinations', and had been 'a staunch supporter of the privileges of Convocation'.[21] Among those listed as his sponsors was J.W. Grieg, who later emerged as the third candidate, simply to make up the trio necessary for presentation to the Home Secretary; but he would attract a mere thirty votes.

It was soon clear what a bad error of judgement had been made by those wanting the Cowper reforms. At the end of April there was some obvious consternation in their camp, and Cozens-Hardy himself wrote to Rosebery:

We have been waiting anxiously for the introduction of the promised Bill in the House of Lords . . . the Annual Meeting of Convocation is to be held in about a fortnight; and . . . it will be a matter for observation if nothing is done before that date. May I, therefore, venture to suggest that there are special reasons why – if possible – the Bill should be at once introduced. This will greatly assist the action

[20] UL RC25/7a.
[21] UL RC25/7c.

of those graduates – I believe the large majority – who thoroughly approve the policy to which the Government is pledged. Convocation may not be, and in my opinion is not, a really important body, but to a certain extent it holds the key of the position, and if nothing has been done when we next meet, I rather fear the effect will be bad.[22]

But by this time, Napier was poised to launch an unequivocal attack on the Cowper proposals. On 3 May his committee of eighteen, which boasted six QCs and most of the old established objectors, including Collins, Baines, Moulton, and Sansom, issued a strong pamphlet, spelling out the case against the Scheme at length. Two additional circulars were also issued, and 'an extensive canvass in the provinces was undertaken . . . by local Committees of the London University correspondence classes'. The Press was sent a letter, signed by Baines, Robert Bryant, Mears, Eliza Orme and P.F.L. Stokes, in the hope that it would be publicised and reach graduates, who were urged

> . . . to vote against this attempt of the London teachers to appropriate to themselves the reputation of London University and its degrees. If the Gresham Scheme becomes law the present *status* of graduates . . . will be lost, for the value of the existing London degree will deteriorate to the level of the degrees of the new University, and a valuable incentive to education, especially self-education, will be destroyed.[23]

In response to this very professional onslaught, all that emerged, from Cozens-Hardy's Secretaries, was a card urging his supporters to turn out and vote, as 'There is reason to believe that the contest . . . will be a close one.'[24] It was far too little, too late.

Whether Cozens-Hardy's plea to Rosebery speeded the proceedings or not, on 6 May, Playfair announced that a Bill would be introduced three days later, and on 9 May the London University Commission Bill received its first reading, in the House of Lords.[25] It was very short, simply authorising the appointment of a Commission, but containing provisions which showed that some of the main concerns of Convocation and of those particularly anxious about the future of the existing work of the University had been taken on board. The relevant directions were that

> The Commissioners shall make statutes and ordinances for the University of London in general accordance with the scheme of the report [of the Cowper Commission] . . . but subject to any modifications which may appear to them

---

[22] NLS Ms 10149, fol. 121, Cozens-Hardy to Rosebery, 29 April 1895.
[23] UL RC25/7e; *Times*, 15 May 1895.
[24] UL RC25/7d.
[25] HL Bill 106/1895; 4s Parl. Deb., vol. 33, cols 483, 777–9.

expedient after considering any representations made to them by the Senate or Convocation . . . or by any other body or persons affected.

. . . the Commissioners shall see that provision is made for securing adequately the interests of non-collegiate students.

Playfair stressed the favourable reception which the scheme of the Cowper Commissioners had received 'by almost all the colleges and bodies having an interest' in it, and promised that the Statutory Commissioners would be named before the Bill came up for its second reading. The space which would contain the names of the Commissioners was left blank, apparently because of the difficulty being experienced in getting people to serve.[26]

Playfair told the Peers that the second reading of the Bill would be taken on 23 May, but here again there was to be delay. May 23 was Ascension Day, and the House did not sit then, or during the Whitsuntide recess which followed. It was not until the beginning of June that the House met again. All its members then received a copy of a printed but unsigned *Statement of the Case against the London University Commission Bill*, similar in length and content to Napier's pamphlet of 3 May. Lord Reay sent a copy to Allchin, who noted that it was 'undoubtedly issued by Messrs Bompas and Napier' and that 'the arguments adduced were known to have influenced several Lords'.[27]

As will soon be seen, there was to be no second reading. It is very unlikely, however, that the Bill's appearance, less than a week before the postal votes of members of Convocation were to be counted, would have made much difference to the outcome of the election of a nominee for the appointment of a Fellow of the University.

The awkward potential consequences of the manoeuvrings within Convocation do not seem to have been given any more credence by the London Colleges than they were by the Cozens-Hardy Committee and their adherents. On the very eve of the Annual Meeting of Convocation, a letter from Sir George Young of UCL showed that passage of the Government's Bill was being taken for granted. Young wrote to Playfair:

> I have been doing what I can, and am able to say that there will be no obstructive opposition offered by the Tories who may be swayed from King's College. They regard themselves as pledged to this by their being allowed to come with us on the deputation, and will stand by it. They 'may have something to ask by way of security, either in the shape of "explanation" or amendment.'
>
> I know that Dr Wace's principal fear is, lest at any time, in the animosity which sometimes prevails among academic circles, a professor at King's College – say one who was thought to have been preferred to a better man because this better man

---

[26] UL RC25/9a.
[27] UL RC25/9a & 10a.

was an agnostic – should by an abuse of the power of the University be kept out of the Faculty. This fear I think one that can be disregarded, but it is at least an honest one.

The great anxiety with us all, now, is as to the composition of the Commission.[28]

Meanwhile, Bompas seems to have been confident that his cause had not suffered any fatal defeat by Convocation in January. He gave notice that he intended to have the resolutions passed on 22 January rescinded, by moving that Convocation was 'of opinion that if a local teaching University for London be desirable it ought to be constituted apart from the existing University of London'. But the 436 members of Convocation who turned out on 14 May rejected his motion by 238 votes to 116. Moreover, on the same day, those attending showed no wish to change the majority of the Annual Committee favourable to the appointment of a Statutory Commission: they returned twenty-six of the thirty-two who had been members in 1894–95, and turned away challenges by Bompas himself, as well as those by his prominent allies Napier, Moulton, Baines, Lemon and Heber Hart.

However, given that he was unlikely to attract all those who supported the more moderate opposition of Collins and Napier, the defeat of Bompas's motion to rescind, though severe, was not crushing. But the result of the election for a nominee for appointment to the Senate was sensational. Napier was preferred to Cozens-Hardy by 1231 votes to 733.

The outcome of the voting on 14 May was generally, and almost certainly correctly, interpreted as revealing a clear gap between the London-based and the provincial members of Convocation. The London contingent included many university teachers, most of whom were in favour of the proposed reforms and the establishment of a Statutory Commission to put them into effect. But the majority of the provincial members of Convocation who voted rallied to one or both of the causes being pressed by the two groups headed, respectively, by Collins and Bompas. It is very probable that a high proportion of the provincial members had graduated after private study, or study at provincial institutions, and were apprehensive about the threat to the interests of the external students which was perceived by Collins and Bompas.

It is also probable that the majority by which Napier won was disproportionately large because the Cozens-Hardy camp were simply too confident, and failed to take their case persuasively to the bulk of the membership. Allchin admitted that 'we relied too much on Mr Hardy's name and did not canvass enough'.[29] An official paper prepared in the Privy Council Office suggested – perhaps over-kindly to the losers – that 'In some quarters it is contended that the election was not fought on [the Cowper Commission]

---

[28] Imperial College, Playfair Ms 704, Young to Playfair, 13 May 1895.
[29] UL RC25/7a.

... issue at all, and there can be no doubt that the supporters of Mr Hardy were taken by surprise and failed to poll their full strength.'[30] This is borne out by the fact that those who nominated the candidates some weeks before the votes were cast, and who were later listed in the Minutes of Convocation, numbered 841 for Cozens-Hardy, which was 108 more than the votes cast for him; whereas only 607 nominated Napier. But Napier's supporters at the poll had grown to more than double that figure.

The publication of the Bill, and Napier's victory, re-energised the opposition. But immediately after the meeting on 14 May, Cozens-Hardy seems to have been peculiarly blind to the significance of his own defeat and Napier's election. Perhaps out of pride, or humility, he concentrated only on Bompas's failure to get the resolutions rescinded, told Allchin that he was 'well satisfied with the results of to-day's proceedings', and went on

> Had Bompas been enough of a general to abstain from forcing a battle upon us, the effect would have been bad. But the victory over him by two to one is the only important feature, and everything else is of no moment.[31]

Silvanus Thompson felt much less comfortable about 'everything else', and even saw the possible need to abandon the attempt to secure a Bill:

> What do you say to the following suggestion? In the event of the Bill being stranded in Parliamentary shoals, have a *Draft Charter* ready on the lines of the Gresham Scheme (but with modifications in detail), and pass it through Senate and Convocation. This would be reverting to procedure by *Charter*. We could certainly pass it through Convocation. I think I shall suggest the course to Anstie.[32]

Collins, on the other hand, saw the possibilities of the new situation as so favourable to his chances of success that he resigned from the LCC's Technical Education Board in order to 'more actively oppose the scheme of reconstruction of the University', ignoring the opinion of Sidney Webb, who did not '*much* mind what happens to the Bill, but think *on the whole* it might as well pass with amendments'.[33]

Dr Wace concentrated on the legislative possibilities, and turned to Lord Salisbury, whom he had been keeping informed on the problem of finding some way to relieve King's from the threat of losing its Treasury grant. He now put to Salisbury two modifications of Playfair's Bill which the College wanted. First was to have included a right of appeal to the Privy Council from the

---

[30] PC1/1756.
[31] UL RC25/4j, Cozens-Hardy to Allchin, 14 May 1895.
[32] UL RC25/4j, Thompson to Allchin, 3 June 1895.
[33] UL RC25/4j, Thompson to Allchin, 3 June; UL Ms 812/90, Webb to Collins, 19 May 1895.

decisions of the Statutory Commission. Secondly, he pointed out that the Statutory Commission was to act 'in general accordance' with the Report of the Cowper Commissioners, who had recommended that

> . . . in the assignment of Funds for University purposes, the action of the Senate 'will be subject to a condition forbidding the grant of money for any purpose in respect of which any privilege is granted or disability imposed on account of religious belief.' Such a clause would exclude this College from assistance . . .

Six of the thirteen Royal Commissioners had dissented from the proposal, and Wace hoped that Salisbury would promote an amendment.[34]

Salisbury responded quickly, and instructed Wace to work with Sir Richard Webster, the past and future Conservative Attorney General, on drafting an amendment to the London University Commission Bill. The draft was duly approved by the College's Council, to which Webster had been elected.[35] Thus by mid-June, KCL was well prepared to defend its interests before Parliament, when second reading and committee stage of the Bill was reached.

King's were not alone in turning to the Opposition, though both Collins and Bompas tried the Government first, claiming the election of Napier by Convocation as evidence of convincing opposition to the Cowper Commissioners' Scheme. Collins wrote that

> The election turned upon the Gresham scheme of reconstruction . . . If . . . you desire to consult the true feeling of Convocation you have it in that vote rather than in that of a small London section of graduates such as you get in meetings of Convocation . . . because the Bill introduced into the Lords is alienating some of the Government's most loyal supporters . . . I beg most earnestly and most humbly that it may not be passed.

Bompas, not a supporter of the Government, wrote a letter in broadly similar terms, and combined with Collins in sending their view of the situation to Acland and Harcourt. The letters were acknowledged, without comment.[36]

Bompas then turned to the Duke of Devonshire, with whom he had 'a long talk', and afterwards told Collins that

> [Devonshire] said it was . . . a matter on which the House of Lords ought to make up its own mind: he asked if the two parties in the University represented two sides in politics or religion and I told him certainly not that it did represent a difference between town and country but otherwise that there was merely a difference of opinion not upon party lines. I told him what Lord Salisbury had said. He said he

---

[34] Hatfield House 3M/E, Wace to Salisbury, 18 May 1895.
[35] Hatfield House 3M/E, Wace to Salisbury, 16 June 1895.
[36] NLS Ms 10149, fol. 123, Collins to Ramsay, 26 May; fol. 125, Bompas to Rosebery, fols 130–2, Bompas and Collins to Acland and Harcourt, 28 May 1895.

thought Lord Salisbury did not know anything about the question and that he should write and tell him that it was a matter that must be considered on second reading. I have seen a letter from Lord Salisbury since showing that this is so and saying in effect that he will follow the Duke of Devonshire who for his father's sake has a special interest in the London University . . . My own belief is that if we come and argue out the matter carefully with them they will probably throw out the Bill but that they will be very anxious to do this on the merits and not to make it a party matter.[37]

Bompas and Napier met Salisbury and Devonshire on 13 June, and probably presented them with copies of the pamphlet which had been circulated to the House of Lords just after the Whitsuntide recess.[38] As a result of this meeting, Devonshire must have written to Herschell, as both Lord Chancellor and Chancellor of the University, and put to him the case which had been made by Bompas. Herschell replied on 18 June:

The 2nd Reading of the University of London Bill will certainly not be taken this week and I should much like to have a talk with you about it. I shall be much mistaken if I do not remove any impression which Bompas has made. The *weight* of authority in the University I believe to be increasing in its favour whatever the *numbers* may be on which I shall have something to say. When would it be possible for us to meet?[39]

It was a meeting which almost certainly did not take place. For on the afternoon of 21 June 1895, a snap vote of censure – the Cordite Vote – on the Secretary of State for War, Campbell-Bannerman, led to a long debate in Cabinet next day, and the decision of a tired and fractious Government to resign, rather than ask for a dissolution of Parliament. The fate of the London University Commission Bill would be settled in a very different political atmosphere.

[37] UL Ms 812/91, Bompas to Collins, 11 June 1895.
[38] UL RC25/10a.
[39] Devonshire Mss, Chatsworth: letters 2nd series, 340.2615, Herschell to Devonshire, 18 June 1895.

# 32

# *The pre-emptive strike of Sir John Lubbock*

At almost the same time that the Government was being defeated in the Commons, on 21 June 1895, news reached Cozens-Hardy and Ramsay, from Lord Playfair, of the approach by Bompas and Napier to the Opposition leaders.

> Bompas, Collins and Co have persuaded Lord Salisbury and the Duke of Devonshire that an amendment to the University Bill should be introduced making it incumbent that Convocation should have a veto and *should be consulted by voting papers*.

Cozens-Hardy was contemptuous but worried: he told Allchin that

> This is childish nonsense. It seems that Napier's victory has been made great use of to impress the Duke. Can you get any Liberal Unionist to approach the Duke? Lord Playfair hopes the Bill will be read a second time on Monday week.

And he added a postscript which foreshadowed future concern: 'Lubbock is so weak in the knees that it is useless to expect any help from him.'

Ramsay summoned a meeting of 'our former committee', – the Cozens-Hardy Committee – for 24 June, and told those invited that he had been advised by Playfair that they should send an 'immediate deputation to Lord Salisbury and the Duke'. Ramsay felt that 'if we fail, our Bill will be mutilated and useless'.[1] Playfair had also written to Sir George Young, and Young sent him a reply which certainly gives an impression of his and UCL's general support for the Bill, and of sensible suggestions for moderate amendment of it.

> If there is anything to be done, it had better be by institutions, than by individuals. The Council of University College have appointed a small committee, consisting of the President, Vice-President and Mr Haldane, MP, to deal with any communications, such as might be expected from those in charge of the Bill. I have just met Lord Reay, and ventured to tell him the contents of your letter, and he has

[1] UL RC25/4i, Cozens-Hardy to Allchin, and round robin letter from Ramsay, 21 June 1895.

undertaken to see you about it. He thinks Lord Cowper is the best man to see the Duke of Devonshire. I hardly know how Lord Salisbury is to be approached, and do not like to speak to Dr Wace without authority.

This opposition of Convocation is certainly no new thing, but it is very serious that the Opposition leaders should declare themselves impressed by it. No doubt, a veto on the work of the Commission, to be exercised by Convocation through voting papers, would as you say defeat the Reform we have in view.

But is the appeal to the Privy Council omitted? You can't expect that there will be no opposition on this head from Lord Salisbury, after what was said by Dr Wace at the deputation: and you must remember that we think exactly the same about this at University College, though we abstain from embarrassing you by a protest. Why not concede this at once, as Huxley promised for the University, and appeal to the precedents of similar legislation against Convocation?[2]

Rosebery resigned on 22 June. Salisbury kissed hands on 25 June; he wanted an early dissolution, but there followed some negotiation over arrangements for completion of outstanding legislation. A coalition Administration of Conservatives and Liberal Unionists was set up, but it was not until 6 July that it was possible to announce, simultaneously, the prorogation and the dissolution of Parliament.[3] The dissolution was gazetted on 8 July: the new Parliament was summoned to meet on 12 August.

This abrupt change of Government, with the following delay before dissolution and the ensuing General Election, greatly disturbed the atmosphere in which the London University Bill was being considered. In the few days which passed before the committee summoned by Ramsay met, on 24 June, there had been time for the hope of some reversion towards the acceptability of a separate Teaching University to have revived in some quarters. The meeting was chaired by Erichsen, the President of UCL. Allchin noted that

> Mr Anstie advised action . . . but every proposal to do anything was resisted by Young and Wace on every possible pretext. Finally on motion of S. Boyd seconded by WHA [Ilchin] it was resolved (Wace dissenting and Young not voting) to request Lord Cowper as Chairman of Commission to endeavour to convince Lord Salisbury and Duke of Devonshire that the proposal mentioned would be fatal to the University.[4]

Uncertainty as to how long the existing Parliament would remain active is the only explanation of Ramsay's patently unrealistic suggestion to Playfair, only three days before the announcement of dissolution.

---

[2] Playfair Mss, Imp. Coll. 704, Young to Playfair, 21 June 1895.
[3] 4s Parl. Deb., vol. 35, cols 303–4.
[4] UL RC25/4i, Allchin's note on round robin letter by Ramsay of 21 June 1895.

I saw Lord Cowper last Friday, and he tells me that it is by no means as serious as you think. He had half an hour's conversation on the university question with the Duke of Devonshire, and said that he had more than half persuaded him that the claim of Convocation was preposterous.

I write to ask: Why is it not possible to get the Bill passed this Session? I see that many measures are passing, and if you were to move the second reading in the House of Lords on Friday, it would pass the Commons on Monday. Mr Balfour is well disposed, as he has frequently assured me, and I will write to him the moment I receive your reply, and remind him of his promise to help us. If we don't carry this now, the whole affair will be done for.[5]

On the very next day, Lord Kelvin sent the Duke of Devonshire a letter, drawing on his convictions and his experience with the Scottish Universities. His may well have been the first private, written approach to the man who was soon to have charge of the whole issue, inside Government, for the next few years. Arguing the case for those who were supportive of Lord Playfair's Bill, Kelvin wrote:

I hope very much you will not let them put into the new London University Bill any clause giving a veto on the Commissioners' Ordinances to the Convocation by individual voting, or in any way. There was no such provision in the Scottish Universities Bill. But the Commissioners' Ordinances had to run the gauntlet of oppositions by the University Councils, Courts, and Senates in the first place; and after that could be stopped by either House of Parliament, and after that by the Privy Council. Surely securities against mistakes by the Commissioners, and assistance to their judgment on all points, might be provided in the London University Bill as in Scottish, much better than by the proposed plebiscite of the Convocation. Indeed, I cannot conceive how men capable of doing the work to be given to the Commissioners could accept the duties under such a condition as the veto by plebiscite.[6]

But if Lord Cowper thought he had weakened the Duke of Devonshire's sympathy for the Bompas/Napier argument; and if Lord Kelvin hoped that his protest would stop Devonshire in his tracks; neither outcome seemed the least likely to Thomas Hudson Beare, Professor of Engineering at UCL, who claimed that he had been in touch with the Duke, on the day before Parliament was dissolved. He told Allchin that,

. . . it is quite clear that [Bompas and Napier] made a great impression on him; this must be removed. It was a gross mistake that the deputation from our side after

[5] Playfair Mss, Imp. Coll. 704, Ramsay to Playfair, 3 July 1895.
[6] Devonshire Mss, Chatsworth: letters 2nd series, 340.2616, Kelvin to Devonshire, 4 July 1895.

going to Lord Rosebery did not later on ask for an interview with the Duke and Lord Salisbury.

My own opinion is that Ramsay ought to be asked to get the deputation together again and to go to the Duke. I am told Salisbury has intrusted the matter entirely to the Duke. This must be done at once then if (*as I hope*) the Unionists come back into power the Bill might be re-introduced into the House of Lords immediately after the Elections.

We must convince the Duke that the weight of Academic authority is unquestionably on our side, and no hole and corner work will do. It must be a powerful deputation representing every body of influence in the academic world in London.[7]

Playfair's Bill died with the dissolution of Parliament, but not before a Petition of Graduates of the University of London, praying that the Bill 'may not pass into law', was laid on the table.[8] By then, however, the long-expected and now forthcoming General Election had pushed all other considerations aside. Not least among the effects of the sudden appeal to the country was the pressure it exerted on Sir John Lubbock to define his position on the proposed change in the constitution of the University of London.

We have recorded two instances when Lubbock's attitude to the reform of the university situation in London seems to have been recognised as equivocal. He was, in fact, in an unenviable situation. He was a recognised figure in the City and in London's intelligentsia, an ex-Vice-Chancellor of the University whose election as the University's MP, as a Liberal, and then as a Liberal Unionist, gave him a position of relatively comfortable, political independence, which he had used admirably to support measures which would have had little chance of success if they had been dependent entirely on more partisan sponsorship. He might, with some justification, before the mid-nineties, have regarded himself as having demonstrated that he had been a Burkean representative, rather than a delegate. But we do not have enough evidence to judge whether, in 1895, he was really convinced of the justice and validity of the argument of those in Convocation who were demanding retention of the power to exercise an effective veto on proposals for change, or whether he simply feared that, if he espoused the opposite view, his constituents would not return him to Westminster. Whatever mixture of motives moved him, he chose to go with the apparently conservative and provincial members of Convocation, to the anger and consternation of the metropolitan, intellectual and academic elite with whom he had been working to form a new University.

Lubbock had been unconcerned about the forthcoming election, and in the context of the major political questions of the day he was probably quite

---

[7] UL RC25/11z, T.H. Beare to Allchin, 8 July 1895.
[8] H of L Jnl, 5 July 1895.

Sir John Lubbock, 4th Bt, 1st Baron Avebury. Liberal MP for Maidstone 1870–1880. Liberal/Liberal Unionist MP for the University 1880–1900. Crown-chosen Member of Senate 1865–1900. Vice-Chancellor 1872–1880.

entitled to have been so. The weaknesses of the Liberal Government; the fact that on Ireland he was firmly Unionist; his good reputation as an active parliamentarian; and the apparent lack of any strong challenge from either the Liberals or the Conservatives in the University constituency, all conspired to re-assure him that he would be unopposed. It was not until the day after Lord Salisbury had accepted the Queen's invitation to form a Government that he recorded in his diary how he had seen 'Benson and arranged matters about the University election'. But within twenty-four hours he recorded that Busk had come to tell him, 'much to my surprise, that a contest was threatened mainly on the Gresham question'.[9]

Lubbock went on: 'I explained to him [Busk] that I think his friends will be satisfied when they see my address.' This implies that he had already drafted a statement which would give encouragement to those opposing the new Scheme and the virtual abolition of Convocation's existing veto. But as it seems that he only learned of the possibility of being opposed by a repre-sentative of the Collins-Napier-Bompas camps from Busk, it is quite likely that he may have strengthened his statement as a result of another meeting with Benson and Busk on the following day, after which he 'settled' the Address.[10] It was published on July 1.

It was Benson, whose ear was close to the ground, who reported to Lubbock on the general situation, and gave the first hint of disagreement between Busk, on the one hand, and Collins and Napier on the other.

I am glad that your address is being posted to-day [July 1] and could wish it had been out on Saturday. The situation is not yet clear. I gather that the Collins-Napier group are not wholly satisfied, and that, Busk failing them, they will not determine until Wednesday whether or not they will run a Gladstonian anti-Greshamite. They are not best pleased with Busk for drawing your attention to the necessity for your anti-Greshamite paragraphs without which they are confident, and in this I believe Busk concurs, that their task would have been easy. If Collins and Napier had not been otherwise engaged one of them would have stood with in their opinion the certainty of success. This I cannot admit. I trust however that with your address our more moderate counsels will prevail. In any event Busk is a true friend and will give us his best assistance.[11]

Collins and Napier, it may be noted, were both fighting as Liberals – unsuccessfully, as it turned out – for London seats in West St Pancras and North Islington, respectively.

Lubbock had apparently discussed his policy only with Busk and Benson. He did not even consult his Chairman, Professor Michael Foster, before

---

[9] BL Add Mss 62684, Diary entries 26 & 27 June 1895.
[10] BL Add Mss 62684, Diary entry 28 June 1895.
[11] BL Add Mss 49661, Benson to Lubbock, 1 July 1895.

publishing the Address. It was brief and brusque about his anti-Home Rule position and his other policies, which he felt sure his constituents knew so well that he did not trouble to summarise them. Most of the Address was devoted to the controversy over the University's future affairs. Lubbock made no mention of the views of Bompas's Defence Committee: but he was plainly supportive of the ideas put forward by Collins.

> The Gresham Scheme (1894) Amendment Committee, which is opposed to the Scheme without substantial amendments, have expressed the opinion . . . that 'such a University might be created as would give the Teachers all they ought to have and yet not injure the present work of the University.' We ought . . . to make every effort to accomplish this object, before we adopt a course which would lead to the establishment of a second University in London, and probably of others elsewhere, a result which would invitably tend to a general lowering of the standard of degrees.
>
> I concur with the two 'conditions' laid down by the Gresham Scheme (1894) Amendment Committee . . . 'First, the Scheme must not have in itself any tendency to cause a lowering of the standard of the existing degrees of the University, and secondly, it must contain sufficient securities that the functions of the University as an impartial examining Board for the Empire shall not be impaired.'
>
> I should wish to see an increased representation of Convocation on the Senate; and the addition of certain members to the Academic Council to be nominated partly by the Senate and partly by Convocation.

Had Lubbock left it at that, it is highly improbable that any serious objection would have been taken to his Address. Whether his original draft may have stopped at this point cannot be established: nor can we know whether he added the following paragraph on his own initiative, or only after consultation with Benson and Busk. But the final version went on:

> Feeling that Convocation ought to be consulted on a matter so vitally affecting the University, I should strongly urge, and would do my best to secure, that the scheme, when arranged, should be submitted to Convocation for their approval, to be signified as at a Senatorial election, and would oppose the Bill unless this were conceded.[12]

Senatorial elections involved postal voting or, as it was then called, 'voting papers'. Under existing rules, they could only be used to elect the University's MP, and one of the three candidates whose names would be submitted to the Home Secretary for selection of a new Fellow. Lubbock's suggestion, in effect, called for a new constitutional provision. Whatever his real motives, Lubbock had made a brilliant, pre-emptive strike, which was to contribute greatly to creating an *impasse* over the future of the University.

[12] UL RC25/11c.

Lubbock's Chairman, Michael Foster, then Secretary of the Royal Society, was much troubled.

> You seem to go in rather strong for Convocation. I should not like to do it myself – it is a detestable body but since it elects you I suppose you must humour it – but I wish it were not necessary. Do you really approve of its having a veto on the scheme – would not more general assurances be enough. In truth I don't like it, but I shan't interfere.[13]

Foster made the same points to Benson, and hoped 'to goodness that there will be no contest'.[14]

Meanwhile, if Collins and Napier had thought of running a 'Gladstonian anti-Greshamite', others were exploring the possibility of putting forward Ray Lankester as 'a Liberal and a supporter of the Royal Commissioners' Scheme for reconstruction of the University'. Lankester was Carey Foster's nominee, and was willing to stand, 'if we can show him he will get serious support'. Carey Foster knew, however, that 'The difficulty is the probably very short time', but felt that 'a stroke now if unsuccessful may help towards next time'. His fears were all too quickly proved valid, and he abandoned the attempt on discovering that 'we are not likely to get sufficient support'. It had been put to him, 'that if we get badly beaten after raising the University question at the Election it will only strengthen Lubbock in the anti-academical position he has taken up. We have no organization and no time to create one'.[15]

Lubbock was well aware of his situation. He wrote on 1 July, 'I am threatened with two oppositions in the University of London: both about the Gresham Scheme; one for going too far one for not going far enough.'[16] But neither opposing group could bring the matter to a vote. As Lubbock recorded on 13 July: 'Was elected without opposition. The Radicals did their worst, but could not find a candidate.'[17] 'Radicals' was an odd word to use, if it covered not only the Collins and Bompas groups, but also a large and pro-fessionally prestigious contingent of his academic constituents in London, which included even his own Chairman. He recorded that Michael Foster was 'strongly against the part of my address dealing with the Gresham Scheme, but will propose me all the same'.[18] Which Foster did, seemingly out of personal loyalty and friendship, but not without joining in a formal protest and making a final plea that Lubbock should change his mind, as we shall see.

---

[13] BL Add Mss 49661, M. Foster to Lubbock, 30 June 1895.
[14] BL Add Mss 49661, M. Foster to Benson, quoted in Benson to Lubbock, 1 July 1895.
[15] UCL Ms Add 89/38, G.C. Foster to Oliver Lodge, 4 & 6 July 1895.
[16] BL Add Mss 62684, Lubbock's Diary, 1 July 1895.
[17] BL Add Mss 62684, Lubbock's Diary, 13 July 1895.
[18] BL Add Mss 62684, Lubbock's Diary, 6 July 1895.

The election in 1895 of the Member for the University of London was the only such election in the nineteenth century in which the principal concern was the affairs of the University. The importance of Lubbock's election Address, for the future of the controversy about the University, was that it greatly strengthened the opposition to a settlement along the lines of the Playfair Bill. And in the process it generated some bitter comment, not least among scientists. Oliver Lodge found the Address 'absurdly weak and hedging'. Carey Foster felt that Lubbock had been 'sitting on the fence during the whole discussion of the University question and has shown throughout that he had no grasp of it'.[19] There was a sharp exchange between Lubbock and the particularly aggressive Silvanus Thompson, Professor of Physics at the City and Guilds Institute, who was

> amazed that you should *without qualification* have indicated your disposition to oppose the reconstitution Bill unless it contains a clause which would obviously prevent any independent or self-respecting man from serving on the Statutory Commission.
>
> Do you suppose any first rate man would serve on a commission, to hear and weigh claims and settle conflicting interests, and adjust differences with care and judgement, if he knew that his most careful judgement was liable to be upset by the vote of a lot of provincial graduates who had never heard the evidence, and had no real means of judging? The thing is too absurd. No Parliament would ever put the vote of Convocation above the authority of Parliament in such a way. An appeal to the Privy Council (who *would* hear and weigh evidence) would be quite reasonable and in accordance with precedents. But such a clause as you propose would be both unconstitutional and against all precedents. Can you not, before it is too late, recall or modify the phrase you have used? It commits you to a quite untenable position, and exposes you to ridicule . . .[20]

Lubbock replied to Thompson that 'Surely it is natural that the Graduates should wish to be consulted in a matter so vitally affecting their own University?' Thompson insisted that he was

> . . . not opposed to a reference to Convocation: on the contrary I worked hard last year to obtain it. But what I say and say emphatically is that the proposal to make the reference to Convocation *after* instead of *before* the judicial decisions of a Statutory Commission is absurd . . . The absurdity of it must be painful to many who would otherwise have supported you.[21]

---

[19] UCL Ms Add 89/38, Note by Lodge on Carey Foster to Lodge, 4 July; Carey-Foster to Lodge, 6 July 1895.
[20] BL Add Mss 49661, S. Thompson to Lubbock, 2 July 1895.
[21] BL Add Mss 49661, Lubbock to S. Thompson, 3 July; S. Thompson to Lubbock, 4 July 1895.

But it was not only the scientists who were upset. Richard Quain refused to have anything to do with the election because he disapproved of the proposal that voting papers should be used – he was not the only one to object to any notion of a plebiscite or referendum.[22] And Owen Whitehouse, head of the Theological College at Cheshunt, felt that Lubbock's 'action has gained nothing for him and will I imagine loosen his hold of his constituency in any future Election contest'.[23]

Inevitably, the row was carried to the correspondence columns of the press. The heaviest disapproval was contained in a letter signed by 'most of the members of Council of the Royal Society', headed by its President, Lord Kelvin. Nineteen signatures were added to the text, part of which read:

> You state that you would 'do your best to secure, that the scheme [for the reorganization of the University] when arranged should be submitted to Convocation for their approval, to be signified as at a senatorial Election, and would oppose the Bill unless this were conceded.'
>
> You must allow us to point out that this proposal would confer upon Convocation a right, which is without precedent, to supervise the acts of a Commission entrusted with the re-organizing of the University of which Convocation itself is a part.
>
> The scheme of the 'Gresham Commissioners' has been approved not only by all the institutions concerned but by the great body of educated public opinion. It is, however, certain that very grave difficulties will arise if the ultimate fate of the scheme is to depend upon the voting papers of Convocation. We, therefore, believe that the proposal you support, if adopted, will result in the failure of another attempt to establish a teaching University in London and will indefinitely postpone the solution of a question which after prolonged discussion, seemed to be on the eve of settlement.[24]

Carey Foster told Lodge that Michael Foster had 'been obliged to send Lubbock' this protest, which had Foster's name among the signatories. Foster told Lubbock that

> My various friends are urging me to press you to meet their views by modifying in some way the statement in your Address, but I do not think that I ought to do anything more than say that if you do feel able to do so I shall be very pleased.[25]

There were numerous letters and articles in the press, including the medical and scientific journals, during the election and in July and August, practically all taking Lubbock to task for his position. But he remained unmoved.[26]

---

[22] UL RC25/11j, Quain to Benson, July 1895.
[23] UL RC25/11bb, Whitehouse to Allchin, 17 July 1895.
[24] Copy in BL Add Mss 49661, 6 July 1895.
[25] BL Add Mss 49661, M. Foster to Lubbock, 10 July 1895.
[26] UL RC25/11 contains cuttings from *Nature*, *Standard*, *Pall Mall Gazette*, *Speaker*, and *Daily News* in July 1895.

In the midst of the legislative trauma, Sir James Paget resigned as Vice-Chancellor. He had been in office since 1883, was now eighty years of age, and had apparently made it known, privately, by the spring of 1895, that he was unwilling to continue. Joshua Fitch, eager to ensure that the forth-coming vacancy was not filled 'at some chance meeting and without due consideration', took upon himself the role of king-maker and put to Lubbock – and perhaps to others – his list of preferred candidates. If rumour was to be believed, and Lubbock was to go to the Lords, then Fitch wished he could be persuaded to return to the office of Vice-Chancellor. But putting that desirable outcome aside, Fitch then deplored the unavailability of Lord Justice Fry, who 'had chosen to bury himself in Arcadia for bucolic pursuits'.

Fitch then came to grips with his version of the realities. He thought Grant Duff was 'a Scholar, a good speaker and a man with large academic and public experience . . . But he seldom attends; he has never shown any strong interest in the details of the University's work; and it is doubtful whether he would be able to give the necessary attention to those details or to spare the time.' Then came Sir Julian Goldsmid, who

> . . . cares a good deal about the University and its work; he has served on the University College Council; is, as you know at the House of Commons, an excellent Chairman and man of business; and what is more . . . would like the post; and would devote himself not only with assiduity but with some enthusiasm to the discharge of its duties. Against him, it may be said that he has no special academic or literary distinction, and that outside of the Jewish communion he is not personally very popular.

Fitch put forward Sir Henry Roscoe as a third possibility. His

> . . . scientific position and general ability and public usefulness are well known. But he has not been long with us. The interest he has shown in our affairs has been mainly turned towards the new Scheme of Reconstruction, and rather towards physical science than towards the larger concerns of learning and the usefulness of the University generally.[27]

It was not until June, 1895, however, that the matter came to a head. Paget allowed himself to be re-elected on 26th, but at the same time expressed to the Senate his wish to resign. His formal letter of resignation was dated 20 July, and, on 24th, the Senate met to elect his successor. By this time, though Fitch's quartet of possibilities – Grant Duff, Goldsmid, Roscoe and Fry – were all sponsored, at least two other candidates appeared. The more formidable was James Bryce: scholarly eminent and lately President of the

27 BL Add Mss 49661, Fitch to Lubbock, 20 April 1895.

Board of Trade in Rosebery's Cabinet, he had joined the Senate on the advice of Asquith, in May, 1894, and had been pressed to stand for the Vice-Chancellorship by Carey Foster. There was, perhaps, a hint of straight political partisanship in Carey Foster's casual remark to Bryce, that 'Goldsmid wishes to be elected', Goldsmid being a Liberal Unionist.[28] The second new candidate was Rucker, Professor of Physics at the Royal College of Science, who had stood, unsuccessfully, as a Liberal Unionist at Pudsey, in 1886.

How many names were put forward for the first ballot is not known, but all six who have been mentioned came through to the second round of voting. The result of that round was: Goldsmid thirteen, Grant Duff ten, Bryce nine, Roscoe nine, Rucker eight, and Fry three. In the run-off, Goldsmid won, eleven to ten.[29] We have a rather nonchalant memory of the contest from Grant Duff:

> Seeing, in the agenda, that there was to be an election of a Vice-Chancellor at the London University in room of Sir James Paget, I went up yesterday afternoon to the Senate to vote for Sir Julian Goldsmid, who seemed to me the person best fitted for the office. I had not, however, had an opportunity of talking over the matter with any of my colleagues, and was not a little surprised to find, when the result of the first ballot was announced, that many of them wished to elect me. After the second ballot, this became still more evident, and at last I only escaped from a highly dignified but somewhat embarrassing position by my own vote, for the numbers in the final ballot were: Goldsmid eleven, Grant Duff ten. I voted throughout for Goldsmid.[30]

Whatever the motives of those who voted – and surely none can have been entirely unaffected by the excitements aroused by the General Election – none of them could have expected that Goldsmid would serve for less than six months. He died, after a long illness, on 7 January 1896, when in his forty-eighth year. He had presided, as Vice-Chancellor, over only three meetings of the Senate. There is less information available about the choice of his successor, but Fitch was again active in the matter. He wrote to Collins that he had again failed to persuade Grant Duff to stand.

> His plea that he lives too far off – at Twickenham! – is I fear only to be interpreted as a sign that he does not care quite enough about the fortunes of the University to give himself much trouble in helping to guide them . . . I suppose Sir Henry Roscoe is now inevitable. He has some excellent qualities but he does not fulfil my ideal altogether.[31]

---

[28]  Bod. Bryce Mss H23 fol. 105, Asquith to Bryce, 6 May 1894; H58 fols 144, 148, Carey Foster to Bryce, 18 & 22 July 1895.

[29]  Bod. Bryce Mss H58 fol. 154, Carey Foster to Bryce, 24 July 1895.

[30]  Sir Mountstuart E. Grant Duff, *Notes from a Diary 1892–95* (London, 1904), p. 233, 25 July 1895.

[31]  UL Ms812/95, Fitch to Collins, 11 February 1896.

The Minutes of the Senate record that a ballot was held, for the Vice-Chancellorship, on 19 February 1896, but does not list the candidates, and no details of a contest have been found. Roscoe, eminent scientist, raised in a strong Nonconformist family, a leading member of the Association for the Promotion of a Professorial University, who had just finished a ten-year stint in the Commons as the Liberal, Home Rule Member for South Manchester, was elected, and would see the University through to the twentieth century.

While the well-publicised protests against Lubbock, in the summer of 1895, tended to smack of a degree of despair, as well as anger, among their writers, the hard business of keeping the possibility of implementing the Cowper reforms alive was tackled by members of UCL and the new Cozens-Hardy Committee. Cozens-Hardy himself had been reluctant, during the electoral contest, to promote any public protest in London constituencies. He doubted 'the expediency of giving a political tone to our proceedings. The average metropolitan elector has never heard of the University of London, and the average candidate cares nothing about it.' At the end of June, he felt that 'it is idle to imagine that attention can be secured for any counterblast' to the pamphlet which had been circulated to the Lords by the anti-Cowper faction. He thought it better 'to save our powder until a later date'.[32]

But early in July, Cozens-Hardy must have come to believe, or have been persuaded, that the time was ripe to prepare an approach to the Duke of Devonshire. Several meetings of the Committee were held during the month, and the main business was putting together a comprehensive statement, designed to refute the arguments made in the opposing faction's pamphlet. Anstie prepared the draft, and a final version was approved 'after considerable discussion', on 26 July. It was intended that the paper should be sent to the Duke of Devonshire, and that Cozens-Hardy should ask the Duke to receive a deputation.[33] But in fact these moves did not take place until early September.

In the meantime, the case for re-introducing the Playfair Bill and implementing the Cowper Commissioners' Report had been pressed, publicly, by Lord Cowper himself, in the Debate on the Address in the House of Lords on 15 August. Cowper stressed the high level of support which existed for the Bill in the academic community. The Duke of Devonshire insisted that the Government was strongly supportive of the establishmnet of a Teaching University for London, and promised that the matter would receive careful attention. But he revealed how strongly he had been influenced by Bompas and Napier, when he stated that

[32] UL RC25/4j, Cozens-Hardy to Allchin, 27 June 1895.
[33] UL RC25/4j, Allchin's record of action, January–July 1895, by the Cozens-Hardy Committee. RC25/10b, Allchin's note on copy of the Statement in support of Playfair's Bill, September 1895.

Lord Cowper had rather exaggerated the degree of unanimity that existed as to the mode in which that University was to be established. Very strong objection had been taken to it by a large and by no means unimportant section of Convocation.[34]

Less than two weeks later, Balfour told Rollit that there would be no legislation in the present session, and that he could not forecast what action the Government might take in the matter.[35]

In fact, Parliament was prorogued on 5 September, and did not meet again until 11 February 1896, by which time there had been several significant developments. In late October, there was a press report, possibly related to the likelihood of the Secondary Education Commission, then sitting, and headed by Lord Bryce, being in favour of a single Teaching University based on the existing University of London, that the Government was 'willing to supply facilities for the passing of Lord Playfair's Bill . . . whilst reserving liberty of action in regard to its details'.[36] But the main factors, in the negotiations over the next stage in the Bill's career, included the financial affairs of King's College; the relations between King's and the anti-reform faction within Convocation; the renewed pressure of those supporting the Bill and their meeting with the Duke of Devonshire; the influence of Sir John Lubbock; and another major vote in Convocation.

[34] 4s Parl. Deb., vol. 36, cols 54–8, 15 August 1895.
[35] 4s Parl. Deb., vol. 36, col. 915, 27 August 1895.
[36] UL RC25/8c, Daily News, quoting Athenaeum, 25 October 1895.

# 33

# *The doubts of the Duke of Devonshire*

Dr Wace was not slow to follow up his success, just before the fall of the Rosebery Government, in persuading Lord Salisbury to arrange for draft amendments to be put forward for inclusion in Playfair's Bill which would protect KCL from the threat of losing its grant of public money, and to ensure that there should be an appeal to the Privy Council from decisions of the proposed Statutory Commission. Those were matters for the longer term, but Dr Wace arranged a meeting with the Prime Minister for 14 August 1895, to discuss the College's immediate financial problem, and sent a letter on the previous day, reminding Lord Salisbury that KCL had been deprived, since March, 1894, of £1700 a year, while grants were being paid to both UCL and Bedford College.[1]

It is highly likely that Lord Salisbury made clear to Wace, on 14 August, that some re-instatement of the grant would be forthcoming. But any early payment was not a prospect welcomed by the Treasury. When Gorst, the Vice-President of the Council, was told by his officials that 'No application has been made by King's College to the Treasury with reference to the suspended grant', he noted on the file that 'The Chancellor of the Exchequer does not wish any hint to be given to King's College to make a formal application.'[2] In part, the Treasury's reluctance may simply have reflected the fact that there was no money left in the allocation for grants in 1895–96, and the known success of KCL in having appealed for more funds from Church sources.

There was, however, a more significant factor at work. The Prime Minister appears to have accepted that some gesture would have to be made by KCL to modify its insistence that almost all its personnel be of the Anglican persuasion. Sometime in late September or early October, Webster, the Attorney General, told the Chancellor of the Exchequer, Sir Michael Hicks Beach, 'that the authorities of King's College had pause, and were willing, to adopt a Conscience Clause for students'. Hicks Beach then told Webster, 'with the full concurrence of the Prime Minister, that this must be a condition of the renewal of the grant'.[3] And in an interview with Hicks Beach, Wace was

---

[1]  Hatfield House 3M/E, Wace to Salisbury, 13 August 1894.
[2]  ED/54/1.
[3]  T1/14110/1895, Hicks Beach to Hamilton, 12 October 1895.

told that 'it would be impossible permanently to subsidize the college unless it should relax its religious requirements'.[4]

Whose idea it was to introduce a Conscience Clause, to give those students whose parents or guardians requested it, exemption from the religious instruction and ceremonies of the College, and safeguarded their rights to scholarships or exhibitions, is unclear. But the irony of the proposal was that, in the words of the Secretary to the Treasury, E.W. Hamilton, 'the only obstacle to the receipt by King's College of its share in the grant was the statutory test relating to Governors and Professors, not students'.[5] As the historian of the College has suggested, 'it was hoped that' the introduction of the Clause 'would be sufficient to pacify the nonconformist conscience, and satisfy the secularist demand'.[6] The grant was renewed for KCL for the last three years of the quinquennium, beginning on 1 April 1896. But the controversy over the religious tests for Governors and Professors was to continue.

The financial wrangling over KCL caused little or no delay in the efforts of the pro-Cowper Commission's forces to begin serious lobbying of the new Government. But it is difficult to establish exactly when, and through what channels, a meeting was arranged between the Duke of Devonshire and a large deputation drawn from all the institutions and interests supporting the passage of Lord Playfair's Bill. Roscoe must have been involved, for he received a letter from the Duke, probably very early in November, saying he was 'actually desirous of receiving a deputation between 23 November and 9 December'. Ramsay, on hearing of this, 'sent round the fiery cross', and alerted Kelvin, who would 'fix' a preliminary meeting of all those who had appeared before Rosebery early in the year. At that meeting there would be a draft resolution on the table, which would include a proposal to insert in the Bill a provision to allow for an appeal from the Statutory Commissioners' recommendations to the Privy Council. Again, who drafted the resolution, and with whom it had already been discussed, is unclear, but it must have been done before 6 November. It might well be that the ubiquitous Anstie was the draftsman. Ramsay, who may also have had a hand in its preparation, felt sure that 'This addendum will . . . conciliate King's College, and probably also many of the members of Convocation.'[7]

The preliminary gathering was scheduled for 21 November, at the University. The Annual Committee of Convocation only learned of it, formally, on 15 November, when they appointed four delegates – Anstie, Murray, Silvanus Thompson and Waring – to attend and to join any subsequent deputation which would interview the Duke of Devonshire. They discussed

[4] Hearnshaw, *Centenary History*, p. 360.
[5] T1/14110/1895, Hamilton to Chancellor of Exchequer, 11 October 1895.
[6] Hearnshaw, *Centenary History*, p. 360.
[7] UL AL304/3, Ramsay to Thompson, 6 November 1895.

the proposed provision for appeal to the Privy Council, and it was agreed to recommend the following text to Convocation:

> ... this House desires the early introduction into Parliament of a Bill for the reconstitution of the University, similar to that introduced last year by Lord Playfair, but with an inserted clause securing to the Senate, to Convocation, and to other bodies affected, the right of appeal to the Privy Council on any of the provisions which may hereafter be settled by the Statutory Commission.

Sir James Paget presided over the meeting on 21 November, when two Fellows of the University, Rucker and Rollit, carried a motion similar to that which the Annual Committee were proposing Convocation should adopt. It is worth quoting that part of the motion which called for the added clause, because it is wider but more specific in its application than that recommended to Convocation. The new Clause should give

> ... to all Institutions or persons directly affected by any Statute or Ordinance proposed by the Statutory Commission, a right of appeal to the Privy Council for the disallowance or alteration thereof, previous to such Ordinance being laid before Parliament for confirmation.

The deputation was to meet the Duke on 28 November. A week earlier, there is clear evidence of potential alliance between the two anti-Playfair Bill groups. In a meeting with Napier, Wace admitted that KCL 'cannot take any steps to revive the old Gresham scheme whilst they assent (although reluctantly) to the new Scheme'. Napier told Collins how Wace thought that

> ... the Government will bring in substantially the old Bill and that the crux of the situation lies with Convocation. If Convocation through its country members worry the Government so that it will become a matter of difficulty to force the Bill, Dr Wace thinks the Government would probably not force it through but try to settle the matter by an alternative scheme in which case the influence of King's would be brought to bear in the direction of a revival of the old Gresham. I pledged nobody to anything but told him that the bent of our minds was that rather than have the present scheme we would have a second university. Dr Wace was candidly of opinion that the scheme would give the whole control of our University to the London teachers.[8]

Sir John Lubbock had seen the Duke at the end of October, and may then have left with him suggested amendments to Playfair's Bill.[9] On the day before he was due to meet the large delegation at the University, Devonshire wanted to know, from Lubbock, whether those 'Amendments which should

---

[8] UL Ms812/92, Napier to Collins, 21 November 1895.
[9] BL Add Mss 62684, Lubbock's Diary, 26 October 1895.

conciliate Dr Busk and his friends' had been published and 'whether they would be accepted by those whom the Deputation represent'. The Duke rightly assumed that the amendments had not been published, and asserted that, 'as half of them are in manuscript . . . there would be no use in my referring to them and endeavouring to ascertain whether they would be accepted by those whom the Deputation represent'. He did reveal to Lubbock, though, a sense that some limits of possible action were being reached.

> Dr Busk appears . . . to beg the question when he says that if Convocation refuses its assent, there would be no Charter lost. The result apparently would be the establishment of two Universities which the Commission expressly reported against, and he can hardly expect the Government to adopt this course in the face of the Report of the Commission and the body of opinion in favour of it.[10]

The meeting of representatives of the London institutions in favour of the Cowper Commissioners' Scheme, with the Duke of Devonshire, on 28 November 1895, must have seemed, to those who were present at the earlier meeting with Rosebery, a re-run of familiar arguments but with a very different reception of them. Lord Kelvin introduced the delegation, and the presentation of the reformers' themes, fully reported in the *Times* of the following day, contained all the usual points which had been raised so many times before. KCL again reserved their position, claiming the right 'to press for material modifications' of the Scheme 'before any Statutory Commission that might be appointed'. Dr Wace, however, while admitting a preference for the 1892 Scheme, said King's College recognised that

> . . . with certain material amendments, the scheme proposed by the second Royal Commission might do much to remedy the disadvantages and injustices of the present situation: and, therefore, with due security for the consideration of such amendments, both by the Statutory Commmission and by the Privy Council, they beg to unite themselves with the rest of that deputation in the petition addressed to Her Majesty's Government.

Roscoe, a member of the Secondary Education Commission which had just reported, claimed that its Chairman, Bryce, and at least eight members of that Commission 'were in favour of the general tenour of the memorial' being presented by the deputation.

But the Duke of Devonshire's reply, interspersed with some sharp interjections by members of the Deputation, was dominated by his insistence that 'some approach to agreement and unanimity should be arrived at, and . . . this Scheme which you desire to see substantially adopted should be adopted,

---

[10] BL Add Mss 49661, Devonshire to Lubbock, 27 November 1895.

if possible, without encountering the strong opposition of a large and important section of the graduates of the existing University'. He had 'received some information – I cannot say whether it is absolutely accurate or not, I only give it for what it is worth', about the state of opinion in Convocation. And, apparently on the basis of that information, he was unwilling

> . . . to regard as unimportant the opinion of the majority of even country graduates. The opinion which they hold may be mistaken, but at all events they think that they represent, and to some extent they do represent, that large class of external students . . . who think that, however valuable for London and for those who will have access to it this new teaching University may be, the functions hitherto possessed and discharged with a considerable amount of satisfaction by the London University as an examining board, will be injured and defeated, and that a severe blow will be struck at educational interests which have hitherto derived so much advantage from the existence of the London University.

The Duke was

> . . . not in a position to say how much time the Government may be able to give to the consideration of such a proposal as this. I have no doubt that in the House of Lords we shall have plenty of time to discuss thoroughly this Bill; but it is possible that a very small amount of opposition in the House of Commons to such a Bill as this might under very conceivable circumstances be fatal to its passing through Parliament in the next Session . . . it is extremely desirable that the Bill . . . should come before [Parliament] in a shape which should excite as little opposition as possible.

The great majority of the Deputation went away, unhappily, to ponder their next move. But Dr Wace, however pleased he may have been to see a proposal to include an appeal to the Privy Council in Playfair's Bill, was quite ruthless in pushing his other institutional ambitions. He wrote to the Prime Minister, on the day after the Deputation had met the Duke. 'I earnestly trust it may be found possible to avoid the difficulties involved in any proposal to transform the existing University of London, by reverting to the Charter for establishing a new University, passed by the Privy Council in 1892, with any requisite amendments.'[11]

As for the Duke of Devonshire, it would seem that at least some of the arguments he had heard expressed by the Deputation had impressed on him the complexity of the issues, and perhaps had raised in his mind some doubt as to any easy acceptance of the Napier and Lubbock propositions. Clearly he felt the need for help, and told Salisbury that he wanted

[11] Hatfield House 3M/E, Wace to Salisbury, 29 November 1895.

. . . a small Committee to decide what is to be done about the London University and Playfair's Bill. You, A. Balfour, James, Goschen and Lord Halsbury? with Gorst would I think be enough. It would probably not be necessary to mention it to the Cabinet till the Committee had met and decided what to recommend. It would keep if necessary till after Christmas.[12]

And the Duke also turned back to Lubbock, telling him of the proposed Cabinet Committee, but also questioning the notion of altering the Charter. 'The petition for a revised Charter can only come from the University itself, and to wait for that seems to be going back to the very beginning of the proceedings. If there is really any approach to agreement possible, why not trust to a fair selection of Commissioners under Playfair's Bill who would under the proposed amendment have power to hear parties interested, and amend the scheme subject finally to an appeal to the Privy Council?'[13] Lubbock's immediate response, if any, may not have survived, but he responded, almost certainly at the very end of December, to a long memorandum issued by the Deputation.

The memorandum was put together after much rapid research and consultation, initiated by Ramsay, who called on those who had spoken at the meeting on 28 November to prepare a statement, which would

. . . correct the impression in the mind of the Duke of Devonshire that the rights of the graduates of London University will be in some way interfered with by the appointment of a Statutory Commission, and that due provision will not be made for the examination of 'external' students.[14]

Fifteen representatives came together on 4 December, with Lord Cowper in the Chair. Dr Wace was not present, but the others nominated Anstie, Allchin and Silvanus Thompson to draft a statement. The final version was thrashed out at meetings on 16 and 20 December.[15] In the course of its preparation some interesting data was produced.

Ramsay was able to obtain from the Duke of Devonshire the paper which he had been given by Bompas and Napier, and to which he had referred as 'some information' which he had received. It turned out to be a copy of the Minutes of Convocation of July, 1894, with some additions whose most important item was the demand that the approval of any Scheme should depend on the verdict of Convocation, using voting papers. Ramsay also revealed that

---

[12] Hatfield House 3M/E, Devonshire to Salisbury, 29 November 1895.
[13] BL Add Mss 49661, Devonshire to Lubbock, 30 November 1895.
[14] UL RC25/12a, Ramsay to members of deputation to Duke of Devonshire, 29 November 1895.
[15] UL RC25/12d & h.

Messrs Bompas and Napier have been calling on and writing to Professor [Carey] Foster, trying to make terms: suggesting that they will help us [i.e. UCL] if we give up our scheme and go for two universities. What help can such people give? However our Council is staunch, and on Saturday reaffirmed our adhesion to the plan of the Commission . . .[16]

Napier, meanwhile, had kept in touch with Dr Wace.[17]

The statement which the Deputation eventually sent to the Duke of Devonshire towards the end of December, 1895, included a full and accurate account of the progress of the whole controversy. It stressed that Convocation had already approved the Cowper Commission's Scheme twice, and that the Charter restricted the use of voting papers to the choice of nominees for appointment as Fellows. The position of the University of London was contrasted with the problems experienced by Parliament in reforming the University of Oxford and the Queen's University of Ireland, 'where the deliberately expressed adverse opinion of the graduates in convocation assembled was set aside by the Acts reconstituting the Universities'. Analysis of recent voting in Convocation showed that in a total electorate of about 3800, only a little over two thousand votes were cast, and it was accepted that some nine hundred graduates were irreconcilably opposed to change. But in the case of the election of Napier, who received 1231 votes in an election involving postal voting, it was argued that if the nine hundred irreconcilables were deducted there was 'a residue of only 330 who may, so far as is known, be willing to cease from opposition on the embodiment in the Act of some modifications of the Scheme of the Commission'.

Among the papers on which the formal response to the Duke was based, there is additional, relevant information. Of the 3800 members of Convocation, 430 lived abroad and could not be contacted. In the opinion of the recently elected Registrar, Dickins, about a thousand to eleven hundred of 'the more eminent graduates and most of the Masters and Doctors strongly approve reform'. Dickins felt sure that 'Napier's majority was largely due to his popularity as an old and diligent member of Convocation', and that his supporters were chiefly 'BAs, small country schoolmasters who take no part in University affairs'. The Bompas and Napier group was, in Dickins' view, 'hopeless', but he believed that the demands of those led by Collins could be met.[18] At the same time, the reformers recognised that their strength lay in London. On 23 December, Henry Frank Heath, who would become Assistant Registrar in 1896, told Allchin, with the forthcoming meeting of Convocation no doubt uppermost in his mind, that 'We are making arrangements for a house

---

[16] UL RC25/12g, Ramsay to Allchin, 10 December 1895.
[17] UL Ms812/93, Napier to Collins, 5 December 1895.
[18] UL RC25/12c & h.

to house visitation of the graduates in London who have not yet expressed an opinion upon the University question. There are actually over six hundred! Would you have believed it?'[19]

The memorandum was published and received the strong support of the *Times*, on 30 December. Lubbock, having read the memorandum, wrote to the Duke, ignoring everything in it except the significance, for him, of the attitude of the provincial graduates. He pointed out that the 'Country Colleges, which send us the great majority of our candidates, were almost unrepresented' on the Deputation which had met the Duke; and complained that

> The only answers given to your question why a Bill should be necessary were
> 1. The difficulty of drafting a Charter. This would be the same in any case.
> 2. The difficulty of consulting so scattered a body. This is evidently no reason, because the vote would be taken at a meeting of Convocation.
> If the reconstruction is effected as I have suggested, I believe everything might be amicably arranged, and the dangers feared may be avoided; but if a bill is forced through it will certainly be strenuously fought in the House of Commons, and I fear much resented by numbers of my constituents. I cannot but feel that this will give rise to a very unnecessary amount of friction, and much dissatisfaction, which might easily be avoided . . .[20]

It is interesting that Lubbock was still arguing in favour of a Charter, but it is unclear whether he envisaged retention of the existing practice whereby the essential vote on any new Scheme would be taken in a meeting of Convocation. He had proposed, in his electoral address, that any scheme should be decided by postal voting in addition to the voting at a meeting. He must have known that the chance of a London-based meeting turning down the Cowper Commissioners' Scheme was slight. And if he had hopes of this being disproved, they must have been dashed by the gathering of Convocation which took place on 21 January 1896.

The basic issue was put plainly before the largest gathering ever held of Convocation hitherto – 784 members attending. Perhaps Heath's door-to-door canvass had contributed to the increased turn-out. Silvanus Thompson and Cozens-Hardy had given notice of motion,

> That this House desires the early introduction into Parliament of a Bill for the reconstruction of the University similar to that introduced last year by Lord Playfair, but with an inserted clause securing to the Senate, to Convocation, and to other bodies affected, the right of appeal to the Privy Council on any of the provisions which may hereafter be settled by the Statutory Commission.

[19] UL RC25/121, Heath to Allchin, 23 December 1895.
[20] BL Add Mss 49661, Lubbock to Devonshire, nd 1895.

Napier and Bompas had given notice that they would move for an alternative resolution:

> In view of the fact that Convocation numbers about four thousand members, most of whom are precluded by their avocations and distance from town from attending a meeting in London, and of the desire recently expressed by the Lord President of the Council to ascertain the opinion of country graduates, it is inexpedient for this House to express any opinion as to the desirability of legislation for the reconstruction of the University of London, until, in compliance with the desire of the Lord President of the Council, the views of all members of Convocation have been ascertained.

After long debate, the alternative proposal was defeated by 460 to 239. There were eight Tellers, so that seventy-seven of those who were recorded as attending the meeting must either have abstained or have left before the vote was taken. The first motion was then carried, presumably by a show of hands, for there is no record of a count being demanded.

No formal meeting of Convocation during the remainder of the century attracted an attendance of more than 160. Most meetings drew many fewer, and two were abandoned for lack of a quorum. Though controversy over the reconstruction of the University continued, with considerable bitterness, for two and a half years after 21 January 1896, Convocation in formal session had no more to offer towards a solution. For a third time, in strict accordance with constitutional rules, majorities had expressed general approval of the Scheme of reconstruction put forward by the Cowper Commissioners. To the friends of those majorities, the matter of principle had been settled; its apparent settlement was celebrated in the February, 1896, issue of the *Journal of Education*.

> It would be rash to prophesy that this century will see a Teaching University for London duly constituted and organized, but the last barriers have fallen, and we are within sight of the goal. At the last meeting of Convocation, the party who were in favour of a paper University administered by post-cards, the Napier-Bompas-Collins cabal, were smitten hip and thigh, and Sir John Lubbock will now regret that he had not the courage to defy a small but noisy minority of his constituents. The Duke of Devonshire's preliminary question has been answered, and the banns of the new University have been published for the third time. The most cautious of modern statesmen can now find no just cause or impediment why a Statutory Commission should not be appointed to join together an examining and a teaching University.

But the Duke of Devonshire was not yet persuaded.

# 34

# *The strength of bishops and provincials*

Four times, between 21 February and 9 April 1896, Ministers were asked – thrice by Rollit – what steps were to be taken in the Session to implement the Scheme of reconstruction. Each time, either Gorst or Balfour simply replied that the matter was under the consideration of the Lord President: on 9 April, Gorst told Rollit that the Duke was abroad and there would be 'no final decision until he returns'.[1] But as early as 10 February, Wynne had been 'led to understand that the Duke would like to know how the country members voted', on 21 January. Wynne asked Gregory Foster, at UCL, to let him have an analysis. 'Two sets of numbers should be prepared, one regarding all those outside the administrative County of London as country members, and a second regarding all those resident beyond say twenty-five or thirty miles as country members.'[2]

Foster's analysis does not seem to have survived, but, several months later, Bennett sent Wynne his version of the vote, in which he had included 'outlying districts such as Kew Richmond Croydon Blackheath and Woolwich as parts of London'. The analysis showed that there was doubt whether twenty-six voters were Londoners or countrymen. But of the others present on 21 January, 384 Londoners and fifty-eight countrymen were in favour of reconstruction, and 181 Londoners and fifty countrymen were opposed.[3] No doubt there were many analyses, and certainly there was continuous correspondence in the press, both sides being well represented. In Manchester, the opponents set up a Manchester District University Defence Association. The actual numbers were often mere accompaniments to a conviction well expressed by one opponent of reconstruction, who claimed, with almost certainly a high degree of accuracy, that the vote did not 'represent the views of the majority of . . . members [of Convocation], but rather the views of those engaged in teaching in the metropolis'.[4]

[1] 4s Parl. Deb., vol. 37, cols 802, 950, 1462–3; vol. 39, col. 581 – 21 & 24 February, 2 March, 9 April 1896.
[2] UCL Coll. Corresp. 2c/36, Wynne to Foster, 10 February 1896.
[3] UCL Coll. Corresp. 2c/52, Bennett to Wynne, 2 November 1896.
[4] From a collection of cuttings from the *Manchester Guardian*, in UCL Coll. Corresp. 2c/38.

While it is unlikely that the Duke of Devonshire was greatly interested in other aspects of the vote, it is worth looking briefly at two breakdowns by degrees. Of those in favour of reconstruction, roughly 55 per cent held degrees in Medicine or Science, as opposed to 45 per cent who had Arts, Laws or Music degrees. In contrast, only 30 per cent of the opposition were medicos or scientists, while 70 per cent had degrees in Arts, Laws or Music. Another analysis, by Lord Playfair,[5] showed that 74 per cent of the holders of Doctorates, and 76 per cent of those with Masters degrees, were in favour: in contrast, support for change by those who held only Bachelor's degrees was 60 per cent. These figures tend to strengthen the view that the majority represented, strongly, teachers in higher education in London, many of whom would be highly qualified. Moreover, it was the scientists and medical people who were keenest, and also, because of the large hospital Medical Schools, the more numerous. And the analyses suggest that, even in London, the opposition no doubt represented many Arts graduates who had taken their degrees 'externally', while working as schoolteachers, or before becoming barristers or solicitors without taking a degree in Law, and were as much perturbed as their provincial counterparts by fears of the results of what was being proposed.

The pro-reconstruction side could do little except wait for the Government to move, but the ever-energetic Silvanus Thompson began to press the Annual Committee to approve of certain changes to the Scheme in order to make it more acceptable to the opposing forces in Convocation. He moved, on 20 March, for increased Convocation membership of the Senate; an enlargement of the Academic Council; a strengthening of the Board for External Students; and a couple of other minor amendments. But the Committee postponed discussion to the next meeting, when such detailed proposals were replaced by a resolution to give a Special Committee full powers 'to prepare amendments to the London University Commission Bill, to be proposed in either House of Parliament, on behalf of Convocation'.

More aggressive tactics were adopted by the opponents of the Bill. They at once began to take their own poll of Convocation opinion countrywide. An undated official document, prepared in the Privy Council Office, probably in the early spring of 1896, reported that the organisers of the poll had 'already received 1100 favourable replies'.[6] And a circular from Bompas and Napier, asking for further support, again undated but most likely sent out in the late spring, claimed that fourteen hundred out of seventeen hundred replies had been 'antagonistic to the Cowper scheme'.[7] But the most favourable opportunity for the opposition came when the veteran Fellow, R.H. Hutton, resigned from the Senate, leaving a vacancy which had to be filled by a nominee of

[5] 4s Parl. Deb., vol. 43, cols 439–44.
[6] PC1/1756.
[7] UCL Coll. Corresp. 2c/4.

Convocation. The call for nominations was announced on 22 April, with the result to be known on 23 June.

Well before then, however, the Duke of Devonshire, on his return to the country, decided to push for progress on the University's future. He called a meeting of his Cabinet Committee for 28 April, and invited Lord Herschell and Lubbock to attend, 'to discuss suggestions which might obviate opposition to the proposed Bill'.[8] In the following week Gorst told Rollit that a Bill was being prepared in the Privy Council Office 'but has not yet received the sanction of the Government'.[9] In fact it was not until the end of June that Balfour told Bryce that the Bill would be introduced in the House of Lords. A week later the Duke presented it for first reading. Much had happened in the interim.

While the Lord President and his colleagues were seeking a formula which might guarantee peaceful acceptance of a modified version of Playfair's Bill, the Prime Minister was giving discreet encouragement to the objections being raised by King's College. After the grant of money to King's had been restored, and the College had introduced its Conscience Clause, Salisbury told Wace that it was

> . . . a source of great gratification to me that for the present at least the College is protected from suffering in consequence of its resolute adhesion to the duty of giving a definite religious education which is impressed upon it by its Charter of foundation.[10]

The critics of any State help for King's did not drop the topic, however. In mid-April, Carvell Williams challenged Balfour about it, and the latter, who had received a delegation of protest, explained that he had appointed a three-man committee to examine the grants to all universities and colleges, which was yet to report.[11]

That Dr Wace was determined to support the attack on reconstruction, on several grounds, is made plain in a letter to Salisbury, sent after the two had met, with which he included a copy of his Council's view of the future.

> You will see that they express a decided preference for the establishment of a separate University, such as that approved by the Privy Council in 1891. I do not think I used too strong an expression in saying that important Faculties in the College are dying for lack of a satisfactory solution of this question. Both our Arts Faculty and our Medical Faculty are being drained of students, simply because they

[8] BL Add Mss 49662, Devonshire to Lubbock, 24 April 1896; 62684, Lubbock's Diary, 28 June 1896.
[9] 4s Parl. Deb., vol. 40, cols 741–2, 7 May 1896.
[10] Hatfield House 3M/E, Salisbury to Wace, 3 December 1895.
[11] 4s Parl. Deb., vol. 39, cols 898–9, 14 April 1896.

cannot obtain in London the kind of degrees which are open to them in Scottish Universities and the Victoria University. It follows that no alteration in the existing London University would be of any avail, unless it ensures the provision of a class of degrees different from the present ones; and there is certainly great danger that the Cowper Scheme, unless materially guarded by any Bill which may be introduced, may be ineffectual to make this provision.[12]

The Prime Minister replied cautiously, but not discouragingly.

I think it very desirable that if any of the parties interested have grounds for apprehending that the legislation proposed by Lord Cowper's Commission will not be satisfactory in its results, they should lose no time in bringing their views before the President of the Council.[13]

The Lord President was soon to be grappling as much, or more, with the defenders of KCL as he was with the largely self-appointed champions of the interests of external students. Which takes the story back to the replacement of Hutton on the Senate.

Eleven years after the events of 1896, Silvanus Thompson recalled them in the course of a vitriolic attack on 'the *Graduates' Association*, under Collins, Napier, etc.', which in his view had 'always shown a sort of vindictive hatred of "teachers", and . . . opposed the election of any teacher on the Senate'. Thompson believed that the Association had 'got the ear of the provincial graduates, and of the proteges of the "Correspondence College"'. This was a generic title probably describing several bodies offering services which would have been helpful to non-collegiate candidates for London degrees, but Thompson may have been pointing, particularly, at the University Correspondence College, founded in Cambridge in 1887, which advertised a 'comprehensive range of textbooks, model answers, tutorial classes, revision classes, tutors, library facilities and correspondence courses'.[14] In 1907, Thompson argued that the Association 'has absolute control over the graduates in the Arts Faculty, owing to the immense preponderance of illiterate B.A.'s who have come in through the cram shop; and it further has much weight in the Laws Faculty, which is very small'. Though he was writing in the present tense, one may fairly assume that he was also applying his opinion retrospectively. In any event, in a direct reference to the election of nominees for the vacant seat on the Senate, in May/June, 1896, he claimed that the

---

[12] Hatfield House 3M/E, Wace to Salisbury, 10 June 1896.
[13] KCL F8, Salisbury to Wace, 15 June 1896.
[14] R. Bell and M. Tight, *Open Universities: A British Tradition?* (Buckingham, 1993), pp. 50–1.

Graduates' Association 'put in a nobody named ——(M.D) in opposition to Lord Lister'.[15]

Sir Joseph Lister, Bt., who would be ennobled in 1897, and who had retired from the Professorship of Surgery at KCL in 1892, was currently President of the Royal Society, and the Establishment's candidate. The 'nobody' of Thompson's letter, was another surgeon, Walter Rivington, a long-serving member of the staff of the London Hospital, who had been Dean of the Medical School for some years, and had been elected for two short spells to the Annual Committee of Convocation. The contest between the two generated intense lobbying of Convocation members, and correspondence in the press. Joshua Fitch, in a letter to the *Times* supporting Lister, declared that Rivington

> . . . has been put forward avowedly on the ground that he is pledged to use any influence he may have as a Fellow . . . to resist such a change in the constitution as has been recommended by Lord Cowper's Commission.[16]

The progress of the election is but scrappily recorded. The result was a further disappointment for those supporting change. Rivington received 963 votes against Lister's 846, with thirty-two going to the third candidate, Stephenson. The turnout was 153 down on the previous year's election, won by Napier. Rivington's 963 perhaps underlined the claim of the Cozens-Hardy group that there was only a hard core of about 900 'irreconcilables'. There may have been special reasons within the medical community why Rivington prevailed – perhaps because of grass-roots medical desires for a less rigorous London degree – but the *Lancet* insisted that the 'contest was throughout carried out on strictly political, as distinct from professional, lines'.[17] Lister improved on the performance of Cozens-Hardy. But it is unlikely that the Duke of Devonshire felt any clearer in his mind about opinion within Convocation as a result of the vote.

There is a certain irony in what followed. Within a few months another Senate vacancy occurred: this one fell to be filled by the Crown directly, with no Convocation involvement. Lister was appointed. The unfortunate Rivington took his seat in the Senate at the end of July, 1896, but he died in the following May. Lister never attended a meeting of the Senate.

Whatever discussions had taken place within Devonshire's small circle of colleagues and advisers, the Bill which he placed before the House of Lords

---

[15] J.S. and H.G. Thompson, *Silvanus Thompson, His Life and Letters* (London, 1920), pp. 177–8.
[16] UCL Coll. Corresp. 2c/50, 26 May 1896, quoting *Times*. There are numerous letters and press cuttings on the matter in 2c/38, 43a & b.
[17] *Lancet*, 27 June 1896.

on 6 July 1896 made two important additions to what Playfair had offered in the previous year. In the original Bill, the Statutory Commissioners were required, in framing statutes and regulations, to see that provision was made for securing adequately the interest of non-collegiate students. The new Bill called for the same interests to be secured for both collegiate and non-collegiate students. The major innovation, however, was that interested parties, led by Senate and Convocation, were given the right of appeal to the Privy Council against proposals of the Statutory Commission; and either House of Parliament could negative any such proposal.

The Duke's speech on the First Reading made very clear that it was the Government's intention to seek a legislative solution to the need to extend the functions and reorganise the structure of the University. Indeed, he stressed that

> It has been almost conclusively proved that the intervention of Parliament through the appointment of a Statutory Commission is necessary, and is the only means by which this desirable end can be effected.

But the Duke did claim that there was some dissatisfaction with the present scheme of reconstruction on the part of UCL and KCL, and that

> ... still more formidable opposition has manifested itself, not on the part of the Convocation of London University as formally constituted, but on the part of a considerable body of members of Convocation residing for the most part in the provinces.

And the Lord President showed that he was fully informed of the nature of the objections taken, by the unhappy graduates, to the reconstruction proposals. They were apprehensive that

> ... the teachers of the affiliated institutions and colleges will exercise a large and perhaps undue influence over the examinations of the University, and that students who have prosecuted their studies in independent colleges or privately will in future be placed at some disadvantage ... either the high standard which ... has always been maintained by the London University will be lowered, or else that in the examinations arranged by the new body external students will compete on unfair terms as compared with students in the recognised teaching institutions.[18]

There was widespread disbelief in any possibility of the Bill passing in 1896, after being introduced so late in the Session. The British Medical Journal, a few days after the First Reading, felt that

---

[18] 4s Parl. Deb., vol. 42, cols 757–60, 6 July 1896.

The Duke . . . is so little sanguine as to the fate of his Bill, that he regards its function to be little more than to give a definite shape to the instruction to a statutory commission, in order to ascertain the real character and extent of the opposition which will be offered to the proposals for reconstruction . . . The Government is now . . . pledged to introduce the . . . Bill early next year, to give it Government support, and to afford facilities for its discussion in the Commons so that it may pass into law before this time next year.[19]

Be all that as it may, the Lord President certainly pressed on with the detailed arrangements. He had been careful not to raise hopes that the Commons would pass the Bill in the current session, but he asked the Prime Minister for his suggestions – before the Bill's Second Reading – of who should be proposed as members of the Statutory Commission. Lord Knutsford had been thought of as Chairman, but Devonshire felt it more likely that Lord Davey, by now recovered from illness, would accept.[20]

Confidence that the Bill might be found acceptable, if not immediately passable, was given a big boost by the Second Reading, which took place on 23 July. In the short term, the debate justified Lister who, a few days earlier, could 'hardly suppose that there will be serious opposition raised in the Lords, now that the Duke is in earnest in favour of the bill'.[21] Indeed, in opening the debate, the Duke showed little sympathy with those who were opposing the Bill. He admitted that the opposition to reconstruction could not be 'compared for a moment, either in weight or as regards scientific or educational experience' with the pro-reform bodies. And he disassociated himself from the claim by the authors of a paper circulated before the Second Reading – almost certainly members of the Collins-Napier-Bompas group – that the unofficial canvass of Convocation had been conducted in order to provide him with information which he needed, and that 'the papers issued for the purpose were first submitted through the Member for the University to the Lord President, and were not disapproved by either'. The Duke admitted 'very frequent communication' with Sir John Lubbock, but denied any recollection of seeing such papers.

No peer spoke against the Bill. Herschell, Cowper, Playfair, Reay and Kimberley were all supportive. Kelvin, who had joined with Stokes and Welldon to express, in a note to the Cowper Commission Report, their preference for a separate University, announced that 'On his own behalf and, he believed, on behalf of his colleagues in the note, he could say they would only have been too glad to have accepted what was now proposed by this Bill.' A Second Reading was given, and the Bill was referred to a Committee of the

---

[19] *BMJ*, 11 July 1896.
[20] Hatfield House 3M/E, Devonshire to Salisbury, 13 July 1896.
[21] UL AL 304/8, Lister to Thompson, 19 July 1896.

Whole House on 27 July. The Committee reported the Bill without amendment, and it went for Third Reading on 30 July.[22]

Alas for the Duke's hopes. Opposition was quickly at work after the Bill was
made public. The rebellious Convocation men were first. Busk, Collins, Napier
and Benson were soon involved in drafting protests and amendments,
and Napier, looking ahead to debate in the Commons, was much concerned
with delaying the Bill until it would die with the end of the session. He told
Collins that

> T.P. O'Connor ought to help us in the House, as Stuart is on the other side. Wace
> has just told me that he has heard on good authority that Balfour is a two University
> man . . . Would it not be possible for you to write to him in the name of the four
> dissentients and ask him to see us. If we could get his ear we should yet ride the
> session.[23]

Busk complained to Collins about what he regarded as the high handed
conduct of the new Vice-Chancellor, Roscoe, in the Senate. More immediately
relevant to the Bill, he reported that Sir John Lubbock had apparently been
discussing possible amendments to the Bill with Haldane, but felt sure the
University's MP would 'not accept any amendment without our knowledge
and approval'. Busk went on to assert, of Lubbock, that

> The only amendment he can accept of his own motion is the insertion of a clause
> giving Convocation a veto upon any Statutes or Ordinances that may be made,
> such veto to be signified as at a Senatorial Election.[24]

We have already come across Haldane and Sidney Webb being interested,
since the publication of the Cowper Commission's Report, in shaping legislation to take care of the University's future. Haldane had been a member
of UCL Council for some years by then, but in the University context,
unlike Webb, who was Chairman of the London County Council's Technical
Education Board,

> He had no official standing . . . He worked backstage. Plans were hatched
> over austere dinners in the Webbs' house, in co-conspiracy with the indefatigible
> Sidney.

There is not much documentary evidence of Haldane's participation in
the early bargaining which set in seriously in 1896, but Haldane told his

---

[22] 4s Parl. Deb., vol. 43, 2nd Rdg, cols 429–51, Cmte stage, col. 673.
[23] UL Ms 812/98, Napier to Collins, 16 July 1896
[24] UL Ms 812/101, Busk to Collins, 17 July 1896.

mother in the summer, that 'All day long, I have been working at the London University Bill trying to get cantankerous people to agree', and claimed, prematurely as it turned out, that 'we are now in sight of a settlement but it has been a tough job'.[25]

There are no letters which might illuminate Webb's involvement in these negotiations, but he did warn Thompson, at a late stage, that 'some of the most extreme supporters of the existing Colleges *as separate institutions* are expecting to get their own way from the present Government'.[26] And his apprehension was justified, because the main obstacle which was to prevent the success of the Bill of 1896 was not the outright opposition of the 'irreconcilable' rebels of Convocation, who never had the chance of testing the extent of their support in the House of Commons. What ruined the Bill's chances – apart from the fact that it was introduced too late in the Session – was the failure to reach an agreement with King's College over how to deal with the recommendation, carried by only seven out of the thirteen members of Cowper's Commission, that the Senate of the University should not have the right to make grants to institutions which imposed any denominational tests.

Dr Wace had kept the Prime Minister informed of the negotiations which he was trying to carry on with the Duke of Devonshire, but after the Bill was published he took the advice of the Attorney General, Sir Richard Webster, and asked Salisbury for an interview, 'before the Bill goes further in the House of Lords', because

> It does not contain one or two provisions for the protection of this College which your Lordship kindly undertook last year to propose as amendments to Lord Playfair's Bill.[27]

It seems probable that Salisbury referred Wace to the Duke, and Wace duly handed three proposed amendments to the Lord President, on the same day as the Second Reading of the Bill, 23 July.[28] But by this time, Devonshire was not prepared to make many concessions.

The Duke reacted firmly to the three amendments proposed by KCL. He consulted the eminent lawyer Lord James of Hereford, now Chancellor of the Duchy of Lancaster, and the Parliamentary Draftsman, C.H. Ilbert. The latter told him that one of the amendments 'would raise the theological test question in the crudest form, and if adopted would certainly wreck the Bill in

---

[25] Eric Ashby and Mary Anderson, *Portrait of Haldane at Work on Education* (London, 1974), p. 33.
[26] UL AL 304/9, Webb to Thompson, 5 August 1896.
[27] Hatfield House 3M/E, Wace to Salisbury, 17 July 1896.
[28] Hatfield House 3M/E, Wace to Salisbury, 26 July 1896.

the House of Commons'. Devonshire then told Wace that the Statutory Commissioners

> ... will possess sufficient powers to deal with both the questions raised by the Amendments, and that it is undesirable to fetter them by instruction on special points; and therefore I could not undertake to move any of them except the second. Of course the others can be moved by any Peer, and I will consult Lord Salisbury as to the view which he would take of them if moved. Personally, however, I should be unwilling to accept them ...[29]

Wace immediately appealed again to the Prime Minister, asking his advice on what course to take. He reminded Salisbury

> ... that the theological test question has been raised, not by us, but the Commissioners, against the protest of six of their number, and that the Amendment desired by our Council simply gives effect to that protest. I doubt not that, as the Duke says, the [Statutory] Commissioners will have sufficient powers to deal with both the questions raised by the first and third amendments, but we have no guarantee how they will deal with them. Lord Davey will in many respects command great confidence, but he is not likely to look with favour on the religious conditions of the King's College Foundation.
>
> To run the risk of 'wrecking the Bill', as the Duke apprehends, by dealing with the religious question which the Commissioners have raised is, no doubt, a very serious responsibility; but it is also a most serious responsibility to leave this College without protection against a regulation which would debar it from a share of any funds entrusted to the administration of the University.[30]

Whether or not Salisbury asked the Duke about the Bill, Devonshire sent him two letters explaining the situation, on 27 July. He told the Prime Minister that an amendment had been agreed with James and Herschell, and that copies had been sent to Wace and the Bishop of London in 'the hope that it may satisfy them'. The Duke felt that 'It might be acceptable to King's College as the words are taken from the Committee of Bishop Barry and others to the Report of Cowper's Commission.' He, James and Herschell thought it 'might be accepted without much risk to the Bill in the House of Commons'. Devonshire, however, was still quite firm in rejecting the first and third amendments. He also confirmed that Davey had accepted the Chairmanship of the Statutory Commission, but that one place remained to be filled. He had been told that a person 'acceptable to the London County Council would be desirable, as they are prepared to give £10,000 a year to the new University

---

[29] Hatfield House 3M/E, Devonshire to Wace, 24 July; Devonshire to Salisbury, 27 July 1896.
[30] Hatfield House 3M/E, Wace to Salisbury, 24 July 1896.

on certain conditions'. The man suggested was Llewellyn Smith, formerly Secretary to the Academical Education Association, and presently Labour Correspondent of the Board of Trade.[31]

All these exchanges took place as the Bill made its way towards and through the Committee and Report stages, by 27 July. It was only in the course of debate on the Third Reading, which began on 30 July, and was completed on the following day, that battle was joined on the floor of the House of Lords. In the opening Session, the Bishop of London, Frederick Temple, moved an amendment which provided that no statutes or regulations proposed by the Statutory Commissioners should 'inflict any disability on any college or institution on account of its religious character'. He was supported by the Archbishop of Canterbury and the Bishop of Salisbury. The Duke of Devonshire refused to accept it, but on the second day of the debate offered, in its place, a form of words based on Bishop Barry's formulation: 'no statutes or regulations shall preclude the University from accepting, if it sees fit, the administration of funds offered for University purposes, whatever may be the conditions attached to such administration'. This was carried, almost certainly without the blessing of the ecclesiastical members. The Bill was passed and sent on its way to the Commons.[32]

The Session was now dangerously advanced. The Bill had its entirely formal First Reading on 4 August. Exactly a week later it was withdrawn, and on 14 August Parliament was prorogued. But though this was the outcome so clearly seen as inevitable, earlier in the summer, the final days of the Bill's life were quite dramatic. An absolutely accurate narrative is probably impossible to construct, but what seems likely is that both streams of opposition operated separately, with Haldane seemingly moving between them in the effort to find a solution acceptable to both. Neither group, however, would yield.

On the evening of 30 July, between the two Sessions of the Third Reading debate in the Lords, Lubbock and Napier met the Vice-President, Gorst, to discuss the Bill. This may have led to a crucial 'long conference', which must have focussed on the claims of the Convocation objectors, because no representatives of KCL were involved. It took place on 4 August, the day of the First Reading of the Bill in the Commons. Those present, according to Lubbock, were, in addition to himself, Cozens-Hardy, Haldane, Busk, Benson and Napier. Lubbock's only, brief record, was that 'if Bompas Committee had been satisfied I think a compromise might have been arrived at'.[33] The failure to agree must have been seen as a final signal that there would be opposition in the Commons from the 'irreconcilable' camp. But the messsage may also have been the first intimation that the united front put up so far by the Collins-Napier and Bompas groups was likely to collapse.

---

[31]  Hatfield House 3M/E, Devonshire to Salisbury, 27 July 1896.
[32]  4s Parl. Deb., vol. 43, cols 1000–8 & 1231–2.
[33]  BL Add Mss 62684, Lubbock's Diary, 4 August 1896.

The struggle between the two factions in Convocation may not have been widely appreciated by the press. But the determined opposition of King's College was publicised, very colourfully, by the *Daily Chronicle* on 7 August. Whether the writer's information was completely true or not, he gave a vivid account, claiming that as the Bill had

> come down almost unscathed from the Lords, all parties in the Commons are willing to let it pass, as alone it can pass at this period of the session – unopposed . . . negotiations have been going on during the past week, in which Mr Haldane has taken a leading and indefatigible part. Finally, all parties have agreed to consent to its passage, except, I am informed, the Church party. My information is that this section of the House, headed by Lord Cranborne, [the eldest son and heir of the Marquess of Salisbury] refuses to allow a London University to be formed without clamping on to it a religious test clause which will be a set-back in the Test Act of 1872. The fight has arisen round King's College which . . . still has a Church of England test for its professorships. The supporters of the Bill in the Lords accepted an amendment allowing the University to hold trust funds in favour of King's College, but not to administer public funds under a 'test' provision. But the Church party . . . are not content. They want to resuscitate the Bishop of London's amendment and to force the new Commission to endow King's. Of course if such an amendment is pressed, the Opposition could not accept it, and the Bill is lost.

Haldane certainly gave the Church party the credit for defeating his efforts, whether or not he thought the Convocation objectors were also serious opponents. The Second Reading was abandoned on 11 August – appropiately enough, on the motion of the Attorney General, Sir Richard Webster, who had drafted King's amendments. Haldane lamented to his mother: 'Alas the University Bill is dead. The Bishops have killed it'.[34] In its issue of the same day, the *Chronicle* produced a piece of splendidly purple invective.

> The Bill might have passed the House of Commons and received the Royal Assent, if the smallest and least considerable section of the Tory party had not intervened. Lord Cranborne and Mr Talbot declared that the time had come for making a stand, and that the 'denominational' principle must be asserted at all costs. They therefore announced their intention of opposing the Bill unless the University of Grote and Mill were made sectarian. Mr Disraeli would have flung them a stinging epigram, and kept them up until they were sorry for themselves. Sir Michael Hicks Beach would have told them to go to the place which they believe to have been designed for those who differ with them in opinion. Mr Smith would have smiled and gone on as if nothing had happened. Mr Balfour, with the weakness which is his least variable quality, at once surrendered to a faction which in the last Parliament was the butt of Mr Hanbury and the laughing stock of Mr Gibson Bowles. The strongest

---

[34] Ashby and Anderson, *Portrait of Haldane*, p. 33.

Government of modern times allows Lord Cranborne to deprive London of a teaching university.

In all the argument and publicity which went on over this and later Bills, the threat of opposition in the House of Commons was frequently cited but rarely assessed in any detail. The problem for the Bill was that, though sponsored by the Government, it was not high in priority, and those concerned with the greater issues of the day were perhaps not so much worried about defeat as they were about how much parliamentary time would be consumed by debate. Thus the emphasis on the need for an agreed formula. But even if Balfour had agreed to try to go ahead with the Bill, there was no likelihood of heavy whipping being applied to the Government's supporters. In a situation where attendance was uncertain, the intervention of the Church party alone would certainly have caused trouble, and, together with opposition from quite other quarters than KCL, could well, if put to the test of a divison, have proved fatal. That the Church party and the rebel members of Convocation were not the only threats, was forecast as early as April, 1896, just as the Duke and his Committee were about to discuss the legislation, by the Liberal MP, Augustine Birrell, who would shortly take up the Quain Professorship of Law at UCL for a spell. He thought that hope for a Bill was already dead, because even if there was some leisure later in the Session, other legislation would be too pressing. But, in addition, he believed that

> ... there are a quite a number of curious creatures who are or think they are mightily concerned to kill this London University Bill. Not only are there graduates of the existing London University but there are a few who think that there are not at present in and about London the *materials* out of which a Teaching Body of due authority can be constituted.[35]

---

[35] UCL Coll. Corresp. 2c/46, Birrell to Hill, 27 April 1896.

# 35

# A compromise refused

Exactly fifty-one weeks after Sir Richard Webster announced the withdrawal of the Bill of 1896, the same fate befell its successor. But the London University Bill of 1897 was a substantially different piece of potential legislation, its content reflecting major shifts of attitude among the interested parties. In the tortuous negotiations which preceded its introduction into the House of Lords, the possibility of compromise was more pervasive than ever before.

That possibility, unsurprisingly in retrospect, was due to a recognition by some of those most opposed to the Bill in its existing, though recently rejected form, that the Government had no intention of allowing the restructuring of the University to disappear from their agenda. Busk realised

> . . . that the opponents [of the Bill] cannot maintain their opposition for an indefinite period. Money runs short and enthusiasm cools. Meantime authority is always urging the Government to pass the Bill recommended by the Commission and it seems to me that unless we can take some decided step an Act of Parliament somewhat similar to that already introduced will be passed, and a Statutory Commission forced upon us . . .[1]

Lubbock, Busk and Napier saw the desperate need to produce a viable alternative proposal, and decided to go back to the idea of pressing for a new Charter, and to try to persuade the Chancellor and the Vice-Chancellor to support them. Busk told their ally, Collins, early in October, 1896, that

> . . . we must be stirring if we wish to avoid a Statutory Commission. Will it not be best to prepare certain heads for a draft Charter and confer on them with Herschell, Roscoe and Lubbock? Lubbock will assist in preparing the heads . . .
>
> If it were possible to agree with Herschell and Roscoe we might obtain a majority on the Senate and it would at any rate be worthwhile to prepare a draft Charter . . . and . . . to secure the consent of Convocation before laying the matter before the Senate.
>
> Unless Herschell would support in the Senate, I am afraid our labour would be

---

[1] UL Ms 812/104, Busk to Collins, 13 November 1896.

lost; but it might be worthwhile to get the draft Charter prepared and approved by Convocation notwithstanding.[2]

Lubbock and Busk worked on a Charter and sent a draft to Collins, Napier and Benson for their reactions.[3] But Collins must have had some doubt about the whole exercise, and Busk wrote to him again, in mid-November, spelling out his own tactical view,

> . . . it seemed to me that the only plan was for us to apply for and obtain a Charter. I agree that although we might be made to accept what is objectionable by a Statutory Commission if appointed, yet we ought not to make a proposal which seems to us to be objectionable, and the idea which Napier and I had in preparing the draft Scheme (for most of which I am responsible) was to suggest a Scheme which would not be objectionable and yet might have a chance of success . . .
>
> The general idea of the Scheme was to make the Senate too unwieldy, but to give it supreme executive power, making the Boards for internal and external students merely advisory and palpably subordinate owing to their being merely committees of the Senate itself. If any other method of obtaining this result, which you have at heart as much as I, occurs to you, or if you desire any modification in the draft Scheme, I shall be very glad to have your suggestions . . .[4]

The idea of proceeding by Charter had been suggested by Silvanus Thompson in June, 1895, when he feared that Lord Playfair's Bill might be 'stranded in Parliamentary shoals', because he was confident, then, that the majority in Convocation would authorise a Charter which would embody the ideas of the Cowper Commissioners.[5] But now a Charter was being envisaged in order to stop a Bill and to preserve Convocation's veto. The idea was almost certainly unknown to Thompson when, at a meeting of Convocation on 26 October 1896, he tried to move consideration of an amendment to the 'Reconstitution Bill', which would have given some ground to its opponents by calling for increased Convocation representation on the Senate, a bigger Academic Council, and a stronger Board of External Studies. He was ruled out of order on a technicality by the Chairman – Busk.

Between November 1896, and June, 1897, there were intense, protracted discussions and bargaining sessions among a relatively small number of men, but such records as are available do not make it possible to present the full content of the arguments or an exact chronology. And while the prime movers are easily identified, the extent of the influence of each is by no means clear. Busk and Napier went ahead with the drafting of a new Charter. Lubbock

---

[2] UL Ms 812/102, Busk to Collins, 6 October 1896.
[3] UL Ms 812/103, Busk to Collins, 9 November 1896: BL Add Mss 62684, Lubbock's Diary, 7 November 1896.
[4] UL Ms 812/104, Busk to Collins, 13 November 1896.
[5] See Chapter 31, p. 379.

was supportive, though he was always his own man, politically, and, as a main channel to the Duke of Devonshire, was somewhat constrained by his appreciation of the ministerial and parliamentary situations. Collins was certainly much consulted, but he was doubtless heavily involved in his duties as Vice-Chairman of the LCC, of which he was to become Chairman in 1897–98. William Ramsay was an important figure from UCL. Sidney Webb kept the interests of technical education to the fore. And while it seems clear that Haldane was, from the outset of the 1896–97 operations, a most significant negotiator, his liaisons – no doubt because of their discreet nature – are not a little opaque. And all these leave aside the spokesmen for King's College, mainly Dr Wace, whose concerns had still to be met; and Lord Herschell, Chancellor of the University, whose authority as spokesman for the majority of the Senate was seemingly accepted without question. Before the end of 1896, Busk seems to have warned Lubbock against approaching the Ministers about the idea of a Charter. He feared that 'the Duke may talk unguardedly and too soon and . . . Gorst's opinion carries so little weight that it may be hardly worth while to obtain it at such a risk'.[6]

It seems likely that Napier and Busk, and possibly Collins, met on 21 December, and had preliminary discussion on the principles which they should adopt to govern what would be given prominence in a new Charter. A major focus was on whether they should accept the notion of 'duality' – which implied the acceptance of a single University with dual responsibility for internal and external students. Napier declared that

> If we are going for duality (and in my view nothing else is left us) the first and main consideration is to get a strong Board for External students and a good Convocation representation on the Senate. A strong external side will force up the Internals – or kill them. We may therefore, it seems to me, in consideration of a strong representation and External Board, give the Teachers their head in their own arrangements . . . insistence on any other conditions except those relating to these two matters (except for purposes of bargaining) is unwise.

And he added, 'I will see Haldane as soon as I can.'[7]

Two other major concerns of the Bill's opponents were the question of which Institutions should be included within the University, and whether there should be different degrees for internal and external graduates. As early as mid-January, Busk was reporting to Collins an agreement that the idea of 'Schools of the University' should be abandoned, and that only Teachers should be recognised. This was seen as a way to deflect Webb's insistence on

---

[6] UL Ms 812/106, Busk to Collins, 5 December 1896.
[7] UL Ms 812/111, Napier to Collins, 4 January 1897.

the inclusion of Polytechnics. Wace and Ramsay, speaking for KCL and UCL, were adamantly against such inclusion, and Napier reported that

> Webb must be persuaded. To name the Polytechnics in the Charter would kill the Scheme . . . Perhaps we may have to go on Webb notwithstanding. He has little influence with either this Government or Convocation or the Senate. It is critical. A good shove now and Charter will hold the field . . .[8]

Webb came round, after discussions with Ramsay and Haldane, and accepted that Teachers, rather then Schools, should be recognised. He was soon said to be 'at work on . . . a list, and thinks it will contain about 500 Teachers, mostly medicals'.[9]

There was also progress on the matter of different degrees for internal and external graduates. On 9 January 1897, the Council of UCL passed a resolution in support of the Bill, but Haldane told Napier that this was merely 'tactics'. Clearly, Haldane was in close touch with Napier, who wrote that

> Haldane thinks University College will not object to differentiation of the degrees. *He* personally doesn't like it. Between us we suggested something of this kind: 'The degrees will be differentiated etc unless the Senate otherwise determines.' Charter progresses merrily, Lord Reay is half converted. Ramsay also . . .

Haldane, however, must have made clear to Napier that there would be no compromise on the single university, for Napier pressed Collins to see Busk 'at once, and urge definite *dualism strongly*. If he does not positively and immediately concede this it is useless going on'.[10]

Lubbock apparently heeded Busk's advice not to risk letting Ministers know about the Charter idea. He tried to see the Duke in mid-January, but had been told that it was not convenient. The Lord President did tell Lubbock that there would be nothing about the Bill in the Queen's Speech at the beginning of the new Session, and that nothing would be done until he had heard from him. To this, Lubbock responded, briefly, that 'Some negotiations are in progress which may perhaps lead to an amicable settlement.'[11]

But while Charter preparations were going on within the opposition group, the committed supporters of the Bill were not idle. On 13 February it was reported that the Cozens-Hardy Committee had met and resolved to press for the re-introduction of the legislation, but that the Duke of Devonshire, while

---

[8] UL Ms 812/113, Napier to Collins, nd 1897.

[9] UL Ms 812/108, Busk to Collins, 19 January 1897; Ms 812/112, Napier to Collins, nd 1897.

[10] UL Ms 812/112, Napier to Collins, nd 1897.

[11] BL Add Mss 49663, Devonshire to Lubbock, 13 January; Lubbock to Devonshire, 14 January 1897.

'not indisposed to accede to this request', was unlikely to take any initiative unless the proposal was uncontentious and had a large measure of support 'not only within, but also outside Parliament'.[12] Undeterred by any such doubt, James Anstie moved in the Senate, on 24 February, a resolution urging HM Government to 'take immediate steps for the constitution of a Statutory Commission'. This provoked a challenge: Busk, seconded by Rollit, moved to postpone consideration of Anstie's proposal until the next meeting. When put to the vote, this amendment was defeated by eighteen to five, and the original motion was passed by the same margin. The division may well have defined the extent of opposition to the Cowper Scheme among the working Fellows. Busk, Collins and Napier were joined by the recently elected Rivington, and by Grant Duff. Though Rollit had seconded Busk's motion, he did not vote.

The Senate, in expressing their keenness to see progress made, were able to count on the declared support of many of the other institutions which had associated themselves with the earlier Bills. The Lord President politely acknowledged their letter early in March. By then, what was going on had become sufficiently recognised for the *University College Gazette* to report that a meeting of 'various institutions concerned in the Reconstruction scheme', chaired by Lord Reay, had given unanimous support for the Scheme. At the same time, the *Gazette* had heard about the idea of a new Charter, but wrote, dismissively, that 'Rumour says (and truly says we believe) that this is merely a new device of the party of obstruction.' And those members of UCL who had shown themselves attracted to the notion of a Charter were upbraided.[13]

There are few details available of what must have been, thereafter, many weeks of tough debating and bargaining, and the exercise of much diplomacy. In the middle of May, Balfour told the Commons that the Lord President hoped to introduce a Bill 'shortly' in the House of Lords, and said 'there is some reason to expect that the difficulties which prevented it from passing last year will be removed and certain negotiations are going on with that object'.[14] A month later, on 16 June, Pye-Smith gave Notice of Motion in the Senate that the Lord President should be urged to receive a deputation which should press for a speedy introduction of the Bill. He never moved it, for the situation had changed dramatically by the time the Senate next met, in mid-July.

Whether or not the proposal to press for a new Charter, instead of a Bill, was seen by its authors entirely as a tactical move to force concessions from those in favour of the Cowper Scheme, that was its effect. The demand for a Charter seems to have been dropped quite quickly once the possibility of compromise

---

[12] *BMJ*, 13 February 1897.
[13] *University College Gazette*, vol. 1, no. 9, 22 March 1897.
[14] 4s Parl. Deb., vol. 49, col. 632, 17 May 1897.

began to take shape seriously. Much credit for the progress made must be given to Haldane. Such documentary evidence as there is, and some of his own letters, support the view that he was a brilliant intermediary. But Beatrice Webb, while praising him, recorded on 16 July, how

> Sidney and Haldane [had been] rushing about London trying to get all parties to agree to a Bill for London University. If it goes through, it will be due to Haldane's insistence and his friendship with Balfour, but the form of the Bill, the alterations grafted on the Cowper Commission, are largely Sidney's.[15]

At the beginning of July, Haldane wrote to Devonshire's Private Secretary, Almeric Fitzroy.

> I still have hopes of the negotiations. A month ago I got the Convocation party to agree to accept the Bill if the enclosed amendments were inserted. I took them at once to Lord Herschell. He was favourably disposed towards them. The delay has been with the Senate party, but I understand that Lord Herschell has convened a meeting of their representatives . . . If they will agree to the substance of the amendments and the Lord President is disposed to adopt them, in the House of Lords, I think I can get the Bill accepted in the Commons with very little discussion. Mr Balfour tells me he can find time on this hypothesis . . . I enclose – as a private document from myself – the amendments which embody what has been accepted by the Convocation opposition and which are before Lord Herschell.[16]

But Haldane was rather worried over the composition of the Statutory Commission. Lord Davey was acceptable to the Convocation rebels as Chairman. But the appointment of Lord Lister as a member would arouse their suspicions, and Haldane felt those suspicions might best be allayed if he, himself, were put on the Commission, claiming that he had the confidence of the opposition party. A week later, however, when he thought full agreement was very near, he insisted that, to counterbalance Lister, it was essential to have a Convocation man, and recommended Busk, 'a gentleman', who 'knows probably more about the details of the matter than anyone else'. Haldane also suggested the new Bishop of London, Mandell Creighton, and, 'if an outsider is wanted, Mr Llewellyn Smith, or Dr Garnett would be acceptable to the Technical Board'.[17] Llewellyn Smith had already been championed by Sidney Webb.

Exactly when the draft amendments were circulated to members of Senate and others is unclear, but Herschell carried the Senate with him on 14 July, when they were discussed. The only point in the proposed amendments

---

[15] *The Diary of Beatrice Webb, 1892–1905*, ed. N. and J. Mackenzie (London, 1983), vol. 2, pp. 119–20.
[16] ED 24/5, Haldane to Fitzroy, 3 July 1897.
[17] ED 24/5, Haldane to Fitzroy, 9 July 1897.

which caused concern was the idea that 'the degrees of external and internal students should be differentiated in the titles conferred on them'. But Herschell himself, like Haldane, had anxieties about the membership of the Statutory Commission. He told the Duke of Devonshire:

> I do not think the proposed constitution of the Commission satisfactory. I could not myself support it anxious as I am for a settlement. The University of London is the leading medical and science school in England. The names you suggest include only *one* representative of medicine and science – viz. Lord Lister – whilst there are three lawyers and two representatives of classical scholarship. The substitution for one of the names of a representative of medicine and science is I think essential. The agreement practically come to will I think render the constitution of the Commission less vital to the opponents (hitherto) of the Bill. It occurs to me that for the name of Sir F. Jeune that of Sir William Roberts, MD, FRS, might well be substituted. He is the representative of the University on the General Medical Council.[18]

Senate had at least had a chance of discussing the new Bill before it was introduced to the House of Lords. It is inconceivable that Convocation was not also provided with copies of the amendments, but they only came before the Special Committee on 23 July, and that Committee found itself prevented by a procedural technicality from making any motion on the new Bill. In plain fact, though, the Bill had long passed out of the control of either Senate or Convocation, and had become almost entirely a subject of governmental and parliamentary manouevre.

The new Bill listed the Statutory Commissioners – Lord Davey as Chairman, Lister, Mandell Creighton, Busk, Jebb, Owen Roberts, and William Roberts. Davey accepted with some reservations: he wanted to know who his colleagues were going to be, and he was concerned as to whether there would be any changes in the Bill which might offend his consistently held position of having nothing to do with any reconstruction 'on anything like a denominational basis'. King's had seen him, correctly, as unlikely to be sympathetic to their special causes.[19]

It is only when the text of the new Bill appeared that the full extent of the shifts which had been made by various parties were revealed. Whether Haldane, or Webb, or officials in the Privy Council Office, or Parliamentary Counsel, were primarily responsible, the short and limited Bills of 1895 and 1896 had been re-cast. In their place was a Bill which was not unduly longer than its forerunners, but attached to it were two Schedules. Lord Herschell's comment that the constitution of the Statutory Commission would be 'less

---

[18] ED 24/5, Herschell to Devonshire, 15 July 1897.
[19] ED 24/5, Davey to Devonshire, 20 July 1897.

vital to the opponents (hitherto) of the Bill', is thoroughly understandable when it is seen that the Schedules laid down the basic structure of the University, and had to be accepted by the Commissioners before they began their task of drafting Statutes and Regulations. Almost all the contentious issues had been resolved by negotiation, and the solutions included in either the Bill or its Schedules. And the Statutory Commissioners were given power to take into account changes in the overall situation which had occurred since the Cowper Commission reported in 1894.

King's College's objections to the earlier drafts were settled in all but a few details by the inclusion of an amended clause which read:

> The Statutes or Regulations . . . shall not authorise the assignment of money for any purpose in respect of which any privilege is granted or disability imposed on account of religious belief. Provided that they shall not prevent the University from allocating funds, on such conditions as it thinks fit, for the payment of any person appointed or recognised by the University as a University teacher, or for his laboratory expenses, or for apparatus to be used by him, notwithstanding any conditions attached to any office held by him in any school of the University.

The Archbishop of Canterbury assured the Duke of Devonshire that he had 'no intention of putting obstacles in the way of the . . . Bill which is on the whole from my point of view a very satisfactory proposal', but wanted further small amendments which were negotiated successfully after some intensive correspondence.[20]

There were to be Schools of the University, listed; and there were to be two categories of Teachers – those appointed directly by the University as Professors, Readers or Lecturers, and those Recognised by the University who were members of the staffs of public educational institutions situated within a thirty-mile radius of London. Though Sidney Webb lost his battle to have the Polytechnics included within the University, the Technical Education Board nonetheless formally approved the Bill.[21]

The new legislation gave Convocation more weight in the Senate and introduced

> an ingenious distinction in the way in which the Academic Council (for internal students) and the Council for External Students, are respectively formed, [which] places the control of the one in the hands of the faculties (the teachers) and the other in that of Convocation.[22]

---

[20] ED 24/5, Archbp of Canterbury to Devonshire, 24 July 1897; Bp of London to Devonshire, 19 July; Ilbert to Devonshire nd [24/5 July]; Haldane to Wace, 26 July 1897.
[21] ED 24/5, Garnett to Devonshire, 27 July 1897, enclosing Minute of Technical Education Board dated 26 July.
[22] ED 24/5. Note on suggested amendments, nd 1897.

The Chairman of Convocation was to be an *ex officio* member of Senate and a member of the Statutory Commission. But, as the *Journal of Education* stressed,

> The principle of uniformity and identity of test for all candidates is not only given up, but it is provided that (unless the Senate shall otherwise determine) separate examinations shall be held for external and internal students respectively, and each certificate or diploma shall state whether the candidate has passed as an internal or external candidate.[23]

And of course, Convocation would lose its veto.

The opposition within Convocation, for some time shared by the Gresham (1894) Scheme Amendment Committee, which originally had supported the idea of a unified University, and the London University Defence Committee, which had always opposed it, was split. Napier, who had succeeded Collins as Chairman of the Amendment Committee, and Busk, Chairman of Convocation, who had also defended the unified institution, accepted the new draft Bill as 'the best compromise now obtainable'. Both Committees held meetings on 16 July. There was apparently some confusion in the meeting of the Amendment Committee, which was reported as having only supported the Bill on the understanding that 'further specified safeguards should be inserted'. The London University Defence Committee, however, roundly condemned the Bill. It did not

> ... secure that the same high standard of graduation shall be impartially required alike for collegiate and non-collegiate students as heretofore, and ... the sacrifice of the veto of Convocation is not compensated by any adequate guarantees for securing the continuance of the present work of the University as an independent Examining Board for all candidates.

And the meeting called upon 'the Member for the University to oppose the Bill, if introduced'.[24]

The Secretaries of the Defence Committee asked the Duke of Devonshire, whom they had 'reason to believe ... had been imperfectly informed' of the extent of the strong opposition to the Bill, to receive a deputation.[25] The request was not met. No figures of attendance at the protest meetings were reported, and they were in all probability not large. But a new, moving spirit had appeared among the protesters, in the person of John Fletcher Moulton, QC, who took the chair of an *ad hoc* Committee of Graduates 'for the purpose

---

[23] *Jnl of Education*, August 1897.
[24] *Jnl of Education*, August 1897.
[25] ED 24/5, J.G. Joseph and A.L. Moore to Devonshire, 22 July 1897.

of strenuously opposing the Bill'.[26] Moulton had been Liberal MP for Battersea, Clapham, in 1885–86, and for South Hackney in 1894–95; and he had been a colleague of Collins on the LCC from 1893–95. He would become MP for N.E. Cornwall in 1898.

Late in July, Collins aligned himself with Moulton in a long letter which was widely circulated. It contained a succinct statement of what he felt was the opinion of the majority of 'those members of Convocation who have placed Mr Busk, Dr Napier and myself on the Senate', and is worth reproduction as representative of the views of the 'irreconcilables'.

> They favour the assumption of teaching powers by the University, but deprecate the principle of a teacher conducting degree examinations for his own pupils; they would regret the establishment of a second university in London but believe that unity can be purchased at too high a price by the surrender of the distinctive features of the University's present work. They think the infusion of representatives of Convocation into the Senate in 1858 was wise, and that the time has come for largely increasing their proportion; they distrust any change which would directly or indirectly work to the disadvantage of the private student; they believe the high standard of the pass degree and graduation thereon independently of collegiate certificates – which were 'abused and misused' in the past, and may be so again – do supply a public want; they fear that the adoption of the Cowper scheme must inevitably lead either to lowering or to variability of the standard of degrees, and they feel that the surrender of the veto of Convocation, in which the Chairman of Convocation and Dr Napier now concur, must inevitably facilitate undesirable and reactionary results.[27]

The Duke of Devonshire introduced the Bill in the Lords on 20 July. Only he and Kimberley spoke. Both stressed their hope that on this occasion the Bill would go through unopposed. The Duke assured the House that last year's problems over denominational colleges had been overcome, and that King's 'practically accepted' the solution offered. Kimberley took the view that the Bill was now in 'probably the only form in which it would be acceptable to all parties concerned'.[28] Their Lordships approved this and the Second Reading without further debate. The Bill went to Committee on 26 July, when minor amendments were made to meet most of the points which had been raised by the Archbishop of Canterbury. On the following day the bill was reported, received its Third Reading, and was sent to the Commons.[29]

---

[26] *Jnl of Education*, August 1897.
[27] UL Ms 812/153/18, Collins to Moulton, 26 July 1897.
[28] 4s Parl. Deb., vol. 51, col. 556.
[29] 4s Parl. Deb., vol. 51, cols 1062–4, 1205.

It would seem that, at this stage, the Ministers felt that the only real danger to the Bill in the Commons was the possible hostility of Sir John Lubbock. It is very likely that the acceptance of the compromise offered in the Bill by the Chairman of Convocation, and by so fierce a previous opponent as Napier, would have swung at least a clear majority of the membership of Convocation in favour of abandoning opposition. Lubbock was well aware of that likelihood, but he was on record as promising to oppose the legislation unless it was first approved by a vote open to all members of Convocation. Lubbock had been with a University delegation to Windsor on 10 July, and on 19 July he recorded in his diary a 'Conference with Busk, Benson, Napier, Haldane and Hopkinson about the University of London Bill. The Government are going to introduce it and I fear I must oppose.' On 22nd he saw the Duke and 'urged him to make [the Bill] subject to the approval of Convocation', and five days later, when the Lords passed the Bill, he met and pressed the same view on Balfour.[30]

Devonshire made a direct appeal to Lubbock.

> I understand that the fate of the University Bill now rests with you. I quite see the difficulties of your position but after the concessions which have been made to the Convocation party and the withdrawal of the opposition of Mr Napier and Mr Busk, I trust that you will be satisfied with an explanation and a protest if necessary. I hope that Balfour will be able to give the necessary time for this.[31]

But Lubbock maintained his position. And it became clear that he was by no means the only MP who would have to be persuaded to abstain from opposing the Bill. Even if he had withdrawn, it is by no means certain that others would have followed him into silence on the matter. And only silence would have allowed the Bill through: there was no time for extended debate. Lubbock wrote to Balfour on 30 July.

> My constituents are very keen about their right of being consulted before any change in the Charter is made. You have I know been told that the great majority of Convocation would support the present compromise. I am not prepared to deny this; but I feel satisfied that they would keenly resent its being carried without their consent; their rights being moreover swept away for the future.
>
> Even if the Bill is dropped I should be glad in the general interest of the University cause, if you could see your way to say that you would have inserted the few words necessary. My constituents as you know are scattered all over the country, and take a very active part in politics. I have spoken to Dilke as to whether the reference to Convocation would remove his opposition. He will consult those with whom he is acting and let you know.[32]

---

[30] BL Add Mss 62684, Lubbock's Diary, 10, 19, 22 & 27 July 1897.
[31] BL Add Mss 49663, Devonshire to Lubbock, 28 July 1897.
[32] BL Add Mss 49663, Lubbock to Balfour, 30 July 1897.

When Balfour introduced the Bill in the Commons on 29 July, he claimed that a majority of Convocation were in favour of the Scheme, and declared that he would 'greatly regret if opposition in this House should prevent [the Bill] being passed'. But immediately afterwards, Sir Charles Dilke gave notice that on Second Reading 'he would move that this House declines to proceed with the Bill in the present session, inasmuch as Convocation of London University has not yet assented to its provisions in their present form'.[33]

With whom Sir Charles Dilke was acting is by no means clear, and it is most likely that he was only one of several MPs who may well have been strongly influenced by Collins, but did not necessarily work together. Certainly Mears retailed to Collins how he had persuaded two legal colleagues who sat in the Commons – Atherley Jones and Lawson Walton – to be prepared to move the Second Reading of the Bill 'this day three months' hence. It is interesting that Mears had first written to Lubbock, but 'Not thinking him very reliable', had turned to others.[34]

As it happened, there was no need for Dilke or any of the other MPs to move against the Bill, for on 2 August the Government withdrew it.[35] Parliament rose four days afterwards.

[33] 4s Parl. Deb., vol. 51, cols 1483–4, 29 July 1897.
[34] UL Ms 812/14, Mears to Collins, 2 August 1897.
[35] 4s Parl. Deb., vol. 52, col. 168.

# 36

# *The insistence of Arthur Balfour*

It is very understandable that, after three Bills had been lost in successive years, there were those who felt reform of the University was not a priority of Government, and without being given that priority would always be thwarted in the House of Commons. Such feeling produced the last alternative Scheme to be publicised: it was proposed and supported, almost exclusively, by a sizeable group of teachers in the London Medical Schools.

The 'moving spirit' of the Scheme, which envisaged the establishment, by Charter, of a federal University of Westminster, quite separate from the existing University of London, was Dr J. Kingston Fowler, Physician to the Middlesex Hospital. One of his more influential colleagues in the venture was Isambard Owen of St George's Hospital Medical School.[1] The idea came from a suggestion made in October, 1895, by the Lord Chief Justice, Lord Russell of Killowen, to the Council of Legal Education.[2] Russell had proposed an Inns of Court Law School, separately or in connection with a University, to grant degrees in Law. Kingston and his collaborators – 'representative members of the teaching staffs' of nine Medical Schools – built on the notion, and planned a University which was in effect a federation of Faculties. A printed prospectus was widely circulated, and attracted a good deal of correspondence in the *Times*. By early December, 1897, a list of 153 supporters was published. All but a very few were doctors; among them one or two Deans, signing in their personal, not their official, capacities.[3]

But this grass-roots medical initiative came too late. The governing bodies of the Medical Schools and the Royal Colleges were unmoved by it. The *Lancet* gave it little coverage, and proclaimed that 'It would serve no practical purpose to discuss the scheme in detail.'[4] The *British Medical Journal*, mouthpiece of the British Medical Association, reported the Scheme at length without supporting it. And the *Journal* carried an exchange of letters between

[1] UL Ms 812/119, Poore to Bompas, 13 December 1897. UL RC/43/21, Owen to Dickins, 10 November 1897.
[2] *BMJ*, 8 January 1898.
[3] For the printed Scheme, see UL RC 43/21. For lists of supporters, see *BMJ*, 20, 27 November & 4 December 1897.
[4] *Lancet*, 4 December 1897.

Kingston Fowler and Pye-Smith, in which the latter dismissed the University of Westminster idea as 'inchoate' and 'stillborn', stressing the strength of agreement among institutions in favour of the Bill, and arguing that only a unified University would attract endowments for research.[5]

What influence the University of Westminster proposal had on the actual course of events is difficult to judge. As the *British Medical Journal* commented,

> If . . . its promulgation shall have the effect of impressing upon those who are in favour of the compromise contained in the Bill of last year, it will at least have served a useful purpose.[6]

Unfortunately, there seems to be no record of when or how the University of Westminster idea was received at the Privy Council Office. But as the printed version of the Scheme was not sent to the University until early November, it is unlikely that any hint of it had reached Ministers as early as mid-October, when Haldane wrote to Balfour. Nor did Haldane then make any mention of it.

Haldane may well have already had an understanding with Balfour and Devonshire about the need to re-introduce the Bill early in the next session, by the time he wrote to Balfour on 16 October 1897.

> . . . I gather that the Senate stands firm in its approval of the Bill as arranged, and that the majority of Convocation takes the same view. There are one or two trifling changes that may be made with advantage in the clauses, one especially which would please Wace and King's College, and which the other people would concede. However, I have no reason to think that King's College is otherwise than friendly.
>
> Now as to the opposition. Dilke told me that he should probably not oppose the Bill if brought in fairly early next session. However I never believe a word he says. The real opposition comes from Dr Collins and Fletcher Moulton. I do not think they can get any substantial support in the House, for the Bill is strongly supported by Herschell, Bryce, Acland, Stuart, Cozens-Hardy and all our leading people, now that the Church difficulty has been satisfactorily settled. Lubbock is of course in two minds, and he will have to make some show of opposition but I believe he would be heartily glad to see the matter disposed of. The attitude of Collins and Moulton is that they do not want any change at all – a position which the Cowper Commission negatived with the approval of every learned body in London . . .
>
> As regards time two hours ought to do for the Second Reading, and a night for the Committee. The grounds on which substantial opposition can be made are few. Dillon says his Irish will not oppose and I think I can do something with Healy, whom I saw before the House rose. As for Redmond he hates the Irish priests and is probably unconcerned – but I have not sounded him.[7]

---

[5] *BMJ*, 20 November, 18 & 25 December 1897; 1, 8 & 15 January 1898.
[6] *BMJ*, 4 December 1897.
[7] BL Add Mss 49724, Haldane to Balfour, 16 October 1897.

As will be seen, Haldane was a little over sanguine about both timing and opposition. But immediately, he must have been happy with Balfour's response. The latter would 'much like to put this London University question out of the way', and thought that Haldane's view 'seems satisfactory and re-assuring'. He would talk to Devonshire in November.[8]

Convocation had seemingly lost interest, at least for the time being, for a meeting called for 15 October did not attract a quorum. Senate showed more concern, and on a motion of Anstie resolved, on 1 December, to request the Chancellor to convene a meeting of the delegates of the institutions backing the Bill, and the Special Committee of Convocation, to consider what to do next to promote the legislation. But the main event of the period was the Duke of Devonshire's speech to the Royal Society, on 30 November, perhaps shaped after discussions with Balfour, in which he put 'in the forefront' of Government intentions the creation of a Teaching University for London.[9] Whether or not the Ministers had been persuaded of the need to make a firm commitment by the prospect of agitation for an alternative scheme, the Duke's announcement may have been the cause of a declaration, a week or so later, by the 'University of Westminster organization' that they had decided not to oppose a Bill if it were introduced in the coming Session, but would urge a 'more decided course of action' if no settlement was reached.[10] In fact, after the first week or two of the New Year, no more was heard of the University of Westminster. As the University College Gazette put it, rather brutally, at the beginning of February, 'It may well be doubted whether the scheme ever had any life, at all events it is dead now.'[11]

The meeting of representatives of all the institutions supportive of the legislation, which met at the University in mid-December, passed no resolutions, but decided to send a deputation to the Duke of Devonshire, to press for the re-introduction of the Bill. In the weeks following the December meeting, the Senate, the Royal Colleges and several Medical Schools each met and reiterated their support, combining that, in the case of the Medical Schools, with provisos about the desirability of seeking some minor amendments to the Bill of 1897. On 17 January 1898, 156 members turned out for the meeting of Convocation, at which Benson carried a motion in support of legislation by seventy-six to forty-two, defeating an amendment which called for delay and consultation with Convocation.

On 24 January, the Duke of Devonshire met the delegates of the interests supportive of legislation and assured them that a Bill would be introduced. But

---

[8] BL Add Mss 49724, Balfour to Haldane, 18 October 1897.
[9] BMJ, 4 December 1897.
[10] BMJ, 18 December 1897.
[11] University College Gazette, 3 February 1898.

he still did not give an unequivocal assurance of Government backing. As the *British Medical Journal* put it,

> The Duke . . . is pledged to introduce the Bill and to urge upon his colleagues (by which paraphrase we may suppose that he meant the Leader of the House of Commons) so to arrange the course of public business . . . as to find time for discussing the Bill at an early date.

And as there was no guarantee that the Bill would be forced through the Commons, the *Journal's* Editor recomended that

> . . . those who are actively engaged in promoting the passage of the Bill would be well advised at once to seek the support and enlist the interest of the metropolitan members of Parliament . . . this is not a party question, and it is understood that Mr Balfour has even relied upon this fact to excuse him from the necessity of making a House and carrying the Bill on a division. It is pretty certain that if the metropolitan members of Parliament could be brought to see that the passage of the Bill into law would redound to the credit and honour of London, time would be found for its discussion and a majority in its favour.[12]

This advice was taken, initially by the Royal Colleges and the Medical Schools, who were reported, on 19 February, as 'arranging to interview the metropolitan members of Parliament'. It was considered likely that the first contact would be with the London Unionist MPs, who were 'organized as a Committee for dealing with questions affecting the welfare of London', but that 'the deputation will seek to enlist the sympathy of London members of all parties . . .'[13] Whether or not other parties were contacted, a widely representative deputation, made up of Allchin and Frederick Taylor from the Medical Colleges and Schools; Rotton from UCL; the new Principal of King's, Rev. Archibald Robertson, successor to Dr Wace; Rev. Vincent Price from the Theological Colleges, and Dr Thomas Boor Crosby from the Corporation of the City of London, met twenty Unionist MPs, with W.F.D. Smith in the Chair, on 28 March. It was well timed, for the Bill had by then reached the House of Commons.[14]

The Duke of Devonshire does seem to have been quite uncertain about the prospects of the Bill in mid-January, for he told Lubbock that though he was due to meet the deputation from the interested parties on 24th he did 'not know that I shall have any definite statement to make to them'. Lubbock met him on 21st and pressed his opposition to the proposed legislation, no doubt quoting the relatively modest vote in Convocation, a few days earlier,

---

[12] *BMJ*, 29 January 1898.
[13] *BMJ*, 19 February 1898.
[14] *BMJ*, 2 April 1898.

which had turned down consultation of the whole membership. But all he received was a promise from the Duke that the matter would be considered.[15] And when the Duke introduced the Bill in the Lords on 21 February, it contained no significant concessions to the opposition.

The Lords gave the Bill its Second Reading on 4 March.[16] The Duke spoke strongly in its favour, and was supported by Herschell and Reay. A week later, in Committee, the Duke announced that Lord Lister, who 'was, for certain reasons, not anxious to be re-nominated', as a member of the Statutory Commission, would be replaced by Michael Foster. Three peers pleaded for the inclusion of Wye College among Schools whose students would be regarded as internal. Wye, a specialist agricultural College, lay well outside the area defined in the Bill for such Schools. The Duke resisted amendment, but promised to consider the problem. The Archbishop of Canterbury successfully moved an amendment to ensure that the Academic Council would be consulted in regard to the appointment of University teachers; but he failed to persuade the House to modify the clause which required that separate examinations for internal and external students should represent the same standard of knowledge and attainment, by adding the words 'as far as possible'.[17] On 17 March, when the Committee's report was received, the Duke moved a tiny technical amendment, which was accepted; on the next day the Bill was read a third time, without debate, and was sent on its way to the Commons.[18]

But five days earlier, and for the second time in three years, the opponents of the Bill were given an ideal opportunity to take the battle to the whole Convocation electorate. On 13 March 1898, the veteran Fellow, Sir Richard Quain, died, creating a vacancy which would be filled after an election by Convocation. And to the consternation of the sponsors and supporters of the Bill, though the First Reading in the House of Commons took place on 21 March, the crucial debate on the Second Reading was delayed until 14 June. The election was decided on 24 May.

In the interval between Readings, an indication of what the opposition regarded as a very controversial aspect of the Bill was the notice given by Ellis Griffith of his intention to move rejection, 'on the grounds that under the scheme the same degree would be obtained after two different sets of examinations'.[19] Two petitions against the Bill were laid on the table; one in the name of Clair James Grece, a solicitor from Redhill, who had served on

---

[15] BL Add Mss 49664, Devonshire to Lubbock, 16 January, Collier to Lubbock, 18 January; Add Mss 62684, Lubbock's Diary, 22 January 1898.
[16] 4s Parl. Deb., vol. 54, cols 589–96.
[17] 4s Parl. Deb., vol. 54, cols 1162–70, 10 March 1898.
[18] 4s Parl. Deb., vol. 55, cols 83, 227.
[19] BMJ, 9 April 1898.

the Annual Committee from 1876–79, and the other from Nottingham. There were anxious questions to Balfour about the date of the Second Reading. Lord Kimberley was worried enough to press the Duke of Devonshire about progress. The Duke explained that the Irish Local Government Bill was dominating work in the Commons, and that as soon as it was out of the way the London University Bill would 'have a prominent place amongst those measures which the Government intend to endeavour to pass during the remainder of the Session', – which was a rather stronger assurance of determination than he had ever given before.[20] It came on 9 May, just five days before the election of the new Fellow.

Collins was not in the Commons, and John Fletcher Moulton would re-enter the House only in August, 1898, as a Radical MP for Launceston, too late to take any part in the debates on the London University Commission Bill. But Moulton was the natural candidate for election to the University's Senate, as a leader of the opposition to the Bill. It is a mark of the break between the moderate opponents of the earlier Bills, now supportive of the compromise Scheme, and the 'irreconcilables', that one of the former, rather than a long-term proponent of legislation, was chosen to contest the vacant seat. Moreover, that candidate was J.B. Benson, who was Lubbock's agent, and the peculiar mix of personal motives and relationships involved in the whole affair is illustrated by the fact that Lubbock offered to help to meet Benson's election expenses. Benson, however, was 'not sure it would be right as I gather you are not altogether at one with us in recommending the compromise to Convocation'.[21]

Benson was both self-deprecatory and unconfident about the election. In the same letter to Lubbock, he explained that

> I have lent my name, under protest, to Busk and Napier, who considered that this vacancy must be fought for the compromise and could not find another candidate. In doing so I felt and still feel myself something of a victim to circumstances, expecting to be beaten, altho' we ought to win, because in this contest we cannot hope to do more than lay the foundation for the future conversion of the constituency to a dual University with separate examinations for the two Sides, an idea not yet generally grasped.

And he complained bitterly, and was not alone in doing so, about the tactics of the 'irreconcilables'. Mr Moulton 'has just written an absolute misrepresentation of the purport and effect of the Bill which will doubtless catch many votes'. Benson was a Fellow and Member of Council of University

---

[20] 4s Parl. Deb., vol. 546, cols 301, 644, 1185, 1403; vol. 57, col. 657; vol. 58, cols 1249–50; vol. 59, col. 59.
[21] BL Add Mss 49664, Benson to Lubbock, 12 May 1898.

College London. The College's *Gazette* criticised Moulton, who had 'suddenly come upon the scene' and whose address showed that 'he has not had time to master the ordinary facts of the case and fails to understand the aim of the reform'.[22]

Convocation's regular attenders were clearly unenthusiastic about the whole situation. At the Annual Meeting on 10 May, there was a delayed start because of the lack of a quorum. With only eighty present, it was resolved, by twenty votes to thirteen, many members abstaining, that Convocation should recommend Government to take the sense of the House of Commons on the Bill in a division.[23] The poor attendance may well have indicated indifference – or even an acceptance of probable defeat in the impending election – by the overwhelmingly London-based members. Three days before the votes were to be counted Moulton was seen as the favourite, attracting 'a very considerable majority of country graduates whilst almost every graduate who is a London teacher is supporting Dr Benson'. A count of signatories in support of candidates gave, at that stage, 1315 to Moulton and only 538 to Benson.[24]

The forecast was correct, but by a far smaller margin. When the votes were counted, Moulton had 1344, Benson 1139, and the make-up candidate, Pasco Daphne, fifteen. In the three elections of 1895, 1896 and 1898, the 'opposition' candidates had recorded 1231, 963 and 1344 votes: the candidates supportive of the Bill received 733, 846 and 1139. In 1898, with a turn-out a quarter larger than in 1895, the opposition majority was reduced from five hundred to two hundred. The 'irreconcilables' claimed a moral as well as a numerical victory. But the result was fairly close: that, and voting by not much more than half the members of Convocation, made subsequent appeals to it, from either side, relatively innocuous.

The London University Commission Bill came before the House of Commons for its Second Reading on 14 June 1898.[25] For the first time, after three Bills had been withdrawn, the issue of principle was put before the elected House. The occasion has been described frequently as momentous, principally because of the praise heaped upon Haldane's speech, which received no special notice in the papers, but certainly impressed Asquith and Chamberlain, and probably influenced MPs who may have been uncommitted to become supporters of the Bill. There is no room for doubt about Haldane's major contribution to the whole process of seeking a compromise and helping to have it confirmed. But in the most measured account of his role, the debate on 14 June was judged

[22] *University College Gazette*, 10 May 1898.
[23] *BMJ*, 14 May 1898.
[24] *Lancet*, 21 May; *BMJ*, 21 May 1898.
[25] 4s Parl. Deb., vol. 59, cols 233–304.

to have been 'not quite as dramatic as Haldane (and some of his biographers who followed Haldane's own version of it) made out'.[26]

The debate began at about 5.30 p.m. and ran for five hours. There were thirteen speakers. Sir John Gorst opened with a comprehensive survey of the saga of the previous decade and a reiteration of all the arguments in favour of the Bill, in the course of which he briefly denied the validity of the claim for any special consultation of the full membership of Convocation. Then followed the main opposition speeches by George Harwood, MP for Bolton, and J.H. Yoxall, MP for Nottingham West. Harwood owned a cotton spinning firm, was a graduate of London, educated at Owens College, and described himself as an Independent Liberal. Yoxall, a Liberal, was General Secretary, and a previous President, of the National Union of Teachers, and had been a member of the recent Royal Commission on Secondary Education.

The main thrust of their arguments was based on their conviction that any kind of federal or confederal arrangement was weak and impracticable. For them there was no sign of appropriate financial provision, and, for them, the institution proposed did not feel like a University – it had no imposing buildings. More in line with many subsequent speakers' concerns, they were acutely anxious about what they saw as the impossibility of degrees being comparable for students preparing for examinations under very different conditions. In short, they despaired of the enterprise and thought that it should be dropped altogether. But, interestingly, neither made any mention of Convocation.

It was at this point that Haldane

> . . . weighed in with a powerful defence. The context of his speech was predictable. It was a careful and reasoned argument for a teaching university in London: to bring distinguished professors into the metropolis; to extend to the 'working classes' opportunities for higher education already enjoyed by their European cousins; to improve technical education so that Britain could stand up better against foreign competition in trade; a bill essential for 'catching up' (as he put it) with other capital cities.[27]

Like Gorst, Haldane played down the opposition from within Convocation, describing it as a 'diminishing majority'. And he, too, denied Convocation's right to override a necessary reform. Lubbock followed, put up his strongest plea for further consultation with Convocation, and deplored the proposed loss of their veto. Bryce responded, criticised Lubbock quite sharply, and supported the Bill as only a start on a long reconstruction of the University.

Of seven remaining speakers, only Captain Norton (Newington West) was unequivocally hostile. Carvell Williams took the opportunity to rail against

---

[26] Ashley and Anderson, *Portrait of Haldane*, pp. 36–8.
[27] Ashley and Anderson, *Portrait of Haldane*, p. 37.

the denominational aspects of KCL; Ernest Gray (West Ham North), who was Secretary to the Education Committee of the NUT and also a previous President of that body, though generally supportive, emphasised Yoxall's worries about the possibility that separate degrees might disadvantage external students; and Robert Wallace (Edinburgh East), a one-time Professor of Church History, rambled around the subject uncertainly, but without showing definite hostility. Two others spoke in strong support as, briefly, did Balfour, who tactfully suggested that the debate might conclude.

At once, the amendment to postpone the consideration of the Bill was withdrawn, and the Bill was given its Second Reading, without a division. This tame outcome does not seem to have been commented upon, subse-quently, by any of those who have written about the passage of the Bill. But it is surely worth asking why, after all the doubts expressed in previous Sessions about the likely fatal effect of opposition in the Commons, was that opposition so pitifully weak?

There is no indication anywhere of attendance in the House during the debate. There was some further business to come after the Bill, and doubtless the Whips were alert to avoid any likelihood of loss of quorum. And despite Balfour's earlier reported reluctance to ensure that a House should be 'kept' for the purposes of seeing the Bill through, there is a hint in his speech at the end of the debate that this reluctance was something of a pretence. Balfour commented that the debate had been dominated by Liberal speakers; in fact the only exceptions, Balfour apart, were Gray, a Conservative, and H.C. Richards, MP for Finsbury East, who described himself as a Democratic Tory, and was in favour of the Bill. Balfour went on to say that the supporters of the Government present, were 'almost to a man . . . supporters of the Bill'. Perhaps, therefore, it is not unreasonable to think that some quiet pressure was in fact exerted on his followers by the Leader of the House. It may well be that those opposed saw themselves to be so heavily outnumbered by Conservative and Unionist Members, that they wished to avoid the humiliation of heavy defeat in a division.

But if the Second Reading was an apparent disaster for the opponents, it did not reveal their full extent in the House, nor did it deter them from an intense and persistent campaign to have the Bill modified. On the other hand, neither did the Second Reading debate indicate, except in Balfour's rather cryptic remarks, that, once the Bill had been accepted in principle, it would seem to have become a measure which the Government were determined to see through to the Statute Book. Even though it was not a formal part of the political programme of the Conservative and Liberal Unionist Coalition, the Bill's subsequent stages were marked by a ruthless determination to concede nothing to those who wished to amend or delay it.

What was possibly the most serious threat to the Bill came from Irish inter-ests, but was negotiated outside the Chamber and the Committee Room, and will be dealt with a little later. In the House, the Bill was sent to the

Standing Committee on Law, Courts of Justice and Legal Procedure. The initial, core membership of Standing Committees was decided by a Committee of Selection at the beginning of the Session, and the Committee on Law had sixty-eight members. But for each Bill to be considered, it was normal practice to add fifteen members, and it can safely be assumed that MPs who had a particular interest in the Bill could usually persuade the Selection Committee to include them in the fifteen. In this case, Haldane and Norton were already core members. Those added included Bryce, Gorst, Harwood, Lubbock, Brynmor Jones, Sir Albert Rollit and Yoxall, so that ten of those who had spoken in the Second Reading debate were members of the Standing Committee, whose total membership was eighty-four. Party strengths in the House were proportionate in the Committee, so that there were fifty-one Conservatives and Liberal Unionists, as opposed to thirty-three Liberals, Radicals and Irish Nationalists.

But like the University's Senate, the Law Committee's meetings did not attract its full membership. At the three sessions at which the Bill was debated, on 12th, 15th and 19 July, there were attendances of forty-four, forty-one and forty-three respectively, shared between fifty-two MPs. All fifteen of the additional members attended. Government supporters were still clearly dominant – thirty-four Conservatives and Liberal Unionists, against eighteen Liberals, Radicals and Irish Nationalists.

In the clause-by-clause discussion, there were thirty-three proposed amendments, and on sixteen the Committee divided. All but the Chairman and three other members voted at least once. The results were as disastrous for the opponents of the Bill as had been the Second Reading. No change of any substance was made, and the only close vote was over the requirement that 'each certificate and diploma shall state whether the candidate has passed as an internal or as an external student'. Those opposed to its inclusion numbered fifteen, but the Government had seventeen supporters. In the other fifteen divisions the votes of the opponents of the Bill only twice reached double figures. There was but a small group who offered most resistance – Harwood, who moved no less than sixteen amendments, Dilke, Lubbock, Norton, Healy, Yoxall, Atherley Jones (Durham North West), Charles Hare Hemphill (Tyrone North), and John Lloyd Morgan (Carmarthen). The three last named were Home Rule Liberals. Lubbock and Norton were the only Londoners. They were joined quite often by two Conservatives, Sir Albert Rollit and Sir Barrington Simeon (Southampton), who divided their votes almost equally between majority and minority positions.

Those trying to amend the Bill, with the exception of Lubbock, were thus predominantly non-London Liberals, Radicals or Irish Nationalists. Those defending the Bill were a mixed group in political party terms. Persistent Liberal support came from Bryce, Cozens-Hardy, Lord Edmund Fitzmaurice, Haldane, Brynmor Jones, and Arthur Pease. At the same time, Gorst and the Solicitor General, Sir Robert Finlay, led a Conservative and Liberal Unionist contingent among whom F.S.W. Cornwallis (Maidstone), H.R. Graham (St

Pancras West), Augustus Helder (Whitehaven), Staveley Hill (Staffordshire), C.J. Monk (Gloucester), Sir William Priestley (Edinburgh and St Andrew's Universities), W.F.D. Smith (Strand), J.G. Talbot (Oxford University), and A.F. Warr (Liverpool East Toxteth), were present at most divisions.

But despite Liberal support, the hard fact is that there were about thirty Conservative and Liberal Unionist members of the Committee who voted to protect the Bill against amendment. How many of them were acting as genuinely non-partisan supporters of a reformed London University, and how many were Government MPs simply giving instinctive loyalty to a Government measure, cannot be estimated with any real accuracy. Excluding Rollit who, as we have seen, picked and chose between amendments, there were only six London Conservative MPs who took part in the Committee's proceedings. They gave their support to the Bill, but again, whether they were voting as Government supporters or were responding to the pleas of the delegation which had sought their votes, is matter for conjecture.

Such doubts about motivation can be dismissed in the context of the last Commons' stages of the Bill. Harwood, Lubbock and their friends were determined opponents, and when the Bill was reported out and brought forward for its Third Reading, on 25 July, they mounted a rearguard action which lasted until 2.30 a.m. on the following morning. They moved many amendments, and forced the House to divide no less than eleven times. And they demonstrated that their support in the House was limited but by no means negligible, though every challenge they made was defeated. The votes they delivered on the ten amendments they proposed were, in order, eighty-seven, eighty-one, forty-four, thirty, forty-one, forty-six, sixty-eight, seventy-two, forty-eight, forty-six, and twenty-four. Only on the Third Reading did they drop to nineteen. In contrast the majority votes ranged from 198 to 104.

It is quite clear that the Government was determined to have the Bill passed unamended, and was able to put as many as 198, and never less than 104, supporters into the division lobbies. Moreover, though a press report credited the minority with having 'gallantly if hopelessly renewed' the points they had raised in the Committee, it also recorded an unflattering account of the legislative process:

> The figures in these . . . divisions during the long debate do not . . . represent the members present through the sitting and likely to be influenced by the arguments submitted. At sound of the division bell the majority streamed in from the tea room, the terrace, the smoking room and other places of popular resort, unhesitatingly voting on the instruction of the Whips. Mr Labouchere frankly confessed that in common with the large majority of members he knew very little of the Bill. In fact, according to this authority, the only persons who thoroughly understood the question were Sir John Gorst and Mr Haldane.[28]

[28] *Daily News*, 28 July 1898.

Examination of the largest votes cast – eighty-seven and 198 – for each side, reveals only very limited cross-party voting. Of the eighty-seven votes for an amendment, only six were cast by Conservatives, and one by a Liberal Unionist – Lubbock: the rest were overwhelmingly cast by Liberals, together with eight Radicals, eight Irish Nationalists of various kinds, and one Welsh Nationalist – David Lloyd George. The majority vote of 198 included only twenty Liberals and one Irish Nationalist: there were, however, some thirty London MPs among them – all but one Conservatives – which may indicate that the attempt to lobby them was entirely justified.

Given that the whips were on, it is dangerous to read too much into the figures of voting on individual items. But it is worth notice that the largest defeat was inflicted on the proposal that two London graduates, nominated by Convocation, should be added to the Statutory Commission. And Lubbock's attempt to have Convocation's veto preserved was defeated by 158 to thirty – after attracting one of the lowest of the minority's votes. Lubbock remained true to his promise and voted against the Third Reading: he was the only Government supporter to do so.

The Bill went back to the House of Lords, where the Commons' amendments were accepted without debate on 2 August. The Royal Assent was given on 12 August.[29] The Bill became the University of London Act, 1898, 61 & 62 Vic ch 62.

Balfour must have made the decision to ensure that the Bill was forced through the House of Commons at the latest after the successful Second Reading and Committee stages, and possibly before. He certainly had the power to overcome much heavier opposition than was encountered, but he may have been relieved of much harder defiance by the diplomacy which Haldane exercised in dealing with a potential revolt by the Irish Nationalists. For many years the latter had been increasingly aggrieved by the failure of attempts to achieve the establishment of a National University which would meet the aspirations of the Roman Catholic majority, who did not wish, or were unable, to enter Trinity College, Dublin, and wanted more than was offered by the Royal University of Ireland, an examining board similar in its basic operation to the University of London.

A sign of the possibility of trouble was reported in the *Lancet* of 30 April 1898, quoting an article in the *Daily Nation*, Dublin, which made a 'passionate appeal to Irish representatives to unite in strenuously opposing the University of London Bill'.[30] By early July, in the course of some largely technical quibbling about whether a money clause in the Bill should have been sanctioned by a Committee of the Whole House, T.M. Healy told Gorst that

---

[29]  4s Parl. Deb., vol. 63, col. 811; vol. 65, col. 4.
[30]  *Daily Nation*, 26 April 1898.

We have again and again been refused a University for Ireland, and therefore we are adopting now this 'dog-in-the-manger' principle to the effect that if you will not allow us to have a University we will not allow you to have yours.[31]

This was only a few days before the Bill was due in Standing Committee. According to Haldane's biographers,

Tim Healey appeared at the head of the Irish members of the committee, and in private parley with Haldane made it clear that the vital Irish vote would be witheld unless something was done to improve higher education in Ireland. Haldane, with evident relish, describes the sequel in his autobiography. Very well: if this was to be the price of the Irish vote, he would pay the price. He would himself go to Ireland privately and of course unofficially, to discuss and work out reforms in the Irish Universities acts, and he would steer them through parliament . . . He approached Balfour and secured his authority to try his hand at direct negotiations with the Irish. During the summer of 1898 he made himself familiar . . . with the problem; and early in October he slipped away to Dublin with a plan . . . in his pocket.

And the plan, after meetings which were described as 'bizarre even for Ireland', proved acceptable and 'laid the foundation for a reform of Irish higher education which was enacted ten years later'.[32]

While Haldane's success in Ireland was clearly remarkable, the account given above of what happened in the Committee stage of the Bill in June, 1898, raises some questions. There were only five Irish MPs on the Standing Committee, and, of them, only Healey attended its meetings on the Bill. Thus one wonders about the 'vital Irish vote', and how much of a threat its witholding would have constituted in the Committee. There were about eighty Nationalists in the House, but of various persuasions, and if – a rather large if – they had all turned out to vote at Report stage, a serious threat might have been posed. Even so, Balfour's whips, who ensured the presence of as many as 198 supporters, and never less than 104, during the final debate, could surely have guaranteed success for the Bill. In fact, only seven Irish Members were among the eighty-seven MPs who made up the largest minority vote in favour of amending the Bill at Report stage, and only four voted against the Third Reading.

No doubt a deal was done with Healey and his friends, before the Committee stage began, and a promise was given to consider the Irish University question. But whether, if the deal had been refused, Healey could have brought a halt to the Bill's progress, as opposed to causing one more

---

[31] 4s Parl. Deb., vol. 61, col. 79, 7 July 1898.
[32] Ashley and Anderson, *Portrait of Haldane*, p. 38.

parliamentary row; and whether such a prospect worried Balfour very much, must be a matter for considerable doubt.

In retrospect, the London University Act of 1898 was a messy compromise, reached after a tiresome delay compounded of official timidity and the persistent reiteration of what the *Morning Post*, in a passage which probably reflected accurately the increasing boredom of the national press with the whole affair, described as 'threadbare arguments' against the proposals for change.[33]

Insofar as those arguments concerned Convocation, its moderate defenders could claim, fairly, that by comparison with what had been offered in the first Bill, introduced in 1895, they had achieved a notable strengthening of its position in terms of its representation in the Senate and in the protection which was built-in to the structure of the University for the continuation of the status, the examination and the award of degrees to external students. But the 'irreconcilables' were left with little to comfort them. In constitutional terms they lost the one major power which Convocation had hitherto possessed – the veto; and they lost it emphatically, to the bitter and scornful criticism of the great majority of the political establishment. Nonetheless, it is interesting to wonder, had Convocation not cast its vote against the changes proposed in May, 1891, how long the University of London might have remained a chartered institution with the possibility that its graduates could hold a veto to its head.

But it is significant that while Convocation did not attract the sympathy of Parliament and of much official and academic opinion, the discontent of the 'irreconcilables' over what they saw as the problem of the relationship between internal and external degrees was genuine, heart-felt, and did not go away. The proposal, which was carried into effect, that the same degrees could be given to candidates who had studied and been examined for them in quite different modes, had been argued at length for years. By 1897, the *Educational Times*, journal of the College of Preceptors, encapsulated the opposition thus:

> With two different examinations for the same degrees – an unheard of and a fantastic device – it would be inevitable that one would be pitted against the other. There would be comparisons, and rivalries, and confusions, and a constant derogation from the dignity of the University.[34]

Three years later, just before the old order would give way to the new, a letter was sent to the incoming Chancellor, Lord Kimberley, almost cetainly by the Registrar, warning him of problems ahead.

---

[33] *Morning Post*, 15 June 1898.
[34] *Educational Times*, 1 September 1897.

... there are very serious and deep divisions of opinion in circles professedly and really academic, and in particular there exists a strong feeling opposed to the development of the internal side of the University, which is the very object of its reorganization under the Act of 1898. This feeling ... rests only or mainly on two suppositions (a) that the interests of the present Graduates will be affected by a lowering of the Standards of Examination (b) that the interests of the so-called private student will be sacrificed to those of the internal or professorial student in other words to the interests of the professoriate. I do not believe there is the slightest justification for this feeling, but it exists and is certain to lead to discussions that may become both factious and embittered, to discussions also in which for various reasons the party adverse to the internal or collegiate side may have the advantage, commanding as that party does the votes of the great majority of Graduates in Arts who are mostly non-collegiate and little interested in the collegiate side of the University. The question is indeed less one between external and internal Graduates or students than between Graduates or students in Arts and Laws on the one hand and in Science and Medicine on the other.[35]

After a century of tremendous development of the extent, facilities and techniques of external study, by correspondence, by distance learning, through the Open University and the internet, the anxieties of the private Arts and Laws Graduates and their champions in 1900 may seem irrational and exaggerated. And so, perhaps, they were. But even today there is plenty of discussion of the varying merits of different types of study and of educational organisation. As in the past, much of it is politely concealed from public discourse. But while the scorn with which, in the 1890s, the 'provincial Arts graduates' were regarded by the collegiate enthusiasts of the metropolis, has been greatly diluted, can one deny that doubts are still expressed, at least informally, in academic circles as to the the comparability of standards achievable in 'internal' and 'external' contexts?

Perhaps it was the real achievement of those who fought against the reform of the University of London that by doing so they gave protection – maybe too much protection – to the interests of the 'private students' at a time when the development of provision for them on a larger scale was still in its relative infancy. The Registrar, in 1900, was justified in defending the integrity of the professoriate against the doubts of the sceptical supporters of the private students: but he was, surely, also wise in recognising that the feelings of the sceptics existed and should be recognised. He was in good company.

Beatrice Webb tells how

Haldane ... would willingly have scrapped the system of external examinations by which alone London University awarded its coveted degrees. In his eyes, even the

---

[35] UL RC 27/16, 1 August 1900. Copy of letter to Kimberley, on official University paper, unsigned. Not from the Vice-Chancellor, and therefore almost certainly from the Registrar.

best equipped public library, and the most highly organized evening classes, counted for nothing in comparison with the inspiration he had found in personal intimacy with Stuart Blackie and Lotze [his teachers at Edinburgh and Gottingen]. But he realised, under Sidney's influence, if not the undesirability, at any rate the political unpracticability, of overthrowing what had already taken deep roots . . .

[Sidney Webb] on the other hand, with little formal schooling, had known what it was to gain education in adolescence whilst earning a livelihood; he realised the advantages of guidance and attraction that were, by a series of university examinations, brought to bear on myriads of lonely students, to most of whom a full-time undergraduate career, not to mention a residential university, was not within sight.[36]

Sophie Bryant, one of the earliest women graduates of the University, its first female DSc, and successor to the formidable Miss Buss as Head of the North London Collegiate, might be allowed the last word on understanding the passions of the 'irreconcilables'. In a short memoir of her, the writer recalls

. . . the long tussle concerning the two classes of students in The University, The Internes and the Externes. In this matter she was inclined, from the circumstances of her life, to hold the balance very steadily, to regard the two classes as equally important, but to maintain that the original motive of The University made Externes its special feature.[37]

[36] Beatrice Webb, *Our Partnership* (London, 1948), pp. 99–100.
[37] An Old North Londoner, *Mrs Sophie Bryant* (London, 1922), p. 19.

# 37

# *New era – old divisions*

It took twenty-six months, after the Royal Assent was given to the London University Act, to complete all the subordinate legislation and to make the final arrangements for the launch of the redesigned University. The country was at war in South Africa throughout most of that period, but that does not appear to have delayed the academic realignment. The Senate and Convocation each had their own interests to protect when the Statutory Commission was drawing up Statutes and Regulations, though the inclusion of so many basic constitutional provisions in the Schedule to the Act made the task of the Commission far less controversial and much less time-taking than it might have been.

The Commission suffered the loss of Sir William Roberts, who died in April, 1899: he was replaced by another prominent medico, Thomas Barlow, Professor at UCL. The Commissioners invited comment from Senate and Convocation, among other bodies, as they began their work, in the early autumn of 1898, and concentrated, initially, on the establishment and representation of Faculties. They presented a first batch of draft Statutes and Regulations in May, 1899, and received recommendations from Senate and Convocation on them and later additions, until the autumn. They finished their task early in the New Year, and submitted the Statutes and Regulations, together with a Report and some Correspondence, during February, 1900.[1]

Both Senate and Convocation set up Committees to pursue their concerns. The Senate's was called the Special Committee for Assisting the Statutory Commission. It was appointed on 3 August 1898; and it was clear that the majority present were unforgiving of the 'irreconcilables', for when Napier proposed the inclusion of Collins he could not find a seconder. The first meeting of the Committee did not take place until 25 November, and, two days before, Magnus was added to its membership. There were only five sessions – in November, December and January, and then in May and June, 1899. Roscoe, Anstie, Fitch, Milman, Magnus and Rucker were almost

---

[1] Report to accompany Statutes and Regulations made by the Commissioners appointed under the University of London Act, 1898, together with an Appendix of Correspondence. PP lxvi, Cd 83, 1900.

always in attendance; Pye-Smith, Routh and Thorpe less so. The Chancellor (Kimberley) came to the last two sessions.

Convocation's experience in this context was somewhat embarrassing. They had appointed, as long ago as May, 1895, a Special Committee on a Memorandum to be presented to the Statutory Commission, and had extended its life in 1896, 1897, and again in January, 1898. After the new Act was in place, the Committee met six times before the end of January, 1899. On accepting membership of the Statutory Commission, Busk had to relinquish his place, and the Committee elected Napier as their Chairman in November, 1898. Napier was the only Fellow, and he was not a member of the parallel Senate Committee, so the two bodies were quite separate.

Under Napier's Chairmanship, the Committee delegated to a sub-committee composed of himself, Benson, Cave, Hart, Sansom and Silvanus Thompson the drafting of representations to be made to the Commission by Convocation. Not without disagreement, as will be seen, a well-argued document was produced and sent to the Commission on 2 February 1899. There was then a lull in proceedings, because the Commission was drawing up the first draft Statutes and Regulations, which were sent to Senate and Convocation for their consideration, on 18 May. Nine days earlier, however, Convocation's Annual Meeting had been held, at which election of the new Standing Committee had taken place. That Committee met on 19 May, the day when the Commission's proposals reached them. At that meeting, Busk declared that in his opinion the Special Committee's powers were exhausted, and that the Standing Committee should take over the business of advising Convocation on the progress of negotiations with the Commission.

It may well be that the Chairman was correct in arguing that the Special Committee had not been formally renewed and was therefore no longer in existence. Even if he had spoken 'off the cuff', it is likely that Busk was simply wanting to ensure that protecting the interests of Convocation in the matter of the Statutes and Regulations was not delayed or weakened. And certainly his position as a working member of the Commission must have made his position as an adviser and leader of Convocation extremely delicate. Nonetheless, it was somewhat odd that either he appeared to have simply abandoned the members of the Special Committee – who had been doing all the work, and were fully in touch with the current issues before the Commission – or that he was overruled by the Standing Committee. But there is no record of debate or disagreement within the Committee, which went ahead with the appointment of a sub-committee to take over the apparently defunct Special Committee's responsibilities. Its members were Beare, Bradford, T.G. Foster, Hopkins, Mears, Morley, Ryalls and Waring. Of the old Special Committee, Boyd, Napier and Odgers were currently members of the Standing Committee, and Boyd was present, but none of them was put on the new sub-committee.

Whether or not there were hidden political tensions which would explain what happened at the 19 May meeting, it is certain that the Standing

Committee was unanimous in realising the importance of the draft Statutes and Regulations which had been received from the Commission, and agreed on the need for Convocation to consider them. All members signed a requisition for an Extraordinary Meeting of Convocation to be held, and such a meeting was subsequently called for 27 June. In the intervening weeks, the new sub-committee met four times to prepare a report for the Standing Committee to present to Convocation. As had happened in the Special Committee, there was considerabe disagreement, which continued when the Standing Committee met on 9 June to approve the final version of a report.

However, Busk's opinion that the Special Committee had expired, and could make no further contribution, was not acceptable to its members. Seven of them met on 12 June – Napier, Cave, Hart, Odgers, Sansom, Thiselton-Dyer and Thompson – and resolved, unanimously, to request that they should be continued with full powers to represent Convocation before the Commission. Standing Orders prevented them from presenting a report to the Extraordinary Meeting, but they were able to submit the Minutes of their meetings.

Thus when Convocation met on 27 June, with only eighty-five present, the Minutes of the Special Committee and the Report of the Standing Committee were put before the House. Bradford moved that the Report of the Standing Committee be received, and after that was done he immediately moved that the Standing Committee should be empowered to make representations to the Commission on the basis of its Report. But he was rebuffed. On a show of hands, by thirty-six to twenty-eight, the Special Committee was given full powers to make representations on behalf of Convocation to the Commission, and to confer with that body. Perhaps as some sort of compensation, two leading members of the Standing Committee, Bradford and Mears, were added to the Special Committee in the places of Busk and Cozens-Hardy, who had resigned. The Special Committee only held two meetings thereafter, at the end of June and the beginning of August, 1899.

In the absence of a division list, it is hard to estimate whether the supporters of the Special and Standing Committees were representative of the groupings within Convocation which had differed over the fundamental question of reform. Nor does the membership of the Committees themselves give any clear answer to that question. What seems more likely is that the divisions within both Committees were not related to the basic question which had, effectually, been settled by Parliament, but revolved around the desired internal arrangement of Faculties within the redesigned University. And the arguments about that arrangement were not confined to Convocation, nor did they imply clear-cut disagreement between Senate and Convocation. In fact, the whole episode reflected the controversies and ambitions inherent in the development and relationships of academic disciplines, which inevitably chafe against established organisational frameworks.

The Act of 1898 provided that the Chairman of Convocation would sit in the Senate *ex officio*, and that Convocation would elect sixteen members. But the election would be by Faculty, and graduates would have a vote in each Faculty in which they had taken their degrees. Thus, in electoral terms, quite apart from the basic importance of academic organisation, the number of Faculties and their allocation of places on the Senate would be politically significant. And it was the case that, while the discussions of the draft Statutes and Regulations in the Senate's and Convocation's committees touched on many topics, the matter of Faculties dominated their sessions.

Arts, Medicine and Science were uncontestable Faculties. The University had not attracted substantial numbers of students to its Law degrees, and the Inns of Court were refusing to accept the invitation of the Statutory Commission to become Schools of the University and to accept places on the Senate. But the Commission was sympathetic to the Senate's wishes, and would have been well aware of the strength of the legal profession in Convocation, mainly due to the presence of lawyers who had taken only Arts degrees. The Commission acknowledged that there were shadows over a Faculty of Laws; but in effect they did not prevent its inclusion.

In a queue behind the original four subjects were several new disciplines craving recognition – Agriculture, Applied Science, Economics (including commerce, social studies and politics), Education, Engineering, Music and Theology. The Commission solved this problem by considering it in terms of Degrees as well as Faculties. Agriculture was kept within Science, and neither it nor Education gained either separate degrees or Faculty status. Theology had been recommended by the Cowper Commission, and though a petition was lodged against it on grounds of principle it was withdrawn; the Faculty of Theology would prepare students for the degrees of Bachelor and Doctor of Divinity. Music, with degrees already well established, survived the refusal of the Royal College and Royal Academy to become Schools of the University. The story of the London School of Economics and Political Science has been told many times, and its establishment and diplomatic support, in which the Webbs played so large a part, doubtless influenced the decision to include in the University a Faculty of Economics and Political Science.

If there were conflicts over most of the decisions about Faculties, they were seemingly resolved discreetly. But a much more visible struggle took place over the claims of Applied Science and Engineering. In Convocation's Special Committee, on 28 November 1898, it took the Chairman's casting vote to recommend that there should be a separate Faculty of Engineering, but a strong majority agreed that if Engineering was included in Science, there should be a separate Enginering Degree. However, at the next meeting, on 5 December, the separate Faculty was denied, being supported only by Silvanus Thompson, who showed his frustration by trying, unsuccessfully, to have the proposal for a Faculty of Economics deleted. The idea of a separate Engineering Degree within the Faculty of Science seems to have remained the favoured proposal of Convocation.

In the Senate Committee, the early position was to refuse a separate Faculty of Applied Science. But there followed heavy lobbying from leading applied scientists, including the Presidents of the Institutes of Mechanical, Civil and Electrical Engineers, joined by professors from Cambridge, UCL, KCL and the Central Technical College, and supported by the ubiquitous Silvanus Thompson, writing from his base at Finsbury Technical College. In January, 1899, the Committee recommended a Faculty of Engineering. The chief antagonists among the Fellows were Magnus, head of the City and Guilds Institute, in favour, and Rucker, Professor at the Royal College of Science, against.[2] The Commission settled for a Faculty of Engineering, but only for an indication, on Science Degree certificates, that Engineering had been a specialism.

The new version of the University of London would begin, therefore, with eight Faculties – of Arts, Economics and Political Science, Engineering, Laws, Medicine and Surgery, Music, Science, and Theology. But while each of the eight Faculties would have, from the outset, a membership of teachers who could be entrusted with the election of representatives to the Senate, only five Faculties had graduates who could form electorates for Convocation elections. What should be the distribution of seats between Faculties, and what provision should be made for graduates from new Faculties, were matters over which Convocation's Committees haggled at length. And much of this argument was carried on while it was assumed that there would be Faculties of Music and Theology, but no certainty about the future for Economics or Engineering.

The first draft proposal, from Benson, for the sub-committee of the Special Committee, argued that Arts and Laws graduates were predominant, that there were very few Medical and Science external graduates, and that graduates from the other disciplinary groups would increase only slowly. He suggested, therefore, that either no less than twelve of the Convocation places on Senate should go to Arts, Laws, Music, Economics and Theology, and only two each to Medicine and Science; or that Arts, Economics, Music and Theology should have eight, Laws four, Medicine two and Science two. The sub-committee compromised, obviously after strong opposition from the medicos and scientists, and put forward eight for Arts and Laws, three each for Medicine and Science, and one each for Music and Theology.

But there then developed a debate over the desirability of providing that 'no Faculty shall be entitled to separate representation on Senate until the number of its registered Graduates shall amount to at least fifty'. This was proposed by Cozens-Hardy and Thiselton-Dyer, and eventually carried, but only by four to three, after amendments to reduce the figure to twenty, and to increase it to a hundred, were defeated. No sooner had this been done, than Hart and Thiselton-Dyer moved for a distribution of five to Arts, and

[2] UL RC 27/3–6.

three to each of Laws, Medicine and Science, with the provision that another place should go to each of Arts and Science until graduates in Theology and another new Faculty had become 'numerically sufficient' to constitute electoral bodies. This was amended on the motion of Thompson and Sansom to retain the scheme but to give Arts and Science each four places.

In February, 1899, therefore, Convocation's official guidance to the Statutory Commission was Arts four, Laws three, Science four, Medicine three, with an initial increase of one each to Arts and Science; the extra place in Arts should go, in due course, to Theology, while the presumption must have been that the other would go to graduates in Applied Science/Engineering.

The Commission was much less generous to Laws, and in their first draft of the Statutes, made available on 18 May, they suggested a distribution of Arts six, Laws one, Music one, Medicine and Surgery two, and Science six. But they also lowered the number of graduates needed to constitute an electoral body. They provided that when there were thirty graduates in Divinity they should elect a representative of the Faculty of Theology, and that the contingent from Arts should then be reduced to five. In the interim, graduates in Divinity should vote in the Faculty of Arts.

The Commission's proposals were argued about in the sub-committee of the Standing Committee, which took over from the Special Committee in May, 1899, and then again in the reinstalled Special Committee at the end of June. There were many divisions, settled on several occasions only by the Chairman's casting vote; all related to attempts to make small shifts in the representation of Faculties. The outcome was a request for very small transfers of places, and these were sent to the Commission on 4 July 1899, but seemingly made no impression.

Thiselton-Dyer was no doubt correct in claiming, in October, 1899, that the Special Committee of Convocation did not represent any particular party.[3] A great deal of their concern was for the wider interests of the University, and often the special pleadings were narrowly disciplinary, rather than reflective of the broader splits between Arts and Science, and between the London collegiate and the provincial, non-collegiate graduates. But as will be seen, voting for Convocation places on the new Senate was the first occasion when the future alignment of forces became apparent; and the results reflected the strengths of the various Faculties and the continuance of tensions between the Internal and External sides.

'I have lately heard', wrote the Duke of Devonshire to the Prime Minister, early in December, 1898, 'that Sir John Lubbock wants a Peerage'.[4] The likelihood of Lubbock going to the Lords had been hinted at on several occasions in the past few years. Whether the affairs of the University of

---

[3] *Times*, 11 October 1899.
[4] Hatfield House, 3M/E, Devonshire to Salisbury, 3 December 1898.

London, and in particular his stand against the loss of Convocation's veto, was an important element in his seeking a peerage, is quite unclear. Lubbock was a successful political figure, with many more public and popular concerns than the University of London. It is entirely possible that his wish for preferment had nothing whatever to do with the University: at the same time, it is not impossible that he may have been wearied by the controversy over the institution's future, and perhaps a little apprehensive that his seat might be at risk because of the stand which he had taken, and on which he had been defeated.

Whatever his motives, he was to get his wish, but it was not granted without strings. Devonshire had gone on, in his letter to Salisbury:

> I should think that [Lubbock] would make an excellent Peer, but as it would involve a vacancy for the University of London, I do not think it can be without consultation as to the probable successor. I should like to be able to tell him that if this can be satisfactorily [arranged] he may hope for his promotion before long.

How long it was before the Duke received the Prime Minister's approval, and what steps Lubbock must have taken, after he was given a conditional blessing, are not apparent in surviving data, published or unpublished. But late in October, 1899, Devonshire reassured Salisbury.

> I understand that Lubbock would guarantee a safe successor to his seat for the University of London, and subject to his satisfying us on this, I should like to tell him his name could be submitted for the next New Year.[5]

What Lubbock did to satisfy Devonshire is unclear. But he had certainly consulted Benson, who had been the Secretary of his election Committee and would have been very knowledgeable about Convocation opinion, at least in London. Lubbock must have told Benson almost at once that his move to the Lords was definite, for on 30 October Benson wrote:

> Your Committee has always been largely personal, and from the Unionist point of view it is, I think, most important that we should be prepared with a candidate and the nucleus of a Unionist Committee ready to address the University as soon as a public announcement is made of your going to the House of Lords.

And Benson went on to reveal that he had discussed the matter with Busk, and was already pushing Busk's candidature. He asked Lubbock whether 'the contingency' of his move to the Lords might be mentioned

---

[5] Hatfield House, 3M/E, Devonshire to Salisbury, 23 October 1899.

. . . confidentially . . . to individual members of Convocation whose views must be ascertained and whose assistance must be sought in order to secure a Unionist succession . . .

Busk and I are inclined to think that, everything considered, he is probably the strongest (and I say certainly the best) candidate on our side under present circumstances. We think his most formidable opponent probably Sir Henry Roscoe.

Would it be your wish to help Busk's friends to establish a Committee to promote his election as your successor, and would it be possible for you and agreeable to you at the proper time to sound some of the influential members of your Committee in Busk's interests?[6]

There is no correspondence available for November and December; and there is no evidence of whether or not Lubbock gave Busk's candidature his blessing. Lubbock's peerage was duly announced on New Year's Day, 1900, when he became Baron Avebury. But on the same day, a letter from Benson shows that there had certainly been contact made on the matter of a successor, with Sir Michael Foster, who had been President of Lubbock's Committee. Benson and Foster were concerned that Lubbock's Committee should circulate 'some suitable response' with any letter which Lubbock wished to send to his constituents. Much more significantly, both immediately and for developments in the near future, Foster had declared that as his Chairmanship of Lubbock's Committee had been 'a purely personal consideration', he did 'not propose to take any active part in the pending Election'. In the light of his decision, Benson and his colleagues had turned, for a Chairman, to 'Mr Osler as the oldest representative of Convocation in the Senate, and the Chairman of the first Liberal Committee of the University'.[7]

Busk's campaign began with the publication of his Address and accompanying letters in the *Times* of 3 January. Benson's letter to graduates lauded Busk's long service to the University, quoting his having been a secretary of the original Liberal Committee in 1868, and of the Committees which had sponsored both Lowe and Lubbock. Benson made no mention of Busk's political affiliation, but Osler's letter of invitation to Busk made the latter's allegiance clear: 'This is a Liberal Unionist seat and you are a Liberal Unionist.' And Busk, in his letter of acceptance to Osler, made no bones about it. 'As a Liberal Unionist', he would support the Government, particularly its determination to win the Boer War, and he would give vigilant attention to the affairs of the University in Parliament. In another letter to the *Times*, on the following day, Osler – perhaps regretting that he had not said enough about Convocation's affairs, stressed

---

[6]  BL Add Mss 49664, Benson to Lubbock, 30 October 1899.
[7]  BL Add Mss 49666 Pt I, Benson to Lubbock, 1 January 1899.

... the valuable assistance Mr Busk gave to the reconciliation of divergent views respecting the future constitution which issued in the University of London Act, 1898, and obviated what appeared to be the risk of deadlock.

The Liberals were off the mark almost as soon as the Liberal Unionists. The University Liberal Association invited Collins to stand, and he was formally adopted at a meeting on 8 January. In his Address he was critical of the handling of the conflict in South Africa. He expressed his 'earnest desire that a satisfactory termination of the war may be speedily achieved, and a just and generous settlement of outstanding grievances and disputes be effected'. On education, he acknowledged that the University of London Act, 1898, 'had closed a long-standing controversy', and went on:

> As the right of the graduates in Convocation to accept or reject any fundamental change in the constitution of the University was abolished by the Act, it will be the duty of their representative in Parliament to exercise the greater vigilance on behalf of his constituents. If elected I should . . . endeavour to maintain the present high reputation of our degrees and imperial character of our University, while welcoming and promoting the better organisation of secondary, technical and University teaching in the Metropolis upon unsectarian lines.[8]

But by the time these two relatively orthodox partisan candidatures had been floated, both were denounced in non-partisan quarters, and Collins was also attacked from within his own profession. The outcome was the first three-cornered contest for the University's seat.

One could only guess at where, within the academic and scientific Establishment in London, the first doubts were expressed about the declared candidates, and where the doubts were translated into a conviction that some drastic action should be taken to introduce a new element into the election. But perhaps the earliest manifestation, in print, of a mood of discontent, appeared in the *British Medical Journal*'s issue of 6 January. An anonymous article claimed that 'Busk . . . has been put forward somewhat hastily as a Liberal Unionist candidate', and went on to report that

> . . . there is a widespread desire that the scanty band of men of science in the House of Commons should not be diminished, but that Sir John Lubbock should be succeeded by a man known to the scientific world.

Two days later, a Dr E.J. Chinnock wrote to the *Times*, calling on medical and scientific graduates to find a 'suitable candidate'. But the first expressions of concern by heavyweights appeared in the same journal on 9 January. Sir

---

[8] UL Ms 812/153/17.

Edward Fry and Sir Joshua Fitch, while carefully avoiding any names, argued the case for having, as candidates, men of 'distinction and personal influence', who would avoid the excesses of university and party politics. The editor was less disposed to be diplomatic. A long and rather tortuous leader endorsed the notions of Fry and Fitch, called for the nomination of a London graduate, was respectful but unenthusiastic about Busk and Collins, and wanted a 'big' figure – while clearly hoping that he would be a Conservative.

For another week, the public focus on Busk and Collins continued. The University Conservative Association, chaired by Rollit, discussed tactics at length on 11 January, and decided to confer with the Liberal Unionist Association. On the next day, Benson, no doubt aware that Busk's candidacy was under pressure, wrote to the *Times*, warning Convocation voters of the danger of ignoring the extent of Collins's support as the leader of the anti-reform group. He quoted the successes of Collins himself, Napier, Rivington and Moulton in Senate elections from 1893 to 1898, and claimed that,

> In all these contests the real victor was Dr Collins, who appealed mainly to the natural affection of the country graduates, numbering perhaps two thirds of the constituency, for the system under which they had taken their degrees . . . the force which . . . carried Dr Collins to victory is still a living force . . . it has life enough left to crush any candidate who cannot appeal to it.

While Collins was seen as a danger to the internal peace of the University by supporters of the current Chairman of Convocation, he was also seen as an unsuitable candidate by the *Lancet*. That journal also took a dismissive view of Busk, as an unwanted additional lawyer, and propounded interesting doctrines of University representation and of the necessity for professional orthodoxy.

> . . . what may be called the domestic side of London University requires no voice in Parliament, while St Stephen's has certainly little need of further legal acumen. Dr Collins . . . is certainly a strong candidate, but we do not consider that he possesses exactly the qualifications to fit him to sit in the House of Commons . . . As is well known he is at variance with accepted scientific belief on the question of vaccination. Whether he is or is not opposed *in toto* to vaccination or whether it is only compulsory processes of inoculation that are distasteful to him is beside the point. The general feeling among medical men that the University of London ought to be represented by a medical man surely implies that the Member of Parliament for the University should be an embodied expression of the highest medical opinion. That is what Dr Collins – an extremely clever man, a tried administrator, and an earnest worker in the cause of medicine and public health – is not; and the objection is a serious one.[9]

---

[9] *Lancet*, 13 January 1900.

But the sparring between Busk and Collins was put in the shade by the announcement, on 19 January, that, despite his earlier disclaimer, Sir Michael Foster would be a candidate. The *Times* hailed him enthusiastically, and pressed Busk and Collins to withdraw. Foster was a shrewd choice. He met fully the demands of the scientific and medical lobbies. The son of a surgeon, he attended University College School and graduated from UCL. He had been an eminently successful Professor of Physiology at Cambridge since 1883, Biological Secretary of the Royal Society since 1881, and had become President of the British Association as recently as 1899. But he also had qualifications which would widen his appeal to some other sections of the Convocation electorate. He had been raised 'in an atmosphere of fervent nonconformity';[10] he was a member of the Statutory Commission; and he was a Liberal turned Liberal Unionist in 1886, though he carried no party label fourteen years later. In his acceptance, he supported the Government over the Boer War, and declared himself against Home Rule for Ireland, but insisted that in other respects he was 'Liberal'.[11]

Foster had been invited to stand 'as the result of a meeting of some influential members of Convocation', chaired by John Rotton, QC.[12] His other sponsors included Waring, then Secretary of the University Conservative Association. That Association, while not claiming Foster as their official candidate, nonetheless gave him their support, on 23 January. As did a group of Fellows and members of Convocation from across a wide spectrum of political opinion,[13] and as did the *University College Gazette*, which, faced with a choice of three UCL men, plumped firmly for Foster.[14]

Given Foster's promise to support the Government on the two crucial policy issues of the Boer War and Home Rule, his appearance on the scene can only have been greeted gladly by Collins. The overwhelming vote of the medicos for the Liberal Unionists in 1886, together with the antipathy of the orthodox over vaccination, meant that Collins's attractiveness to the medical graduates must have been very limited. At the same time, though science was now attracting equal numbers of students, the number of scientific graduates was still relatively small, and those of them who might have been lured into Foster's ranks were probably not numerous enough to worry Collins. He depended mainly on the traditional Liberal Party supporters who were opposed to the Government on national policy lines; in addition, he no doubt was seen by the 'irreconcilables' in Convocation as the candidate, in a strictly University context, most deserving of their vote. And remembering the less than flattering opinions expressed in the recent past about the provincial BAs, it is not

---

10  *DNB*.
11  *Times*, 29 January 1900.
12  *BMJ*, 27 January 1900.
13  *Times*, 5 February 1900.
14  *UC Gazette*, February 1900.

surprising that the Executive of the National Union of Teachers recommended their members to vote for him.[15]

The Busk camp, on the other hand, must have been devastated by Foster's nomination. The Chairman of Convocation was no match for Foster in intellectual and academic standing; he was a lawyer when influential forces were proclaiming a superfluity of lawyers in Parliament and demanding more representatives of medicine and science; and, though he led the majority of the few hundred who regularly attended Convocation meetings, his views on the reform of the University were not accepted happily by large numbers of provincial graduates. Moreover, he had upset many people by being 'so quick in obtaining the support of an electioneering association with which he had for a long time been working'.[16]

At an early stage of the campaign, Benson had suggested that Busk would be willing to give way to 'an eminent candidate',[17] but he and others showed themselves to be bitterly opposed to Foster's bid. Benson pointed out that Foster had 'described external graduation as "a disadvantage" and external students as "a clog" upon the work of a real university'.[18] And Blake Odgers asked

> What has [Foster] done for the University of London? He has been for more than thirty years a Professor in the University of Cambridge – a University which already has two representatives in the House of Commons and does not need a third. He has never shown any sympathy with that which is the distinctive feature of our system of graduation – viz., the inclusion of students who are not attending lectures at any London college. Compared with Mr Busk, or even Dr Collins, Sir Michael Foster has done no work for the University of London, and I shall be much surprised if either of those gentlemen withdraws in his favour.[19]

These and other emphatic protests were no doubt responsible for the caution with which the *Lancet* welcomed Foster's candidacy, of which it approved strongly. The journal warned that Foster might not win, 'for there are parties within this particular constituency over and above the ordinary political division everywhere to be found'.[20] And the *Journal of Education*, while sure that 'no more fitting representative of the reformed University could be found' than Foster, feared that his 'outspoken views as to the necessity of developing the teaching side of the University will not commend him to a constituency that rejected Lord Lister in favour of Mr Rivington'.[21]

[15] *Times*, 5 February 1900.
[16] *Lancet*, 17 February 1900.
[17] *BMJ*, 27 January 1900.
[18] *Times*, 20 January 1900.
[19] *Times*, 27 January 1900.
[20] *Lancet*, 27 January 1900.
[21] *Jnl of Education*, February 1900.

But when polling took place, over five days from 7th to 12 February, the other 'parties within' did not stop Foster. He took 1271 votes, 47 per cent; Collins won 32 per cent, with 863; and Busk 21 per cent with 586. It was never likely that Collins could have overcome the support given by a largely professional class electorate to a Government committed to the Boer War and steadfastly opposed to Irish Home Rule. In a straight fight with Foster, though, it is likely that an uncertain proportion of those who voted for Busk would have come across to Collins, because of the latter's undoubted sympathy for Convocation's rights and for the interests of the External side of the University. Collins and Busk, between them, took 53 per cent of the vote. Those who voted for Busk must have included many whose support for the External work of the University may have been passionate enough to have overcome their qualms, on the grounds of national policy, of voting for Collins. Almost certainly, not enough to have foiled Foster; but certainly enough to have indicated that the domestic affairs of the University of London had been a genuinely significant – and just possibly, a crucial – factor in the election.

The final version of the Statutes was laid before both Houses of Parliament on 16 February 1900, and the Regulations followed on 1 March. The Report of the Commissioners which accompanied them was signed on 27 February and laid on the tables on 5 March. Objections to the Statutes and Regulations could have been received and considered over the following forty days. But the only formal opposition came a little later, in a Petition by a graduate aggrieved over the establishment of a Faculty of Theology; and that Petition was withdrawn at the last moment. Printing delays, and the absence of the Court in Balmoral, prevented the Statutes and Regulations coming before the Queen-in-Council until 29 June, at Windsor, when they were approved and came into effect. But by then the Long Vacation was so near that there was no way in which elections to the new Senate could be held until the early autumn. The old order continued, therefore, until October.

During this long interval, the negotiations between the Government and the University over the latter's new headquarters were completed, and on 9 May the Senate held their first meeting in the Imperial Institute in South Kensington. And after apparently protracted internal arguments, the Inns of Court, who had refused to accept the invitation embodied in the 1898 Act, to send representatives to the new Senate,[22] changed their minds and made the appointments late in September. On 1 October, Michael Foster was returned unopposed at the General Election – the Khaki Election, called to take advantage of military victories. The members of all parties in Convocation were seemingly exhausted by the struggle earlier in the year: no attempt seems to have been made to find candidates to oppose Foster.

---

[22] For the earlier negotiations between the Statutory Commissioners and the Inns of Court, see the Commissioners' Report, PP lxvi, Cd 83, 1900.

In passing, it is worth looking ahead in this context. Foster's streak of independence prevented him from becoming a reliable supporter of the Conservative-Liberal Unionist Coalition: he crossed the floor after the Government's Education Act of 1902, and thereafter voted with the Liberals. But in the landslide election of 1905, he lost by twenty-four votes to Sir Philip Magnus, who stood as a Unionist.

The last event to be recorded here is the election of the sixteen members of the new Senate by Convocation. It was decided on 9 October 1900, but electioneering began months earlier. The whole episode underlined the fact that, far from disappearing or even being discreetly concealed from public view, the division between the devotees of the External side of the University, and the champions of the new order with its provisions for Internal students, would continue, noisily, in the new era.

It was the old 'irreconcilables' who took an aggressive lead. Late in April it was reported that 'activity is already being displayed in various directions in regard to the composition of the new governing body of the University'.[23] A circular was sent to graduates,

> ... inviting them to join the 'University of London Graduates Association', formed under the presidency of Mr Fletcher Moulton to secure the return by Convocation of Senators 'who, while desirous of aiding the development of University teaching in London, are anxious to preserve the existing worth of the University.'[24]

The founders of the Association were reported as expressing 'the desire that its membership should not be confined to graduates who have in the past taken any particular line'. Nonetheless, 'it would be inconsistent with the objects of the Association to ask for the co-operation of those who would regard the interests of the external students as of secondary importance, or subordinate them to those of the internal students'.[25]

Moulton and his colleagues must have pursued their task with zeal, for they claimed a thousand members by the end of May, and fourteen hundred by the beginning of July.[26] Their avowed intent was to select a list of sixteen candidates to contest every Convocation place on the Senate. And, inevitably, this provoked an organised response. Once again, the origin of that response is unclear, but, by the beginning of June, 'various sections of Convocation' were 'actively engaged in endeavouring to agree upon a strong representative list which shall fairly reflect the views of that composite body'. And a month later negotiations were 'on foot for the selection of a strong "ticket" in each

[23] *BMJ*, 25 April 1900.
[24] *Jnl of Education*, May 1900.
[25] *BMJ*, 28 April 1900.
[26] *BMJ*, 26 May, 7 July 1900.

of the Faculties which will command the respect and support of all sections of Convocation'.[27] Formal opposition took shape as the University of London Graduates Union, whose President was Pye-Smith, with Gregory Foster as General Secretary and with Secretaries for each of the Faculties.[28] Later in the year, it was claimed that the Union was 'partly formed' in the 'interests' of University College. This was probably not wholly inaccurate, but Foster demurred, insisting that 'The Union is opposed to the division of the University into sections, and thinks such division detrimental to its best interests.'[29]

The election was at last fixed for 9 October, with nominations closing on 17 September. All sixteen seats were contested except that for the Faculty of Music, where a single name, that of J.W. Sidebotham, who was supported by both the Association and the Union, was put forward. But in the other four Faculties – Arts, Laws, Medicine and Surgery, and Science – there were thirty-one candidates for the fifteen seats, and most of them were sponsored by either the Association or the Union.

The result was a strong confirmation of the continuing power of the provincial graduates, especially in the Arts Faculty, where all six seats went to men blessed by the Association, though one of them, J.D. McClure of Mill Hill School, was also endorsed by the Union. The other five were Moulton, who led the field with 1140 votes, Rollit, Napier, Benson and Mears. It is a little ironic that all five were practising lawyers; it was remarked that 'Literature and the humanities are well nigh unrepresented . . . Law, Science and Medicine seem likely to have it all their own way.'[30]

In the Science Faculty, five of the six elected were candidates on the Association's list, though three of them – Magnus, Sophie Bryant, and C.W. Kimmins, were also supported by the Union. F. Clowes and F.S. Macauley were the others listed by the Association. Silvanus Thompson was the only candidate who reached the Senate apparently without the endorsement of either the Association or the Union. The Union's candidates carried the day in the Faculties of Laws and of Medicine and Surgery. Cozens-Hardy won the seat for Laws; Thomas Barlow, one of the Statutory Commissioners, and J.F. Payne, who had been appointed to the Senate in 1899, represented Medicine and Surgery.

Thus of sixteen new Convocation Senators, five – Sophie Bryant, McClure, Magnus, Kimmins and Sidebotham – had been supported by both Association and Union; seven others were nominees of the Association; only three had been put forward by the Union alone; and Silvanus Thompson remained sturdily independent. There is no doubt that

[27] *BMJ*, 2 June, 7 July 1900.
[28] *Times*, 24 August 1900.
[29] *Jnl of Education*, November & December 1900.
[30] *Jnl of Education*, November 1900.

The election of Convocation members was practically a large majority for the nominees of a ticket issued by Mr Fletcher Moulton, Dr W.J. Collins and Mr Willis, who secured all the seats (six) in Arts and four out of the same number in Science ... [Others] were rejected because of their supposed approval of the changes from the old University.[31]

Convocation had lost its veto power, but its more traditional members had fought for and had now ensured a significant influence, not merely on the External side of the reformed University through their dominance of the External Council, but within the Senate itself. How that influence was used should be one theme of another volume of this history.

Those who stood for the new Senate and were defeated included five members of the old Senate – Fitch, Carey Foster, Osler (who had served continuously since January, 1859), Routh, and Sydney Howard Vines. Carey Foster was subsequently nominated as a Senator by UCL, but the others, while retaining their Fellowships, were no longer involved in the governance of the University.

The old Senate met for the last time on 10 October 1900. The Vice-Chancellor, Roscoe, presided, and there were twelve others present. Roscoe would continue as Vice-Chancellor; Busk, as Chairman of Convocation, would become an *ex officio* member of the new Senate. Magnus, Rollit and Rucker would also belong to the new body. But for the remaining eight, this was their last appearance as Senators – Fitch, Lubbock (now Lord Avebury), Milman, Osler, Parry, Thorpe, Tilden and Williamson. That evening, Avebury wrote in his diary:[32]

Attended my last meeting of Senate of the University of London. My father and I have been on from the beginning! It is rather sad but I did not wish to undertake the work of the new institution. The new rooms at the Imperial Institute seem very good.

The new Senate met for the first time on 24 October.

[31] *Lancet*, 30 October 1900. There are small discrepancies in the allocation of seats due to the lack of any official documentation. The results used here have been taken from various newspapers and journals.
[32] BL Add Mss 62684.

# *Appendix*

The University of London in 1901
Schools, and Institutions Having Recognised Teachers

Compiled from the first Statutes of the University, issued in 1900, and the
*University Calendar for 1901-02*, vol ii.

## Schools

All Faculties: University College London
King's College London

Arts & Science: Royal Holloway College
Bedford College

Economics: London School of Economics and Political Science

Engineering: Central Technical College of City and Guilds of London
Institute for the Advancement of Technical Education

Medicine: Medical Schools of
St Bartholomew's Hospital
London Hospital
Guy's Hospital
St Thomas's Hospital
St George's Hospital
Middlesex Hospital
St Mary's Hospital
Charing Cross Hospital
Westminster Hospital
London (Royal Free Hospital) School of Medicine for
Women

Science: Royal College of Science
South Eastern Agricultural College, Wye

Theology: Hackney College
New College
Regents Park College
Cheshunt College
Wesleyan College, Richmond
St John's Hall, Highbury

## Institutions having recognised teachers

Westfield College
Birkbeck Institution
Borough Road Training College
St John's College, Battersea
St Mark's College, Chelsea
City of London College
Jews' College
Goldsmiths' Institute
Northampton Institute

Finsbury Technical College
East London Technical College
West Ham Municipal Technical Institute
Battersea Polytechnic
Northern Polytechnic
South Western Polytechnic
Woolwich Polytechnic

Royal Academy of Music
Royal College of Music
Trinity College

College of the National Dental Hospital
London School of Dental Surgery
Institute of Dental Technology and School of Mechanical Dentistry
Hospital for Sick Children Medical Classes
National Hospital for the Paralyzed and Epileptic Medical School
Hospital for Consumption and Diseases of the Chest Medical Classes
Pharmaceutical Society School of Pharmacy
Royal London Opthalmic Hospital Medical Classes
London College of Tropical Medicine of the Seamen's Hospital Society

# Index

Abbott, Arthur Robert, 235
Aberdare, Lord, *see* Bruce, H.A.
Academical Education Association, 415
Acland, A.H.D., 330, 333, 359–61, 364, 366, 368–9, 371–2, 380, 431
Acton, Lord, 16, 104, 114–15
Airy, George Biddell, 161
Albert University, 244, 270, 273, 285, 288, 298, 305, 308–9, 311, 313–14, 316–17, 322, 324, 326
Allchin, William Henry, 170, 225, 248, 261–3, 285, 293, 295, 303–4, 306, 325, 355, 358, 361, 374–5, 377–9, 383–4, 401–2, 433
Allen, Henry Ebenezer, 27, 40
Anderson, Elizabeth Garrett, *see* Garrett, Elizabeth
Anderson, J.G.S., 95n.18
Anson, Sir William, 277, 340
Anstie, Francis Edmund, 102
Anstie, James, 135, 156, 166, 175, 192–4, 233–5, 238, 249–50, 255–6, 258, 266, 280–1, 289, 292, 297, 299, 302–3, 334, 336–7, 341, 343, 346, 348, 351, 353, 357, 360–1, 371, 379, 383, 394, 397, 401, 422, 432, 446
Arnold, Matthew, 185
Arnott, Neil, 96
Ashbourne, Lord, 334
Aspland, Lindsey Middleton, 194–5
Asquith, Herbert Henry, 333, 349, 393, 436
Association for Promoting the Higher Education of Women, Bristol, 113
Association for the Promotion of a Professorial University, 283, 338, 341, 343–4, 365, 370, 373, 394
Association for the Promotion of a Teaching University for London, 42, 243–50, 252, 256, 259–63, 266–70, 279, 333, 373

Association of General Practitioners, 268
Association of Headmasters of Endowed and Proprietary Schools, 216
Association of Headmistresses, 214
*Athenaeum*, 92n.11
Avebury, Baron, *see* Lubbock, Sir John, 4th Bt.

Bagehot, Walter, 38, 151, 153–4, 160–3, 165–8
Baines, Matthew, 102, 148, 156, 281, 293, 302–3, 310–11, 313, 320, 336, 342, 349, 353, 358, 360, 363, 376, 378
Balfour, Arthur James, 217, 317, 326–30, 337, 369, 384, 395, 401, 405, 407, 412, 416–17, 422–3, 428–9, 431–3, 435, 438, 441–3
Balfour, Gerald William, 374
Ball, John Thomas, 276
Barford, Alfred Henry, 287n.3
Barlow, Thomas, 446, 460
Barnes, Robert, 118, 128–9
Barry, Bishop Alfred, 254, 333, 346, 368, 414–15
Bartley, G.T.C., 319, 322, 328–30, 337
Basing, Lord, 308
Bastian, Henry Charlton, 129
Bath High School, 110
Baxter, Evan Buchanan, 235, 240
Beach, Sir Michael Hicks, 396, 416
Beale, Dorothea, 211
Beare, Thomas Hudson, 384, 447
Bedford, 9th Duke of, 18
Bedford Charity, 210
Bedford College, 40, 80, 97, 110, 130, 309, 316, 328, 342, 360, 370, 396
Bedford Modern School, 208, 210
Belcher, Rev. Robert Henry, 208
Benn, John, 364n.28
Bennett, Alfred William, 111, 128–30,

465